OLAP Solutions

Building Multidimensional
Information Systems

OLAP Solutions

Building Multidimensional Information Systems

Erik Thomsen

Wiley Computer Publishing

John Wiley & Sons, Inc.

New York • Chichester • Brisbane • Toronto • Singapore • Weinheim

Executive Publisher: Katherine Schowalter

Editor: Robert M. Elliot

Managing Editor: Brian Snapp

Electronic Products, Associate Editor: Michael Green

Text Design & Composition: SunCliff Graphic Productions

Library of Congress Cataloging-in-Publication Data

Thomsen, Erik, 1959-
    OLAP solutions : building multidimensional information systems /
Erik Thomsen.
      p.   cm.
    Includes index.
    ISBN 0-471-14931-4 (paper/CD-Rom : alk. paper)
    1. Decision support systems. 2. Database design. 3. System
design. I. Title.
T58.62. T485 1997
658.4'03'0285--dc21   96-46688
                                                CIP

Printed in the United States of America
10 9 8 7 6 5

Contents

v

Chapter 13 OLAP Models for Improving Operations 351

Chapter 14 Cost/Benefit Analysis for Infrastructure 381
Investments

Appendix D   Glossary   **505**

Appendix E   Case Study and Software Providers 513

Appendix F   The OLAP API   **517**

Appendix G   What's on the CD-ROM   **521**

Appendix H   Vendor List and Descriptions   **525**

Foreword

Computer software for the enterprise is hard enough to understand; it gets worse when competing software vendors, all striving for a position in users' minds, muddy the waters further with misleading claims. This usually happens when a new category of software is born which challenges older technologies and paradigms. Such has been the case with OLAP: On-Line Analytical Processing software.

The new paradigm that OLAP brings to us is the ability for the user to think of data logically as multidimensional. Business people, when they're thinking analytically, think of their enterprises in dimensions: sales by region; profit by product; expenses by cost center; market share by market, etc. The elegance of matching the user's mental model of the data with the logical organization of the data opens a whole new world of analysis, navigation, and visualization.

So where's the argument and the confusion? Some haven't understood the need; others haven't appreciated why it takes special and sophisticated software approaches to deliver analytical processing multi-dimensionally and with interactive responsiveness. Even some of the well-known IT (Information Technology) advisory firms, who have tended to look at the world through a bottom-up, relational-data-base lens, missed an early comprehension of OLAP and its missionary vendors.

This book sets the record straight: not as a debate but as an impressive, scholarly work. You are embarking on a narrative and a text book, all in one. The book should be the basis for college business school and computer science curricula. It is must reading for any IT analyst, expert, developer, procurement decision maker and consultant working in the fields of decision support, financial reporting, sales and profit analysis, and quality management. It is equally important for those who work in the more generalized IT fields of data management, data warehousing, and Intranets. The book helps you understand OLAP and where it fits and what it does.

This book does it all. It presents the academic theory and the pragmatic case studies. Parts of it are a quick read and parts must be studied in multiple passes. By the end of it, You will know OLAP and you will be a better practitioner, advisor, or user of Information Technology for having read it.

Congratulations to Erik for the patience, skill, and steadfast commitment to de-mystifying a hotly-contested segment of enterprise software.

So where do you begin to talk about OLAP? Since a lot of people feel their best thinking is done while on airplanes with little distractions, let's start there.

Can you describe OLAP to a stranger on an airplane?

I'm sitting next to a total stranger on an airplane. He looks over and notices some papers I'm holding, one of which says "OLAP" in bold print. "What is OLAP?" he asks. I respond, "It is a type of computer software that helps business managers assess what's good and what's bad about business performance."

"That's interesting. I'm a business-unit manager, and we use PC spreadsheets to do that," he says. I respond, "Well then, you may be exactly the type of person who could benefit from OLAP software. We can test that out with a few questions. Are you game?" "Sure, at least until the movie starts," says he, agreeably.

Q: "About how many spreadsheets does it take for you to understand your business unit's performance?"

A: "That could be a loaded question, but I'll try to answer it. There are actually a fair number of spreadsheets around. We have one for each product we sell. They track units sold, prices, discounts, etc., for each month and quarter. We have 30 products so that's 30 spreadsheets.

More recently we've expanded geographically into eight regional offices, so we've created a spreadsheet of sales, expenses, and profit for each office."

Q: "Have you seen the need to look at the matrix of sales for each product in each region?"

A: "Yes, we just finished that—it resulted in more spreadsheets—these list products down the side and regions across the top. We need one for every month and quarter, so that's a growing number of spreadsheets. The information is invaluable in understanding where we have management problems, compensation plan problems, market differences, and differences in product promotion by region. In fact, now that I think of it, the problem is magnified by our multiple organization structure. We have a hierarchy of sales offices that consolidate into districts, which are consolidated into regions, then countries, global regions and total world. Each of these consolidated levels needs a spreadsheet and it's a bit difficult to keep them linked. Recently we've implemented a second overlay hierarchy for internal commissioning purposes that in places overlaps the geographic hierarchy and in others regroups territories differently. We haven't computerized that problem yet."

Q: "I see you compute profitability by regional office. Will you do the same by product across all offices?"

A: "That's exactly the project we have under way at the moment. The problem is that the current suite of spreadsheets are not set up to support that because we need to allocate some expenses such as marketing costs and overhead. These allocation rules need to apply across spreadsheets, and they differ depending on whether we're allocating a cost across offices or across products. The number of spreadsheets and the coordination among them are getting to be a mess. I'm not even sure the calculations I've seen are correct."

"Bingo," I say. That's where OLAP comes in. It's like using a typewriter for letter writing—then the letters get longer and the uses broaden into full papers, status reports, and so on. The typewriter becomes too limiting, so you upgrade to a PC-based word processor and everything gets easier.

Managing a business means tracking information in any number of dimensions—sales, expense and profit by product, by region, and by time period. A spreadsheet shows only two dimensions with its columns and rows. Every two-dimensional subset (a "slice") from the real multidimensional picture of your business is a compromise view of what the business really looks like. If you look at enough spreadsheet combinations, you eventually construct a view of what is happening. Meanwhile, someone had to create all those spreadsheets, load them with data, maintain them, and check them. Like the typewriter, the spreadsheet wasn't ever designed to do this multidimensional analysis, hence the advent of OLAP software.

"So now I can answer the question, 'What is OLAP?' in terms common to both of us. *OLAP is the* process of creating and managing *multidimensional enterprise data for analysis and viewing by the user* who seeks an *understanding of what the data is really saying.* OLAP gives the user the analytical tools to visualize the data. The user can see what's good, what's bad, what's changed, and what's about to change by using comparisons to see the numbers in context. Typical comparisons are these:

❑ Product sales and profit by geography (product profitability)
❑ Product sales by channel (sales, promotion analysis)

❑ Profits by business unit (business unit profitability)

❑ Budget versus actual performance over time (trend and variance analysis)

These examples are from the world of business, which is where OLAP has been most often deployed. However, the benefits of multidimensional structuring of data extend beyond business modeling into economics, chemistry, quality information systems, and more. The multidimensional characteristic of OLAP systems presents a logical view of data that fits closely to the mental model that users have of the data. Any business person, when asked to describe the perspectives with which he or she would like to see data about enterprise performance organized for best comprehension, will usually describe the inherent dimensions of the business.

The "A" in OLAP

The real power of OLAP comes from both comparative and projective calculations such as variances, consolidations, ratios, and trends applied across any dimensions. Using the richness of a multidimensional model, the user can see the data in context by comparing and contrasting the data with similar data taken from a different context.

For example, usually it is difficult to gain an understanding of the profitability of an enterprise by looking at its absolute profits by contributor. It is not clear what is good and what is bad in absolute terms. But by calling for a profit *margin* calculation (that is, the ratio of profit to sales) it becomes much more meaningful to scan regions or products or channels to see where margins are unusually high or low. Without even charting, comprehension is greatly improved by computing profit relative to sales and looking at this across dimensions.

Once the analytical component of data is known, further enhancement via graphical charting can be used to add clarity to the numbers. Beyond that, OLAP systems can help the user project into the future with time-series analysis, forecasting, and "what-if" modeling functions. Without the "A" in OLAP, the user is only navigating data; with the "A", the user is exploring information.

History: Where Did OLAP Originate?

Often it is not very productive trying to pinpoint the exact origin of a new technology, but in the case of OLAP, its 30-year evolution helps us to understand the strengths of the technology in its modern client/server form. *OLAP was not an outgrowth of database management*; rather it was an outgrowth of business modeling and the need for the analytical strengths of matrix algebra.

However, while there is a strong emphasis on analysis in OLAP, it was not until data management was added to modeling functionality enabling larger data bases with greater than two dimensions, that we saw the emergence of OLAP. Today, the popular OLAP systems are all grappling with traditional DBMS issues such as multiuser performance, scalability, and backup and recovery.

Historically, the two primary development efforts for the type of software technology now called OLAP were the Express development from Management Decision Systems (later acquired by Information Resources and most recently acquired by Oracle) and the System W development from Comshare. The coining of the current market term OLAP is due in large part to the more recent efforts of Arbor Software. What follows are some brief descriptions of how these three companies were motivated to create multidimensional analytical software tools.

Express—Multidimensional Analysis for Consumer-Packaged Goods

The Massachusetts Institute of Technology Sloan School was the breeding ground for the advent of Express. Toward the end of the 1960s John Little, a Ph.d. in physics, and a young marketing academic at the Sloan School, Len Lodish, now a professor of Marketing at Wharton, and Glen Urban, then a young assistant professor and now Dean of the Sloan School, all were looking into the use of computers in mathematical and analytical applications. They gravitated toward the use of analytics in marketing, particularly in consumer product marketing. This was an ideal area of investigation because there is so much raw data to process and such high-impact decisions that could be improved with better understanding of the data. This early work led to the formation of Management Decision Systems in 1974. MDS was initially in the business of creating mathematical models for marketing analysis. It was all custom work, programming in FORTRAN. The FORTRAN language was a good starting place due to its matrix capabilities, but it had severe limitations in that all the work and data had to be done in real memory, which limited the scope of the applications.

A software development effort was funded to create FORTRAN-based subroutines that resulted in a library of analytical functions and disc-based matrix-handling capabilities. John Wirts had joined the effort as the key architect. He realized that the subroutine library could be generalized and that the analytical facilities could be greatly improved for the end user by adding data management capabilities including the disc-based matrix handling and metadata handling that allowed the use of names and logical addressing to the matrix, instead of row and column numbers. This was an important jump-off point into early OLAP. By 1972 this software mix of analytical functions and data management was wrapped in a language and Express was born: a software tool for creating matrix algebra models for marketing analysis.

In its first years, Express was not a commercial offering. It was a development productivity enhancer for consultants who were creating marketing models. By 1974, customers began asking how MDS consultants were so productive creating these custom models, and that became the impetus to mount Express on commercial time-sharing services for sale as a commercial offering. Its features and the skills of those most familiar with the tool combined to position Express as a marketing analysis tool. It was different from other tools and early database systems in that it presented the very multidimensional view that fit users' mental model of the marketing scenario represented in the data. In other words, the tool was built from the user's mindset, and just enough data management was added to the matrix algebra to enable a systematized approach to performing the desired modeling, analyses, and forecasting. The origins of Express were the *pragmatic* needs of market researchers.

System W—Multidimensional Analysis for Financial Planning, Analysis, and Reporting

Comshare was one of the very first vendors in business to serve end users directly with computing power. It was one of the first time-sharing firms, conceived in 1965 and founded in early 1966 in conjunction with the early research into time-sharing operating systems conducted at the University of California, Berkeley. Comshare's early focus was on bringing the power of interactive computing to the workplace. The 1960s saw the rise of interactive third-generation programming languages such as Basic, FORTRAN, and CAL (California Algebraic Language). While neither particularly knew it, Comshare and MDS were on a parallel track toward OLAP, but in different user specialties.

In the early 1970s Comshare chose financial analysis, reporting, and modeling as its core competence. This choice arose from a strategic decision to push the benefits of time-sharing into the hands of the business professional—a different audience from the scientists and engineers who were the early adopters of time-sharing use. Comshare licensed a financial modeling language called FCS from a small British software firm (EPS Consultants) and was instrumental in popularizing the product throughout the world all through the 1970s. FCS was not OLAP in that it had no internal support for multidimensionality, but it was a highly capable analytical tool. Comshare implementation consultants were stretching FCS more and more to meet real market needs for what would eventually be recognized as multidimensional analysis. This entailed lots of custom add-on implementation and maintenance, but there were indeed many successful financial reporting and analysis systems installed. FCS competed with IFPS from Execucom, and together these two products led the way to form a market niche for financial modeling.

In 1978/1979 Comshare had concluded that it had pushed FCS too far beyond its limits in pursuit of market requirements and engaged in extended design sessions to conceive the "next-generation" financial modeler. The conclusion of those sessions was that the next generation would be achieved by combining the analytical functions of modeling with enough data management technology to manage the much greater data volumes associated with multidimensionality. The concept of adding data management to analytical modeling functionality is what turned algebraic languages into "decision support systems" as they began to be called in the early 1980s. The resulting product produced by Comshare was System W DSS. Its primary positioning was financial decision-support uses including financial consolidation, budgeting, forecasting, strategic planning, product and customer profitability, and more. As Express had grown to be a major product force in marketing analysis applications, System W became the force in financial planning, analysis, and reporting applications all through the 1980s.

Arbor Software's Essbase—Coining "OLAP"

At the onset of the 1990s almost all software product companies were facing the challenges of redesigning their products to utilize client/server principles. As with any major technology shift in the computer industry, the move to client/server opened opportunities for new vendors, and there was no exception for decision-support systems. Arbor Software was formed in 1991 with the singular business purpose of creating a multiuser multidimensional database server that it called Essbase.

Essbase was introduced to market in 1992. It ran on the OS/2 and Windows NT server operating systems. In an attempt to gain market recognition for multidimensional servers, Arbor provided education and demonstration to Edgar Codd, who is known for having created the concepts behind the relational database model in 1970 at IBM. Codd had created the now famous 12 rules for defining relational databases. His conclusion after seeing Essbase as an example of multidimensional databases was that SQL was never meant for this kind of analysis.

Codd saw the logic in differentiating this technology from online transaction processing systems and hence coined the phrase "Online analytical processing systems" (OLAP) to describe this awakening software product category. While the use of multidimensional decision-support systems had been growing, the combination of newly rearchitected mainframe products as client/server offerings and brand new entrants such as Essbase combined with increased market awareness of the OLAP category to light a fire under the category.

What does history teach us about OLAP?

❑ OLAP is an outgrowth of modeling and analysis software and the mathematics of matrix algebra rather than database management technology.

❑ OLAP is a good example of "finding tactics that work and then making a strategy out of them." Pragmatic consultants from Management Decision Systems created Express to make multidimensional model building for marketing analysis a productive exercise. Likewise, Comshare created System W as a packaged software tool to solve the multidimensional financial analysis, modeling and consolidation problems that were too difficult in two-dimensional financial modeling systems.

❑ The most important letter in OLAP is the "A" for analysis.

❑ The two most common application areas for OLAP are financial analysis and modeling and marketing research and analysis.

❑ The single architectural principle that characterizes OLAP is true multidimensionality.

❑ OLAP has been a growing part of the computer industry's tool kit for nearly 25 years—it's about as old as relational database management. OLAP has taken longer to develop than RDBMS, perhaps due to its being closer to the use of data in an application, rather than the creation of data. Applications usually come after tools in this industry. However, with the introduction of client/server architectures in OLAP products, the growth curve has accelerated in the past few years.

The OLAP Council

The computer industry has a reputation for short product lifecycles, yet ironically many of its technologies have experienced long incubation periods. Relational databases celebrated their twenty-fifth birthday in 1994, a year in which they had just recently hit their growth stride. Similar observations can be made of the personal computer, object-oriented development methodology, graphical user interfaces, and online analytical processing.

Multidimensional analysis has been around for a long time. Throughout the 1970s and 1980s, customers installed thousands of systems before they were ever known under the OLAP name. Lacking a common identity, there were only pockets of multidimensional awareness in the overall marketplace. This is finally beginning to change. January 1995 marked the announced formation of the OLAP Council, which was to play a key role in establishing OLAP as an acknowledged and better-understood software category. After eight months of work prior to announcement, four software vendors whose revenues and customer bases comprised the bulk of the emerging OLAP market, dropped their competitive swords long enough to form the OLAP Council. *Its charter purposes were to establish the OLAP category and eliminate confusion in the mind of the market via education and to make the category more appealing to the market by establishing open standards.*

The initial announcement of the council included some real deliverables in the form of a glossary of terms and a position paper discussing OLAP's role. Despite its good intentions, the council was born in controversy that centered on whether the physical data store needed to be specially structured for multidimensional analysis or whether standard (relational) data structures would suffice. The arguments were unfortunate because they were at a technical level and they temporarily clouded the more important issues of where OLAP was truly needed and how it fit in end-user computing architectures.

The early days of the OLAP Council were spent dealing with a very excited press, which always loves controversy (more than 100 articles mentioned the Council in 1995). A single official spokesman was appointed so the council would speak in a unified voice to keep the message clear. This allowed council members and their chief technologists to move forward with the next round of real deliverables.

There were two early targets for deliverables from the council: one was predisclosed to the public, and the other was not.

The OLAP API

The very first council press release announced that members would work on a standard of interoperability (the OLAP API) between OLAP clients and OLAP servers. This would be based on an ODBC-like model of data access. In the case of the OLAP API, the goal was to allow any conforming client to access a previously unfamiliar OLAP server, learn its metadata, and then allow the user to navigate via slice and dice. This would be accomplished even though the client had not been explicitly designed to access that server. The OLAP API project was intended to be the acid test as to whether the council was real and whether the vendor-competitors would work together for a common accomplishment of significance to the customer.

The API effort bore fruit. The technical specifications had been agreed by early 1996, and an outside expert was retained to finalize the specifications for public review by the summer of 1996. The public review period is intended to accommodate external commentary from customers, analysts, and experts. Then the final API will be manifested in code that will be given to any and all developers for use in their products and software applications.

OLAP Benchmark

The second project undertaken in the Council's first 18 months was potentially more sensitive because it entailed creating a realistic and objective benchmark for measuring the performance of systems that claim to solve OLAP problems. The need for a benchmark in educating the market as to how to tell a real OLAP system from brochureware and spurious claims was felt to be critical. A system that claims to be capable of OLAP will disappoint its users if it does not deliver fast and consistent response time, almost regardless of query and analytical complexity. The reason for this demanding performance standard stems from the very interactive nature of an OLAP user experience. Unless the system responds to the user in seconds consistently, even if cross-dimension, cross-hierarchy computational operations are involved, then the user will quickly get bored waiting between interactions, and usage will cease.

The database world talks of query, but rarely does it speak of *interactive* query with *embedded analysis*. It is much more typical in the database world to assume the user knows what is being sought up front, then uses that knowledge to create a query. The response to the query comes in whatever elapsed time it takes, whether seconds, minutes, or hours. Clearly, the response is quicker than manual methods for sifting the data, but that doesn't mean that the query response is amenable to interactive exploration.

In an OLAP application, the user typically does not know what he or she is looking for, and so interactive exploration is the normal mode of accessing the data. The OLAP requirement for interactive response needs to be defined and measured to provide a clear understanding of the user requirements. That was one of the purposes of the OLAP benchmark project. The existence of this project was not predisclosed because there was the risk that the sensitivities within the growing council membership might not be overcome. However, by contracting with an outside independent, and through perseverance, the benchmark was produced and was disclosed for public comment in April 1996.

The concept behind the benchmark project is to specify a realistic problem the customer would typically look to solve with an OLAP system and to measure performance using objective, fully disclosed, and audited procedures.

The focus of the benchmark is on the customer having a useful tool to help assess whether a problem is best solved with OLAP technology rather than another approach. The benchmark is not intended to make fine differentiation between competitive OLAP systems, but rather to help the customer assess whether OLAP is applicable at all.

Looking back over the first 18 months of the OLAP Council, the expansion of membership from 4 to 16 vendors, the release of the glossary, the position papers, the OLAP API, and the OLAP benchmark all point to a productive body of vendors who defied the odds and the early claims of the leading analysts and nay-sayers. During the 1995/1996 period the OLAP Council was clearly established and takes its place among other cooperative efforts and standards bodies. The council continues to work to improve the understanding of OLAP and to improve the technology itself.

Rick Crandall
Chairman, Comshare Inc.
OLAP Council Spokesman
May 13, 1996

Preface

Why read this book? You should read this book if you are interested in technologies like:

- ❑ OLAP
- ❑ Multidimensional information systems
- ❑ Data warehousing
- ❑ Databases
- ❑ Decision support systems (dss)
- ❑ Executive information systems (eis)
- ❑ Business or visual intelligence

or if you have goals, like

- ❑ Synthesizing knowledge from data
- ❑ Modeling and analyzing large data sets
- ❑ Using information systems for real competitive advantage
- ❑ Thriving on (rather than being burdened by) lots of fast changing data and information
- ❑ Thinking clearly about business, economic and social issues

This book is written for business analysts, IT workers, IT managers, executives, computer science and business students, economists, and researchers of all kinds. It teaches you everything you need to know about designing and using a multidimensional information system and comes with software and tutorials to give you hands-on experience. The book is accessible to any intelligent person with a basic understanding of computers. There is a glossary at the end and an extensive index. It also helps if you have some understanding of spreadsheets. The greater your background in relational databases, logic, linear algebra, statistics, cognitive science, and/or data visualization, the fuller will be your appreciation of the advanced material.

How the Book Is Organized

The book is grouped into four sections plus appendices and a CD-ROM. Section I explains what analysis-based, decision-oriented information processing is all about and why we need OLAP and multidimensional technology. Toward that end, it shows where traditional spreadsheets and databases run aground when trying to provide analysis-based decision-oriented information.

Section II, the longest section, describes the features and concepts of multidimensional technology. It is composed of a logical and a physical part. In the logical part, basic and advanced features are explained. You will be taken in a clear, step-by-step fashion from the world of ordinary rows and columns to a world of multidimensional data structures and flows. After going through the chapters on basic features, you will have your first opportunity, in Chapter 5, to use the enclosed multidimensional software. Chapter 5, like the four hands-on case studies in Section III, is written as an illustrated narrative with tutorial asides so that you can learn the essential material without using the software, but, of course, you will gain hands-on experience by following along with the software. The last chapters in the logical part cover advanced features and concepts. The physical part covers, as you might guess, physical features from storage and indexing to client/server architectures. (The level of detail in the physical chapters is enough for you to understand the differences between products and their relative strengths and weaknesses. It is not enough for you to go out and build a multidimensional software package.)

Section III presents a practical set of steps for designing and using multidimensional information systems. Then it presents four different hands-on case studies: sales and marketing, portfolio analysis, cost/benefit analysis for civil engineering, and operations analysis for an airline. Each chapter represents a case study in the sense that the model structure and data for each chapter is based on a real situation, as submitted by the consulting firm with whom each chapter was developed. My hope was to capture some of the real-world irregularity that is frequently absent from invented examples. Each chapter is also hands-on in the sense that there is a running sidebar tutorial that allows you to follow along with the enclosed multidimensional software. Chapters 11 and 12 provide the most coaching. You are essentially taken through every software step. In contrast, Chapters 13 and 14 assume you have by that point learned the basics and are ready for more advanced problem solving.

Section IV extends and summarizes what you have learned from the first three sections. Chapter 15 explores further issues in dimensional analysis including issues of ordering within dimensions and independence between dimensions. Chapter 16 looks at the logical grounding of multidimensional information systems, compares what is required with what is offered by canonical logic, and points to an alternative logic that provides a better grounding for multidimensional functionality. Finally, Chapter 16 presents a comprehensive set of guidelines for comparing products and assessing your own needs.

The appendices provide further material related to some of the chapters, a glossary of key terms, introductions to the multidimensional and visualization software enclosed with the book, descriptions of OLAP software vendors, the case study and software providers for this book, and the emerging OLAP API.

Using the Enclosed Software

Two software packages are enclosed with the book: TM/1, a multidimensional database engine from TM/1 Software, and Diamond, an analytical data visualization program developed by IBM and sold through SPSS. An introduction to TM/1 is in Appendix I on the CD-ROM; the introduction to Diamond is in Appendix J on the CD-ROM. Wherever software is used in the text, it is always optional. All the case studies, plus the multidimensional tutorial in Chapter 5, are fully developed models included on the CD-ROM.

Elements of Style

Although the tone of the book is informal—like a narrative—its content is well grounded—like a textbook. The book is heavily illustrated. If you are thinking about OLAP concepts (some of which can be fairly abstract) for the first time, you will benefit from working through the figures in Section II. Technical information is provided in sidebars. You will find interactive training tutorials based on genuine applications of OLAP technology in Section III. The typographical conventions used during the tutorials are presented at the beginning of each tutorial.

Acknowledgments

I could not have written intelligently about multidimensional information systems without the many engaging discussions and debates that I have been privileged to have over the past 15 years. Although there are far too many people to name, my special thanks go to Joe Bergman, Herb Bernstein, David McGoveran, Steve Shavel, John Silvestri, Mike Sutherland, and Stephen Toulmin, for the quality and longevity of their dialogue. I also wish to thank Praxis International for giving me the time to write the early portions of this manuscript.

And I wish to thank the persons and firms whose participation made it possible to include the hands-on case studies. (A description and full contact information for each of the participating firms may be found in Appendix E.) They are

Dan Gilmore and Rob Peterson of the Planning Technology Group, Tracy Peck of MIS AG (special thanks go to Tracy for her technical assistance with TM/1), Steve Elkins of Elkins Economics, and Peter Cook of GIS/Trans.

Thanks also go to the interns for their assistance with the diagrams and tutorials, and for their positive attitudes throughout the project: Edith Chan, Dakota Pippens, and Acacia Gorman. And thanks go to TM/1 Software, and to Bernice Rogowitz at the IBM Data Visualization Center for assistance in providing the enclosed software.

I am also very thankful to the formal reviewers—Paul Anderson, Rick Crandall, Ron Kalin, David Kirkdorffer, David McGoveran, Will Martin, Nigel Pendse, Andria Rossi, George Spofford, Mike Sutherland, and especially Marie Kelly—for their constructive criticisms while reviewing all or parts of the manuscript.

Many thanks go to Nigel Pendse for numerous lively discussions and for his contributions as principal author of Chapters 8 and 9. Extra special thanks (too many to enumerate) go to George Spofford for providing invaluable criticism and assistance during the final weeks and for being the principal author of the Links section in Chapter 7 and the OLAP API description in Appendix F. I assume full responsibility for any errors or ommissions in those sections. Special thanks go to David Friend for providing the original opportunity to write this book.

Thanks finally to my partner Marjorie Schwartz, for her wonderful patience during this time, and to my parents, for their living examples.

Section I

The Need for Multidimensional Technology

A basket trap is for holding fish; but when one has got the fish, one need think no more about the basket. Words are for holding ideas; but when one has got the idea, one need think no more about the words.

—Chuang Tzu

CHAPTER

Functional Requirements of OLAP Systems

The purpose of this chapter is to define the essential characteristics (otherwise known as the functional requirements) for any **OLAP** or **On-line Analytical Processing** system. The requirements of OLAP systems share many of the standard requirements of any information system such as timely, accurate information. Beyond that, OLAP systems are unique in their attempt to provide you with fast, flexible, friendly access to large amounts of derived data whose underlying inputs may be continuously changing. To accomplish these demanding goals, OLAP technology was forced to overcome the challenges of information overload that have arisen, especially during the past ten years. They include increases in the amount and complexity of data needed to make decisions, increases in the number of people who currently read and write to a common pool of data, increases in the amount of decentralized decision making, and increases in the distribution of data and processing that may pertain to a single query.

This chapter begins with an historical look at why most corporations (and other large-scale information users) maintain separate databases for transactions and for analysis. Then it looks at analysis-oriented information systems, and positions OLAP within this category. Finally, the chapter describes the essential characteristics of any OLAP system. If you are not interested in the origins of OLAP's requirements, you may safely skip the first three sections of this chapter and move straight to a detailed description of the functional requirements for OLAP.

Appendix A describes the relationship between OLAP and data warehousing.

Defining the Term OLAP

The term OLAP sprang up more in a marketing than in a technical context. It lacks the definitional rigor of such neighboring terms as "the relational data model." I debated for a while whether to even use the term OLAP in this book. After all, the fundamental technology behind OLAP is multidimensional. Yet there is an essential activity or process that corporations around the world perform every day. And that activity, which consists of analyzing business operations with an eye toward making timely and accurate analysis-based decisions, has no official name. It's as if you wanted to talk to people about the benefits of a good mattress in a language that had no word for sleeping. For this reason, I take the time to define analysis-based decision-oriented information processing as the natural, larger, and more general category of processing within which OLAP and data warehousing each refer to complementary components. By defining OLAP within the scope of a well-grounded category, OLAP becomes well grounded.

Defining terms is a process of connecting what is new to what is already understood. As you will see, we build toward a definition of analysis-based decision-oriented processing by passing through the general requirements of good information processing and decision-oriented analysis with which everyone has some familiarity, even if that familiarity is more passive than active. I make it as easy as possible to understand OLAP by showing it as an extension of common sense, and by showing that the roots of OLAP are solidly grounded. Therefore, OLAP, like transaction processing, deserves to be a permanent part of our computing environment.

"OLAP" is not the only process term to have emerged in the last few years; "data warehousing" is another. As you can see in Appendix A, the two terms have at various times been defined in nearly identical ways. Are they identical? Is OLAP just another word for data warehousing? I believe they are complementary, and it is useful to understand their differences in order to appreciate the full range of processes required to create high-quality analysis-based decision-oriented information systems.

Basic Requirements of Information Processing

The cornerstone of all business activities (and any other intentional activities, for that matter) is information processing. This includes data collection, storage, transportation, manipulation, and retrieval (with or without the aid of computers). From the first sheepherders, who needed to tell when sheep were missing, to the Roman empire, which required status reports on its subjugates, to the industrial barons of the nineteenth century, who needed to keep track of their rail lines and oil fields, to modern enterprises of every variety, good information processing has always been essential to the survival of the organization.

The importance of good information can be thought of as the difference in value between right decisions and wrong decisions, where decisions are based on that information. The larger the difference between right and wrong decisions, the greater the importance of having good information. For example, poor information about consumer retail trends results in poor buying and allocation decisions for a retailer, which results in costly markdowns for what was overstocked and lost profit-making opportunity for what was understocked. Retailers tend to value accurate product-demand forecasts very highly. Good information about world events helps financial traders make better trading decisions, directly resulting in better profits for the trading firm. Major trading firms invest heavily in information technologies; good traders are very handsomely rewarded.

Regardless of what information is being processed or how it is being processed, the goals are essentially the same. Good information needs to be accurate, timely, and understandable. (Completeness is another essential attribute. It is left out here—no pun intended—because it is less applicable to computing systems than to humans, at least as long as computing systems are presumed to be incapable of intentionally withholding information.) All of the requirements are important. Imagine, for example, that you possessed the world's only program that could accurately predict interest rates. Would you suddenly become fabulously wealthy? It depends on the timeliness and understandability of the information. The program would be worthless if it took so long to access the predictions that by the time you had them they were already in the newspaper or if you could access them with sufficient time to act but received the information in some unintelligible form (like a typical credit report).

The first component of the functional requirements for OLAP comes from these general goals for good information processing: accuracy, timeliness, and understandability.

Differences between Operational Systems and Decision-oriented Systems

This section introduces a second component of the functional requirements for OLAP. It comes from the specialized requirements for analysis-based decision-oriented information processing relative to operational information processing.

The Source of These Differences

Buying, selling, producing, and transporting are common examples of business operations. Monitoring, evaluating, comparing, budgeting, planning, projecting, and allocating resources strategically are common examples of the business thinking that generates analysis-based decision-oriented information.

The information produced through these thinking activities is analysis-based because some data analysis, such as the calculation of a trend or a ratio or an aggregation, needs to occur as part of the activity. The information is also decision-oriented because it is in a form that makes it immediately useful for decision making. Knowing which products or customers are most profitable, knowing which pastures have the most lush grass, or knowing which outlets have slipped the most this year is the kind of information needed in order to make decisions such as which products should have their production increased, or which customers should be targeted for special promotions, or which fields should carry more sheep, or which outlets should be closed. The decision orientation of the analysis is essential. It serves to direct analysis toward useful purposes.

In contrast, many operational activities are decision-oriented without being based on analysis. For example, if a credit-card customer asks for a credit increase, a decision needs to be made. If the customer's record states that the customer is at his or her credit limit, the decision is no. The credit information was decision-oriented, but no analysis was involved in the decision.

Together, operations and decision-oriented analysis are at the core of all business activities, independent of their size, industry, legal form, or historical setting. Figure 1.1 highlights a number of diverse businesses in terms of their operational and analysis activities. Figure 1.2 shows the relationship between operations and analysis-based decisions for a merchant in fifteenth century Venice. Analysis-based decision-oriented activities take normal operating events such how much fabric is purchased on a weekly basis, or weekly changes in the internal inventory of fabrics, or sales of spices as inputs and return changes to operating events, such as changes in how much fabric is bought on a weekly basis, or changes in what clothes are produced, or changes in the selling price for spices, as decision outputs.

For small businesses, it is common for the same inputs, including software, to be used in multiple ways. For a small book shop, a software consultant, or a donut stand, one person with a single program may effectively run all operating and analysis aspects of the company. Such a program might be a spreadsheet, a desktop database, or a prepackaged solution. For midsized to large businesses and organizations, however, the world is significantly more complex, thereby creating a natural tendency for specialization.

Business	Operation	Decision-oriented Analysis
-Sheep farming 5000BC	-Raise sheep for milk, wool, meat	-Grow/shrink herd, stay or move on
-Trader in Venice 15th century	-Buy/sell fabrics and spices	-Pricing, suppliers, product line
-Railroad 19th Century	-Transport goods and people	-Track location, labor source
-Bank 20th Century	-Lending/borrowing money	-Interest rates -Target industries -Target customers -Portfolio analysis
-Retail clothing 20th Century	-Buy/sell consumer goods -Stocking, transporting	-How much shelf space/ product -When to mark down -How much to buy

Figure 1.1 Operations and analysis activities for a variety of businesses.

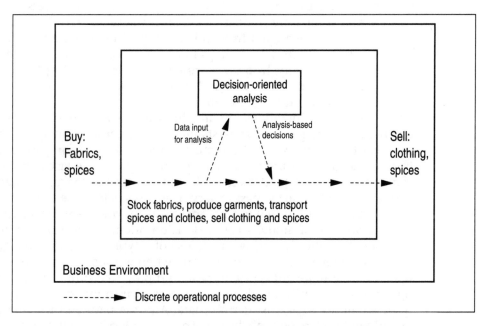

Figure 1.2 Operations and analysis activities for a merchant in Venice.

Current Differences between OLTP and Analysis-based Decision-oriented Processing

In a typical flow of daily operating events for an even moderately complex company, potential customers may ask sales staff questions about available products and make product purchase decisions that result in sales transactions. In parallel with sales events, products are produced, their inputs are purchased, and all stages of finished goods are transported and stocked. The sales, production, and cost information, which is constantly being generated, would be recorded and managed in one or more database(s) used for operational purposes. To answer customer questions, perform sales transactions, and do other operational tasks, employees query these databases for operational information.

Operational software activities tend to happen at a relatively constant rate (during periods of normal operations and excepting certain peaks). Data is updated as frequently as it is read. The data represents a current snapshot of the way things are, and each query goes against a small amount of information. Operational queries tend to go against data that was directly input. And the nature of the queries is generally understood in advance (or else you'll be talking to a supervisor). For example, when a customer tells you her account number and you've pulled up her record from the database, you might ask that customer to tell you her name and address, which you would then verify against your record. Verifying a name and address involves re-trieving and comparing nonderived data in the sense that the address information was not calculated from other inputs. The address was more likely furnished by the customer, perhaps in a previous order. The set of operations queries that are likely to be performed, such as retrieving the customer's record and verifying the name and address, is knowable in advance. It frequently follows a company procedure.

In contrast to operations-oriented information activities, and on a less frequent basis, managers and analysts may ask higher-level analytical questions such as what products have been most profitable for the company this year, is it the same group of products that were most profitable last year, how is the company doing this quarter versus the same quarter last year, or what kinds of customers exhibit the greatest loyalty. The answers to these types of questions represent information that is both analysis-based and decision-oriented.

The volume of analysis-based decision-oriented software activities may fluctuate dramatically during the course of a typical day. On average, data is read more frequently than written. And when written, it tends to be in batch updates. Data represents current, past, and projected future states, and single operations frequently involve many pieces of information at once. Analysis queries tend to go against derived data. And the nature of the queries is frequently not understood in advance. For example, a brand manager may begin an analytical session by querying for brand profitability by region. Each profitability number refers to the average of all products in the brand for all places in the region where the products are sold for the entire time period in question. Literally hundreds of thousands or millions of pieces of data may have been funneled into each profitability number. In this sense, the profitability numbers are high level and derived. If they had been planned numbers they might have still been high level, but directly entered instead of derived, so the level of atomicity for a datum is not synonymous with whether it is derived. If the profitability numbers looked unusual, the manager might then begin searching for why they were unusual. This process of unstructured exploration could take the manager to any corner of the database.

The differences between operational and analysis-based decision-oriented software activities are summarized in Table 1.1.

As a result of these differences between operational and analysis-based decision-oriented software activities, most midsize and larger companies use different software products for operations and for analysis, essentially for two reasons:

1. More demanding companies need software that is maximally efficient at operations processing and at analysis-oriented processing.

2. Fast updating is necessary for maximally efficient operations processing, and fast calculating (and the associated need for fast access to calculation inputs) is necessary for maximally efficient analysis-oriented processing, require mutually exclusive approaches to indexing.

In a nutshell, whereas you and I can get by with the same car for cruising around country roads and transporting loads, large corporations need race cars and trucks.

Software products devoted to the operations of a business, principally large-scale database systems, have come to be known as online transaction processing systems or OLTP. The development path for OLTP software has

Table 1.1 A Comparison of Operational and Analysis-based Decision-oriented Information Processing Activities

Operational Activities	*Analysis-based Decision-oriented Activities*
More frequent	Less frequent
More predictable	Less predictable
Smaller amounts of data per query	Larger amounts of data per query
Query mostly raw data	Query mostly derived data
Require mostly current data	Require past, present data and projections
Few, if any, complex derivations	Many complex derivations

followed a pretty straight line for the past 30 years. The goal has been to make systems handle larger amounts of data, process more transactions per unit time, and support larger numbers of concurrent users with ever greater robustness. Large-scale systems process upward of 1,000 transactions per second. Some, like the airline reservation system SABRE, can accommodate peak loads of more than 10,000 transactions per second.

In contrast, software products devoted to supporting analysis-based decision-oriented processes have gone under a variety of market category names. The market for these products has been more fragmented, having followed what may seem like a variety of paths over the past 30 years. In addition to the power analyst–aimed decision support system (DSS) products of the 1970s and the executive-aimed executive information systems (EIS) products of the 1980s, spreadsheets and statistical packages and inverted file databases (such as M204 from CCA) have all been geared at various segments of the analysis-based decision-oriented processing market. To conserve ink, I will use the acronym ABDOP.

Figure 1.3 represents the ABDOP category. It shows the chain of processing from source data to final end-user consumption. In between there may be multiple tiers of data storage and processing. Let's look at this more closely.

At one end there are possibly several data sources. These may include transaction systems and/or external data feeds such as the Internet or other subscription services. Note that the actual data sources, including the Internet, straddle the boundaries of the category—the boundary-straddling data also participates in some other functional category. For example, the transaction data also belongs to an OLTP system. Because the source data is generally copied into the ABDOP category, data and *metadata*, or data about the data, from the source(s) need to be kept in sync with data in the ABDOP data store(s).

Because there may be multiple data sources, it may be necessary to integrate and standardize the information coming from the different sources into a common format. A common type of integration that needs to be performed is that of data type. Of the more obvious kind, a string-encoded male/female category variable from one source may need to be integrated with a Boolean-encoded 1/0 from another. Of the less obvious kind, an integer-encoded number from one source may need to be integrated with a floating point–encoded number from another.

The raw data for analysis may be real or virtual. If it is real this means there is an actual data store. If it is virtual, there may be only links to the real source data that get invoked at request time so the requester may not know whether the data requested is actually present in a single data store. (Of course, the time it takes to process a query may be an indication.) If the data store is real, there needs to be at least one data server.

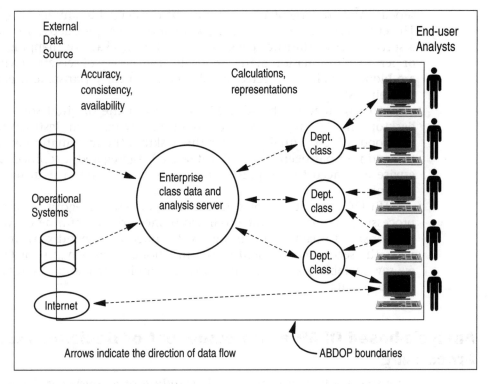

Figure 1.3 The ABDOP category.

Assuming that the organization in question is of moderate to large size, it is reasonable to assume that there exist two or more tiers of servers. An enterprise-class data and analysis server is one that is in the relative category of most powerful server in the organization. ("Relative" is used because one company's enterprise-class server may be another company's PC.) There may be one enterprise-class data server or many. Regardless of their numbers or power, data and analysis servers are more than just file servers. As their name implies, they need to perform analytical calculations. Some of the calculations may be associated with loads and performed in bulk; others may be initiated by end users.

Again, assuming the organization is of moderate to large size, a single enterprise-class data and analysis server will connect to a number of department-level data and analysis servers. Network wires, if not WANs, may be used here, and (as you will see in Chapter 9) bandwidth may pose a problem.

Finally, end users are connected to departmental servers and other servers. The connection between end users and servers is more n to m than n to 1. In words, any one of N end users may be connected to any m of M

servers. And any one of *M* servers may be connected to any *n* of *N* end users. The end users may be running any kind of personal productivity tool such as a spreadsheet or statistics package or graphics package or mapping program or personal information manager. Ideally, the variety of servers to which they are bidirectionally connected should serve as nearly transparent extensions to their desktop.

At each stage in the ABDOP chain, from the original sources to the desktop, the data is refined like any other raw material destined for product-hood. When it finally reaches the desktop, the information available to the end user has been cleansed, integrated, aggregated, extended, and otherwise enhanced to the point where it is immediately useful for decision making.

ABDOP is a natural, or software independent, category of information processing that serves as the grounded framework for defining OLAP (and its relationship to data warehousing, as described in Appendix A). It also provides the second component of the functional requirements for OLAP that we saw in Table 1.1: fast calculations of complex derivations and fast access to lots of data.

Analysis-based OLAP as a Component of Decision-oriented Processing

Now that we have a general understanding of analysis-based decision-oriented processing, let's zoom in on the main goals and challenges of ABDOP. We will then identify the functional requirements for OLAP in terms of a subset of the goals and challenges for ABDOP.

The Goals of ABDOP

Timeliness:

To ensure timeliness, an ABDOP system needs to guarantee the following:

1. Raw data has already been preprocessed or prepared for analysis. This refers to the data cleansing and integrating described earlier.
2. Data access is fast.
3. Data calculations are fast.

Accuracy:

To provide for *accuracy*, an ABDOP system needs to ensure that raw data is accurate and that calculations are accurate.

Understandability:

To provide for *understandability*, ABDOP systems need to ensure that views are easily reorganized and that interfaces are friendly or intuitive.

The biggest challenges of ABDOP are as follows:

❑ *Lots of data*—Very large data stores measuring in the tens, hundreds, and thousands of gigabytes

❑ *Many levels of detail*—From SKU codes to individual products, groups of products, product lines, brands, and more

❑ *Many data analysis factors*—Products, location, company organization, market, time

❑ *Lots of users of the same data*—Hundreds and thousands

❑ *Lots of sites*—Hundreds, thousands, and more

❑ *Decentralized decision making*—User-analysts who do not follow predefined procedures; they make autonomous decisions as to what data to access and how to analyze it

A given challenge can affect the ability to achieve multiple goals. For example, large amounts of data can increase the likelihood that some data is anomalous. Because it is not possible to manually check large amounts of data, routines must be run to scan for anomalous data. But this requires that someone state what constitutes anomalous data in order to define the routine.

Calculating with large amounts of data has its own complications that may introduce errors. Missing and meaningless data are likely, and they need to be properly dealt with. And there are likely to be differences in the way existent data need to be treated. For example, sales tax rates may need to be applied differentially to stores as a function of the cities and states where they are located because of differences in tax rates. Different cities in an economic analysis may need to be weighted as a function of their population.

The presence of lots of data clearly affects speed of data access. This could have an impact on basic retrieval or on calculations that depend on large numbers of inputs. This may become more important if certain calculations are performed only at request time.

The abundance of data can affect the understandability of that data. Getting a feeling for the whole of the data set requires more compression than with smaller data sets. There is thus a greater risk of compressing the data to the point where its essential features are no longer recognizable. The challenge of large amounts of data affects all the goals of ABDOP.

Because most of the challenges affect multiple goals, a useful (and, I might add, multidimensional) way to think about the functional requirements for ABDOP is as a matrix of goal challenges. Not every intersection of a

Table 1.2 The Goal Challenges for OLAP Relative to All of Analysis-Based Decision-Oriented Processing.

Goals/challenges	Lots of Data	Lots of Levels	Lots of Factors	Lots of Users	Multiple Sites	Decentralized
Timely	Preprocessed	dw	dw	dw		dw	
	Fast access	OLAP	OLAP	OLAP	dw	dw	
	Fast calculations	OLAP	OLAP	OLAP	OLAP	dw	
Accurate	Accurate raw data	dw	dw	dw	dw	dw	
	Computational expressiveness	OLAP	OLAP	OLAP		OLAP	
Understandability	Friendly interface	OLAP	OLAP	OLAP			
	Flexible views	OLAP	OLAP	OLAP		OLAP	dw

goal and a challenge is equally important. Unimportant cells are left blank. OLAP, as a set of functional requirements, is defined in terms of a subset of ABDOP's important goal challenges. The other important goal challenges, as discussed in Appendix A, are the focus of data warehousing and are marked "dw" in Table 1.2. In all fairness to, and from my own personal experience with, OLAP, there are many times where building or using an OLAP application highlights, and can help to resolve, problems with data accuracy.

Table 1.2 is indicative of the major emphases in OLAP activities, as evidenced by the vendors and users of OLAP software. It is not meant to be taken as a static or controversial description.

Functional Requirements of OLAP Systems

In the last section we saw that the main goals for OLAP are fast access, fast calculations, computational expressiveness, user-friendly interfaces, and flexible viewing, given the challenges of lots of data with many levels of detail and multiple factors in a decentralized multiuser environment. Achieving these goals, given the various data and environmental challenges, constitutes the essential functional requirements for OLAP. After illustrating how typical challenges, if they are not addressed, cause problems when performing decision-oriented analytical processing, we will end this chapter by looking more closely at OLAP's functional requirements and how they need to overcome these challenges.

Answering particular queries may take too long because every time a manager asks a question about a class of customers defined in terms of a set of attributes, a whole SQL routine needs to be written by a database programmer. Or it may take too much disk space to store all the relevant analytical data. Or it may just be impossible to allocate certain costs below the department level. Or it may be dangerous for more than a handful of users to be on the system at once. Or it may be impossible for end users to edit the data. Or the company might want to perform nightly incremental computes, which means that all changes from operations need to be reflected in the analytical data within something as small as a four-hour window. Or reports, once generated, may be hard to reconfigure. Or the network may get jammed every time a client makes a request for data from a server.

In short, end users are usually trying to get at more data and calculations based on that data, faster, and with greater viewing flexibility than can be achieved with traditional technologies, which are generally a combination of SQL databases, SQL-based data query tools, and spreadsheets.

Any software product claiming to fulfill the functional requirements for OLAP should give you fast, flexible, shared access to all analytical information. It should allow you to view and browse through information any way you like. It should be powerful enough to calculate profits and allocations across products, divisions, and currencies. It should be friendly enough to be learned by a nontechnical person with a minimum of effort. And it should be integrated in both a user sense—integrating multiple users by allowing them simultaneous access to the same data—and a data sense—integrating data from across the enterprise and its environs.

Requirement 1: Fast Access and Calculations

Speed is a crucial component of OLAP. It's more than just the thrill—it's about maintaining your train of thought. OLAP requires supporting ad hoc analytical queries, some of which may require computations performed on the fly. For example, someone might start a session by querying how overall product profitability was in Europe last quarter. Seeing that profitability was lower than expected, he or she might navigate down into individual countries while still looking at overall product profitability. Here a person might see that some countries were significantly below the others and so would naturally navigate further down into product groups for these countries, always looking for some data that could help explain the higher-level anomalies. First glance might not reveal anything unusual. Sales were where they were supposed to be, as were returns and manufacturing costs. But wait, indirect costs were substantially higher for the errant countries. Further navigating into indirect costs might reveal that significant taxes were recently levied on those products (possibly the result of a trade dispute), which served to sharply reduce their profitability because prices remained stable due to market competition.

Each step in this train of thought constituted a query. Each query was iterative in the sense that it followed the result of the previous one. Anyone engaged in this sort of querying wants to maintain the momentum. It would be difficult to follow this type of analytical thread if the mean response time per query were measured in days, hours, or even tens of minutes. The stated goal of OLAP systems is to provide a mean response time of five seconds or less regardless of the type of query or the size of the database.

In the past, analysts who needed quick response time placed data extracts in local, single-user applications that were fully dedicated to a single user/analyst. Today's challenge is for systems to provide blazing response time to access and computation requests, while working with large data sets in a multiuser environment distributed across a network. Some tools provide for this by precomputing all aggregates. This can, however, lead to database explosion (as described in Chapter 7). Even if you could store all the precomputed results, the increase in the size of the database can actually offset any gains made to query response time by precomputing. For maximally efficient access, tools need to provide the right combination of precomputed and query-time computed results.

Requirement 2: Powerful Analytical Capabilities

As stated earlier, there is a lot more to analysis than simply aggregating numbers. Sure, it is important to be able to correctly sum and average large quantities of data, but most of the important information results from the intelligent comparison of ratios and inferred trends over time and other dimensions. In other words, a good part of the querying that takes place in analytical processing contains embedded analysis. And as you will see in Chapter 3, where we get into the technology, the combination of aggregating and comparison analysis can get pretty tricky. Once again, this is why the category is called analysis-based decision-oriented processing.

For example, imagine you are the sales director for an electronic products company that just finished its first year of international operations. You might want to know which product categories had profit levels abroad that differed the most from their profit levels in the United States. And you might want to see the results ordered from most positive to most negative. To answer this query, the system needs to perform a variety of calculations. Profits need to be calculated per product. Profit values need to be normalized so they can be compared across products. Normalized profit levels need to be aggregated to the product category level. This needs to be done across time for the United States and for the new foreign market. Time aggregations may need to be adjusted for differences in reporting periods and/or number of days per period. The profit level for each product group then needs to be compared between the two markets, and finally the differences in profit level need to be ordered from most positive to most negative. In an OLAP system, these types of calculations should be as straightforward to define as they are to say.

To provide true OLAP functionality, a software tool needs to contain a sophisticated calculation language. It must be possible, for example, to define exceptions to such things as unit costs, productivity rates, rent, or head count without resorting to programming.

Requirement 3: Flexibility

Flexibility is another crucial component of OLAP functionality. It carries a variety of meanings—flexible viewing, flexible definitions, flexible analysis, flexible interfaces. Systems need to be flexible in all these ways. They need to support a full range of unplanned calculations because analysis-based decision-oriented thinking is inherently difficult to automate or specify.

We can present or look at information in many ways. View flexibility means the user can easily choose to see information in the form of graphs, matrices, or charts, and within any form, such as matrices, and in any orientation of row and column headers.

In terms of definitions, users (whoever has the relevant authority) should be able to change the names of descriptors, the formatting of numbers, the definitions of formulas, the triggers for automatic processes, and the location of source data, all without incurring any undue penalty.

In contrast, the DSS systems of the 1970s and the EIS systems of the 1980s were often very fast and powerful but at the cost of being rigid. Usually a team of developers needed to custom-write decision support or aggregation routines. Thereafter, these routines were simply called. Although they performed well, they were hard-coded and thus inflexible. If an end user wanted to change the way an aggregation routine was performed, it required programmatically editing the application. Generally, the categories of data to be processed, such as the names of departments or the names of countries, were hard-coded as well.

Interface flexibility is a more general form of what is sometimes called an "intuitive interface." Intuitiveness or friendliness is so important it almost deserves its own category. I have elected to keep it under the more general heading of flexibility because not everybody has the same concept of what's intuitive. Thus, to allow everyone the ability to interact with a system in the way that makes the most sense for that person, a flexible or friendly interface is needed.

Having a fast, powerful system is no good if you cannot figure out how to use it and you don't understand what it is telling you. On the input side, friendliness affects the user's ability to quickly define what the user wants to do. Like other types of flexibility, friendliness (interface flexibility) applies to a variety of areas such as model definition, model browsing, formula specification, direct data input, and external data source links. The friendlier the software, the less time you spend thinking about how to do something and the more time you spend actually doing it.

This is especially important in today's world. In earlier times, analysis tended to be performed by small groups of individuals within the organization who devoted most of their time to analysis. These people could afford the steep learning curves associated with DSS-style analytical systems. Today, however, analysis is increasingly performed by a wider scope of persons, each of whom devotes only a small percentage of her or his time to analysis. These people need to be up and running quickly. They need an analytical environment that allows them to maximally leverage what they already know so they can be up and running very quickly. The standard paradigm for friendliness these days, on the input side, is a graphical user interface. Of course, friendly is whatever appeals to the end user. Many people still prefer a command-line interface supporting a well-documented 4GL for its greater speed and power of expression.

Requirement 4: Multiuser Support

Corporations are collaborative work environments. As a result of downsizing and decentralizing, the relative number of employees who need read and write access to decision-empowering analytical data is on the rise. Problems discovered by a regional sales manager, for example, may need to be communicated to a distribution or manufacturing manager for prompt resolution. Forecasts examined by senior executives may reflect data that was generated from a dozen or more separate departments. For global corporations, some of those departments may not even share the same country or language.

As with any complex issue, multiuser support is not a black-and-white issue. It is a question of degrees. There can be multiuser read based on separate caches for each user with no write-back capabilities. This may satisfy some applications like sales reporting, where the source of the data came from operational systems. There can be multiuser read/write with all the processing done on the server. This may satisfy budgeting applications where the budget is centrally controlled on the server. And there can be multiuser read/write where the processing and data are distributed between client and server, where the server is intelligent enough to know when data should be processed on the server and when on the client, and where the server offers a multiuser cache. Because it holds out the promise of the most efficient use of enterprise computing resources, the last and richest form of multiuser computing is in most vendors' sights.

Conclusion

Information processing is a part of all organizations regardless of whether they use computers. The major subdivisions in information processing reflect the major subdivisions of organizational activity: operations and decision-oriented analysis. The terms OLAP and data warehousing are complementary terms, each of which refers to a component of the overall functional requirements of analysis-based decision-oriented information processing. Whereas data warehousing represents a server-centric or supply-side view of analysis-based decision-oriented information processing, OLAP represents a use-centric view of the same function. The major requirements for OLAP are fast data access, fast calculations, computational expressiveness, user-friendly interfaces, flexible views, and multiuser support.

In Chapter 2 we will look at why the two main traditional technologies for providing OLAP functionality—SQL and spreadsheets—are inadequate for the job. Following that, in Chapter 3, we will look at the main features offered by multidimensional technology and see why it is more naturally suited for creating decision-oriented analytical information systems.

The Limitations of Spreadsheets and SQL

In Chapter 1 we defined analysis-based decision-oriented processing as a natural category of information processing that stems from the general goals of good information, the age-old business distinction between operations and analysis, and modern-day information challenges such as large amounts of data and multiple users in a decentralized environment. Relative to this category, OLAP was described in terms of the following functional requirements:

- ❑ Speed of data access
- ❑ Speed of calculations
- ❑ Computational sophistication
- ❑ Flexible interfaces (views and controls)
- ❑ Multiuser support

During the past 10 years, the two most commonly used product technologies for delivering analysis-based decision-oriented information to end users have been databases and spreadsheets. Spreadsheets have been predominantly end user–oriented, while databases have usually been set up and administered by IT professionals. Typically, end users were given access either to canned query templates or, more recently, to easy-to-use query tools existing within a managed query environment.

This chapter explores why traditional spreadsheet and database approaches to organizing, managing, and querying data are inadequate for meeting the functional requirements of OLAP applications. We will start with a quick review of the last 10 years, during which time both spreadsheet and

21

database vendors have added significant amounts of OLAP functionality to their products. You will see that technology producers have been aware for quite some time that the traditional tools in their original form did not satisfy end users' analytical requirements. Then we will get into specific examples of where spreadsheet and database technologies break down. To provide direct evidence of the problems, I will focus this section on the functional requirements of computational sophistication and view flexibility. In other words, we will examine the difficulties that spreadsheets and SQL/relational databases have in specifying the calculations required for OLAP and in specifying the views required for using the data. We will not try to compare calculation or access times. (Comparisons of access and computation methods occur in Chapter 8. Also, there is a section on the OLAP benchmark in Appendix C.) For those readers uninterested in the historical evidence that spreadsheets and SQL/relational databases have evolved toward supporting increasing amounts of OLAP functionality, you may safely skip the first section in this chapter.

Limitations of Traditional Spreadsheet and Database Technologies

Spreadsheets and OLAP

Spreadsheets were originally positioned against the calculator by promoting their ability to perform what-if calculations. Instead of having to rewrite a series of interdependent numbers, such as a total of line items in a budget, just to see what would happen if one or more inputs were changed and then manually reperform the computation, the spreadsheet allowed users to define the result in terms of a formula. In this way, users could simply change the value of an input and the spreadsheet would automatically recalculate the total. The need for spreadsheets was a no-brainer.

In the 1980s, as personal computers became more powerful and increasing numbers of people were performing analysis on their desktops, the demand increased for higher-level functionality, to which the spreadsheet market responded in a variety of ways.

First there came the spreadsheet add-ins such as Panaview, Look 'n' Link, and Budget Express. These add-in tools were designed to compensate for the difficulties that spreadsheets had with aggregating data and combining worksheets. For example, Budget Express enabled users to create a multilevel spreadsheet outline that they could then collapse and expand. This helped with aggregations. Look n' Link allowed users to link aggregations from one worksheet into a cell of another worksheet. This also helped for working with larger amounts of data.

The functionality embraced by the market in the form of add-ins eventually became incorporated into the spreadsheets themselves.[1] Packages like Lucid 3D offered linked worksheets. Version 3 of Lotus's 1-2-3 added addressable pages to the rows and columns. In this way, if rows represented *products* and columns represented *stores*, pages could represent *weeks* and the total yearly sales of all products for all stores could be defined as the *sum across weekly pages for the all product by all store cell.*

Even with increased functionality, creating near-OLAP style functionality in a spreadsheet is still very cumbersome. In the early 1990s I worked at Power Thinking Tools, which had developed a desktop multidimensional analysis tool. We were frequently asked the question, "Why can't I create a multidimensional model with a spreadsheet?" We intuitively felt that spreadsheets weren't suited for multidimensional modeling, but we did some direct testing to better understand the obstacles.

We defined a small, yet typical multidimensional model for comparison testing. It consisted of *stores, time periods, products,* and *measures. Stores, time periods,* and *products* each contained several hierarchical levels. The test actions consisted of defining and performing simple aggregations, more complex aggregations that contained weighting and inferencing schemes, and a variety of views. Ad hoc queries were conducted as well. No serious analysis was performed.

It took an experienced spreadsheet macro programmer eight hours to define the macros and lookup tables necessary to create all the aggregation levels, calculations, and views. (The test was performed using Lotus 1-2-3, Quattro Pro, and Microsoft Excel.) Using our product, FreeThink, the entire model could be defined and calculated in less than 15 minutes.

Nowadays, products such as Excel offer pivot tables. Pivot tables, or *n*-way cross-tabs, are multidimensional. And any survey of the OLAP market space would have to include a product like Excel because it offers some OLAP functionality. However, at this time, Excel's pivot table functionality is not integrated into its core spreadsheet structures. Because you have to import data from your Excel worksheet into the Excel pivot tables, functionally speaking the pivot table is not a spreadsheet.

OLAP, the Relational Model, and SQL Databases

SQL databases are the commercial implementations of the Relational Data Model, which was initially defined by Edgar Codd in his 1970 paper, "A Relational Model of Data for Large Shared Databanks."[2] The conceptual schema of the Relational Data Model is largely derived from set theory (and theory of relations) and the predicate calculus. The relational model defines, among other things, a declaratively oriented relational calculus and a procedurally oriented relational algebra. The combination of the calculus and the algebra defines a complete data definition and data manipulation language. While the relational model freed the database designer/user from having to think about the physical storage and access of data, the relational model turned out to be overly focused on low-level detail for the higher-level work of programmers and end-user analysts. It was particularly difficult to define decision support applications (or any other kind of application) that depended on complex data aggregation. As a result, soon after Codd published his original paper, work began on building higher-level abstractions into the relational model.

All through the 1970s and into the 1980s, many academic papers were written on adding abstraction capabilities to the relational model. Abstract data types are one approach to looking at the problem of aggregation. In many approaches such as ADABPTL[3] and DAPLEX[4], notions of hierarchy were added to relational concepts. In one groundbreaking article, Smith and Smith wrote about adding two new abstraction types—aggregates and generalizations. Aggregate objects were complex data types or what today would be called objects (though interobject "messaging" was not a part of the aggregate type). For example, "hotel reservation" might be an aggregate consisting of the fields *date, time, reservation taker, confirmation number, name of reserving party, date of reservation, number of days of stay, number of persons in party, type of room requested (bed types, smoking or non-smoking, floor, etc.),* and *price per night.* Another aggregate could be "airline reservation," consisting of the fields *date, time, reservation taker, confirmation number, date of flight, time of flight, flight number, number of seats, position of seats, fare class, method of payment, special requests.* A generalization of hotel and airline reservation might be "reservation." The fields associated with reservation might be *date, time, name of reservation taker, reservation number, date of reservation, name of person in whose name the reservation is made,* and *number of parties in reservation.* The fields associated with the generalization "reservation" would be passed on to or inherited by any aggregate that was a child/specialization of the generalization "reservation."

Even Dr. Codd wrote academically on the topic when in 1978 he published "Extending the Database Relational Model to Capture More Meaning."[5] His focus in that paper was on defining hierarchical data types and a variety of hierarchical relationships, such as subtypes and supertypes as extensions to the basic structures of the relational model. The work on database semantics led to the development of object-oriented, or OO, programming methods, OO databases, entity-relationship data modeling, and knowledge bases.

By the early 1980s with the release of SQL database products from Oracle and IBM, relational databases were becoming a commercial reality. As a part of that reality, SQL, which had evolved from experiments with database languages that attempted to implement the relational model, became the de facto standard commercial relational database language. By the early 1990s, more than 100 commercial database products supported some dialect of SQL.

Although SQL's original goal may have been to be an end-user query language (hence the original name SEQUEL from "Structured English Query Language"), the language proved too abstruse for typical end users. In the same way that products were built to extend the capabilities of spreadsheets, products were built to extend the capabilities (or at least hide the syntax) of SQL. Query by example, graphical queries, natural language queries, and arranged end-user queries were all attempts to hide the complexity of SQL generation from the end user. This occurred because *analyzing data and exploring relationships are not part of the SQL vocabulary*. For example, *A Guide to the SQL Standard* by Chris Date and Hugh Darwin and *Instant SQL Programming* by Joe Celko do not even treat the most basic operations of analysis such as comparisons.[6] As you will see in the next section, there is a good reason for this. Most types of comparisons are very difficult to specify in SQL.

Plenty of circumstantial evidence suggests that neither spreadsheets nor SQL databases adequately meet users' needs for OLAP functionality.

Proving the Point: Some Examples

Indirect evidence is fine to whet your appetite. But now let's follow some specific examples so you can see first-hand why it is so difficult to provide OLAP-style functionality with spreadsheets and SQL databases. The best way to judge the performance of SQL and spreadsheets is to put them to work on the same problem.

One metaphor for looking at the problem of generating analysis-based decision-oriented views from base data is to think of the entire process as an information economy, as illustrated in Figure 2.1. We have a common supply function; this refers to our base data and the rate at which it is refreshed. And we have a common demand function; this refers to analytical reports and views and the rate at which end users consume/view them. In between we have a manufacturing logistics or production problem. The key production question may be phrased as "What is the most efficient method to define and produce the consumer information goods demanded by our end users in an accurate, timely, and understandable fashion?"

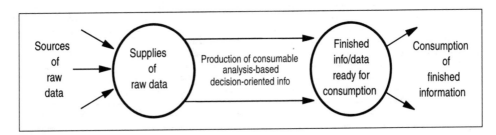

Figure 2.1 The information economy.

	Jan		Feb		Mar		Quarter 1	
	actuals	variance	actuals	variance	actuals	variance	actuals	variance
skin care	4,156	1.01	4,572	1.01	5,034	1.01	13,846	1.01
soap	2,517	1.00	2,769	1.00	3,051	1.00	8,391	1.00
rose water soap	1,342	0.99	1,476	0.99	1,629	0.99	4,472	0.99
olive oil soap	1,175	1.02	1,293	1.02	1,427	1.02	3,919	1.02
lotion	1,639	1.03	1,803	1.03	1,988	1.03	5,455	1.03
hypoallerg. lotion	1,639	1.03	1,803	1.03	1,988	1.03	5,455	1.03
furniture	4,953	1.06	5,448	1.06	5,998	1.06	16,484	1.06
office	3,796	1.09	4,176	1.09	4,598	1.09	12,625	1.09
bookshelves	1,501	0.99	1,651	0.99	1,821	0.99	4,998	0.99
dividers	2,295	1.16	2,525	1.16	2,782	1.16	7,626	1.16
home	1,157	0.99	1,273	0.99	1,405	0.99	3,860	0.99
mattresses	1,157	0.99	1,273	0.99	1,405	0.99	3,860	0.99
All products	9,109	1.04	10,020	1.04	11,027	1.04	30,331	1.04

Figure 2.2 Product manager's quarterly sales report.

A Common Starting Point

Let's start with the desired outputs or finished consumable information. Imagine that you are the sales director for a retail organization and that you are responsible for the ongoing analysis of sales for all the products sold in all your stores. As a part of your normal analysis process, you want to see monthly sales totals by product and product category. You also want to see monthly total product sales broken down by region and store. In addition to cumulative totals, you want to see how the actuals vary from plans. These views or reports are illustrated in Figures 2.2 and 2.3.

Figures 2.2 and 2.3 represent typical decision-oriented information. For example, knowing that the sale of desks has been falling for the last four weeks relative to plan may help you decide that there should be a midwinter sale on desks. On the other hand, even if sales are slow this month relative to last month, if sales have been consistently slower this month for the past three years it might indicate that it's some sort of as-yet-unaccounted-for seasonal variation, not indicative of a longer-term slowdown, and thus not cause for a sale. Regardless of how these views were generated, they are common to any decision-oriented analysis process.

Sales	Jan		Feb		Mar		Quarter 1	
All products	actuals	variance	actuals	variance	actuals	variance	actuals	variance
Northeast	4,369	1.02	4,806	1.02	5,291	1.02	14,551	1.02
Ridgewood	1,985	1.04	2,184	1.04	2,407	1.04	6,600	1.04
Newbury	1,824	1.01	2,006	1.01	2,212	1.01	6,067	1.01
Avon	560	0.97	616	0.97	683	0.97	1,884	0.97
Midwest	4,740	1.06	5,214	1.06	5,740	1.06	15,779	1.06
Francis	2,643	1.11	2,907	1.11	3,203	1.11	8,778	1.11
Nikki's	1,390	1.00	1,529	1.00	1,687	1.00	4,631	1.00
Roger's	707	1.00	778	1.00	860	1.00	2,370	1.00
All Company	9,109	1.04	10,020	1.04	11,027	1.04	30,331	1.04

Figure 2.3 Regional manager's quarterly sales report.

Now let's consider the raw data from which these views were constructed. It is not as easy to define a common starting point as it is a common end point. Different production techniques, notably SQL and spreadsheets, have such radically different logic that the source data will tend to be structured differently between them.

The Difficulty of Defining a Common Source Data Set for Spreadsheets and SQL

SQL, if thought of as a language for defining and manipulating relational tables, is supposedly application-neutral when it comes to structuring base data. Base data, in a relational sense, is supposed to be structured or normalized on the basis of its own internal relationships. This facilitates the database update operations that characterize transaction processing. But for many decision-oriented applications, SQL tables are intentionally denormalized (or physically optimized) to speed up queries.

When thinking through a problem with spreadsheets, the way base data is structured (which is to say, the form of the data) has a great impact on what can be done with it. This will become even clearer as we get into the specific examples. It is important to bring up now because it isn't possible to define a realistic starting point where the data has the same form for both spreadsheets and SQL. Rather, our common starting point will be defined in terms of the content of the data.

Imagine that all the data has been collected, refined, and now resides in a large base table. In addition, there may be some adjunct lookup tables. A "star" schema for this base data is shown in Figure 2.4.

This table schema is called a star schema because the central "fact" table is usually depicted as surrounded by each of the "dimension" tables that describe each dimension. In this example, the base sales data table is the fact table and each lookup table is a dimension table.

Notice how the stores, weeks, and products columns in the "fact" table in Figure 2.4 contain numeric values. Fact tables can grow to a huge number of rows. Because each value of the store, weeks, and product column is repeated many times, using a simple value in the base table and storing the full name only once in the dimension's lookup table saves space.

The lookup tables also contain hierarchy information relating each *store, week,* and *product* with its higher-level aggregations. For example, *store 1* in the base table of Figure 2.4 connects with the *'Store Lookup'* table where it has the name *Ridgewood* and rolls up to the *Northeast region. Product 2* in the base

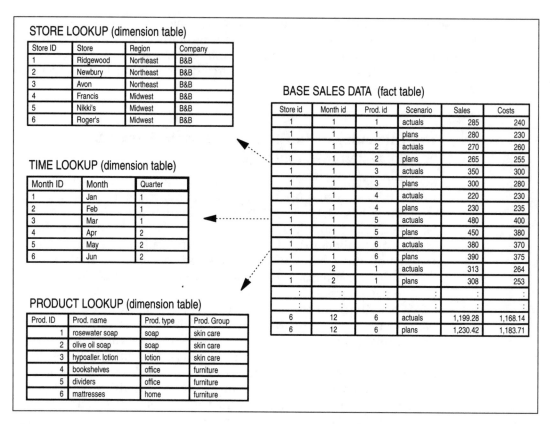

STORE LOOKUP (dimension table)

Store ID	Store	Region	Company
1	Ridgewood	Northeast	B&B
2	Newbury	Northeast	B&B
3	Avon	Northeast	B&B
4	Francis	Midwest	B&B
5	Nikki's	Midwest	B&B
6	Roger's	Midwest	B&B

TIME LOOKUP (dimension table)

Month ID	Month	Quarter
1	Jan	1
2	Feb	1
3	Mar	1
4	Apr	2
5	May	2
6	Jun	2

PRODUCT LOOKUP (dimension table)

Prod. ID	Prod. name	Prod. type	Prod. Group
1	rosewater soap	soap	skin care
2	olive oil soap	soap	skin care
3	hypoaller. lotion	lotion	skin care
4	bookshelves	office	furniture
5	dividers	office	furniture
6	mattresses	home	furniture

BASE SALES DATA (fact table)

Store id	Month id	Prod. id	Scenario	Sales	Costs
1	1	1	actuals	285	240
1	1	1	plans	280	230
1	1	2	actuals	270	260
1	1	2	plans	265	255
1	1	3	actuals	350	300
1	1	3	plans	300	280
1	1	4	actuals	220	230
1	1	4	plans	230	235
1	1	5	actuals	480	400
1	1	5	plans	450	380
1	1	6	actuals	380	370
1	1	6	plans	390	375
1	2	1	actuals	313	264
1	2	1	plans	308	253
⋮	⋮	⋮	⋮	⋮	⋮
⋮	⋮	⋮	⋮	⋮	⋮
6	12	6	actuals	1,199.28	1,168.14
6	12	6	plans	1,230.42	1,183.71

Figure 2.4 Common base table for sales data and lookup tables for stores, times, and products.

table connects with the *'Product Lookup'* table where it has the name *'olive oil soap'* and rolls up into the product type *'soap'* in the *skin care products group*. In practice, the lookup tables may also contain additional attribute information about the individual stores, times, and products such as the square footage per store.

This base data content, though not necessarily the base data form, would be the same regardless of whether you were going to build your analytical model with a spreadsheet, with an SQL database or, as we will see later on, with a multidimensional tool. Consider it a common starting point.

Trying to Provide OLAP Functionality with a Spreadsheet

Now let's explore how we satisfy end-user information demands using spreadsheets.

The first problem you face with spreadsheets is deciding the form of the base data. Would you build one gigantic worksheet? And if so, how would you organize it? Would you nest weeks within stores within scenarios along the rows and then nest measures within products along the columns? Or, perhaps, you would nest measures within stores within products along the rows and nest weeks within scenarios along the columns? The possibilities are numerous. And the method you choose affects the ease of defining subsequent structures. For example, the auto-sum function in a spreadsheet will only work with contiguous cells, so cells that you want to sum need to occupy such contiguous ranges. You definitely have to think about how you are structuring your base data.

Probably, for manageability reasons, you would distribute the base data across a variety of worksheets. Here again, there are many options. You could create a separate worksheet for each product and/or each store and/or each week. Theoretically, any method will work. Of course you will be faced with the unpleasant task of integrating data from many worksheets, perhaps hundreds or even thousands. For example, if you decide to break up the base data into groups of simple worksheets so that each worksheet can be managed more easily, and toward that end you decide that all base data worksheets will be organized with stores along the rows by weeks along the columns, with a separate worksheet for each product, scenario, and measure, and if you assume there are 100 products, 3 scenarios, and 10 measures (not an overly complex model), then you will have 3,000 separate base data worksheets.

The next major problem you face is trying to aggregate the base data. Each of the worksheets will need to have the rollup information embedded for the purposes of defining aggregates. Or, you could define even more worksheets. In either event, there will be massive amounts of structural redundancy. For example, you will need to define city and regional aggregates for stores. Given that there are 3,000 worksheets, all organized by store, you will have to make 3,000 copies of a store-city-region hierarchy, one for each worksheet.

Hierarchies are not the only structures that are massively duplicated—so too are formulas. After all, spreadsheets work with cell-based formulas. Every aggregate cell needs to be defined with a formula. Not only do you have to repeat the store hierarchy information 3,000 times, but for each of those 3,000 times you would have to repeat, for example, the formula that sums stores 1 through 3 into the Northeast region for each of 52 weeks. So the formula that says "compute the value for the Northeast region as the sum of stores 1 through 3," which in a multidimensional model is defined once, would be defined 3,000 × 52 or 156,000 times across all your worksheets!

Defining hierarchies for the nonrepeated dimension values, in this example, *products, scenarios,* and *measures,* is no less complicated. Creating product

Sales
Actuals

		Quarter 1	Quarter 2	Quarter 3	Quarter 4
Northeast	skin care	7,191	9,556	12,857	17,889
	furniture	7,360	9,780	13,157	18,305
Midwest	skin care	6,655	8,843	11,905	16,565
	furniture	9,124	12,126	16,291	22,662

Figure 2.5 An aggregated spreadsheet view.

aggregates requires linking each underlying product worksheet to the appropriate aggregate worksheet, *on a cell-by-cell basis.* With 100 stores and 52 weeks in a one-year model, this means creating 5,200 links for each aggregate worksheet. Can you think of anyone who really wants to do this?

Assuming that, through some combination of perseverance and luck, you have managed to create all the necessary aggregations, the question remains: How are you going to view the aggregates? As long as you are viewing information in the form that you defined it for the purposes of aggregation, there is no problem. For example, if you defined your low-level spreadsheets with products nested within stores along the rows and variables nested within time along the columns, your aggregate view would look like that shown in Figure 2.5.

What if you wanted to compare how different regions performed for the same products? In other words, what if you wanted to see how toys sold in the Northeast as opposed to the Southeast? You would want to see a view, such as the one shown in Figure 2.6, where regions were nested inside of products along the rows. The view shows the same information as the one in Figure 2.5, but the arrangement is different. Unfortunately, the spreadsheet offers no simple way to rearrange views. As any spreadsheet user knows all too well, you need to build the view from scratch. The fastest way (and the word "fast" is definitely misleading here) to build the new view is to create a

Sales
Actuals

		Quarter 1	Quarter 2	Quarter 3	Quarter 4
skin care	Northeast	7,191	9,556	12,857	17,889
	Midwest	6,655	8,843	11,905	16,565
furniture	Northeast	7,360	9,780	13,157	18,305
	Midwest	9,124	12,126	16,291	22,662

Figure 2.6 View reorganization.

new view template with just the margins filled in, then bring in the data through intersheet references. Because the organization of the two sheets is different, you will need one formulaic link per cell. Spreadsheets have problems with both aggregation and view reorganization.

The central reason why spreadsheets have such problems trying to create a multidimensional model is that spreadsheets cannot separate the structure of a model from the views of that model. For example, there is no way in a spreadsheet to capture the model's dimensional hierarchy information apart from creating worksheets that embody the dimensions in views.[7] As a result, the same worksheets that represent your base data limit the aggregate views that can be created. And each view, such as the ones shown in Figures 2.5 and 2.6, represents a separate grid of numbers. The cell-based formula logic of a spreadsheet and the need to massively duplicate structural information are both consequences of this lack of separation.

Although it is theoretically possible to create hierarchical multidimensional views with a traditional spreadsheet, it is practically infeasible. Add to this the fact that today's challenge is enterprise-wide and requires server and client resources combined across a network, and you can see why RAM-based spreadsheet solutions are simply out of the question.

Using Spreadsheets as Display Vehicles for Multidimensional Systems

Before closing the book on spreadsheets, it is fair to say that spreadsheet and multidimensional products share the same display grid or matrix metaphor. This is why (as you will see in the next chapter and in Section III) spreadsheets make such a fine vehicle for displaying views or slices of a multidimensional model. Because almost everybody is familiar with how to perform analysis with a spreadsheet, many vendors of multidimensional tools have intentionally used spreadsheet products as interfaces.

Trying to Provide OLAP Functionality with SQL

As we have seen, it is not so easy to deliver OLAP-style functionality with a spreadsheet. Let's take a look at doing it with SQL. After all, SQL is a database language based on structured English. It is supposed to be powerful and intuitive.

Look again at Figure 2.4. These are the base tables for our example model. If SQL were being used to perform the aggregations, it would create one aggregate table for each unique combination of aggregation levels. With 4 levels for time, 3 for stores, and 3 for products, there are 36 unique aggregation

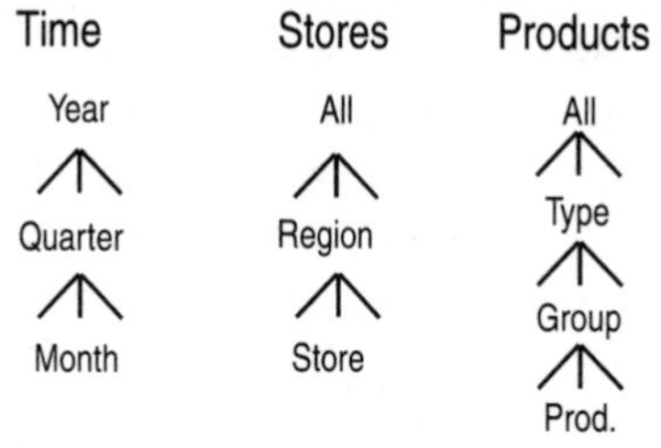

	Time			Stores			Products	
	Year			All			All	
	Quarter			Region			Type	
	Month			Store			Group	
							Prod.	

1	month.store.product	13	qtr.store.product	25	year.store.product
2	month.store.pr group	14	qtr.store.pr group	26	year.store.pr group
3	month.store.pr type	15	qtr.store.pr type	27	year.store.pr type
4	month.store.all prod	16	qtr.store.all prod	28	year.store.all prod
5	month.region.product	17	qtr.region.product	29	year.region.product
6	month.region.pr group	18	qtr.region.pr group	30	year.region.pr group
7	month.region.pr type	19	qtr.region.pr type	31	year.region.pr type
8	month.region.all prod	20	qtr.region.all prod	32	year.region.all prod
9	month.all strs.product	21	qtr.all strs.product	33	year.all strs.product
10	month.all strs.pr group	22	qtr.all strs.pr group	34	year.all strs.pr group
11	month.all strs.pr type	23	qtr.all strs.pr type	35	year.all strs.pr type
12	month.all strs.all prod	24	qtr.all strs.all prod	36	year.all strs.all prod

Figure 2.7 Thirty-six unique aggregation levels.

levels (including the base level), requiring 36 unique aggregate tables. The combinations are enumerated in Figure 2.7.

Each of the tables would have to be created with a separate "Create Table" statement. For example, the following SQL fragment would create the table for the quarter by region by product type aggregation level:

```
CREATE TABLE quarter-region-prodtype
( quarter (CHAR 16),
  region (CHAR 16),
  prodtype (CHAR 16),
  scenario (CHAR 16),
  sales (DOUBLE FLOAT),
  costs (DOUBLE FLOAT) )
```

Then, to set up for populating the Quarter-Region-Prodtype table, views that contain only the relevant aggregation levels would be created for each of the three lookup tables in Figure 2.4. For example, in order to create the *quarter-region-product type* table shown above, a view would first be created of the product lookup table that contained only product IDs and product types. Otherwise there would be a lot of unnecessary data replication because the columns of the original lookup tables that contained information about the columns that were not going to be used in the quarter-city-prodtype table, such as the product names and product groups columns in the product lookup table, would needlessly be expanded upon joining with the base table. The SQL to create these three lookup views is as follows:

```
CREATE VIEW quarter-name (quarter, month-id) AS
SELECT quarter, month-id
FROM time-lookup

CREATE VIEW region-level (region, store-id) AS
SELECT region, store-id
FROM store-lookup

CREATE VIEW product-type (prodtype, prod-id) AS
SELECT prodtype, prod-id
FROM product-lookup
```

Then each of the three lookup table views would be joined with the base table to create a modified view of the base table containing the aggregate identifier columns "quarter ID," "city ID," and "prodtype ID," in addition to the base-level columns of store, month, and product.

month id	quarter	store id	region	prod id	prodtype	scenario	sales	costs

The modified base table view would be defined by the following SQL statement:

```
CREATE VIEW qrp-modified-base-table (month-id, quarter, store-
        id, region, prod-id, prodtype, scenario, sales, costs)
AS
SELECT month-id, quarter, store-id, region, prod-id, prodtype,
        scenario, sales, costs
FROM base-table JOIN time-lookup JOIN store-lookup JOIN prod-
        lookup
```

The actual aggregate table is then populated by the following SQL statement:

```
INSERT INTO quarter-region-prodtype
SELECT quarter, region, prodtype, scenario, SUM (sales),
        SUM (costs)
FROM qrp-modified-base-table
GROUP BY quarter, region, prodtype, scenario
```

The aggregation functions for the variables would have to be defined within each of the aggregate tables. Repeating this process a total of 35 times will generate all the basic aggregate values such as the sum of products across all stores. (We started off with the month-store-product level table, so 1 of the 36 was already there.) But how about generating some of the comparisons that were shown in Figures 2.2 and 2.3? Alas, this is not a trivial exercise.

Let's calculate the ratio between actuals and plan that is shown in the rightmost column of Figures 2.2 and 2.3. The problem is that the difference between actuals and plans for any measure is defined across the rows of the base table. For example, referring back to the base table in Figure 2.4, to calculate the ratio of actuals to plan for the sale of rose water soap for the Ridgewood store in the first quarter (store 1, time 1, product 1), you would need to calculate the ratio between the sales figure in row 1 (the actuals value) and the sales figure in row 2 (the planned value). SQL has no good way for defining interrow comparisons or inserting new rows that are defined in terms of arithmetic operations performed on other rows. SQL processing is very column-oriented. So, you need to somehow put plans and actuals in separate columns.

The way to place actuals and plans in separate columns is to create two views for each of the 36 already existing aggregate tables. One of the views will hold just the actual values, and the other will hold just the planned values. This is shown in the following SQL statements. (For simplicity, the remaining examples pretend that the base data is joined with the appropriate names found in the lookup tables).

```
/* create view of actuals */
CREATE VIEW actual-quarter-region-prodtype (quarter, region,
        prodtype, act_sales, act_costs)
AS
SELECT quarter, region, prodtype, sales AS act_sales, costs AS
        act_costs
FROM quarter-region-prodtype
WHERE scenario = 'actuals'
/* create view of plans */
CREATE VIEW plan-quarter-region-prodtype (quarter, region,
        prodtype, plan_sales, plan_costs)
AS
SELECT quarter, region, prodtype, sales AS plan_sales, costs AS
        plan_costs
FROM quarter-region-prodtype
WHERE scenario = 'plans'
```

Figure 2.8 shows the view returned by selecting rows from the *actual-quarter-region-product type* view.

Quarter	Region	Prod. Type	act_sales	act_costs
1	Northeast	soap	4,217	4,019
1	Northeast	lotion	2,974	2,474
1	Northeast	office	5,313	4,839
1	Northeast	home	2,047	1,918
2	Northeast	soap	5,603	5,339
2	Northeast	lotion	3,952	3,288
2	Northeast	office	7,060	6,431
2	Northeast	home	2,720	2,549
1	Midwest	soap	4,174	3,883
1	Midwest	lotion	2,481	2,266
1	Midwest	office	7,312	6,667
1	Midwest	home	1,812	1,342
2	Midwest	soap	5,546	5,159
2	Midwest	lotion	3,297	3,011
2	Midwest	office	9,718	8,860
2	Midwest	home	2,408	1,783

Figure 2.8 Table of actual values.

Notice that *we haven't done anything useful yet in terms of calculating variances. All we've done is reorganize the data in order to get around SQL's limited interrow math* by converting what had been row differences into column differences. To begin to use these columns, you now need to join them together in a query. The following SQL code will perform that join:

```
SELECT quarter, region, prodtype, act_sales, plan_sales
FROM actual-quarter-region-prodtype JOIN plan-quarter-region-
        prodtype
```

The join creates a table view that contains the shared store, quarter, and product type columns, and separate columns for actual sales and planned sales, as shown in Figure 2.9. This table is suited for the intercolumn arithmetic required for SQL computations.

Now that the columns are suitably arranged, we can divide values across columns in a straightforward way. For example, the following SQL view will generate the table shown in Figure 2.10.

```
CREATE VIEW var-quarter-region-prodtype (quarter, region, prod-
        type, act_sales, plan_sales, variance)
AS
SELECT quarter, region, prodtype, act_sales, plan_sales,
        act_sales/plan_sales AS variance
FROM actual-quarter-region-prodtype JOIN plan-quarter-region-
        prodtype
```

Quarter	Region	Prod. Type	act_sales	act_costs	plan_sales	plan_costs
1	Northeast	soap	4,217	4,019	4,316	3,995
1	Northeast	lotion	2,974	2,474	2,779	2,349
1	Northeast	office	5,313	4,839	5,081	4,634
1	Northeast	home	2,047	1,918	2,117	1,961
2	Northeast	soap	5,603	5,339	5,735	5,308
2	Northeast	lotion	3,952	3,288	3,693	3,121
2	Northeast	office	7,060	6,431	6,752	6,158
2	Northeast	home	2,720	2,549	2,813	2,606
1	Midwest	soap	4,174	3,883	4,068	3,777
1	Midwest	lotion	2,481	2,266	2,498	2,266
1	Midwest	office	7,312	6,667	6,551	5,948
1	Midwest	home	1,812	1,342	1,769	1,322
2	Midwest	soap	5,546	5,159	5,405	5,018
2	Midwest	lotion	3,297	3,011	3,319	3,011
2	Midwest	office	9,718	8,860	8,706	7,905
2	Midwest	home	2,408	1,783	2,351	1,756

Figure 2.9 View of the joined tables containing a column for actual and planned sales and costs.

Repeating this process a total of 35 times will generate all the correct views from which to compute variances for all the aggregate levels in the model. To generate the data values for our reports, using only summary tables, we will need to join up to 8 or 12 of them together, as the reports contain quarters and months combined with either products, product types, product groups, and all products, or stores, regions, and the entire chain of stores.

Note how the months, products, and stores are all displayed along the rows. This is not how the information was displayed in Figures 2.2 and 2.3. In those figures, the months were displayed, in a natural way, across columns. It is common and useful to be able to organize data across rows and columns. It is done all the time with spreadsheets and in presentations. What about with SQL? How would you rearrange the view to show months along the columns? Basically, *SQL has no way to rearrange views by transposing rows and columns.* You can write a special-purpose view to transpose a particular column on a table whose values for that row are known to you, but it will be tricky to code, and it will require recoding if the values in the column change.

You can see that SQL has no natural way to define comparative functions or provide flexible view reorganizations that involve the transposing of rows and columns. Something as simple as the ratio of planned sales to actual sales, which can be defined in a minute or two with a typical spreadsheet by copying a formula across a new "variance" column or, as you'll see in the

Quarter	Region	Prod. Type	act_sales	plan_sales	variance
1	Northeast	soap	4,217	4,316	0.98
1	Northeast	lotion	2,974	2,779	1.07
1	Northeast	office	5,313	5,081	1.05
1	Northeast	home	2,047	2,117	0.97
2	Northeast	soap	5,603	5,735	0.98
2	Northeast	lotion	3,952	3,693	1.07
2	Northeast	office	7,060	6,752	1.05
2	Northeast	home	2,720	2,813	0.97
1	Midwest	soap	4,174	4,068	1.03
1	Midwest	lotion	2,481	2,498	0.99
1	Midwest	office	7,312	6,551	1.12
1	Midwest	home	1,812	1,769	1.02
2	Midwest	soap	5,546	5,405	1.03
2	Midwest	lotion	3,297	3,319	0.99
2	Midwest	office	9,718	8,706	1.12
2	Midwest	home	2,408	2,351	1.02

Figure 2.10 An end-user view of variance data.

next chapter, even more quickly with a multidimensional tool, is undefinable without going through a whole sequence of complicated maneuvers like the ones we just went through in this section. Ralph Kimball put this well when he said that a freshman in business needs a Ph.D. in SQL.[8]

SQL has other analytical limitations as well. Common analytical functions such as cumulative averages and totals, subtotals as found in typical spreadsheets, and rankings of data are not supported in standard SQL, though vendors have implemented extensions to support them. The topic has received some interest from notable relational experts.[9] Convenient expression of multidimensional aggregation, including partial aggregations across multiple dimensions at once, has also received attention.[10]

One fundamental source of complication for SQL in performing analytical operations is its weakness at interrow computations, as shown above. The future SQL-3 standard will likely support user-defined (DBA-defined) "stored functions" that can be coded in procedural logic, allowing many of the current shortcomings to be overcome. However, while any application can be created in a simple procedural language, the point is not *if* something can be done but *how difficult* it is to do it. To code an interrow ratio function in a SQL-3 stored function would be akin to programming it in COBOL. Adding intrinsic row functions to SQL would make it extremely different from the SQL of today.

The organization of definitions in a SQL database is another limitation of SQL that affects even the proposed extensions for handling analytical functions and user-defined functions. All views (stored queries) and stored functions (in the SQL-3 proposal) would be organized by database schema, just as tables and indexes are. They are placed in a flat list structure, just like any one table. The structures that they would be called on to define and compute, however, would be hierarchical and multidimensional. The disparity of structure between the analytical elements and the operations that define them will cause them to be difficult to manage. (Even though a spreadsheet function does not have the general expressive power of a SQL query, you at least know where to go in a spreadsheet to view or modify a formula for a particular cell.) If you altered the definitional structure of a SQL database to give its catalog the same hierarchical and dimensional structure as the analytical information stored in its data tables, you would have gone a long way to metamorphose SQL into a multidimensional data language.

Instead of using complicated procedures to contort SQL into providing analysis-based decision-oriented information, it is also possible to issue multiple simple SQL commands and perform the analytical functions on the client. The problem with this strategy is that frequently the amount of data that gets returned is too large for the client and overloads either the client or the network or both. For example, what if you worked for a large retail organization and you wanted to see your top 20 products in terms of cumulative sales? If you had 500 stores and weekly sales totals for 50,000 products, and you were 20 weeks into the year, you would have to send 500 million numbers across the network (dubious) to your desktop (highly dubious), to calculate 20 numbers. Rankings are an important class of comparative function. When large amounts of data are involved, it is not the kind of operation to be performed on the desktop.

Conclusion

It is normal to want to be able to phrase analytical queries in a natural or near-natural way. If what you want to see are product totals and subtotals or this year/last year comparisons or moving 52-week averages or top-selling products or changes in market share between this year and last year or percent change in margins, that's all you should have to ask for. Spreadsheets let you phrase analytical queries in a near-natural way but only for small amounts of data that can be organized in a two-dimensional grid. SQL lets you phrase simple queries based on columns of data in a near-natural way as long as they do not involve any analysis or interrow comparisons. Neither approach lets you easily phrase analytical queries against large amounts of complexly organized data.

The best approach for providing analysis-based decision-oriented processing and meeting the requirements for OLAP is multidimensional.

Endnotes

1. There were also a number of forward-looking desktop products during this time. Javelin, eventually bought by IRI, had the concept of time series and understood how to translate variables between different time periodicities. And TM/1 (for Table Manager 1) was the first multidimensional desktop spreadsheet, though at the time it called itself a relational spreadsheet.

2. Codd, E. F., "A Relational Model of Data for Large Shared Databanks," *Communications of the ACM*, February 1974.

3. David Stemple, Adolfo Socorro, and Tim Sheard, "Formalizing Objects Using ADABPTL," *Advances in Object-Oriented Database Systems*, 2nd International Workshop, 1988.

4. David Shipman, "The Functional Data Model and the Data Language DAPLEX," *ACM Transactions on Database Systems* 6 (March 1981): 140–173.

5. E. F. Codd, "Extending the Database Relational Model to Capture More Meaning," 1978.

6. Joe Celko, *Instant SQL Programming* (Chicago: Wrox Press, 1995). C. J. Date and Hugh Darwin, *A Guide to the SQL Standard*, 3rd ed. (Reading, MA: Addison Wesley, 1994).

7. Technically, it is possible through the use of many lookup tables and macros to drive the whole process. However, the resulting model is very fragile and very difficult to define and maintain. I know this from experience—my former company created such macro-driven models for all the popular spreadsheets to show just how difficult the process was.

8. Ralph Kimball, "A Freshman in Business Needs a Ph.D. in SQL," *DBMS* (January 1996): 16.

9. Red Brick Software's Red Brick Warehouse implements a proprietary variant of SQL called RISQL that explicitly supports computation of cumulative sums, and selection of rows based on ranking (top- or bottom-*N*) and quartile criteria. Chris Date, in a series of articles published in *Database Programming and Design*, explores the area of "quota queries" (queries based on ranking criteria) on how SQL might be extended to support them

10. Data Cube paper; Jim Gray and Microsoft Tech.

Section II

Explanation of Multidimensional Features and Concepts

Laws like the principle of sufficient reason, etc. are about the net [of language] and not about what the net describes.

—Ludwig Wittgenstein

Basic Multidimensional Features, Part 1

If OLAP were music, then multidimensional software would be the musical instruments and multidimensional data sets would be the scores. After reading Chapters 3 and 4, you should be able to pick up any multidimensional dataset as if it were sheet music and create analytical music all day long with your favorite software.

Multidimensional software, unlike spreadsheets or SQL databases, is specifically designed to facilitate the definition and computation of sophisticated multilevel aggregations and analysis. The types of common business or OLAP problems, which in the previous chapter were seen to be difficult for spreadsheets and traditional databases, are straightforward to define and resolve in the multidimensional world.

Chapters 3 and 4 explain the major features common to any multidimensional software product or tool. The major features include hypercubes, dimensions, hierarchies, formulas, and links. Chapters 6 and 7 describe advanced features. (An in-depth treatment of dimensional structures is presented in Chapter 16.) Let's begin with a quick overview of the key multidimensional features and their problem-solving benefits.

The first key feature of any multidimensional tool is the ability to define a dataset in terms of multiple dimensions. Loosely speaking, dimensions may be thought of as major perspectives, entities, factors, or components. For example, the major dimensions in a sales tracking system might be time, location, salesperson, customer, and measure. The major dimensions in a loan application might be time, branch, customer, and loan type. In database terms, a good analogy for a dimension is a key. So a multidimensional dataset may be thought of as a multikey or multiattribute dataset. The benefit of handling multiple dimensions is in being able to represent the full richness of a dataset in a single model or cube. Also, as you will learn by reading further, this multidimensional aspect is something of a generally enabling feature.

The second key feature of any multidimensional system is the ability to display the model dimensions in any three-dimensional grid configuration—consisting of rows, columns, and pages—on a computer screen. In other words, any model dimensions such as time, store, customer, and measures can be shown in any row by column by page screen configuration. This is extremely useful for all kinds of ad hoc querying and analysis, especially when the number of dimensions exceeds two or three.

The third key feature of any multidimensional tool is the hierarchical nature of the dimensions. Any dimension such as time, products, and stores can have multiple levels of granularity. For example, the time dimension may have a day-level granularity, a week-level granularity, a month-level granularity, a quarter-level granularity, and so on. This is indispensable for working with larger data sets that invariably need to be aggregated, analyzed, and viewed across multiple levels of aggregation.

The fourth key feature of any multidimensional tool is the ability to attach formulas to members of dimensions. Because a single member of one dimension, say the "sales" member from a variables dimension, interacts with every single member from every other dimension, a single-dimensional formula has a powerful application range frequently doing the same work that would otherwise take thousands of spreadsheet formulas. Also, unlike SQL formulas, multidimensional formulas work equally well in all dimensions. Multidimensional formulas dramatically simplify the process of defining aggregation and analysis calculations.

The combination of multiple dimensions, flexible screen representations, multilevel dimensions, and dimension formulas represent the heart of any multidimensional system.

Dimensions, Hypercubes, and Their Representation

The notion of a **hypercube**, or a cube with more than three dimensions, is fundamental to an understanding of multidimensional software. Multidimensional tools use hypercubes in the same way that spreadsheets use worksheets and databases use tables. All browsing, reporting, and analysis are done in terms of hypercubes.

Typically, introductions to hypercubes begin with a description of lower-dimensional surfaces such as lines, planes, and cubes. They then leave it to the reader to visualize, by analogy, a higher-dimensional cube.[1] This is not the best approach because the path to understanding hypercubes does not pass through the length, width, and height of a physical cube. As a result of this and other confusions, hypercubes (and multidimensional analysis) may seem hard to understand.

The correct approach to understanding hypercubes recognizes three main points:

1. Screen displays are not the same as visual metaphors.
2. Logical dimensions are not the same as physical dimensions.
3. Logical dimensions can be combined.

These points will be brought up and clarified during the course of incrementally building on something understood by everyone: a two-dimensional row by column arrangement of data. Once you understand these points, hypercubes and the rest of multidimensional modeling and analysis will appear forthright and intuitive.

Lower-Dimensional Data Sets

Let us start with some simple examples of two-dimensional data. Anything that you track, whether it be hours per employee, costs per department, balance per customer, or complaints per store, can be arranged in a two-dimensional format. Figure 3.1 shows sales data organized by month in a two-dimensional grid. This grid could easily be created in any spreadsheet program and displayed on any computer screen. Months are arranged down

Months	Sales
January	790
February	850
March	900
April	910
May	860
June	830
July	880
August	900
September	790
October	820
November	840
December	810
Total	10180

Figure 3.1 Sales data by month.

the rows. The total for all months is displayed on the bottom row. The grid is very narrow. It has only one data column: the sales column. But the data set has two dimensions: a row-arranged month dimension and a column-arranged sales dimension.

Now let us add some additional data to the grid in Figure 3.1, as shown in Figure 3.2. Notice how Figure 3.2 is still arranged in a two-dimensional format. But instead of there being just one column for sales, there are now five columns: one for sales, one for indirect costs, one for direct costs, one for total costs, and one for sales minus total costs (or margins). Figure 3.2 shows sales, cost, and margin data organized by month. Individually, sales, costs, and margins represent variables. Variables are the items we are tracking. If someone were to ask you the question, "What are you measuring or tracking?" you would respond, "Sales, costs, and margins." Collectively, all the variables form a variable dimension. (For an in-depth discussion of variables see Chapter 16.) Each member of the variable dimension is a variable.

In contrast, the months represent how we are organizing the data. We are not tracking months. We are using months to individuate sales and cost values. If someone were to ask you the question, "From where are you getting your data?" or "How often are you making measurements?" you would respond, "We are tracking sales on a monthly basis." Months are a type of key or identifier dimension. Our simple data example has two dimensions: one identifier dimension and one variable dimension.

What happens when we add a third dimension, say products? It seems easy enough to visualize. After all, it is just a cube. Figure 3.3 shows a three-

Month	Sales	Direct Costs	Indirect Costs	Total Costs	Margin
January	790	480	110	590	200
February	850	520	130	650	200
March	900	530	140	670	230
April	910	590	150	740	170
May	860	600	120	720	140
June	830	490	100	590	240
July	880	500	110	610	270
August	900	620	130	750	150
September	790	300	90	390	400
October	820	540	100	640	180
November	840	570	150	720	120
December	810	600	120	720	90
Total	10180	6340	1450	7790	2390

Figure 3.2 Sales, costs, and margin by month.

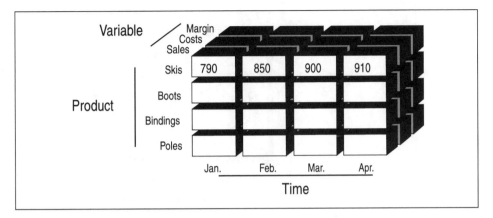

Figure 3.3 Three-dimensional cube: product by variable by time.

dimensional cube that represents product variables by month. But where is this cube that we are showing? Is it on a computer screen? Is it "out there" in the world? Is it in your mind? Where is it?

As Magritte might have said, the cube cannot be a part of the computer screen any more than an apple can be a part of a piece of paper (see Figure 3.4). The computer screen, like a sheet of paper, has only two (usable) physical dimensions. We can create a two-dimensional representation of a three-dimensional cube on a computer screen. It is done all the time. But we cannot create a three-dimensional representation of anything as part of a two-dimensional surface.

Figure 3.4 This is not an apple.

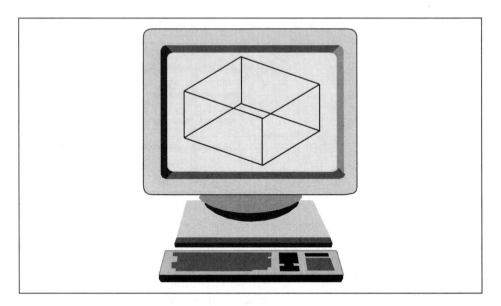

Figure 3.5 Flat screen display of a cube.

This raises the first of our above-mentioned points. *The actual two-dimensional screen display of data is separate from the metaphors we use to visualize that data.* The cube we visualized in Figure 3.3 is just that, a visual metaphor. It could have even been a real cube. But it is not the same as the two-dimensional display shown in Figure 3.5. Now why is this an important point? It is important because there are natural limits to what can be done with a two-dimensional computer screen. This limitation made software developers think long and hard about the optimal way of representing numerical structures of more than two dimensions on a flat computer screen for the purposes of viewing and manipulation.

Figure 3.6 shows a spreadsheet-like display of the three-dimensional data set visualized in Figure 3.3. Most of the display looks the same as for the two-dimensional display shown in Figure 3.2. It is essentially a two-dimensional grid except, in the upper-left portion of the display, there is an icon called page with the label "Product: Shoes." The page icon stands for a third "page" dimension.

The three-dimensional data set consisting of variables, time, and products is displayed on a computer screen in terms of the three display dimensions, row, column, and page. The row and column display dimensions correspond to the row and column screen dimensions. We can see.as many rows and columns of data as the screen's rows and columns permit. Given a large enough screen, we could see the whole of any two-dimensional data

		Sales	Direct Costs	Indirect Costs	Total Costs	Margin
page Product: shoes					columns Variables: all	
	January	520	320	110	430	90
	February	400	250	130	380	20
	March	430	300	120	420	10
	April	490	320	150	470	20
	May	520	310	180	490	30
	June	390	230	150	380	10
	July	470	290	160	450	20
	August	500	360	150	510	-10
	September	450	290	140	430	20
	October	480	290	140	430	50
rows	November	510	310	150	460	50
Time: months	December	550	330	160	490	60

Figure 3.6 Typical three-dimensional display.

set. In contrast, the page dimension doesn't correspond to anything that is actually on the screen. No matter how big the screen, all that is seen is an indicator saying which page is currently visible: shoes, socks, shirts, and so on. Still, it is easy to visualize the relationship between the data shown on the screen and the whole of the data set stored in the computer. All you have to do is imagine a three-dimensional data cube and a screen display showing one slice of that cube, as illustrated in Figure 3.7.

Beyond Three Dimensions

Suppose that you are tracking different measures of different products by month for a chain of stores. *You've now got a four-dimensional data set. What kind of visual metaphor should you use to form a picture of the whole?* And how should the relevant information be organized on the screen? Trying to use a cube as the basis for a four- or higher-dimensional visualization can get very messy, very quickly. Figure 3.8 shows a picture of a tesseract, the technical name for a four-dimensional cube. Something seems wrong. It looks too complicated. The cube metaphor shown in Figure 3.3 seemed easy to understand. And adding the notion of stores to the data set in Figure 3.2 didn't

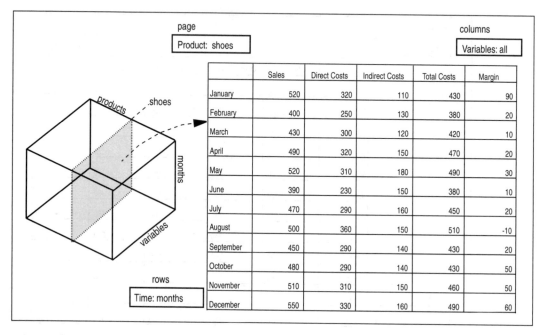

	Sales	Direct Costs	Indirect Costs	Total Costs	Margin
January	520	320	110	430	90
February	400	250	130	380	20
March	430	300	120	420	10
April	490	320	150	470	20
May	520	310	180	490	30
June	390	230	150	380	10
July	470	290	160	450	20
August	500	360	150	510	-10
September	450	290	140	430	20
October	480	290	140	430	50
November	510	310	150	460	50
December	550	330	160	490	60

Figure 3.7 Slice of cube.

seem to add that much more additional complexity. So why, when we add just one more factor to the data set, does the complexity of its visualization skyrocket? This brings us to the second major point: the difference between logical and physical dimensions.

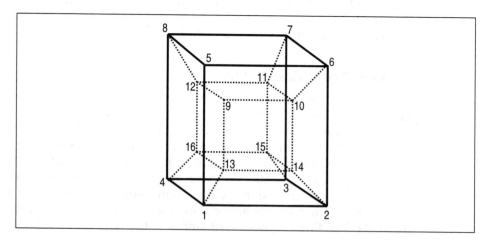

Figure 3.8 A view of a tesseract.

The cubes that most of us studied in a high school geometry class were implicitly physical because Euclidean or standard textbook geometry is based on the physical notions of length, width, and height. (Incidentally, the Greeks inherited their geometry from the Egyptians, who used it for surveying.) In textbook geometry, the *x* axis is perpendicular to the *y* axis is perpendicular to the *z* axis. The three perpendicular angle-related axes translate perfectly into the physical dimensions of length, width, and height. Physical geometry is very practical, and it has served humankind well for over two millennia.

Now what does angle have to do with the relationship between variables, stores, and products? *Does it make any sense to say that stores are perpendicular to products?* Think about it for a minute. It makes no sense. What does make sense is to say that the display of stores on the computer screen is perpendicular to the display of products (but that is totally different). Figure 3.9 is a simple sketch of an event that could have generated the data shown in Figure 3.7. It is a picture of a retailer selling a product to a customer in exchange for money and buying supplies from a supplier. It certainly doesn't look like a cube. Figure 3.10 displays a series of these pictures: one for each month and their correspondence with a cube arrangement of data. Yet there is something about the relationship between the cube and the event pictured by the cube that makes the cube an intuitive representation of the event. We need to explore this further.

Every point in the cube represents a particular measurement taken from the event. For example, one point in the cube might represent the fact that $1,000 worth of shoes were sold in February. Another point might represent the fact that $500 worth of pants were bought in March. Notice that each fact in the cube is identified by one value from each dimension.

Going back to the event image in Figure 3.9, every dimension of the event is a coexistent factor. For each sales transaction, one can always identify a product sold, a dollar amount, and a time. (Where there is smoke there is fire.) Furthermore, each of the coexistent factors is independent of all the others. In other words, any product could be sold at any time. And at any

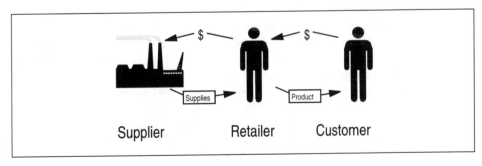

Figure 3.9 A retailer-centric view of the world.

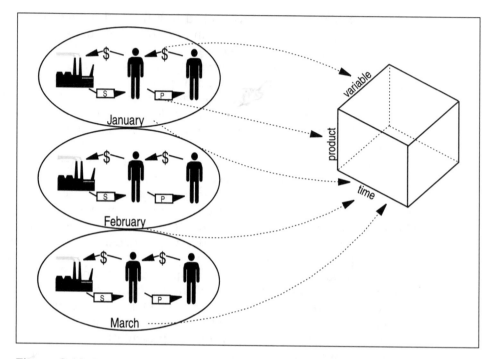

Figure 3.10 Events that could generate the data in Figure 3.7.

time, any product could be sold. (Actually, the condition of independence does not hold for the variables, but it is safe to ignore that now. For a full treatment of this see Chapter 15.)

The cube works so well as an intuitive representation of the event because all of the dimensions coexist for every point in the cube and they are all independent of one another. Figure 3.11 shows how any point *(xn,yn,zn)* in three-dimensional space is identified by its *x* value, its *y* value, and its *z* value (or its *product, time,* and *variable* values). From any point in the cube, one can move in any value in any dimension independent of any other change in any other dimension. This is shown in Figure 3.12. The problem with the cube is that, physically speaking, there are only three independent dimensions. So the cube breaks down as a metaphor for visualizing more than three dimensions.

Even though there is nothing wrong with using an angle-based cube for representing up to three dimensions of an event, the angle-based definition of a dimension is not necessary for a useful representation of the event. A useful representation requires coexistent and independent dimensions regardless of how that coexistence and independence are defined. These two properties are logical properties, not physical properties. Any metaphor that provides a consistent definition of independent and coexistent dimensions will work.

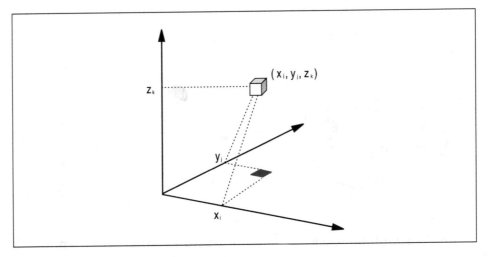

Figure 3.11 Points are identified by their *x, y, z* values.

Multidimensional Domain Structures

Let's introduce a new metaphor for representing events that is not based on angle-defined dimensions and that is capable of representing any number of event dimensions. If you want to give it a name you may call it a multidimensional domain structure (MDS). The new metaphor is shown in Figure 3.13 along the path between data-generating events and data cubes shown in Figure 3.10. Each dimension is represented by a vertical line segment. Every

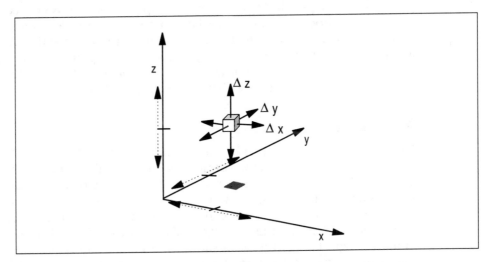

Figure 3.12 Change can occur by any value of any dimension.

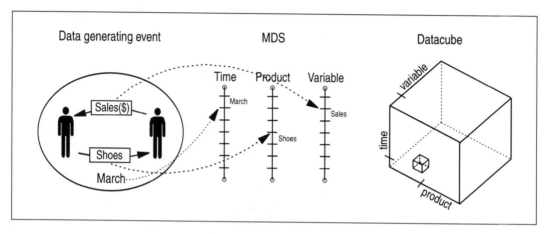

Figure 3.13 Multidimensional domain structures are a way of representing events.

member within a dimension is represented by a unit interval within the segment. As we are starting with a three-dimensional example, there are three line segments: one for time, one for products, and one for variables. Any union of one interval from each of the three line segments is connected to an element in the event and in the cube. For example, in Figure 3.13, the MDS highlights March shoe sales as does the cube. In the same way that one can move independently in each cube dimension, one can move independently in each MDS dimension, as shown in Figure 3.14.

In Figure 3.14, where there are 12 time periods, 10 products, and 5 variables, there are 12*10*5 = 600 hypercube intersections or potential data points. In this sense, an MDS is more descriptive than a physical cube. However, an MDS doesn't show actual data points, just possible combinations of dimension members. So here it is less descriptive than a cube that can at least allude to (though it cannot actually show) all data points. Then again, the purpose of a visual metaphor is to give a useful picture of the whole structure of a model. It is the job of the display to show the data.

Adding a Fourth Dimension

Using an MDS, it is easy to add a fourth dimension to the model. Remember when we tried to add a store dimension to the cube? That's when things started to break down. But not with an MDS. It's a cinch. Just add a fourth line segment called stores, as shown in Figure 3.15. The MDS is not a pictorial representation of the data-generating event, but then neither was the cube. The MDS shows the number of data points extracted from the event and their logical organization. It shows all the dimensions one can browse in and how far one can go in any dimension. It shows more structural informa-

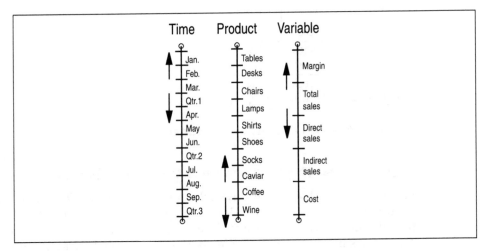

Figure 3.14 You can move independently in each MDS dimension.

tion than a cube, and it can show it for an arbitrary number of dimensions. If you want a more realistic picture of the event, you should consider some enhanced version of the simple images I used in Figure 3.13 or perhaps even a camera. If you want a useful computer screen representation of the data, you need to use some version of the three-dimensional spreadsheet interface shown in Figure 3.7. (This will be discussed later in this chapter.)

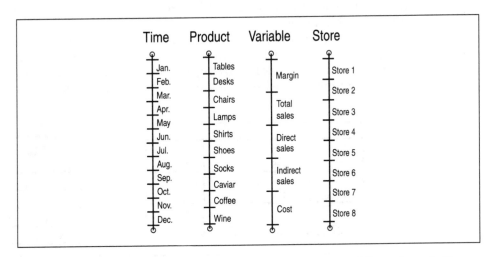

Figure 3.15 The fourth dimension may be represented by a fourth line segment.

	sales	cost	margin
shoes	shoe sales	shoe cost	shoe margin
socks	sock sales	sock cost	sock margin

Figure 3.16 A two-dimensional arrangement.

Representing Hypercubes on a Computer Screen

We've figured out why the physical cube metaphor breaks down, and we've introduced a logical visualization principle for representing the structure of N-dimensional data sets. We still need to see them on the computer screen. This brings us to our final hurdle: mapping multiple logical dimensions onto a single physical (screen) dimension. Look again at the image of a three-dimensional grid-style interface, as shown in Figure 3.6. *How are we going to represent four or more logical dimensions given our three display dimensions of row, column, and page? The answer is we combine multiple logical dimensions within the same display dimension.* Let's examine this more closely.

Look at Figure 3.16. It shows a two-dimensional arrangement of products by variables with the name of each intersection explicitly written. Notice how each point or intersection in the two-dimensional grid is formed from one member of each dimension. And notice how each member of each dimension combines with each member of the other dimension. In this simple example there are two products and three variables for a total of six product variable combinations.

Mapping the two dimensions into one dimension means creating a one-dimensional version of the two-dimensionally arranged intersections. Although any one-dimensional arrangement will work, the typical method is to nest one dimension within the other. For example, Figure 3.17 shows how

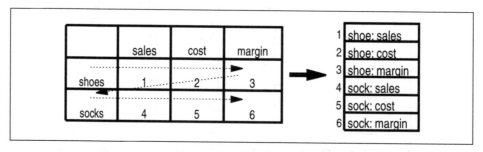

Figure 3.17 Nesting variables within products.

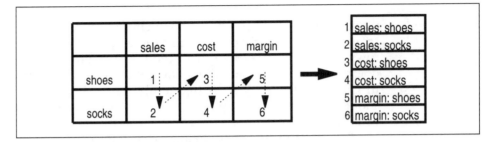

Figure 3.18 Nesting products within variables.

to create a one-dimensional list of variables nested within products from the two-dimensional grid originally shown in Figure 3.16. Notice how the list scrolls through every member of the variables dimension for each product as it is scrolling through products. You can think of it as a generic code loop:

```
For variables = 1 to N

    For products = 1 to N
    End products


End variables
```

This is what it means for variables to be nested within products. In contrast, Figure 3.18 shows how to create a one-dimensional list of products nested within variables from the same two-dimensional grid. Notice how in both figures, the number of elements is the same for the one- as for the two-dimensional arrangement. No data is lost by combining dimensions. (Actually, some information is lost as you will see later.) Any number of dimensions can be combined.

The Effects of Combining Dimensions

Two main things change as a result of combining dimensions: axis lengths and neighborhoods. One main thing does not change: truth criteria.

The first thing that changes is the shape of the viewable data. As you can see from either Figure 3.17 or Figure 3.18, the length of the one-dimensional list is equal to the product of the lengths of each of the two dimensions in the two-dimensional arrangement. When the lengths are as small as they are in these examples, the impact is negligible, but when the axis lengths are in the hundreds or thousands it can make a real difference. For example, browsing through a two-dimensional grid of 100 by 100, which may fit all at once on your screen, is considerably easier than browsing through a list of 10,000 rows, which most certainly will require substantial scrolling. This doesn't mean you shouldn't combine dimensions (as you will learn in Chapter 10, doing so is frequently desirable), but simply you should be aware of how you are changing the shape of the data by combining them.

The second thing that changes as a result of combining dimensions is the set of neighbors surrounding any point. *In two dimensions, each two-dimensional point has four immediate neighbors, when the two dimensions are combined; each point in a one-dimensional list has just two immediate neighbors.* This is shown in Figure 3.19. Notice how in the top panel, where the data is arranged in two dimensions, the sales value for Newbury in February has four neighboring cells. Compare this with the lower panel, which shows the exact same data, only in one dimension. Here, the sales value for Newbury in February has only two neighbors. The changing of neighbors can affect analyses and graphical visualizations because they make use of information about neighbors. (For a discussion of multidimensional visualization, see Chapter 6. For a discussion of multidimensional analysis, see Chapter 15.)

(Note the difference in adjacency)

	Jan	Feb	Mar
Ridgewood	555	611	677
Newbury	490	539	598
Avon	220	242	271

Jan	Ridgewood	555
	Newbury	490
	Avon	220
Feb	Ridgewood	611
	Newbury	539
	Avon	242
Mar	Ridgewood	677
	Newbury	598
	Avon	271

Note:

A ▢ highlights the adjacent cells

Figure 3.19 Two different dimensional structurings of the same data set.

One important thing does not change during the process. No matter how dimensions are combined, and no matter how the data grids are arranged, they make the same statements, claims, or propositions about the world whose truth or falsehood are a function of the same criteria. (For a discussion of dimensions, variables, and truth conditions, see Chapter 15.)

Now that we have learned how to combine dimensions, let us more fully demonstrate the process by adding two dimensions to our previous four-dimensional example. Figure 3.20 shows a six-dimensional data set consisting of products, times, stores, customers, variables, and scenarios. Figure 3.21 shows each dimension of Figure 3.20 connected to either a row, column, or page role of a three-dimensional grid display. Notice how multiple dimensions are combined in the row, column, and page dimensions of the grid display. The same visual display that works for three dimensions can easily be extended to work with N-dimensions. From here on, we will call this type of display a multidimensional grid display. Figures 3.22 and 3.23 show two different ways that the same six model dimensions can be mapped onto row, column, and page axes.

If you look at Figures 3.21 through 3.23 you will notice that there is always exactly one member represented from each model dimension shown on pages of the screen. There is no way around this fact. Try it. You will see that if you attempt to show more than one member from a dimension represented as a page, you will need to choose how to arrange the two or more

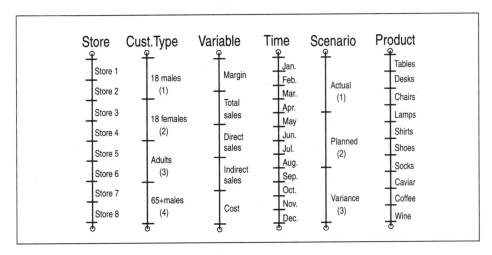

Figure 3.20 A six-dimensional MDS.

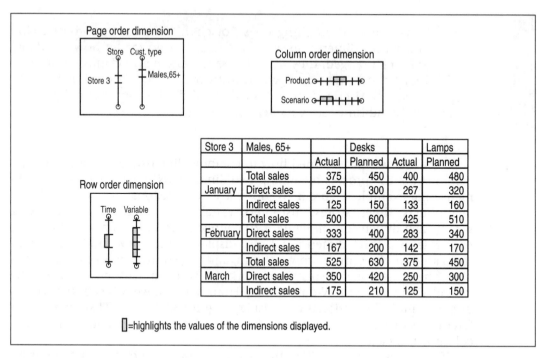

Store 3	Males, 65+		Desks		Lamps
		Actual	Planned	Actual	Planned
	Total sales	375	450	400	480
January	Direct sales	250	300	267	320
	Indirect sales	125	150	133	160
	Total sales	500	600	425	510
February	Direct sales	333	400	283	340
	Indirect sales	167	200	142	170
	Total sales	525	630	375	450
March	Direct sales	350	420	250	300
	Indirect sales	175	210	125	150

[]=highlights the values of the dimensions displayed.

Figure 3.21 A six-dimensional data display.

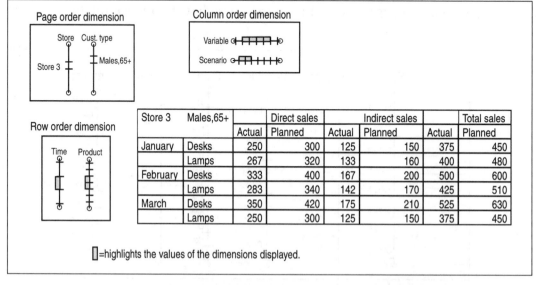

Store 3	Males,65+		Direct sales		Indirect sales		Total sales
		Actual	Planned	Actual	Planned	Actual	Planned
January	Desks	250	300	125	150	375	450
	Lamps	267	320	133	160	400	480
February	Desks	333	400	167	200	500	600
	Lamps	283	340	142	170	425	510
March	Desks	350	420	175	210	525	630
	Lamps	250	300	125	150	375	450

[]=highlights the values of the dimensions displayed.

Figure 3.22 A different six-dimensional data display of the same MDS.

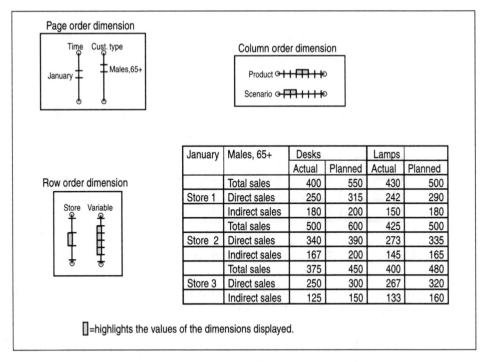

Figure 3.23 Yet a third six-dimensional data display of the same MDS.

members. And the only choices you have (in a flat static screen display) are across the rows or across the columns.

Multidimensional grids are so flexible that they can mimic any kind of (regular) table. After all, a table is just a special case of a grid where all or most of the dimensions are represented as columns. The table shown in Figure 3.24 can be thought of as a spreadsheet-like grid where five dimensions are represented as column headings whose members are the column values. And one dimension, in this case the variables dimension, has its members represented as column headings. Tables, such as the one shown in Figure 3.24, where one of the dimensions has its members represented as column headings and where the rest of the dimensions have their members represented as row values, are frequently (and in this book will be) called type one tables.[2] (Using this same nomenclature, Figure 3.25, which is discussed below, would be called a type zero table because it has zero dimensions whose members are represented as column headings.)

Notice how every instance of a sales variable in the type one table is associated with an instance from every dimensional attribute. The identifier dimensions of the situation are represented as primary keys in the table. The variables of the situation are represented as nonkey attributes. Relationally

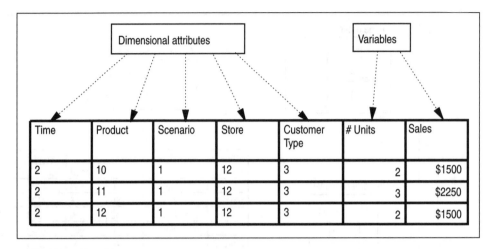

Figure 3.24 Electronic capture of point-of-sale data in a type one table.

speaking, this grid is a table in third normal form. This means that all of the nonkey attributes, in this case sales and costs, apply to or are uniquely identified by all of the primary or dimension keys. There are no sales variables that are not associated with a product and store and time. For every unique dimensional combination there exists one and only one instance of a variable.

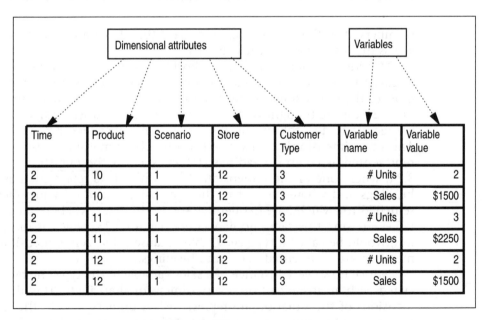

Figure 3.25 A type zero table.

Finally, look at Figure 3.25, which shows a different table-like representation of the same data found in Figure 3.24. Although both table forms allocate one column per dimension, notice how in Figure 3.25 the individual variable names, "sales" and "units," are treated as the values of a column called variables. Also notice the addition of a "value" column whose row entries are the data values that, in the preceding table, were situated in each of the variables columns. (For an in-depth discussion of the value dimension and how it relates to the dimensionality of a multidimensional model, see Chapter 15.)

As a practical matter, the table in Figure 3.24 will be shorter in rows and wider in columns than the table in Figure 3.25. The long and narrow table in Figure 3.25 will use more space for storing keys because it has an extra key column.

The ability to easily change views of the same data by reconfiguring how dimensions are displayed is one of the great benefits of multidimensional systems. It is due to the separation of data structure, as represented in the MDS, from data display, as represented in the multidimensional grid. The actual method will be different from tool to tool, but the essence is the same. For example, the commands or actions to create Figure 3.21 are as follows:

1. Show variables nested within months along the rows of the screen.
2. Show scenarios nested within products along the columns of the screen.
3. Show stores and customer type along the pages of the screen.

Analytical Screens

While there is no such thing as a right or wrong grid display, there are some rules of thumb that you should keep in mind when analyzing multidimensional data in grid form. First, nesting dimensions across rows and columns consumes lots of screen resources relative to putting dimensions into screen pages. And because we still live in an age of limited screen realty, the more screen space is consumed displaying dimension members, the less space is left for displaying data. The less space left for displaying data, the more scrolling you need to do between screens to see the same data. And the more scrolling you need to perform, the harder it is to understand what you are looking at.

To maximize the degree to which everything on the screen is relevant, try keeping dimensions along pages unless you know you need to see more than one member at a time. And when you do need to nest multiple dimensions across rows and columns, since there is generally more usable vertical screen space than horizontal screen space, it is generally better to nest more dimensions across columns than across rows. For example, Figure 3.26 shows total sales by month with products, stores, and scenarios in the page. Imagine how

Page:		Month	Sales
product: toys		January	790
stores: store2		February	850
scenario: actual		March	900
customer type: 3		April	910
		May	860
		June	830
		July	880
		August	900
		September	790
		October	820
		November	840
		December	810
		Total	10180

Figure 3.26 Looking at a page of total sales by time in a six-dimensional model.

much more sales data you can see this way as compared with showing all the dimensions across rows and columns, as shown in Figure 3.22.

Second, ask yourself "What do I want to look at?" or "What am I trying to compare?" before deciding how to display information on the screen. For example, you may want to look at and compare actual costs across stores and time, for some product and customer type. If this is the case, you should set your page dimensions to that product and customer type you are analyzing and organize your display to show stores and times for actual costs, as shown in Figure 3.27.

Now, what would you do if you were trying to compare the ratio between sales and advertising costs for low- and high-priced products across stores and times? You could try to see whether the returns on advertising for low- and high-priced products varied across stores or times. Perhaps it costs less to sell expensive products in high-income area stores, or perhaps there were better returns on advertising cheaper products during holiday time periods. How would you want to set up the screen to look at this? The complicating factor here is that what you are looking at—variables by product category—is itself a two-dimensional structure.

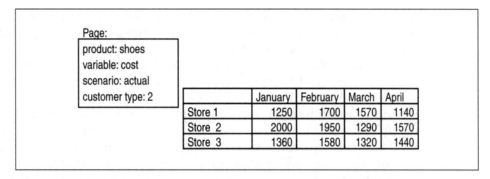

Figure 3.27 Arranging data to compare costs across stores and time.

The way to show this type of information on the screen is to put one of the looked-at dimensions in the most nested position along one visible row or column axis and to put the other looked-at dimension across the other visible column or row axis, as shown in Figure 3.28. The more you think in terms of complicated multidimensional structures, such as the one shown above in Figure 3.28, the more you may want to use graphical visualization techniques for displaying the information. (These techniques are discussed in Chapter 6).

Although any combination of dimensions may be mapped to any combination of rows, columns, and pages, you will be most productive when you think about what you are trying to learn before defining screen representations for your data.

Summary of Dimensions

We have seen that dimensions are logical factors or identifying attributes of measurable events or things that we track. We call these dimensions **identi-**

		December		January		February	
		High Price	Low Price	High Price	Low Price	High Price	Low Price
Store 1	Sales (000)	450	200	340	280		
	Costs	267	160	265	200		
Store 2	Sales	402	400	350	450		
	Costs	283	315	310	325		
Store 3	Sales	250	460	200	500		
	Costs	225	300	165	356		

Figure 3.28 A two-dimensional comparison.

fier dimensions. We have also seen dimensions that identify what we track in a situation. We call these **variable dimensions**. The things tracked are called **variables** or **members** of the variables dimension. As distinguished from physical dimensions, which are based on angles and limited to three, logical dimensions have no such limit.

Frequently, the number of dimensions in a data set exceeds the three dimensions found in a typical row, column, and page screen display. Fortunately, multidimensional software enables multiple dimensions of information to be combined onto each row, column, and page axis of a display device, thus making it possible to visualize and understand a multidimensional data set in terms of information presented on a flat computer screen.

The ability of multidimensional software to model multiple dimensions of information and to handle the user representation of the information makes it better suited for working with complex data sets than either SQL databases or traditional spreadsheets.

Hierarchical Dimensions

Hierarchies Are the Backbone of Aggregating

The second major feature common to most multidimensional software tools, after that of support for multiple dimensions, is that of support for hierarchies. A hierarchy is an attribute of a dimension. Most dimensions have a hierarchical or multilevel structure. Similar concepts include abstraction, grouping, aggregation, and consolidation.

In an informal way, everybody is familiar with some hierarchical dimensions. Time, which we think of, for example, in hours, days, weeks, months, quarters, and years, forms a multilevel hierarchical dimension. Geography, which we may think of in terms of neighborhoods, cities, states, and countries, forms a multilevel hierarchical dimension. And corporate reporting structures, which frequently include a task, project, department, business unit, and company level, form a hierarchical dimension as well.

In contrast, a scenario dimension, which is common to most business models, typically has a small number of members such as an actual member, a planned or perhaps several planned members, and a variance member for each combination of planned and actual members. It would almost never be portrayed hierarchically.

In business, as in most types of activity, hierarchies are a necessity of life. It would be impossible to run a company effectively if all the company's data were confined to the transaction level. Whether it is done in the computer or in your head, you need to track the performance of different types of product aggregations. Even if you ran a small company with a small number of products working out of a single storefront, you would still need to aggregate product sales over time and view your business in terms of larger time scales than that of your sales transactions in order to have the information required to decide which products are selling well and which are selling poorly. Here again, the benefit of multidimensional software tools is that they are geared for directly handling hierarchical dimensions.

The categories by which data are aggregated for analysis and reporting should be the same as the categories in terms of which you act or make decisions. If you make product pricing decisions to maximize sales, then you need to look at product sales data aggregated by product price. As your analytical and decision-making criteria change, so too must your aggregation routines. Aggregation routines need to be flexible to support unplanned analysis.

Managers and analysts spend most of their time thinking about groups of things: groups of products, groups of customers, groups of accounts, and so on. Even when we think we are thinking about particulars such as particular sizes, colors, and widths of a specific men's shoe, we are usually considering a tight grouping such as the group of all individual shoes of the same size, style, color, and width. Where data is concerned, groups of things, such as all men's shoes, frequently mean derived things, such as the sum of men's dress and casual shoe sales (unless the data flow is top down, as discussed later in this chapter). In this regard, OLAP-style derived data queries are different from transaction queries as the latter generally return the same data that was input, such as the address of a customer, as data was originally supplied by the customer. Furthermore, groups are frequently changing. It is especially important for analysis-based decision making to have strong support for flexible as well as deep and wide-fanning hierarchies.

Finally, the ability of multidimensional software to reference things according to their position along a hierarchy is incredibly useful for managing real-world applications. Hierarchical referencing may be more common than you think. In corporate organizations, for example, security and privileges are often defined along a hierarchy. Persons below a certain level may not be allowed to see certain data, or they may need authorization to make certain purchases. Budgeted resources are frequently allocated along a hierarchy. Some amount for total overhead that applies to a whole division may be allocated down the corporate hierarchy as a function of headcount or sales. In fact, a typical term for a corporate reporting organization is a reporting hierarchy!

The remainder of this section will explore the anatomy of a dimensional hierarchy.

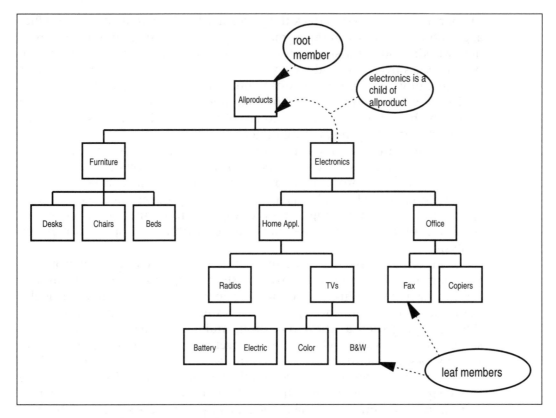

Figure 3.29 Product hierarchy for a manufacturer.

Dimensional Hierarchies

The best way to come to an understanding of dimensional hierarchies and how they can vary is to see them. Let us begin with a hierarchical product dimension, as shown in Figure 3.29.

Individual elements or nodes are called members. Furniture is a member, electronics is a member, office equipment is a member, and so on. By convention, hierarchies are shown with the root on the top and the branches on the bottom. Typically, though not always, data flows from the leaves toward the root.

Most members have connections up and down the hierarchy. Upward connections are many-to-one and are frequently called **parent connections**. Downward connections are one-to-many and are frequently called **child connections**. Electronics, for example, is the parent of office equipment and home appliances. Faxes and photocopiers are the children of office equipment. Generally speaking, a member can have no more than one parent. (For an example of where this does not hold see Chapter 7.)

A member that has no parent is called a **root member**. In Figure 3.29, the allproduct member is the root member of the product dimension hierarchy. Members that have no children are called **leaf** or **outermost branch members**. Desks, lamps, beds, chairs, battery radios, electric radios, color and black and white TVs, fax machines, and photocopiers are all leaf members of the product dimension hierarchy.

In multidimensional applications there is frequently a need to reference members relative to some other member. For example, one might wish to run a sales report for all products in the electronic products group including any relevant subtotals plus the totals for the group. In a dimensional hierarchy, you would request to see the sales figures for the electronics member of the product dimension and all its children or descendents.

Relative referencing within a hierarchical structure is more complicated than relative referencing within a row and column structure. In a row and column structure, such as the flat file shown in Figure 3.30, every row has the same set of columns, so the same collection of elements or fields can be referenced in any row above or below any other row of interest.

Due to the grid representation, the set of all fields that are the same distance from the top of the file as the field "shoes" (column 3) in row 3 (namely, the fields store "3", week "4", "variable sales", and value "$1000") is the same as the set of all fields that are the same distance from the bottom of the file as the field "shoes" in row 3.

	Store	Week	Product	Variable	Value	
1	4	3	shoes	sales	$675	9
2	4	4	shoes	sales	$1025	8
3	**4**	**5**	**Shoes**	**sales**	**$1000**	**7**
4	4	6	shoes	sales	$850	6
5	5	1	shoes	sales	$775	5
6	5	2	shoes	sales	$550	4
7	5	3	shoes	sales	$690	3
8	5	4	shoes	sales	$475	2
9	5	5	shoes	sales	$900	1

Top-down counting

Bottom-up counting

Note: The set of all fields the same distance from the top of the file as the field "shoes" in row3, column3 is the same as the set of all fields the same distance from the bottom of the file as the field "shoes" in row3, column3.

Figure 3.30 Referencing within a flat file.

Because it does not matter in which direction we count, we need only one method of counting. By convention, we count down from the top. So row 3 means the third row down from the top. In fact, the whole concept of row as a specific collection of elements would lose its meaning if it could not be identified in a direction-independent way. (I only mention the obvious to serve as a point of comparison.)

With hierarchical structures it usually does matter in which direction we count. Referring back to Figure 3.29, let us say we wanted to reference all the elements that were the same distance from the root as home appliances, as shown in Figure 3.31. The collection includes the elements desks, chairs, beds, home appliances, and office equipment. All the elements in this collection are two levels down from the root.

Whereas in the flat file example above we could reference the same collection of elements either from the top or the bottom of the file, the members of the hierarchical dimension that are two levels down from the root are not all the same distance from the leaves. This is shown in panel A of Figure 3.32, which is composed of the same product hierarchy as Figure 3.31, but where the collection of members the same distance from the bottom of the hierarchy as home appliances are highlighted. Home appliances is two levels

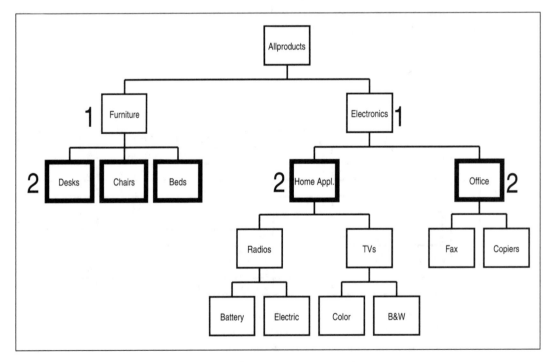

Figure 3.31 Referencing from the root within a hierarchy.

down from the root and two levels up from the leaves. However, when counting up from the leaves, no other member is the same number of levels up as home appliances.

You may have noticed that there is more than one way to count up from the leaves. Essentially, you can count the maximum distance, as was done in panel A, or the minimum distance, which is shown in panel B. Both counting methods are useful. The maximum distance method is the one more commonly used. (This is discussed further in Chapter 7.) In any event, the collection of elements that are the same distance from the root of the hierarchy as home appliances is not the same collection of elements that are the same distance from the leaves as home appliances.

Dimensional hierarchies, like the product hierarchy shown in Figure 3.32, for which the collection of members some distance from a vertical edge of the dimension depends on whether one started counting from the top or bottom edge, are called **asymmetric** or **ragged**.

Although asymmetric hierarchies are common, not all hierarchies are asymmetric. Hierarchies, like the time hierarchy shown in Figure 3.33, where the collection of members some distance from the vertical edge of the dimension is the same regardless of which edge you started counting from, are called **symmetric hierarchies**. With symmetric hierarchies, you can refer to members by their level. (Levels are discussed in Chapter 7.) Thus, quarters as a collection is the set of all members two levels up from the bottom and one level down from the top.

Because the relative referencing of members within a hierarchy is generally sensitive to the direction in which you count, most OLAP vendors use different terms to identify distances down from a member versus distances up from a member. Not only do they use different terms, but (given that they developed products independently of one another) some use the same terms

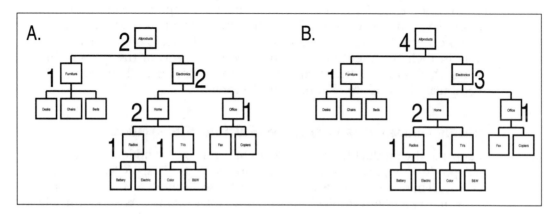

Figure 3.32 Referencing from the leaves in a hierarchy.

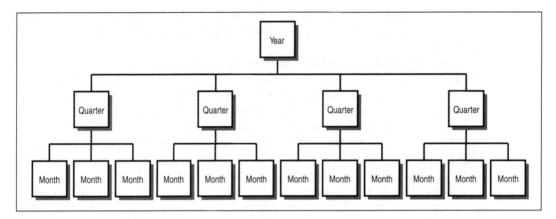

Figure 3.33 A symmetric hierarchy.

to mean opposite things. (For example, some vendors use the term "genera-tion" to mean distance down from a member and use the term "level" to mean distance up from a member. Others use the term "level" to mean down and the term "generation" to mean up.)

To be clear with terms, I will use the terms "up" and "down" combined with the term "level" and the terms "minimum" or "maximum" (when nec-essary) to signify the direction and way in which one is counting along a hi-erarchy. Distances counted from a member toward the leaves will be called "levels down." In Figure 3.31, for example, furniture is one level down from allproduct and home appliances is two levels down. The distance from a nonleaf member to the nearest leaf member will be called "minimum levels up." Looking again, in panel B of Figure 3.32, allproducts is just two mini-mum levels up from some leaves. In panel A, the root is four maximum levels up from some leaves. That said, and in order to simplify the terminology, the term "levels up" will mean the maximum levels up because it is the most common way that levels up are counted. OLAP vendors do differ consider-ably in their treatment of hierarchies, both in terms of the types of hierar-chies they support (there are still more to come) and in terms of the vocabulary they use to refer to them. Be careful.

Single Dimensions May Have Multiple Hierarchies

Return to the product hierarchy shown in Figure 3.31, and look at the individ-ual products represented at the leaf nodes: beds, TVs, VCRs, and fax ma-chines. There are other ways to group these individual products than by furniture versus electronics. Take pricing, for example. As shown in Figure 3.34, the categories "bargain," "typical," and "deluxe" represent another equally useful method for organizing the members of the product dimension.

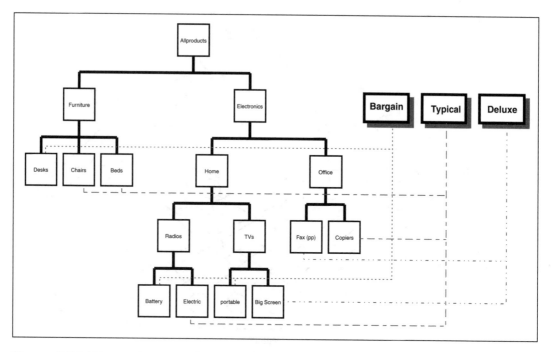

Figure 3.34 Dimensions can have multiple hierarchies.

Choosing the appropriate middle levels of grouping or aggregation are critical to our understanding and our ability to make decisions because data has only one detail level and one fully aggregated level but many intermediate levels. As shown in Figure 3.35, there are many paths to Nirvana. Each path highlights some factors and hides others. For example, aggregating store-level product sales into cites, states, and countries will highlight factors that are differentiated by region, such as economic zone-based differences in sales. The same aggregation path will hide other factors such as store size–based differences in sales. The nearly limitless number of intermediate levels, such as product price groups, product margin groups, product type groups, and product producer groups, allows us to experiment with different ways of looking at and understanding our data. This is one of the areas of convergence between dimensional structures and statistics. For example, techniques such as cluster analysis can help to identify the natural groupings in the data which then serve as useful intermediate levels of aggregation. (More on the relationship between OLAP and statistics in Chapter 15.)

Alternate methods of grouping do more than just rearrange the members, they create entirely different aggregate numbers.[3] (Compare this with the view reorganizations shown in Figures 3.21 and 3.22.) Figure 3.36 shows two spreadsheets in two panels. Both spreadsheets are two-dimensional and are

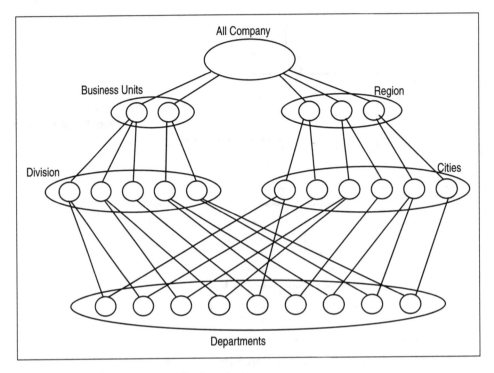

Figure 3.35 The many paths to nirvana.

composed of a variables dimension and a product dimension. The variables dimension is identical between the two spreadsheets. The product dimensions share the same leaf nodes between the two spreadsheets; however, Figure 3.36A rolls up into furniture, home, and office products whereas Figure

A				B		
	Sales	Costs			Sales	Costs
Beds	500	450		Tables	350	200
Tables	350	200		Fax	275	275
Furniture	850	650		Radios	150	125
Radios	150	125		Bargains	775	600
TV's	550	400		Beds	500	450
Home	700	525		Photocopiers	600	500
Fax	275	275		TV's	550	400
Photocopier	600	500		Deluxe	1650	1350
Office	875	775				

Figure 3.36 Different rollup paths produce different aggregate numbers.

3.36B rolls up into bargain and deluxe products. Not only are the numbers different, the number of numbers is different. Price and customer are two equally valid ways of grouping individual products. For most multidimensional products, the two rollups would be treated as separate hierarchies within the same dimension.[4]

In this sense, a dimension may be thought of as a collection of leaf members and the set of hierarchy or group members created from that collection. In other words, all the members of a dimension—leaf members, intermediate level members, and root members—form a single collection of members of the same type, which, as a whole, constitutes one factor/dimension in a multifactor/dimensional situation. Keep in mind that all members of a dimension, from leaf to root, can vary from analysis to analysis.

Looking again at Figure 3.34, if a dimension has multiple hierarchies, when traversing up the hierarchy from any node (child) that has two or more parents, it is necessary to specify the parent or root toward which you are navigating. For example, if from the member fax machines, you wanted to navigate up to office equipment, it would be necessary to indicate that you wanted to move in the direction of allproduct rather than in the direction of deluxe products.

Summary of Hierarchies

Hierarchies are the foundation for aggregating data and for navigating between levels of detail within a hypercube. Relative referencing within a hierarchical environment is more complicated than within a row and column environment as the former is direction-specific. Although hierarchies are not a necessary part of any dimension, all real-world applications of moderate or greater complexity involve some hierarchical dimensions such as time, geography, product, customer, or market.

Multilevel Hypercubes

The combination of multiple dimensions and multiple levels per dimension constitutes the essence of a multidimensional cube or hypercube. A cell in a hypercube is defined by the intersection of one member from each dimension. The more dimensions and hierarchies are in the cube, the more complex is the neighborhood surrounding any cell, and the more directions along which you can go browsing. In an N-dimensional hypercube (with one hierarchy level per dimension), each cell has $2N$ immediate neighbors or browsing directions (an immediate neighbor to a cell differs from that cell by one unit of one dimension). A cell in a two-dimensional spreadsheet, for example, has four immediate neighbors; a cell in a three-dimensional cube has six.

Calculating the Number of Cell Neighbors

When you add hierarchies to the situation the number of browsing directions gets even larger. Figure 3.37 shows how to calculate, for any given cell, the total number of neighboring cells. (The total number of neighboring cells includes all cells other than itself that are zero or one unit away in any combination of dimensions.)

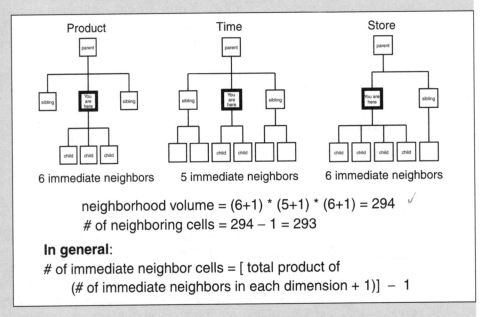

Figure 3.37 Calculating the number of neighboring cells.

Navigating in a direction is one way to browse a hypercube (or any structure, for that matter). Every time you use your cursor key or scroll bar, you are directionally navigating. Another way to move is by explicit statement of where you want to go. I call this an **endpoint navigation**. Stating that you want to see data for New York, or see last month's total sales, or see projections for next year's labor force are examples of navigating to a particular endpoint or view as opposed to navigating in a particular direction.

The term "drill down" refers to the process of navigating either directionally or by endpoints toward greater detail. That greater detail can come from moving down along any dimension. In other words, if you were looking at the screen shown in Figure 3.38A, you could drill down in any of the model's dimensions for which greater levels of detail existed. Figure 3.38B shows the

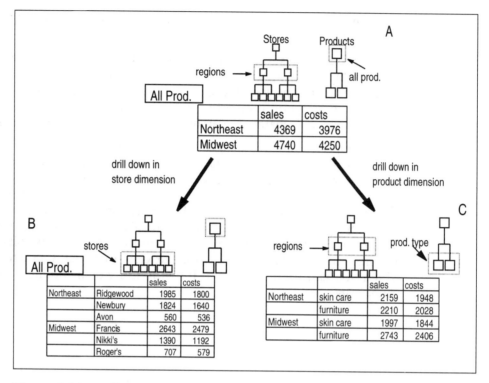

Figure 3.38 Drilling down.

result of drilling down in the products dimension. Figure 3.38C shows the result of drilling down in the geography dimension. The term "drill up" is simply the reverse of drill down.[5]

Endnotes

1. Abbott, Edwin, *Flatland*, HarperCollins Publishers, Inc., New York, 1983.

2. This term was first mentioned, I believe, in *The OLAP Report* published in 1995. See Nigel Pendse and Richard Creeth, *The OLAP Report: Succeeding with Online Analytical Processing* (London: Business Intelligence ltd., 1995), pp. 52–64.

3. The number of distinct hierarchies in a multidimensional structure is equal to the product of the number of hierarchies in each dimension. Thus, if there were 3 in time (calendar, fiscal and project), 3 in store (regions, types

and sizes), and 4 in product (type, price, margin and volume), and 1 in variables there would be 3*3*4*1 = 36 distinct hierarchies.

4. Some products can support only one hierarchy per dimension. Such products would have to treat each hierarchy as a separate dimension (that is, product price groups would form one dimension and product type groups would form a second dimension, which is how most statistics packages work), or add the separate hierarchy members to the original dimension.

5. In this respect, I disagree with Ralph Kimball where he states (page 38 in *The Data Warehouse Toolkit*) that "An explicit hierarchy is not needed for drilling down." Although you can drill down in any dimension, there needs to be some hierarchy in any dimension that can support or be used for a drill down. If there weren't a hierarchy for a dimension, you would always be in the drill-down position. In Figure 3.38, for example, you need to have a product hierarchy where individual products collapse into an allproduct in order to generate the view in panel 3.38A relative to which you can then drill down into the individual products shown in panel 3.38C.

Basic Multidimensional Features, Part 2

In the last chapter we began our story of the basic features of multidimensional information systems. You learned how to think about data sets, problems, and solutions in terms of hypercubes composed of multiple hierarchical dimensions. In this chapter, you will learn about the data that populates and flows through hypercubes:

❑ What kinds of data there are

❑ How different kinds get into a hypercube

❑ How simple and complex derivations are specified

Data

What kinds of data belong in a hypercube? Can hypercubes be populated with nonnumeric data? Or are they strictly numbers-oriented? Although the majority of data residing in real-world implemented hypercubes is numeric, any kind of media from text to graphics, and even sound, may be multidimensional. Imagine an audio cube consisting of bird songs (as variables) organized by species, region, and time. The key issues related to data and whether they belong in a hypercube are as follows:

❑ Identifying the value of bringing the data into a hypercube

❑ If the value is there, finding a tool that can do the job

Beyond numbers, many tools provide the ability to populate hypercubes with textual data. But if you wanted to create a more exotic hypercube now, you would need to find an object database.

79

The two main ways that an OLAP tool adds value to data is through organization and aggregation (in multiple levels and dimensions). Numeric data is so well suited for OLAP applications because it has a dimensional organization and because we know how to aggregate it. Other data types may benefit from a dimensional organization, but the issues surrounding their aggregation (with the exception of counts or other match-based processes performed on string data) go well beyond the numeric computation abilities of today's OLAP tools. For example, how would you aggregate bird songs across species or time?

Most of the corporate data held in databases around the world is character- or text-string-based.[1] For this reason, I believe that character string data will become increasingly important for OLAP tools to handle properly. Character string data like color, address, package type, customer type, and reason for return are essential factors in analysis. You may want to analyze whether product sales are a function of package type or color. Or you might want to know if there is any correlation between the type of complaints your chain receives and the location of the store where it was made. (See Chapter 15 for a discussion of analysis with nontraditional data.)

Attributes

So far, all of the data we have talked about (with the possible exception of the data we just finished talking about), numeric and nonnumeric, have been cell-based. Data may also attach to the members of a dimension. This type of data is called **attribute data**. For example, a store dimension may contain information about the address, phone number, and square footage of each store. These pieces of information would be called attributes of the store dimension.

From a data warehousing perspective, most of the attribute data exists in the dimension tables like the one shown in the Star Schema in Figure 2.4. Attributes can be just as important as cell-based data for the purposes of analyzing a hypercube. For example, you may want to see sales broken down by stores grouped according to the attribute's square footage, or number of floors, or the existence of parking, or whether it plays music, or its opening date. Dimensions may have dozens of attributes. Most multidimensional tools provide for a way to store and analyze attribute information.

Beyond Simple Attributes

We can further distinguish between definitional and property dimension member information. Although few tools support the distinction, there is a big conceptual difference between information related to the definition of a member and information that reflects a state or property of the member (usually at some point in time and/or space). An example of definitional information could be the location and ownership of a store. Generally speaking, if the location and ownership of a store were to change, the store would no longer be considered the same store. An example of property information would be the square footage of a store. In the latter example, the square footage of a store, which is usually indistinguishably treated from definitional information, could change one day as a particular store expands or contracts. But the store would (generally speaking) continue to be regarded as the same store.

There is also attribute information that does not neatly belong to one particular dimension. To understand this, think of "belonging to" a dimension as meaning "varying with respect to" a dimension. In other words, typical data in a hypercube varies as a function of all the identifier dimensions. Sales may vary as a function of store and time and product. What the industry calls attribute information can be thought of as data that varies only as a function of the dimension to which it belongs. For example, "address," which above was called an attribute of the stores dimension, may be thought of as a variable that varies only along the store dimension but remains constant across all other dimensions. Thus, the value of the address variable varies from store to store but does not vary from product to product or from time to time. In reality, few if any dimensions are static. Allowances must be made for the fact that dimensions change. (Such allowances are discussed in Chapter 10 in "Practical Steps for Defining a Multidimensional Information System.")

What about variables whose variance pattern falls in between typical variables and attribute variables? These are multidimensional attributes or variables that vary as a function of some but not all the dimensions in a hypercube. Price may vary as a function of product and time but not store. Rent may vary as a function of store and time but not product. Even square footage, which we safely called an attribute above, when looked at closely may be seen as a variable that varies predominantly across stores but also across time (though less frequently). In fact, by calling square footage an attribute of the store dimension, we need to version it or update it when square footage changes. This is precisely the transaction-oriented current-data-only approach that OLAP was supposed to transcend. Admittedly, it is difficult to model these situations, but if you want to think precisely about your data you need to keep them in mind.

Links

You have now seen the basics of a multilevel hypercube with its variables and attributes, and how to drill through and pivot one. It is time to see how hypercubes get data. Then, in the next section, we will see how that data formulaically flows through the cube. This section introduces the linkages between a hypercube and its data sources.

Need for Links

Hypercubes need some linkage to the external data world if they are going to receive data. Those linkages may be as simple as a table import facility that is periodically invoked. All data processing products, from spreadsheets to statistics packages, have these capabilities.

Unlike typical data processing products, however, OLAP products are regularly called upon to process large amounts of periodically refreshed data. A manual approach to maintaining synchronicity between data sources and hypercubes is unacceptable in the long run. OLAP tools need to have the ability to establish persistent links with external sources of data (and dimensions and attributes), such that when changes occur in the external data sources, they are automatically brought into the hypercube. And any dimension modifications or data calculations are automatically and incrementally performed.

Because OLAP products and implementations are generally separate from the systems that generate the data to be manipulated and analyzed, links serve essentially as transformation functions. They indicate how to transform table- or spreadsheet-formatted data and metadata into dimensional data and metadata.

Links can be read only or read/write. Although we are focusing here on the traditional read aspects of links, there is certainly a need for bidirectional links. As OLAP systems become more integrated with transactional systems, the results of analyzing data, such as finding an optimal price point for a product, will want to be fed back into operational systems, or at least the data warehouse, if there is one. Some products do support read/write links. (More on this theme in Chapter 16.)

Links can be static or dynamic. Static links are not capable of processing changes made to the source. They are used only by the multidimensional tool when it loads or refreshes its information from the source. Dynamic links maintain an open connection between the source and the hypercube wherein changes to the source are propagated to the hypercube.

Even though I was recently involved in developing an OLAP product that had as one of its goals the creation of extensive link capabilities, as of the time of this writing, few tools offer such links. Whether the tools that you use support links that you can just declare and have work, or whether you need to code the transformations by hand, the transformations would be the same. If your tool supports the ability just to declare the links without procedural code, then they should map cleanly to the ones described here. If you need to code a script or program by hand, then the descriptions of link types can serve as its high-level design.

Links provide a persistent infrastructure for importing and exporting data and metadata. They vary as a function of the type of information brought into the cube and the type of table from which the information is obtained. The limiting factors for linking are the hypercube's ability to process small amounts of change efficiently and the link processor's ability to detect changes efficiently. As illustrated in Figure 4.1, change may come from a variety of sources. The remainder of this section focuses on table links. (Importing data is covered in the hands-on case studies of Chapters 12 and 13.)

Types of Links

There are three basic kinds of links: structure links, attribute links, and content links. (Member attributes, essentially data that is associated with the

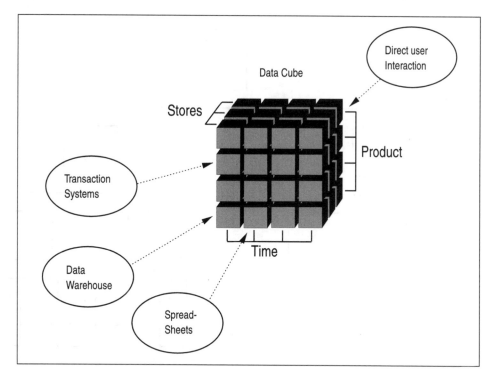

Figure 4.1 Changes may come from many sources.

structure rather than the hypercubes, do not fall cleanly into either metadata or data.) A **structure link** is used to extract structural information for a dimension, identifying the members and their referential or hierarchical structure (if any). An attribute link is used to map attribute information to the members of a dimension. (Note from the preceding discussion on attributes in Chapter 2 that the choice of defining a quantity to be an attribute as opposed to cell data ought to be made with care.) **Content links** are used to map data into the hypercube. Figure 4.2 shows a classification scheme for links. (They will treated in depth in Chapter 7. For now, Figure 4.2 should help you see the whole.)

Tables that contain structural information (member identity and hierarchical relationships) are linked to a dimension with structure links. A structure link connects a dimension with one or more structuring columns in a table. There are two basic forms of such tables. In one form, called "parent-child," a member may appear as the child of another member in one row and as the parent of other members in other rows. In another form, a table may contain two or more columns that identify members at different hierarchical levels, for example, company name, SIC code, industrial sector, or city, state, and region. It is possible (particularly for variables) that no hierarchy is speci-

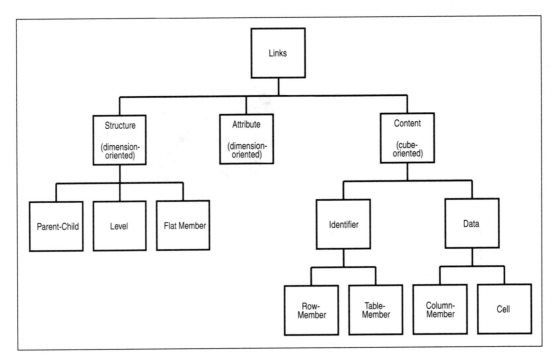

Figure 4.2 Classification of link types.

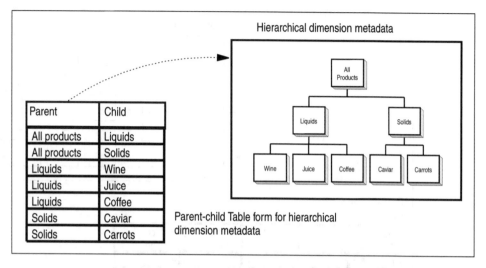

Figure 4.3 Parent-child structure inputs to hierarchical dimension of an OLAP model.

fied. In this case, having all the members and being able to tell them apart is as much structure as is required from the table. Figure 4.3 shows structure links between a parent-child table representing the product dimension and the product dimension of the model. Note the hierarchical members of the product dimension. Figure 4.4 shows structure links between a lookup table and the levels of a dimension.

Tables containing information other than structural relationships that are associated with members can have that information brought into the dimensional model of the multidimensional tool through attribute links. Frequently, this attribute information will be part of a metadata table that also contains structural information, and the one table would be connected to the multidimensional model with both types of links. Each attribute link will connect an attribute associated with the members of a dimension with a column identifying the members and a column identifying values for the attribute. Attribute links are shown in Figure 4.5.

Tables containing values for variables in the hypercube's dimensional space need to be attached with content links. While the structure and attribute links connect a dimension and a table independently of any cube, the content links all connect to a table in the context of a cube. Two of the different types of content links are required to connect a table to a cube[2] because different links extract member identifiers and variables' values from rows. Figure 4.6 shows the content links between a multidimensional model and an input table.

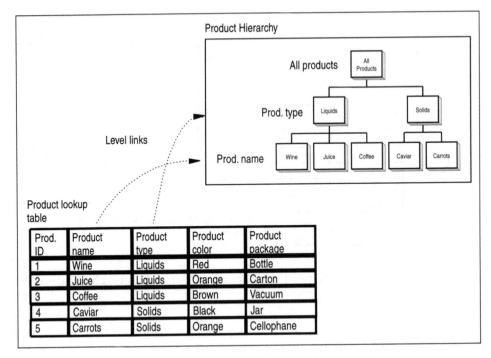

Figure 4.4 Level links.

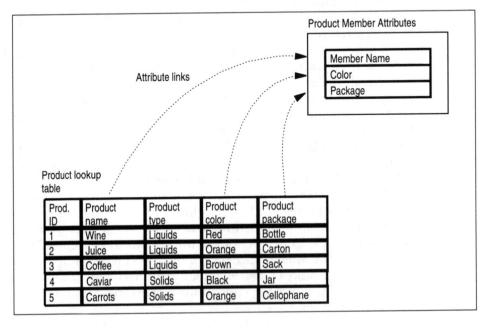

Figure 4.5 Attribute links.

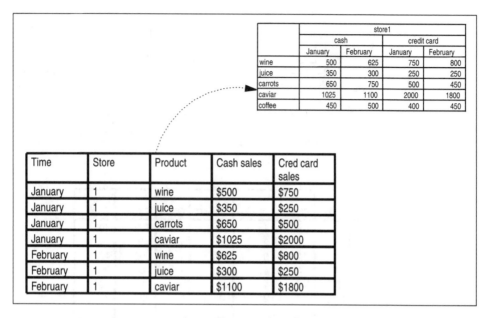

Time	Store	Product	Cash sales	Cred card sales
January	1	wine	$500	$750
January	1	juice	$350	$250
January	1	carrots	$650	$500
January	1	caviar	$1025	$2000
February	1	wine	$625	$800
February	1	juice	$300	$250
February	1	caviar	$1100	$1800

Figure 4.6 Content links from an input table to a hypercube.

Tables may require aggregation prior to entry in a cube. For example, a multidimensional model that has weeks as its lowest level of time may need to link to a data source that has daily summaries or individual transaction information. In this case, the necessary aggregations would be included in the overall link information. In general, if there end up being duplicate combinations of members in the rows, the data-bearing fields should be aggregated. For example, take a cube with sales variables and store, time, and product dimensions, and a linked data table containing transaction number, store, time, product, quantity, and sale price. We would not link the transaction number field. We expect more than one sale transaction for some store, day, and product combination (there may be six different records that all contain "store 3," "May 11, 1997," "Dom Perignon"), so we would want to specify summing of the quantity and sale price fields as part of the links.

It is also possible to link in data and hierarchical metadata from the same table, as illustrated in Figure 4.7. Certainly, if this is the form of your data tables, a multidimensional tool should be able to make use of the information. However, it is not recommended to maintain your data tables in this form because any organizational changes to your source data, such as reorganizing your product groups or changing the reporting structure for the corporation, will result in a need to define new links between the input tables and the multidimensional cube. This occurs because the particular form of the hierarchy is defined by the columns, that is, stores, cities, regions. Any change to the hierarchy, such as adding a new product group, needs to be reflected in a

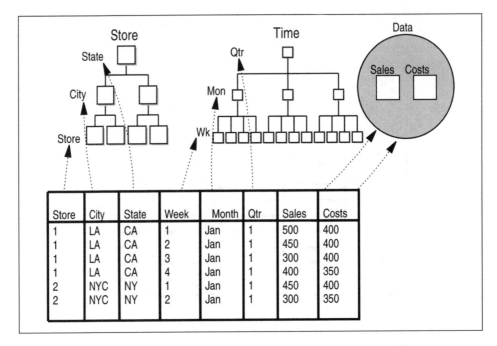

Figure 4.7 Linking in data and metadata from the same table.

change to the column structure of the input tables, which in turn requires a redefinition of the links between the cube and the input tables. It does provide a convenient form for packaging a client-sized hypercube of data, though.

Even if the table is providing multiple kinds of information, each link is to one kind of information only (structure, attributes, or content). One reason for this is that a structure link is used to define the members of a dimension, while the attribute and content links extract information for members already in a dimension. Procedurally, the dimension must be constructed before data values can be identified with its members. In some notation, a single construct could represent both, but we would say that it represents the combination of a separate structure link and content link.

Summary of Links

Links between separate multidimensional and operation systems are a fact of life. They define the method for maintaining a persistent bidirectional connection between the hypercube and a changing external data set. We discussed content links, structure links, attribute links, and mixed-type links.

We focused on the import capabilities of links in this section because they are the most critical and because most commercial hypercubes are import-oriented. Nevertheless, links will become more bidirectional as the results of multidimensional processing gets automatically fed back into production databases. Although there is nothing inherently multidimensional about links, the need to have robust dynamic links and the ability to incorporate incremental changes efficiently into a hypercube are important features for successful multidimensional systems. Multidimensional systems deal with sufficiently large quantities of data that a manual approach to maintaining synchronicity between data sources and hypercubes is unacceptable in the long run. As of the time of this writing, most of the multidimensional vendors were working hard to improve the seamlessness of the links between their hypercubes and the typical relational database-as-source.

Formulas

For any multidimensional model, as we saw in the "Data" section, the intersection of some member from each dimension identifies a cell. Some cells contain input data, such as individual product sales. All other populated cells contain derived data. Derived data values are defined in terms of formulas. Formulas are used for aggregating, allocating, analyzing, explaining, and inferring. For example, net sales may be defined by a formula such as gross sales minus returns. And, business products may be defined as the sum of computer products, fax machines, and photocopiers. Next year's projected sales may be defined as the average sales growth multiplied by the current sales.

Referential Versus Formulaic Hierarchies

As we saw in Chapter 3, most dimensions have a hierarchical structure. This is true even with a simple example. Figures 4.8 through 4.10 show all the members for each of four dimensions in a simplified, though representative, sales example. Notice that all the dimensions except for variables (in Figure 4.8) have a hierarchical structure. Stores and time have single hierarchies. And products, with two separate hierarchies, have the most complex structure.

What exactly do these hierarchies represent? In Chapter 3 we spoke about the way hierarchical dimensions facilitated calculating (especially aggregating) and navigating or referencing. For example, all the store-level sales data may aggregate up the store dimension. And you can refer to all the stores in a particular city (assuming that stores connect to cities) as the children or first-level members below that city. In other words, it seemed that the hierarchical structure of a dimension determined both aggregations and ref-

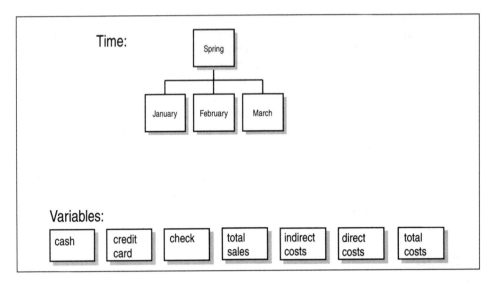

Figure 4.8 The dimensional structure for the time and variables dimensions.

erencing. Although this is frequently true, it is not always true. The way data is calculated within a hypercube need not share the same paths or structure as the way data is referenced. This is a very important point, one worth exploring.

The data associated with the city Columbus in the store dimension of Figure 4.9, for example, is the sum of the data associated with the three stores in Columbus:

Columbus = sum (store1, store2, store3)

Another way of saying this is that the value for Columbus is the sum of the values of its children. This is an example in which the calculation structure for a member is the same as the referential structure.

Now look at the "New Chicago Store" member of the store dimension in Figure 4.9. It represents a store that is being built but has not yet opened. Let's say you want to project what the revenues for this store might be. Figure 4.11 shows the formula for calculating the value of projected sales in the new Chicago store as the average of the known revenues for other nearby cities (perhaps modified by an appropriate weighting function). Notice that the dependency relationships for this formula also look like a hierarchy (otherwise known as a dependency tree). Thus, the formula hierarchy for a dimension member need not be the same as its referential hierarchy (that is, the formula for a member can use inputs that do not come from that member's children in the hierarchy).

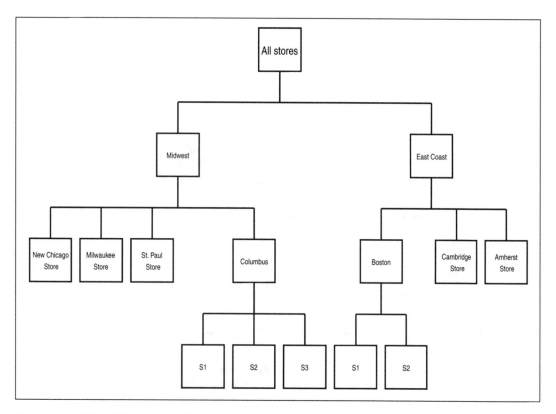

Figure 4.9 The dimensional structure for the stores dimension.

Look closely at Figures 4.8 to 4.11. Can you spot another instance where the formula hierarchy for a member is not the same as the referential hierarchy? How about total sales and total costs in the variables dimension? Total sales and total costs are both functions of their respective individual sales and costs, yet they coexist on the same level as a variables dimension.

When you define your dimensions in a multidimensional tool, you are initially defining the referential structure of the dimensions. For all but the variables dimension, that referential structure will frequently, though not always, be the same as the formulaic structure. In contrast, the formulas in the variables dimension may deviate substantially from their referential structure.

Finally, the dependency relationships between the members of a dimensional hierarchy may vary as a function of the other dimension members with whom they are intersecting. In fact, the distinction between measured and derived data applies to cells and not members. (In this respect, many vendors and journalists refer to input and derived members. Even the glossary published by the OLAP Council, as of the time of this writing, refers to

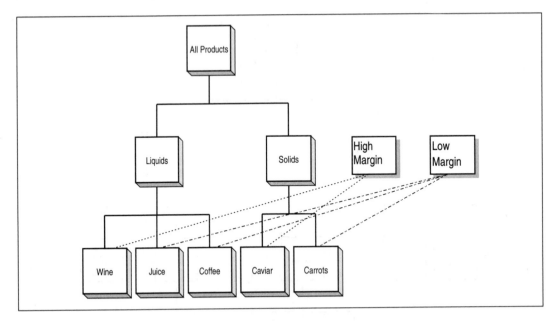

Figure 4.10 The dimensional structure for the products dimension.

input and derived members.) An extreme example of this is shown in Figure 4.12. For the variables dimension member "sales," the derivation path goes from the leaves to the root of the product hierarchy path. On the other hand,

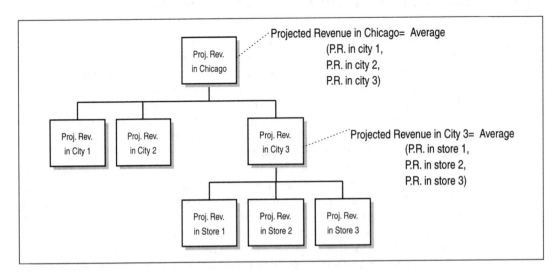

Figure 4.11 Dependency relationships form a hierarchy.

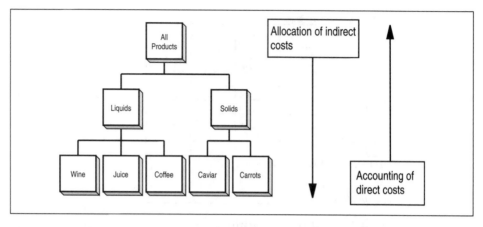

Figure 4.12 Derivation paths may flow in any direction.

the variable "allocated indirect costs" takes the opposite derivation path, going from the root of the hierarchy toward the leaves because costs are allocated from the top down.

Given the variable nature of dependency relationships within a dimension, the most precise way to represent them is relative to actual data points. Figure 4.13 shows the relationship between input and derived values for a portion of the example model.

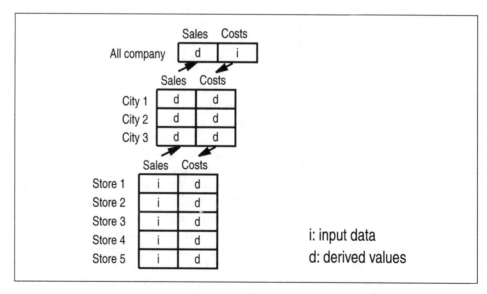

Figure 4.13 Input and derived values.

Sales of Ski Equipment by Region					
	C	D	E	F	
	West	North	East	Total	
skiis	450	750	800	2000	11
bindings	150	300	250	700	12
boots	300	450	500	1250	13
poles	50	125	100	275	14
goggles	75	200	150	425	15
total	1025	1825	1800	4650	16
Every aggregated cell carries its own formula					
For example:					
The total in cell c13 = sum(c8:c12)					
The total in cell d16 = sum(d11:d15)					

Figure 4.14 Cell-based formulas.

Now that we've seen how the term "hierarchy" has both a referential and a dependency meaning and that formulas define the dependency hierarchies for a cube, let us explore how formulas operate in a multidimensional environment.

Cell- and Axis-based Formulas

In a traditional spreadsheet environment, the formulas in terms of which derived cells are defined apply directly to the cell. In Figure 4.14, the value for total sales appearing in cell F16 is defined in terms of a formula for the contents of cell F16; specifically, F16 = sum F11 - F15.

It is no secret that cell formulas can get very numerous and messy as worksheets become complex. Given that OLAP applications can easily produce tens of millions of derived numbers, only a certified trouble worshipper would try to create and manage that many cell-based formulas.

In a multidimensional environment, formulas are usually defined in terms of the dimensions or axes. (Statisticians sometimes call these margin formulas.) Referring again to Figure 4.14, instead of creating one formula for the cell that defines the value of total sales for all products (that is, the formula for cell F16), you would define a formula for total sales in terms of each type of sale (along the variables dimension or axis) and a formula for all product in terms of individual products (along the product dimension or axis). The formula for total sales might be equal to the sum of direct plus indirect sales. The formula for all product might be equal to the sum of skis through goggles. The formula for total sales of all products is defined by the combination of the two separate formulas. An example of axis-based formulas is shown in Figure 4.15.

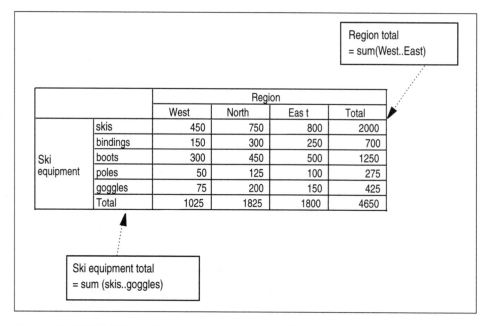

Figure 4.15 OLAP tools use margin or axis-based formulas.

Precedences

The formula for any particular cell is a function of the combination of all the dimension-specific formulas that apply to the cell. In many cases, as with the example above, the order in which dimension-specific formulas are applied to a cell does not affect the result of the calculation because the above calculation was defined purely in terms of sums. In general, when a cell is computed purely through addition, subtraction, multiplication, or division, then the formulas from each dimension may be computed in any order.

The following series of examples in Figure 4.16 shows how sums, differences, and ratios may be taken in any order. The left panel in each case performs the calculation with the column dimension first. The right panel performs the same calculation with the row dimension first. Note that, in all cases, the same result is achieved.

When a cell is defined in terms of combinations of different operators, then the result of the calculation may depend on the order of the operations. In general, you can combine addition with subtraction in any order; and you can combine multiplication and division in any order. But you cannot combine addition or subtraction with division or multiplication without paying attention to the order. Look at the following examples to see this clearly.

Columns before rows　　　　　　　**Rows before columns**

A. Pure summation

	Store1	Store2	BothStores
Skis	80	30	110
Boots	40	60	100
BothProducts			210

	Store1	Store2	BothStores
Skis	80	30	
Boots	40	60	
BothProducts	120	90	210

B. Pure differences

	Actual	Planned	Actual / Plan
Sales	120	90	30
Cost	60	30	30
Profit			0

	Actual	Planned	Actual / Plan
Sales	120	90	
Cost	60	30	
Profit	60	60	0

C. Pure ratios

	Actual	Planned	Actual / Plan
Sales	120	90	1.33
Cost	60	30	2
Margin			0.67

	Actual	Planned	Actual / Plan
Sales	120	90	
Cost	60	30	
Margin	2	3	0.67

Figure 4.16 Pure operations may be computed in any order.

Figure 4.17 shows actual sales, planned sales, and the difference between actual and planned for two products. Notice that whether we obtain the variance by first summing the actual and planned product sales and then taking the difference of the sums, or whether we obtain the variance by taking the difference of actual and planned sales for each product and then summing the differences, we get the same variance values.

Figure 4.18 shows actual and planned total purchase price, tax rate and tax paid, and the ratio between the actual and planned values for each of these. Notice how, again, it doesn't make any difference whether we multiply

Columns before rows　　　　　　　**Rows before columns**

	Actual	Planned	Actual / Plan
Skis	120	100	
Boots	50	60	
BothProducts	170	160	10

	Actual	Planned	Actual / Plan
Skis	120	100	20
Boots	50	60	-10
BothProducts			10

Figure 4.17 Mixing sums and differences.

Columns before rows					Rows before columns			
	Actual	Planned	Actual / Plan			Actual	Planned	Actual / Plan
Price	150	120			Price	150	120	1.25
Tax Rate	.3	.25			Tax Rate	.3	.25	1.2
Tax Paid	45	30	1.5		Tax Paid			1.5

Figure 4.18 Mixing products and ratios.

the tax rate by the product price and then divide actual by plan, or whether we take the ratios of the actual and planned values first and then multiply them.

Figure 4.19 shows actual sales, planned sales, and variance in sales, except that this time variance is defined as actual divided by planned. Note how it does make a difference for the derived cell "variance in total costs" whether it was calculated as the ratio between total actual and total planned costs or whether it was calculated as the sum of the ratios of individual product variances.

Finally, Figure 4.20 shows actual tax, planned tax, and variance in tax, except that this time variance is defined as the difference between actual and planned. Notice how it makes a difference whether the derived cell "variance in tax paid" was calculated as the difference of products or as the product of differences.

Columns before rows					Rows before columns			
	Actual	Planned	Actual / Plan			Actual	Planned	Actual / Plan
Skis	120	100			Skis	120	100	1.20
Boots	50	60			Boots	50	60	.83
BothProducts	170	160	1.06		BothProducts			2.03

Figure 4.19 Mixing sums and ratios.

Columns before rows					Rows before columns			
	Actual	Planned	Actual / Plan			Actual	Planned	Actual / Plan
Price	150	120			Price	150	120	30
Tax Rate	.3	.25			Tax Rate	.3	.25	.05
Tax Paid	45	30	15		Tax Paid			1.5

Figure 4.20 Mixing products and differences.

Measurements that derive from other quantities are frequently sensitive to the order in which they are calculated. Ratios (including **flows**, or measures of one type per unit of another type), aggregate percentages, normalized indicators, and multiplicatively combined variables are all sensitive to calculation order.

Ratios, aggregate percentages, and normalized indicators are usually calculated on summarized data or averaged instead of summed. For example, if you had a data set describing the market penetration of your product in a variety of countries, you would not sum the percentages to a regional level to determine market penetration on a regional basis. You would either sum the data that went into computing the market penetration to the regional level and calculate market penetration at that level, or, if perhaps you possessed only market penetration figures, you would define the market penetration per region as the average of the penetrations per country. If you went with averages, they would most likely be weighted where the weighting was a function of the market size in each country. But this tendency is not a rule. For example, there may be instances where a ratio, such as profitability, is computed before being averaged. This produces an unweighted average profitability which, in some cases, may be what you need.[3]

Multiplicatively combined variables need to be combined before they are aggregated. For example, if you want to calculate the lost productivity across all workers in your organization as a result of local area network downtimes, assuming you track downtime and system users, you would want to first multiply the length of downtime per system failure by the number of persons affected and then sum that number for lost productivity per failure across all system failures. You would get the wrong answer by first summing the number of downtime hours and the number of system users and then multiplying those two sums together.

Although tendencies exist, since almost any ordering of operations will produce a mathematically meaningful result, you really need to know what you are trying to calculate before assigning precedences to formulas.

Default Precedence Orders

When using a multidimensional tool, if the value for a derived cell depends on the application order of the formulas that apply to the cell, you need some method for deciding which formulas to apply in which order. For example, precedence may be set on a dimension-wide basis, that is, time before products before variables, and then overridden (as you will see in the next section) on a member-by-member basis.

There is no golden rule for deciding what precedence order to apply in every case. In practice, of course, as with the example above involving the sum of a set of ratios or percentages, rules of thumb can help you decide the order in which to compute aggregates. But once again, rules of thumb are no substitute for knowing what you are trying to calculate.

The practical methods offered by vendors vary widely. Some tools are fairly intelligent and do a good job of guessing the order in which to apply formulas. Other tools are not as intelligent but offer a simple declarative method for users to specify the type of number any derived cell should contain. For example by declaring that the cell for "all-product sales variance" is a ratio, the tool would know to calculate the variance ratio last. Still other tools, though flexible, are unintelligent and offer no more than a procedural approach for defining formula precedence.

Assigning Default Precedence

Several complications are involved in algorithmically assigning the "correct" precedence for a series of dimension formulas that overlap at a cell. Before you can determine which dimension formula should be evaluated in which order, you need to assign some sort of precedence ordering to each dimension formula. In other words, there needs to be a table of precedences stating that addition comes before division (this being the type of rule that would enable a multidimensional tool to guess that an allproduct margin is to be calculated by taking the ratio of allproduct sales and allproduct costs rather than the sum of individual product margins). However, dimension formulas may themselves be complexes of formulaic clauses. For example, the formula:

Variance = (Actual - Plan) / Plan

contains both a subtraction operator and a division operator. Given that subtraction and division have different precedence, how do you assign a precedence to the formula as a whole? There is no right or wrong answer for the general case that vendors can use to ensure that the right thing happens in all cases. But somewhere (in the tool or in your head), there need to be rules for assigning precedence for dimension formulas that contain multiple formulaic clauses, each of which has a different precedence level. If you create complex formulas in your dimensions, and if you are using a tool that does not force you to specify the order of calculation of the formulas, you should be aware of how the tool automatically assigns precedence levels to overlapping formulas. And you should verify that aggregate values represent what you are trying to calculate.

What follows are some general classifications of formulas into precedence levels. The higher the level, the later the formula is calculated. These are listed in Table 4.1. Following the table, note the listing of several operators that cannot be assigned a precedence level without knowing what is being calculated. For example, the operator "max" has no natural precedence level. Imagine that you keep track every month of which week during the month had the greatest sales. Each month would have a sales value for the maximum weekly sales. And suppose that you stored this information in a simple cube composed of a variable and time dimension where time consisted of weeks, months, quarters, and years. Furthermore, you defined time so that all its members sum up to the next highest level. At the year level, the maximum sales could tell you two equally useful things depending on its precedence level relative to the sum operator associated with the time dimension. If the summation operator of the time dimension were calculated first, it would tell you the greatest weekly sales value during the past year. But if the maximum operator were calculated first, it would tell you the sum of the 12 weekly maximums.

Table 4.1 General Rules of Thumb for Assigning Precedence Levels

Operator	*Precedence Level*
Input values for which there are no formulas	1
Count of nonmissing cells in a range	2
Multiplication Unary minus	3
Addition Subtraction Sum	4
Average	5
Division Exponentiation	6

Logical and relational operators such as
   Equal to, not equal to
   Less than, greater than
   And, or
	7

Operators whose precedence level needs to be assigned on a case-by-case basis:

- ❏ Max
- ❏ Min
- ❏ First
- ❏ Last
- ❏ Rcoefficient
- ❏ Variance
- ❏ Least squares intercept and slope
- ❏ Standard deviation

In practice, most multidimensional calculation engines apply only one rule to calculate a particular cell because the inputs to the derived cell are, relatively speaking, intermediate results from yet other calculations as opposed to raw data. For example, as shown in Figure 4.19, the total variance cell (actual/plan), as seen in each of the two panels, is calculated in two different ways using two different inputs. In the left panel, it is calculated by applying the one formula "ratio" to the sum of actual product sales and the sum of planned product sales. In the right panel, it is calculated by applying the one formula "sum" to the ratio of actual to planned ski sales and the ratio of actual to planned boot sales.

Conditional Formulas

Axis formulas may be looked at as category- or set-based formulas. In a three-dimensional cube consisting of 10 members per dimension, a single formula applied to a single member, such as a formula for the allproduct member of the product dimension, applies across all the cells in the cube that have an allproduct component. Specifically, this would amount to 100 cells. The number 100 is reached by taking the product of the number of members in each of the nonstore dimension as shown in Figure 4.21.

It is only natural, given such generality of application, that many members should have formulas that vary as a function of where they apply relative to the other dimensions in the cube. For example, the all-plant member (that is to say, manufacturing plant) of a plant dimension might be defined as the sum of the individual plants. This works fine for the variables output, number of employees, costs, and so forth. It doesn't work for all the members of the variable dimension.

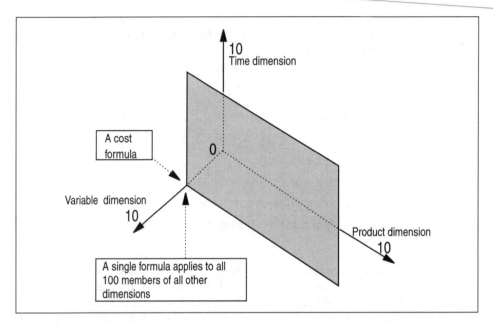

Figure 4.21 Formulas for a given member apply to all members of all other dimensions.

As you saw in the previous section, normalized indicators, or measures that have been converted to range between 0 and 1, such as quality or productivity indexes, need to be averaged instead of summed. This amounts to defining an exception that overrides the axis-based formula for the intersection of the quality index member of the variable dimension and the all-plant member of the plant dimension. The exception would look something like the following:

```
Allplant = sum (individual plants)
except
If variable = quality index
then allplant = average (individual plants)
```

A robust multidimensional system would let you specify the exception conditions with any combination of relative dimensional referencing such as if member is the child of some member, or if member is the parent of some member, and so on. For example, the indirect cost member of the variables dimension may vary as a function of the type of product (along the product dimension) for which the indirect cost is being calculated. The indirect costs for producing furniture may be different from the indirect costs for producing clothing.

Using relative referencing, a multidimensional language would need to allow for formulas that state roughly the following:

- ❑ If product is a descendent of furniture, then the indirect cost is total salary divided by 2;
- ❑ If product is a descendent of clothing, then the indirect cost is total salary divided by 3.

The other major type of formula exception is data-driven. For example, the formula for the pool of funds available for bonuses may vary as a function of the percentage variance in direct sales between actual and plan.

Roughly stated, a formula for this type of variance would look something like the following:

```
If variance of actual/plan direct sales < 0.95
then the bonus pool is 0

If variance of actual/plan direct sales is between 0.95 and 1.20
then the bonus pool is 0.1% of total direct sales revenue

If variance of actual/plan direct sales > 1.2
then the bonus pool is 0.15% of total direct sales revenue
```

Both types of formula exceptions are needed.

Note that different products may provide different techniques for specifying where functions should apply based on location in the dimensional space of the model. One possibility is to use if-then tests in the formula language, which would follow the form of the preceding examples. Another possibility is to organize the formulas into a structure which associates formulas with regions of the cube, so that dimensional formulas are associated not with dimensions as a whole but with those subsets of the hypercube over which the formula will apply. So, the capability of overriding dimensional formulas with specific formulas for subsets of the cube may be provided either in formula syntax or in the structure of the formulas.

Summary of Formulas

Formulas operate in a more abstract fashion in a multidimensional environment than in a traditional spreadsheet environment. Instead of being defined in terms of individual cells, multidimensional formulas are defined in terms of members of dimensions, which means they apply to all cells in the cube sharing that particular member. As the number of cells to which a formula may apply can be very large, it is common for member formulas to be conditional upon the values of members in other dimensions. Because there can exist one formula per member per dimension, frequently more than one formula applies to a particular cell. In these cases a precedence rule needs to be invoked to determine which formula (or ordering of formulas) will be evaluated for the cell.

Conclusion

Through this chapter, you have explored the basic data-oriented concepts associated with multidimensional multilevel hypercubes. We looked at data, links, and formulas. The formulas that are used to calculate data cells are defined in terms of members of dimensions. Although this regularized approach is very powerful, data sets are rarely so homogeneous. As a result, there is usually a need to define exceptions based on the values of intersecting dimensions and precedence rules for choosing between multiple formulas applying to the same cell.

Some advanced multidimensional issues remain to be covered in Chapters 6 and 7, most notably multicube models, sparsity, and visualization (and further issues still in Chapters 10 and 15). If you read Chapters 6 and 7 carefully, you should have a solid understanding of the basics of any multidimensional model. And you should be able to pick up any OLAP instrument and improvise a few tunes.

Endnotes

1. Private conversations with international officials.

2. Strictly speaking, it is possible to define a table that would take only one kind of data link to extract the data into the cube, but you would never see such a table in real-world use. As a frivolous exercise, after reading the advanced discussion on links in Chapter 7, you may try to create such a table for a cube.

3. Thanks to Rick Crandall for pointing out this example.

The Benefits of a Multidimensional Approach

In the last two chapters, we explored the main features of multidimensional tools. These included dimensions, hierarchies, viewing hypercubes, linking to data, and axis formulas. Although the feature descriptions indicated how and why they might be used and examples were given along the way, the focus was more on understanding the features in a conceptual way than on seeing them in action.

This chapter focuses on the benefits of using multidimensional tools to design and work with analysis-based decision-oriented systems. Specifically, we will use the same example that was introduced in Chapter 2 to show how multidimensional tools overcome the problems of spreadsheets and SQL that were identified there.

The three main problems for spreadsheets and SQL Databases are these:

❑ Defining multilevel, multidimensional aggregates

❑ Defining multidimensional analytical calculations

❑ Defining ad hoc view reorganizations

Please note that this chapter contains a live example in a running sidebar. If you have been reading sequentially, this will be your first exposure to the enclosed multidimensional software. If you want a quick taste of what it is like to define and browse a multidimensional model, you are invited to follow along. For help on how to install TM/1 from the CD-ROM, please refer to Appendix G. Past this point, and assuming you wish to follow along, it is assumed that you have successfully installed the software. If you do not wish to follow along on your computer, simply ignore the sections in this chapter between

<u>**heading**</u>

and

_____

Typographic Conventions for Following the Interactive Example

As you follow along, you will be asked to open up different windows in the TM/1 program. Each time that you are supposed to see a new window on your screen, we will print the name of the window in **bold** and [bracket] it in the text. Everything that you will be asked to click on with your mouse will be <u>underlined</u> in the text. Key words that you will see or type on the screen will be *italicized*.

<u>**Getting Started**</u>

Click on the <u>TM/1</u> menu and select <u>Options</u>.

[TM/1 PERSPECTIVES - OPTIONS]

Click the <u>Select</u> button.

The normal Windows dialog box will appear. Point to the subdirectory *C:\TM1DATA\CH5MODEL*.

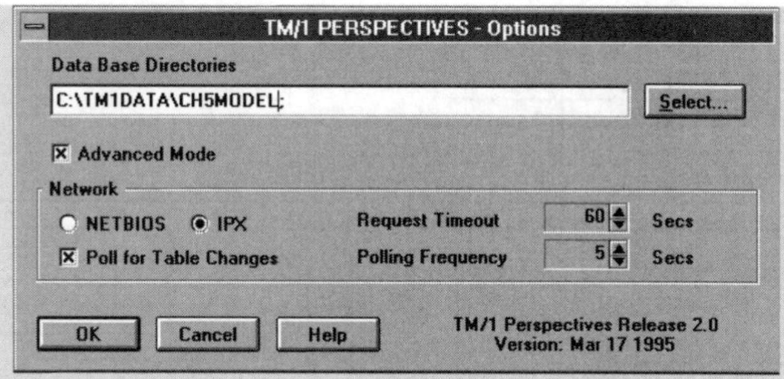

Figure 5.1 Selecting the example directory.

Click <u>OK</u>.
When asked whether you want to update the file *TM1.INI*, select <u>Yes</u>.

The Common Example

Recall the example described in Chapter 2. You are the sales director in a retail organization and you are responsible for analyzing sales and cost data for all the products sold in all of your stores. All the data has been collected and refined and it now resides in a large base table with some adjunct lookup tables. The schema for this base data, which was shown originally in Figure 2.4, is shown again in Figure 5.2.

Recall that the lookup/dimension tables also contain hierarchy information relating the members of each store, week, and product dimension with their respective aggregation paths. For example, store 3 in the base table of Figure 5.2 connects with the store lookup table where it has the name Ridgewood and rolls up to the Northeast region. Product 2 in the base table of Figure 5.2 connects with the product lookup table where it has the name rose water soap and rolls up into the product type soap in the skin care products division.

Building the Model with a Multidimensional Tool

Let's see how you would build a model with a multidimensional tool making use of the features learned in the previous two chapters. Remember, the goal is to define and compute aggregates for all sales and cost data and to calculate variances between plan and actual.

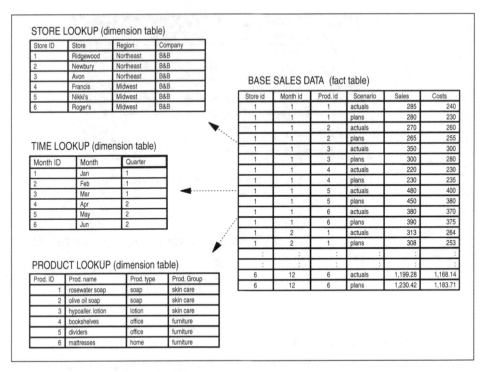

Figure 5.2 Common data and dimension tables for sale data.

Define Your Dimensions and Links

The first thing you need to do is define the dimensions. In this example there are five dimensions: stores, weeks, products, scenarios, and variables. Begin with the four identifier dimensions. You need to define a list of all the members in each identifier dimension. As you can see, the essential information for each of the identifier dimensions is contained in the corresponding lookup table. For example, the identifier dimension "products" is defined by the lookup table that includes *products, product types,* and *product lines.* The one difference is that the dimensional definition doesn't need the numeric identifiers.

Recall that we spoke about links in Chapter 4. We discussed how most multidimensional tools had features for connecting to source data and metadata either in level form or in parent/child form. In this example, the metadata for the identifier dimensions is expressed in the form of dimension-level tables with one column per dimension level.

A simplified view for each of the four identifier dimensions is shown in Figures 5.3 through 5.7. There is no "right" way to list the members of a di-

Company	Region	Store
B&B	Northeast	Ridgewood
B&B	Northeast	Newbury
B&B	Northeast	Avon
B&B	Midwest	Francis
B&B	Midwest	Nikki's
B&B	Midwest	Roger's

Figure 5.3 Hierarchical presentation of the store dimension.

mension. Different multidimensional products use different methods. The two most common ways, however, are the list method and the indented outline method. In Figure 5.3, the stores dimension is presented in indented outline form. In Figure 5.4, all the members of the stores dimension are listed in a single column. In addition, every nonleaf member has its children listed underneath.

Ridgewood
Newbury
Avon
Francis
Nikki's
Roger's
Northeast
Ridgewood
Newbury
Avon
Midwest
Francis
Nikki's
Roger's
B&B
Northeast
Midwest

Figure 5.4 Linear list of the store dimension.

Jan
Feb
Mar
Apr
May
Jun
Quarter 1
Jan
Feb
Mar
Quarter 2
Apr
May
Jun

Figure 5.5 Linear list of the time dimension.

rose water soap
olive oil soap
hypoallergenic lotion
bookshelves
dividers
mattresses
soap
rose water soap
olive oil soap
lotion
hypoallergenic lotion
.
.
skin care
soap
lotion
.
.
all product
skin care
furniture

Figure 5.6 Linear list of the product dimension.

actual
plan

Figure 5.7 Linear list of scenario dimension.

Seeing Dimensions in TM/1

Click on the TM/1 menu and select Cubes.

[TM/1 - CUBES MENU]

Click Browse. A list of available cubes will appear.

[SELECT CUBE TO BROWSE]

Click on ch5model, then click OK. The browse box for ch5model appears.

[VIEW: [UNNAMED] - CUBE: CH5MODEL]

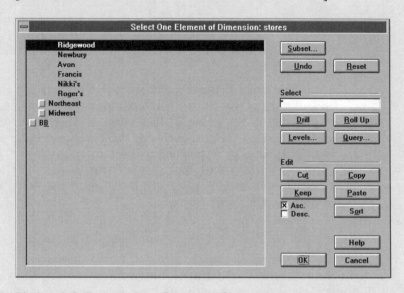

Figure 5.8 Examining dimensions.

Click on the raised box labeled stores.

[SELECT ONE ELEMENT OF DIMENSION: STORE]

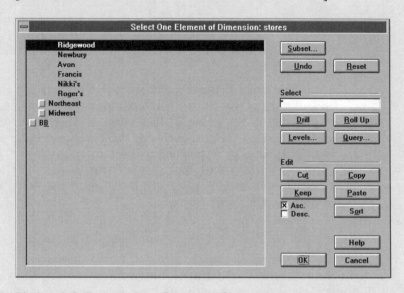

Figure 5.9 Examining the store dimension.

Now double-click on <u>B&B</u>, and see that it is made up of <u>Northeast</u> and <u>Midwest</u>.

Double-click on each of those to see the individual *stores* that sum up to each *region*.

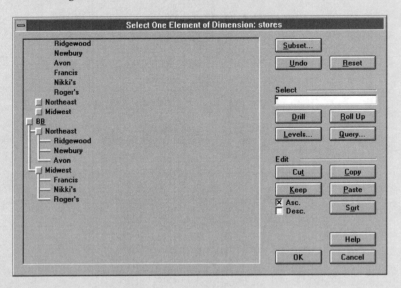

Figure 5.10 Examining the stores hierarchy.

Click on <u>Cancel</u> to return to the browse box.

You can view any of the other dimensions shown in the browse box the same way.

In the browse box, the dimension "tags" are listed in three columns. The dimension(s) in the first column—products, variables, and stores—define the pages in this view (recall from Chapter 3), with one element selected for each—in this case "rose water soap," "sales," and "Ridgewood," respectively. The dimension(s) in the second column—scenarios—will be set in the rows of the view; the dimension(s) in the third column—months—will be set in the columns of the view.

In contrast with the identifier dimension metadata, the variables dimension metadata is mixed in with the base data. The two members of the variables dimension are defined in terms of nonkey attribute headings in the base table:

❑ Sales

❑ Costs

To bring the data into the defined cube, we need to specify the import links. Relative to a view that joins month names, store names, and product names to the base data table, the links will establish that the month, store, product, and scenario columns contain names of members that will help identify data values and that each row's fields for the sales and cost columns contain data for variables of the same name.

(In this chapter, whose purpose is to highlight the ease of defining calculations and views with a multidimensional approach, we are not going to perform the step of actually transforming the data into multidimensional form. We will wave our hands at the process here; data import steps are examined in detail in the case studies that appear later in the book.)

Even though no formulas have been defined to aggregate the data, there is still enough structure in the multidimensional model to flexibly view the data and gain an appreciation for its dimensional metaphor.

Browsing a Table

In the browse box, drag the raised box labeled <u>variable</u> to the right-most column with your mouse. Then drag the <u>products</u> box to the middle of the dialog box such that it appears next to *Rows*. Then move all the other dimension boxes to the top-left corner. It should read <u>actuals</u> next to <u>scenarios</u>, <u>Ridgewood</u> next to <u>stores</u>, and <u>Jan</u> next to <u>months</u>.

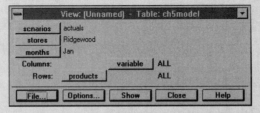

Figure 5.11 Arranging the dimensions.

Now click on the <u>Show</u> button in the browse box.

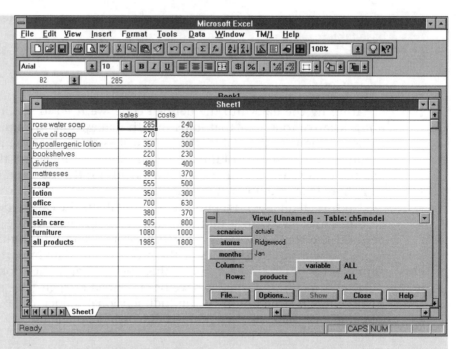

Figure 5.12 Seeing cube data.

Now we have a view of *actual sales* and *costs* data by product for *January* in *Ridgewood*.

What if you want to see a comparison of *rosewater soap sales* across *stores*? You just move the *product* dimension from a row display to a page display, making sure to have *rosewater soap* as the current element, and move the *store* dimension from a page display to a row display. As with most functions, there are many multidimensional tool-specific ways to achieve this, such as dragging an icon across the screen display or editing a view control window, but the logical simplicity is always the same. Return to the browse box and move <u>stores</u> to the middle of the dialog box and <u>products</u> to the top-left corner.

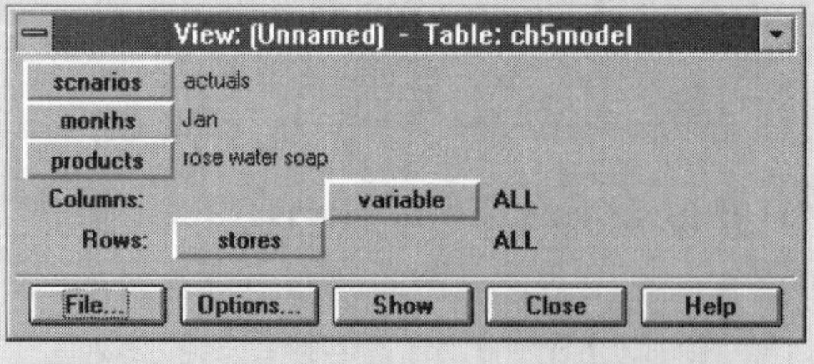

Figure 5.13 Rearranging dimensions.

Click on the <u>Show</u> button.

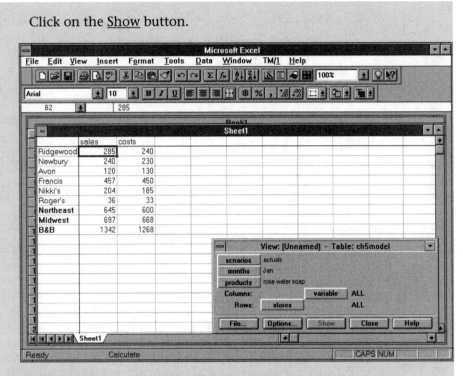

Figure 5.14 Seeing a different view of data.

Now you see January's actual sales and costs of rose water soap by store. Thanks to the fact that the dimensional structure of the model is separate from how those dimensions are connected to the screen, it is incredibly simple to change views with multidimensional tools. Recall from Chapter 2 that you certainly could not perform these types of operations with spreadsheets or SQL.

Duplication

Some readers may have noticed that the dimensions we just defined are essentially a duplication of previously defined information. We started with base data in table form, which consisted of fact tables and lookup tables. Then we duplicated this information as a part of our dimension-defining process.

Duplication is an unavoidable byproduct of creating separate databases for transaction processing and for decision-oriented processing. The important questions are how much information is getting duplicated, how hard is it to ensure consistency between duplicated copies, and what are the benefits of this duplication.

As regards the first question, it is important to keep in mind that the amount of data-based information is orders of magnitude larger than the amount of metadata-based information. For example, in a three-dimensional model with 1,000 members along each dimension (and with a perfectly dense cube), there are 1 billion (1,000*1,000*1,000) data-based pieces of information, but there are only 3,000 (1,000+1,000+1,000) metadata-based pieces of information. Metadata duplication such as the dimensional duplication described above is very inexpensive relative to the cost of duplicating data. Also, the need for metadata duplication is technology neutral. The only reason why it seemed that the SQL option in Chapter 2 did not require any duplication is because the source data set was already in SQL form (a reasonable assumption). However, that SQL-structured base metadata and data was already a duplicate of some operations-based metadata and data.

Data duplication is another matter, and a more tricky matter at that. Data is duplicated, for better or for worse, throughout most information systems, transaction-oriented and decision-oriented. Customer data, for example, is frequently duplicated between different transaction applications such as credit and sales. Data is frequently duplicated between transaction systems and the base level of decision-oriented applications. Here, that duplication may be called replication because the duplication is intentional and consistency between duplicates is maintained via a change management system, usually through the detection and replication of changes rather than through the wholesale copying of data. (To be fair, some people prefer copy management to replication.)

In a world of data warehouse databases plus multidimensional databases, duplication gets trickier still. For here, data is duplicated from the transaction systems into the data warehouse database. And from the data warehouse database, data may again be duplicated into a multidimensional database. This may seem a bit much. And it does not need to occur. Typically, when there is a data warehouse database between the transaction systems and the multidimensional database, data is aggregated from the warehouse database into the multidimensional database. The aggregation of data as it is fed into the multidimensional database was discussed in Chapter 4.

As regards the second question, consistency gets harder to maintain the more copies are laying around, the less time you are willing to allow for inconsistent states (that is, the amount of time between duplication of changes), and the less computing energy you are willing to expend on detecting changes. It is not too hard to reread a source data file every so often and recreate a multidimensional model, but it is a very inefficient process. It is harder to detect new dimension members than it is to recreate a dimensional structure. It is harder to detect new cells than it is to detect new dimension members. And it is harder to detect an updated cell than a new cell.

As regards the third question, there are benefits to duplicating data and metadata. The benefits to duplicating metadata are the clearest. By storing a complete metadata set in the hypercube, the costs for which are very low relative to the amount of data involved, it is possible to drill through the hypercube into the underlying data sets. This is an important benefit.

The benefits to duplicating decision-oriented data are less clear-cut (as opposed to the benefits of duplicating operations data to provide for analysis-based decision-oriented processing, which are clear-cut). For efficiency's sake, it may be best to aggregate the source data before loading it into the multidimensional model and then reach back for the detail data only when necessary. Or, depending on the product, you may be able to aggregate directly from the table-stored data.

It is realistic and beneficial to see metadata duplicated from a source data set into a hypercube. It is realistic but somewhat less beneficial to see data duplicated. If the above example (which was intentionally simplified so as to highlight essential points) were more life-like, and if the source data were really found in the form of fact tables and lookup tables, then it is reasonable to assume that the source of the data was a data warehouse database. If this is the case, then it is also reasonable to assume that the granularity of the data in the warehouse database was below the level required for the hypercube, and thus the data from the warehouse database would be aggregated into the hypercube (regardless of whether the hypercube were created by a so-called multidimensional database or a relational OLAP tool), so that there would not be any data replication. (More on this in Chapter 9.)

Defining Formulas

Defining dimensions and linking in base data was easy. The next step in building a model is to attach formulas where aggregations are to take place.

Assume that initially you need to summarize the variables' data across times, stores, and products. In other words, the first order of business is to determine how much was bought and sold for each product, product type, and division; for each store, city, and region; and for each week, month, and quarter.

There are many ways to represent this formulaic information, depending on the product. One way that is frequently used, is to attach formulas directly to the members of each dimension. This approach, which is shown in Figures 5.15 through 5.18, defines formulas using the same structure as the referential hierarchies. (Recall that in Chapter 3 we distinguished between referential and formulaic hierarchies.) Remember, the attribute of being an input data value or a derived data value pertains to cell-specific data and not members of dimensions. Nevertheless, for many applications where most of the data is input at the base level and most of the measures aggregate in the same way, it is efficient to first define the cube as a completely regular structure by attaching formulas to dimension members and then define either member-based or cell range-based overrides. (In practice, many OLAP tools assume you are summing across your hierarchical dimensions so the act of defining your dimensions gets you your basic aggregations as well. I broke out the two processes here purely for explanatory purposes. For a discussion of hypercube defining strategies, see Chapter 10.)

Ridgewood
Newbury
Avon
Francis
Nikki's
Roger's
Northeast
Ridgewood =
+Newbury
+Avon
Midwest =
Francis
+Nikki's
+Roger's
B&B =
Northeast
Midwest

Figure 5.15 Store dimension aggregation formulas.

Jan
Feb
Mar
Apr
May
Jun
Quarter 1 =
Jan
+Feb
+Mar
Quarter 2 =
Apr
+May
+Jun

Figure 5.16 Week dimension aggregation formulas.

rose water soap
olive oil soap
hypoallergenic lotion
bookshelves
dividers
mattresses
soap =
rose water soap
+olive oil soap
lotion =
hypoallergenic lotion
:
:
skin care =
soap
+lotion
:
:
all products =
skin care
+furniture

Figure 5.17 Product dimension aggregation formulas.

actuals
plans
variance =
actuals/plan

Figure 5.18 Scenario dimension aggregation formula.

Although the formulas for each of the hierarchical nonvariable dimensions (stores, weeks, and products) were defined with one token per derived member, many tools assume that dimensions sum across members so that you do not have to state anything as long as you want things to sum. Once again, this is so much simpler than defining formulas was for either spreadsheets or SQL. Recall from Chapter 2: With spreadsheets, the problem was that the formulas could not be separated from the data. And with SQL, the problem was that formulas work in terms of columns and were separated too far from the structure of the data. What you want and what you get with a multidimensional tool is the ability to attach formulas to members of dimensions.

Defining Simple Dimension Formulas

Close the browse box by clicking <u>Close</u>.

Click on the <u>TM/1</u> menu, then click on <u>Dimensions</u>.

[TM/1 - DIMENSIONS MENU]

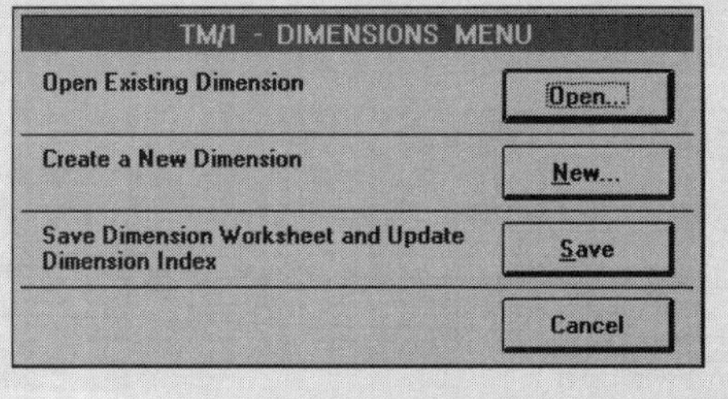

TM/1 - DIMENSIONS MENU	
Open Existing Dimension	Open...
Create a New Dimension	New...
Save Dimension Worksheet and Update Dimension Index	Save
	Cancel

Figure 5.19 Opening a dimension.

Now click on <u>Open</u>.

A dialog box will appear with a list of all the dimensions.

[SELECT DIMENSION WORKSHEET]

Figure 5.20 Selecting a dimension to open.

Click the <u>stores</u> dimension, then click on <u>OK</u>.

[STORES.XDI]

TM/1 distinguishes between leaf-level members (denoted by an <u>N</u>) and nonleaf-level (denoted by a <u>C</u>). Data values associated with the members listed under a <u>C</u> member are summed to define the data associated with the <u>C</u> member. For example, Ridgewood, Newbury, and Avon all sum up to Northeast.

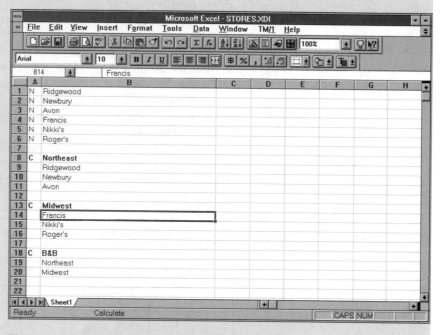

Figure 5.21 The stores aggregation hierarchy.

All regions							
	Quarter 1			Quarter 2		
	actuals	plans	variance	actuals	plans	variance
skin care	3,000.55	2,801.95	1.07	3,988.91	3,724.85	1.07
furniture	3,579.80	3,546.70	1.01	4,759.08	4,715.07	1.01

Figure 5.22 High-level view of aggregated data broken down by product groups.

Press the Compute Button

You have now defined a multilevel hypercube and may compute the derived values for your model. (Actually, you may not even need to do that. For reasons we will explore in the next chapter, many of the values that are defined as calculated values are only calculated at request time.) You can drill through your model and pivot it any way you like.

Figure 5.22 shows a high-level view of the aggregated data. Sales data is shown organized along the rows by product group, along the columns by scenario and quarter, and in the pages by region. This is the kind of view that someone analyzing products would want to see.

What if you saw a strange number for actual Q2 sales in region 1? How would you navigate or drill down to the details behind the cell? In a multidimensional environment, the referential hierarchies that are defined as a part of the model serve as the basis for all browsing. Here, for example, both quarters and regions are high-level members of their respective dimensions. Quarters sit on top of months and weeks. Regions sit on top of stores. From the company-year level (and ignoring products and scenarios), eight lower levels are available for navigation, as shown in Figure 5.23.

The actual gesture for drilling down may differ among software products, but the concept is always the same. Just state, or click on, what you want. This is a declarative approach to querying. Figure 5.24, for example, shows

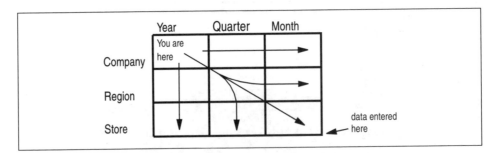

Figure 5.23 Drill down possibilities.

All products		Jan	Feb	Mar	Apr	May	Jun
Ridgewood	actuals	1,985.00	2,183.50	2,406.85	2,640.05	2,910.56	3,201.61
	plans	1,915.00	2,106.50	2,322.15	2,546.95	2,808.15	3,088.96
	variance	1.04	1.04	1.04	1.04	1.04	1.04
Newbury	actuals	1,824.00	2,006.40	2,212.04	2,425.92	2,675.01	2,942.51
	plans	1,800.00	1,980.00	2,183.00	2,394.00	2,639.90	2,903.89
	variance	1.01	1.01	1.01	1.01	1.01	1.01
Avon	actuals	560.00	616.00	682.60	744.80	825.78	908.36
	plans	576.00	633.60	701.96	766.08	849.19	934.11
	variance	0.97	0.97	0.97	0.97	0.97	0.97
Francis	actuals	2,643.00	2,907.30	3,203.03	3,515.19	3,873.21	4,260.53
	plans	2,380.00	2,618.00	2,884.80	3,165.40	3,488.44	3,837.28
	variance	1.11	1.11	1.11	1.11	1.11	1.11
Nikki's	actuals	1,390.00	1,529.00	1,686.90	1,848.70	2,040.07	2,244.08
	plans	1,385.00	1,523.50	1,680.85	1,842.05	2,032.76	2,236.03
	variance	1.00	1.00	1.00	1.00	1.00	1.00
Roger's	actuals	707.00	777.70	860.47	940.31	1,040.84	1,144.93
	plans	705.00	775.50	858.05	937.65	1,037.92	1,141.71
	variance	1.00	1.00	1.00	1.00	1.00	1.00

Figure 5.24 Drilling down to stores by month.

the store-by-month view of all products sales data that results from drilling down on quarters and regions. Vendors employ two basic methods: gesturing directly on the matrix view and selecting members from a dimension view. I prefer the direct method whenever possible. Both methods within the multi-dimensional approach, though, are dramatically simpler than any methods based on spreadsheets or SQL.

Browsing Calculated Hypercubes.

Go back to the TM/1 menu and select Cubes again.

[TM/1 - CUBES MENU]

Click on Browse.

[SELECT CUBE TO BROWSE]

Click on ch5model, then click OK.

If you have followed all the steps so far, you should have stores in rows, variable in columns, and all other dimensions in the page.

Move months to the right-most column of the browse box (where variable is), and move variable to the top left.

Now click on the raised box labeled <u>products</u>.

[SELECT ONE ELEMENT OF DIMENSION: PRODUCTS]

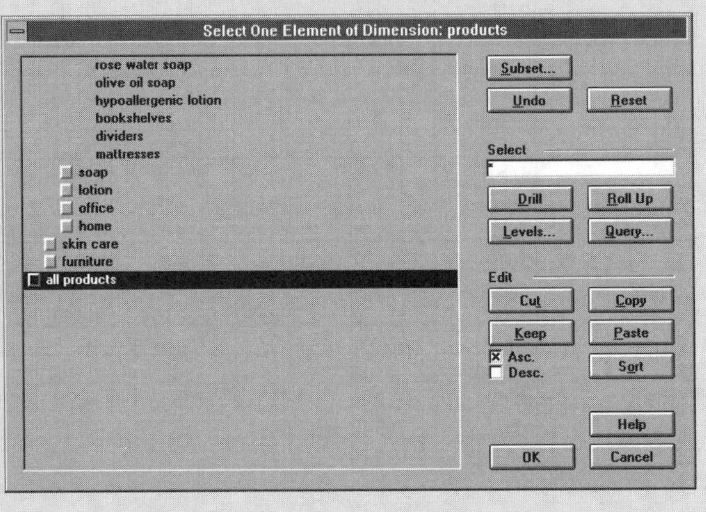

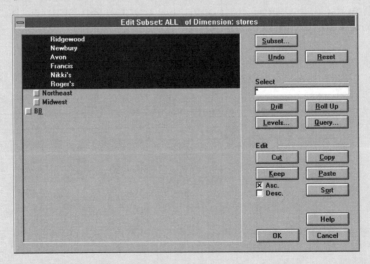

Figure 5.25 Selecting all-product aggregations.

Click on <u>all products</u> and click on <u>OK</u>.

Now click on the raised box labeled <u>stores.</u>

[EDIT SUBSET OF DIMENSION: STORE]

Figure 5.26 Selecting a set of stores.

Highlight all the store names (from Ridgewood to Roger's), click on <u>Keep</u>, then click on <u>OK</u>.

Next, click on the raised box labeled <u>months</u>.

[EDIT SUBSET:[UNNAMED] OF DIMENSION: MONTHS]

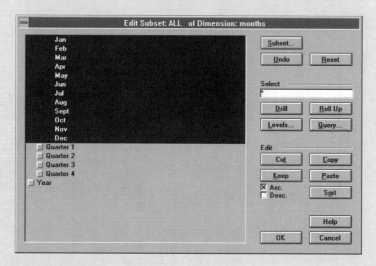

Figure 5.27 Selecting a set of months.

Highlight all the months (from Jan to Dec), click on <u>Keep</u>, then click on <u>OK</u>.

Your browse box should look as follows:

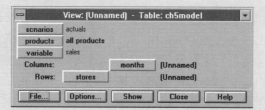

Figure 5.28 Orientation of report.

Now click on <u>Show</u> and you should be able to see store-by-month sales data.

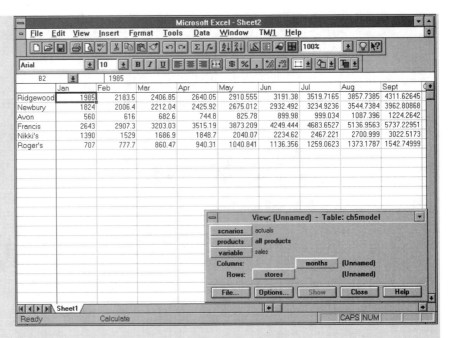

	Jan	Feb	Mar	Apr	May	Jun	Jul	Aug	Sept
Ridgewood	1985	2183.5	2406.85	2640.05	2910.555	3191.38	3519.7165	3857.7385	4311.62645
Newbury	1824	2006.4	2212.04	2425.92	2675.012	2932.492	3234.9236	3544.7384	3962.80868
Avon	560	616	682.6	744.8	825.78	899.98	999.034	1087.396	1224.2642
Francis	2643	2907.3	3203.03	3515.19	3873.209	4249.444	4683.6527	5136.9563	5737.22951
Nikki's	1390	1529	1686.9	1848.7	2040.07	2234.62	2467.221	2700.999	3022.5173
Roger's	707	777.7	860.47	940.31	1040.841	1136.356	1259.0623	1373.1787	1542.74999

Figure 5.29 Generated report.

Return to the browse box and click on <u>months</u>.

[EDIT SUBSET:[UNNAMED] OF DIMENSION: MONTHS]

Click under <u>Subset</u> and open <u>ALL</u>.

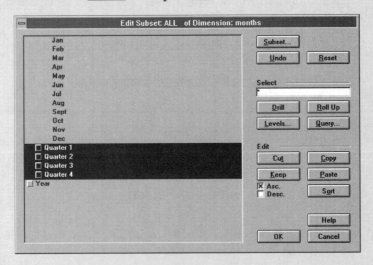

Figure 5.30 Selecting months for the report.

Now highlight <u>Quarter 1-4</u>, click on <u>Keep</u>, then click on <u>OK</u>.

Then click on <u>Show,</u> and you should be able to see store by quarter sales data.

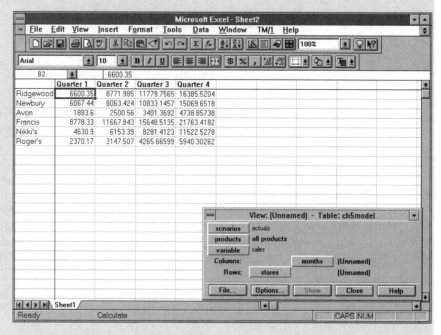

Figure 5.31 The revised report.

Beginning Analysis

Let's see how to define some of the analytical calculations we mentioned that we would want to perform. If you go back to Figure 5.18, you can see that we created an additional member of the scenario dimension: *variance*. *Variance* is defined as the ratio between *actual* and *plan*. You may recall from Chapter 4 that when formulas are attached to the members of dimensions and those members cross at a cell, the resulting combination of formulas may not be commutative, thus making it important to decide which formula takes precedence. In this model, for example, where the hierarchies created from *stores*, *weeks*, and *products* are all defined with summation, simple variables, such as *sales*, encounter no ambiguity when aggregated across the three hierarchical dimensions because sums are commutative. Recall that it makes no differ-

All products All stores			
	actuals	plans	variance
Quarter 1	6,575.35	6,343.65	1.04
Quarter 2	8,741.99	8,433.92	1.04
Quarter 3	11,689.08	11,277.51	1.04
Quarter 4	16,250.58	15,678.47	1.04

Figure 5.32 All product sales by quarter by scenario.

ence whether you sum *sales* across *stores* and then sum *stores* across *time* and *regions* or whether you first sum *sales* across *time* and then across *products* and *regions.*

In contrast, the ratio called *variance* is sensitive to its order of computation. It makes a huge difference whether *actual* and *planned* sales are first summed across *stores*, *time,* and *products,* followed by taking the ratio of the sum of *actual sales* to the sum of *planned sales,* or whether the ratio of *actual* to *planned sales* is taken at the bottom level of *stores*, *time*, and *products,* followed by summing the ratio. Thinking back to the discussion of formula precedence in Chapter 4, you would usually want to take the ratio of the sums and not the sum of the ratios.

In one way or another, the precedence of the formula for *variance* needs to be set relative to the other formulas it crosses at cells. Most multidimensional tools are pretty savvy in this respect and would guess that you would want to perform the sums first, followed by the ratio of sums. Figure 5.32 shows allproduct sales by quarter by scenario. Remember how difficult it was to define a simple variance with SQL. The actuals and planned data first had to be separated into separate tables.

Creating a Variance Calculation

Most multidimensional tools provide for simpler calculations to be attached to dimension members while more complicated ones are defined in a special scripting (and generally procedurally) area. The dividing line varies from vendor to vendor. With the enclosed software, anything beyond weighted sums needs to be defined in "rule worksheets." This is what we need to use for our variance calculation.

Close the browse box by clicking on Close.

Go to the TM/1 menu and select Rules.

[TM/1 RULES MENU]

Click on <u>Open</u>.

Figure 5.33 Selecting a TM/1 rules sheet.

Select <u>ch5model</u> and click on <u>OK</u>. The rule sheet shown in Figure 5.33a will appear.

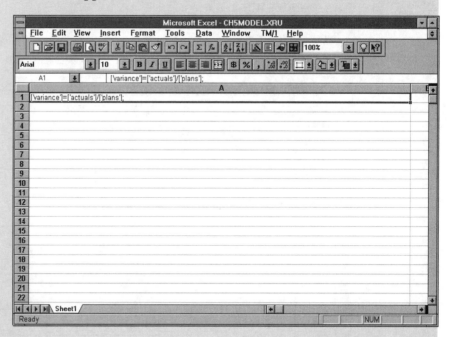

Figure 5.33a The variance rule.

You can see that *variance* is set to equal *actuals* divided by *plans*.

Now go back to the <u>TM/1</u> menu and select <u>Cubes</u>.

[TM/1 CUBES MENU]

Click on Browse.

[SELECT CUBE TO BROWSE]

Once again, choose ch5model.

Now move the raised box labeled scenarios to the right-most column, move variable directly above scenarios, and move months to the top left. The browse box should look as follows:

Figure 5.34 Selecting a dimension arrangement to examine all scenarios.

Now click on Show.

You can see that variance is indeed the ratio between actuals and plans.

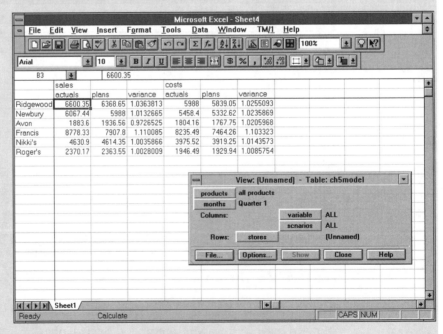

Figure 5.35 Report showing all scenarios.

You can now create the analytical reports that will help you make decisions. (Actually, you could have created them sooner, but this chapter also served to take you on a quick OLAP tour.)

Creating the Quarterly Product Report

In the browse box, drag the raised box labeled <u>variable</u> to above the <u>products</u> box, in the page area.

Now, drag the raised box labeled <u>stores</u> to above the <u>products</u> box, in the page area. Click on the <u>stores</u> box.

[EDIT SUBSET:[UNNAMED] OF DIMENSION: STORES]

Click on <u>Subset</u> and open <u>ALL</u>, then click on <u>B&B</u> and click on <u>OK</u>.

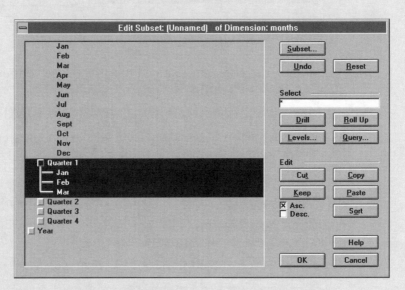

Figure 5.36 Selecting quarters and months.

Now, drag the <u>products</u> raised box to the rows, and click on it.

[EDIT SUBSET:[UNNAMED] OF DIMENSION: PRODUCTS]

Double-click on <u>skin care</u> and <u>furniture</u>, then double-click on <u>soap</u>, on <u>lotion</u>, on <u>office,</u> and on <u>home</u> to show all of the individual products. Select the rows from <u>skin care</u> to <u>allproducts</u>, and click on <u>OK</u>.

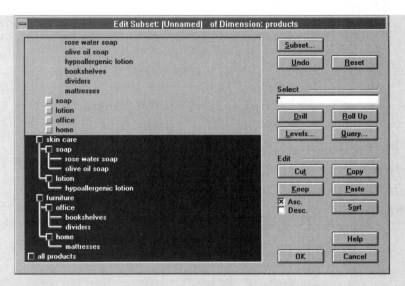

Figure 5.37 Selecting entire hierarchy of products.

Now, drag the raised box named <u>months</u> to the columns, above <u>scenarios</u>. Click on <u>months</u>.

[EDIT SUBSET:[UNNAMED] OF DIMENSION: MONTHS]

Click on <u>subset</u> and open <u>ALL</u>. Double-click on <u>Quarter 1</u>, and highlight the times from <u>Quarter 1</u> through <u>Mar</u>. Click on <u>OK</u>.

Now, click on the raised box named <u>scenarios</u>.

[EDIT SUBSET:[UNNAMED] OF DIMENSION: VARIABLE]

Click on <u>Actual</u>, control-click on <u>Variance</u> (which will select <u>Actual</u> and <u>Variance</u> without <u>Plan</u>) and click on <u>OK</u>.

Your browse box should now look like Figure 5.38:

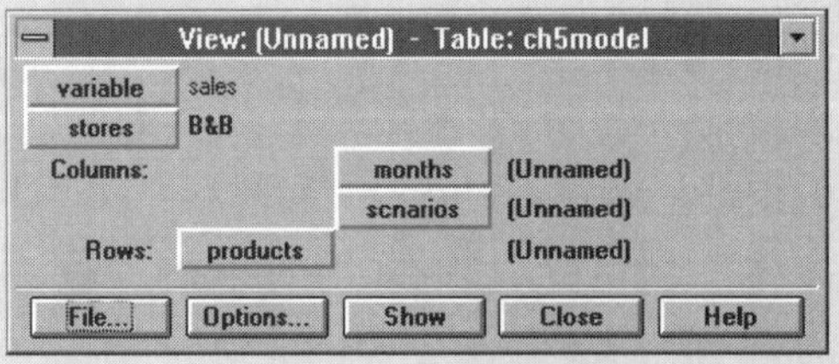

Figure 5.38 The arrangement of dimensions for the product report.

Now, click on <u>Show</u>.

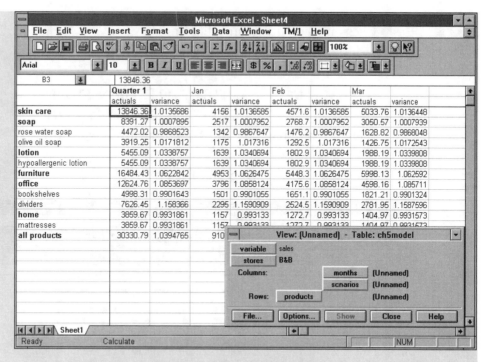

Figure 5.39 Product manager's quarterly report.

This is the first report that we were trying to develop. Though it is not as neatly formatted as the version in Figure 2.2, the content is present and the relevant adjacencies are in place. It is now convenient to look at the sales information across products at each time, and to compare actual and variance to plan for each product and time. The ability to structure data and functions to match our analytic need, combined with the friendliness and flexibility of the interface, has greatly reduced the amount of effort we needed to spend to create this report on the original data.

Now, let us create the second report.

Creating the Quarterly Region Report

In the browse box, drag the raised box labeled <u>products</u> from the rows to the pages under <u>variable</u>. Click on it.

[EDIT SUBSET:[UNNAMED] OF DIMENSION: PRODUCTS]

Click on <u>all products</u>, and click on <u>OK</u>.

Now, drag the raised box labeled <u>stores</u> to the rows area in the browse box. Click on it.

[EDIT SUBSET:[UNNAMED] OF DIMENSION: STORES]

Double-click on <u>Northeast</u>, and double-click on <u>Midwest</u>, to show their stores. Highlight all of the rows from <u>Northeast</u> to <u>B&B</u> and click on <u>OK</u>.

The browse box will appear. Click on <u>Show</u>.

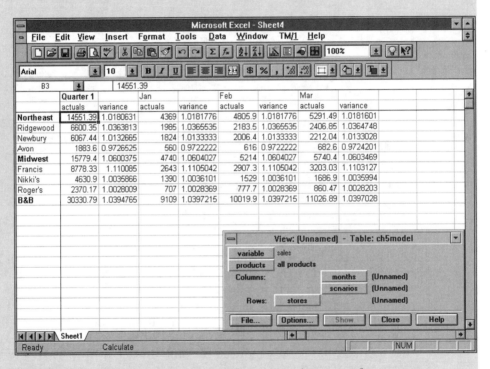

Figure 5.40 Looking at the regional manager's quarterly report.

Once again, though not as nice looking as the version of the quarterly region report in Figure 2.3, it is essentially the same. The report immediately shows us that if there is a store we should look at first, it's in Avon. The fact that Avon is the only store selling less than planned, and consistently so, is made quite plain by the line of variances stretching across all time periods at

Avon. This fact would take longer to glean from looking at the summary table of variances that we developed in Figure 2.10. Being able to transpose time to the columns, which creates the ability to look at a cross-section of stores over time, makes the difference here.

Conclusion

Typical business models require multiple levels of data aggregation across multiple dimensions. End-user analysts need to be able to browse the data while changing the configuration of its display on the screen. And they need to be able to analyze data, looking most often at comparisons along dimensions.

A multidimensional approach offers many clear advantages over spreadsheets and SQL for both defining and using such models. The separation of data structure (defined in terms of dimensions) from data representation is a big advantage of the multidimensional approach. It serves to minimize the need to duplicate any structural information and it provides direct support for easily changing views on a screen. The direct support for multilevel dimensions, and the ability to assign formulas directly to the members of dimensions, makes it easy to define multilevel aggregates and multidimensional calculations with a multidimensional tool.

In the next two chapters, we will turn our attention to more advanced features of multidimensional tools.

CHAPTER

Advanced Features, Part 1

In Chapters 3 and 4, you explored the basic features of a multidimensional model. You should understand that dimensions are factorable attributes of any real-world situation, that dimensions frequently have a hierarchical structure, that models are fed through links to data and metadata, and that the formulas that get attached to members of dimensions that need to be combined at cell intersections in order to calculate the values of derived cells. In Chapter 5, you saw the advantages that these types of features bestow on the builder and user of analysis-based decision-oriented models. Specifically, you saw how easy it is to define a multilevel, multidimensional model, complete with formulas for derived values. And you saw how easy it is to browse and reconfigure views. Of course, the real world isn't quite as tidy as it was made out to be in the last three chapters, and neither are multidimensional models.

Chapters 6 and 7 examine further multidimensional features within the same categories presented in Chapters 3 and 4: hypercubes, views, formulas, links, and hierarchies. (More about dimensions is presented in Chapter 15.) The features are described in roughly descending order of likelihood that you will need to use them for typical modeling efforts. As a result, the ordering of the features in these next two chapters is not the same as in Chapters 3 and 4.

More about Hypercubes

So far in this book, we have been treating multidimensional models as single, logical hypercubes created by taking the Cartesian product of a set of dimensions. For example, the model in Chapter 5 was created by taking the Cartesian product of a store, product, time, scenario, and variables dimension. Can everything be represented in a single hypercube? What happens if we

137

need to add dimensions to a model? Is there a limit to the number of dimensions in a hypercube? Are there any natural cube structurings? If there are, how do you decide whether a new dimension belongs in an existing cube or in some new cube?

When a New Dimension Belongs to a New Cube

Consider Figure 6.1, which shows a grid of implicitly actual values. Let's imagine that we now need to track actuals against plans and variances. The best way to do this is by adding a scenario dimension and explicitly reclassifying prior data as actuals. Because the new dimension reflects new data and connects to the old data, it works well as an addition to the initial dimensional structure. The modified cube is shown in Figure 6.2.

Now imagine we started tracking employees and the number of hours they spend on each type of task: customer help, stocking, and cash register. In addition to an employee dimension and a set of variables denoting "hours worked per task," the data would also contain the dimensions store and time. Should this data be added to the original cube in the same way that planned data, with its associated scenario dimension, was added? Or should the data go into a separate cube? Does it make a difference?

Let's try adding this new information to the original cube and see what happens. Figure 6.3 shows the list of dimensions for the modified model. So

	Jan	Feb	Mar	Apr
Store1 Shoe Sales	200	250	150	270
Store1 Shoe Costs	180	200	200	270
Store1 Shirt Sales	320	350	400	300
Store1 Shirt Costs	300	300	350	270

Figure 6.1 Table of implicitly actual values (in thousands of dollars).

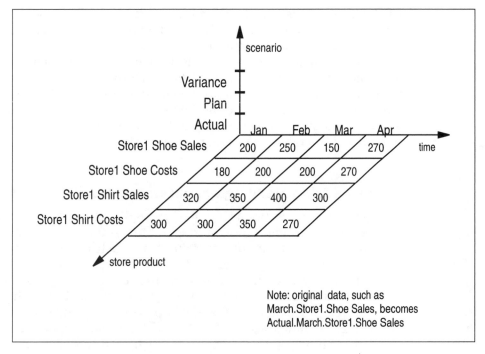

Figure 6.2 Adding a scenario dimension to a cube.

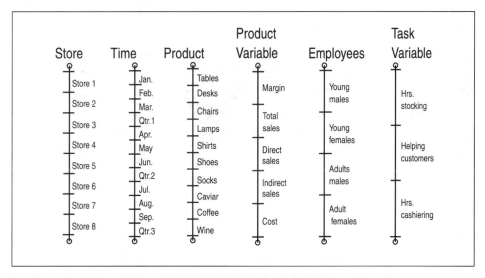

Figure 6.3 List of dimensions for the modified model.

far it looks fine; it is hard to tell without seeing how data points are referenced in the new model. Recall that for the original sales data, each variable was identified by its store, time, and product.

In the modified model, sales measures continue to be identified by their store, time, and product, in addition to which they are further identified by an employee and task variable. On the face of it, this doesn't seem to make a lot of sense. According to the modified cube, sales are now a function of store, time, product, employee, and task. But measured sales values are not differentiated by employee or task per employee.

Visualizing Meaningless Intersections

Figure 6.4 shows (for a simplified version of this example that leaves out the two dimensions—stores, and time—that both data sets share and that just treats one variable from each of them—total hours worked per employee and total sales per product) how for all but the allemployee and alltask members, the regions defined by employee and task are empty. Look at the bottom right panel of the figure. You will see two tables composed of one column each. The one on the left shows hours worked for each of 10 employees, plus a total. The table on the right shows sales for each of 10 products, plus a total. We are thus starting with 22 data points.

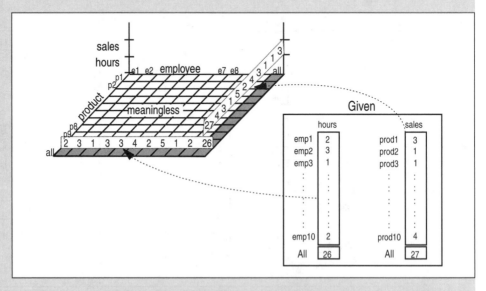

Figure 6.4 Except for allemployees and alltasks, regions defined by employee and task are meaningless.

In the upper left part of the figure is the cube that results from combining the two data sets. I concatenated, as you realistically would, the two variable dimensions from the original data sets. Hours and sales form the members of the *z* axis. Products form the depth axis, and employees form the horizontal axis. Hierarchies were left out of the cubes. An allemployee and an allproduct member were added to each of their respective dimensions along a single level. The resulting cube is 11 by 11 by 2, giving it 242 intersections. There are only 22 data points in it: 11 product sales values and 11 employee hours values. Figure 6.4 shows where the numbers from the two original tables fit into the combined cube. And it shows all the meaningless intersections. The employee hours data fits along the employee by allproduct by hours region. The product sales data fits along the products by all employee by sales region. The rest of the cube is meaningless.

It would seem that employee task data describes a different situation from the product sales data (even though the two situations share some dimensions) and thus ought to be defined as a separate data cube. This contrasts with the planned and variance data which, though generated by a separate situation from that of the actual sales data, fit cleanly into the original model.

What is the difference between these two modifications? Why does one modification seem to fit and another seem not to fit? For one thing, the plan and variance data have the same dimensional structure as the original data. The original (actual) data and the new plan data are both dimensioned by store, time, and product. In addition, you can reclassify the sales variables (units sold, dollar value sold) as actual variables. Thus, the original data could have been dimensioned by store, time, product, and scenario where scenario had only a single member, the actuals member. In this way, the addition of plan and variance can be seen as the addition of new members to the scenario dimension. In contrast, the employee and hours data do not share the same dimensional structure as the original data. The original data is not dimensioned by either employee or hours per task, and the new data is not dimensioned by product or sales variables.

It would be useful to define a logical hypercube such that there are limits to what fits in it. As a consequence, you would need a way to determine when additional information belongs in a new hypercube.

A logical hypercube is a set of variables, defined along a variables dimension, that all share the same identifying dimensions. According to this definition, the act of adding a scenarios dimension does not violate the definition of a cube because the new variables data share the same identifier dimensions as the old variables data. In contrast, the addition of an hours variable and employees identifier dimension does violate the definition of a cube because the new variables do not share the same identifier dimensions as the old sales variables.

If two data sets belong in the same logical hypercube, the density of their combination will equal the weighted average of their densities prior to being combined, where the weighting is a function of the number of data points per data set. For example, if a perfectly dense cube is defined in terms of 100 stores, 10 time periods, 100 products, and 5 sales measures, it will contain 500,000 data points. And if a second cube is defined in terms of 100 stores, 10 time periods, 100 products, 5 measures, and 3 scenarios where the 3 scenarios are plan, actual, and variance and data exist only for plan, it will also contain 500,000 data points but be only 33 percent dense. The combination of the two cubes would contain 1,000,000 data points and be 67 percent dense.

If two data sets do not belong in the same logical hypercube, the density of their combination will be less than either of the two original data sets. For example, if a perfectly dense cube is defined in terms of 100 stores, 10 time periods, 5 sales measures, and 100 products, it will contain 500,000 data points. And if a second perfectly dense cube is defined in terms of 100 stores, 10 time periods, 200 employees, and 5 task measures, it will contain 1,000,000 data points. As separate cubes, they are each perfectly dense.

The density plummets, however, if the two cubes are combined. The combined cube would have 100 stores, 10 times, 100 products, 5 sales measures, 200 employees, and 5 task measures. This defines 500 million intersections, but we have only 1.5 million data points. By combining two perfectly dense cubes we created one cube that was 98.5 percent empty!

Joining Cubes

Because many applications involve data from more than one type of situation, such as financial and marketing or manufacturing and distribution or demographic and sales, there will frequently be a need to use more than one logical hypercube in an application. How does data move between cubes? You can reference data between cubes in the same way that you can reference data between tables. (Intercube referencing is treated in all of the hands-on case studies.) Generally speaking, the cubes need to share one or more dimensions.[1]

Look again at the two cubes we defined above: the sales data cube and the employee tasks cube. The two cubes share two dimensions: stores and time. In addition, the sales cube has a product, scenario, and measures dimension; none of them are shared by the employee cube. The employee cube has an employee and a task variable dimension that it does not share with the sales cube.

Imagine you are trying to analyze whether there is any relationship between the amount of time that employees are spending at various tasks and the amount of products sold. For example, maybe certain employees are better than others at showing customers clothing and thus customers are more likely to purchase clothing when those employees are working with customers.

How would you go about this? To compare the values of measures originating in two separate cubes, we first need to define a common denominator or analytical framework. By analogy, if you want to compare $\frac{2}{3}$ with $\frac{3}{4}$ you need to define both fractions in terms of a common denominator such as twelfths, that is, $\frac{2}{3} = \frac{8}{12}$ and $\frac{3}{4} = \frac{9}{12}$. Once both fractions share the same common denominator, their numerators may be compared directly; that is, you can directly compare the 9 in $\frac{9}{12}$ with the 8 in $\frac{8}{12}$. And because 9 is greater than 8, so $\frac{3}{4}$ is greater than $\frac{2}{3}$.

Returning to our sales and employee cubes, the common denominator between the two cubes is the union of their shared dimensions: store and time. Conversely, the union of the nonshared dimensions in each cube form the numerators. This holds true for the comparison of single values, one dimensional series, or any dimensional volume. Figure 6.5 shows a schema for this multicube model. Notice how the model contains the global dimensions store and time and how each hypercube is a branch off the global dimensions. Figure 6.6 shows a schema for displaying the two cubes on a single

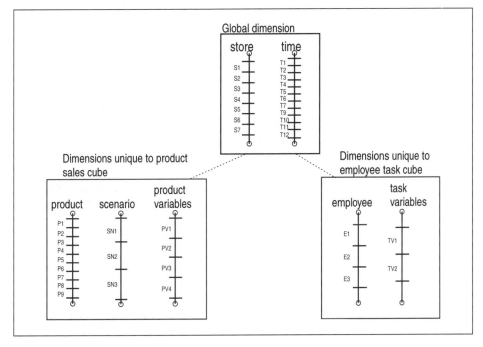

Figure 6.5 Model schema.

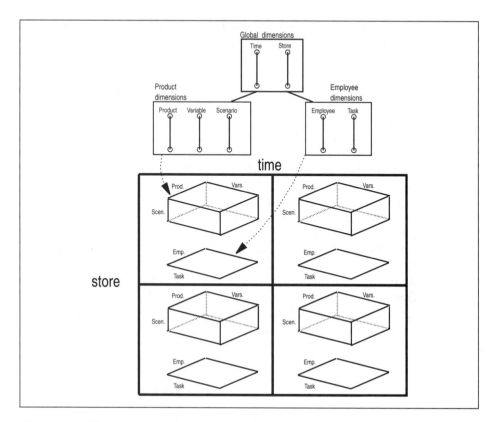

Figure 6.6 View schema.

screen. Notice how the (Cartesian product of the) nonshared dimensions of each hypercube appear as subcubes within each cell defined by the Cartesian product of the shared dimensions. Think of each of the subcubes as a collection of variables and each subcube intersection as a variable. Figure 6.7 shows a sample multicube data view.

For example, to compare the sales of all products made at the Cambridge store for the month of March with the amount of hours that young men spent working the aisles, you define and compute a ratio like the following:

```
allproduct sales/young men's hours working the aisles.
```

And then you look to the cell for the Cambridge store, March for the value. The result is a single data point. Although this ratio is perfectly valid, you probably want to explore whether there is any pattern to the relationship between changes in the number of hours young men spend working the aisles and changes in allproduct sales.

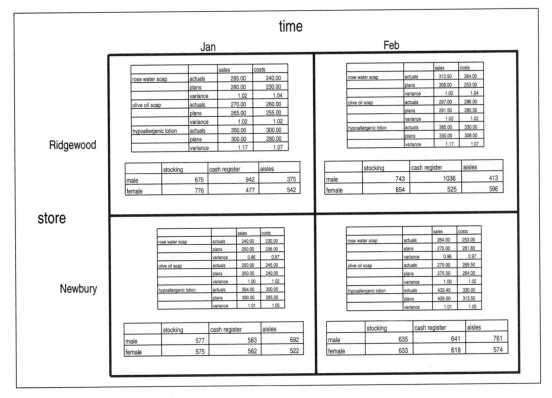

Figure 6.7 Sample view.

To analyze the relationship between changes in product sales and changes in young men's hours working the aisles, you could define and compute a time series like the following:

```
(allprod salest / young men's aisle hourst), t = t0, t1, t2, ... , tn
```

And then you look to Cambridge for the numerical results. Or you could graph the three component time series:

1. `allproduct salest, t = t0, t1, t2, ... , tn`
2. `young men's aisle hourst, t = t0, t1, t2, ... , tn`
3. `(allproduct salest / young men's aisle hourst), t = t0, t1, t2, ... , tn`

This is illustrated in Figure 6.8. Clearly, young men make good aisle workers.

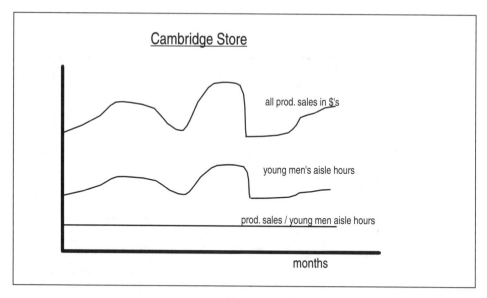

Figure 6.8 Comparison of data from two different cubes.

Using Multicubes to Integrate Irregular Spreadsheets and Records

Using multicubes, it is possible to integrate irregular data sets composed of records or spreadsheets. Irregular data sets are commonly found at the more detailed levels of a data warehouse, in operational systems, and when trying to combine data from across multiple departments. (If you are working with very large data sets measured in the hundreds of millions or billions of rows, that possibility may still be more of a logical one than a physical one. Large-scale integrations require a combination of SQL database capacity plus multidimensional structuring down to the detail level. Although I was involved in a project to integrate a multidimensional and SQL database, such an integrated tool does not yet exist in the commercial domain. This issue is discussed in Chapter 8.)

Think about the integration of spreadsheet-based sales and financial reporting. Typically, the data belong to two departments; sales and finance, and each maintains its own set of spreadsheets. Figure 6.9 shows a multicube view of an integrated sales and financial reporting model for a retail corporation composed of two types of stores: low-cost consumer goods (Five 'n' Dime) and furniture (Furniture Land). Stores and months compose the base level of the shared dimensions, with stores aggregating into chains of stores and months aggregating into quarters. The sales and financial reporting information coexist within each store-month cell. The financial information consists of a two-dimensional grid of financial indicators by planned/actual/variance. The sales information consists of a three-dimensional grid of product type by sales/cost information by planned/actual/variance. Computationally, the sales and cost figures from the sales spreadsheets are ready to be brought into the financial indicators spreadsheet where they drive the calculation of the financial indicators. Visually, the two hypercubes may be integrated as shown in Figure 6.9. Note how the two types of stores share the same financial subcube while the members of their product subcubes are different.

Consider the irregularity of detailed operational information. Figure 6.10 shows a multicube view of individual transactions and aggregate data records for the same stores discussed in the example above. (In order to manage this information correctly, your tool needs to recognize when a variable, such as *clerk*, does not apply to an aggregation level such as *chain by month* so that only meaningful variables are shown in the grid display.) A furniture store may sell 5 units of furniture in 5 transactions one day and 60 units in 15 transactions the next. Different business rules, and thus fields, apply to the two chains: the furniture stores allow credit accounts for customers, whereas the Five 'n' Dimes are strictly cash-and-carry. Several types of records are being organized: at the store-by-month level there is employee payroll information, line-item sales information, and overall sales information. At the chain by month level, the furniture chain tracks account balances. And all stores track aggregate sales data. The multicube model (when issues of sparsity have been properly worked through) provides a general method for relating different sets of measurement complexes with each other.

More About Views: Graphic Multidimensional Visualization

Graphical visualization is a complex subject. Many excellent articles and books have been dedicated to it, a number of which are cited in this chapter. This section is in no way meant as a substitute for a complete treatment of the subject. Rather, it is meant to give you some practical knowledge of how graphical images work, in the sense of how they bear meaning, and to serve as an introduction for using that knowledge to squeeze as much meaning out of your data as possible when working in a multidimensional environment. The literature does not adequately deal with latter issue. I suspect it is because most of the sophisticated graphical programs currently in use are more multivariate than multidimensional. In other words, they are oriented toward displaying many variables at a time, anywhere from 1 to 10, usually in a one-, sometimes in a two-, but rarely in even a three-dimensional context. What do you do with a data set that seems to have six identifier dimensions? Read on, and you will find out.

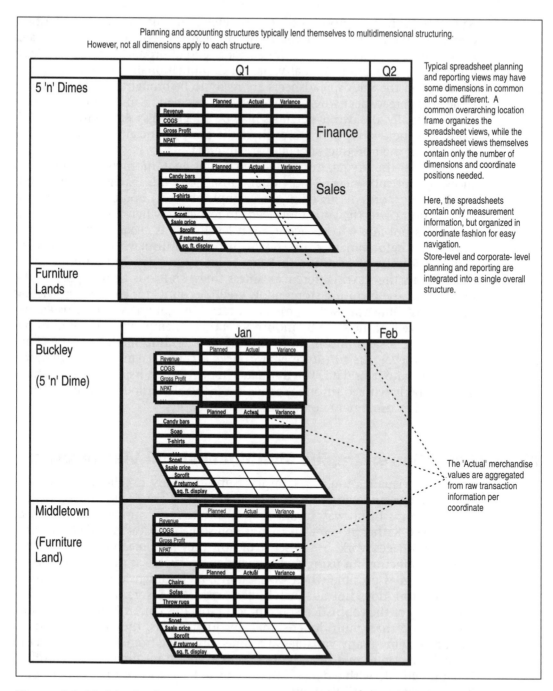

Figure 6.9 Multicube framework for organizing irregular spreadsheets.

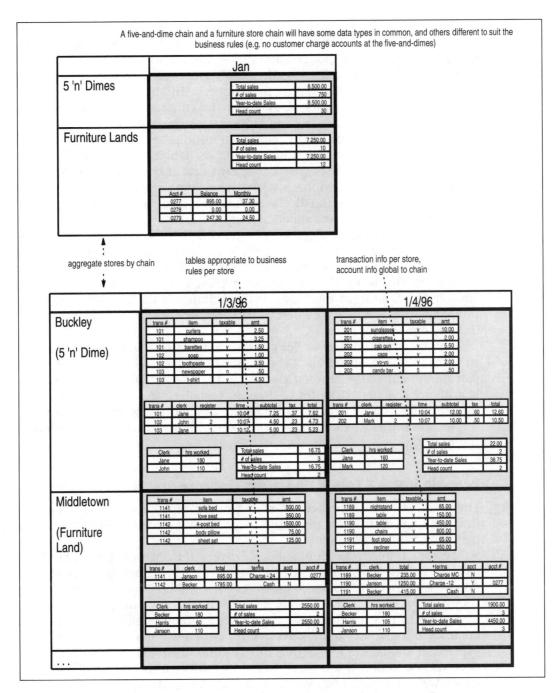

Figure 6.10 Multicube framework for organizing irregular records.

In Chapters 3 and 4, we examined how higher-dimensional structures could be represented in terms of variations to traditional tables and spreadsheet-style matrices. Although multidimensional grid-based views are more powerful and more flexible than their spreadsheet antecedents, they are still composed of grids of data, primarily numbers. Grid-based number representations satisfy many business uses where the emphasis is on knowing how much or in seeing exact values—in essence traditional reporting.

Whether in business or in science, traditional analyses are concerned with such things as finding upper and lower ranges, like top and bottom quartiles, group attributes (such as means and modes), correlations, and trends. When end-user emphasis is on performing analysis, especially exploring relationships within the displayed data, graphical views are more popular and more productive than numeric views.

Why do graphical displays work better than tabular, numeric ones for exploring analytical relationships? Is there any connection between the way data is structured in a hypercube and the way it ought to be displayed for maximum effectiveness? Furthermore, typical graphics such as line graphs and pie charts show at most two or three dimensions. This raises the additional question, "What is the best way to graphically visualize more than two or three dimensions of data?"

This section takes a closer look at multidimensional graphic visualization with the intent to answer all of the questions we have raised. It begins by exploring the difference between graphic and tabular visualization. Then, after identifying the key attributes of graphic visualization, connecting them to the structure of a hypercube, and looking at a variety of graphic examples, the section finishes by exploring how to graphically visualize higher-dimensional spaces.

Graphic Versus Tabular-numeric Representation

The term "graphical" has been used in a variety of ways so let's spend a little time distinguishing these meanings before trying to define the relationship between graphical and tabular.

Edward Tufte, in his seminal book *The Visual Display of Quantitative Information*, defines data graphics in the following way. "Data graphics visually display measured quantities by means of the combined use of points, lines, a coordinate system, numbers, symbols, words, shading and color."[2] In other words, for Tufte, everything visual qualifies as graphics, not necessarily good graphics, but graphics nonetheless. Although I agree that all forms of visual expression should come together in the graphical presentation of information, this definition is too broad to help us distinguish graphic displays, for which we all have an intuitive feel, from tabular displays.

A little less broadly, you may interpret graphics as visual displays that contain no numbers or words. Although numbers and words frequently make their way into the header and legend of a graphic, this definition holds for the body of most business graphics. Pie charts, bar charts, line graphs, and the like are composed of lines, points, colors, symbols, and shapes. We will come to use this definition by the end of the section, but to understand the essence of why graphics work, we need first to develop a more restrictive or essential definition.

In its most essential form, graphics may be interpreted as visual displays that contain only points and sets of points (lines, shapes, areas, volumes). Graph theory operates within these bounds, as do unadorned maps and typical geometric plots. We will begin our discussion with this definition because the essence of what makes graphical displays better for certain types of information may be found by exploring the properties of points and lines.

To see how much easier it is to spot analytical patterns when the data is graphically portrayed, and to see why this is so, consider Figures 6.11 and 6.12. Each of the figures is divided into two panels: an *a* panel that represents a tabular display and a *b* panel that represents a graphic display of the same data.

Figure 6.11 shows sales data in conjunction with cost data for the purpose of break-even analysis. See how much easier it is to identify the changing relationship between sales and costs over time when the information is portrayed graphically. Although your eye might be able to scan the table in Figure 6.11a to discover that break-even occurred in July, it is unlikely that you would notice from just looking at the numbers that at the break-even point, costs were leveling off while sales were accelerating.

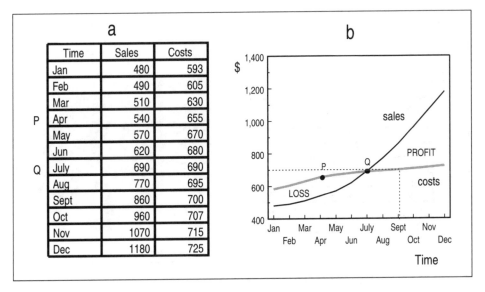

Figure 6.11 Break-even analysis.

It is easier to describe the relationship between sales and costs over time from a graphic perspective because with the graphic display, the relationship information is explicitly given. For example, a natural description of the line segment between points P and Q on the cost curve of panel 6.11b would say something like "Costs are continuing to increase, but at a decreasing rate of increase." You would never see this relationship at a glance from looking at the rows between P and Q in the panel in 6.11a.

In contrast to looking for relationship information, if your goal were to know for any particular time the exact value of sales or costs, that information would be more immediately given with a tabular-numeric display. For example, to see what the company costs were in September, you would have to draw a line from September to the cost curve to find the cost point for September, then draw another line from that point on the cost curve to the y axis to see the dollar value of the costs at that time. In the tabular display you would locate the row for September and immediately read the associated cost value.

Let us look at another example. Figure 6.12 shows cities in the top quartile of sales growth with their corresponding longitude and latitude. Once again, simple inspection of the tabular view in panel 6.12a does not reveal any pattern to the cities with sales growth in the top quartile. In contrast, with the graphical view in panel 6.12b recognizing the pattern (location relationship between the cities) that sales are growing fastest in the Northwest and Southeast, is trivial.

Why is it so much easier to see location relationships with a graphic map display than with a tabular numeric display? There are three reasons:

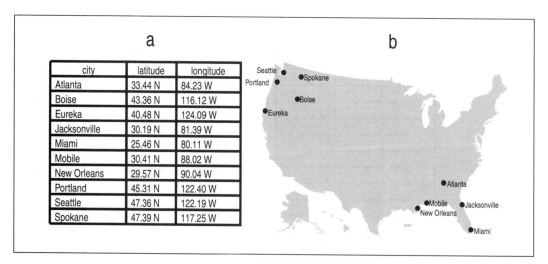

Figure 6.12 Cities with high sales growth.

1. The map display uses locations on the computer screen to display location information about the data.

2. The dimensionality of the location information about the data is preserved in the dimensionality of the location information on the computer screen. In other words, the two-dimensional longitude/latitude relationship between cities is preserved in a two-dimensional map display but lost in a one-dimensional tabular one. For example, with the map display, moving vertically on the screen corresponds to moving in latitude; moving horizontally corresponds to moving in longitude. With the tabular display, however, there is no correspondence between moving up and down rows and moving in either longitude or latitude. This dimensional preservation is sometimes (and in this book will be) called an analog, as opposed to symbolic, representation. See the sidebar "Graphical Misrepresentations" for more information.

3. The quantitative properties of the map display, such as the relative distance between points, which can be processed with minimal effort by the brain, correspond to quantitative properties of the data. For example, the distance between Jacksonville and Atlanta, which appears to be about the same on the map as the distance between Jacksonville and Miami, represents the fact that those distances are, in reality, roughly equivalent.

Graphical Misrepresentations

The most serious problem associated with graphical representations is the ease with which they can misrepresent the underlying data.[3] Two major causes of misrepresentation are described here—both are avoidable.

1. Collapsing multiple data dimensions into a single location-based display dimension, as shown in Figure 6.13, when the graph and the data do not share the same structure, the graph can create false impressions about the data.

   The apparent periodic dip in sales across the x axis in Figure 6.13b is caused by the collapse onto one dimension of two dimensions worth of identifier information: stores and months. By representing the data in two identifier dimensions, as a series of line graphs with one for each store, as shown in Figure 6.13c, or as a plane in the z dimension, as shown in Figure 6.14, it is easy to see a constant upward trend over time for all stores.

A straightforward graphing of the data in (a) produces the graph shown in (b); more meaningful picture presented in (c)

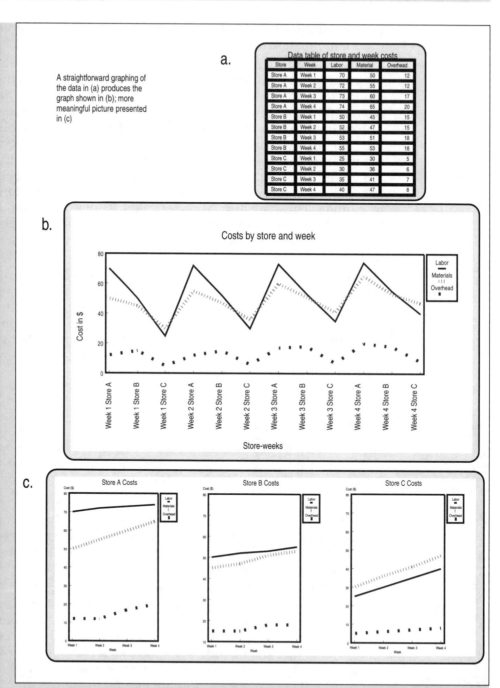

a.

Data table of store and week costs

Store	Week	Labor	Material	Overhead
Store A	Week 1	70	50	12
Store A	Week 2	72	55	12
Store A	Week 3	73	60	17
Store A	Week 4	74	65	20
Store B	Week 1	50	45	15
Store B	Week 2	52	47	15
Store B	Week 3	53	51	18
Store B	Week 4	55	53	18
Store C	Week 1	25	30	5
Store C	Week 2	30	36	6
Store C	Week 3	35	41	7
Store C	Week 4	40	47	8

b.

Figure 6.13 False graphical impressions.

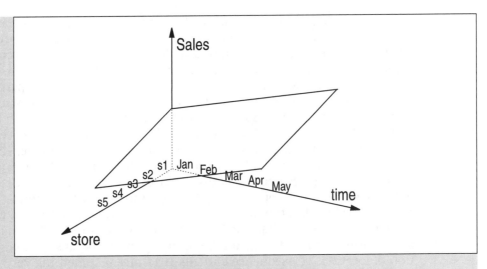

Figure 6.14 Using the *z* dimension.

2. Using any display technique, especially areas, that changes apparent value in amounts or proportions that are different from the changes to the underlying data. Tufte illustrated his book with many fine examples of misleading graphics. Figure 6.15 purports to show changes in sales of apples using the height of an apple to represent the sale of apples. Note how much larger the apple looks for 1996 than for 1995 even though sales just doubled. It is because the area of the apple quadruples when its height doubles.

Figure 6.15 Beware of the big apple.

Summarizing this short excursion into the difference between graphic and numeric displays, we can say that the meaning of a graphical token (in the essential sense as described earlier) is its location on the display screen. The meaning has nothing to do with the content or form of the token. In other words, each point, whether in isolation as in Figure 6.12b or as a part of a line segment as in Figure 6.11b, has the same content or internal structure or form. Every point is the same as every other point. The difference in meaning between the points comes from the location of the point on the screen.

In contrast, the meaning of a numerical token is entirely dependent on the form of the token and has nothing to do with its placement on the screen. Every number token is distinct from every other. In other words, what makes the number 2 different in meaning from the number 1 or the number 3 is just that the form or shape of the number 2 is distinct. It doesn't matter where the number 2 is located; it always means 2. (The one pseudo-qualification is that of base number. I say "pseudo" because it is not a question of location. The sequence of digits 1011 means something very different in base 2 than in base 10. Nonetheless, given a base number for a string of digits, their meaning is entirely location-independent.)

Thus, there are two fundamentally different ways of using tokens to represent or bear meaning on a display screen: using screen location and using screen content or form. *Numbers bear meaning by virtue of their form. Graphic tokens bear meaning by virtue of their location.* A token may represent two fundamentally different types of expressions: value and relationship. As we saw in Figure 6.11, *numeric tokens represent their values more directly than the relationship between their values, while graphic tokens represent the relationships between their values more directly than their actual values.* Figure 6.16 summarizes these key distinctions.

Colors and shapes, although frequently associated with graphical displays because they show relationship information more easily than value information, work like numbers in that they derive their meaning more from their

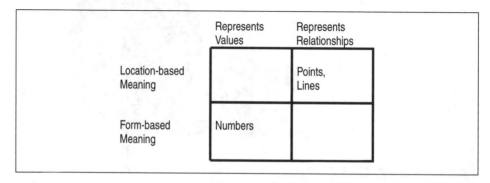

Figure 6.16 The key distinctions between numeric and graphic displays.

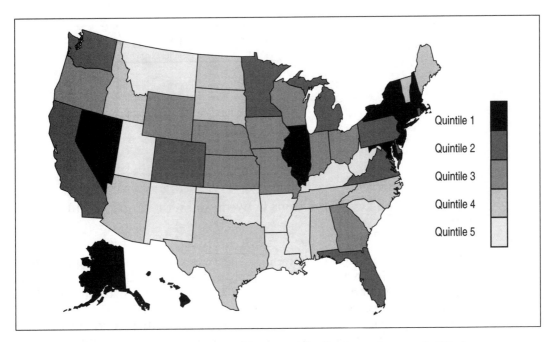

Figure 6.17 U.S. per capita income by state (shades based on quintiles).

form on the screen (that is, the particular color or particular shape) than from their location. They were left out of the initial discussion because they have attributes of both numbers and graphics, as shown in our next example.

Figure 6.17 shows another map of the United States, this time colored on a state-by-state basis according to per-capita income quintiles. (In the world of geographic information systems, or GIS, these are called **thematic maps**.) As stated in the legend, the lowest quintile is shown by the lightest shade of gray, the next lowest quartile by the next lightest shade of gray, and so on. Light gray in Georgia means the same as light gray in Montana. The meaning of each shade is independent of the location of the shade on the map. Instead, it is entirely a function of the shade itself. The shades are directly analogous to groupings or low-order numbers, in this case quintiles. However, unlike numbers, it is easy to detect relationships between states by looking at shades. In this example, it is easy to see that zones of high per-capita income occur in clusters along the East Coast, the West Coast, and the Great Lakes. In this sense, shades are analogous to points and lines. Figure 6.18 shows a version of Figure 6.16 updated to reflect the properties of shades, shapes, and symbols.

Looking back over the last two figures, you should notice that although Figures 6.11b and 6.12b were both graphical, they seemed to convey differ-

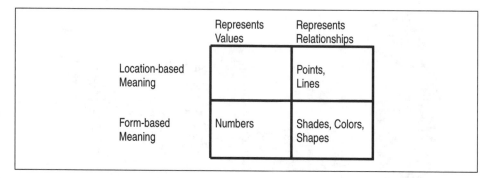

Figure 6.18 The key distinctions between numeric, graphic, and colored displays.

ent kinds of information. Figure 6.11b answered a comparison question. It used two lines in an *xy* plot to accomplish that. In addition to *xy* plots, bar graphs and pie charts like the ones in Figures 6.19 and 6.20 are useful for showing comparisons between values.

Figure 6.12b identified certain cities that met a particular criteria by using a map to display city indicators. In addition to maps with symbolic indicators, topographic maps (and isosurfaces) like the one shown in Figure 6.21 are useful for identifying value ranges. The topographic map is ideal for identifying peaks, valleys, flat areas, and steep areas. Note, by the way, that any variable, not just geoaltitude, can have peaks and valleys, steeps and flats. The map could just as easily portray sales volume per booth in a large trade show, or pollution levels, or economic zones.

In addition to comparing and identifying values and value ranges, it is common to want to identify value changes over space and time. "What part of our network has the most bottlenecks during the course of a typical day?"

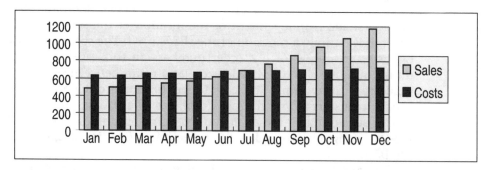

Figure 6.19 Comparison of sales and costs over time.

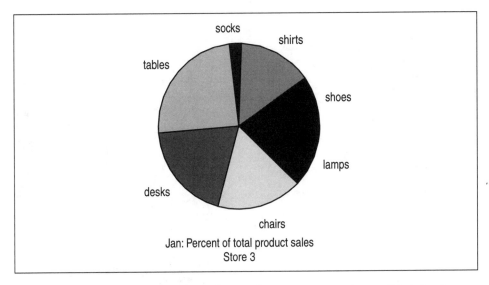

Figure 6.20 Comparison of product sales as a percentage of total sales.

is a question about value changes over space and time. "Where do our products go after they leave the warehouse?" is a question about the direction and volume of shipments over space and time. Arrows and directed graphs (especially when superimposed on maps), such as the one shown in Figures 6.22, are useful for showing value changes over space and time. Figure 6.22 shows, for each of PTT's warehouses, the relative volume of product shipments in

Figure 6.21 Topographic map of the Lost River Valley.

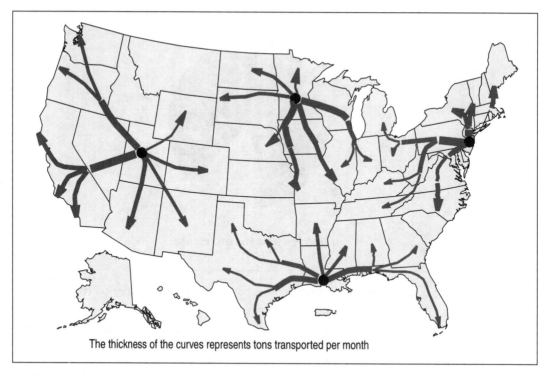

The thickness of the curves represents tons transported per month

Figure 6.22 The volume per path of PTT product shipments.

each direction. Arrow locations represent where the shipments go. And arrow thickness represents the transported tonnage per month.

Finally, in preparation for visualizing hypercubes, we need to look again at grid displays in the light of the previous discussion. Grid displays, like colors, bear some of the characteristics of graphics. For example, Figure 6.23 represents a data set of store profits by store and time. In the table display, the rows are ordered by time and within time, by store. For the graphical display, the stores on the store axis are arranged in descending order of average customer traffic per unit area of store space. And the time axis is ordered chronologically. In both panels the store-times with highest profitability are highlighted.

Looking at the grid in panel 6.23b, it is easy to see that profitability is highest around December and around medium traffic stores. You would never detect this in the table shown in panel 6.23a. Why is that? As long as the two dimensions in the grid represent two key dimensions of the data, and *as long as the grid dimensions are ordered according to some meaningful criteria*, such as the chronological and store traffic criteria shown in Figure 6.23B, *the grid behaves like an abstract map* or coordinate system. (The exact proper-

A

Time	Store traffic	Profit margin
Aug	1	2.0%
Aug	2	2.4%
Aug	3	2.6%
Aug	4	2.9%
Aug	5	2.7%
Aug	6	2.5%
Aug	7	2.2%
Sept	1	2.4%
Sept	2	2.7%
Sept	3	2.9%
Sept	4	3.2%
Sept	5	2.8%
Sept	6	2.6%
Sept	7	2.3%
Oct	1	2.8%
Oct	2	2.9%
Oct	3	3.1%

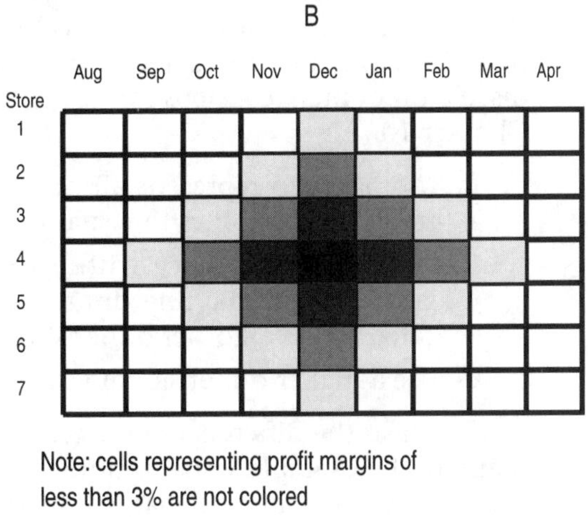
B
Aug Sep Oct Nov Dec Jan Feb Mar Apr
Store
1
2
3
4
5
6
7
Note: cells representing profit margins of
less than 3% are not colored

Figure 6.23 Store profits by store and time.

ties of the grid are a function of the ordering characteristics of the dimensions, such as whether the dimensions are ordinally or cardinally ordered. This is addressed in Chapter 15.)

We have now covered enough preliminary groundwork to explore how graphical techniques may be applied to the visualization of multidimensional hypercubes.

Visualizing Multidimensional Hypercubes

We have seen what makes graphic images work and when to use form- or content-based images versus location-based images. We turn now to the graphic display of higher-dimensional structures. There are no magical techniques guaranteed to capture the essence of any hypercube. The larger the number of dimensions or data points in a cube, the harder it is to capture it in a single graphic display.

The question isn't "How do I visualize everything?" because the answer to that is "You don't." Nor is the question "How do I decide what to visualize?" because the answer to that is "You visualize what you need to see." (Of course, once you have initiated the process of discovery, a visual display, like a numeric query result, may direct you toward your next visualization.) The real question when it comes to visualization is "How do I decide the best way to visualize what I need to see?" What follows here is a description of the three main techniques for graphically visualizing hypercubes along with a brief discussion of how to decide how to visualize the data. (A more complete discussion of practical steps for deciding how to visualize data is presented in Chapter 10.)

1. Use pages to represent all but two or three dimensions and then use traditional graphics to visualize the rest.
2. Represent a subspace within the overall structure and then create a grid of the remaining dimensions wherein the base graphic is replicated across all other dimensions.
3. Use a higher-dimensional visualization technique.

To make the differences between these techniques as clear as possible, as many of the example visualizations as possible are drawn from the same data set, namely the same one that was used in Chapter 5, with the exception that customer types are not included. This leaves us with a five-dimensional retail-based data set consisting of stores, times, products, scenarios, and variables.

Using Pages

This option amounts to subsetting the hypercube and using normal visualization techniques for the lower-dimensional subcube. For example, you could slice out a one-variable time series from the hypercube by putting store, products, scenario, and variables into the page dimension. This leaves time as the only dimension for which multiple members are shown. Figure 6.24 uses a two-dimensional graphing technique to display time across the x axis, dollars across the y axis, and the values of the sales variable in terms of a line. Of course, the graphic represents only a small portion of the hypercube. But that is fine if it is all you need to see. The important point to remember is that traditional graphics work perfectly well on a lower-dimensional subcube.

Nontraditional image techniques, while still portraying only a lower-dimensional space, reveal more of the data's hierarchical structure than is typical of lower-dimensional images. Figure 6.25 shows network traffic loads for a telecommunications company organized by day and time of day. Surface height and color represent network load. Dimensionally the image depicts two identifier dimensions—day of month and time of day—and one variable—traffic. Notice the back panels in the figure; they represent average hourly loads and average daily loads. The graphic lets you visually explore relationships on two levels simultaneously.

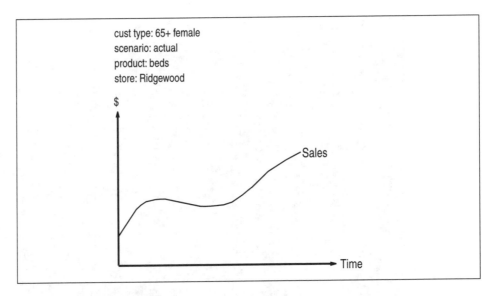

Figure 6.24 Sales by time.

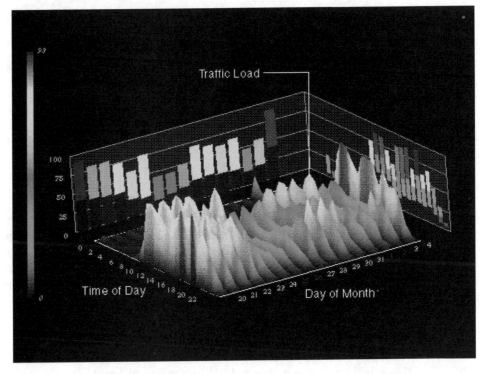

Figure 6.25 Network traffic loads.

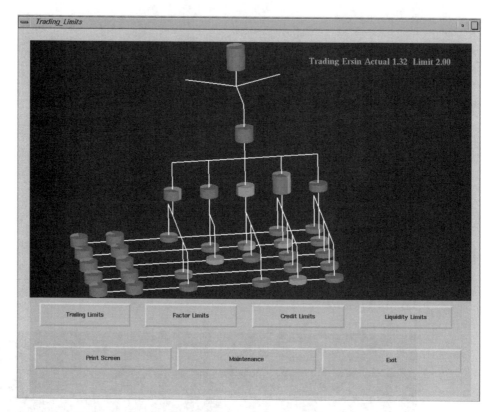

Figure 6.26 Risk management.

Figure 6.26 shows risk exposure for a currency trading operation. The horizontal edge of the hierarchical form represents the individual traders, or managers, and their place in the three-level reporting hierarchy. At the leaf level, the depth-wise edge of the hierarchy represents currencies. The circular shapes represent the position of each trader in that currency. The size of the shape represents the dollar value for the position. The color of the shape represents the riskiness of the trader's position. Dimensionally, the figure shows two identifier dimensions—trader and currency—and two variables—position size and position risk. The hierarchical figure makes it very easy to see at a glance the position of individual traders, individual currencies, and trading units as exemplified by the manager's position.

Using Repetition

What if you were interested in how sales and costs varied across stores and times and you were interested in how the variance of sales across stores and times varied across products and scenarios? You might be trying to spot prod-

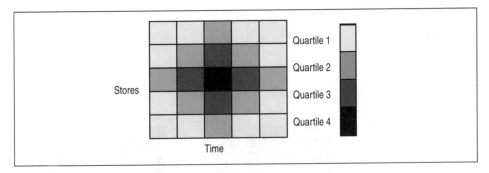

Figure 6.27 Sales data for beds in quartiles for store by time.

ucts for which there was less seasonal variance in sales. To do this, you would need to visualize a much greater percentage of the hypercube. And what if you still wanted to use lower-dimensional graphic images? You would have to show many lower-dimensional images. Figure 6.27 shows the same product sales variable shown in Figure 6.24 but with the addition to the visual display of a store dimension. In the process, we have also changed our method of portraying sales. Instead of a line showing all sales values, a set of shadings shows sales quartiles. We made this change for two reasons: a two-dimensional grid with shade-values in cells takes up less space than a three-dimensional grid where the height of the *z* dimension (the sales dimension) is used to represent value, and shades or other relative form-based representation techniques work best for low cardinalities.

Figure 6.27 is about as far as you can go with traditional graphics. So how do we get the other dimensions in the picture? Figure 6.28 shows the image of Figure 6.25 as the contents of a higher-dimensional cell composed of the product, scenario, and variables dimension.

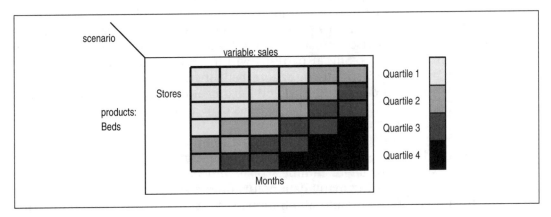

Figure 6.28 Sales data by stores and time nested in a higher-dimensional cell.

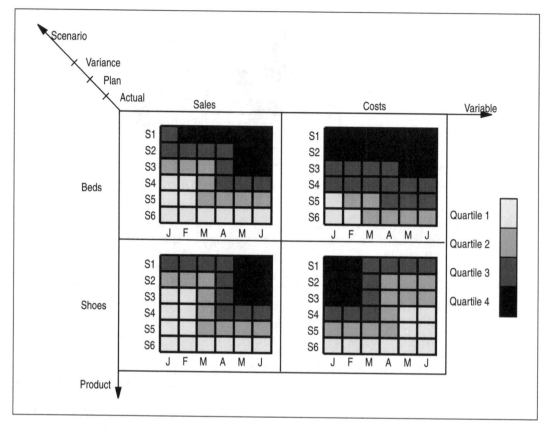

Figure 6.29 Sales data by stores and time nested in a higher-dimensional grid.

In other words, the graph of sales by stores and times may be thought of as a complex content of a subsuming cube composed of products, scenarios, and variables. There is one sales by stores by time image for each product-scenario-variable intersection, as shown in Figure 6.29. Notice how your eye can switch between looking at patterns within each of the complex grid cells (such as discovering that the sale of beds increase toward the lower traffic stores and toward later months) and looking at patterns across multiple grids (such as discovering that traffic patterns may have less of an impact for shoe sales than bed sales).

How do you decide which dimensions to put on the inside and which to put on the outside? Generally speaking, you want to put on the inside those dimensions with larger numbers of members because graphic images are good at compressing many data points onto a single image. For example, if there were 500 stores and 500 time periods, a two-dimensional grid of sales quartiles (that used one pixel per sales value), like the one shown in Figure 6.28 would do an excellent job of displaying the data in an informative way. In contrast, if you were to put the dimensions with the highest cardinality on the outside, it would increase the number of repetitions of the inside graphic to the point where it would be difficult, if not impossible, to understand.

Using Higher Dimensional Visualization Techniques

Most uses of multidimensional visualization rely on the techniques shown in the previous two sections. Keeping dimensions as pages serves to simplify the multidimensional space so that it can be visualized with normal-dimensional visualizations. Repeating a normally dimensioned graph across a grid serves to extend the dimensional reach of a display. (Actually, most multidimensional visualization still relies on the graphing of subcubes.) In contrast, higher-dimensional visualization techniques attempt to show multivariate multidimensional relationships in a single, nonpartitioned image. They demand powerful hardware and software, and sophisticated users, and are still uncommon, especially in the corporate world. They are most often used in science and engineering (and, to some degree, in finance).

This last section briefly touches on the main issues surrounding the use of higher-dimensional visualizations. Due to the lack of available tools, consider this food for thought rather than immediately usable knowledge. The visualization software that is included in this book and used during the hands-on case studies, like other statistics-oriented tools, is more multivariate than multidimensional. However, even without software, I find it useful to picture higher-dimensional visual spaces because it helps me think about relationships within data sets when I am mulling them over in my mind. Also, this is a rapidly evolving field. Products may be out before too long that bring higher-dimensional visualization to commercial analysts.

Unlike with lower-dimensional visualizations where you can use location-based techniques to display either identifier dimensions or variable values, with higher-dimensional visualizations, you will need all the location-based dimensions you can use (three or four) to display the identifier dimensions of your data.

Figure 6.30, reprinted with the permission of AVS, is a geospatial image that depicts relative humidity, temperature, wind speed, and air pressure over the continental United States. The figure uses three location-based dimensions on the screen to portray the three identifier dimensions in the model: longitude, latitude, and altitude. And it uses shape, colors, and lines to represent the variables in the model. The figure uses what is called an *isosurface* (the worm-like shape in the figure) to identify all the locations that have the same relative humidity. Then, relative to this region, colors and lines are used to depict the temperature, pressure, and wind speed within the isosurface.

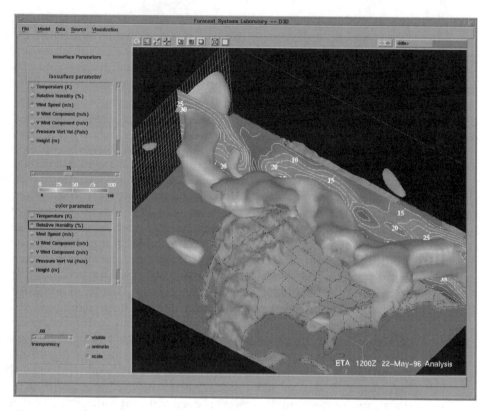

Figure 6.30 Multidimensional visualization of geospatial data.

The isosurface clearly identifies the jetstream as a region of constant relative humidity.

The technique of using colors and lines in conjunction with isosurfaces embedded in three-dimensional spaces is useful for representing any kind of data that is defined in terms of three or four identifier dimensions. (Actually, the identifier dimensions should at least be ordinally ordered. This is discussed in Chapter 15.)

If you were trying to compare peak actual sales and peak actual purchases between products and stores over time, you would need to see if peak sales or purchase periods vary from store to store or from product to product. You would also want to look at the time span between peak purchases and sales of products to see whether there is an ideal lead time. You are not sure of where to look for correlations: between stores, products, or times, so you want to represent stores, times, and products at the same time on the screen along an *x*, *y*, and *z* axis. You probably also want to represent peak sales and peak costs as two separate isosurfaces and represent facts about sales and costs as attributes associated with the isosurfaces.

Table 6.1 Visualizing higher-dimensional commercial data.

Logical	*Geospatial*	*Commercial*
Identifiers: *x y z* axes	longitude, latitude, altitude	stores, products, time, scenarios
Principal variables: isosurfaces, glyphs	relative humidity	sales, purchases
Secondary variables: colors,lines, textures, patterns	temperature wind velocity air pressure	cost of transation labor component energy component

Table 6.1 shows how a commercial data set could be visualized in terms of a geospatial modeling metaphor.

Summary of Section on Visualization

In this section, you explored multidimensional visualization from a variety of perspectives: core graphical tokens, representing lower-dimensional slices, iterating slices in other dimensions, and using higher-dimensional visualization techniques.

Summary of Chapter

In this chapter, you have explored how to define individual hypercubes and how to use multicube structures to join the information belonging to multiple hypercubes. You have seen the differences between form-based and location-based visualization techniques. You have also seen techniques for displaying dimensional information, and how to combine these techniques to create higher-dimensional visualizations.

Endnotes

1. It is not strictly necessary for there to exist any dimensions in common. One can always create a formula that says *x = cube z dim1a, dim2a, dim3b + 150*measure 'w'*. Only when you are trying to perform analysis (which is nearly all of the time) do you need to compare a series in one cube with a series in another cube.

2. Edward R. Tufte, *The Visual Display of Quantitative Information* (Cheshire, CT: Graphics Press, 1983), p. 9.
3. See, for example, the discussion on misleading graph types in Edward Tufte, *The Visual Display of Quantitative Information* (Cheshire, CT: Graphics Press, 1983), pp. 69–72.

Advanced Features, Part 2

In the last chapter, we explored hypercubes and visualization. Here we take a closer look at formulas, hierarchies, and links.

More about Formulas

This section explores two important issues related to formulas in a multidimensional environment that were not treated in Chapters 3 and 4:

1. The storage of derived data computed in advance of any query and its relation to huge increases in database size

2. How formulas should treat sparse data, which requires an understanding of the difference between repeating zeros, missing data, and meaningless cells

Pre-query Versus Post-query Calculation: Controlling the Explosion of Derived Values

In addition to the issues of formula definition and precedence, which were discussed in Chapter 4, there is another aspect to formulas that is important to understand. If all the formulas you define in a multidimensional model are computed and their results stored at the time the data set is loaded (as opposed to at the time their outputs are requested by a user), you may discover that your database has expanded by a factor of two or even three *orders of magnitude*!

Let us put this in perspective. One million input numbers requiring a mere 20 megabytes of storage, which could easily fit on your notebook, could

171

create one billion derived numbers that would require 20 gigabytes of server disk. And one billion input numbers, which could safely fit online on your server, would generate an output data set requiring 20 terabytes to store. This would almost certainly require some degree of offline storage.

The factors that influence the creation of derived data values and what can be done to manage them will be explored in the following sections.

Factors Influencing the Explosion of Derived Values

In the spreadsheet and database worlds, there is no mystery to the creation of derived values. For example, as we saw earlier in Figure 4.13, derived spread-sheet values are generated by defining a formula that directly applies to the derived cell. In the SQL database world, as we saw in Chapter 2, derived values are generated by creating a view whose attribute columns are explicitly defined in terms of a formula.

In contrast with these explicit or hands-on approaches, the creation of derived values in the OLAP world is relatively hands-off or implicit. Recall from Chapter 3 how OLAP formulas were specified along the margins or dimensions of the cube. Typically, you attach aggregation formulas to nonleaf members in each nonvariables dimension. (The variables dimension does not usually have a hierarchical form, and its formulas attach to the leaf variables.) The member formulas then combine when the dimensions are intersected to form the cells that actually contain (or point to) the data. Thus, unlike spreadsheet or SQL database formulas, multidimensional formulas do not attach directly to the data. That action takes place when the dimension formulas intersect within the context of a cube. One formula defined in each of four dimensions could create thousands of derived data values when the dimensions intersect.

The indirect approach is not a problem as such. It does make it easier for problems to occur, as when giving someone directions and hoping they are interpreted correctly rather than taking her or him there yourself, which requires no interpretation. One problem can occur when you compute some formulas, expecting that your database grows by a relatively small factor of perhaps 2 to 3, yet you discover, when all the derived cells are calculated, that the number of output cells is 1,000 times larger than the number of input cells. Where do all these derived numbers come from? Are they necessary? Is there some way to keep things under control?

For a typical hierarchical dimension under normal circumstances (and most dimensions such as time, stores, products, and customers are defined with hierarchies), the ratio of total members to leaf-level members is a small number in the area of 1.5 to 2.5. Assuming that data is entering at the leaf level and propagating upward, we can, for the purpose of this example, treat leaf members as input and nonleaf members as derived (This approach is like

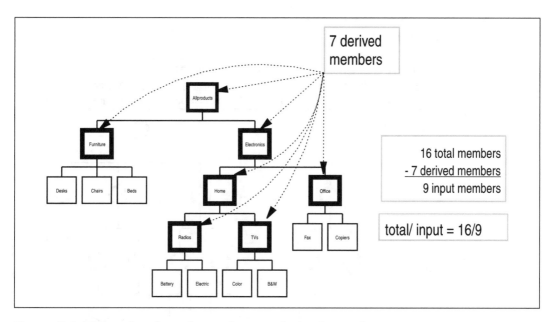

Figure 7.1 The ratio of total members to derived members.

ignoring friction for the purposes of studying gravitational forces). Figure 7.1 shows the ratio of total members to input members within a single product dimension.

What happens when a model has two or more dimensions? If a three-dimensional model has a ratio of total to leaf-level members, or an inflation factor of 2 in each dimension, what is the inflation factor for the model as a whole? Dimension-specific inflation factors are multiplicative, so the total inflation factor for a three-dimensional model with an inflation factor of 2 in each dimension is 8 or 2*2*2 or 2^2. In other words (and assuming all the dimensions have the same inflation factor), the number of derived cells in a multidimensional model inflates or grows exponentially with the number of dimensions.[1]

Let's examine this point more closely. Look at Figure 7.2, which shows all the members for each of two dimensions in a simple two-dimensional model composed of products and measures. Counting the members of the product and the stores dimension we see that for each dimension, there are 1.8 times as many total members as there are base members. Figure 7.3 shows the number of all base and derived values in the model. Subtracting the base data from the store by product level reveals 224 derived values. The ratio of total values to input values is therefore $324/100 = 3.24 = (1.8)^2$. Thus (we can infer), *the inflation factor for a model equals the average ratio of total to input members raised to the power of the number of dimensions.*

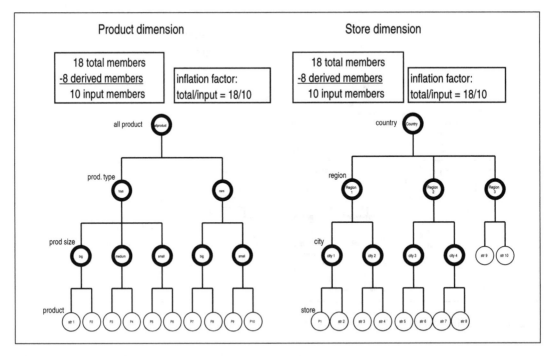

Figure 7.2 All the members for each of two dimensions.

	10 products	5 sizes	2 types	1 allproduct
1　country	10	5	2	1
3　regions	30	15	6	3
4　cities	40	20	8	4
10　stores	100	50	20	10

Note that there are 16 distinct matrices of numbers representing the cross-product of each of the four levels in the two dimensions. The number in each cell represents the number of data cells in that matrix. For example, there are 10 stores and 10 products so there are 100 measure values in the store-product matrix.

Figure 7.3 The number of values for each aggregation level in a two-dimensional example.

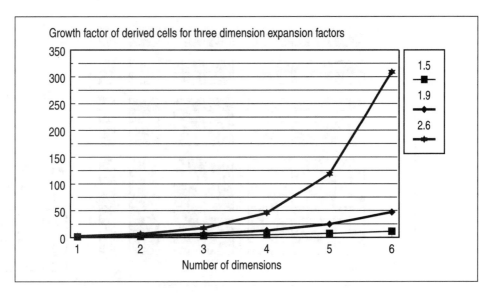

Figure 7.4 Derived cell inflation factor as a function of the number of dimensions.

Assuming that most dimensions have a similar ratio of total to input members, the expansion in derived values is largely a function of the number of dimensions. Stated otherwise, the larger the number of dimensions in your model, on average, the greater the ratio of derived data to input data. For example, a three-dimensional model with the same average inflation factor per dimension would grow by a factor of 5.8, and a four-dimensional model by a factor of 10.5. So far, this still seems manageable. But like any other exponential function, it eventually gets out of hand. Figure 7.4 shows how the growth of derived data in a model increases with the number of dimensions and with the inflation factor per dimension, for up to six dimensions. Notice how a six-dimensional model with an inflation factor of 1.9 per dimension experiences a total growth of almost 50, and the same number of dimensions with a growth factor of 2.6 expands by a factor of more than 300. A 10-dimensional model expanding at that rate would grow by a factor of more than 14,000!

The degree to which a database inflates as a result of precomputation may also be affected by the sparsity of the base data. If computations are run anywhere there is at least one data point available for input, then the database explosion will be exacerbated by sparsity.

Look, for example, at Figures 7.5 and 7.6. They represent the same two-dimensional model. The base data in Figure 7.5 is 50 percent sparse. The base data in Figure 7.6 is 90 percent sparse. See how the ratio of derived to input

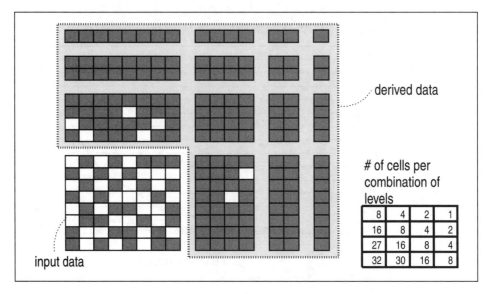

Figure 7.5 Derived data, from a 50 percent sparse data set.

data grows from 1.8 per dimension (when the input data is perfectly dense), to 2.5 (when the input data is 50 percent sparse), to 4 (when the input data is 90 percent sparse). At an inflation factor of 4 per dimension, the derived data

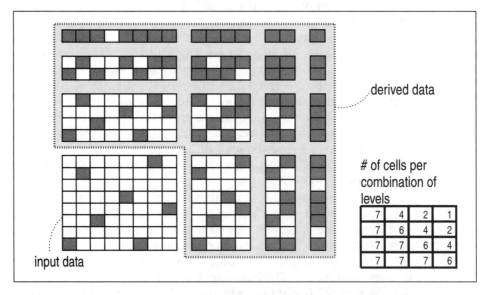

Figure 7.6 Derived data, from a 90 percent sparse data set.

in a ten-dimensional model would propel the database to over 1 million times its original size! Although few models have either 10 hierarchical dimensions or an average inflation factor of 4, it is not uncommon for databases to balloon by a factor of several hundred.

It has been stated elsewhere that the way to reduce the explosion problem is to use fewer dimensions when modeling the data[3] because a five-dimensional model will create less derived data than a seven-dimensional model. Although generally a good rule of thumb, it is still possible to create all the same derived values in a five-dimensional model as in a seven-dimensional model. It just requires the creation of more multipath hierarchies, as shown for a simple case in Figure 7.7, where a two-dimensional model consisting of stores and products is represented in a single dimension. In two dimensions, stores and products would each have four members at the base level, followed by two intermediate-level members and one root member. Their inflation factors would therefore be 7/4. As you can tell by inspection,

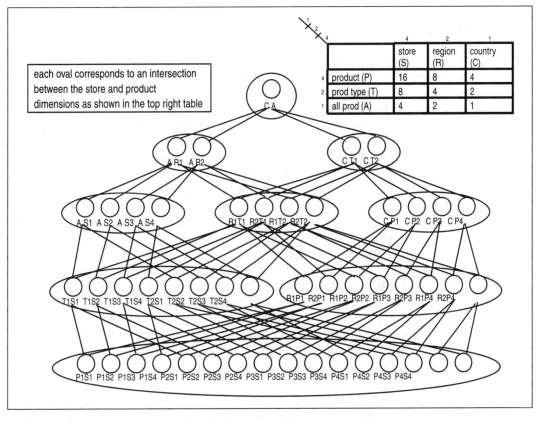

Figure 7.7 High inflation in a single dimension.

the inflation factor for the one dimension shown in Figure 7.7 is 49/16, which equals $(7/4)^2$.

The key question is, are you computing aggregates on an as-needed basis, or are you defining dimension formulas and letting them loose onto a data set? If you are defining them on an as-needed basis, then changing the dimensional structure of your data set will have no significant impact. If, however, you are defining them by stating your needs in terms of dimensional formulas, then changing the dimensional structure of your model may serve to reduce the amount of unneeded aggregates and thus the size of the derived data space.

Even if you are defining aggregates on an as-needed basis (and assuming your tool allows you to do this), there will still be a lot of aggregates. The inflation factor may be in the tens rather than in the hundreds, but it will still be significant. This brings us to the next issue associated with the management of derived data: computing (and storing) data when it is defined, as opposed to when it is requested.

Controlling the Explosion of Derived Data Values

Partial Precalculation   The discussion we have had so far about the growth of derived values has assumed that data, once defined, was calculated and then stored in anticipation of eventual queries. But there is no logical reason why all derived data needs to be precalculated. Although the press has frequently characterized multidimensional tools as somehow needing to precalculate everything, in reality, multidimensional tools differ widely in this area. (See Chapter 8 for more detail.) Although some tools do insist that all data is precomputed, others (like the one enclosed with this book), usually working in RAM, calculate everything at request time. In contrast to tools that decide for you whether derived data is to be precalculated, some tools offer you the ability to decide whether a data value is to be precalculated and stored or calculated at request time.

A number of academic papers have been written in this area.[4] It is clear that an ideal system provides the ability to choose whether a data value is or is not precomputed. Essentially, it is best to precompute and store those aggregates that are most often used as inputs to other calculations and those aggregates that themselves depend on the greatest number of inputs. It is best to compute at request time those aggregates that are cheapest to compute, that are least used by other calculations, and that use analysis has shown to be least requested by end users.

End-user-defined Formulas   Finally, there is no way that a model designer can anticipate all the formula-based queries that end users might want to pose to the system. Just think, for example, of all the different types of ranking formulas or ratios that can be created. In a typical retail model, you might wish to see stores ranked by this year's sales, this month's sales, this week's sales, this year's costs, this month's costs, number of employees, sales per employee (again, this year, this month, or this week), sales per square foot, sales of some particular product or group of products, profit margin per store, variance from plan, change relative to some milepost, and so on—the list is virtually endless.

The solution is to let end-user analysts (who are probably working on a client machine connected through a network to the server) define their own formulas. Many tools work like this. (Of course, once you have tools from different vendors communicating through an external API there is plenty that can go wrong.) The problem is that many of the interesting end-user queries involve large amounts of data. Passing them across the wire to the client could easily choke the network or the client.

Ideally, the client should be capable of formulating unanticipated queries that are executed on the server. For example, the query "Find the five products that sold the most in one month during the past year," in a company that sells tens or hundreds of thousands of products, would potentially require a scan of millions of records, for a result set of just five lines. This is exactly the type of query that is best executed on the server. The issue of client-defined calculations is important and will be discussed further in Chapter 8.

In summary, multidimensional models naturally create large amounts of derived data. If the base data is sparse, or if the hierarchies are deep, or if there are many dimensions, the amount of derived data created can be quite large relative to the amount of input data. By precomputing and storing only what is needed, it is possible to control the growth of derived values.

The Problem of Logical Sparsity

The term "sparse" or "sparsity" is frequently associated with multidimensional data sets. It was used in the previous discussion in "Controlling the Explosion of Derived Data Values" in the context of exacerbating the problem of database explosion. Figure 7.8 is a view of a sparse four-dimensional matrix. The four dimensions are stores, time, product, and variables. The view shows variables and products along the columns, and stores and times along the rows. Notice all the sparse or blank cells.

Why are the sparse cells sparse? Does a sparse cell mean that data for the cell is missing but potentially forthcoming, like a late sales report? Does a sparse cell mean that data could never apply to the cell, such as the name of an unmarried employee's spouse? Or does a sparse cell simply mean that all zeros are being suppressed like the zeros associated with individual product

		Indirect Sales			Direct Sales			Total Sales		
		Chairs	Tables	Total	Chairs	Tables	Total	Chairs	Tables	Total
Avon	January	150		150	250		250	400	0	400
	February	120	220	340	300	150	450	790	370	790
	March		300	300				300	300	300
Milwaukee	January	600	800	1400				1400	800	1400
	February	760			1200	1350	2550	2550	1350	2550
	March	300		300				300	0	300

Figure 7.8 Viewing a sparse four-dimensional model.

sales in a store that carries many products but that only sells 5 percent of its items on any one day?

The term "sparse" has been indiscriminately used to mean missing, inapplicable, and zero. The first two cases fall under the heading of what in the database world is thought of as invalid data. It is an important topic. E. F. Codd, in his expanded 18 features for OLAP, suggests that OLAP models follow the relational model version 2 rules for handling missing data.[5] These entail what is called four-valued logic. This will be treated in depth later in this section.

The third case, where the term "sparsity" has been used to mean the existence of many zeros, is a special case of how to handle large numbers of repeating values where the repeated value happens to be a zero. The existence of many repeating zeros is not really an example of sparsity. Zero is just as valid a number as any other number. (It actually took thousands of years of human mathematical development before we recognized the need for a number that meant zero.) It is a perfectly well-formed statement to say that store x sold zero units of product y. It carries as much value as to say that store x sold 15 units of product y. You can sum and average zeros. You can compare them to other quantities and so on. (Of course you can't divide by zero, but that's another topic.)

The confusion has arisen because OLAP applications frequently encounter large numbers of repeating zeros and large amounts of missing and meaningless data. And the techniques for physically optimizing the storage of large numbers of repeating values are similar to, and sometimes the same as, the techniques for physically optimizing the storage of large amounts of missing and meaningless data.

Once again, the physical techniques for compressing repeating values, be they zero, missing, or meaningless, should be treated separately from the logical techniques for computing with missing and meaningless data. We take a look at some of the physical techniques for compressing repeated values in Chapter 8.

Missing and meaningless values are not valid data. They cannot be treated in the same way as any other value. You cannot take the sum of three integers plus two missing values. You cannot compare the value of an integer with that of an inapplicable token. Special logical techniques are required to handle these cases. Improper treatment of nulls can cause inaccurate calculations. Mistaking a missing value for a zero, or mistaking a zero for a missing value, or assigning a proxy value where none is applicable will all create incorrect results. For example, if a missing value is treated like a zero then the sum of 3 + 6 + "missing" will be called 9, which is wrong. The right answer, in the absence of a proxy value, is "missing."

The accuracy of calculations is of crucial importance to the analysis of any data sets, whether or not they are multidimensional. The issue of how formulas should work with sparse data is a very important one and is frequently debated in the database world. As it relates to the accuracy of calculations, especially in the sense of database queries and computations, it is a question of logic.

For most of its history, logicians have believed there were two logical values: true and false. Logical rules that apply to databases are expressed in terms of these two values. For example, querying a database to list all salespersons who sold more than $50,000 of product in March may be thought of as posing, to each salesperson's record for March, the question "Is it true that this salesperson sold more than $50,000 of product?" and listing all the records where the answer is "yes, the statement is true." This is illustrated in Figure 7.9.

Problems arise, however, when invalid data enter a logical system or database. Look again at Figure 7.9. Notice the blank entry for the commission field in row five. And now imagine the same query, "Is it true that the value

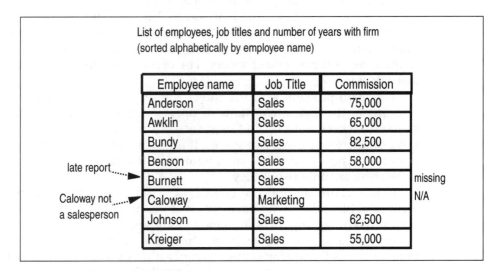

Figure 7.9 Record sparsity.

of the commission field in this row is greater than $50,000?" What would the answer be?

You could be a wise guy like Aristotle and say the statement is false; that is, it is false that the value of the commission field is greater than $50,000, simply because there is no value. But there is a problem with this answer.

The problem is that the truth value of the answer is a function of how the question was phrased. In other words, if the query had had the form "Is it true that the value of the commission field is less than or equal to $50,000?" the answer would still, according to the same logic, be false. But according to logic, a proposition and its inverse cannot both have the same truth value.

More likely you would say, "I don't know whether it is true or false because the data is missing." This is tacit acceptance of your inability to process the missing data as if it were existent. In the same vein, and answering the same query, if an employee did not draw a commission because that person was salaried, then the commission field would be inapplicable as shown in row 6 of Figure 7.9. That is, commission does not apply because the employee draws a salary. "Not applicable" is similar to "missing" in that you cannot process it like a valid data value, but it is different from "missing" in that it would be wrong to assign it a value.

Toward a Solution to the Problem of Logical Sparsity

Logic has no rules for handling invalid data. (In Chapter 16, you will see that logic ought to have such rules.) Yet such things as missing and nonapplicable data regularly enter all kinds of databases including multidimensional ones. Logicians are divided over the best way to deal with invalid data.

Some prefer to use logical systems that work with three or more logical values. Terms such as "unknown" and "not-applicable" are frequently given to these beyond-two-valued values. The extra values then enter into the formal calculus.

The main problem with the three—and higher—valued logics is that the meaning of the logical constants or operators, such as the "negation" term, which have been built up and used successfully over the last 2,000 years, depend on there being just two values. It is inconsistent to add a third or fourth term to the pool of logical values while continuing to use operators that assume there are only two values.[6,7]

In the relational model, version 2, Codd advocates the use of four-valued logic. And like others who have gone before, he changes the meaning of the negation term, giving it two different meanings.[8]

For true and false propositions, the negation of a term yields a different term with a different truth value. The negation of true is false, and the negation of false is true. For missing and inapplicable propositions, the negation

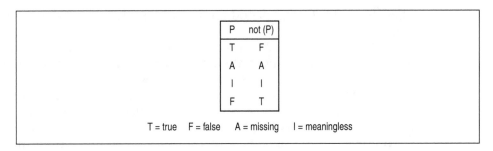

P	not (P)
T	F
A	A
I	I
F	T

T = true   F = false   A = missing   I = meaningless

Figure 7.10 The four-valued logic of the relational model, version 2.

of a term is itself. So the negation of missing is missing and the negation of inapplicable is inapplicable. This inconsistency in the definition of negation produces several problems that have been described elsewhere.[9]

Some prefer to retain two-valued logic because of its desirable inferencing properties and exclude invalid data from entering the system.[10] They generally characterize invalid data as either the result of poor database design or as data about the data, sometimes called metadata. For example, rather than entering the null value for "spouse's name" into an employee database when an employee has no spouse, it would be better to enter the valid data value "no" into a field called "is married." A separate spouse table would contain the relevant spouse information. The improved database design would eliminate the invalid data.

The problem with this two-values-plus-metadata approach is that it conflates two general classes of invalid data: missing and meaningless.[11] The two classes need to be individually treated because they affect computations in different ways. They just don't need to be treated as logical values on a par with true and false. Consider the following example.

Imagine you are the general sales manager for a chain of 100 department stores. And imagine you need to calculate the average monthly shoe sales per store for all 100 stores. In the simple case, all 100 stores sell shoes and all 100 stores reported their sales of shoes. The arithmetic is clear.

If all 100 stores sell shoes, but only 80 out of the 100 stores reported their sales, and the average for those 80 stores was $20,000, the arithmetic is no longer straightforward. It would not be accurate to state without qualification that the average shoe sales per store was $20,000. Any statement about shoe sales that applies to all stores in the chain must, implicitly or explicitly, assign a default value to the nonreporting stores. Saying that the average sales per store is $20,000 assumes that the average per nonreporting store is $20,000 as well. This default value for the nonreporting stores need not equal the average value of the reporting stores, however. For example, it may make more sense to assume that nonreporting stores sell a dollar value equal to what they sold the last period modified by some function of their previous growth rate.

If the reason why 20 stores did not report shoe sales is because they recently stopped selling shoes, then no statement should be created about shoe sales that applies to all 100 stores. In other words, no default value for shoe sales should ever be assigned to stores for whom the value is meaningless. In this situation, it would be accurate to state that the average sales for the 80 stores that sell shoes is $20,000.

However, in the same way that a proxy value may be substituted for a missing data point, there are times when an applicable measure or variable, such as slippers, may be substituted for the inapplicable variable, shoe sales. For example, it may be that shoes are thought of as footwear and, although most stores sell shoes, some specialty stores do not sell shoes but do sell slippers. In this instance, it would make sense to report on the sale of slippers (modified by some appropriate function relating the average sales of shoes to slippers) where a store does not sell shoes.

Thus, when a measure or variable, such as shoe sales, is applicable but data values are missing, regardless of the reason, the missing values need to be assigned some type of default if they enter into operations with other data. (It is always possible to stipulate that missing data values be eliminated from a calculation as, for example, when a manager's bonus is tied to his or her store's sales figures and the bonus cannot be assigned until the actual sales figures are known.)

When a measure or variable, such as shoe sales, is not applicable to a location for whatever reason, such as a particular store that stopped selling shoes, and substitute variables are not being used, no default data value should ever be assigned to it for that location.

In general, the existence/nonexistence of data such as sales reports and the applicability/inapplicability of measures, such as the dollar value of shoe sales, may vary from location to location, or cell to cell, in a model. For example, if sales reports are late, then applicable data is missing for those stores. If a store changes its product lines, then certain variables may become inapplicable and/or applicable between time periods.

The ideal approach is to combine a two-valued logic engine embedded within a shell that provides special procedures for detecting missing and inapplicable data on an instance-by-instance basis.[12] This approach lets the user freely incorporate user-defined rules for substituting measures and data whenever invalid cases are found. And for those situations where the system is left with missing and/or inapplicable data, formal rules are used to convert the mixed expressions containing missing and/or inapplicable data into two-valued form where they can be processed via the use of traditional logic. (A detailed description of such an approach, which I call an L-C approach, is presented in Appendix B). It provides a powerful platform for squeezing knowledge out of incomplete data sets without stepping beyond the boundaries of logic.

More on Hierarchies

In Chapter 3, we began to discuss what hierarchies are and described different kinds. Here, we will explore some of their details in more depth. Support for structuring hierarchies within dimension varies quite a bit from product to product, and it is useful to know which types of hierarchical structures allow you to perform what types of activities.

The concept of level within a hierarchy is very important to determining what kinds of navigation you can perform within it and what types of computations it directly supports. In this discussion, "level" means a grouping of members across the dimension that are not so much at a hierarchical level in the dimension as at a level of scale or resolution. Typically, you would want to name these levels something meaningful like "month" or "city," instead of referring to them as "one level up from the leaf level in the hierarchy." Relationships between members in these levels tend to be symmetric.

A tool might not support named levels on any dimension, or it may only support named levels on one dimension such as the time dimension, or it may support them on all dimensions. If a tool supports named levels as an explicit construct, various types of formulas will be easier to code (particularly time-related functions) than if it does not. A tool that does not support named levels (providing only parent-child-defined hierarchies) will support asymmetric hierarchies. A tool that supports only named levels may require you to force all of the asymmetry of your model into a symmetric set of levels.

Named levels in a hierarchy may be represented in one of two ways (with any tool perhaps supporting only one of them). In one way, a level is a named group of members. For example, the named level "City" would contain the members "Chicago," "Milwaukee," "Columbus," and so on. In the other way, a name level is simulated by introducing a member into the model that serves as a root for the level and making all members belonging to a common level immediate children of that root. To represent the cities in the preceding example this way, a root member named "City" would be added to the dimension and be made a parent of "Chicago," "Milwaukee," and "Columbus." We will call this latter technique "pseudo-levels," as they create the grouping of members, though without any semantic connection as levels. Figure 7.11 illustrates the two different representations.

When using named levels, referencing data at particular levels in formulas can become much easier. For example, a formula can divide sales by the "year"-level or the "country"-level sales without having to know how far away in the hierarchy the "year"-level value is from the current time member

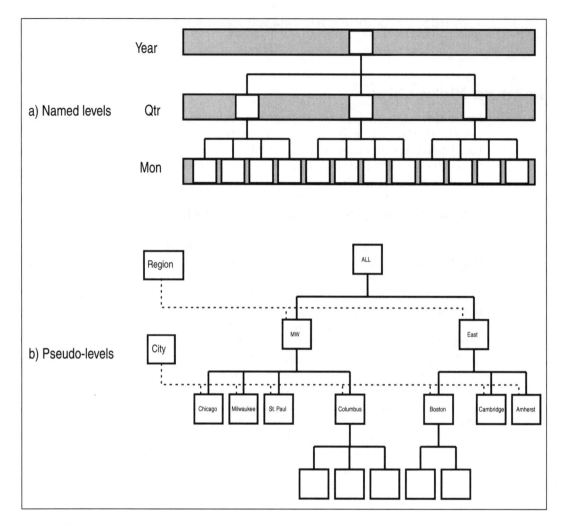

Figure 7.11 Named levels and pseudo-levels.

or how far away the "country"-level value is from the current geography member. In an asymmetric hierarchy, named levels help this even more because the appropriate "country" might be two hierarchical steps away from one city and three away from another. They help the person writing the formula concentrate on the meaning of the level as opposed to the structure of the hierarchy.

As another example, you may wish to compute a running average of the last three months' values for some variable. If the tool you are using cannot express months as a level independently from whatever parent members each month has, then you would have to express taking the average of each month and its prior two months as separate, specific formula clauses (one clause taking the average of months 1, 2, and 3, the next one taking the average of months 2, 3, and 4, and so on). You would then either attach these to new members added to the time dimension expressly for this purpose or attach them to existing members on the time dimension or variables dimension using some conditional logic to make sure the right average is performed on the right variable. If the tool you are using can express named levels of time, you ought to be able to create one formula that simply takes the average of the last three time members at the appropriate level. The multidimensional tool itself will then take care of averaging months 1, 2, and 3 or months 2, 3, and 4, and so on, as appropriate. Even though time is the dimension that is most frequently associated with levels for the purpose of analysis, levels can apply to any dimension.

When using pseudo-levels, it is not straightforward to find out how the level for a member relates to other levels, or even to find the next level above or next level below, because the tool does not directly support this notion of level. (The adjacent-level information might be coded as an attribute of the level's root member; see Chapter 4 for a discussion of attributes.) Accessing members from one level to the next can be a little difficult as well. Say that a geography dimension is modeling countries, provinces/states, and cities using level root members of "country," "province," and "city." To get the cities for the country "France," you will have to obtain "all children of the member 'city' that are also children of the member 'France'." A tool may or may not be able to express this easily.

Ideally, a tool provides clean support for both irregular hierarchies and named levels that are semantically understood to be like levels of scale.

More on Links

In Chapter 3, links between table sources of metadata and data were briefly described. Here, we build on the earlier discussion to explore more fully the variety of links necessary to connect dimensions and cubes to tables. Remember that links may describe structural relationships, member attributes, or hypercube contents. (Attribute links were adequately discussed in Chapter 4 and will not be further treated in this section.) You should also keep in mind that the variety of links required to process tables is a reflection of the variety of tables used to store data and structural information. Tables and links will frequently be described together in this section.

Structure Tables and Links

There are two basic forms of structure tables and links: parent-child and level.

A parent-child table can define any type of member hierarchy, symmetric or asymmetric, and it is the easiest type of table for maintaining dynamic metadata definitions. All the information about the hierarchical structure of the dimension is defined in terms of the values of rows in the parent-child table, so a hierarchy can be completely rearranged just by tweaking the rows of the table. (The dimension tables in a star schema may contain a column for "parent" member, providing the necessary information for a single hierarchy. In this case, they function as a parent-child table as well as providing other attribute information.)

A parent-child table connects to a dimension via a single parent-child structure link between the dimension and the parent and child columns. Variations on the basic parent-child link can occur, as required by specific tools. For example, if a tool required hierarchies to be named, then each link would also need to connect to the named hierarchy of the dimension (if all rows of the table were for the same hierarchy) or to a column of the table whose field values contain the appropriate hierarchy name.

Recall the discussion of dimension hierarchies in the previous section. Note that parent-child relationships alone do not indicate semantic levels such as month/year or store/city. They can indicate that January, February, and March are all children of Quarter One; but they cannot define January, February, and March as months that collectively share a relationship with quarters and with days. Thus, the table columns in a pure parent-child table can not fully specify levels in a multidimensional model.

A table of model structure information, such as a lookup or dimension table of the kind we saw in Chapter 2, could contain separate columns wherein each column connected to a different level in a symmetric hierarchy. For example, separate columns for city, state and region, or company name, SIC code and industry can very clearly identify not just hierarchical relationships between members but also how the levels relate to each other. In this type of table, the names of the columns involved in identifying hierarchy levels will correspond to the levels in the multidimensional model. While these are flexible enough for moving members around in a given set of levels, they are less flexible than parent-child tables for adding and removing levels of hierarchy. Of course, the flexibility of the parent-child tables comes at the expense of not being able to express inter-level relationships adequately.

Tables containing named levels need level structure links, one link for each level. If the levels in the table are not mapping into named levels in the dimension but simply a member hierarchy, then each link connects from a level's column to the dimension. If the levels in the table correspond to named levels in the dimension, then each level link connects from a level's column to the corresponding level in the dimension.

Occasionally, a dimension simply won't have any hierarchy (for example, a dimension of scenarios, nonhierarchical variables, and so on). If it is necessary to link this dimension to a table, then a level link for a single level will suffice. For a table containing only two named levels, like county and state, that is connected to a dimension without named levels, parent-child and level links can be used interchangeably.

The hierarchy pseudo-levels described previously may be represented in a parent-child link table because they are described in terms of parents and children. Defining pseudo-levels through parent-child links may significantly add to the number of parent-child links in the table because each member that is part of a pseudo-level will have a record for its connection to the pseudo-level root member as well as a record for its referential hierarchy. (Fortunately, using encoded values to identify members, each parent-child record is quite small.)

Data Tables and Content Links

Four different types of content links are required to connect any table to a cube for the purpose of mapping data into the cube: row-member, column-member, cell, and table-member.

Row-Member Links

Row-member links are required to associate member names contained in each row of the table with the right members in the model. A row-member link connects a dimension of the cube and a column in the table whose field value in each row contains the name of a member in that dimension. If the dimension is a variable dimension, then it is quite likely that the table is a type zero table and that a cell link would also be used (see below). It is also possible to see a type one table with the variable names occupying their own column. *It is most likely a grave semantic error to make more than one member link between a particular field and any cube, as this would mean that the data is associated with members in two dimensions that share the same name.*

Variations on the basic member links may be required from time to time. For example, denormalized data warehouse summary tables may contain multiple levels of members, one per column. For example, company, SIC code, and sector would each be in their own column. Rows containing company-level summary data will have values in each of these columns. Rows containing an SIC-code-level summary will have a NULL company name and values for each SIC code and sector, and rows containing sector-level summaries will have NULL in both the company name and SIC code fields. There may be an additional column that gives the name of the level to which the summary data pertains. This would assist the SQL programmer to query the table. The column containing the relevant member name varies from row to row in the table, and a member link that conditionally examines fields (perhaps based on the level name contained in another field) would be used.

Column-Member Links

Whereas *row-member links* associate columns with dimensions and the field values with members, a *column-member link* is required to associate a table's column with a particular variable and its field values with values for that variable. Each column-member link will connect a member of a dimension and a column of a table bearing data for a particular variable. Examples of such columns would be ones named "number of units sold," "total sales," and so on. Column-member links are used to identify the data-bearing fields in type one or type two tables. Column-member links and cell links (see below) are mutually exclusive (because a table cannot be both a type zero and a type one); if a cube uses even one column-member link to connect to a table, then it cannot use a cell link, and vice versa. If a table has columns that do not correspond to one variable but rather to a multidimensional intersection (type two tables), then one column-member link per dimension is required. For example, to link a table containing the columns "Actual Sales," "Planned Sales," "Actual Costs," and "Planned Costs" to a model that had a scenario dimension with "Actual" and "Planned" members requires two column-member links for each of these columns. Each column would have a column-member link to the appropriate scenario member and a column-member link to the appropriate variable.

Figures 7.12 and 7.13 show member and column-member links connecting two different types of type one tables to a cube.

Cell Links

Sometimes, the column bearing data in a table will not correspond to any dimension that you have defined in the model, and all of the dimensions of the cube link to the table with member and table-member links (see below). Even the variable names are in a column. This would correspond to a type zero table. In order to associate the values with the variables, you need to create a *cell link*. A cell link connects the cube as a whole to a table column whose field values are data for cells that are otherwise completely specified by the other links. (Logical implications to this, are explored in Chapter 15.) Figure 7.14 shows a type zero table connected to a cube via row-member links and a cell link.

Table-member Links

One more type of link is required to connect data-bearing tables to a cube—a link that represents information that isn't in the table at all! Let's call this a *table-member link*. What kinds of information wouldn't be in a table? Well, a data table extracted from an operational system will generally contain actual values from the operations (we hope!). If this is feeding into a planning cube

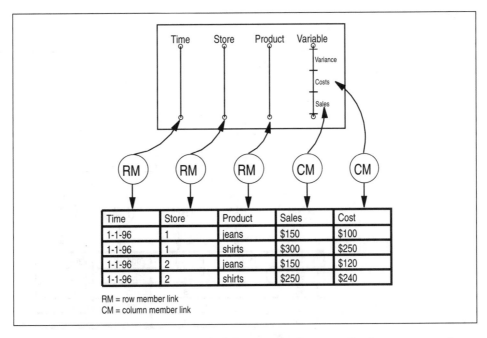

Figure 7.12 A typical type one table attached to a cube by row-member and column-member links.

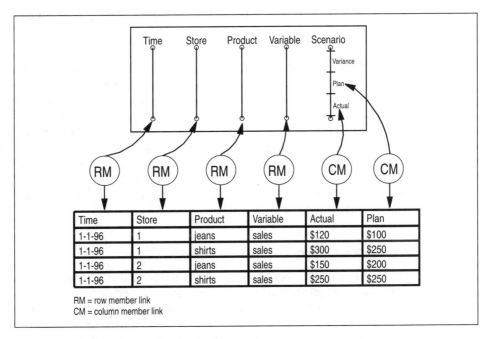

Figure 7.13 A less typical type one table attached to a cube by row-member and column-member links.

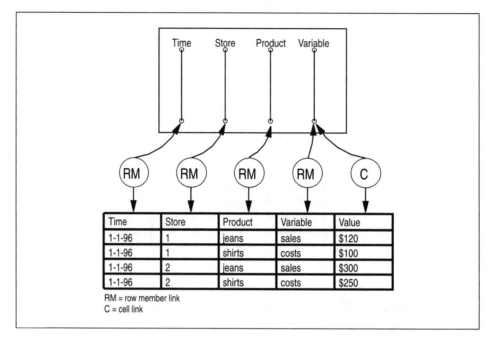

Figure 7.14 A type zero table attached to a cube by row-member links and a cell link.

that contains a scenario dimension having "Plan," "Actual," and "Variance" members, then the entire table is associated with the actual member in that cube. But there is nothing in the table, probably not even in its name, that we can use to assign it to its place in the model. Hence, we need this fourth type of link. It may be that more than one table-member link is required to connect a table to a cube. For example, each table may contain the actual data for an individual line of business within the corporation, and the cube consolidates their results into the planning model. Figure 7.15 shows a type zero table of actual values connected to a cube containing scenarios using a table-member link.

Pre-aggregation

If the table being linked needs to be aggregated during the process of reading, then the aggregation can be specified as an extension to the linking process. The aggregation should be specified as part of the linking to ensure that the same aggregation is performed each and every time the links are used. However, the aggregation operation to be performed is not strictly a part of the link. Think of it as an attachment to the linked field or fields. All that needs to be specified is the aggregation operator (sum, average, and so on) on each

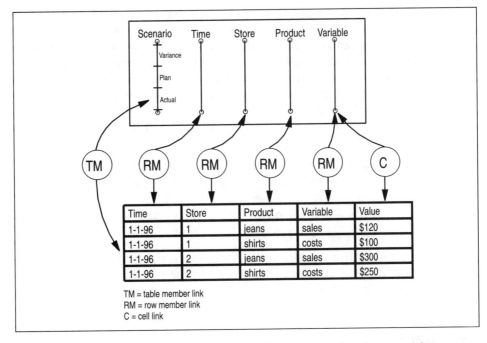

Figure 7.15 A type zero table completely connected using a table-member link.

field to be aggregated. The fields to be aggregated are the data fields. If you have already established links, they are the ones with either a column-member link or a cell link.

The reason why aggregation operations need to be kept separate from individual links is most apparent when considering the column-member links of a type two table. For a type two table, which will have two column-member links connecting each table column to members in two different dimensions, it would be inconsistent to specify one pre-aggregation for one dimension and a different pre-aggregation for the other. What is being aggregated is the data of a column. It makes more sense to attach the aggregation to the columns of the table rather than to any specific link.

Summary of Links

When a linked data table is read, the process of using the links can be summarized as follows. Any table-member and column-member links determine a set of model members that stays the same throughout the entire reading of the table. These members may be extracted from the model side of the link for use in identifying values of variables. Then, for each row, the fields for each column linked by a row-member link are examined and the members that they name determined. If the table has a cell link, then that column contains a single identified value for the variable identified through one of the row-member links, and the variable's value can be extracted from this field. If the table has column-member links instead, then for each column containing a column-member link, the members for its link (or links in case of a type two table) are collected, and an identified value for a variable can be extracted from the column's field.

A cube cannot be considered fully linked to a data table until the following occurs:

❏ Each dimension of the cube either is directly connected to a column or has some member connected to either a column or to the table itself.

❏ Each metadata field and each data field of the table, deemed relevant to the cube, have been connected.

Given the types of links discussed in this chapter, you should be able to describe how to move virtually any type of data from tables to multidimensional structures.

Summary

In this chapter you have explored some of the finer details of formulas, hierarchies, and links. You have seen when precalculating formulas can create huge amounts of derived data and how to alleviate this potential problem through run-time computations and enduser-defined queries. You have seen that sparsity has a variety of meanings and that it is necessary to distinguish missing and meaningless data. And you were shown how dimensions can have named or pseudo-levels. Finally, you were exposed to a detailed description of the types of links required to bring data into multidimensional information systems.

Endnotes

1. This topic was first given serious treatment in Nigel Pendse and Richard Creeth, *The OLAP Report: Succeeding with On-Line Analytical Processing* (London: Business Intelligence Ltd., 1995), p. 69.

2. Based on a study conducted in Pendse and Creeth, *The OLAP Report.*

3. Pendse and Creeth, *The OLAP Report*, vol. 1, p. 75.

4. See, for example, Venky Harinarayan, Anand Rajaraman, Jeffrey D. Ullman, "Implementing Data Cubes Efficiently," ref. 15.

5. *The OLAP Report*, p. 116, contains a description of Codd's 18 rules.

6. For example, in a logical system with three values True, False, and Unknown, there is no good way to say "not" to all three values. In most systems offered, Not(True) will be defined as False, Not(False) will be defined as True, and Not(Unknown) will be defined as Unknown. Unfortunately, that means that sometimes Not(x) does not equal (x), and sometimes Not(x) does equal x! In other systems where Not(Unknown) is defined as False, then Not(Not(x)) will sometimes equal x and sometimes not. All of a sudden, logic is not something that can be consistently applied. See S. Shavel, and E. Thomsen, "On Three Valued Logics," from a paper presented at the 16th Wittgenstein International Symposium on Cognitive Science.

7. See E. F. Codd,. "Missing Information (Applicable and Inapplicable) in Relational Databases," *ACM SIGMOD Record 15* (December 1986): 53–78, and E. F. Codd and C. J. Date, "Much Ado About Nothing," *Database Programming and Design 6* (October 1993): 46–53.

8. E. F. Codd, *The Relational Model for Database Management: Version 2* (Reading, MA: Addison Wesley, 1991), p. 182.

9. S. Shavel and E. Thomsen, "On Three Valued Logics" unpublished paper presented at the International Wittgenstein Symposium on Cognitive Science, 1993.

10. See the series of articles by David McGoveran in *Database Programming and Design*:

    David McGoveran, "Nothing from Nothing (Or, What's Logic Got To Do With It?)," *Database Programming and Design 6* (December 1993): 32–41.

    David McGoveran, "Classical Logic: Nothing Compares 2 U," *Database Programming and Design 7* (January 1994): 54–61.

    David McGoveran, "Nothing from Nothing: Can't Lose What You Never Had," *Database Programming and Design 7* (February 1994): 42–48.

    David McGoveran, "Nothing from Nothing: It's in the Way That You Use It," *Database Programming and Design 7* (March 1994): 54–63.

11. The need to formally distinguish between missing and meaningless data was shown in the paper "On Three Valued Logics." Stated briefly, if two truth values (true and false) are employed, then missing data may be thought of as either true or false, while meaningless data may be thought of as neither true nor false.

12. That approach was described in "On Three Valued Logic," cited above. As a consultant, I developed a prototype system for performing these substitutions for a large institutional client.

Storage, Access, and Computing

The last five chapters of this book have focused on the logical aspects of multidimensional models. In Chapters 3 and 4, for example, we explored the features that are basic to any multidimensional model such as hypercubes, hierarchical dimensions, dimensional formulas, and feeder links. In Chapter 5, you got a chance to get your feet wet using the enclosed multidimensional software. And in Chapters 6 and 7 we covered advanced multidimensional features. If you carefully read these last chapters, you should be able to think about a problem in multidimensional terms and figure out how to use any particular product to build a solution. This is what you get from an understanding of the logical aspects of multidimensional architectures.

If it were possible to store unlimited amounts of data, and if it were possible to perform any search, external data fetch, or computation in an instant, there would be no need for users of multidimensional information systems, whether end user or administrator, to pay any attention to physical architectures. (Of course, anyone attempting to build a multidimensional product will always pay attention to these issues.)

As many SIMMs, MIPS, gigabytes, and wires as we purchase, we still run out of main memory, fill disk space, and choke networks. Thus, it should come as no surprise that you should indeed pay attention to physical architectures when choosing a multidimensional tool. The choice of physical architecture can have a dramatic impact on overall system performance.

As you will see in Chapters 8 and 9, there is a wide variety of physical architectures. Ultimately, you will need to decide what range of physical architectures makes the most sense for your situation and explore which products

197

offer the appropriate range. Most products, as you will learn, offer some choice of physical architecture. But few, if any, can run the gamut.

Introduction

The purpose of this chapter is to examine the variety of ways in which multidimensional data is stored and accessed. This, in turn, affects the performance not only of browse and query operations but of calculations as well. Many calculations access large numbers of data points. The faster the data access, the faster the calculating.

Toward that end, this chapter covers the following topics:

- ❏ Sparse data storage
- ❏ Memory versus disk-based storage of live session data
- ❏ Persistent storage in SQL tables
- ❏ Persistent storage in physically optimized multidimensional databases
- ❏ Choosing the best method for storing live session data
- ❏ Comparing products
- ❏ Supporting ad hoc calculations
- ❏ Indexing options

The multidimensional conceptual model is the most natural way to view business information. But, handling large volumes of multidimensional information in a practical way on a computer is far from easy, and the "obvious" solution is certainly not the only way and is rarely the best.

The obvious way to store multidimensional data (on disk or in memory) is as a simple array, which is how the user visualizes it. That is, space is reserved for every possible combination of dimension members, and the location of any cell can be computed with some very simple arithmetic. Such a simple array has many benefits because it is extremely fast to identify the location of any cell (to read it or update it), and cells can be populated for the first time or updated without affecting the physical location of any other cells. Consequently, many OLAP products do indeed use simple arrays for part of their data storage, either in memory (quite frequently) or on disk (relatively uncommonly).

However, although it is natural for human beings to think of business information in this way, it is rarely efficient to store the data on disk using a simple multidimensional format that directly reflects the user view. Even when the data is in memory for fast, random access, it is often necessary to lay out the data in a more complex format than a simple array. This complexity is due largely to the sparsity (recall the discussion in Chapter 7) that usually occurs with multidimensional data. However, another factor is the requirement to modify dimensions without having to recreate the whole array.

The main performance problem with the disk storage of sparse data is that data is read off the disk in blocks (rather than cell by cell), and if each block is likely to be very sparsely populated, large numbers of empty or near-empty blocks will have to be read into memory for little benefit. As far as data in memory is concerned, RAM is still a relatively scarce commodity, and it would be very wasteful to use, say, 100 times the memory that is truly required.

Expected Performance of Multidimensional Information Systems

Multidimensional data not only has to be stored, but has to be viewed, updated, and used as the basis for calculating many other results—preferably in less than five seconds. How it is stored will affect the performance and functionality of each of these other requirements. The user is not interested in how large the underlying database is and is unlikely to want to wait 10 seconds or more just because the data has been structured as a single large database rather than many smaller ones.

This expectation puts pressure on the products to deliver a fast, reasonably predictable response, regardless of the amount of data that must be used to support a single query. Ideally, products achieve this by determining the minimum amount of information needed to fill a screen (rather than the number of results that the full query might call for) and then asking the application server for only this amount of information. The server should then be smart enough to do the minimum work necessary to service the query. For consistency, the response time for a query should largely depend on the number of results displayed on the screen, not the size of the database, the amount of data that supports the query, nor even the size of the potential result set defined by the query. If this is achieved, users will get a genuinely interactive response (of not more than a few seconds), regardless of what is happening behind the scenes.

Storing Sparse Data

In practice, most realistic OLAP applications are very sparse. Typically, fewer than one in a thousand potential cells are actually occupied. In some cases, fewer than one in a million potential cells are used. Wasting megabytes of disk or RAM to store a single cell that actually contains only 8 bytes worth of data is clearly nonsense, so OLAP product designers have come up with other, more ingenious ways of storing multidimensional data that still provide fast access and the ability to maintain the structures.

Because OLAP applications are meant for interactive decision support, it is important that they remain fast, even if the database is large and sparse. The key issue, therefore, is that you need to get at cells anywhere in multidimensional space, but you do not want to waste too much physical space storing nonexistent information or indexes. Simply storing them as a list of identified cells might eliminate any wasteful storage of nonexistent cells, but it would not provide fast access, easy updating, or efficient indexing, so more sophisticated solutions are usually needed. Many possible solutions to this conundrum exist, each with its own strengths and weaknesses. The "right" choice depends on the size and other characteristics of the application.

Some of the factors that affect the choice include the following:

1. The amount of actual data to be stored. If the overall quantity is relatively small, a totally RAM-based approach is likely to be best; larger amounts will require some of the active data to be accessed directly from disk, which is slower and more complicated.

2. The natural data sparsity. If the data is very sparse, more complex indexing and data compression may be needed, which will make the product slower and potentially less reliable.

3. How often data needs to be updated, and whether this is in large batches or individual cells. Batch updates are simple because only a single task has to be run, and all the updates can be merged at once and any database restructuring can occur at the same time; individual cell updates are much more complex, because they need fast random write access, even to hitherto empty cells, which not all structures can support.

4. Whether random read and/or write access is required. Reading and/or writing individual cells to disk files is much more complex than creating and reading the whole database in a single operation, and some of the more compressed file structures are therefore unsuitable if this type of access is needed.

5. Whether immediate recalculations based on user input are required. This requires tracking which previously computed and stored results have been invalidated by data changes and will therefore need to be recomputed, and doing so immediately; few products can do this.

6. Whether the data is to be shared with other users (with multiple read and/or write access). This requires a multiuser database with security; if multiple write is required from the OLAP application, then few products have adequate database technology.

7. Whether data is to be shared dynamically with other products. This will require either a well-supported API or storing the data in simple relational tables.

8. The style of client-server architecture being used. This depends on where the multidimensional processing is being carried out; different data structures may be appropriate. See Chapter 9 for a discussion of options.

9. The amount of "real" and virtual RAM available. This will determine how much active data should be held in memory.

10. Disk and CPU performance. This will affect how much is precalculated and where such information is kept: disk or RAM.

11. Disk space available. This will affect the degree of precalculation and the amount of indexing.

12. How often the database dimensions change. This will affect the extent to which the dimensions are made "data driven."

OLAP product designers always have particular applications in mind when they create their products, and they therefore have some idea of the range of the factors listed above. Using this knowledge, they preselect the techniques they will use to store and manage sparse multidimensional data effectively *for these applications*. Thus, no single product is optimum for every possible OLAP application, despite the claims made in the glossy marketing materials.

All products use a combination of techniques internally; some offer explicit choices to the application builder while others prejudge which techniques are likely to be generally suitable for the types of application for which their products are intended. It is obviously simpler if the product selects appropriate structures itself, but unless its choices are smart, the resulting application will not perform well. Ideally, you might hope that a really clever product would make an informed, dynamic choice of structures based on the criteria described above, but this does not currently happen.

I do not suggest technical ignorance on the part of product developers, but I do say that each company focuses on what its existing customers are demanding, without having the opportunity to see the bigger picture. Each product, therefore, tends to get better at solving one class of problems, without necessarily becoming more versatile, and it becomes all the more necessary to select a product that was designed to implement the kind of application that you need.

Memory versus Disk-based Model Processing

The first decision that must be made is where the data of an active model is kept while it is being processed and accessed. A few products, like desktop spreadsheets, hold all live data in memory. The disk files are used simply to hold the data between sessions and for safe storage. In some other products, this is an option, but it is also possible to keep the rest of the active database on disk, at some cost to performance.

There is one huge advantage in holding all active data in memory: it is *very* fast—perhaps 200 times faster than even the most highly optimized disk storage, which, in turn, is faster than standard RDBMS storage.

This performance advantage can be seen in many ways:

1. It is possible to do far more calculations "on the fly" because the ready availability of all relevant data in memory makes this an almost instantaneous process; the main "cost" of OLAP calculations is the time taken to read all the necessary supporting data off disk, not the CPU time taken to perform the actual arithmetic. If this disk access time can be eliminated, it is possible to perform many more calculations on demand, rather than as a batch process in advance. This makes the product suitable for interactive ("what if?") analysis, with significant calculations being performed in real time; this is a prerequisite for some planning applications.

2. The intrinsically fast performance means that even if the database is not optimally designed, the users may not notice any significant performance degradation. This means that it is less important for applications to be tuned well, and product designers can risk presetting more database structures automatically without having to provide additional tuning facilities for expert users. This has the effect of making the product simpler to deploy, which greatly reduces the overall cost of ownership.

3. The reduction, or even the elimination, of the need to perform large amounts of precalculations can greatly reduce the time taken to load and preprocess large amounts of new data. This means that more can be done within a given update window, or shorter time windows can be used. This may be important if data changes often and only the application can be unavailable for only short periods.

4. Finally, the great reduction in the need to perform large precalculations means that the size of disk files required to hold the database is greatly reduced (practical experience of different products in use today shows that memory-based products typically use between 10 percent and less than 1 percent of the disk space required by disk-based products).

There is, of course, one big snag with pure memory-based processing: even with the smartest compression techniques, the size of data that will fit into memory is much smaller than will fit on disk. Memory is very fast, but it is also much more expensive than disk; the particular ratio may vary over time, but RAM is typically 80 times more expensive than disk (per megabyte). It is also more limited: The maximum memory that can be installed on a particular machine may be measured in the hundreds of megabytes whereas the maximum disk that can be installed may be in the hundreds of gigabytes.

This means that although RAM-based storage of active multidimensional data provides an excellent technical solution for many applications, it is either too expensive or simply not viable for many others. Although these other applications will still hold some of the active data in RAM, they will also have to keep the active database on disk, stored either in optimized proprietary structures or in conventional relational tables. This disk-based approach is obviously slower, but it may reduce hardware cost because the server does not need enough memory to hold the complete active database. Very large applications become possible on relatively modest servers. However, if a multigigabyte database is to be processed, then the server is still likely to need plenty of available real memory for best performance (because indexes and some of the active data will still need to be held in RAM or disk caches if performance is not to suffer unduly).

Some of the more complex multicube products allow the data storage and indexing structures to be chosen at the subcube level, so a single database may use a variety of structures on disk and in memory. Usually, this choice is transparent to the application and can be easily altered after the application has been built. This allows expert tuners to determine which parts of the application are RAM-based, disk-based, RDBMS-based, or combinations of all of them. This flexibility may seem attractive, but tuning facilities are a double-edged sword: They require effort to use, and it is just as likely that they will be used incorrectly as optimally.

This may seem complex enough, but in the real world of computer hardware, the distinction between disk and RAM is often fuzzier than you might expect because of the effects of disk cache and virtual memory.

All disk-based products (and operating systems themselves) include some form of memory-based cache; there is often DBA control over how large this should be, sometimes even at the subcube level. This means that even "disk-based" data structures will actually be stored partly in memory-resident disk caches, and it could happen that a product that offers dynamically compressed sparse structures on disk will be able to fit all the data into memory with smaller applications, thus transparently turning a disk-oriented structure into a memory-based one! On the other hand, a memory-based product may require more memory than is available in real RAM, and it will therefore use virtual memory, thus holding a memory-based structure partly on disk. Each of these will deliver a less optimal performance than would be the case had a structure more appropriate to the physical characteristics of the computer been chosen.

This may all sound more complex than OLAP is meant to be, but multidimensional applications can soon become alarmingly sparse and they may also need to hold many millions of real data cells (apart from all the defined, but nonexistent, items). We have found that quite minor changes in underlying structures can dramatically alter the data load, calculation, and reporting performance of large-scale multidimensional applications, as well as the disk space requirement, so ignoring the realities of multidimensional storage may not be wise.

How (and Where) to Store Multidimensional Data on Disk

As mentioned previously, and despite the confusions of virtual memory and disk caching, live multidimensional data structures can be stored, in principle, in RAM, proprietary multidimensional databases, or in general-purpose databases. These are listed in descending order of performance and ascending order of data capacity. Although RAM is much faster, it is usually scarce, so most larger OLAP applications keep a large proportion of the active database in some form of disk files. These are so much slower than RAM that they will usually be more highly indexed to minimize the access steps, even if it means that relatively more disk space is used. Conversely, memory-based structures must use less index space even if it means that more steps are required to locate a cell.

Traditionally, OLAP products have used their own proprietary databases, optimized to suit the particular applications for which the products were intended to be used. The vast majority of installed OLAP applications work this way. However, recently a number of products have begun to offer the option for some—or all—of the active database to be held in conventional SQL tables.

Although an organization's data may be held in SQL tables, the SQL tables are a part of the organization's analysis-based decision-oriented information processing system, not a part of its operational systems. Thus, even if an OLAP application stores all its data in a relational database, it will be working on a separate copy of the data, not the live transaction database. This allows it to be structured optimally for OLAP, rather than for some other application.

Storing Multidimensional Data in SQL Tables

In principle, it is not difficult to store multidimensional data in SQL tables; after all, this is often how the data originated. The problem is to provide fast access and flexible multidimensional manipulation. (Recall that we looked at the problems of defining multidimensional aggregations and analyses in Chapter 2.) A variety of techniques can be used, and the resulting structures are usually quite complex, involving many tables.

The most common form of relational storage used for OLAP is what is called a "star schema." (Recall the discussion of star schemas in Chapter 2.) This apparently simple structure is inadequate, however, for most real-world applications for a number of reasons.

The single fact table is an inefficient way to store large amounts of base data. If there are many variables, it may not be possible to store them all in a single fact table (because of column limits in the underlying relational database). It may also be very inefficient because the sparsity may differ greatly between groups of variables or not all the dimensions may apply to all the variables, and the data may also come from multiple applications, making updates to a single large table inefficient. Thus, in large applications, it is quite common to partition the fact table between groups of variables based on their sparsity, which dimensions apply to them, and where the data in them comes from.

It is also sometimes desirable to partition the fact table on one or more of the other dimensions. For example, if there is a "scenario" dimension, with budget/actual data, it is common to split the fact table(s) along this dimension also (so that there would be separate tables for budget and actual data). Furthermore, if several years of history are included, then it is quite normal to split it by year, so that each year's data forms a set of tables. Thus, the base data is typically partitioned along several of the dimensions in large applications, so that in a large system, there could easily be 10 or 20 base fact tables.

A further complication then arises. For best query performance, as we described in Chapter 7, at least some of the aggregations and other calculations usually need to be performed in advance. Thus, a decision needs to be made about which calculations should be done at data load time and which at query time. In order for the system to make best use of the stored calculated results that are available, when deriving any other dependent ones, the precalculated values should be clearly identified and readily accessible. If SQL "group by" operations are to be used to generate these derived values, it is most efficient not to mix multiple levels of consolidation together in a table. This means that for each combination of hierarchical level in each dimension that is deemed to be worth precalculating, a separate summary table will be needed. However, these, in turn, are likely to be partitioned on the same lines as the base tables, so the potential number of precalculated summary tables can rise very rapidly. In the largest applications, there can be thousands of summary tables. These need to be kept in line with the data and comprehensively revised if, for example, product structures change.

Once the table layout, or schema, has been designed, the base tables populated, and the summary tables created, the problem of multidimensional manipulation still needs to be resolved. The major impediment, as we saw in Chapter 2, is that standard SQL is not equipped to specify multidimensional operations. In essence, vendors take three approaches to add multidimensional functionality to data stored in SQL tables. The first approach is only an option for SQL database vendors as it involves changes to the way the SQL database works. The latter two options, because they are external to the database, may be taken by OLAP vendors.

1. Integrate multidimensional processing into the relational database management system. This can occur either by extending SQL or by adding multidimensional functionality into the core of the database system. Although some vendors have extended SQL to offer more analytical functionality, no vendor, as of July 1996, has a commercially implemented version of an integrated multidimensional/SQL database.

2. Perform a series a separate steps in SQL, sometimes known as multipass SQL. In this approach, the OLAP query tool issues a whole series of SQL Select statements, with the outputs of the early statements going to temporary tables that are then used by the subsequent tables. As most of these intermediate tables are small, they tend to remain in cache and the process need not be as inefficient as it sounds; however, it still has higher overhead than a simple multidimensional retrieval and can never be as fast.

3. Retrieve the relevant data from the appropriate tables to an intermediate application server where the multidimensional processing is performed.

Because of the complicated way that data is stored on disk, relational OLAP tools always provide a read-only view of the data, and other tools must be used both to update the base data and (usually) to update the summary tables as well. This means that these products cannot be used for "what-if" type calculations or any other applications where users can update certain data items.

SQL Aggregate Query Processing

Optimizing the management of aggregate tables in a SQL database is an area of active research. Aggregate tables take up storage space and reduce the time it takes to return aggregated results to a query. Given some knowledge of how big the base and aggregate tables are, a judicious compromise between storage and computation can be made. The ideal location of this knowledge would be in the SQL optimizer itself, but this would require either extending SQL to describe the relationships between the aggregated views and the base table or overhauling the internal catalog and optimizer to automatically recognize these relationships. However, this knowledge is also useful to products that know the structure held in the tables and generate their own SQL. "Implementing Data Cubes Efficiently," a paper by Harinarayan, Rajaraman, and Ullman, describes results of research into optimization techniques.

Storing Multidimensional Data in a Physically Optimized Database

The more common way to store multidimensional data is in a specialized database designed for the purpose. Typically, the data is held in the form of a collection of small, relatively dense arrays; in some products these themselves can be compressed, so that only nonnull values are stored at all. Other designers felt that this would save only a small amount of disk space and would lead to slower retrievals, so that they do not compress the lowest level arrays. Often these low-level arrays have one or two dimensions only, and in this sense, they resemble records in a typical fact table.

Only arrays that contain data are physically stored; because of the inevitable sparsity in large multidimensional databases, most of the possible arrays are never created, thus saving large amounts of disk space. In most cases, any access to even a single cell in such low-level arrays requires that the whole array be brought into memory, so it is best if they are not too large. For best performance, the dimensions of these disk arrays should be ones that are commonly accessed together, so that a single file access operation brings back a whole collection of relevant cells, not just a single one.

This raises an important note: Disk storage is ultimately two-dimensional; memory ultimately one-dimensional. There is no way around this. Although multidimensional products will let you treat all dimensions as logically equivalent, physically speaking, dimensions cannot all be treated equally (and clustering must favor one dimension). There will always be some dimensions across which data are more easily retrieved than others. Even when records are Z-ordered, the clustering is spread out but not eliminated.

Z-ordered Records

In *Z-ordering*, a single numerical key is synthesized from each dimension's member key to form a number that assists range searching in a hypercube. Rather than combining the keys one after another, the bits that compose the keys from each dimension are interleaved to form a binary-coded "Z-number." When the records are sorted by this Z-number, it tends to cluster records that are near each other in the dimensional space near each other on disk, in all dimensions. This technique was first developed to support spatial querying for geographic and image databases. The clustering has the interesting property that no dimension is poorly clustered, and no dimension is ideally clustered either. (Contrast this with one-dimensional arrays, which do a great job of clustering on one dimension but provide no clustering on any other dimension.) All points within a subhypercube are found between the corner of the hypercube with the lowest Z-number and the corner with the highest Z-number. With Z-ordering, certain types of multidimensional range queries will get more optimal access than they would with arrays, and no dimension should suffer badly compared with other sortings of records. However, there will be some bias toward the dimension that appears first in the order of interleaving, and some bias away from the last dimension in the order of interleaving. (See [Orenstein 84] for more information on Z-ordering.)

Z-ordering is one of a set of spatial ordering techniques which, in general, linearize records in a multidimensional space by placing all records on a "space-filling curve" (basically, a line which meanders in a predictable way throughout the entire multidimensional space so that no record gets left out). Z-numbering is one of the simplest of these in computational terms, and has found its way into commercial spatial-data management systems.

Some multidimensional databases have a built-in knowledge of time. They understand the concept of time as a series and can automatically do time conversions with full knowledge of the complications of the calendar (weeks into months, fiscal years, leap years, and so on). Such products often store a whole time series as a compressed single entity rather than as an array of values, so that they can compress out the periods when no activity occurred (and do not need a key for each time period). There is a cost associated with storing time series as entities—it is slower to perform cross-section aggregations.

Because multidimensional databases use the same engine for both storing and processing the data, and this engine has full knowledge of multidimensional data structures and manipulations, it is relatively easy for the product designer to provide full function multidimensional security, data manipulation (including multiuser read-write), and application calculations right within the engine. This can lead to high-function, fast products. However, because the multidimensional database vendors are responsible for all the technology and cannot use the strengths of standard databases, they are forced to build their own DBMS engine. This is no trivial task, and many of the vendors have skimped on it, so most multidimensional databases do not offer the same capacity, error recovery, or hardware exploitation as the top RDBMSs.

Physical Optimization of Structures

In addition to optimizing the storage of cell data, it is very important to optimize indexing of the cell storage. Multidimensional indexing has been an active area of research for a long time, for geographic and spatial systems, for knowledge bases, and for other domains with multiple independent keys. The basic B-tree index has been extended to multiple dimensions with Kd-trees and R-trees, for example. Efficient multidimensional hashing can be implemented using grid files, and BANG files (balanced and nested grid files) form a tree-like hash index.

Merging the structures for indexing with computation processes, the hierarchical cube forest structure stores aggregate values in a clustered index (an index structure that contains the actual data as opposed to pointing to the data in a separate table). It also determines a storage/computation trade-off in a fashion similar to that described in "Implementing Data Cubes Effectively."

While these may be implemented in a specialized multidimensional database, they are just indexing techniques similar to those in use in all commercial RDBMSs. They index records in the same way that simple B-trees and one-dimensional hash indexes do already, so they could be applied and accessed through SQL in an RDBMS.

Where Is It Best to Store Active Multidimensional Data?

This is a controversial area, and much disinformation has been propagated. There is no single "right" answer, and the choice of database technology should depend on a number of factors.

Generally, as might be expected, specialized technologies will perform better and provide more comprehensive application facilities than is possible by adding external facilities to a general-purpose database. However, there are cases where storing some or all of the multidimensional data in a relational database may be the right solution:

1. The amount of data in total is too large to duplicate, so very detailed data is not copied into a multidimensional database, but is kept in the

source RDBMS and read as required. The precalculated summaries may be stored in either the RDBMS or in a multidimensional format, either disk- or memory-based.

2. Multiple concurrent write access is needed, and an OLAP product is used that does not have an engine capable of managing this. In this case, the RDBMS engine's concurrent read/write access capabilities are used instead. Although a proper multiuser multidimensional engine will do this faster and will allow better integration with the multidimensional application logic, if this need is only a small part of the overall application, then there may still be reasons to implement it in the RDBMS.

3. Data in the underlying RDBMS feeder system changes very frequently, and it is better read in real-time rather than in staged copies.

4. Data, calculated results, and calculation logic are shared with other applications or reporting tools, and an RDBMS is the best common storage mechanism (even if both products have their own more highly tuned proprietary formats).

5. The site has a policy of not duplicating data into other file structures for security or other reasons, even if this leads to less efficient applications. As long as the performance and cost implications are understood, then a site may choose to make any decision it likes, presumably because other advantages outweigh them.

Really large or sparse applications will, ideally, use a combination multidimensional RAM, multidimensional disk, and SQL databases. The data that is being used most will be deliberately kept in memory-based structures (this is more efficient than simply using disk cache algorithms). Data that is used regularly, but not frequently, might be kept in optimized proprietary multidimensional data files. Finally, large amounts of detailed information may be read and processed when required from the feeder RDBMS without being kept in the multidimensional environment.

This can be illustrated by a simple chart (Figure 8.1), showing the optimum storage strategy for different application sizes and sparsities. Of course, the scales are only approximate guides and will depend on the hardware being used. Applications and products can be mapped into this space and the degree to which an application fits a product's capacity and style can be checked. Products that allow multiple or hybrid structures will cover more of the area, and some might cover the whole surface, although other factors (not least, price) may still make them unsuitable for some applications.

The area of the chart in which memory-based applications are the best fit is based on the reckoning that a memory-based system will always outperform (and provide more dynamic calculations than) a disk-based system whenever it can hold everything in real RAM. However, for very dense exam-

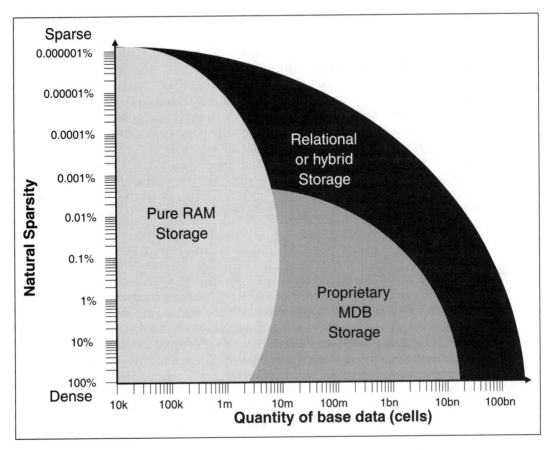

Figure 8.1 Optimum storage architecture.

ples, disk-based products will be nearly as good, but will require less (expensive) RAM and are therefore cheaper. Conversely, for very, very sparse applications, a hybrid solution of memory plus disk and/or RDBMS is probably best. Very sparse data typically has a higher overhead for indexes and pointers, even if held in memory, so the available RAM capacity is consumed faster.

The area of the chart in which proprietary disk-based systems are recommended reflects their ability to handle medium to large quantities of data most efficiently. For fairly large, but very sparse data or very, very large databases, an RDBMS storage strategy may be the only feasible option, possibly boosted by memory and multidimensional database-based storage of some of the most frequently used information. Even if it is desired that most data be kept in RDBMS storage, some memory-based structures are desirable for good performance. The option to keep some data in a proprietary structure allows intermediate or temporary results to be held within the OLAP application with better access performance than would be possible with the RDBMS alone, and it allows more application control over data structures that do not need to be shared with other applications.

Mapping any proposed early application into the chart is not a bad idea, just to check that you understand it and how it relates to OLAP. Note that the log scales used on both axes make the memory area look somewhat larger than reality and the other two areas are somewhat compressed; however, this is not misleading because there are far more small OLAP applications than large. The horizontal axis shows the number of real *base* data cells stored, not the theoretical number that could be stored or those that are calculated from the base data. The position of the scale will depend on the amount of RAM available, so the scale should be regarded as an approximate guide, not a precise measure.

Product Differences

Comparing the capacities of different OLAP products by listing the disk space occupied by their largest applications is very misleading. It is hardly an advantage to require 50 gigabytes to store a database if another product requires much less than 1 gigabyte for exactly the same application. This may seem an unlikely range of outcomes, but I have found even wider variations in disk efficiencies, based on the choice of structures described below and whether products precalculate results. Despite this, many vendors still seem to prefer to quote their capacities in terms of the disk space used rather than the amount of actual base level data stored. This would be rather like a new truck being promoted on the vast amounts of fuel it consumes rather than its cargo capacity. Trucking firms would not be fooled by this ploy, and OLAP buyers should be no less perceptive. Always compare applications and products based on what they hold, not how much space they take to hold it.

The usual reasons that one product might take far more much disk space than another are simply that the bulkier product probably precalculates results, devotes more space to indexes, or fails to exclude all empty values. While all of these are wasteful, the product using more disk space could still be faster because of its use of more sophisticated indexing, minimal run-time calculations, and simpler data structures. The better performance may be more important to the user than the wasted (but cheap and plentiful) disk space. It may also use smaller amounts of expensive and scarce memory, at the cost of more of the cheap and plentiful disk space, and thus it may still be the cheaper solution. This may cease to be true if the disk consumption is more than 50 times as much.

In general, simpler products do not offer a choice of data structures and locations, whereas the more versatile products allow combinations of memory, disk, and RDMS (at the application developer's discretion) and allow the application builder to control the degree of precalculation. For very large or particularly complex applications, this versatility is almost essential, but it does have a price: The products that offer such capabilities are far more complex to implement, and they are usually more expensive to buy. Furthermore, misusing options is usually easier, so that applications built using the versatile products can often end up in a nonoptimized state and may actually perform worse than the simpler products that attempt to optimize automatically.

In general, if you are buying a product to implement a single application, it is more cost-effective to select a simple product that is particularly designed for that application. Conversely, if you are buying a product for strategic purposes and many applications, it may be necessary to acquire one of the complex, versatile products.

Indexing Options

Depending on the database, you may have to make choices about the indexing technique to be used. Most multidimensional databases handle this automatically, but the system designer sometimes has a choice. Generally, multidimensional databases do not have a concept of joins, or if they do, they are all handled transparently. This is never true of relational databases, and star joins with large data volumes may not be handled efficiently by the optimizers in some RDBMSs (although this situation is improving).

Table 8.1 is a partial list of the basic multidimensional structures I have used in the products I surveyed. I have left out or been deliberately vague about highly specialized ones where I was specifically asked to keep them confidential pending the granting of patents. This list starts with the most basic multidimensional structures and moves to some of the more unusual, dynamic structures.

Most products use at least one of these techniques; some use others not listed; many use more than one. Anyone planning to build an efficient OLAP engine, either from scratch or hosted by an RDBMS, must have an excellent understanding of how multidimensional data clumps in practice, the updating, calculation, and retrieval characteristics of the target applications, and the kind of performance with large quantities of data that the best OLAP engines can provide.

When performing multidimensional analysis, multidimensional databases are usually between 2 and 10 times faster than relational databases running on the same hardware, depending on the relative quality of the implementations. However, an RDBMS running on more exotic (and expensive) parallel processing hardware could make up for the inappropriateness of the relational model for storing multidimensional data and significantly outperform a multidimensional database running on a simpler machine. Table 8.2 presents a summary of these points.

Table 8.1 **Survey of storage and indexing techniques**

Basic Structure	Compression or Indexing Technique	Speed Efficiency	Space Efficiency	Comments
Array	None.	The fastest possible method for read and write, regardless of the number of dimensions.	Suitable for small or dense structures (>30 percent density). No overhead for keys or indexes.	Very suitable for complex modeling calculations with modest quantities of data. Often used for data temporarily held in RAM.
Array	Empty pages suppressed.	Very fast for read, good for write.	Suitable for "clumpy" data on disk. Good for density >10 percent.	A typical mainframe database technique where large pages of data could be moved rapidly between disk and memory.
Array	Strings of repeated values compressed.	Slow for read, very slow for write. Unsuitable for random access.	Good for planning data (with many repeated or empty values), less good for actuals.	A good way of handling disk-based dynamic compression, with block transfers and unpacking in memory.
Fixed Record table	Hashing.	Good for read and write with moderate data quantities.	Efficient dynamic sparsity in all but one dimension.	Good dynamic sparsity handling in all but the columns dimension.
Fixed Record table	B-Tree.	Good for read and write.	Good for moderately sparse data without too many dimensions.	Good for moderate data quantities.
Fixed Record table	Sorted.	Good for read, very bad for write; unaffected by sparsity.	Best with small numbers of dimensions.	Good for large, very sparse, read-only data sets.
Fixed Record table in an RDBMS	As used in the RDBMS.	Acceptable for occasional read and write. Can be slow for bulk storage.	Effectively no net space used if the data was stored in the RDBMS anyway.	Good for integration with other systems and warehouses and for using the RDBMS's data management facilities.
Variable length record structure	Sorted and compressed records.	Acceptable read, very slow write.	Excellent data compression of randomly sparse data on disk.	An excellent way of storing, but not processing, very sparse data on disk.
Variable length record structure	Sorted records, with only incremental differences stored.	Slow to read, completely unsuitable for write; updates must be stored separately and merged occasionally.	Highly flexible storage of tagged individual cells. Efficient for applications with up to a few million cells.	A specialized technique for storing mixed data types multidimensionally

Table 8.2   **Comparison of Architectures**

Functionality	Memory-based Processing	Proprietary Disk-based MDDB	Standard RDBMS
Net disk space occupied	Very small.	Potentially large if applications are precalculated.	Possibly zero, if existing databases are used unchanged (unlikely), but may be large if new structures are created.
Data retrieval performance	Instant (hundreds of times faster than disk).	Moderately fast.	Slow.
Calculation functionality	Moderately high, in all dimensions.	Can be very high, in all dimensions.	Limited in all but one dimension, although application midtier servers may redress this.
Calculation speed	Very fast.	Slow.	Very slow.
Ability to calculate "on the fly"	Excellent.	Limited, varies by product.	Good; some products provide great flexibility and can exploit MPP hardware.
Data capacity	Small to medium.	Medium to large.	Extremely large.
Openness to live data access by other applications	Minimal.	Limited.	Excellent in principle, but may be limited if a complex schema is used.
Data searching	Fast and often functional.	Slow and often limited.	Moderate performance but usually very functional.
Ease of dimension restructuring	Good and can sometimes be done with live databases.	Good, but databases may have to be taken offline.	Good with row dimensions, bad with column dimensions.
DBMS administration facilities	Minima.	Variable, but usually weak.	potentially, very strong.
Ease of database building by end users	Good.	Moderate.	Near impossible

Conclusion

In this chapter we explored a variety of OLAP storage, access, and computing strategies. We saw the difference between memory and disk-based storage of live session data. And we saw the difference between persistent storage in SQL tables versus physically optimized multidimensional databases. We also briefly touched on some product storage and indexing differences.

Multitiered Architectures

In Chapter 8 we explored the variety of ways in which multidimensional data can be stored, accessed, and manipulated in the computer. We looked at RAM processing, disk processing, and the use of SQL databases as the principal repository for the data. In contrast with this internal view of OLAP architectures, this chapter offers a more external view. Specifically, we will look at how data and processing may be distributed across physical devices within the framework of a client/server architecture and how this affects overall system performance. Toward that end, this chapter will discuss the rationale for a client/server architecture, followed by a description of the pros and cons of typical configurations.

The Rationale for a Client/Server Architecture

In principle, the architecture of all OLAP applications is simple: Data has to be read from a disk, multidimensional transformations and calculation applied, and results presented on-screen. In some cases, users are also able to make temporary or permanent data changes, which may need to be written back to the disk files, either immediately or later.

Despite this apparent simplicity, real OLAP applications have a wide variety of architectures, some very complex. The variety, and the complexity, arise for several reasons:

❑ Many OLAP applications handle large amounts of data, which cannot be duplicated for each user. This requirement to share some or all of it, while serving users with distributed client PCs, means that some form of client/server architecture is likely to be needed.

❏ Once a client/server architecture has been implemented, both a client and one or more server processors are available to do the multidimensional transformations and calculations. Deciding on how the work is split between the two (or more) available processors alters the architecture.

❏ With more than one computer involved, there is a probability that multiple databases and tools will also need to be integrated into the solution. How, when, and how much data moves between these will affect the performance of the resulting system and is a function of the architecture.

The whole point of any client/server solution is to share scarce resources. Cheap or plentiful resources may not need to be shared, so it might be more efficient to duplicate them for each user. Or, if some resource is used constantly, there may not be any realistic chance of sharing it—for example, few users would take kindly to sharing screens, mice, and keyboards, yet until quite recently, it was quite normal for office workers to share mainframe terminals. However, other resources are used infrequently, and it makes good sense for these to be shared among users.

For example, many users in an office can share a network printer, particularly if it is high quality, particularly fast, or color. They may also share other hardware resources over a network, such as modems and back-up tape units. It is therefore natural for them to share large data files on a server, and if the applications are large and infrequently processed, it is cheaper for many users to share some common processor power and memory on a server than to duplicate it into each client PC, where it would lie idle for much of the time. However, if the users are continually processing large applications individually (for example, with graphics work), it may be more sensible not to try and share processing power on a server.

Thus, client/server architectures are not contemplated just because "they are a good thing," but because they allow expensive or scarce resources that are not needed continually by each user, to be shared among many. This is not, of course, a new idea. Even in the 1960s, time-sharing mainframes were available, and they were very popular in the 1970s and early 1980s. The rationale was exactly the same, but they faded in popularity with the advent of the independent PC, which was apparently cheaper and certainly provided more freedom. The reduction in costs was true at the pure hardware level, but overall system costs did not always fall because the corporate PC infrastructure was often harder to support than initially seemed to be the case. The mainframes, of course, shared everything except the basic terminal (which typically had little or no processing capacity). This model may seem very old-fashioned, but it has actually been reborn in a more popular guise: ultra thin, or Web clients, called "network computers." These have no local disk storage and only limited processor and RAM. Everything else is done on the Web server, which, ironically, may even be a mainframe!

The desire for freedom and independence is now usually manifested in the form of notebook computers. By their vary nature, apart from when these are connected to the corporate network (which will not usually be the case), these are not suitable platforms for client/server computing. Thus, whatever the strengths of the client/server model, it cannot fully replace the stand-alone PC model that became so popular in the 1980s.

Modern solutions have to encompass the full range of architectures: stand-alone (roaming) PCs, carefully balanced multitier client/server architectures, with processing distributed between the tiers, and the old (almost) dumb terminal (mainframe) model, now renamed and much hyped as the network computer.

Regardless of the client/server model chosen, one limiting factor that must always be considered is network bandwidth. If bandwidth is limited and traffic is high, the available capacity will be reduced, and the response to requests for anything from the server will get worse. In this case, it may be necessary to ensure that processing happens as near as possible to the data. At any one time, data may be present on the server, the client, or any of the intermediate tiers, so it can get quite complex to ensure that the processing (when the number of outputs is less than the number of inputs) is performed where the data is already located, rather than moving the data to where the processor program resides. Only by doing this can network traffic be minimized.

In its simplest form, a client/server architecture requires that the data be stored on a server and be presented to users via a client PC. In itself, this simple definition says nothing about the degree to which data is actively shared between users and where the processing occurs.

Typical Client/Server Configurations

In principle, you can define several logical tiers in a client/server architecture (see Figure 9.1). Generally, in a particular implementation, not all of these will exist as distinct tiers, as two or more may be combined into a single program. However, in extreme cases, they might all be distinct, separate tiers, running on separate machines. Indeed, even these logical layers may be split between machines.

In Figure 9.1 the relative data volumes transmitted between the layers are indicated by the thickness of the arrows linking them. Of course, the volumes will vary by application and are not fixed.

Although there are many theoretical possibilities, there are a few relatively common examples, as shown in Tables 9.1 to 9.5 and in Figures 9.2 to 9.6.

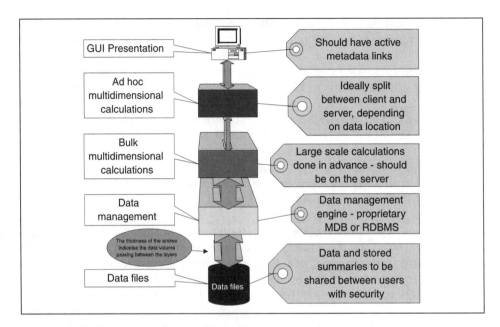

Figure 9.1 Client/server logical layers.

Figures 9.2 to 9.6 illustrate these typical configurations. The arrows linking layers within a single tier are thicker, illustrating the faster links that are possible within a tier, as opposed to between tiers. Bottlenecks often arise between tiers because of network bandwidth limits or because of overheads in the communications protocols. If you compare Figures 9.1 and 9.2 to 9.6, you will see which of the architectures place a high-volume data connection over a low-capacity (networked) link: All except the fourth example place at least one high-volume connection over a low-capacity link, and it is no surprise that all of these architectures require more performance tuning and are less certain to deliver a very fast response in practice. For example, they may need local caches to disguise the slow performance of the client/server architecture.

Data Sharing on the Server

In principle, when a server supports multiple users, it shares not only its processing capacity and memory but data between users. For example, if one user has recently viewed data, it is likely to be retained in memory cache (or buffers), and should be available more quickly to another user who also needs to view it. In a read-only application, this is simply a matter of performance and hardware utilization. However, in an application that allows users to change data, it is even more important that changes made by a user, when

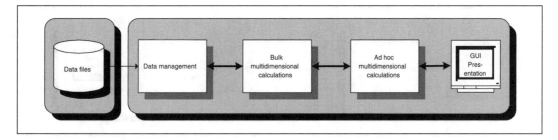

Figure 9.2 Shared file.

confirmed, are immediately available to other users, who would otherwise be working with out-of-date information.

In practice, this level of sharing is *not* always provided. Regardless of architecture, many servers run, effectively, as a series of individual tasks, one per user, without communicating with each other. In this "monolithic" approach, each user operates entirely independently of all the other users, who can neither take advantage of cached data for performance nor have the most up-to-date information available. This is inefficient and particularly unsuitable for multiuser, read-write applications. Some of the more modern products, particularly those that are "multithreaded," usually do provide a true multiuser environment, rather than a set of single users that happen to be sharing one computer, but taking no advantage of so doing.

Table 9.1 Shared file

Description	Strengths	Weaknesses
1. Shared file—only layer 1 is on a file server, with layers 2–5 on the client.	Simple to implement. Independent of network protocols. Cheap server: any LAN file server can be used. Scales well in terms of numbers of users.	Not true client/server. Does not exploit server processing. May require high-capacity client PCs. May generate excessive network traffic, as all data must be moved to the clients for processing. Security must be managed by the client applications and may be weak. Hard to implement multiuser updating.

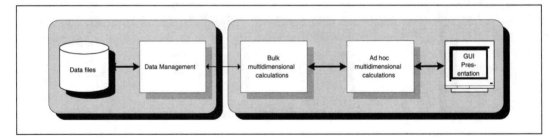

Figure 9.3 Shared database.

Table 9.2 Shared Database

Description	Strengths	Weaknesses
2. Shared database—layers 1 and 2 are on a relational database server, layers 3–5 on the client.	Depending on the application, it may be possible to manage security on the server. Reduced network load, as data can be selected and partially processed by the server database, before sending it to client machines for processing and presentation. Capable of handling large databases; if the client can generate sufficiently sophisticated SQL, most of the processing can be done by the RDBMS, which allows good exploitation of massively parallel processing. Potentially capable of online data updates with better data locking. Better sharing of data between multiple application products.	Does not scale so well as users are added, as the database server may become overloaded. Requires a suitable DBMS on the server, adding to costs and complexity. May generate excessive network traffic if all the multidimensional processing is done on the client.

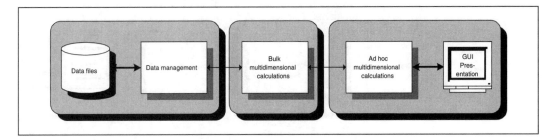

Figure 9.4 Three tier.

Table 9.3 Three tier

Description	Strengths	Weaknesses
3. Three-tier—layers 1 and 2 on a relational database server, layer 3 on one or more application servers, layers 4 and 5 on the client. Layer 3 may also have a local database for nonvolatile storage of multidimensional information.	Flexible distribution of processing across database and application servers. Reduced network traffic through being able to process wherever the data is.	
Potentially high functionality through the use of a sophisticated RDBMS and a powerful application server. Good scalability in terms of application size.	Complex to implement— many design decisions to make, and good networking expertise required. Often less open than the shared database architecture (2). Scalability in terms of number of users can be constrained by limits on either the database or application servers, so tuning is complex.	

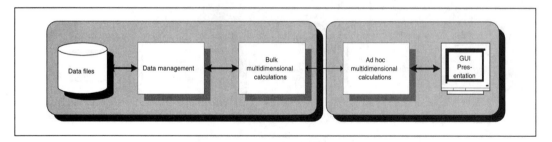

Figure 9.5 Two-tier dedicated OLAP database server.

Multivendor Solutions

In the simplest client/server architectures, all the programs in a single application come from the same vendor. This makes it easy to ensure that they all cooperate by "speaking the same language." It is also possible for these homogeneous architectures to be clever in how they allocate tasks between machines, and they can even vary this depending on the circumstances. For example, depending on what data has recently been displayed, new calculations may be performed on a client or the server. Or, the client may have to do certain calculations when it is running stand-alone, but when connected to a server, it may delegate these tasks.

Such dynamic cooperation is not usually possible when all the programs are not from the same vendor. In such cases, they are more likely to have to

Table 9.4 Two-tier dedicated OLAP database server

Description	Strengths	Weaknesses
4. Two-tier dedicated OLAP database server—layers 1–3 on a multidimensional database server, layers 4 and 5 on the client.	Optimum performance, with minimal network traffic. Low hardware costs. Relatively simple to set up and tune. Easier to implement multiuser concurrent updating of multidimensional data, with fine-grained multidimensional security. Sophisticated application functionality is simpler to implement.	Typically less open. Application scalability may be constrained by multidimensional capacity limits. Products of this type are often more specialized and less suitable for general purpose use.

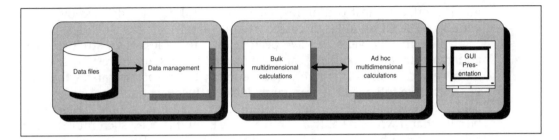

Figure 9.6 Three-tier web OLAP.

work together with a much more formal demarcation of tasks, as one program will know little about the others. They will have to communicate using a standard, agreed language. This may be an "industry standard" language, like SQL, or a set of "calls" defined by one vendor, to which other vendors adhere. Such interface standards are usually known as APIs (application pro-

Table 9.5 Three-tier web OLAP

Description	*Strengths*	*Weaknesses*
5. Three-tier web OLAP—layers 1 and 2 on a relational database server, layers 3 and 4 on an application server, and layer 5 on a Web browser, connected via the Internet or intranet and a Web gateway.	Easy to deploy for large numbers of casual users, including those outside the organization. Low-cost wide-area networking. No dedicated software required on the client, saving software and support costs. Wide range of client platforms supported, including low-cost ones that would not run conventional PC software, with no need to maintain and support separate software versions. Easy switching between, and integration of, multiple applications at the desktop level.	Reduced functionality and performance. Potential security concerns. Reduced client-level data manipulations unless suitable applets are available. Currently, few graphic display options available without transferring bit maps. Requirement to be online, which may be inconvenient or even impossible for some users. Likely to require additional server software. Rapidly evolving standards will shorten the application life before a rewrite is required.

gram interface). Most commonly, client tools link to APIs defined by server vendors. (The OLAP API is discussed in Appendix F.)

Unfortunately, vendors have been known to be less than strict in their adherence to such standards, and it is usually necessary to test such interfaces very carefully—it is rarely good enough to accept assurances that the vendors have followed the standards. Ideally, the exact combination of platforms, networks, products, and versions that is required should be tested to be sure that it works reliably and efficiently. Even if it does, such multivendor solutions are inherently more fragile than a single-vendor approach because if one vendor brings out a new version that is slightly incompatible for all the carefully tested links, the solution may start to fail inexplicably.

Conclusion

Client/server architectures can improve efficiency by sharing scarce or expensive resources. This enables larger applications to be handled with better performance. Furthermore, by splitting applications machines, components from multiple vendors can be used, so that "best of breed" solutions are possible. Most large OLAP applications do indeed have a multiproduct client/server architecture.

But, client/server applications are complex, and more can go wrong so they are much more likely to need performance tuning. Multivendor solutions are yet more complex and more fragile because of the greater risk of incompatibilities between products, especially as new versions are introduced. This means that they need more testing, something that should never be neglected.

Section III

Hands-on Multidimensional Case Studies

All our faculties can never carry us farther than barely to observe that particular objects are constantly conjoined together and that the mind is carried by customary transistion from the appearance of one to the belief of the other.

—David Hume

10

Practical Steps for Defining OLAP Models

Introduction

Many tasks are associated with the design and implementation of a multidimensional information system. At a high level, they can be summed up as problem definition, tool selection, and solution implementation. In an idealized world, tool selection should follow problem definition because, as we saw in the last two chapters, tools are generally optimized for particular uses.

Some tools, for example, do the following:

❑ Work exclusively as a client or as a server

❑ Assume that persistent data is stored in an SQL database

❑ Have built-in knowledge of time

❑ Have built-in knowledge of currencies

❑ Assume that certain dimensions are present like time, location, and products

❑ Have less functionality but are simpler to use within their intended domain

❑ Are harder to use but are more general in their applicability

In reality, however, tool selection may precede a full understanding of the problem and be a function of many things that have nothing to do with either the logical or physical aspects of that problem, including tool price, the geographical representation of the vendor, the friendliness of the sales person, the size and reputation of the vendor, the quality of the vendor's collateral, and the existence of vendor champions within the organization. Thus, how you design and implement an OLAP model may be influenced by your tool selection process.

Regardless of the factors that influenced tool selection, regardless of whether you are building a model for yourself or for others, regardless of whether you are rapidly prototyping a solution or designing a logical model prior to implementation, you still need to go through the sequential steps of defining cubes, dimensions, levels, members, formulas, and data links. Let's call them model building steps. The specific way you think through these steps may differ between tools, especially between tools where the data is stored in SQL tables versus tools where the data is stored in a multidimensional format and between tools that treat all dimensions equally versus tools that make you define variables and then assign identifier dimensions to each variable.

However, you still need to pass through the same basic steps.

This chapter illustrates the practical steps associated with designing and implementing OLAP models. It is written more as a guide than a methodology. As such, it is not meant to generate any of the partisan fervor typified by proponents of methodologies such as De Marco, Yourdon, Martin, Rumbaugh, Booch, Shlaer-Mellor, and so on. The guidelines should serve you regardless of the tools you are using or the type of multidimensional system you are implementing.

For whom are these guidelines written? They are written for the designer and implementer of the OLAP model. They make no assumption about the relationship between the designer/implementer and the end user(s). In other words, you may be designing a model to be used by others, or you may be designing a model for yourself. In either case, you need to design and implement it. And in either case, you need to define the core of the model before defining any ad hoc additions. The guidelines also make no assumptions about whether tool selection has or has not yet occurred. On average, it may be that tool selection has already occurred and you are now ready to design and implement an actual solution (which may not be your first). On the other hand, you may wish to first define your problem space and then specify the requirements that the tool you select needs to fulfill.

The guidelines are more detailed about the attributes of a well-constructed model than on the order in which a model is constructed. As you will see, there are multiple starting points and sequences for building models. Only the specifics of a situation can serve to identify which starting point makes the most sense in that situation. *In general, you want to begin where you are most confident of what needs to be and work out from there.* For example, you might be most confident of the data sources, but you are not yet sure of all the purposes for which people will use them. This would result in a more bottom-up, data-to-function modeling approach. Or you might know the types of calculations that need to be performed, but you are less confident of the data sources to feed those computations. This is more of a top-down, function-to-data approach.

What is critical is that you design a properly connected structure. In this sense, there is no right or wrong starting point. Rather, there are right and wrong connections. (Software model construction enjoys a relative freedom of sequencing in comparison to physical model construction where you cannot, for example, build a skyscraper from the top down. Unlike software model construction, physical model construction has to deal with gravity. In this respect, the construction of the orbiting space station will have more sequencing freedom than any similar physical structures built within the earth's gravitational field.)

Nevertheless, for the sake of readability and to correspond with what I presume the majority of readers will do, the guidelines are presented in an essentially top-down fashion, starting with cubes and ending with formulas that attach to members.

This chapter takes you through the major steps of designing and implementing a multidimensional information system. At a high level those steps include the following:

- ❑ Understanding the current and ideal data flow
- ❑ Defining cubes, dimensions, and links
- ❑ Defining dimension levels and/or hierarchies
- ❑ Defining dimension members
- ❑ Defining aggregations and other formulas

Notice how, with the exception of data links, which appear earlier in this chapter than in Chapter 3, these steps follow the ordering of features presented in Chapter 3. Links have moved up in this chapter because when you are beginning with a pre-identified source data set (as is common), the data set, through the use of links, can serve to define the cubes and dimensions of the model. Also note that physical issues are addressed, whenever relevant, together with logical issues.[1]

Finally, these guidelines are presented as a series of descriptions:

- ❑ Things that typically occur
- ❑ Things you need to do and watch out for
- ❑ Rules of thumb for making certain decisions
- ❑ Questions that you should ask either of yourself or of those for whom you are designing the system

Practical Steps for Defining a Multidimensional Information System

Understand the Current Situation

Regardless of how you go about designing a model, you first need to understand the situation for which you are attempting to provide a solution—in terms of what is actually going on and in terms of what ought to be going on. As you saw in the last section, there are logical and physical aspects to what is going on. You need to be aware of both.

Physically speaking, and ignoring their quantitative attributes, there could be a variety of situations, such as a spreadsheet situation with some number of analysts accessing the same worksheets, or many separate, partially redundant worksheets, and/or a data warehouse database or several linked databases from which analytical data is directly accessed or perhaps staged in a data mart. Or there may be several legacy databases running operational programs from which extracts are taken through the use of home grown routines, or there may only be a SQL database serving as data warehouse with a bunch of SQL report writing tools on the client side, probably with a large supporting IT shop.

On the logical side, for example, you need to see the current applications that end users are using, any schemas relevant to decision support, and any schemas relevant to the source data. You also need to gain an understanding of relevant business rules such as rules about performance thresholds, data access, or the event-based distribution of information. The rules might be encoded or in the minds of key personnel.

As a solution provider, you need to talk with all the persons who have something to do with the system that existed at the time you arrived on the scene, as well as everyone who has a part in the system you are going to design and implement. These may include power end users, casual end users, data entry operators, system administrators, persons responsible for the data sources, and management. You will need to discover not only what people are currently doing but also what they would like to be doing.

As you learn about the situation, you will identify problems and loosely classify them according to whether they have more to do with the availability of data, needed derivations, or representation forms, in which case they are more logical, or whether they have more to do with speed of access, amount of storage required, maximum number of concurrent users, operating system problems, network jams, or where the data is coming from, in which case they are more physical.

Questions About the Actual Situation

1. With what frequency do which types of users use the system? (Questions 1.1 to 1.6 pertain to each type of user.)

1.1 How many users are there for each type?

1.2 What kinds of dialogue does each type of user have with the system?

1.3 How much data does each type of user examine during a typical session?

1.4 How much data travels across the network in response to typical queries for each type of user?

1.5 What categories of information are typically browsed by each type of user?

1.6 What kind of end-user tools are being used to browse/analyze the data?

2. How much data is at the input level of the system?

3. Where does the server's input data come from?

4. What ad hoc computations are typically performed on the server?

5. What computations are pre-performed on the server?

6. What computations are typically performed on the client?

7. What integration/refinement issues were involved with the source data?

8. How frequently is server data updated?

9. What machines, operating systems, and network configuration(s) are used?

Questions about Problems/Solutions

Logical Problems   You need to gain an understanding of the logical problems that users are experiencing. Logical problems are independent of the software they are currently using or the type of machines or operating systems on which the software is running. Logical problems have to do with how models are defined, how users interact with the data, how they browse or make new selections, how they define computations, and how they view data. *For each of the following questions to which your respondents answer "yes," there exists a logical problem.*

❑ Is it hard to define certain multidimensional calculations such as profitability by product, market, and time? If so, how are they currently defined?

❑ Is it hard to drill down from summaries to underlying details?

❑ Is it hard to change views once they are created?

❑ Are users stuck with hard-to-interpret names?

❑ Is a lot of end-user intelligence required to operate the programs?

- ❏ Are the graphics lacking?
- ❏ Are reports filled with zeros?
- ❏ Is there any inconsistent data?
- ❏ Does text need to be, without currently being able to be, associated with data?

Physical Problems   *These questions help determine the existence of physical problems:*

- ❏ Is end-user data access fast enough? How fast does it need to be?
- ❏ Can end users generate queries without too much IT support?
- ❏ Is there enough hardware and software capacity at the server and client ends?
- ❏ Is a lot of client or server processing required for what seem like simple queries?
- ❏ Is there a lot of network traffic in response to client queries?
- ❏ Does the system support an adequate number of users for read/write operations?

Information About Constraints

Some of the relevant information you need to propose a solution may be expressed by participants in the form of constraints on a solution. For example, the people for whom you are working to provide a solution may not think of their operating system as a problem, but if the solution needs to run on AIX, NT, or some other specific operating system, then the operating system is a constraint on or a necessary attribute of any solution.

A typical solution might include the following types of system constraints:

- ❏ Physical machine
- ❏ Operating system
- ❏ Display resolution
- ❏ Network protocol
- ❏ Network tiers
- ❏ Client tools
- ❏ Other software that needs to run
- ❏ Number of system users
- ❏ Data set sizes on the server
- ❏ Server refresh rates
- ❏ Valid data types (numeric and non-numeric)

Information About Proposed Solutions

If you have passed through the last three sets of questions and can answer most or all of them, you have learned what the situation looks like at the source and from the end users' perspective. You should be able to draw or fill in a sources and uses diagram like the one in Figure 10.1. It is a convenient way to picture important information. The sources and uses diagram represents what is important for sources and for end users. It shows what kinds of data enter the system and who is using the data. It is, in effect, a simple logical model of the current situation, known problems, and proposed solutions. You should also have a pretty good idea of what the major problems are with this flow and what needs to be done to improve the current state of affairs.

Note that a logical model in the OLAP world is quite different from a logical model in the relational world. In the relational world, logical data models do not model derived data. But as we've seen throughout this book, one of the main problems for SQL, as the commercial implementation of a relational data definition language/data manipulation language, is its inefficiency for specifying many types of derivations (especially complex, multilevel aggregations and allocations) that need to be performed on a regular basis. In this sense, one of the chief missions for a multidimensional information system is to provide an environment for the easy specification of complex aggregations. And, any logical model of a multidimensional information system has to model the derivations as much as the raw inputs.

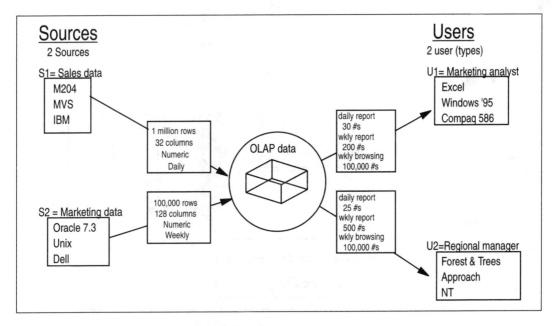

Figure 10.1 A sources and uses diagram.

Define the Logical Model

If you've ever designed an end-user solution before, you must have gone through the previous stage, Understand the Current Situation. There was nothing inherently multidimensional about it. Now we're coming to the multidimensional steps within the more general guidelines.

Given an understanding of existent and desired data flows, how do you define a multidimensional model to serve as an architecture for the desired data flows? Is there a specific order to the steps for defining a multidimensional model? Are there certain things that must be specified?

In a nutshell, you need to define your model in terms of one or more hypercubes so that both data sources (or links to data sources) and data outputs (or user interactions) are represented within each hypercube. This ensures that it is possible to generate the data outputs from the data sources. Figure 10.2 shows a version of the multidimensional data structures presented in Chapter 3, used here to represent data transformations. The vertical line segments still represent dimensions, but this time each segment represents a granularity level rather than an individual member. The connected points

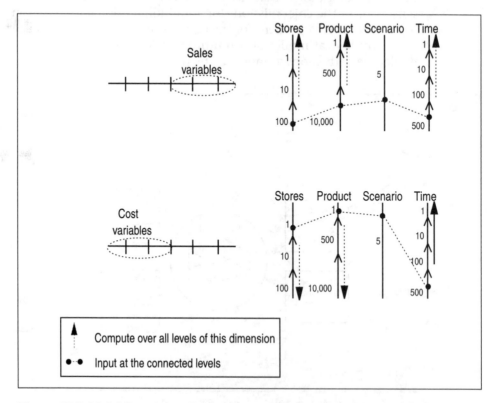

Figure 10.2 Multidimensional data structure represents data transformations.

represent the specific granularity levels where the data entered the cube. and the arrows represent the direction of calculation. For example, in the top panel, sales data can be seen entering the base level of the cube and aggregating upwards. While in the lower panel, costs data can be seen entering the top levels of store and product and the lowest level of time. And it is seen being allocated down stores and products but aggregated up in time.

How do we define such cube structures? The following steps outline one way of defining appropriate cubes. They are presented in an essentially top-down manner, starting with cubes and ending with formulas that attach to members. After all is said and done, the top-down approach is still the most common and fastest way to test whether you have understood all aspects of the users' problems and constraints on a solution. The steps also assume that the base, input, or nonderived data exist and can be identified. This is not a necessary assumption. It is certainly possible to start by defining a model that you would like to build and then going and finding data to populate it. Again, the vast majority of the time some data will already exist when it was decided to improve the current state of affairs by building a multidimensional model.

High- and Low-level Logical Models

A logical multidimensional model spans several levels of abstraction that, if you are coming from the relational world, might be thought of as different things. A high-level logical model represents the essential elements of the model, as understood by its users. For example, a typical entity-relationship diagram represents a high-level logical model outlining the basic entities, attributes, and relationships in a model, as illustrated in Figure 10.3.

A low-level logical model contains sufficient detail to design a physical model. For example, the set of normalized relations shown in Figure 10.4 contains all the logical elements of the model. Every key and nonkey attribute and every datum or data point are represented in this low-level logical model.

Whereas entity-relationship models and table schemas are typically considered to be different models, the high- and low-level logical views that they define are all a part of any one logical multidimensional model. In the multidimensional world, cubes, dimensions, and hierarchies form the high-level, user-oriented picture of the model. Members, their relationships, and formulas paint the low-level logical picture. Furthermore, typical relational schemas, whether high- or low-level, do not depict the data transformations that take place. In contrast, a multidimensional model more explicitly represents the entire data transformation process.

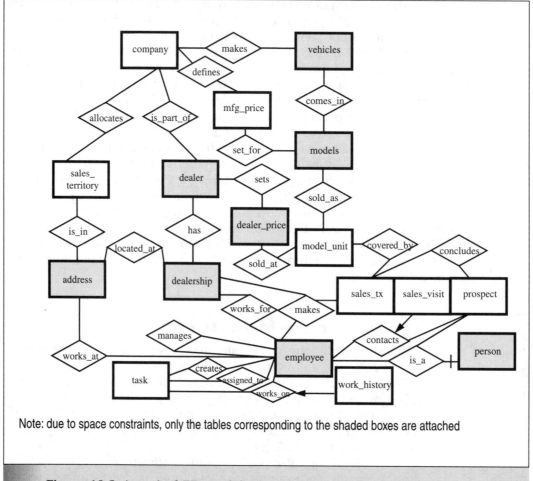

Note: due to space constraints, only the tables corresponding to the shaded boxes are attached

Figure 10.3 A typical ER model.

Cubes and Dimensions

The first thing you want to define is the logical cube and dimension structure for the model. Even if you are using a hypercube product, which may force you to put all data that needs to interact in a single physical cube, seeing the logical cube structure of your data is useful. The benefit to seeing the logical structure is that it reveals more about the representation, transformation, and viewing of data than any physical structure. Logically, is there just one cube, or are there multiple cubes?

dealer

dealer_no	dealer_name	number_of_dealerships
integer4	varchar(30)	integer
1	versailles ford	2

address

address_no	civic_address	city	zip	state	country	tel	fax
integer4	varchar(30)	vhar(30)	char(10)	char(3)	char10	char12	char12
1	123 street 1	city1	123	CA	USA	111.213.3333	111.1112222

dealership

dealership_no	dealer_no	address_no	dealership_name
integer4	integer4	integer4	name
1	1	1	varchar(30)

dealer_price

dealer_no	price_class_no	start_date	end_date	price
integer4	integer4	date	date	money
1	1	1/1/19	1/1/40	$2,000

vehicles

vehicle_no	company_no	vehicle_line_name	launch_date
integer4	integer4	varchar(30)	date
1	1	Cadilac	1/1/89

models

vehicle_no	model_no	model_name	model_options
integer4	integer4	varchar(30)	varchar(30)
1	1	DeVille	OptionPack111

person

person_no	SSN	Lname	Fname	Gender	Age
integer4	varchar(10)	char(30	char(30)	char	integer
1	111-1111-111	Antonuk	Ferengi	M	35

employee

person_no	dealership_no	employee_no	manager_no	hire_date
integer4	integer4	integer4	integer4	date
1	1	1	1	1/1/90

Figure 10.4 A low-level schema.

If your starting point includes base tables, you can pull some, if not all, the basic dimensions from the base tables using links. (Recall from Chapter 7 that there may be dimensional information that is table-wide and thus not captured in any table.) For example, if you are given a table with stores, time, product, sales, and costs, you would most likely define stores, times, and products as dimensions, and define sales and costs as members of a variables dimension. The only difference between types of tools is whether you define stores, time, and products as dimensions in an OLAP system or as lookup table dimensions with a SQL database, and whether costs and sales are members of a variables dimension or whether they are treated as individual variables to be dimensioned by stores, time, and product. Either way, they mean the same thing. Some OLAP products will even build the cube for you once you have the source data in table form. That table form may vary between vendors, but it will generally be either type zero or type one. (Table types were described in Chapter 3.)

Otherwise, if you are thinking through a model structure in the absence of a given data set, or if you are starting one with measurements that are directly input into the model, the way to proceed is to identify the variables or types of things tracked, measured, or otherwise calculated and group them according to the identifier dimensions by which they vary.

For example, with a sales application, the variables might include sales, costs and units sold, while the dimensions might be time, market, and product. With a financial application, the variables might include account balance and credit rating, while the dimensions might be account number, branch number, account type, and time. With a budget planning application, the variables might include projected revenues, head count, overhead, and allocated expenses, and the dimensions might be organizational unit, time, and scenario.

If you are talking to users, they should be able to answer these questions directly. If you are looking at data sources in a table form consisting of key columns and attribute columns, look for the nonkey attributes as indicative of the variables. And look for the keys as indicative of the dimensions. If all the data seems to be in one column, which would likely be called a value column, then look for one of the columns (generally adjacent to the value column) to be a variables dimension consisting of names of variables. (These types of tables and their links to a cube were described in Chapter 3.)

If there are multiple tables, look at them and ask yourself whether the facts in each table belong with each other. Is there some key, like time, place, or scenario, that is implicit in one table but explicit in the other? Are the key columns between the tables related to each other in a way that would make sense to have them combined into a single cube? Does one table deal with the Northwest while another table describes the South? If there are multiple tables and you cannot figure out how to merge their key structures, and the data between the two tables cannot be brought into a common set of dimensions, chances are the tables should be modeled as separate cubes. To be sure, you should perform the density test that was introduced in Chapter 5. (Review Chapter 5 for a discussion of the density test and when a cube is not a cube.)

I prefer to model all variables that share the same dimensions, even when they do not share the same cells, as a part of the same cube. It reduces the number of cubes in my model. (Some multicube models that employ 5 or 10 physical cubes can be logically represented as one or two cubes. In these cases, the physical cubes come closer to representing physical partitions than information content differences.) And it highlights the fact that data residing in the same cube can be compared meaningfully.

For example, consider modeling a data set consisting of international sales data and macroeconomic information. Imagine the sales data is collected at the store level every week while the macroeconomic information is collected at the national level every month. Depending on the multidimensional tool you were using, you may wind up creating a different cube for each data set. Logically speaking, when designing my model, I would always find it simpler to define the data sets as a part of the same cube. Furthermore, being in the same cube, it is easy to see how I can compare the sales data with the macroeconomic data by aggregating my store- and week-level sales data to the country by month level and then meaningfully compare changes in national-level sales with changes in macroeconomic indicators.

You also need to be aware of **attributes**, variables that vary mostly as a function of the members of one dimension. Attributes are usually found in lookup tables associated with, or as a part of, dimension tables.

In a retail model where store, time, product, and variables are dimensions, there will be many facts about the members of each of the dimensions. With stores, for example, the facts might include square footage, rent, address, manager names, phone number, and so on. Logically speaking, these variables or facts belong at the allproduct by store by "sometime" level of the cube. They belong at the store level because facts like address vary from store to store. They belong at the allproduct level because the address of a store is independent of the products carried by the store, but they belong at the "sometime" or not-totally-specified time level because the facts can change over time. Addresses change, managers change, rents change, square footage can change, and you may want to keep a history of the values. You may want to enter these facts initially as constants but be prepared to convert them to yearly or quarterly variables as they change.

If your source data is in spreadsheets, think about how the dimensions are expressed in the spreadsheets. Are there pages or worksheets, or distinct areas within a worksheet? The values that identify each page or sheet or file may form a dimension. For example, each page may represent a separate store. Spreadsheets need not be so regular, however. A single worksheet may contain multiple axes, levels of granularity, and even cubes' worth of data. An example of this is shown in Chapter 13 where an OLAP model is built from an irregular spreadsheet.

At the end of this step you should be able to identify all the cubes that define the model and all the dimensions that make up each cube. Figure 10.5 illustrates what a cube structure may look like. Notice, that this is a high-level logical view of a model. We are not showing any information about the number of levels per dimension nor any information about data flows. We

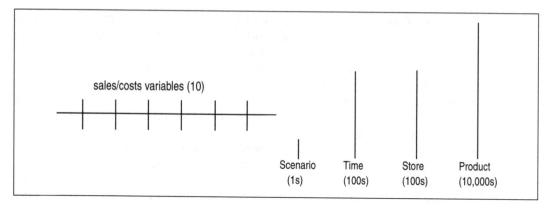

Figure 10.5 A high-level multidimensional data structure view of your model.

are just showing the number of variables, the number of identifier dimensions, and the approximate number of members in each dimension. Recall how the distinction was drawn earlier between high-level logical views and low-level logical views and how for multidimensional modeling, the same model spanned both levels. Figure 10.6 shows the same high-level information for a multicube model.

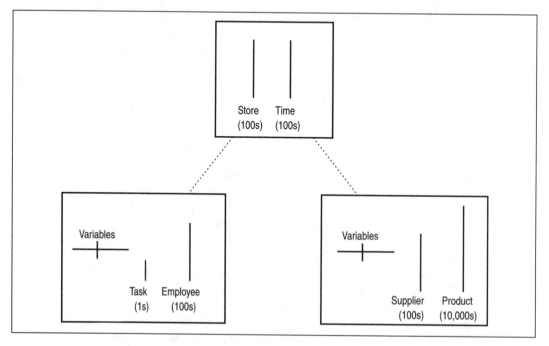

Figure 10.6 A high-level multidimensional data structure view of a multicube.

Choice of Number of Dimensions   Whether you defined your cubes based on existing data sources, or whether you defined them based on what you think you want to model, *you should spend some time reviewing the dimensional choices you made before proceeding to solidify them with hierarchies and members.* The main way you modify the dimensional structure of a cube is by adding and subtracting dimensions. The main reason for subtracting dimensions from a cube is to combine two or more dimensions whose intersections are not universally meaningful and each of whose cardinalities is not very high, into a single dimension composed exclusively of valid intersections and of a higher cardinality than either of the two original dimensions. The benefit of combining dimensions is to eliminate meaningless values and lower the growth of derived data in the cube. The main downside of combining dimensions is the loss of efficiency when dealing with changes that occur in a single dimension (such as needing to make multiple formula entries in a dimension where one entry would have sufficed were the dimensions to have been broken out).

The two main reasons for adding dimensions are to take into account some factor that was previously unaccounted for, such as time or place, and to represent cofactors present in a single list of elements with separate dimensions that can vary independently of one another. Regarding unaccounted-for information, your source data may come from multiple tables where each table represents a different time or place. In such cases, the time or place of the data may be implicit to the data and thus not explicitly included in any fields associated with the table (other than, perhaps, the table name). There is no real downside to taking this information into account. If you didn't, you would not be able to put it into a single cube.

Regarding cofactors, you might have a table whose attribute columns are labeled "actual direct sales," "actual indirect sales," "actual salaries," "actual material costs," "actual other costs," "planned direct sales," "planned indirect sales," "planned salaries," "planned material costs," and "planned other costs." All your sales and cost information is either actual or planned (or a calculated variance). Every actual and planned value is for a sales value or a cost value. Sales and costs, which can be thought of as members of an accounts dimension, are thus cofactors along with actuals and plans, which can be thought of as members of a scenario dimension. By representing this information in terms of the two dimensions, accounts and scenario, it is easier to define formulaic relationships that pertain to accounts or scenarios, it is easier to visually represent accounts and scenarios along separate axes on a display screen, and if the number of original members is very large, say one million, and if the number of members in each of the two created dimensions is roughly equivalent, then the number of members in each of the two new dimensions will be approximately equal to the square root of the number of original dimension members. In other words, one dimension with 1 million members could be represented by two dimensions with a thousand members per dimension.

When Dimensions Change over Time There is a (Buddhist) saying that the only constant is that everything is changing. So, the real question is, and for each dimension, "What is the rate of change?" At one extreme, some dimensions may not change during their lifetime in a single model, especially if that model is a single server-based application of short duration. But for models that evolve with the users, change in at least one dimension is certain. The most dramatic changes usually occur with product dimensions, organization dimensions, and marketing geography dimensions. For example, products are added and subtracted, product lines are reorganized, and corporations change their reporting hierarchies.

There is no one right way to model these changes. You can keep multiple copies of dimensions and build separate cubes for each dimensional version. You can keep a single dimension in a single cube that represents the union of each dimension version. You can keep explicit dimension versions, again in a single cube. The third option requires direct support from a product. The first two you could implement with most any product.

Links

Assuming that you can identify the source data, that the source data corresponds to the leaf level of the model, and that there are no references to higher levels of aggregation in the source tables, it is useful to give the links from the cube to the data source a trial run at this stage. (If your source tables have aggregation levels defined in them, or if some of the source data represents aggregate information, you will need to have defined these levels in the cube prior to linking, or you will need to use a tool capable of defining levels through the linking process.)

The good thing about bringing in some or all of the data at this stage is that it gives you the ability to test the dimensionality of the model you have created before you have gone and defined a lot of other structures that might all have to be revised in the event that the dimensionality of the model needs to be changed. Because the data is there, it also lets you define and test variable formulas. With the hierarchies not yet present, there should be no danger of time- and storage-consuming database explosion complicating the picture.

The more you are sure of the hierarchies that need to be created in each dimension, and sure of the dimensions themselves, the less difference it makes whether you define the links and bring in data before or after defining the hierarchies.

Dimension Levels and Hierarchies

As we saw in Chapter 3, dimensions may have, but do not necessarily have a hierarchical structure. For example, products, time, and place usually have hierarchical structures. The question remains: Are the hierarchical structures symmetric, in which case they may be efficiently represented in terms of levels, or are they asymmetric, in which case it would not be efficient to define them in terms of levels? For example, time is usually representable as a series of levels such as day, month, quarter, and year. Products, on the other hand, sometimes have an irregular structure for which named levels may not apply. Other dimensions, such as a scenario dimension, frequently have no hierarchical structure at all.

You need to look at all the dimensions you defined in the previous step and identify all the dimensions that can be further decomposed into levels. The levels should be named. Geography, for example, may be a dimension to which the named levels country, region, state, county, and city can be applied. Level names can, of course, be numeric.

If you are working from data tables that contain levels, they will be found as the names of columns in the base data tables or in lookup tables associated with the base tables. Any levels that were used in the situation as you found it have to be accounted for somewhere in the system. Users may want you to implement levels that were not a part of their base data. If this is so, you need to learn the parent-child relationships that define each level. For an initial pass, it will suffice to know the dimension to which a level applies and its relative hierarchical position. In other words, region as a geographical level may be defined as in between cities and states.

At the end of this second stage, you will still have a high-level logical model, but it will contain more detail relative to the end of the first stage. Figure 10.7 shows a multidimensional data structure with each dimension broken out into levels where the number of members in each level is specified. Think of the process as similar to increasing the magnification on a microscope that is focused on an onion skin. Starting from a relatively high level where many cells are in view, as the magnification is increased everything initially blurs, but then a new, more detailed view of the interior of a

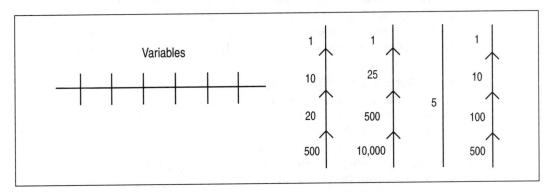

Figure 10.7 Showing levels in the multidimensional data structure.

cell comes into focus. There are fixed levels of detail at which interesting structures appear. The same is true with a dimensional model.

Multiple Hierarchies   When members need to be aggregated by different groupings, you need to create multiple hierarchies. Most tools allow for multiple paths of aggregation in the dimension hierarchies to at least some degree. The grouping principle for each path should be identified and the hierarchies named. (Even in a dimension with a single hierarchy, the principle should be identified.) For example, products may be grouped by generalizations of product type, by classifications of size or color, or by demographic group to which they are targeted. Attributes associated with the members will provide clues to useful hierarchies.

Because tools may support different types of hierarchy structures depending on the type of dimension (for example, variables and time as distinct from all others), identifying the aggregation paths needed will help to form the strategy later on for expressing the structure and computations. Some tools require the designation of one of the hierarchy paths as the consolidation path; other paths can exist to organize members but do not play the same role in computing aggregations.

When forming the hierarchies, depending on a tool's structuring capabilities, you may need to decide whether to create multiple root members to define the hierarchies. For example, you may consider the typical grouping of products by levels of generalization of product type to be the primary aggregation path of interest, and you may be interested in aggregating up to an allproduct member. In the same dimension, you could have other aggregation paths that group products by the demographic group for which they are designed, by pricing or size categories, and so on. If all leaf members feed into the product-by-price-category path, then an allproduct-by-price-category member will generate an aggregation redundant with the allproduct-by-type member's. However, the highest-level by-price-category members will appear in the model to each be a separate path, practically indistinct from the highest-level by-size-category path members as well. The addition of a root member to the top of each hierarchy will be redundant, but it will serve to at least distinguish each hierarchy from the others.

Deciding Between Multiple Levels in a Dimension and Multiple Dimensions   Imagine a data table whose columns consisted of products, stores, and product groups. Clearly you would keep products and stores as separate dimensions. But would you do the same with product groups? What would make you decide? Generally, you want to examine the cardinality relationship between the members of the columns, in this case product groups and products. The more that relationship is M to N, the more it makes sense to treat product groups as a separate dimension. In contrast, the more their rela-

Table 10.1 Products and Product Categories

Product	Product Category
triglets	foobars
spiglets	foobars
derbots	doobars
berbots	doobars
crumpets	goobars
flumpets	goobars

tionship is 1 to N, the more it makes more sense to treat product groups as a separate level of the products dimension.

Cardinality relationships, like dimensionality, are sometimes in the eye of the beholder. Look at the following data set, shown in Table 10.1, for an imaginary company that produces six products belonging to three categories.

At first, it may seem there exists a 1–N relationship between product categories and products, specifically, there are two products for every one product category, and thus product categories belong as a level within an overall product dimension. But notice there are the same number of products within each product category. *Instead of thinking of each product as an individual with a unique name, you could think of each product as a relatively numbered member of a product category.* This is shown in Table 10.2.

By re-representing the products as relatively numbered within each category, we have converted a 1–N relationship between product categories and products to an M–N relationship. And, as an M–N relationship, products and product categories could be represented as two separate dimensions (see Figure 10.8).

Table 10.2 Relative Numbering of Products

Product	Product Category
1	foobars
2	foobars
1	doobars
2	doobars
1	goobars
2	goobars

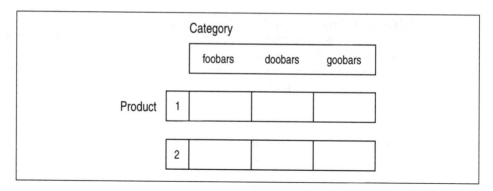

Figure 10.8 Products and categories as separate dimensions.

The thing to watch out for is whether the lower-level members, in this case individual products, can be beneficially represented as relatively enumerated items within a higher-level grouping. To answer yes, there should be some similarity between products that have the same relative enumeration per category. Perhaps products are organized within each category by price or margin, so that it makes sense to talk about "1" or "2" products in general. Also, if adding a product "3" at a later time would mean adding a product "3" to each product category, then products and categories make better candidates for separate dimensions.

One of the potential benefits (assuming you answered yes to the question above) of splitting up levels into separate dimensions is the ability to represent them on separate axes of a display screen. In other words, most OLAP tools are not able to display two levels of one model dimension in two dimensions on a computer screen. You also need to ensure that there are roughly the same number of relatively enumerated items in each higher-level grouping. Otherwise, you will generate a lot of meaningless intersections. Time is an example of a dimension whose levels are frequently represented as separate dimensions, especially weeks and months where weeks are cast as the first, second, third, and fourth week of the month. (See the AirTran case study in Chapter 14 for an example of this.)

Disconnected Hierarchies   So far, the dimensions we have looked at in this book have either been loose collections of elements, such as those found in a variables dimension, or they have been composed of one or more hierarchies. The implicit assumption with hierarchical dimensions that contain multiple hierarchies is that the hierarchies are connected through at least some of the members. You should be aware that this need not be the case. *A single product dimension with a hierarchical structure sometimes splits into two or more disconnected hierarchies.* This could be the result of a product reorganization where, for a period of time, a new product division did not feed into the main product root. It could also be the result of a mistake; perhaps an intermediate product category was inadvertently deleted. In either event, a situation would be produced where the root member of the dimension did not connect to all the leaf nodes in the dimension. This may not be apparent with large dimensions. When you are working with large dimensions, you need to verify that either all the leaf members do indeed connect to the root member or that the dimension contains an intentionally disconnected hierarchy.

When a Dependent Member Is a Parent Versus a Peer How should you represent a dependent member, such as a total cost that depends on a variety of particular costs? Should you represent it as a parent of the individual costs or as a sibling to the individual costs? Does it make any difference? Most of the time, with dimensions like time, products, geography, and employees, you define levels within a dimension and portray dependent members as relative parents within a hierarchy. The biggest single reason why it is worth the effort to define hierarchies is because they funnel the masses of individual members into the higher-level categories that we think about for decision making. In a product dimension with 30,000 individual products, 100 product categories and 10 brands, it is easier and more natural to think about and define rules for the 100 product categories, and 10 brands that are the basis for most of our decision making, than to think about and define rules that explicitly consider the 30,000 individual products.

When there are not too many members in the dimension, you will have more flexibility regarding where you represent members as peers. This commonly occurs in variables and scenario dimensions. For example, some OLAP products make it difficult to have data enter at a nonleaf level. If you have some data that is not normally provided at the most detailed level, or if you needed to hand-enter estimates for some of the dependent members for which you did not yet have data, it would be easier if the member were a leaf member rather than a nonleaf member. Also, it may be easier to compute members without needing to override built-in aggregation formulas if the members are all peers.

Figure 10.9 shows a simple variables dimension in two forms. Figure 10.9a shows all the members as peers, while Figure 10.9b shows the dependent members as parents.

Dimension Members

If you want to think of a dividing line between high-level and lower-level multidimensional models, it occurs (generally speaking) at the boundary between levels and individual members. In a dimension like products or customers there may be 5 or 10 levels of granularity, while there may be

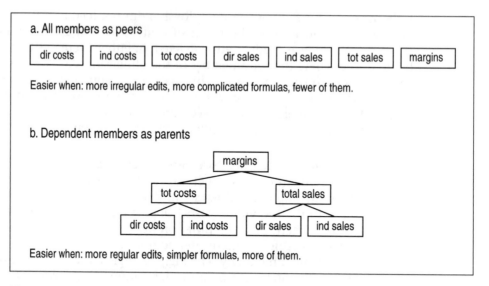

Figure 10.9 Showing dependents as parents or as peers.

thousands or even millions of base-level members. A diagram of all 2 million customers serves no practical purpose, certainly not as an abstraction. There are just too many members. A useful model needs to be a scaled-down version of the real thing, not a replica.

It may be useful to list a representative sample of the members of a dimension to make sure that there is no confusion. Or it may be useful to define a test model with a sample list of members. But when it comes to working with all the members in a dimension with many members, the best you can do is assure yourself that the member list is sufficiently clean. If it is a customer list, for example, you want to be confident that the same customers are not listed more than once. As discussed in Chapter 1, data, or in this case metadata, cleansing is a part of the warehousing process. To reiterate, the techniques presented in this book on multidimensional systems assume that the base data exists and is of good quality.

In a typical large model, no more than one or two dimensions have such high cardinality. This means that most cubes have one or more low-cardinality dimensions. "Scenario" and "Market" dimensions are generally of low enough cardinality that enumerating all of their members is helpful. For example, there may be only 10 markets into which a particular group of products is sold, or there may be only four scenarios for the purposes of budgeting.

In addition to distinguishing between low- and high-cardinality dimensions, keeping the variables dimension separate from all the others is useful. Remember, the members of the variables dimension, whether there are 5 or

500, will have most of the formulas in the cube that are not straight sums. They are, after all, the things whose values you are tracking in the model. Even if there are 500, as, for example, with a large chart of accounts, whoever is using that information will need to be aware of each of the 500 accounts. Variables usually need to be dealt with on an individual basis.

Looking over the base tables, as was shown in Chapter 3, the dimension member information may be represented in two basic ways: embedded within data tables, in which case the dimensional information will be represented by column headings in a level-based way, or free-standing in parent-child tables. (Additional permutations were discussed in Chapter 7.)

The cells defined by the intersections of dimension members will be at least as numerous as the number of base data points to enter the system. In cases where the source data represents transactions such as actual products sold, the number of data points brought in to a model may be only a very small percentage of the total number of cells in the model. The cube in this situation would be called sparse. Recall the issues surrounding sparsity that were treated in Chapter 6.

Relationships Between Members   For each of the dimensions in the cube you are designing, how do the members relate to each other? Assume you are working with a stores dimension. What is the relationship between stores? Are they simply enumerated members in a list? Or does some additional information differentiate them? Recall the example given in Chapter 5 where stores were listed along with longitude and latitude information. Clearly, this kind of information can serve to define distance functions between the members. This would frequently be captured in attributes that accompany the structural identity of the members.

You would want to capture this information for pattern searches, extrapolations, and other analysis. (See the discussion of dimensional analysis in Chapter 15 and the distinction between nominal, ordinal, and cardinal orderings.) For example, if you know how your sales have changed by month for the past three years, you could make a projection for the next month based on your experience because time intervals are cardinally ordered. You can define a formula that says:

$$time\ (x{+}1)\ sales = time\ (x)\ sales + projected\ change\ in\ sales$$

You could not define such a formula for a dimension where the members were just nominally ordered elements of a list. Nor could you explore correlations between variables unless your identifier dimensions were cardinally ordered.

Changing Names of Members   Sometimes dimension members have coded names, like SKU codes, in the source tables that end users do not want to be forced to work with. You should verify for all the dimensions whether the member names need to be given aliases for the benefit of end users. If you feel it is necessary, you should make sure that aliases are supported by whatever OLAP tool you invest in and check to see what the impact is of changing names on your existing model structures. For example, with some products you would need to manually change all formulas that depend on members whose name has changed. In such cases, you want to define your aliases as early in the model design process as possible.

Types of Formulas

The previous steps have led to a dimensional structure for your data. The task of defining formulas remains. It is time to step back for a minute and ask yourself, perhaps more thoroughly than you have before, " What is the purpose of the model I am building? What kinds of formulas am I defining to achieve that purpose?"

Are you trying to construct a picture of what is going on in your company or organization? Are you trying to analyze certain events, such as the decrease in market share of your product, to discover what may have been the cause? Are you trying to predict how sales, costs, and margins are going to evolve over the next 12 months? Or are you perhaps trying to come up with policy recommendations?

Independent of any subject area, the four model purposes just mentioned result from four different types of formulas that you could build: descriptive, explanatory, inferential, and prescriptive. It is not a question of building one type, such as a descriptive formula, as opposed to another type, such as a predictive formula. It is also not a question of building separate cubes for each type of formula. The movement from descriptive formulas to prescriptive formulas represents a series of incremental increases in analytical complexity within the same cube. Prescriptive formulas rely on inferential or predictive formulas, which rely on explanatory formulas, which rely on descriptive formulas. There is no way to build a predictive formula that does not somewhere contain, implicitly or explicitly, an explanatory formula and a descriptive formula. All formulas may share the same cube-defined dimensional structure. You should be aware of these distinctions because the quality of whatever model you build will be limited by the quality of all the formulas. Let's explore them a little further.

Prescriptive formulas represent alternative courses of action. Scenario-based planning for corporations and government entities relies on prescriptive formulas. Frequently, there is a need to decide a particular investment strategy, such as repairing a bridge versus building a new one or expanding market share within a geographical market versus expanding into new markets. All rational or data-based methods for selecting from alternative strategies must have some specified goal (or set of goals), such as minimizing cost, and/or maximizing net social welfare, and/or maximizing dividend returns, and/or maximizing capital appreciation. And all methods must have made some predictions about how events will evolve as a function of each of the possible investment strategies. Without predictions there would be no alternatives from which to pick. And without a goal there would be no way to pick. To create a prescriptive formula, therefore, you need to have a predictive formula already.

Predictive or inferential formulas represent values for locations where no measurement has yet taken place. On average, we create inferential formulas about the future—these may be called predictive. We also create inferential formulas about the past, such as formulas about the origins of capital markets, or of humans, or of the origins of the universe. And we create inferential formulas about situations that exist contemporaneously but at some inaccessible location (not necessarily that far away), such as the inner mantle of the earth.

Any data-based inferential formula (I keep saying data-based because it is always possible to pull predictions out of thin air—just watch a politician) is the combination of a known relationship combined with an extrapolation function. For example, we know from experience that decreases in interest rates are correlated with a lagged time increase in home sales. When you see that interest rates just took a dive, you assume that the correlation between interest rates and home sales remains constant, and you predict that home sales will rise. The prediction followed naturally from your belief in an existing correlation and the constancy of that correlation over time. Without some factor correlating interest rates with home sales, there would be no way for you to make a prediction about future home sales given knowledge of a change in interest rates. This correlation factor is the result of an explanatory formula.

Explanatory formulas represent relationships between data elements already described in the formula. Statistical regressions are a common form of explanatory formula. Given any series (of 30 or more cases) of two or more variables, where one variable is called the dependent variable and the others are called the independent variables, it is possible to calculate the degree to which the variances in the dependent variable are explained or accounted for by variances in the independent variables. Standard business comparisons that consist predominantly of ratios, such as the ratio of this year's sales to last year's sales, or the ratio of new sales to maintenance revenue, or the ratio of domestic worker productivity to foreign worker productivity, or the ratio of male to female employees, are all a part of explanatory formulas. All explanatory formulas presume the existence of descriptive data. You could never calculate the ratio between the different genders of employees or the ratio between foreign and domestic sales unless you had those numbers in the beginning. All explanatory formulas rely on descriptive data and formulas.

A pure descriptive formula has no comparison formulas. It is simply a description of what is. Measured variables represent descriptions. And simple aggregations of data represent descriptions. (In statistics these aggregations such as sum and average are called *descriptive statistics*.) Cubes that contain only input data, or input data plus simple aggregations of input data, are pure descriptions. We frequently lose sight of these descriptive formulas because we tend to focus on the more exciting explanatory and predictive formulas. Yet frequently, problems arise in these more complex formulas because there was a basic quality problem with the descriptions. As was stated all the way back in Chapter 1, OLAP assumes that the base data exists and is of good quality. This just means that most of the basic techniques for refining data, such as integrating data of different types or cleaning up tables where the values in columns do not represent what the column headings say should be in the columns, fall under the tutelage of data warehousing. Nevertheless, you can certainly do things in your OLAP environment to screen your input data for anomalies such as compare data values and changes in data values to a table of acceptable values. This won't capture subtle errors, but it will highlight the more egregious ones.

Given how these formulas build on one another, I suggest that regardless of the kind of formula you are ultimately building, begin with a descriptive formula and incrementally verify what you are doing at each stage. Be confident of your descriptions before looking for correlations. Be confident of your correlations before making predictions. And be confident of your predictions before making strategy recommendations.

Aggregation Formulas

A major factor that affects the analyses you will need to create is whether you are the end user or whether you are defining a system for end users to perform their own analysis. If you are preparing a system to be used by others, your goal should be to create an environment that facilitates analysis. If you are the end user, you will still want to perform your ad hoc analyses on top of more basic, preparatory analysis. Either way, you need to perform basic aggregations and analysis.

A key component of multidimensional modeling is the definition of formulas or derivations, especially aggregation formulas. An aggregation formula can be as simple as the sum of two members or as complex as a system of conditionally weighted equations. For most applications, the majority of aggregation formulas are basic sums and averages. Figure 10.10 shows an MDS view of simple aggregation formulas across three hierarchical dimensions for data entering at the leaf level.

When creating a logical model you want to identify all the dimensions that are used principally for aggregation. With the exception of variables and

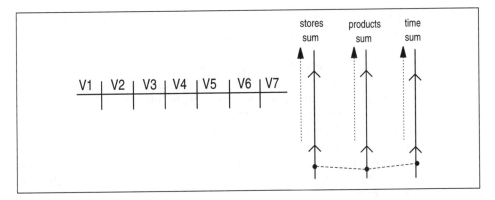

Figure 10.10 Showing aggregation dimension formulas in the multidimensional data structure.

scenarios, most dimensions such as products, customers, time, geography, and departments are hierarchical and responsible for generating simple aggregations. A typical definition for products might state that all products sum into their parent. Recalling that derivation is an attribute of data and not of members, you should realize that what this actually means is that all data (in the absence of overriding formulas) sums across products.

Because OLAP models can become quite complex, I recommend incrementally verifying them (and if need be, debugging them). Toward that end, *I suggest that you test out the basic aggregation functions before putting in the fancier stuff.* A good way to do this is to compute aggregates along dimensions for which the aggregation function is a pure and simple function, like sum, for variables (that is, members of the variables dimension) that have no attached formula.

Basic Variables and Other Nonaggregation Formulas Once you have assured yourself that the basic aggregation functions are working, it is time to add any further formulas that are a part of the core model. The core model in this sense means any data that most users will want to look at, that is most frequently queried, that is a part of your first deliverable, or that might feed further analysis. Typically, such formulas are found in the variables dimension as ratios, products, and differences. They can also occur in the time dimension where it is not unusual to see interperiod ratios.

Unless your formulas are complex within single dimensions, you may not want to test them on a dimension-by-dimension basis except for verifying that the syntax is correct and that they say what you think they are supposed to say. Of course, you may run aground anywhere. But it is more likely that if problems are going to arise, they will arise when formulas in one dimension intersect with formulas in another dimension, as discussed below in the section on "Calculation Precedence."

Functions Attached to Dimensions Versus Functions in Rules/Scripts The decision to attach functions to the members of a dimension, as opposed to a separate calculation rule or script, is related closely to the product that you use, but exists for all of them. This is related to the decision to structure members in a hierarchy or leaving them as peers, discussed in the preceding section on dependent members. Two factors in the decision process include the functions that can be expressed in a tool and whether a formula is the one most commonly used across the members of other dimensions or is more of an exception.

If the computation you wish to express is summation, then the choice is likely arbitrary because products generally support summation in the hierarchies and could be driven by performance considerations. If the computation is a ratio or involves several terms with different operators, it may not be possible to express this in the dimension structure as opposed to a script.

Where one function serves as a default, but other functions are used in certain regions of the hypercube, expressing the default in the dimension and the exceptions in the rules may be desirable. For example, a scenario dimension may be used mostly for examining the quantitative difference between actuals and plans, with a few ratios between plans and actuals taken as well. In products that support subtraction (summation with a negative weight) in the hierarchies, the *Actual – Plan* could be usefully placed in the dimension while the *(Actual – Plan) / Plan* could be placed in the rules.

Qualified Referencing of Data   As you are writing formulas, be aware of all the hierarchically qualified references. For example, the formula *margin = sales – costs* in a two-dimensional cube whose other dimension is geographical, involves nonhierarchical references. If you have any formula writing background, you are probably familiar with these types of references. At the store level, store margins are calculated in terms of store sales and store costs; at the city level, they use city sales and costs. You should also keep in mind when you are making relative hierarchical references, as is the case with the term "parent," and when you are making absolute hierarchical references, as is the case with any named level such as cities or brands.

Consider the formula *contribution = sales/[parent]:sales*. At the store level, in a hierarchy where cities follow stores, this formula calculates the ratio of one store's sales to all the sales made in the city. Conceptually, it is pretty straightforward, but unless you've been writing OLAP applications for a while, it is easy to introduce a mistake. There may be cases in an asymmetric hierarchy where stores connect to cities in some places but to states or regions in others. If what you want to calculate at the store level is the contribution of the store to the city, then you will get the wrong answer for stores that connect directly to states. (The correct answer would be the number one as opposed to the fraction of state or regional sales accounted for by the store.) In such a case, you would want either to add a city node to your geography hierarchy or to define a conditional formula for contribution.

Calculation Precedence   Recall from Chapter 4 that the need to decide calculation precedence arises whenever the formulas that originated in different dimensions produce different results as a function of the order in which they are applied. The common case is a summation formula in one dimension intersecting with a ratio formula in another dimension. The sum of a set of ratios is not equal to the ratio of a set of sums. It is very easy to make mistakes here. On the positive side, when mistakes are made, numbers are usually thrown off by a large factor and are thus easy to spot as erroneous when you perform a manual check. You should initially look for incorrect results in a trial calculation by reviewing aggregates whose values you can associate with a particular range. For example, an average employee age may need to fit between 18 and 65. A value of 2,500 would signal an aggregation error. The most common error is due to incorrect precedence. Usually, a variable that needed to be averaged was summed instead.

As described in Chapter 4, there are many operational combinations such as summing and dividing, multiplying and adding, and subtracting and dividing where the operational precedence makes a difference. Unlike the testing of simple aggregations where the aggregation function is given by the formula attached to the aggregation dimension, the aggregation function needs to be determined in cases where operational precedence is an issue. I suggest working through the calculation of a small number of cells when there is doubt.

To work through a calculation, you can either chain formulas together or follow the calculation order. This is very important, so let's review how it works. Imagine a two-dimensional cube defined by time and sales variables. The relevant variables are sales, costs, and margins defined as sales minus costs. The relevant times are this month, last month, and the ratio between this month and last month. Now imagine that you want to calculate the ratio between the margins for this month and last month. And you want to do it by defining a precedence ordering for the two dimensions.

The relevant time formula is a ratio and the relevant variable formula is a difference. Consider how the two formulas might chain together. If you perform the ratio first you wind up taking the difference between two ratios: *(this month sales / last month sales) – (this month costs / last month costs)*. If you perform the difference first, you wind up with the ratio between two differences: *(this month sales – this month costs) / (last month sales – last month costs)*. Just seeing the algebraic difference between the two different combinations might be enough for you to realize that you want the ratio of the differences and not the difference of the ratios.

If it is not, you will want to follow the calculation order through a simple sequence like the one shown here.

	sales	*costs*	*sales − costs*
last month	40	20	20
this month	80	40	40
this month / last month	2	2	2 or 0

Of course, the correct ratio between this month's margin and last month's margin is 2, not zero.

Conditional Formulas   Unlike formula precedence issues that can arise in an otherwise exceptionless cube, the need for conditional formulas generally arises from the existence of known exceptions. For example, the market value of a stock means something different for a private portfolio (where it is a function of the number of shares held in the stock multiplied by the price per share) than for an industry basket such as the Dow Jones Industrial Average or the S&P 500 (where it is a function of the number of shares issued and outstanding of the stock multiplied by the price per share). In cases of missing values for some variables and not others, tests for existence may be required to combine them or aggregate correctly. A pool of bonus funds may be available only if actual sales exceed plans by a certain amount.

Errors here will usually be more subtle than with incorrect precedence, so you should manually verify, at least for a few cases, that any position- or data-based formula exceptions are working properly, where conditions are triggered and where they are not.

Deciding When to Compute   This topic was first discussed in Chapter 7 and it is one of the areas where a large divergence occurs between types of tools. Tools that work with SQL databases, for example, generally handle issues of pre-aggregation differently from MDDB tools. You may need to create tables of aggregates in SQL and then connect the aggregate tables to the associated OLAP tool. There is unlikely to be any automatic help for you to figure out which aggregates are most worthwhile to precalculate. Most OLAP tools these days (with the exception of those tools that operate entirely on dynamically calculated results) provide an option that lets you define certain aggregations to be performed at request time. Whatever tool you use, you will want to give some thought to which aggregates need to be precalculated and which do not. See Chapter 7 for a discussion of pre- versus post-query computations.

More Complex Aggregations and Analysis

As stated at the beginning of this chapter, there are many different ways you can sequentially proceed with the design and implementation of an OLAP model. Depending on your situation, you may not need to think through more complex issues, at this point anyway, or, something complex, like entering data at a nonleaf level, may be the first issue you have to think through.

On average, however, you most likely will need to work through all the issues of basic aggregation first. Those issues were treated in the last section. The issues placed in this section were the ones that I felt arise for some of the people, some of the time. This section does not treat issues of analytical technique such as how to perform a cluster analysis. Rather, it treats issues that appear in a multidimensional environment and that can hinder the analytical process.

Nonleaf Input Data   Data does not always enter a cube at the leaf or base level. In Chapter 3, we looked at some examples of cost allocations running down the same product hierarchy for which sales information was aggregated. The cost data entered the cube at the top of the hierarchy (in the form of total allocatable costs) and was allocated downward. Remember that the attributes input and derived are a function of data and not dimension members.

From a practical perspective *you need to be able to spot data that does not enter the cube at the base level, and you need to know when formulas rely on input data that comes from a nonleaf level, especially when there exists leaf-level data.*

One reason for being aware of data that needs to enter at a nonleaf level is that not all products are equally graceful at accepting nonleaf-level input data. As discussed earlier in this chapter, there are many occasions when data that all share the same dimensional structure do not all share the same aggregation levels. Recall the example of a sales cube where sales data entered at the store level and where macroeconomic information entered at the national level. Assuming your product can handle nonleaf-level inputs, there shouldn't be any problem here as long as the data enters only at the nonleaf level.

Things get trickier when data for the same variable enter at both a leaf and a nonleaf level. Think about a sales model where sales data normally enters a cube at the store level and aggregates upward. And now imagine that the VP of sales needs to make a presentation that includes current figures for all regional sales and their aggregates but that all of the relevant store-level data has not yet entered the system. The easiest solution is for each regional sales manager to manually enter a best guess for the regional sales totals and then aggregate those regional sales guesstimates to the national level. To do this properly, a multidimensional system would need to be able to aggregate sales from the regional level only where the estimates were placed; if the system took the base-level data it had and ignored the estimates, it would get incorrect results.

You may also need to suppress the aggregation of base-level sales data until all stores have reported their sales. Again, you need to be sure that if this is important to you, the tools you use offer this option.

When formulas need to access data from multiple levels within the cube, I find it useful to write formulas, if only for my own mental model, that include the aggregation level of the inputs to the formula. For the example above, I would write the following formula:

$$National.sales = Sum[regional]:sales.$$

Nominal Versus Ordinal Versus Cardinal Analysis   In a cube with a store, time, product, and sales variables dimension, you could compare sales across any combination of stores, products, and time. In this sense (and as we saw in Chapter 4), all analyses in a cube take place relative to the cube's dimensional structure. The question remains, "What about more sophisticated analyses?"

Your ability to perform more sophisticated analyses, such as correlations, regressions, clusterings, and projections, is limited by the quantitative structure of your dimensions and your data. (See Chapter 15 for a discussion of dimensional analysis.) For example, are your data and dimensions nominal, ordinal, or cardinal? Typically, with the exception of a time dimension that generally has a cardinal or quantitative structure, all your dimensions are nominal. This means that there is no quantitative relationship between the members of the dimension. In contrast, and with the exception of ranks and other groupings, all of your numeric data will be cardinal. Because nominally, ordinally, and cardinally ordered data may look the same, you need to be careful.

To discover the types of data and dimensions that you have ask of whomever is most knowledgeable of the data the following questions for each nonvariable dimension and for each variable:

1. Can you quantitatively rank the members of the dimension or the values of the variable? If the answer is no, then the variable or dimension is nominally ordered. If the answer is yes, then the dimension or data is at least ordinally ordered.

2. Can you assign a numeric value to the distance between any two variable values or dimension members? If the answer is no, then the dimension or variable is ordinally ordered. If the answer is yes, then the variable or dimension is cardinally ordered.

The most important thing is to make sure that you do not try to perform an analysis that requires cardinal dimensions and data, such as a standard regression, with anything other than cardinal dimensions and data. For example, you would not want to run a regression of sales against costs along a typical nominally structured product dimension. You would get a result, but it would be meaningless.

Sparsity   Most multidimensional models contain some sparsity. (You may recall that sparsity was treated in Chapter 7.) When designing and implementing an OLAP system, you need to know the following things:

❑ How sparse is the data?

❑ Which dimensional combinations are the sparse ones; which are the dense ones?

❑ What kind of sparsity exists?

Depending on the tool you are using, you may or may not have to deal with the first two questions. Some tools will automatically figure out the amount of sparsity in the data and adjust the storage accordingly (see Chapter 8). Other tools make you decide whether your data is significantly sparse and, if so, which dimensional combinations are the most sparse.

Regardless of whether your tool can automatically configure storage to handle sparse data sets, it is a good idea for you to be aware of the sparsity of your data because the amount and type of sparsity will affect the analyses you can perform. You cannot, for example, aggregate sparse data where the sparsity reflects meaningless intersections in the same way as sparse data where the sparsity reflects large amounts of zeros.

You can answer the first question by calculating the number of intersections at the base level of the model (which equals the product of the number of leaf elements in each dimension) and dividing that into the number of data points at the base level. This will give you the sparsity at the base level of the model.

The second question is tougher to answer—and there may not be a clean answer. Another way of phrasing it is "What dimensions can you use to partition the cube such that you are left with relatively dense subcubes?" The dimensions of the dense subcubes are then called the dense dimensional combinations, and the dimensions used for partitioning are called the sparse dimensional combinations. In any event, it helps to have an understanding of the data in order to address the question.

Think about the dimensions of retail data: stores, products, time, and variables. And imagine that the cube is a collection of monthly figures so that most stores sold some of most products during the course of the month. Typically, if one variable is evaluated for a store-product-time combination, all variables are evaluated. Chances are, if a product is not sold for a store during a month it is because the store does not carry that product. If this is the case, then the combination of stores and products is sparse, and either stores or products will have to be used as a partitioning dimension. Time and variables will form a part of the dense subcubes along with either stores or products.

What may seem confusing is that sparsity is a function of dimensional combinations. Yet you may be called upon by a product to identify sparse and dense dimensions. Just remember that what you are really doing is partitioning the one cube into groups of denser subcubes. Toward that end, you need to split up sparse dimensional combinations.

You can take a stab at the third question by finding the sparse entries, substituting the terms "zero," "missing," and "not applicable" and seeing which one makes the most sense. As with the second question, you may need to know something about the data in order to figure out what the sparsity means. In a retail model, for example, where you might see a sparse intersection at widgets, January, Florida, sales you might guess that the sparsity meant the number zero. And it probably would. But without a metadata description defining the meaning of sparse intersections, it could have meant anything. It could be that widgets are not sold in Florida or that the data for widgets or for Florida is missing, or that zero widgets were sold in Florida in January.

Typically, for retail data, sparse intersections refer to zeros. If, however, there is a customer dimension, the sparse intersections will most likely denote "notapplicable." This occurs because most customers do business with only a small number of outlets. With financial data, sparse intersections frequently refer to nonapplicable indicators such as "change in share price over the last 12 months" for a company that has been public for only six months. In marketing and transportation models sparsity is also frequently a measure of nonapplicability. Certain products may not be sold through certain channels, and certain transportation segment combinations may exist for which no transportation exists. In socioeconomic models, sparse intersections frequently denote missing data.

As discussed in Chapter 7, the way you work with each form of sparsity is different. You can sum across large expanses of zeros without thought. Summing across nonapplicable values will work in any tool, but you need to understand what the sum means. The same is especially true of averaging over missing values. Where you have both types of sparsity existing, you need special care in interpreting results if not formulating computations. Missing data requires proxies before entering into a calculation, which most tools will provide for you as a zero. Nonapplicable data must not enter into a calculation at all.

Here again, if you are not sure of what you are doing, first check to make sure that there is sparsity in the data. Whereas for storage purposes you can ignore sparsity of less than 30 percent or so, for calculation purposes even one sparse cell can throw off your calculations. And because some products will assume that sparse intersections mean a zero value, you need to verify what they really do mean. Then after you have defined your aggregation functions, manually verify that the aggregates make sense. Because you will need to look at every input number to perform a manual check, you should carve out a small enough slice that you can check each number. Once you have carved out a working slice, check to make sure that if sparse cells are nonapplicable, they were left out of the calculation. This means that they do not enter the denominator in a calculation of averages. In a calculation of sums, you should also do a count of meaningful cells so that the viewer of the aggregate results will know what percentage of the underlying cells went into the aggregate. If you are working with missing data, check to make sure that proxies were used for the missing values or that the missing values were eliminated from the calculation.

Auditing The last topic I will cover is the creation of auditable models. When someone is using the model you want him or her to be able to easily discover, for any piece of data, the following:

- ❑ What are the formulas
- ❑ What kind of weighting scheme was used, if any
- ❑ Where the data originated
- ❑ How often the source data is refreshed
- ❑ Who has write authority for that data
- ❑ Who has read permission
- ❑ If it is a derived data value, who defined the formulas

For economic indicators you want to know if there are multiple sources for the same data. And you will want to know if there are any comments related to any part of the model: dimensional structures, hierarchies, aggregation formulas, and so on.

The best thing you can do is keep track of all relevant metadata as you design the model, and be aware of the metadata you lack and how you intend to acquire it. Because not all products offer the same support for auditing and annotation, you should check to see whether your product offers audit trails in the form of dependency tracking and, if so, to what level of detail dependencies are tracked. *Dependency tracking* is the tracing of inputs to a particular cell and/or outputs from a particular cell.

Summary of Practical Steps

You have, by this point, defined the logical schema for the multidimensional model that will serve as the basis of your proposed solution. During the course of defining the model you will have figured out, or generated the necessary information to figure out, how many distinct cubes will be required, how much base data there is per cube, how much data will be derived, the sources for the base data, how often the base data will be refreshed, how many calculations will be performed, how many of the calculations will be complex, and how much sparsity is at the base level. You are also prepared to document the formulas and the pedigree of your data as it flows through the model.

Endnotes

1. The difference between logical and physical models is crucial and worth exploring further. Logical models deal with structural and semantic relationships independently of how or where those relationships are stored and accessed. Physical models deal with the logistics of how and where data is stored, calculated, and accessed.

   As George Tillman wrote in his book, *A Practical Guide to Logical Data Modeling*, "The major purpose of logical data modeling is to communicate the end-users' view of the organization's data to those who will design the system... The logical data model should not be tied to a particular architecture, technology, or product. Logical design breaks down a problem into its lowest logical components so that physical designers can build it back up into a physical interpretation of the logical problem."

   Furthermore, there is a difference between high-level logical models and low-level logical models. A high-level logical model represents the essential elements of the model as understood by its users. For example, a typical entity relationship diagram represents a high-level logical model outlining the basic entities, attributes, and relationships in the model. This is illustrated in Figure 10.1.

   A low-level logical model contains sufficient detail to design a physical model. For example, the set of normalized relations, as shown in Figure 10.2 contains all the logical elements of the model. In other words, every key and nonkey attribute as well as every datum or data point are represented in this low-level logical model.

   Figure 10.3 represents a physical model of the same situation. Note how the physical model doesn't reveal any additional detail about what the data is, just about how it is stored, computed, and accessed.

CHAPTER

Global Planning for Sales and Marketing

Multinational organizations need a global strategic planning process and information infrastructure to meet their performance goals. The following hands-on case study demonstrates how to use multidimensional modeling for sales and marketing analysis within the context of strategic planning. It was created in collaboration with the Planning Technology Group (PTG), which specializes in the creation of corporate planning strategies. In this chapter, you will learn the basics of building and browsing a multidimensional model. You are encouraged, but not required, to follow along with the optional tutorial. In addition to viewing the model, the tutorial will have you perform some of the steps to modify it.

The Situation at WearCo

WearCo is a global manufacturer and retailer of clothing operating in more than 40 countries on four continents. Manufacturing is performed on a global level and distributed to countries on the basis of projected and actual demand. Margins are slim in the clothing business, and the corporation needs to take local economic factors, such as interest rates, labor rates, and exchange rates, into account before making global distribution plans. Corporate headquarters are in the United States. Forty percent of manufacturing and 25 percent of sales occur in North America. Consolidated corporate financials are calculated in dollars. But each country is treated as a separate business unit having its own P&L.

The Problems with How WearCo Is Currently Doing Planning

Planning was a difficult process. When PTG arrived at WearCo, plans were the outgrowth of budgeting. But budgets were created just one year at a time. They were done at the country level, and were not broken down by product. As a result, WearCo made few attempts to systematically define future market potential. Product life cycles with the commensurate changes to marketing costs and strategies were not adequately taken into account. Without coordination, market estimates and subsequently derived data were frequently inconsistent. Useful planning data was definitely lacking. At best, you could say that planning was taking place once a year in conjunction with budgeting.

PTG's Project Goals for WearCo

After consulting with PTG, WearCo decided to embark on a global project to develop a strategic planning process for sales and marketing activity. Participation and input by key managers around the world was deemed critical to the success of the project.

Specific management goals were to do the following:

1. Define a most likely case scenario that forms the basis for the 1997 budget.
2. Deliver a final 1997 budget that takes into account long-range goals and permits fast, effective adaptation to environmental changes.

Given the need to aggregate market estimates and sales information from all of WearCo's operating countries, and to provide the managers and analysts with fast flexible access to that information, PTG decided that WearCo needed an OLAP solution to its planning problem.

The OLAP Model

The planning model is composed of two hypercubes: a Profit and Loss, or P&L, cube and a market-sizing cube.

Overview of Hypercubes

Overview of Market-Sizing Cube

The market-sizing cube is an multidimensional representation of a standard market-sizing report. Market-sizing reports represent information about a

	1995	1996	1997
Marketable population	505,324,192	510,015,062	514,820,530
Penetration	10.42%	10.76%	11.20%
Segment population	52,646,634	54,860,932	57,664,814
Average annual usage per customer	8	8	8
Segment consumption	414,266,247	428,003,871	445,140,443
Average price per unit	338	333	328
Segment market value	2,688,393,835	2,859,477,384	3,059,088,318

Figure 11.1 Typical market-sizing report.

marketplace. They generally include demographic information such as total population and targetable population; economic information such as per capita GNP, inflation, and unemployment; consumer information such as how much of the product type is consumed by the population; and competitive information such as market share.

The natural dimensions for a market-sizing cube include market variables like the ones we just saw, plus product, country, and time. Figure 11.1 shows a typical market-sizing report.

Overview of P&L Cube

The P&L cube is a multidimensional representation of a standard P&L statement, which represents information pertaining to revenues (sources of profit) flowing *into* the organization and expenses (sources of loss) flowing out of the corporation. In contrast to a balance sheet, which represents a static snapshot of the state of an organization at a given moment in time, the P&L is a representation of a flow of activity over a period of time. Figure 11.2 shows a sample P&L.

The natural dimensions of a P&L cube are accounts, country, and time. The accounts are the line items of expense or revenue; time is the time period of the statement. Typically there is only one time period for a P&L, so the statement looks like a narrow table with accounts running down the rows for just one time period.

Acme Widgets, 1995	
Income	
Net Sales	760,980,907
Expenses	
Distribution	35,473,788
Advertising	136,155,465
Promotion	58,723,907
Cost of Goods Sold	198,627,286
Direct Product Expenses	428,980,447
Sales Force	61,242,961
Other Marketing	9,014,523
General & Administrative	15,186,240
Cost of Money	2,791,240
Other Income/(Expense)	1,317,072
Investment Costs	0
Total Expenditures	515,898,339
Profit / Loss	245,082,569

Figure 11.2 A sample P&L statement.

Multicube Relationship of Market Sizing and P&L

The two hypercubes share three dimensions: time, country, and product. Even though each hypercube stands on its own, having dimensions in common gives them what is called a *multicube structure*. The cubes may be related to each other through these dimensions.

The multicube is exploited by bringing sales and cost information generated within the P&L cube into the market-sizing cube to calculate the corporation's market share in each market and to calculate the profitability of different markets. The two cubes are kept separate for a combination of logical and manageability reasons:

❏ The variables of each cube are organized by different dimensions

❏ The sources of the P&L and market-sizing information are distinct

❏ The two cubes track different kinds of information—the P&L is internal information whereas the market sizing is external industry information

Source Linkages

The models are fed by original research, off-the-shelf data, local market knowledge and assumptions, and in-house financial systems. Most of the information is collected via a Lotus Notes interface. Notes was chosen because it facilitates the widespread collection and replication of qualitative assumptions and data—a critical requirement for gaining consensus and buy-in among the members of the strategic planning team. Where possible—for example, in inputting historical P&L information and audited data sources—data is transferred between the source system and Notes and/or TM/1 through the use of Import Master, a data transfer module used to automate the transfer of data between flat files, relational database, and so on, and TM/1. Quantitative data is regularly exported from Lotus Notes into the TM/1 models through a combination of Platinum Infopump and Import Master.

Dimensional Structure of the Model

The two hypercubes are linked in a multicube structure, in which some dimensions are shared between the cubes and others are particular to a single cube. Figure 11.3 outlines the dimensions of the multicube.

As we begin to examine the dimensions in detail, we will start the hands-on portion of the case study as well. Enclosed with the software is a dataset based on the one used by the company. If you choose not to use the tutorial, you can just read through, ignoring the segments of the text with **bold and underlined headings**, as below:

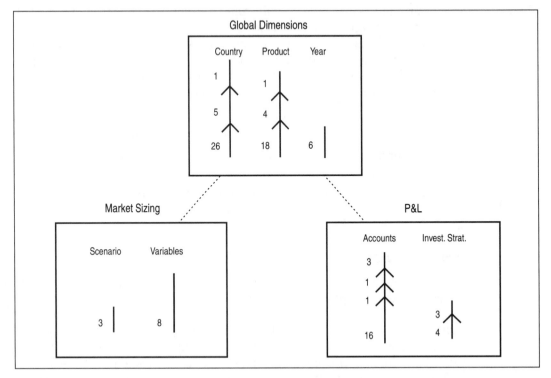

Figure 11.3 Diagram of multidimensional data structure for WearCo model.

Tutorial: Getting Started

As you follow along, you will be asked to open up different windows in the TM/1 program. Each time that you are supposed to see a new window on your screen, we will show the name of the window as **[bold bracketed]** in the text. Everything that you will be asked to click with your mouse will be <u>underlined</u> in the text. Key words that you will see or type on the screen will be *italicized*. This tutorial assumes that TM/1 has already been installed and that you have access to all directories. (To find out how to install TM/1, see Section 1 of the TM/1 manual in Appendix I).

Click on the <u>TM/1</u> menu and then the <u>Options</u> menu choice.

[TM/1 PERSPECTIVES - OPTIONS]

Make sure the database directory is set to *C:\TM1DATA\PTG* and that it is set on *Advanced Mode* (see Figure 11.4). Click <u>OK</u>.

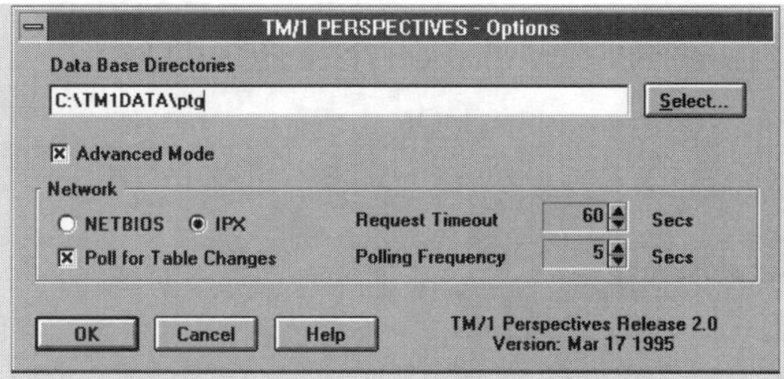

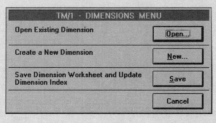

Figure 11.4 Setting the base directory.

[TM/1 PERSPECTIVES]

(It should ask you, "Do you want to update file: tm1.ini?")
Click <u>Yes</u>. You are now ready to begin the tutorial.

Common Dimensions

The common dimensions of the model are the ones that can be used to integrate information from the individual hypercubes. In this case, country, time, and product are common to the two hypercubes. We will first examine them here separately from the cubes. Later on in the case study, we will see how the common dimensions are used to integrate separate cubes' data for analysis.

Country   This dimension is composed of 26 of the countries in which the corporation competes.

<u>Viewing a Dimension: Country</u>

Click on the <u>TM/1</u> menu, then the <u>Dimensions</u> menu choice.
[TM/1 - Dimensions Menu] (See Figure 11.5)
Click on <u>Open</u>.

Figure 11.5 Open an existing dimension.

[Select Dimension Worksheet] (See Figure 11.6.)

Click on <u>country</u> and click <u>O</u>K.

Figure 11.6 Select country.

[COUNTRY.XDI]

We now can examine the country dimensions shown in Figure 11.7. We can use this same procedure to view any dimensions in the database.

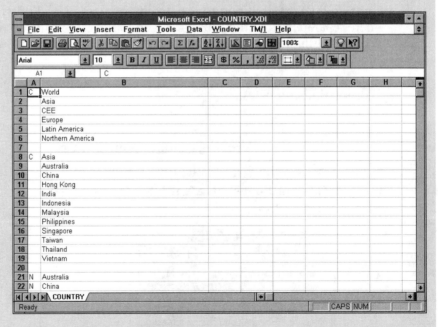

Figure 11.7 The country dimension.

Note the hierarchical structure of the dimension. Consolidated (parent) elements are preceded by a "C" in TM/1. *World* is composed of five regions: *Asia, CEE, Europe, Latin America,* and *Northern America.* Each of these regions is composed of individual countries. In multidimensional terms, each region is a child member of the world and is a parent of its individual countries. Each country is therefore a child member of the corresponding region. No country is a parent of any other members. In hierarchical terms, the countries are leaf members of the hierarchy.

Year   This dimension consists of the years 1995 through 2000 (see Figure 11.8). Note that there is no hierarchy connecting the time members; instead, they are all individuals and logically are as much roots as they are leaves. Because they are not parents, TM/1 requires that we designate them as leaves, so they each have an *N:* next to them. Also, the only values we will see in the cubes from 1996 to 2000 are projected values.

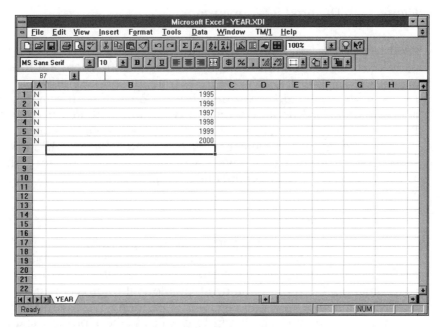

Figure 11.8 The year dimension.

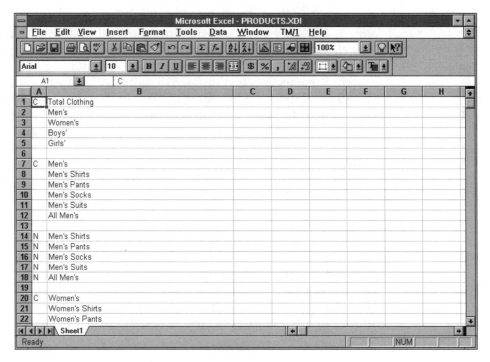

Figure 11.9 The products dimension.

Products This dimension consists of 14 clothing products that the company sells throughout the world (see Figure 11.9). There are four product lines—*Men's, Women's, Boys', Girls'*—that are broken down by product types—*shirts, pants, socks, and suits/dresses*. Some store information is available only on a product-line level and is not differentiated by product type. Because TM/1 does not allow information to be entered at consolidated levels, we have added the elements *All Men's, All Women's, All Boys', and All Girls'* at the product-type level, which then aggregate into the *Men's, Women's, Boys',* and *Girls'* product lines, respectively.

Market-Sizing Report

The WearCo market-sizing report looks at population and market segment variables. Each of these variables is naturally organized by product, country, and time. In addition, WearCo wishes to use this cube for planning purposes, so a scenario dimension was added that allows it to project market sizing under different competitive and economic conditions. We have already seen the country, time, and product dimensions, so let's take a look at the dimensions particular to the market-sizing cube: variable and scenario.

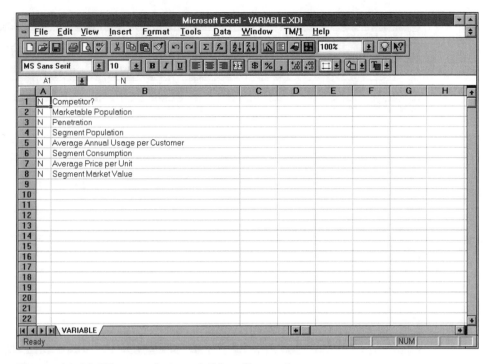

Figure 11.10 The market variables dimension.

Variables   This dimension contains the information involved in determining the state of the market in a particular country (see Figure 11.10). *Marketable Population* is the number of people in a country that could possibly be purchasers of the type of product, independent of which product they purchase. *Penetration* refers to the percentage of the marketable population that is buying the product, from any company in the market. *Segment Population* is the number of people in the country buying the product, so:

Segment Population = Marketable Population * Penetration

Average Annual Usage Per Customer is the number of units of the product the average consumer purchases each year. *Segment Consumption* is the total number of products purchased in the country per year, so:

Segment Consumption = Segment Population * Average Annual Usage Per Customer

Average Price per Unit is the average price that the product is marketed for in the country. *Segment Market Value* is the total value of all the products that have been sold in the country. So:

Segment Market Value = Segment Consumption * Average Price Per Unit

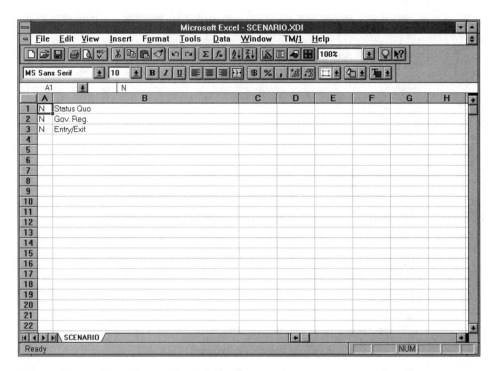

Figure 11.11 The scenario dimension.

Scenario This dimension reflects situations and actions that will have a significant effect on the markets in which the corporation operates (see Figure 11.11). *Status Quo* assumes that the current trends in the market continue. The high government regulation scenario, *Gov. Reg.*, models markets in foreign countries where the government significantly intervenes to protect its domestic companies. *Entry/Exit* reflects the situation where WearCo's major competitor decides to enter or exit a country's market.

The P&L Cube

What's the difference between a traditional P&L and a P&L hypercube? For a global corporation, in addition to an accounts dimension and a single value for a time dimension, there is also a country dimension. In other words, the company can generate a P&L for its activities in each of its countries. Figure 11.12 shows this extension of a P&L by a country dimension.

Recall that one of PTG's goals was to implement a systematic planning process. Toward that end it developed an investment type dimension called "invstrat" for WearCo's P&L statements. Invstrat represents different types of potential investments such as geographical expansion, product line expan-

Acme Widgets, 1995	USA	France	Germany
Income			
Net Sales	760,980,907	4,077,830	554,702,393
Expenses			
Distribution	35,473,788	180,498	28,854,808
Advertising	136,155,465	1,739,250	116,933,509
Promotion	58,723,907	908,898	38,332,558
Cost of Goods Sold	198,627,286	1,352,247	129,761,635
Direct Product Expenses	428,980,447	4,180,892	313,882,510
Sales Force	61,242,961	596,582	47,607,230
Other Marketing	9,014,523	333,318	5,264,258
General & Administrative	15,186,240	301,733	8,492,533
Cost of Money	2,791,240	29,927	0
Other Income/(Expense)	1,317,072	(7,539)	1,243,796
Investment Costs	0	0	0
Total Expenditures	515,898,339	5,449,992	374,002,735
Profit / Loss	245,082,569	(1,372,161)	180,699,658

Figure 11.12 P&Ls across countries.

sion, advertising blitz. Each investment type option defines a new possible P&L.

With these additions, we've taken a simple columnar P&L and fleshed it out into a five-dimensional hypercube. The P&L accounts are organized according to investment strategy, country, product, and year dimensions. They contain forecast P&Ls by product segment and country under different high-level corporate strategies.

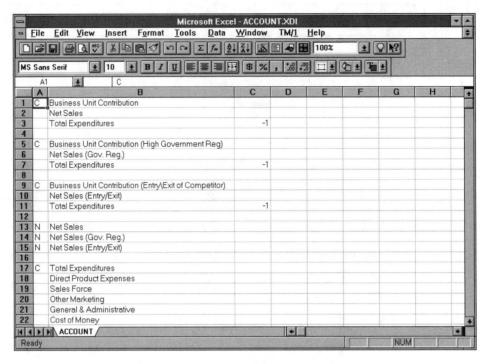

Figure 11.13 The accounts dimension.

Account   The account dimension defines the variables for the P&L cube. It contains all the relevant figures for calculating profits and losses (see Figure 11.13). *Net Sales* represents total income due to product sales. *Advertising, Distribution, Promotion, Cost of Goods Gold, Sales Force,* and *General Administrative* are account variables that contain the expenses from their respective sources. *Other Marketing* and *Other Income(Expense)* contain additional expenses incurred for reasons other than the main budgeting categories listed above. *Cost of Money* involves the losses due to economic transactions and exchanges necessary with the corporation's divisions in other countries. *Investment Costs* are the additional expenditures required for the different investment strategies the company may pursue.

Complex variables in the account dimension are described below.

❑ Direct Product Expenses is the total of Advertising, Distribution, Promotion, and Cost of Goods Sold.

❑ Total Expenditures combines Direct Product Expenses with the Sales Force, General Administrative, Other Marketing, and Other Income (Expense).

❏ Business Unit Contribution is the company's total net profit/loss (Net Sales – Total Expenditures).

There is a *Business Unit Contribution* variable and a *Net Sales* variable for each of the three scenarios from the market potential cube. The external-factors scenario dimension of the market-potential cube could have been added to the P&L cube as well. This would have provided a tighter integration of the P&Ls with the potential combinations of scenarios and investment strategies (described in the next subsection), but it would also have required more work to create all of the rules that would fill in the combinations and would have added to the model size, while the various expense variables were assumed to be the same under each scenario. So, three versions of the relevant variables were created. (If additional scenarios became desired, adding a separate scenario dimension would become more desirable because the tool would automatically keep everything in sync.)

The costs/expenditures are entered at the *All Men's*, *All Women's*, *All Boys'* and/or *All Girls'* members because they can't always be differentiated by product type. For example, the commercial advertising for all types of boys' clothing may be done together, making it difficult to distinguish advertising costs for boys' shirts versus boys' pants. Thus, it only makes sense to view costs/expenditures at the product-line level. The business unit contributions entered for these members cover the overhead costs associated with each of the lines.

Invstrat (Investment Strategy)   The investment strategy dimension (called "invstrat") was designed to evaluate the viability of investing in different ways. Examine the investment strategy dimension (see Figure 11.14). The *Baseline Case* represents what will happen if the company continues on its current course. Three strategies are represented here:

1. The *Product Line Extension Case* projects the effects of increasing profits by creating/selling new types of a product (for example, a new brand of men's shirts).

2. The *Geographic Expansion Case* reflects expanding the number of outlets or regions in a country that sell a particular product.

3. The *Advertising Blitz Case* involves a massive investment in the advertising and promotion of a product line.

Prod. Delta, Geog. Delta, and *Adv. Delta* reflect the *additional* profits/losses accrued in each of the three scenarios. So, for example, the *Product Extension Case* is equal to the *Baseline Case* plus the *Product Extension Delta*. Once again, the summation operation is implicit to the hierarchy in TM/1.

Now that we've looked at the dimensions of the multicube model, let's see how the model works. We will start with the market potential hypercube.

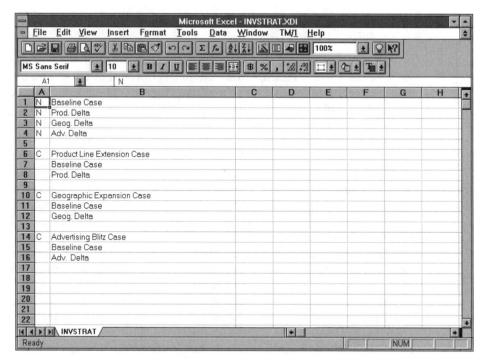

Figure 11.14 The investment strategy dimension.

The Solution in Action

Benefits of Dimensional Organization for Analyzing Market Potential

The market-potential hypercube holds the relevant information about the state of the product markets. Let's examine the cube and discuss its analytical capabilities.

Creating the Market Potential Hypercube

Once the dimensions have been created, we can combine them to form the necessary hypercubes. The following section will step you through the process of creating your own market-potential cube (called *mymarket*) with the prepared dimensions.

Click on TM/1, then click on the Tables menu choice.

[TM/1 - Tables Menu] (See Figure 11.15)

Click on Create.

Figure 11.15 Select "Create."

[Create a Table]

Type *mymarket* (see Figure 11.16), then click OK.

Figure 11.16 Name your table "mymarket."

[Creating Table: mymarket]

Each label represents a dimension that we can use for our hypercube; we will use five. Click on the arrow next to the blank box adjoining to label 1, which will expose a drop-down list box containing the names of the dimensions. Then, click on country (*country* should appear in the box). Repeat this process for the next labels (2 through 5), adding the dimensions products, scenario, variable, and year (see Figure 11.17). Now, click OK and we're done!

Figure 11.17 Selecting dimensions for "mymarket."

We would create any other hypercube in exactly the same manner.

Viewing Your Market Potential Hypercube

Let's examine the hypercube we've just created. Click on TM/1, then the Tables menu choice.

[TM/1 - Tables Menu]

Click Browse.

[Select Table to Browse] (See Figure 11.18)

Click on mymarket and then click OK.

Figure 11.18 Select "mymarket."

[View [Unnamed] - Table: mymarket]

This is the panel used to view the *mymarket* cube. There are three columns in this panel in which the dimensions can be placed (see Figure 11.19). The dimensions in the left-most column (over the *File...* button) are page dimensions for this view. Only one member will be used from these dimensions to form the view. In this case, country is set to *World*, products is set to *Total Clothing*, and scenario is set to *Status Quo*. The dimensions placed in the middle column (over the *Options...* button, currently the variable dimension) form the rows of the view; the dimensions in the right-most column (over the *Show* button, currently the year dimension) form the columns of the view. For dimensions used to form rows and columns, the lower the place of dimension tile in the column, the more nested the dimension. (Review Chapter 3 for a discussion of nesting dimensions for display.)

Figure 11.19 The browse box for the spreadsheet.

[View [Unnamed] - Table: mymarket]

Click <u>Close</u> to end our examination of *mymarket*.

Now we'll open the original market potential hypercube that has already been created, called *markpot*, using the same procedure as above. Click on <u>TM/1</u>, then the <u>Tables</u> menu choice.

[TM/1 - Tables Menu]

Click <u>Browse</u>.

[Select Table to Browse]

Click on <u>markpot</u> and then click <u>OK</u>.

We're ready to view the market potential cube.

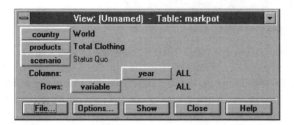

Figure 11.20 The market potential browse box.

The market potential cube is composed of the country, products, scenario, variable, and year dimensions (see Figure 11.20). By specifying which dimensions are placed on the rows and columns of the display (and which are placed in the page area), we can examine particular "slices" of the market information.

Suppose, for example, that we want to examine the status quo state of the men's shirts market in China over the next five years. In terms of the multidimensional tool, this means we want to select the country *China*, the product *Men's Shirts*, and the scenario *Status Quo* as the page elements of the view, with the dimensions variable and year as rows and columns of our view. We will do this by arranging the view box, as shown in Figure 11.21.

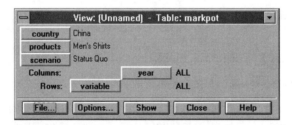

Figure 11.21 Rearranging the browse box.

Viewing the Men's Shirts' Market in China

[View: (Unnamed) - Table: markpot]

Click on the <u>country</u> dimension. This will bring up the dimension subset-editing window, as shown in Figure 11.22.

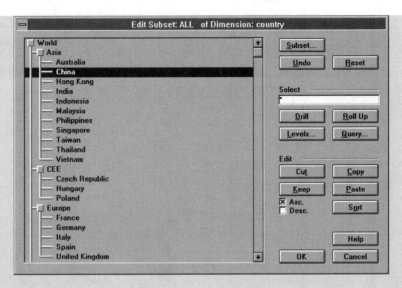

Figure 11.22 The dimension subset editing window.

[Select Element of Dimension: country]

Click on <u>China</u>, then click <u>OK</u>.

[View: (Unnamed) - Table: markpot]

Click on the <u>products</u> dimension.

[Select Element of Dimension: products]

Click on <u>Men's Shirts</u>, then click <u>OK</u>.

[View: (Unnamed) - Table: markpot]

To view this slice, click <u>Show.</u>

This view shows us the projected market variables for Men's Shirts in China over the next five years (see Figure 11.23).

Suppose that as a result of looking at these numbers, we now wish to view them in the context of the Men's Shirts' market in other countries. Let's do this for 1995 first.

In multidimensional terms, we want to keep looking at the product *Men's Shirts* and the scenario *Status Quo*, but we want to focus on the year *1995* while looking at variables across all of the countries. To make it easier to view all the data, we'll move the country dimension to the rows and the variable

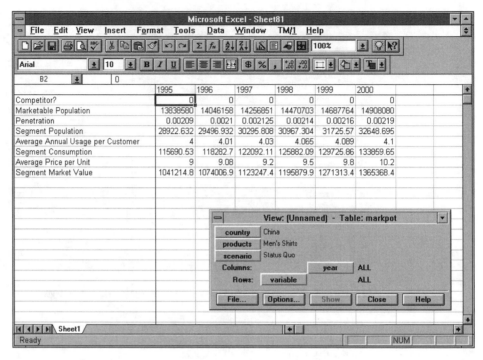

Figure 11.23 Projected market variables.

dimension to the columns. We don't wish to view all the members of the country dimension (which include regions and the whole world), just the individual countries. This means that we want to select only the leaf members of the country dimension for the rows of our "slice."

Viewing the Men's Shirts Market Across Countries

To compare market variables by country, we want to configure the browse box so that all but the country and variable dimensions are held in pages, as shown in Figure 11.24. To do this, we need to "drag" the year dimension into the left-most column. (Place the mouse pointer over the *year* dimension, then press down on the left mouse button; don't release the mouse button until you've moved the mouse pointer into the left-most column. Once you release the mouse button, the *year* dimension should then appear in the left-most column.) The *year* dimension will be set to *1995*, which will show next to the raised box representing the *year* dimension.

Figure 11.24 Defining a view to compare variables by country.

Now, we need to move the variable and country dimensions. Drag the *variable* dimension from the middle column to the right-most column. Drag the *country* dimension from the left-most column to the middle column. Click on <u>country</u>.

[Edit Subset ALL of Dimension: Country]

This is a structured representation of the country dimension. We want all leaf elements, which TM/1 will let us select by their hierarchical level. Click on <u>Levels</u>.

[Select Levels]

TM/1 counts hierarchical levels up from the leaves (see the discussion of hierarchy levels in Chapter 4). Leaves are considered level 0, so click <u>0</u>, then click <u>OK</u>. This lists all the individual leaf elements (our countries) of the country dimension. Click on the scroll bar's down arrow to view the rest of the countries (but don't click on any of the individual countries). Click <u>OK</u> to choose them all as shown.

[View: (Unnamed) - Table: markpot]

Click on <u>Show</u>. You may want to minimize the panel so that you can see the entire screen. (To minimize, click on the arrow in the top-right corner. It will float on top of the spreadsheet; you can't lose it off your screen. To return it to normal size, double-click on the mini-mized box.)

This view allows us to examine the market information for each country in Men's Shirts in 1995 (see Figure 11.25).

We know that many of the Asian countries' economies are expanding, so let's continue our analysis by looking out one year and focusing on Asia. We

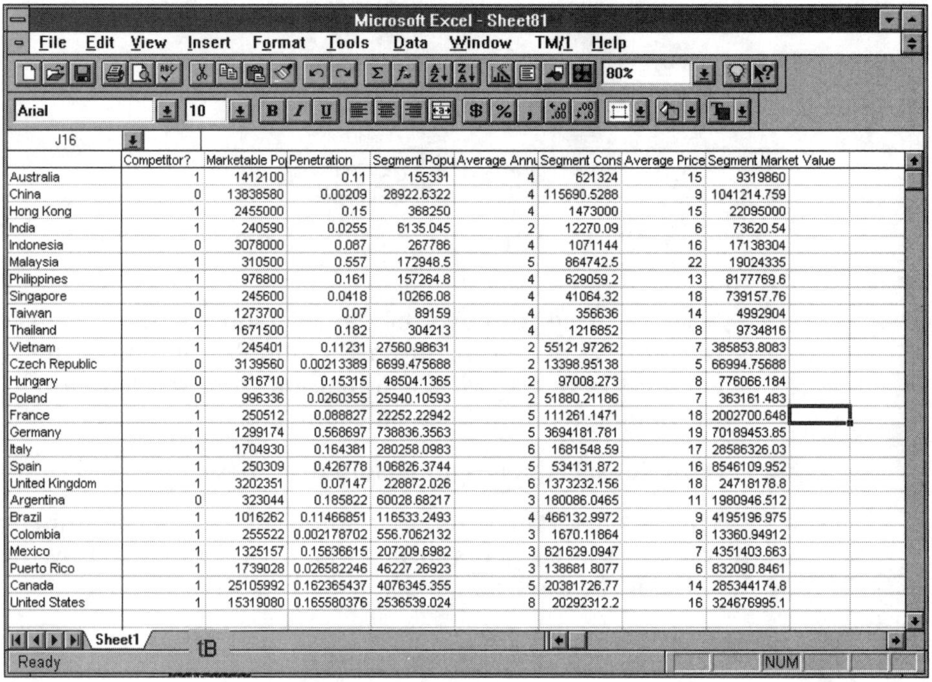

	Competitor?	Marketable Po	Penetration	Segment Popu	Average Annu	Segment Cons	Average Price	Segment Market Value
Australia	1	1412100	0.11	155331	4	621324	15	9319860
China	0	13838580	0.00209	28922.6322	4	115690.5288	9	1041214.759
Hong Kong	1	2455000	0.15	368250	4	1473000	15	22095000
India	1	240590	0.0255	6135.045	2	12270.09	6	73620.54
Indonesia	0	3078000	0.087	267786	4	1071144	16	17138304
Malaysia	1	310500	0.557	172948.5	5	864742.5	22	19024335
Philippines	1	976800	0.161	157264.8	4	629059.2	13	8177769.6
Singapore	1	245600	0.0418	10266.08	4	41064.32	18	739157.76
Taiwan	0	1273700	0.07	89159	4	356636	14	4992904
Thailand	1	1671500	0.182	304213	4	1216852	8	9734816
Vietnam	1	245401	0.11231	27560.98631	2	55121.97262	7	385853.8083
Czech Republic	0	3139560	0.00213389	6699.475688	2	13398.95138	5	66994.75688
Hungary	0	316710	0.15315	48504.1365	2	97008.273	8	776066.184
Poland	0	996336	0.0260355	25940.10593	2	51880.21186	7	363161.483
France	1	250512	0.088827	22252.22942	5	111261.1471	18	2002700.648
Germany	1	1299174	0.568697	738836.3563	5	3694181.781	19	70189453.85
Italy	1	1704930	0.164381	280258.0983	6	1681548.59	17	28586326.03
Spain	1	250309	0.426778	106826.3744	5	534131.872	16	8546109.952
United Kingdom	1	3202351	0.07147	228872.026	6	1373232.156	18	24718178.8
Argentina	0	323044	0.185822	60028.68217	3	180086.0465	11	1980946.512
Brazil	1	1016262	0.11466851	116533.2493	4	466132.9972	9	4195196.975
Colombia	1	255522	0.002178702	556.7062132	3	1670.11864	8	13360.94912
Mexico	1	1325157	0.15636615	207209.6982	3	621629.0947	7	4351403.663
Puerto Rico	1	1739028	0.026582246	46227.26923	3	138681.8077	6	832090.8461
Canada	1	25105992	0.162365437	4076345.355	5	20381726.77	14	285344174.8
United States	1	15319080	0.165580376	2536539.024	8	20292312.2	16	324676995.1

Figure 11.25 Viewing data for Men's Shirts in 1995 by country and variable.

will shift our attention to looking at both the countries within Asia and Asia as a whole, so we can compare countries against the regional aggregate. This means we will want to change the year to 1996 and to select both the region member *Asia* and its country child members for the rows. This will give us the view shown in Figure 11.26.

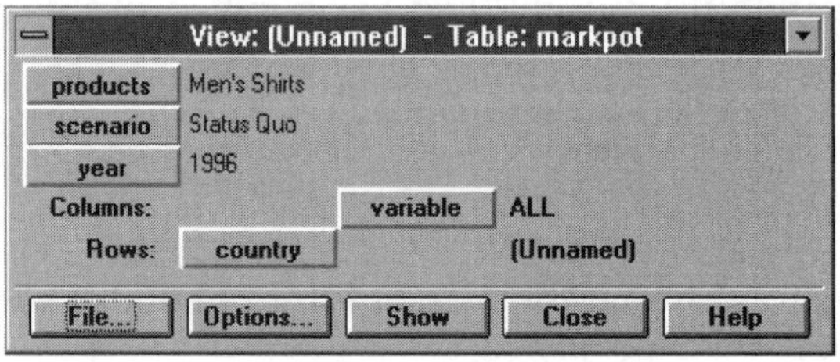

Figure 11.26 Defining a new view.

<u>Viewing the Asian Men's Shirts' Market</u>

(If you minimized the view panel, then double-click on it now to restore it.)

[View: (Unnamed) - Table: markpot]

Click on <u>year.</u>

[Select Element of Dimension: year]

Click on <u>1996</u>, then click <u>OK</u>.

[View: (Unnamed) - Table: markpot]

Now click on the <u>country</u> dimension.

[Select Element of Dimension: country]

Click on <u>Reset</u> to display all the dimension's members. We're only interested in Asia, so click on <u>Asia</u>, then click <u>Keep</u>. (See Figure 11.27.) Asia should be the only element in the dimension "kept." We want all the child elements of Asia. Asia should be highlighted (if it is not, click on <u>Asia</u>), so click on <u>Drill</u> (see Figure 11.28). (If you don't have the Drill function, you are not in *Advanced Mode. See the previous Section, "Dimensional Structure of the Model," to learn how to set all the hypercubes in Advanced Mode from the start.*) We now have all the desired countries.

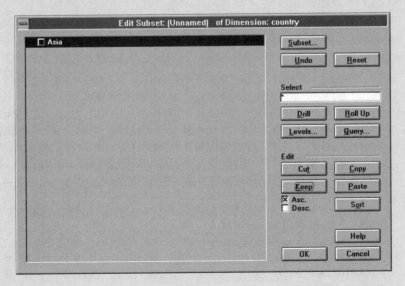

Figure 11.27 Selecting Asia.

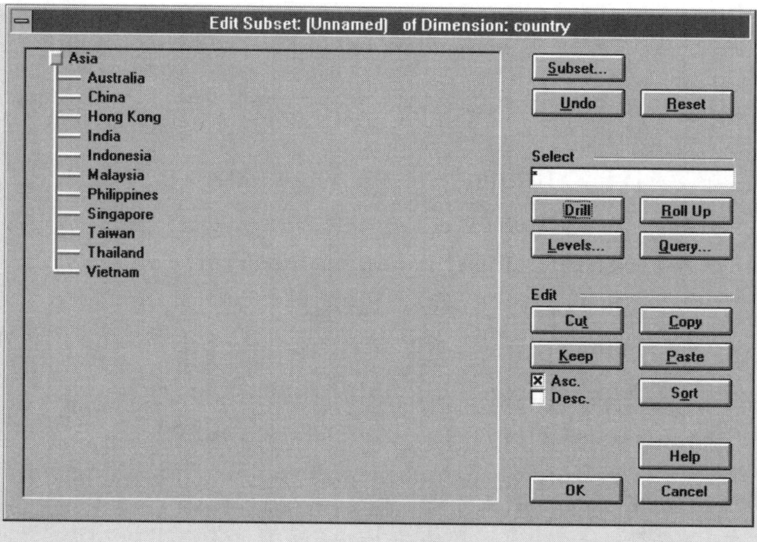

Figure 11.28 Selecting Asia's children.

Click <u>OK</u>.

[View: (Unnamed) - Table: markpot]

Click <u>Show</u>.

Examine this "slice" of the database (shown in Figure 11.29). We notice that two modifications are needed for the model.

First, look at the *Competitor?* variable. It is a flag indicating the presence of a competitor and is supposed to be either 0 or 1; for Asia, it has a value of 8. This is a useless aggregation. Because parent elements are initially set to be the sums of their child elements, the model is summing the *Competitor?* variable for Asia from its component countries. As we look at sums over product lines, this will become a confusing and essentially useless figure. (We will resolve this later on by creating a rule that makes the competitor rule inapplicable for parent elements.)

Now look at the figures for *Average Price Per Unit*. Notice that Asia's average price is much larger than the average prices in each of the individual countries, which can't be correct. As we described before, TM/1 (like most other OLAP tools) automatically sums variables up the dimensional hierarchies. For a value like price that needs to be averaged, this produces an incor-

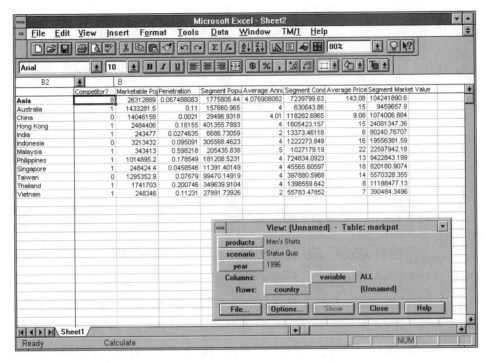

Figure 11.29 Viewing countries in Asia by variable.

rect value. Every parent element will have this same error; thus, we need to create a formula (rule) for calculating average price.

We established earlier that:

*Segment Market Value = Avg. Price Per Unit * Segment Consumption*

The *Segment Market Value* is calculated by computing *Avg. Price Per Unit * Segment Consumption* per country and summing these products up the country hierarchy (the value of a big market is the sum of the values of each part of it). The *Segment Consumption* is likewise calculated by summing from countries because it measures total quantity of product consumed across all consumers. Therefore, the average price per unit at an aggregated level is simply the ratio between these two aggregated values. So, we can devise a rule to divide the segment market value by segment consumption:

Avg. Price Per Unit = Segment Market Value / Segment Consumption

at aggregated levels only.

Adding Rules to a TM/1 Model

[View: (Unnamed) - Table: markpot]

Click Close.

Click on the TM/1 menu, then click on the Rules menu choice.

[TM/1 - Rules Menu]

Click on Open.

[Select Rules Worksheet]

Click on markpot, then click OK. Your rule sheet should appear like that of Figure 11.30.

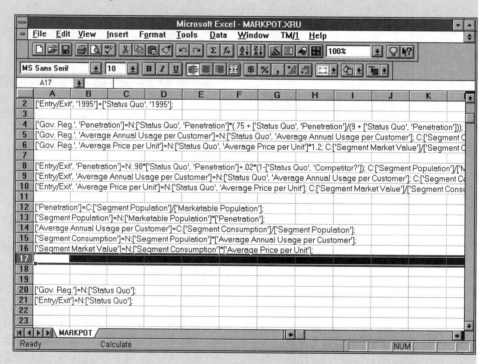

Figure 11.30 The rules sheet.

[MARKPOT.XRU]

We are going to add a rule here. TM/1 requires rules to be in a particular order, which in this case will mean that we want to put the new rule after the first three sections of rules in the rules worksheet. Let's put it in row 17. Click on row 17, on the 17 that is part of the worksheet margin. With the entire row highlighted, click on the TM/l menu, then click on the Edit Formula menu choice.

[Edit Rule Formula] (See Figure 11.31.)

This dialog simplifies the creation of rules to a point-and-click exercise, which is useful in long formulas when the chance of a typo is high. Click on [...].

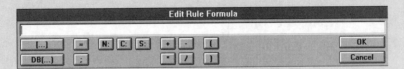

Figure 11.31 Creating a rule sheet formula, step 1.

[Reference to Markpot] (See Figure 11.32.)

This allows us to select elements from the hypercube to be used in our formula. First, we'll select *Avg. Price Per Unit*. Click on variable.

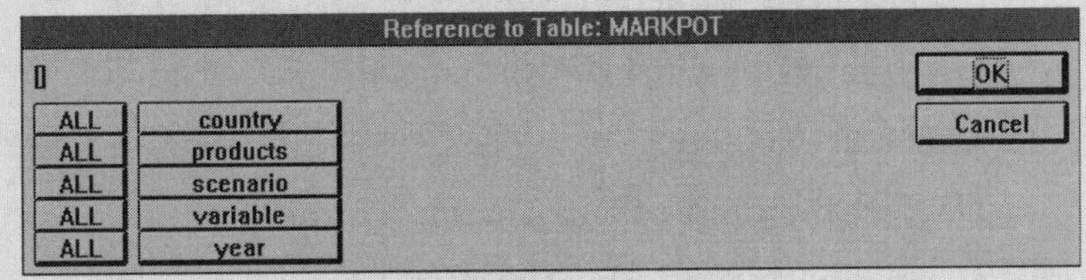

Figure 11.32 Creating a rule sheet formula, step 2.

[Select Element of Dimension: variable]

Click on Avg. Price Per Unit, then click OK. (See Figure 11.33.) Click OK.

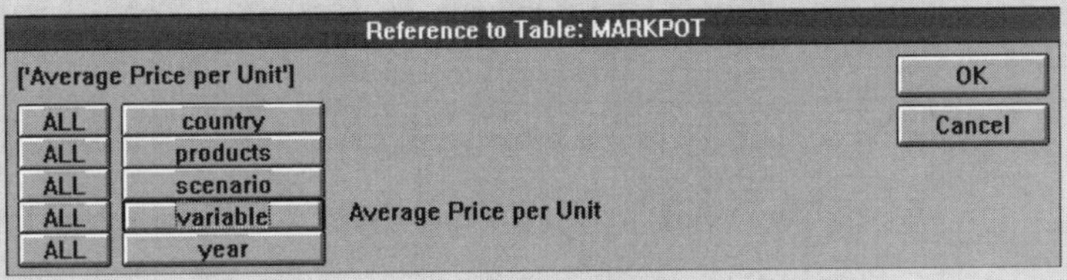

Figure 11.33 Creating a rule sheet formula, step 3.

Click $=$, then click C: (see Figure 11.34). "C:" specifies that the rule be used only for consolidated (parent) elements.

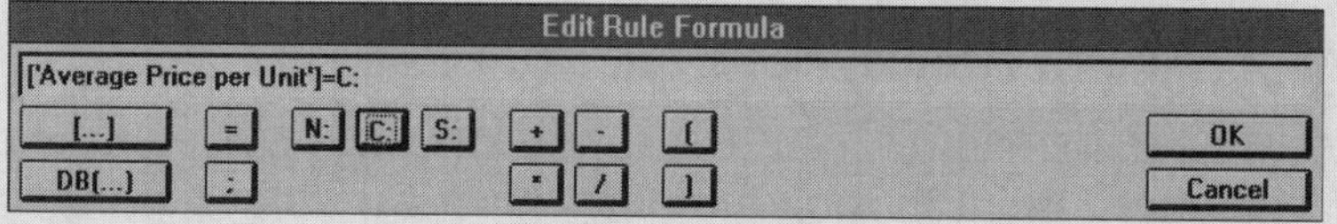

Edit Rule Formula

['Average Price per Unit']=C:

[...] [=] N: C: S: [+] [-] [(]   OK

DB[...] [:]   [*] [/] [)]   Cancel

Figure 11.34 Creating a rule sheet formula, step 4.

Again, click on [...].

[Reference to Markpot]

Click on variable.

[Select Element of Dimension: variable]

Click on Segment Market Value, then click OK

[Reference to Markpot]

Click OK.

Then click on the division sign /. Click on [...].

[Reference to Markpot]

Click on variable.

[Select Element of Dimension: variable]

Click on Segment Consumption, then click OK.

[Reference to Markpot]

Click OK.

Click on the semicolon ; to complete the rule (see Figure 11.35). Click OK. Note that the rule has been added to the worksheet.

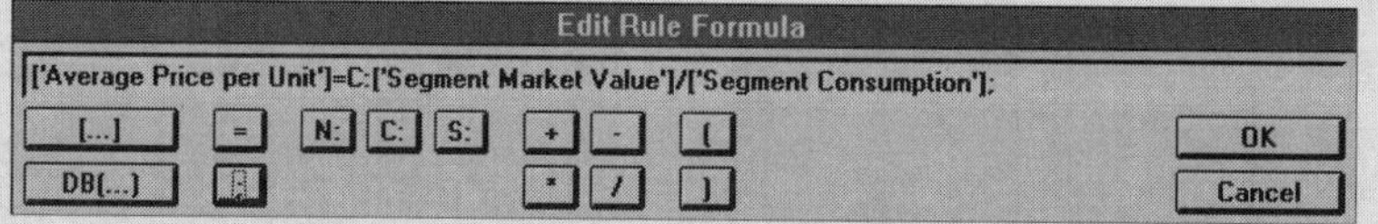

Edit Rule Formula

['Average Price per Unit']=C:['Segment Market Value']/['Segment Consumption'];

[...] [=] N: C: S: [+] [-] [(]   OK

DB[...] [:]   [*] [/] [)]   Cancel

Figure 11.35 Creating a rule sheet formula, step 5.

Now let's add the *Competitor?* rule to prevent the *Competitor?* variable from uselessly aggregating. This rule is short, so we will just type it in. Click on row 22, then type:

['Competitor?'] = C: 0/0;

(In TM/1; *C: 0/0* tells the database that this value is undefined for all consolidated elements.)

Now we must save and update the rules file. Click on <u>TM/1</u> and click on the <u>Rules</u> menu choice.

[TM/1 - Rules Menu]

Click on <u>Save</u>. (If there is an error message, make sure the rules were typed in correctly, then try saving again.) The rules have now been updated. You can close the Excel spreadsheet now if you wish.

Once this new rule has been added, the hypercube will give us the appropriate values. Now we continue with our analysis.

Perhaps sales of imported clothing are surging throughout Asia. Consequently, the market share of their domestic manufacturers is shrinking, and it is prudent to look at how the competitive landscape might change as a result. Let us zoom out to look at the segment market value for the clothing market in general and compare the projected effects of high government regulation with the status quo over the next five years. In terms of the multidimensional tool, we want the products dimension to be set to *Total clothing* and the variable to *Segment Market Value*. We want to view multiple members from three dimensions on our two-dimensional screen and, in particular, to compare the *Status Quo* and *Gov. Reg.* scenarios per country and year. To view the *Status Quo* and *Gov. Reg.* scenarios alongside each other in each country, we will "nest" the scenario dimension in the country dimension; both the scenario dimension and the country dimension will be in the rows of the view (as indicated by Figure 11.36).

Figure 11.36 Browse box for comparing scenarios.

Nesting Dimensions for Comparison Purposes

First, let's reopen the "markpot" cube. Click on the TM/1 menu, then the Tables menu choice.

[TM/1 - Tables Menu]

Click Browse.

[Select Table to Browse]

Click on markpot and then click OK.

[View [Unnamed] - Table: markpot]

Because we have updated the database, all the dimensions are reset to their original positions (which were shown in Figure 11.20). Drag the variable dimension into the left-most column. Click on variable.

[Select One Element of Dimension: variable]

Click on Segment Market Value, then click OK. Drag the country dimension to the middle column. Click on country.

[Edit Subset ALL of Dimension: country]

Click on Asia, then click Keep. Now, click on Drill, then click OK.

[View [Unnamed] - Table: markpot]

Drag the scenario dimension *beneath* the country dimension in the middle column. Click on scenario.

[Edit Subset ALL of Dimension: scenario]

Hold down the *control* key on the keyboard (this allows you to select multiple elements), and click on Status Quo and Gov. Reg. Click OK.

[View [Unnamed] - Table: markpot]

Click Show.

[Browse Options]

Click on the arrow next to *number format*, and select 0. Click on the up arrow next to *Min. Column Width*, until the number showing next to the arrow is *13*. Click OK.

[View [Unnamed] - Table: markpot]

Click Show.

		1995	1996	1997	1998	1999	2000
Asia	Status Quo	1,244,229,590	1,391,597,513	1,572,678,123	1,760,777,720	1,967,328,035	2,220,397,717
	Gov. Reg.	1,244,229,590	1,330,471,689	1,503,940,222	1,684,207,820	1,882,816,426	2,125,994,992
Australia	Status Quo	76,284,001	83,167,473	90,031,753	97,488,784	106,178,127	113,269,955
	Gov. Reg.	76,284,001	76,164,928	82,442,139	89,269,177	97,232,078	103,790,285
China	Status Quo	65,715,277	80,978,713	100,990,209	125,993,881	157,216,474	195,039,869
	Gov. Reg.	65,715,277	74,679,620	93,259,058	116,511,257	145,597,017	180,930,068
Hong Kong	Status Quo	57,832,692	64,426,563	71,859,293	80,095,970	89,240,417	98,733,895
	Gov. Reg.	57,832,692	60,472,278	67,791,610	75,996,897	85,234,644	95,044,782
India	Status Quo	147,884	161,479	175,858	191,839	209,064	228,432
	Gov. Reg.	147,884	145,917	158,959	173,463	189,104	206,702
Indonesia	Status Quo	62,395,651	90,983,720	108,384,400	129,455,286	155,315,203	175,694,408
	Gov. Reg.	62,395,651	83,793,353	99,908,171	119,428,693	143,417,917	162,658,405
Malaysia	Status Quo	107,831,873	120,346,137	134,324,223	150,085,846	167,893,402	187,300,694
	Gov. Reg.	107,831,873	111,716,232	124,935,209	139,898,224	156,875,598	175,513,597
Philippines	Status Quo	291,956,862	314,882,121	366,444,387	414,482,812	459,292,586	543,421,520
	Gov. Reg.	291,956,862	304,964,364	353,967,456	399,927,110	443,427,512	523,425,779
Singapore	Status Quo	23,192,986	26,666,531	30,766,508	36,473,367	43,647,186	53,537,115
	Gov. Reg.	23,192,986	24,505,757	28,298,204	33,579,533	40,211,610	49,380,825
Taiwan	Status Quo	120,262,486	125,040,779	130,137,677	135,132,697	140,850,722	145,935,622
	Gov. Reg.	120,262,486	116,984,556	121,942,760	126,804,276	132,361,181	137,282,870
Thailand	Status Quo	429,236,555	474,281,611	527,661,633	578,218,216	633,185,114	691,657,490
	Gov. Reg.	429,236,555	467,348,538	520,410,525	570,644,778	625,248,503	683,560,674
Vietnam	Status Quo	9,373,323	10,662,388	11,902,180	13,159,022	14,299,740	15,578,717
	Gov. Reg.	9,373,323	9,696,146	10,826,130	11,974,412	13,021,262	14,201,005

Figure 11.37 Comparing scenarios and countries.

It's hard to compare such large numbers in this form. Let's tell TM/1 to format the cells of the spreadsheet differently. To do this, click on Options.

Now for each country we have the high government regulation scenario listed directly below the status quo scenario; we can compare the markets for any country that we choose (see Figure 11.37).

We have seen in this section how analysis of a market-sizing model is made easier through multidimensional organization and the use of an OLAP tool to manipulate and view it. In the next section, we will explore the similar benefits that multidimensional organization provides for analyzing P&L statements.

Benefits of Dimensional Organization for Analyzing the P&L

The P&L hypercube contains the account information for the corporation organized by country, investment strategy (invstrat), products, and year. The five-dimensional structure of the cube allows for analysis against many different factors (see Figure 11.38).

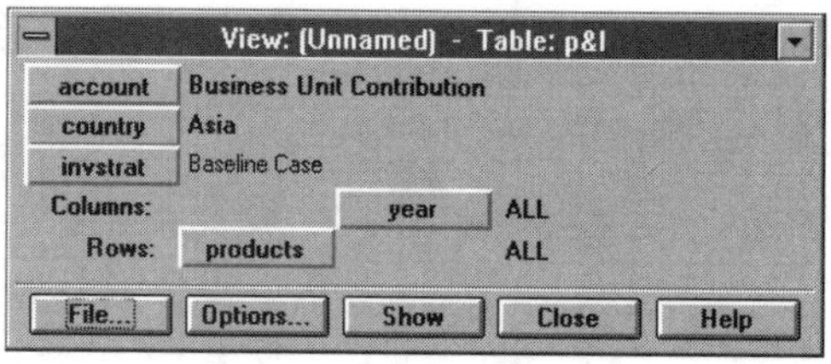

Figure 11.38 The P&L browse box.

Viewing the P&L Hypercube

[View [Unnamed] - Table: markpot]

Click <u>Close</u> to end our viewing of the market-potential cube. Click on <u>TM/1</u> menu, then click on the <u>Tables</u> menu choice.

[TM/1 - Tables Menu]

Click on <u>Browse</u>.

[Select Table to Browse]

Click on <u>p&l</u>, then click <u>OK</u>.

[View [Unnamed] - Table: p&l]

We are now reading to examine the P&L cube.

Analyzing the U.S. P&L

Viewing WearCo's Current P&L in the United States The majority of the company's sales are in the United States. Suppose the company wishes to view the business unit contribution to the company over the next five years, in combination with its net sales and total expenditures components. In

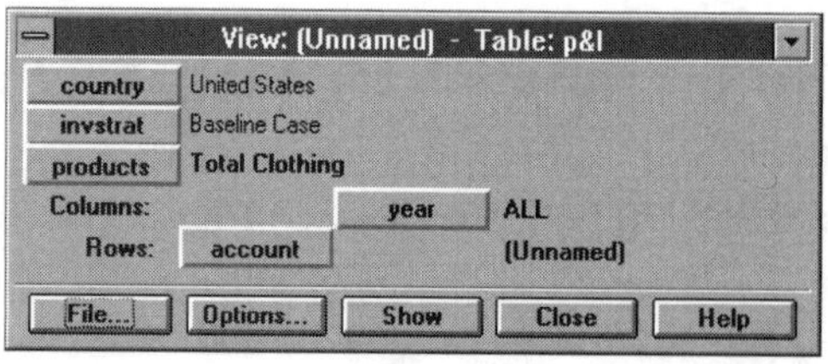

Figure 11.39 Rearranging the browse box to compare accounts.

terms of our multidimensional display, we want the country dimension to be set to *United States*, products to *Total Clothing*, investment strategy to *Baseline Case*, and *account* and *year* set as the rows and columns. Figure 11.39 shows us the view arrangement we are going to construct.

Viewing U.S. Profits/Losses over the Next Five Years

[View [Unnamed] - Table: p&l]

Drag the products dimension into the left-most column. It should say *Total Clothing*. Drag the account dimension to the middle column. Click on account.

[Edit Subset ALL of Dimension: account]

Click on Business Unit Contribution, then click on Keep. *Business Unit Contribution* should be the only element remaining. We want to look at the children of the Business Unit Contribution as well, so click on Drill. You should now have *Business Unit Contribution, Net Sales, and Total Expenditures*. Click OK.

[View [Unnamed] - Table: p&l]

Click on country.

[Select One Element of Dimension: country]

Because this dimension is shared between the two hypercubes, TM/1 has retained the set of members we were last viewing in the market-potential cube. Click on Reset to show all the country dimension members. Scroll down the list of countries until you find *United States*, then click on United States. Click OK.

[View [Unnamed] - Table: p&l]

Invstrat is already set to *Baseline Case*. Because the numbers will be big, click on Options.

[Browse Options]

Click on the arrow next to *number format*, and select 0. Click on the up arrow next to *Min. Column Width*, until the number *13* shows for the width. Click OK.

[View [Unnamed] - Table: p&l]

Click on Show.

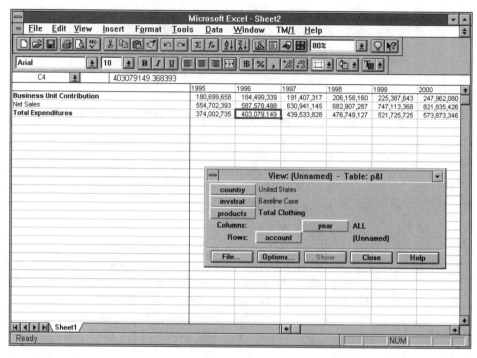

Figure 11.40 Viewing business contributions by time.

We are able to examine the projected profits for the U.S. business unit over the next five years, as shown in Figure 11.40. We can see from this "slice" that the profits are projected to continue to increase over this period. Let's drill down on the total expenditures to get a more complete picture of the P&L.

Drilling Down on Total Expenditures

[View [Unnamed] - Table: p&l]

Click on account.

[Edit Subset ALL of Dimension: account]

Click on Total Expenditures, then click on Drill. This breakdown of total expenditures still has another consolidated element, *Direct Product Expenses*. Click on Direct Product Expenses, then click on Drill. Click OK.

[View [Unnamed] - Table: p&l]

Click <u>Show</u>.

We now have Business Unit Contribution, with all the sales and costs broken down, as shown in Figure 11.41. Numbers in parentheses are negative values.

Which product lines are the major contributors to sales and costs? Let's examine the 1995 P&L, broken down by product. Because cost information is stored only on the product line level, it makes sense to break down total clothing into the four product lines, rather than looking at individual products. We want to set year to *1995* and look at the product dimension broken down into *Men's, Women's, Boys', and Girls'* (see Figure 11.42).

	1995	1996	1997	1998	1999	2000
Business Unit Contribution	180,699,658	184,499,339	191,407,317	206,158,160	225,387,643	247,962,080
Net Sales	554,702,393	587,578,488	630,941,145	682,907,287	747,113,368	821,835,426
Total Expenditures	374,002,735	403,079,149	439,533,828	476,749,127	521,725,725	573,873,346
Direct Product Expenses	313,882,510	337,306,805	366,153,882	395,714,313	432,289,040	474,476,399
Distribution	28,854,808	30,348,971	32,451,229	33,088,030	34,917,562	37,583,185
Advertising	116,933,509	128,187,105	141,249,406	156,505,116	176,835,122	199,994,321
Promotion	38,332,558	41,140,205	46,038,821	51,436,072	56,321,484	61,645,599
Cost of Goods Sold	129,761,635	137,630,525	146,414,427	154,685,094	164,214,872	175,253,294
Sales Force	47,607,230	49,409,627	53,617,294	58,148,805	62,958,184	68,497,488
Other Marketing	5,264,258	6,896,855	8,761,382	10,321,757	12,003,206	14,465,222
General & Administrative	8,492,533	9,294,566	10,779,399	12,278,325	14,104,540	15,951,447
Cost of Money	0	0	0	0	0	0
Other Income/(Expense)	1,243,796	(171,296)	(221,871)	(285,927)	(370,754)	(482,791)
Investment Costs	0	0	0	0	0	0

Figure 11.41 A breakdown of business unit contributions.

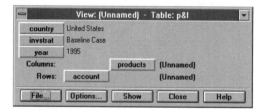

Figure 11.42 Reorganizing the view.

1995 U.S. P&L by Product Line

[View [Unnamed] - Table: p&l]

Drag *year* to the left-most column. It should be set to *1995*. Drag the *products* dimension to the right-most column. Click on <u>products</u>.

[Edit Subset ALL of Dimension: products]

We don't want to view any of the leaf elements. Click on <u>Levels</u>.

[Select Levels]

Click on <u>1</u>, then Control-click on <u>2</u>. Click <u>OK</u>.

[Edit Subset ALL of Dimension: products]

The dialog should look like the one shown in Figure 11.43. Click <u>OK</u>.

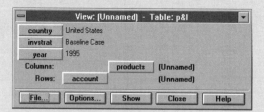

Figure 11.43 Subsetting a dimension.

[View [Unnamed] - Table: p&l]

Click <u>Show</u>.

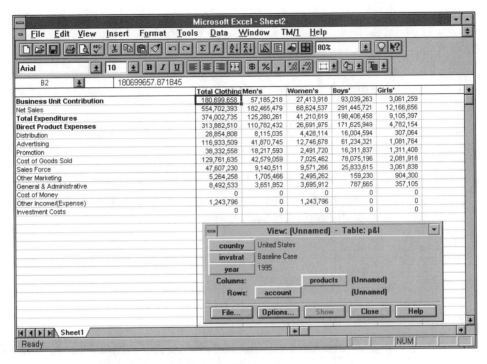

Figure 11.44 Sales and cost breakdown.

Now we can see the breakdown for sales and costs over product lines, as shown in Figure 11.44.

Note that most of the sales and costs stem from the Men's and Boys' product lines. To get a better sense of what's happening in each of these product lines over the next five years, let's examine the trends in the net sales of each of the product lines in that period. The *account* dimension will be set to *Net Sales*, the *product* dimension will be moved to the rows, and the *year* dimension will be moved into the columns (as shown in Figure 11.45).

View: (Unnamed) - Table: p&l		
country	United States	
invstrat	Baseline Case	
account	Net Sales	
Columns:	year	ALL
Rows:	products	(Unnamed)
File...	Options...	Show	Close	Help

Figure 11.45 Reorganizing the view.

U.S. Net Sales by Product Line

[View [Unnamed] - Table: p&l]

Drag the *account* dimension to the left-most column. Click on <u>account</u>.

[Select One Element of Dimension: account]

Click on <u>Net Sales</u>, then click <u>OK</u>.

[View [Unnamed] - Table: p&l]

Drag the products dimension to the middle column. Drag the year dimension to the right-most column. Click <u>Show</u>.

We now have a view of the increasing net sales in each product line over the next five years (also shown in Figure 11.46).

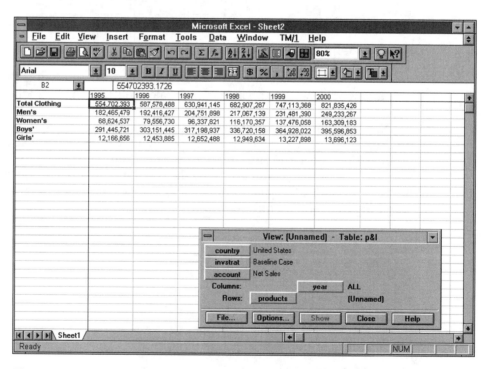

Figure 11.46 Viewing net sales by time.

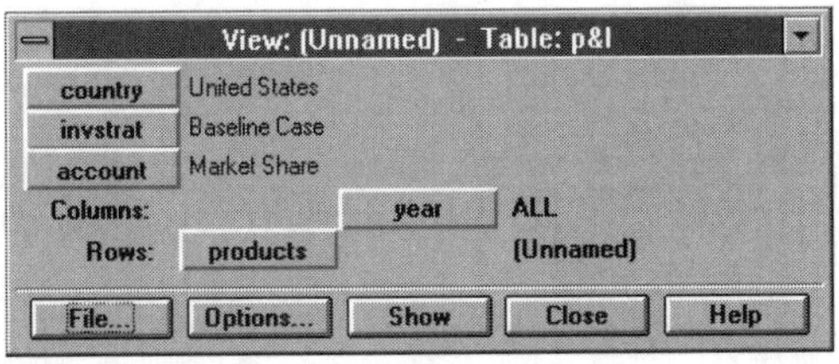

Figure 11.47 Reorganizing the view to view market share.

As with the market-sizing cube, examining forecast P&Ls from many different angles is made straightforward through multidimensional structuring and OLAP viewing and manipulation tools. Although each of these cubes stands on its own, they can feed data to each other to allow analyses that draw on them both. The next section explores some of the results that can be obtained through this approach.

Interlinking the Two Cubes

To evaluate the significance of the net values trends, we need to understand the market. Perhaps the market value has been increasing at a much greater rate than our net sales, and we're really slipping behind. Or the market value could actually be relatively constant, and our increases in net sales are due to winning over our competitor's customers. Essentially, we want to know what is happening to our *market share*. Market share is calculated by dividing net sales (in the P&L cube) by segment market value (in the markpot cube). TM/1 allows us to create rules that calculate figures using values from multiple cubes. The market share account in the P&L cube is computed from the P&L's net sales and the markpot cube's market value.

Let's put this to use in our analysis. We'll view the trends in the U.S. market share over the next five years by product line. Given our last view, we simply need to set *account* to *market share* (as shown in Figure 11.47).

<u>U.S. Market Share by Product Line</u>

[View [Unnamed] - Table: p&l]

Click on <u>account</u>.

[Select One Element of Dimension: account]

Click on <u>Reset</u>. Click on <u>market share</u>, then click <u>OK</u>.

[View [Unnamed] - Table: p&l]

Click <u>Show</u>.

We can't see any of the market share values because we've changed the options to help analyze large numbers. To change this again, click on <u>Options</u>.

[Browse Options]

Click on the down arrow next to *Number Format* to show the format choices, and click on <u>General</u>. Click <u>OK</u>.

[View [Unnamed] - Table: p&l]

Click <u>Show</u>.

Now we have a view of the market share by product line (shown in Figure 11.48). This gives us a clearer sense of what is happening in the U.S. market. The overall market share is increasing slightly in the United States because its market share is increasing in WearCo's two largest product lines: men's and

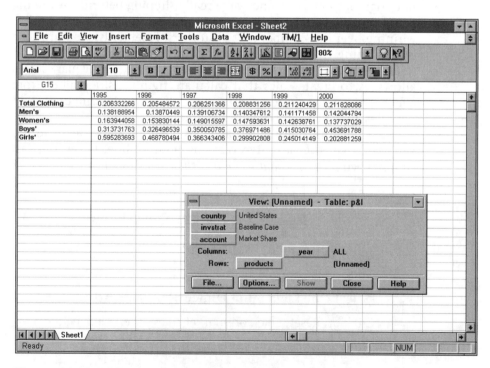

Figure 11.48 **Viewing market share data by product line and time.**

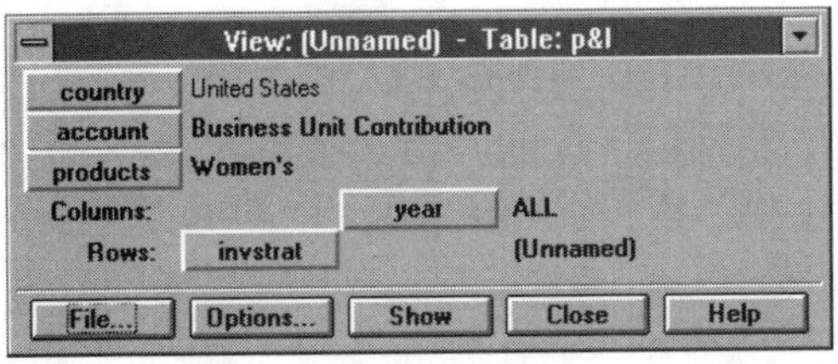

Figure 11.49 Reorganizing the view to compare investment strategies.

boys'. Even though net sales were increasing in women's and girls' clothing, however, they haven't been increasing with the market; in fact, their market shares are actually decreasing.

Our net sales in female clothing aren't keeping up with the expansion of the market. Is it worthwhile then to invest in these markets? If so, which type of investment strategy will be most beneficial?

Analyzing Alternative Investment Strategies   Let's analyze the women's clothing market first. Let's compare the profit from the baseline case against three different investment strategies: product-line expansion, geographic expansion, and advertising blitz. In terms of our TM/1 view, we want to set the *account* member to *Business Unit Contribution* and the *products* member to *Women's*, and to put the *invstrat* dimension in the rows, selecting *Baseline Case, Product Line Extension Case, Geographic Expansion Case,* and *Advertising Blitz Case*. We will construct the view as described in Figure 11.49.

<u>**Comparing Investment Strategies in the U.S. Women's Clothing Market**</u>

[View [Unnamed] - Table: p&l]

Click on <u>account</u>.

[Select One Element of Dimension: account]

Click on Business Unit Contribution, then click OK.

[View [Unnamed] - Table: p&l]

Drag the <u>products</u> dimension to the left-most column. Click on <u>products</u>.

[Select One Element of Dimension: products]

Click on <u>Women's</u>, then click <u>O</u>K.

[View [Unnamed] - Table: p&l]

Drag the <u>invstrat</u> dimension into the middle column. Click on <u>invstrat</u>.

[Edit Subset All of Dimension: invstrat]

Hold the Control key down and click on Baseline Case, Product Line Extension Case, Geographic Expansion Case, and Advertising Blitz Case. Click OK.

[View [Unnamed] - Table: p&l]

We're going to be seeing big numbers again. Click on Options.

[Browse Options]

Set the *Number Format* to 0. Click OK.

[View [Unnamed] - Table: p&l]

Click on Show.

Let's examine the different strategies (shown in Figure 11.50). Product line extension is consistently more profitable that geographic expansion over the next five years, so it's clearly the better of the two. Let's compare it with an advertising blitz. The advertising blitz has an immediate payoff that nets about $9 million more than product line extension over the next two years. However, in the long run, product line extension is significantly more profitable, creating a cumulative net profit of about $40 million over the advertising blitz in the years 1998–2000. Given the company's long-term focus, product line extension is the best strategy in the women's market. But what about in the girls' market? Let's set the product dimension to girls'.

Comparing Investment Strategies in the U.S. Girls' Clothing Market

[View [Unnamed] - Table: p&l]

Click on products.

[Select One Element of Dimension: products]

Click on Girls', then click OK.

[View [Unnamed] - Table: p&l]

Click on Show.

The resulting view is shown in Figure 11.51.

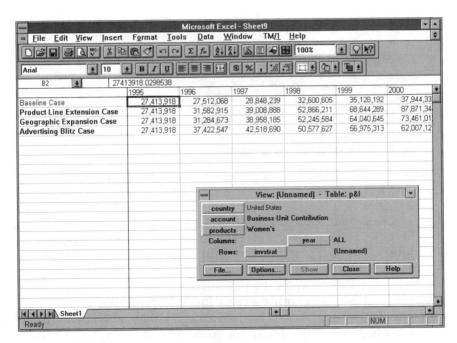

Figure 11.50 Comparing contributions for women's clothing by investment strategy over time.

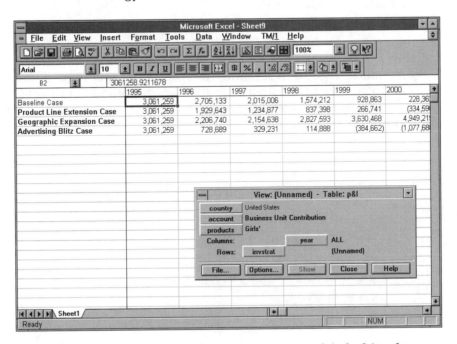

Figure 11.51 Comparing contributions from girls' clothing by investment strategy and time.

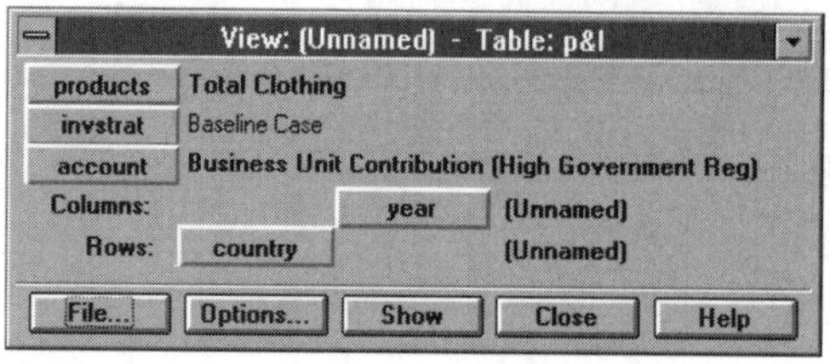

Figure 11.52 Reorganizing the view to compare countries.

The product line extension and advertising blitz are not cost-effective in the girls' market. However, expanding the number of outlets selling girls' clothing, though sustaining an initial net loss of $500,000 over the baseline case in 1996, creates millions in net profits for the company over the next five years. This provides the best strategy for girls' clothing. Referring back to Figure 11.50, geographic expansion was projected to be pretty good for women's clothing as well, so to the degree that geographic expansion would be applied to multiple lines, this could be a good way to go as well.

Analyzing the Asian P&L

Earlier, we examined the effect that high government regulation will have on the markets in the Asian countries, but how will it affect WearCo? Let's examine the corporation's net profits/losses in the Asian countries in the high government regulation scenario. In terms of our multidimensional view, we wish to set investment strategy to *Baseline case*, products to *Total Clothing*, account to *Business Unit Contribution (Gov. Reg.)*, and set Asia and the Asian countries as the rows of the "slice" (as described in Figure 11.52).

Viewing Profits/Losses in Asia Under High Government Regulation

[View [Unnamed] - Table: p&l]

Drag the invstrat dimension into the left-most column. *Baseline case* will automatically be selected. Drag account to the left-most column. Click on account.

[Select One Element of Dimension: account]

Click Reset. Click on Business Unit Contribution (High Government. Reg), then click OK.

[View [Unnamed] - Table: p&l]

Drag the country dimension to the middle column, then click on <u>country</u>.

[Edit Subset All of Dimension: country]

Click on <u>Asia</u>, then click <u>Keep</u>. Asia should be the only element on the screen. Click on <u>Drill</u>, then click <u>OK</u>.

[View [Unnamed] - Table: p&l]

Click on <u>year</u>.

[Edit Subset All of Dimension: year]

Hold down the control key and click on the years 1996 through 2000. Click <u>OK</u>.

[View [Unnamed] - Table: p&l]

Click on <u>products</u>.

[Edit Subset All of Dimension: products]

Click on <u>Total Clothing</u>, then click <u>OK</u>.

[View [Unnamed] - Table: p&l]

Click <u>Show.</u>

Now we can examine our profits/losses in the case of high government regulation (shown in Figure 11.53).

We are continuing to profit in most countries, yet we expect to consistently suffer losses over the next five years in Australia, India, and Singapore with our current strategy. What is the best course of action in these countries? Let's examine the Business Unit Contribution in these countries based on different investment strategies. We want to nest the invstrat dimension in the country dimension, so that we can compare the profits/losses of each strategy within each country. Then we want to select only Australia, India, and Singapore (see Figure 11.54).

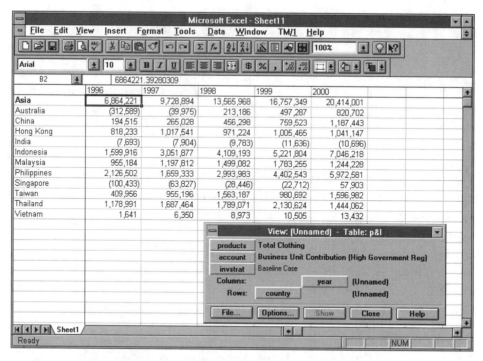

Figure 11.53 Comparing contributions by country under high government regulation.

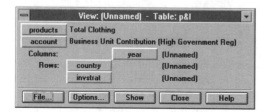

Figure 11.54 Changing the view.

Determining Strategies under High Government Regulation

[View [Unnamed] - Table: p&l]

Drag the <u>invstrat</u> dimension under the *country* dimension. (It was last set to the set of strategy members that we are interested in, so we don't need to pick them out.) Click on <u>country</u>.

[Edit Subset All of Dimension: country]

Hold down the Control key and click on <u>Australia</u>, <u>India</u>, and <u>Singapore</u>. Click <u>OK</u>.

[View [Unnamed] - Table: p&l]

Click <u>Show</u>.

We can now view the strategies by country (see Figure 11.55). In India we lose out in all three scenarios, so we are best off pulling out in the case of high government regulation. In Australia and Singapore, however, it is worth continuing in the market despite high government regulation, if we invest in a mass advertising campaign; the net profit for investment in advertising exceeds the profits of the other two strategies.

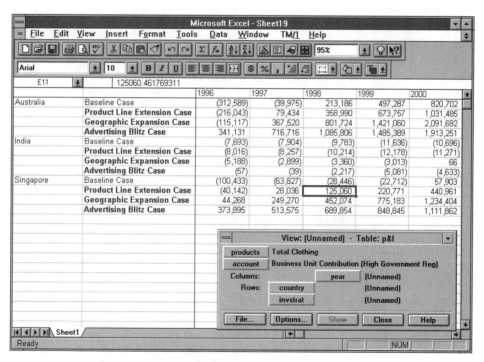

Figure 11.55 Comparing strategies by country.

Conclusion

PTG's client is now using a global strategic planning process and information infrastructure based on multidimensional technology. It helps management meet their global performance goals. Participation and input by key managers around the world is now possible. The OLAP solution facilitates effective team communication, ensuring rapid, broad sharing of information and faster decisions.

If you followed along with the tutorial, you should be familiar with the basic steps for constructing and using a hypercube: defining dimensions and aggregation formulas, defining variable formulas, joining information from two cubes, and organizing views for analysis.

12

Portfolio Analysis

This hands-on case study shows the use of spreadsheets as an interface to a multidimensional model within the context of portfolio analysis. It addresses issues of working with dimensions (stocks and portfolios in this model) that change over time, using conditional formulas, and specialized aggregation functions. The raw material for this chapter was provided by Tracy Peck in conjunction with MIS AG, a software firm specializing in training and support of TM/1 OLAP implementations.

The Situation at Equity Performance Inc. (EPI)

EPI is a provider of an independent third-party opinion as to how well portfolio managers have handled their portfolio during the quarter. Portfolio performances are rated on the basis of individual performance, as well as how they compare to the performance of the S&P 500, a market indicator like the Dow Jones Industrial Average. It represents a basket of stocks from the New York Stock Exchange. The managed portfolios are a collection of stocks held by very large companies. MIS AG was called in by EPI to help it improve its ability to provide that opinion.

Four people are currently involved in this process for EPI. One analyst prepares the tables and the analysis, and three assistants generate the output reports. Reports are prepared on a quarterly basis for 35 separately managed portfolios.

EPI uses two types of information as source data to perform its analysis: stock market data and portfolio holdings data. EPI purchases a stock database

315

from Ford Investor Services for the general stock market information. The Ford database, which is updated weekly, contains information about 3,360 stocks. For each stock there are roughly 110 indicators. Out of these, EPI needs about 16 basic indicators such as price, dividends, and earnings. This makes roughly 40,000 base data points per quarter taking up about three quarters of one megabyte. EPI gets its information about the portfolios directly from each portfolio manager.

The Ford data arrives on disk once a quarter and comes with its own data extraction routines that operate in DOS. The portfolio data comes directly from each of the portfolio managers on a daily basis in either spreadsheet files or hard copy.

As a part of its normal process, EPI needs to create a variety of financial calculations. For example, each stock's indicator provided by Fords needs to be weighted for each portfolio, by the stock's market value in that portfolio (defined as the stock price at time period x multiplied by the number of shares held at time x). When MIS AG was first called in to assess the situation, the Fords and portfolio data were maintained in files on a server to which EPI's staff could serially share access across a network. EPI relied exclusively on spreadsheets to perform the portfolio analyses. For the final client reports, Microsoft Word and Harvard Graphics were also employed.

The Problems with the Current State of Affairs

EPI was experiencing many problems trying to perform its quarterly portfolio management reports. Most, if not all of them, were attributable to EPI's use of spreadsheets as a data store and multiuser analysis environment. The problems listed below are typical of what MIS AG found.

- ❑ EPI had to load the entire Ford database into each Excel spreadsheet for each portfolio. It had no capacity to share the database across portfolios. There were too many files and lots of redundant data.

- ❑ The process was so laborious that valuations could be performed only on a quarterly basis.

- ❑ Reports had been custom programmed years ago and were no longer usable. There was no flexibility in either reporting formats or output items.

- ❑ EPI had problems creating hierarchical views, such as by industry and sector, from the stock data.

- ❑ Quarterly changes to items, such as the number of shares per stock in a portfolio, needed to be manually rekeyed in the analysis spreadsheets. If the number of shares owned by a portfolio or a stock price is incorrectly input, all aggregate calculations are thrown off, and it is very hard to find the cause of the error.

Applications took so long to build that they could offer their services only once per quarter instead of once per month. Out-of-date report macros and the need to rekey data did not make the system very friendly or flexible. The spreadsheet data store didn't allow multiple users to share the data. Working with spreadsheets also made it difficult to add hierarchical categories to their description of stocks and enable updates to flow through into the analysis model.

Recall the functional requirements for OLAP presented in Chapter 1: fast, flexible, shared access to lots of potentially complex derivations. EPI was experiencing problems with every one of the requirements!

MIS AGI's Project Goals for EPI

MIS AG and EPI identified the following attributes of an ideal solution:

- Sufficiently improved processing time should allow reports to be issued monthly, as opposed to quarterly.
- Users should be able to generate annual reports and historical reports.
- Users should be able to generate reports with a minimal amount of data handling.
- Unsophisticated users should be able to input data, access data, and generate output reports with little training or supervision.
- Users should only access the system through an Excel spreadsheet report form, not interact directly with the underlying database system.
- The preparation and population of the model should be simple, so that with the passage of time between quarters intricate and detailed steps would not be forgotten.
- The amount of data to be stored should be greatly reduced.
- Maintenance of applications should be minimal, yet flexible enough to expand in the future.
- Applications should be able to evolve. They may need to include new data items from Fords, may need to change time periods, have data applied to multiple periods, change data providers, and so on. These changes should not render the current application useless.
- Data should be consistent across portfolios. If two portfolios own AT&T, the price should be the same for the two portfolios, but the number of shares owned by each will differ. The calculations need to reflect this.
- Multiple (currently all four) users should be able to be on the system at the same time.

Given the need for complex number crunching, the existence of multiple dimensions, such as stock, portfolio, indicator and time, the need for multiple aggregation levels, and the need for multiple users, it was clear to MIS AG that an OLAP solution was needed to solve EPI's problems.

The OLAP Model

The first step toward implementing an OLAP solution is to gain a high-level view of EPI's data flow and of the cube structure required to provide that flow.

On the input side, data comes from two types of sources: the Fords stock database and from each portfolio that is evaluated. The Fords stock database provides standard measures, such as price and earnings information on 2,600 publicly traded stocks. The portfolio information describes, for each portfolio, how many shares of each stock the portfolio contains. On the output side, EPI's analysts need to work with spreadsheet views that show how each portfolio fared in isolation and against the S&P 500. In fact, EPI requested that its analysts never need to look at the actual multidimensional model.

Overview of the Cube

EPI's needs can be met with a single data cube consisting of four dimensions: stock names, time periods, client portfolios, and variables, as shown in Figure 12.1. (Actually, as you can read in the appendix to this chapter, MIS AG built a system for EPI that consisted of five separate cubes. The reasons for this have more to do with the tool that MIS AG used and the fact that the multi-dimensional model was to be transparent to the user than with the logical nature of the problem. Thus, for the purpose of this hands-on case study, we have simplified things a bit by concentrating on a single, abridged cube containing all the essential structure of the model.) Recall from Chapter 10 the

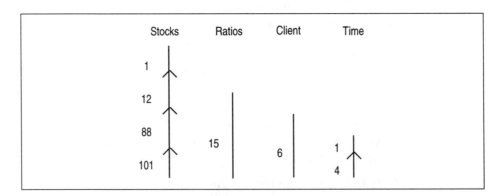

Figure 12.1 MDS view for EPI stocks cube.

basic items that need to be defined in a multidimensional model: cubes and dimensions, levels and hierarchies, basic aggregation formulas, variable formulas, and links.

We will continue by looking at these dimensions.

The Cube Dimensions

Let's explore each the four dimensions of our main cube. The four dimensions of the cube are *stocks*, *time*, *clients*, and *ratios*.

If you wish to follow along on your own computer, open your Excel application now. I assume that you have successfully set up TM/1 Perspectives at this point and that you have experience with Excel. (For help on setting up TM/1 Perspectives, refer to Section 1 of Appendix I.) The step-by-step tutorial is contained within the bracketed sections. If you do not wish to use TM/1, simply read on. The captured screens will still give you a sense of how the multidimensional tool works.

Setting Up Your Directory

Within your spreadsheet, click on the TM/1 menu and then the Options menu choice (shown in Figure 12.2).

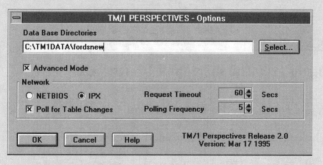

Figure 12.2 Setting the directory.

[TM/1 PERSPECTIVES-Options]

Make sure that your database directory is set to *C:\TM1DATA\FORD-SNEW* (if you have installed the sample data on a different disk drive and/or directory, enter that directory here), and make sure that *Advanced Mode* is checked. Click OK. You will be prompted "Do you wish to make changes to tm1.ini?" Click Yes.

Stocks

The *stocks* dimension consists of the individual stocks and their aggregations into *industries* and *sectors*. Industries and sectors are two different aggregation paths stemming from the individual stocks. Stocks will sum into the industries and sectors.

Viewing the Stocks Dimension

Click on the TM/1 menu, then click on the Cubes menu choice.

[TM/1 -Cubes Menu]

Click on Browse.

[Select Cube to Browse]

In the list, click on share and then OK. A TM/1 *browse box* will appear, as shown in Figure 12.3.

Figure 12.3 The share table browse box.

[View:[Unnamed] - Cube: share]

Click on the raised box labeled stocks.

[Edit Subset: ALL of Dimension: stocks]

On the right-hand side of the dialog, click on the subset button.

[Subsets of Dimension: stocks]

Now select the subset stocks by double-clicking on it.

The individual stocks will be shown, as illustrated in Figure 12.4.

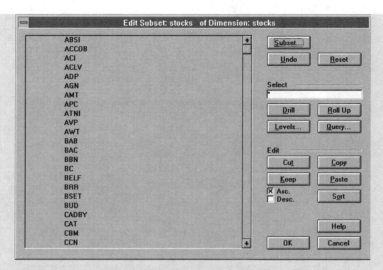

Figure 12.4 The stocks dimension.

Now using the same procedure, click on <u>Subset</u>.

[Subsets of Dimension: stocks]

Double-click on <u>industries</u> to select that subset (shown in Figure 12.5).

This is the industry level of the *stocks* dimension.

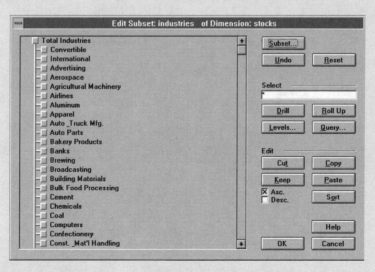

Figure 12.5 Subsetting the stocks dimension.

Finally, use the same procedure to select the <u>sectors</u> subset of the stocks dimension.

This is the sector level, as shown in Figure 12.6.

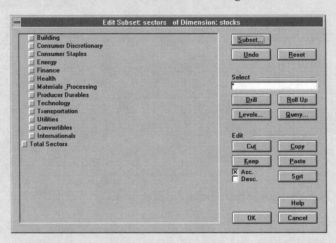

Figure 12.6 The sectors subset of the stocks dimension.

Now, double-click on <u>Building</u>, and see all the industries that belong to the building sector.

Double click-on <u>Cement</u> to see that the *MSA* stock belongs to the cement industry. Your display should look like the one in Figure 12.7.

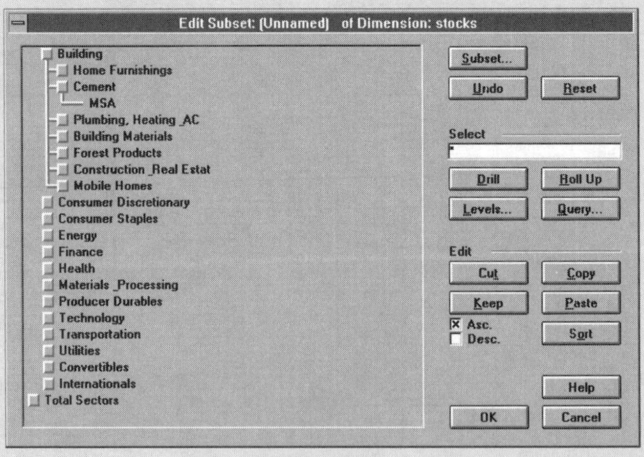

Figure 12.7 Another view of the stocks dimension.

Click <u>Cancel</u> to exit.

———————

Time

The *time* dimension (in our simplified representation) has four quarters that sum into one year.

<u>Viewing the Time Dimension</u>

[View:[Unnamed] - Cube: share]

Click on the raised box labeled <u>time</u>.

[Edit Subset: ALL of Dimension: time]

The dialog shown in Figure 12.8 should appear.

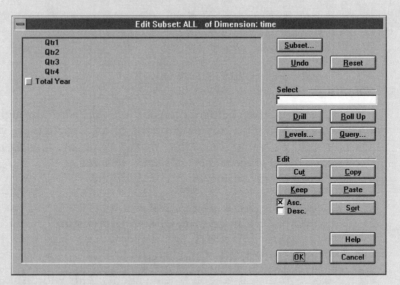

Figure 12.8 The year dimension.

You can see that the members of the time dimension are *Qtr1* through *Qtr4* and *Total Year*. If you double-click on <u>Total Year,</u> you can see that it is composed of *Qtr1* to *Qtr4* (as shown in Figure 12.9).

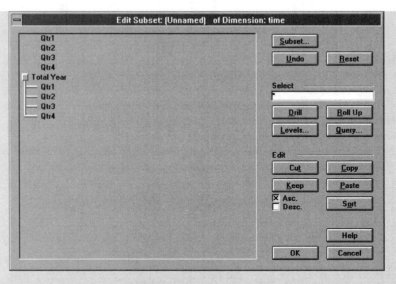

Figure 12.9 The components of Total Year.

Click on Cancel to exit.

Clients

The members of the clients dimension are *Portfolio1* through *Portfolio5* and *S&P500*. The S&P 500 can be thought of as a particular type of portfolio *where, for the purpose of calculating market value, the number of shares held of each stock is equal to the number of shares outstanding.*

Viewing the Clients Dimension

[View:[Unnamed] - Cube: share]

Click on the raised box labeled clients. This will display the list of all the members of the clients dimension, as shown in Figure 12.10.

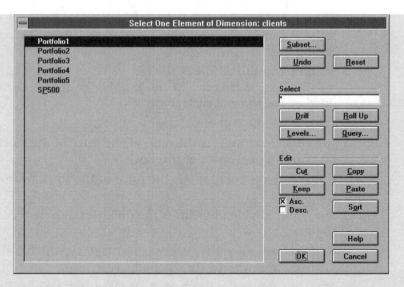

Figure 12.10 The members of the clients dimension.

(Note that the last member in the list is *SP500*, not *S&P500*. This is an artifact of the mechanisms that display the list; when TM/1 internally asks Windows to display the *Sort* button in this dialog, for example, it gives Windows the character string "S&ort" which tells Windows to underline the 'o' in Sort when it draws the button on the screen. Through the rest of this case study, we will ask you to see *S&P500* and click on SP500, as though the '&' were displayed.)

[Select One Element of Dimension: clients]

Click Cancel to continue.

Ratio

This is the variables dimension for the *share* hypercube. It is called "ratios" because financial indicators are frequently based on, and called, ratios. Price/earnings, price to book, dividend yield, and return on equity are examples of ratios. This variables dimension includes those ratios as well as number of shares, market capitalization, price per share, market value, and percent of fund. These ratios are briefly defined below.

❑ **Shares** is the number of shares of each particular stock held by a portfolio. For example, portfolio 1 may hold 10,000 shares of ABC stock during quarter 1, while portfolio 2 may not hold any.

❑ **Market capitalization** is the net value of all of a company's shares outstanding. It is equal to the number of shares outstanding multiplied by the price of each share.

❑ **Price** is the price of one share of a stock.

❑ **P/E** (price/earnings) is the ratio of the price of the stock to the corporate earnings per share of the stock.

❑ **P/B** (price to book) ratio is the price of the stock to the book value of the stock.

❑ **Div yield** (dividend yield) is the dividend as a percent of the price of the stock.

❑ **ROE** (return on equity) is the percentage by which a stock's value has changed over a given time period.

❑ **Market value** is the value of the stocks in a portfolio. For example, the market value of 10,000 shares of ABC stock at $9 a share would be $90,000. For the S&P500, however, market value is equal to shares outstanding (instead of shares owned) times price per share.

❑ **Percent of fund** is the market value of a stock in the portfolio as a percentage of the market value of the entire portfolio.

Viewing the Ratio Dimension

[View:[Unnamed] - Cube: share]

Click on the raised box labeled <u>ratio</u>. The dialog should look as shown in Figure 12.11.

These are all the members of the ratios dimension. Some of the variables here (the ones with **Mkt Val* in their name) are intermediate variables used for calculations, which will be explained later in this chapter. For the end user's analysis, these intermediate variables will never be used.

[Select One Element of Dimension: ratio]

To view only the variables that are final results, click on <u>subset</u> on the right-hand side of the dimension dialog box and open the subset: <u>ratios</u>. This will display the subset shown in Figure 12.12.

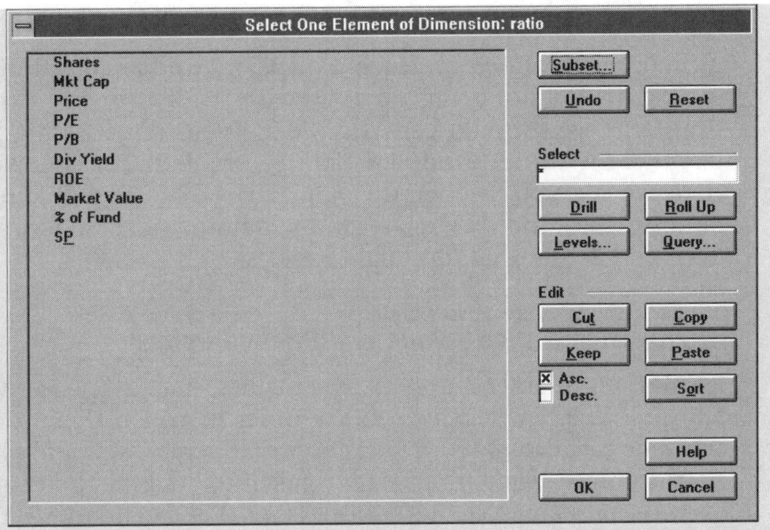

Figure 12.11 The ratio dimension.

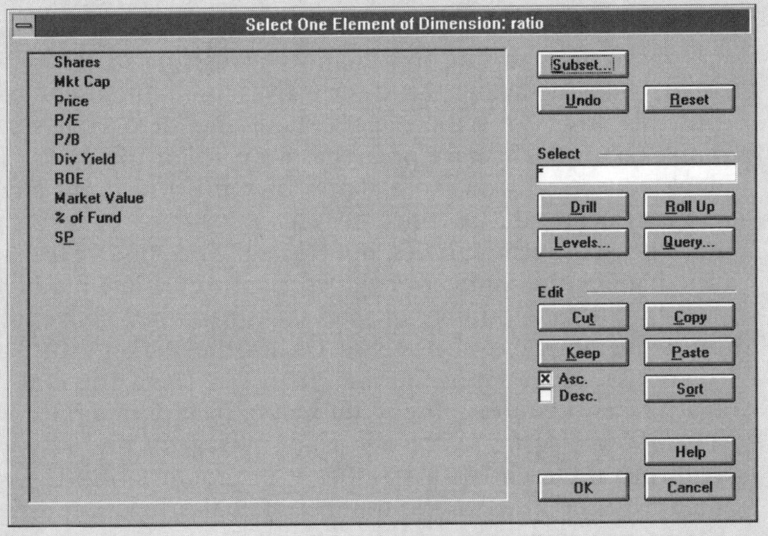

Figure 12.12 A subset of the ratio dimension.

Click <u>Cancel</u> to continue.

Defining Formulas for the Variables Dimension

Although we defined the cube dimensions and aggregations in the previous section, we did not define anything else. As discussed in Chapter 10 on practical steps, you should generally define your dimensional aggregations and test them with nonformulaic data before defining your variable formulas. Here, we take you through the major steps that you would perform to handle ratio variables and their aggregation: defining nonstandard aggregation functions and defining conditional formulas.

Aggregating Ratios—Price and Price/Earnings

Recall from Chapter 3 that many variables, such as those involving quotients and products, are sensitive to the order in which their component dimensions are calculated. In a typical example, actual sales and planned sales need to be summed before their ratio is taken to describe their variance. This is an example of taking the ratio of two sums. For the financial indicators used by EPI, the ratios likewise cannot simply be averaged or summed. The essential factor here is that we are given ratios by stock, yet we are really trying to compute a value per share as opposed to per stock.

Let's start by looking at how to aggregate the ratio of price per share (total stock sale price divided by the number of shares changing hands). It will not make sense to sum this quantity across the stocks in a portfolio or in a sector/industry; taking the average gives us a more useful aggregate measure. However, just taking the average share price across the stocks in a portfolio won't tell us the average price that we paid for the stocks because we've undoubtedly purchased more shares of some and fewer shares of others. To properly aggregate the price per share, we need to take the average of the price per share across shares, not stocks. To do this, we first multiply the price per share by the number of shares, then sum these products and divide the sum by the total number of shares. (As described above, the price per share times the number of shares is also called the market value.)

In the case of ratios such as P/E or P/B, averaging is also the aggregation that makes the most sense to develop a picture of a portfolio or a sector/industry. Once again, taking a straight average of the ratio won't provide the right picture. Each P/E is significant in proportion to the value of the stock holding as opposed to the number of shares held. Multiplying the ratio by the market value per stock, summing these products, and dividing by the number of total shares across all stocks being aggregated will produce the meaningfully weighted result.

Most of the variables in our *ratios* dimension work in a similar way. Let's take the price-to-earnings ratio as an example. All the ratios are fed in from the *descrip* cube (generated from the Fords database) at the base level. Given only the dimensional aggregation formulas, the multidimensional tool will do a straight sum across the stocks dimension. This is not what we need. In order to create the product of P/E and market value, an intermediate variable called *P/E*Mkt Val* was created. At the base level, it is exactly what the name suggests, the product of *price earnings* and *market value*. We allow the multidimensional tool to sum this variable as we aggregate in the stocks dimension, then at each level of aggregation, we set P/E equal to *P/E*Mkt Val* divided by the market value at that level.

Another wrinkle permeates the process, which we will describe here before actually showing the rules as written in TM/1. At any time period, a portfolio (including the S&P 500) may or may not hold any shares of a stock. A ratio that divides some quantity by zero shares will (correctly) produce a result of not-applicable, and in TM/1 any operation done on a not-applicable value will also result in not-applicable.

The actual rules written in TM/1 are as follows:

$$['P/E*Mkt\ Val'\ ]= N:['P/E']*['Market\ Value'];$$

At the leaf levels (indicated by the *N:*), the variable *P/E*Mkt Val* is set to be the product of *P/E* and *Market Value*. It is then summed up the dimension hierarchies as we aggregate, and we are interested in the sum across stocks.

$$['P/E'] = N:if(['Shares']>0,DB('descrip',\ 'P/E',\ !time,\ !stocks),\ 0);$$
$$C:if(['Shares']>0,['P/E*Mkt\ Val']/['Market\ Value'],0);$$

At the leaf levels (indicated by the *N:*), if the number of shares is greater than zero, then the P/E ratio is fed in from the *descrip* cube, which holds data from Fords. At the higher (consolidated) levels (indicated by the *C:*), if the number of shares is greater than zero, then P/E is equal to the variable *P/E*Mkt Val* divided by the *Market Value* at that level.

When we aggregate the P/E ratio across time, if we do not specify otherwise, *Total Year*'s P/E ratio would be equal to the straight sum of the quarterly P/E ratios. This would not make sense. We wrote a separate rule to set the total year's P/E ratio to equal the average of the four quarters' P/E ratios:

$$['P/E',\ 'Total\ Year']=(['P/E',\ 'Qtr1']+['P/E',\ 'Qtr2']+['P/E',\ 'Qtr3']+['P/E',\ 'Qtr4'])/4;$$

Other ratios, such as price to book, dividend yield, and returns on equity, are all averaged similarly. If you are interested in the rules written for each of the other ratios, please feel free at this point to open up the rule worksheet of the *share* cube. The rule worksheet contains comments to help you understand them.

Opening the Rule Worksheet

Close your browse box if it is still open.

Click on the TM/1 menu and select the menu option Rules.

[TM/1 - Rules Menu]

Click Open.

[Select Rules Worksheet]

Double-click on share. This will bring up the rules worksheet for the share cube, as shown in Figure 12.13.

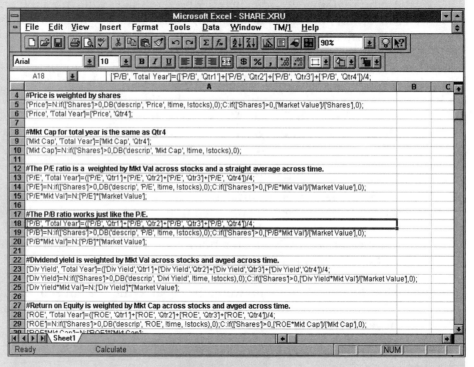

Figure 12.13 A portion of the rules worksheet.

Positionally Conditional Definitions

In order for EPI to evaluate the *percent of fund* variable across individual portfolios and make comparisons with the S&P 500, it was necessary to define *Market Value* (a component of the *percent of funds* variable) differently for portfolios than for S&P 500. This is an example of formulas that are different depending on position in the dimension, described earlier in Chapter 4. While the model is full of rules that change how a variable is calculated at different places in the time or shares hierarchy, this is an example of a definition that subtly alters the meaning of a variable for a given portion of the model (the S&P portfolio information). Whereas each portfolio owns shares of stock, the S&P 500 indicator owns no shares of stock, so the meaning of market value quantities and the *percent of fund* variable are semantically different for the S&P 500.

The market value for a stock in a portfolio is the price of the stock times the number of shares of that stock held by the portfolio. Thus, the market value of the entire portfolio is the sum of the market values of all the individual stocks it contains. Once the *market value* variable is set up correctly, the *percent of fund* variable can be computed from the ratio of an individual stock's market value to the market value of the entire portfolio.

The only way that market value for the S&P 500 can be meaningful and useful for analysis is if it sums, over each stock, the stock's price times the total shares outstanding. This could be done a number of ways. The way it is done in EPI's model is to set the share variable equal to shares outstanding for all the S&P 500 stocks in the S&P 500 portfolio. Then, when the multidimensional tool applies the formula that sets market value to the price times shares owned, it is actually price times shares outstanding for the S&P 500 portfolio. Once this is set up correctly, the market value variable can be used for such things as comparing the percentage change in market value for each portfolio as compared with the change in market value for the S&P 500. The total number of shares outstanding is given in the *descrip* cube as the *Shares O/S Total* variable. Here are the actual rules written in TM/1:

> *['S&P500', 'Shares']=N:if(['S&P']>0,DB('descrip', 'Shares O/S Total', !time, !stocks),0);*

At the leaf level of time and stocks (indicated by the *N:*), if the stock is indicated as an S&P 500 stock by the S&P flag, then extract the *Shares O/S Total* value for the corresponding stock and time. Otherwise, the S&P 500 has zero shares of that stock. This quantity will then sum over stocks (the model contains a rule that prevents the summation over time).

> *['Market Value']=N:['Price']*['Shares'];*

For all portfolios, including the S&P 500, market value is then computed as price times shares outstanding at the leaf levels of the dimensions and will sum over stocks (the model contains a rule that prevents the summation over time).

Having defined the variable formulas, we are ready to explore the multidimensional aggregations.

Viewing and Analysis

Spreadsheet Views

Recall that EPI did not want its analysts working directly with the data cubes. They needed specific views of the data most often for analysis, which Tracy Peck laid out in an advanced spreadsheet view. EPI specifically requested to be able to view all the variables for each sector for each portfolio, to be able to make a few comparisons between an individual portfolio and the S&P 500 stocks, and to generate a list of the 10 largest holdings within each portfolio during a given period.

In this section you will be taken through the interactive spreadsheet views that Tracy Peck helped EPI set up through the multidimensional model whose dimensional structure was defined above. Then in the next section, you will be taken through the cube itself.

Opening the Spreadsheet

Close your browse box if it is still open.

Click on the TM/1 menu, then click on the Options menu choice.

[TM/1 PERSPECTIVES-Options]

Switch your database directory to *C:\TM1DATA\FORDS* and click OK. (If you have installed the sample TM/1 model to another directory, then change to that directory.)

Note: It is very important that you switch directories here because the original, unabridged version of the model is in this directory. The spreadsheet feeds from the original TM/1 model, and the TM/1 database directory must be set to the proper directory for the spreadsheet to work properly.

Within your spreadsheet, click on the File menu, then the Open menu choice.

[Open]

Click on C:\TM1DATA\FORDS\OUTPUT.XLS (substitute the actual directory to which you installed the TM/1 case study if different from C:\TM1DATA) and click Open.

This spreadsheet is linked to the multidimensional model that Tracy Peck created. It allows you to compare each portfolio with the S&P 500. The top section of this spreadsheet displays financial indicators aggregated to the sector level, on a portfolio-by-portfolio basis. Notice that to the far right of the financial indicators column are two price columns, one for the current quarter, one for the previous one. This allows you to see the prices for the current and previous period.

Viewing the Spreadsheet

Click on cell **R7** (which contains *Qtr2*). You can see in the formula area at the top of your Excel screen (and as shown in Figure 12.14) that this cell contains a formula that always references the period before what is referenced in cell B6. This allows you to view changes in the prices easily; entering a new time member name in cell B6 will automatically cause the previous time to be referenced here.

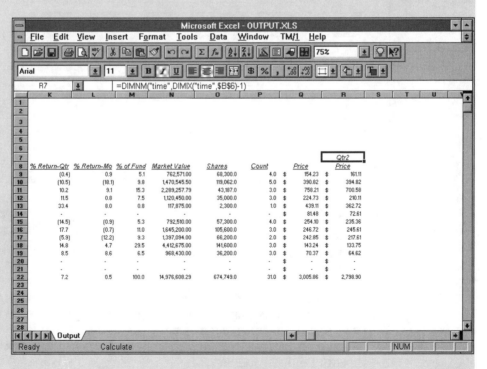

Figure 12.14 Viewing the output spreadsheet.

Now scroll left and down to the box of cells outlined in purple (B26 through G41). The resulting view, shown in Figure 12.15, compares the percent return and percent of fund of stocks in the portfolio in question (*Portfolio 3*) with the *S&P500* stocks. Here we can see that some of the sectors in *Portfolio 3* had higher returns than *S&P500*'s and some had lower. The *Weight* column contains the ratio of the portfolio's *percent of fund* to the S&P 500's *percent of fund*. It shows that, overall, *Portfolio3* had 1.2 percent higher return than the *S&P500* stocks.

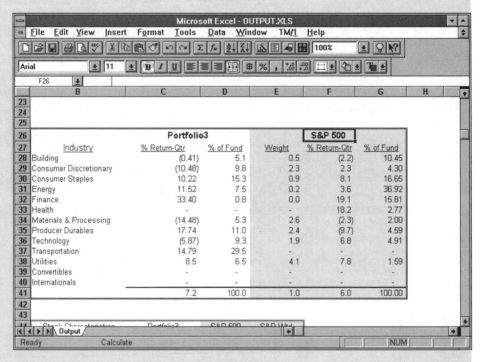

Figure 12.15 Comparisons with the S&P 500.

Now, scroll down to the box of cells outlined in blue (B44 through E51). The resulting view, shown in Figure 12.16, allows you to compare some stock characteristics between *Portfolio3* and the *S&P500*'s. The column labeled *S&P Wtd* gives you the *Portfolio3* number as a percent of the *S&P500* one.

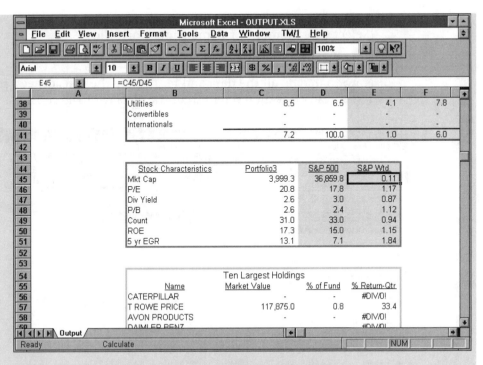

Figure 12.16 More comparisons with the S&P500.

Click on cell <u>E46</u>. You can see that it contains the formula *=C46/D46*. It defines a ratio between *Portfolio3* and *S&P500*'s stock characteristics.

Finally, scroll down to see the last section of this spreadsheet, the box of cells outlined in bright cyan (B54 through E56). In the actual spreadsheet created for B&B, this gives you the top 10 largest holdings in *Portfolio3*, their *market values*, *percent of fund*, and the *percent return* for the period specified. (A spreadsheet macro actually performs the ranking of the stocks so that the top 10 are selected. Because the macros are omitted in this simplified case study version, a static set of 10 stocks will appear, though their holding information in the sheet's active portfolio will still be displayed.)

Now scroll back to the top of the spreadsheet. Double-click on cell *B5*, which reads "*Portfolio 3*." This brings you to the TM/1 dimension dialog box from which you can choose a different portfolio to view.

[Select One Element of Dimension: portfolio]

Choose <u>Portfolio 2</u> and click <u>OK</u>.

Now, to update all the data and recalculate the spreadsheet, press <u>F9</u>. The spreadsheet should refresh to the display of Figure 12.17.

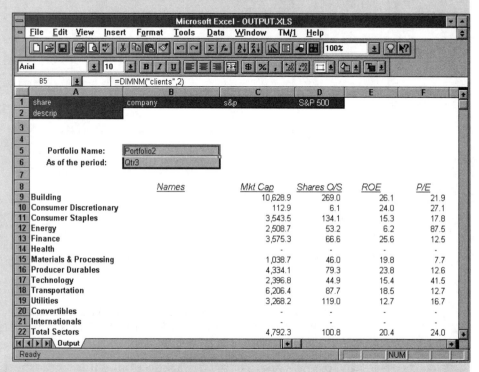

Figure 12.17 Recalculated view.

Performing the same actions on cell B6 will allow you to view the data for a different quarter.

Drilling Up and Down

Not only can you look at the data for different quarters, you can move up a level of aggregation by looking at *Total Year*.

Drilling Up and Down in Time

Return to the top of your *OUTPUT.XLS*.

Double-click on cell *B6*.

This brings you to the multidimensional dimension dialog box, where you can choose which time period you wish to look at. The steps you take to drill up to total year (admittedly not an exciting hierarchical movement) are no different from the steps you take to switch to a different quarter.

[Select One Element of Dimension: time]

Click on <u>Total Year</u> in the dimension dialog box. Click <u>OK</u>.

In the spreadsheet, press <u>F9</u> to recalculate. The spreadsheet should refresh to the display of Figure 12.18.

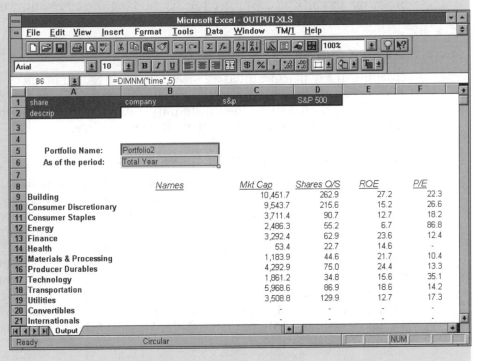

Figure 12.18 Another refreshed view.

You can see that moving between quarter and year levels is quite simple. There could have just as easily been 10 levels of hierarchy. Note that Tracy Peck could have also helped EPI create drill-down capabilities in the stocks dimension. Although EPI did not require this feature, it would be performed in the same way you drilled up and down in the time dimension. As demonstrated by this example, spreadsheets make a reasonable interface to a multidimensional model. It is possible to endow a spreadsheet with hierarchical navigation capabilities in multiple dimensions and to arrange distinct reporting areas.

Limitation of the Spreadsheet Interface

The spreadsheet interface comes with some limitations. Let's say you want to compare indicators across portfolios. You will need to construct a region of cells with the right formulas. Changing the orientation of the cells involves more construction or reconstruction. The spreadsheet is great for browsing reports constructed within a certain set of parameters, but for unrestricted browsing and analysis, you need to be working directly within the hypercube.

Viewing and Analysis in a Hypercube

Browsing in a hypercube interface provides great freedom of selection and dimensional arrangement of information. In this section, we will explore how a multidimensional tool allows us to pursue different lines of thought from different perspectives through its navigational interface.

Comparison of Portfolio Market Values by Quarter

As an analyst, the first things to look at in comparing the individual portfolios are market value changes over time. Let's take a look at changes in market value for each of the five portfolios. We will create a view that provides us with the market value information for each individual portfolio for each quarter. Rather than change the multidimensional model to add this computation, we will use the spreadsheet to find the changes between quarters. In terms of TM/1, we want to set up a view and save it as a "slice" (which is just a normal Excel worksheet), from which we will make the proper variance computation. We will arrange the client portfolios in the rows and quarters across the columns, with the ratio *Market Value* and the *Total Sectors* of stocks forming the slice's page.

Setting Up the View

We need to return to the "Fordsnew" database.

Click on the TM/1 menu, then click on the Cubes menu choice.

[TM/1 PERSPECTIVES-Options]

Switch your database directory back to *C:\TM1DATA\FORDSNEW* (or to the actual directory in which you installed the data, if different) and click OK.

Click on the TM/1 menu, then click on the Cubes menu choice.

[TM/1-Cubes Menu]

Click Browse.

[Select Cubes to Browse]

Click share, then OK.

[View:[Unnamed] - Cube: share]

We are going to arrange the view to show us *clients* in the rows, *time* across, and both *ratio* and *stocks* in the page area, as shown in Figure 12.19.

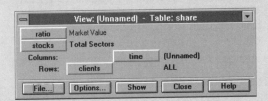

Figure 12.19 The browse box for the share table.

Drag stocks to the page area, in the left-most column of the browse box (above the File... button). Drag clients to the center column of the browse box (above the Options... button) and drag time to the right-most column of the browse box (above the Show button). Ratio should be in the left-most column as well.

Click on the raised box labeled stocks.

[Select one element of dimension: stocks]

Click on Total Sectors and confirm with OK.

[View:[Unnamed] - Cube: share]

Click on the raised box labeled ratio.

[Select one element of dimension: ratio]

Click on <u>Market Value</u> and confirm with <u>OK</u>.

[View:[Unnamed] - Cube: share]

Click on the raised box labeled <u>time</u>.

[Edit Subset: ALL of dimension: time]

Highlight *Qtr1* to *Qtr4* by clicking on <u>Qtr1</u> and holding down your mouse button while dragging down to <u>Qtr4</u>. Click <u>OK</u> to confirm the selection.

[View:[Unnamed] - Cube: share]

You shouldn't need to change any settings in the *clients* dimension.

Your browse box should now look like the one shown in Figure 12.20.

Now, click on <u>Show</u>.

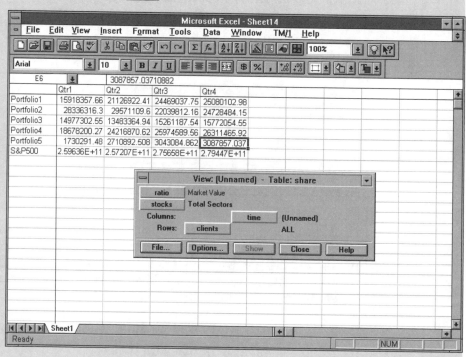

Figure 12.20 Comparing individual *Portfolios* with the *S&P500*.

In order to use Excel to calculate changes in the market value, we now need to save the view as a spreadsheet slice.

Saving the View as a Slice

In your browse box, click <u>File</u>. The browse file menu should appear, as shown in Figure 12.21.

Figure 12.21 The browse file menu.

[Browse File Menu]

Click on <u>Slice</u>.

The view will be recreated as a spreadsheet slice, as shown in Figure 12.22. You now have a regular Excel worksheet to work with.

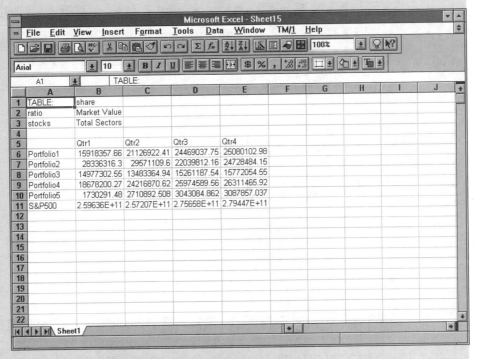

Figure 12.22 An Excel slice of hypercube data.

To judge the performance of portfolio managers relative to the S&P 500, you need to compare relative changes in market value between portfolios and the S&P 500. If you tried to compare absolute changes in market value, results would be biased toward high-valued portfolios like the S&P 500. Although the market value of stocks held in individual portfolios is calculated differently from the market value of stocks in the S&P 500, comparing percent changes in market values will produce a meaningful result. It will tell us in relative terms how much the value of a portfolio changed relative to changes in the value of the S&P 500. If the S&P 500 increased in value by 20 percent during the course of the year and a portfolio only increased by 15 percent, then the portfolio underperformed the S&P 500. We will use quarter 4 and quarter 1 as the basis for our comparison.

Calculating Change of Market Value

In cell F5 of your Excel worksheet, type Q1-Q4. This is the column heading, as illustrated in Figure 12.23.

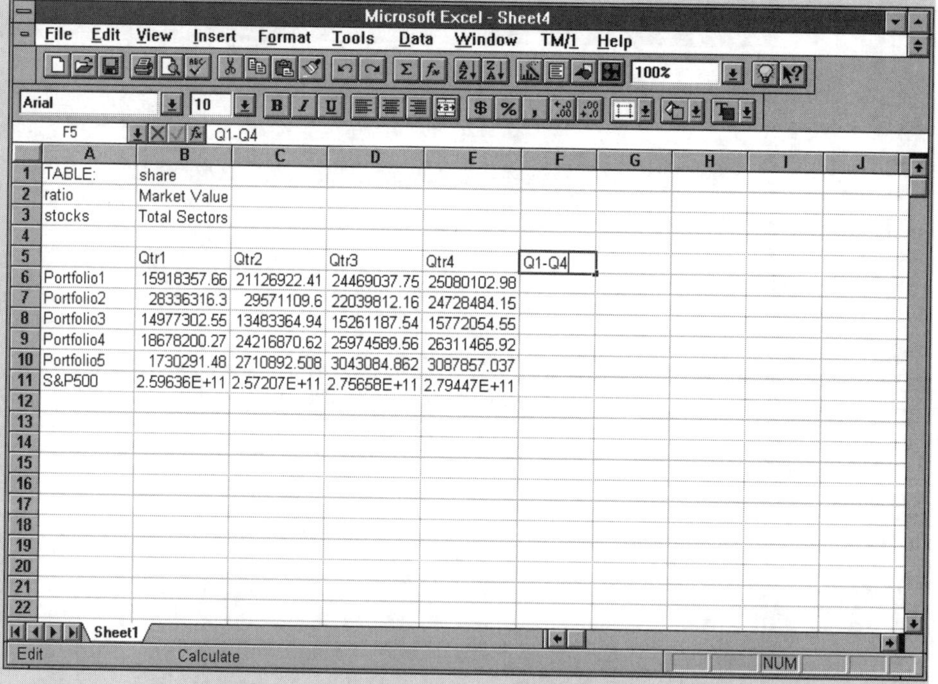

	A	B	C	D	E	F
1	TABLE:	share				
2	ratio	Market Value				
3	stocks	Total Sectors				
4						
5		Qtr1	Qtr2	Qtr3	Qtr4	Q1-Q4
6	Portfolio1	15918357.66	21126922.41	24469037.75	25080102.98	
7	Portfolio2	28336316.3	29571109.6	22039812.16	24728484.15	
8	Portfolio3	14977302.55	13483364.94	15261187.54	15772054.55	
9	Portfolio4	18678200.27	24216870.62	25974589.56	26311465.92	
10	Portfolio5	1730291.48	2710892.508	3043084.862	3087857.037	
11	S&P500	2.59636E+11	2.57207E+11	2.75658E+11	2.79447E+11	

Figure 12.23 Calculating change in market value, step one.

In cell F6, type the formula =(E6-B6)/B6 and press the Enter key.

Highlight cells F6 to F11 with the mouse. Click on the Edit menu and select Fill/Down.

Now, press F9 to recalculate and refresh the screen. The display should look like Figure 12.24.

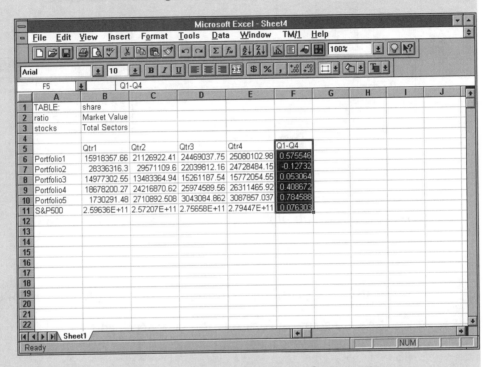

Figure 12.24 Calculating change in market value, step two.

Using the Excel Chart Wizard, you can then easily create a graph like the one shown in Figure 12.25.

We can see that portfolios 1, 4, and 5 did better than the S&P 500 in increasing the market value of their portfolios. But portfolio 3 did a bit worse and certainly portfolio 2 was much worse.

Distribution of Funds by Sectors

At this point, you might ask yourself, "Maybe portfolios 1 and 5 invested on similar stocks and portfolio 3 invested mostly on S&P 500 stocks?" Let's find out how the funds are distributed among sectors in each portfolio.

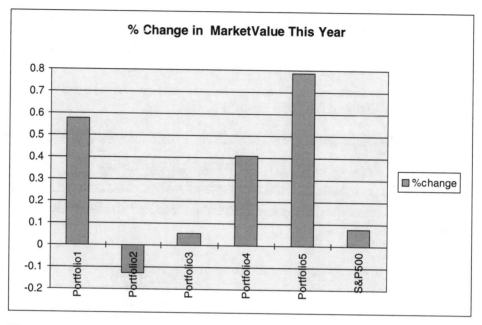

Figure 12.25 Graph of change in market value from Q1 to Q4.

Comparing the Distribution of Funds Between Different Portfolios

We are going to construct the view specified by the browse box as shown in Figure 12.26.

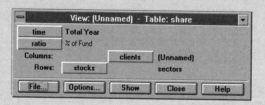

Figure 12.26 A new browse box view.

Click on the TM/1 menu, then click on the Cubes menu choice.

[TM/1 PERSPECTIVE-Cubes]

Press Browse.

[Cube-Browse]

Click on the <u>shares</u> cube.

[View:[Unnamed]-Cube: share]

Drag *time* on the top-left corner. Drag *stocks* to the middle column, and drag *clients* in to the right-most column.

Click on <u>ratio.</u>

[Select One Element of Dimension: ratio]

Click on <u>percent of Fund</u> and then <u>OK</u>.

[View:[Unnamed]-Cube: share]

Click on <u>time</u>.

[Select One Element of Dimension: time]

Click on <u>Reset</u>. Click on <u>Total Year</u> and then <u>OK</u>.

[View:[Unnamed]-Cube: share]

Click on <u>stocks</u>.

[Edit Subset: ALL of Dimension: stocks]

Click on <u>Subset</u>.

[Subsets of Dimension: stocks]

Double-click on <u>sectors</u>.

[Edit Subset: ALL of Dimension: stocks]

Click <u>OK</u>.

[View:[Unnamed]-Cube: share]

Let's first compare *Portfolio1* with *Portfolio 5*. Click on <u>clients</u>.

[Edit Subset: ALL of Dimension: clients]

Select <u>Portfolio 1</u> and <u>Portfolio 5</u> by holding down the Control key and clicking the mouse on these two members. Click <u>OK</u>.

[View:[Unnamed]-Cube: share]

Click on <u>Show</u>.

This will produce a view as shown in Figure 12.27.

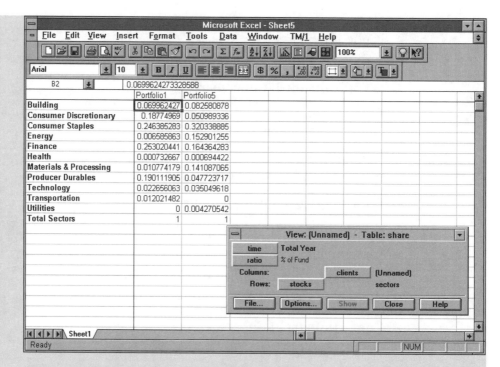

Figure 12.27 Comparing the "percent of fund" variable across sectors and portfolios.

Once again, understanding this data is easier if it is graphed. Let's proceed by saving our view as a slice and using Excel to produce another graph.

Creating a Bar Graph

[View:[Unnamed]-Cube: share]

Click on File.

[Browse File Menu]

Click on Slice.

Once created, the slice looks like Figure 12.28.

Now highlight cells *A5* to *C16*, and use the Excel Chart Wizard to guide you through the steps to create the graph you need.

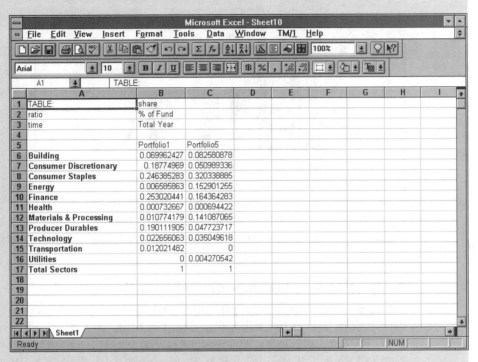

Figure 12.28 A new Excel data slice.

An example of a graph you can create is shown in Figure 12.29. Even though this graph shows only some of sector names in the legend, we can see from it that both portfolios invested heavily in the consumer staples and the finance sector. Also, both invested very little, if any at all, in the health, technology, transportation, and utility sectors. Consumer discretionary, materials and processing, and producer durables stocks show significant differences in relative investment.

Advanced Visualization

We performed a visual correlation analysis of P/E with other market variables. Look to Diamond|Data|Q1Fords.txt for a description of the visual analysis and a pointer to the relevant image file.

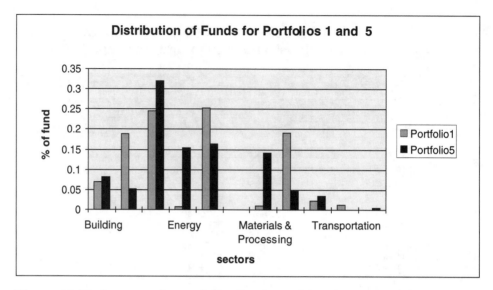

Figure 12.29 A comparison of distribution of funds across portfolios.

Summary of Analytical Browsing Within a Hypercube

While we may wish to use the capabilities of the spreadsheet for additional calculations and other functions like graphing, the multidimensional tool provides the framework we need to easily construct and arrange multiple views of data that support our train of thought in analyzing the portfolios. We have still only scratched the surface of the ability for a multidimensional tool to flexibly rearrange views.

Conclusion

The model built by Tracy Peck in conjunction with EPI is a good example of an OLAP solution. The data is now held in one central place. The amount of overall storage is minimal compared to past storage requirements. Portfolios can be browsed and drilled on easily. Queries are straightforward to define and compute, such as the following:

1. "Who are the 10 largest holdings for the portfolio?"
2. "Who had the highest return for the period?"
3. "Which industry did the poorest?"
4. "Was that poor return driven by a single stock?"

The input table connects to spreadsheets from portfolio managers and can be populated without any rekeying. The output file (OUTPUT.XLS) is in report-ready form. It provides the multidimensional browsing capabilities that EPI needed through a spreadsheet interface.

Appendix: EPI's Actual Model

EPI's functional requirement that its analysts never need to look at the data cubes, combined with its security requirement that its analysts never manipulate the base data, and combined with aspects of the particular tool it was using (that, for example, it did not support dimensional attributes), led MIS AG to follow an implementation strategy that used several cubes to get the job done.

In the description that follows, the status of a dimension is identified as either *shared*, meaning that the same dimension is used in multiple cubes, or *private,* in which case the dimension exists only in that particular cube. The term "# of members" refers to the total number of members in the dimension including aggregate members.

Cube name: "Ford"

Dimension names	Shared/private	# of members
"Base ratios"	private	42
"Stocks"	shared	2,860
"Time"	shared	22

This cube holds the information that is downloaded from the Ford database. It is a densely populated cube. It contains all the financial data items for use in the *"portfolio"* and the *"S&P"* cubes.

Cube name: "S&P"

Dimension names	Shared/private	# of members
"Stocks"	shared	2,860
"Portfolio"	shared	35
"Time"	shared	22
"Ratios"	shared	57

This cube defines the financial indicators or ratios for the S&P 500 stocks. One of the data items in Fords is a flag that indicates which 500 of the 2,600 stocks are included in the S&P 500. This flag is translated into 1 if a stock is included in the S&P 500 and 0 if excluded. The cube is linked to the *"Ford"* cube by an intercube reference that says, "If the flag for S&P = 1, then bring in the Ford data for that stock. If it is =0 then skip." This is an entirely virtual table.

Cube: "Shares"

Dimension names	Shared/private	# of members
"Stocks"	shared	2,860
"Portfolio"	shared	35
"Time"	shared	22
"Ratios"	shared	57

This cube holds the number of shares owned and the financial ratios of each stock for each portfolio. It is also linked through intercube references to the *"Ford"* cube. The rules say, "If the number of shares held by a portfolio for a particular stock is greater than zero, then bring in the Fords data for that stock." Because most portfolios hold only a small percentage of the total number of stocks this cube is highly sparse. The sparsity created here is zero-type sparsity. With the exception of the number of shares owned by a portfolio, this is a virtual table. In addition to the main informational cubes, two additional lookup-style tables were defined.

Lookup cube name: "Company name"

Dimension names	Shared/private	# of members
"Names"	shared	2,860
"Stocks"	private	2,860

This cube aligns a company name in the form of a string with the ticker symbol defined in the stock dimension.

Lookup cube: "Industry Names"

Dimension names	Shared/private	# of members
"Indname"	private	2
"Indnum"	private	105

All of the stocks in Ford are assigned a numeric industry classification. The numeric code is a unique identifier in the same way that an employee ID is more constant than an employee name. During the download process, these numbers are read through the *"Industry Names"* cube and are replaced with the corresponding text name.

The one cube focused on in this chapter is equivalent to the shares cube described here. Although it was actually linked to the Ford cube, we ignored those links for the purpose of this chapter because they did not add materially to an understanding of the basic issues.

OLAP Models for Improving Operations

As part of a data warehousing initiative, Elkins Economics was brought in to design an OLAP model for the analysis and improvement of operations at AirTran Airways. This hands-on case study reflects Elkins' experience. This chapter shows you, among other things, how to work with sparse data and when to split the time dimension.

The Situation at AirTran Airways

AirTran Airways is a low-fare startup airline based in Orlando, Florida. It operates a fleet of 10 aircraft between Orlando and 20 medium-sized cities in the Midwest and East. Its clientele is composed primarily of vacation travelers (over a million a year).

The Problem with the Current State of Affairs

Prior to the commencement of AirTran's data warehouse project, most data analysis was done using the limited reporting tools (mostly standard printed reports) included with the operational systems themselves. The most important elements of summarized data were hand-keyed into an Excel worksheet to provide consolidated reports to senior management. A copy of the reservations system tables, in Microsoft Access, was used as a source for a few SQL programmers to produce additional hard-copy marketing reports on request.

(These had more of an administrative than analytical nature.) The company is growing at a rate of about 1 additional aircraft per quarter, and this style of information gathering is no longer adequate to manage the airline.

Elkins Economics' Project Goals for AirTran Airways

The object of its ongoing data warehouse project is to extract the data required to manage the business from the operational systems, and transform it so that it is easily accessible to the company's managers. Because of the company's relatively small size (both in terms of available staffing and revenue base), the tools selected must fit into the airline's existing client server IT architecture:

❑ They must be versatile enough to support a consistent view of the information across all the departments

❑ They must be easy to deploy and maintain

❑ They must be able to scale up as the airline grows

❑ They must enable *all* end-user managers to satisfy their information requirements without the assistance of nonexistent programmers

The general project approach involves first creating a base level "data warehouse" in the form of a series of denormalized tables or flat files holding the extracted operational data in a format suitable, in turn, for populating a larger number of "data marts" lodged in a multidimensional database (Essbase). The end users access the data marts via either a spreadsheet (Excel) add-in or a graphical user interface designed specifically for the multidimensional database (Wired for OLAP).

The data has now been ported from Essbase to TM/1, so that you can examine it using the software provided with this book.

The OLAP Model

The model is used to support analysis of operations. Discovering flight inefficiencies will help plan flight operations, target maintenance, and allocate training resources. Such information is critical to an airline that must promote its high quality while keeping costs to a minimum. The model supports analysis of flight delays and fuel consumption rates.

There are two hypercubes in the TM/1 model: one for delay information ("delayinf"), and one for fuel information ("fuelinfo"). These hypercubes share most of their dimensions in a multicube model. A diagram of the overall multidimensional data structure is shown in Figure 13.1. In addition, note that some of the variables are shared between their variables dimensions.

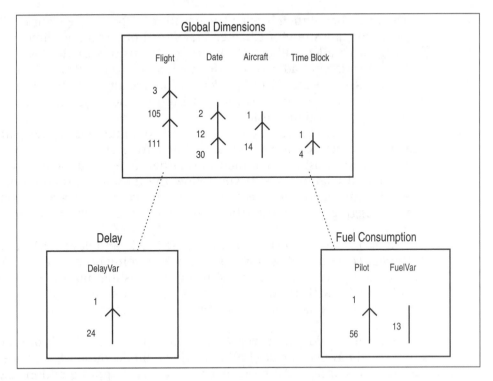

Figure 13.1 Multidimensional data structure diagram of the multicube model.

Common Dimensions

Aircraft

The company's aircraft are listed by aircraft number. There are 14 different aircraft in the model, most of which transport passengers; one transports cargo. To allow us to evaluate data across all aircraft, we created a parent member *All Aircrafts*.

The "Date" and "Timeblck" Time Dimensions

Note that this model contains two dimensions that represent time at different levels of scale or resolution. Recall from the discussions of hierarchies and dimensions in Chapter 7 and in Chapter 10 that a set of potential intersections and aggregation paths can be created either by using two or more dimensions or by combining the dimensions into a single dimension with a greater number of members and aggregation paths. In the Planning Technology Group case study of Chapter 11, instead of a scenario dimension intersecting with all members of all other dimensions in the P&L cube, key scenario variables had a version for each scenario instead. This reduced the overall size of the model and prevented some redundancy between scenarios. Here, there are two reasons for splitting the one physical time dimension into two analytical dimensions.

It is simpler to create all of the desired combinations of aggregations (for each time block across days/weeks/months, for each day/week/month across time blocks) by using two dimensions rather than one dimension with more hierarchical relationships. If you follow the tutorial steps and examine the date dimension, you will see that it already has a fair degree of complexity in the aggregation paths (the original Essbase model was considerably larger).

It also makes it possible to orient time blocks and days/weeks/months on different edges of a view (for example, weeks going down the rows and time blocks going across the columns) using the existing multidimensional tools (Essbase and TM/1 both). This does not reflect computational needs quite so much as it reflects certain view limitations inherent in most multidimensional tools.

Of course, additional cyclical relationships between levels of time resolution could have been placed into additional model dimensions. For example, every year contains 12 months or (to a useful approximation) 52 weeks. These relationships could be the basis for placing years and months in separate time dimensions in the model.

Date   The TM/1 database stores all the company's flight information for the month of June; there are 30 dimension members, one for each day. AirTran was also interested in breaking months down by weeks (for example, in which weeks of the month are we doing most of our business?) and by type of day (for example, are there more delays on the weekends or during the work week?).

Remember that multidimensional modeling allows for multiple hierarchies within a dimension to support multiple breakdowns and consolidations. A sample description of the date dimension with multiple hierarchies is shown in Figure 13.2.

Getting into the Software

The multidimensional model is enclosed, along with the original spreadsheet. You have the option of examining the two models as you read along. If you do not use the spreadsheet and TM/1, you can read through, ignoring the segments of the text with **<u>bold and underlined headings</u>**, as below.

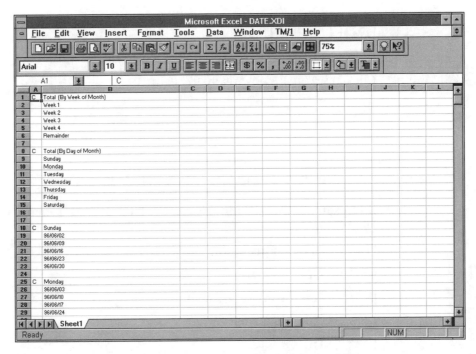

Figure 13.2 Date dimension with multiple hierarchies.

Using TM/1: Getting Started

As you follow along, you will be asked to open up different windows in the TM/1 program. Each time that you are supposed to see a new window on your screen, we will show the name of the window as **[bold bracketed]** in the text. Everything that you will be asked to click on with your mouse will be underlined in the text. Key words that you will see or type on the screen will be *italicized*. This tutorial assumes that TM/1 has already been installed and has access to all directories (to find out how to install TM/1, see Section 1 of the TM/1 manual in Appendix I).

Click on TM/1 and then the Options subheading.

[TM/1 PERSPECTIVES - OPTIONS]

Make sure the database directory is set to *C:\TM1DATA\TRANS* (or the directory to which the sample data set was installed, if different) and that the *Advanced Mode* option is set. Click OK.

[TM/1 PERSPECTIVES]

It should ask you "Do you want to update file: tm1.ini?"

Click Yes. You are now ready to begin.

Multiple Hierarchies in the Date Dimension

Let's examine the *date* dimension. Click on the TM/1 menu, then the Dimensions menu choice.

[TM/1 - Dimensions Menu]

Click on Open.

[Select Dimensions Worksheet]

Click on date, then click OK.

[DATE.XDI]

Note that 96/06/02 is consolidated in two manners: into *Sunday*, and into *Week1*.

You should notice that there are two hierarchies. One breaks the month down by week, then into individual dates; the other breaks the month down by day, then into individual dates. This allows us to examine the data along either hierarchy.

"Timeblck" (Time Block Within Day)   There are four timeblocks, *Morning* (6:00 A.M.–12:00 noon), *Afternoon* (12:00–6:00 P.M.), *Evening* (6:00 P.M.–12:00 midnight), and *Late Night/Early Morning* (12:00–6:00 A.M.). Only nonpassenger flights travel during Late Night/Early Morning.

"Flight" (Flight Routes)

There are 107 different flights routes, labeled by their flight number, destination airport, and arrival airport. For example, flight *101/LGA/MIA* is flight number 101 from La Guardia to Miami. Depending on what it is analyzing, AirTran may be interested in breaking flights down by number, destination, or by arrival airport, so there are multiple hierarchies, one for each different breakdown.

The Delay Hypercube

The "delayinf" hypercube of delay information uses the common dimensions to identify values for the 24 delay variables. These variables are collected in the "delayvar" dimension. Several of these variables are calculated using variable formulas. These formulas are created later in the process (see the section "Creating Formulas (Rules)" later in this chapter). The key variables for our analysis are

- ❑ *Total Passengers*: Total number of passengers on a set of flights
- ❑ *Flight Departures*: Number of flights in a given period
- ❑ *Delayed Flights*: Number of flights that have experienced a delay
- ❑ *Total Delay Minutes*: Total minutes lost to delays in all flights
- ❑ *Average Delay Minutes*: The time lost to delays averaged over all flights
- ❑ *Average Delay Minutes (over delayed flights)*: The time lost to delays averaged only over delayed flights
- ❑ *Passenger-Delay-Minutes*: The delay time for a flight multiplied by the number of passengers, which accounts for the fact that 100 people forced to wait 30 minutes (3,000 passenger-delay-minutes) is more significant than 10 people having to wait 30 minutes (300 passenger-delay-minutes)

Visualizing the Model

As stated in Chapter 6, there is a dearth of software for visualizing the whole of a multidimensional data set. Nevertheless, it is useful to try and create such visualizations as best you can in an attempt to quickly get your arms around a data set. Enclosed on the CD-ROM, you will find two color images (and the associated data files) created with Data Diamond, the enclosed visualization software, that give an overview of the delay cube in a single view. The text that describes the images and points to the diamond data set from which you can interact with the images is located on your CD-ROM under Diamond\data\Air_vis.txt. Grayscale versions of these figures are shown as Figures 13.3 and 13.4.

These images are not crucial for your understanding of the case study. Since they also raise important issues concerning dimensions and variables which are addressed in Chapter 15, you will benefit the most from these images and the accompanying descriptions if you revisit them after having read Chapter 15.

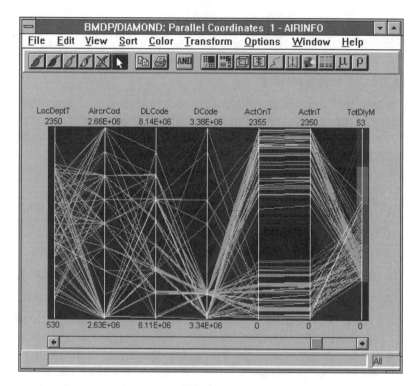

Figure 13.3 Parallel coordinates for the air delay model.

The Fuel Consumption Hypercube

The fuel consumption hypercube is composed of two additional dimensions: a pilot dimension and a fuel variables ("fuelvar") dimension.

Pilot

Pilots are listed by their number. There are 57 members, one for each pilot, and an *Unknown* member, which stores data from flights where the pilot information is incomplete. The consolidation *All Pilots* allows us to sum the values across all of the members.

"Fuelvar" (Fuel Variables)

There are 13 fuel-related variables in all. The key variables include *Flight Departures, Delayed Flights, Total Delay Minutes* and *Average Delay Minutes*, which are also used in the fuel variable dimension. An additional significant analysis variable used here is *Burnoff Variance*, a fraction representing the relative

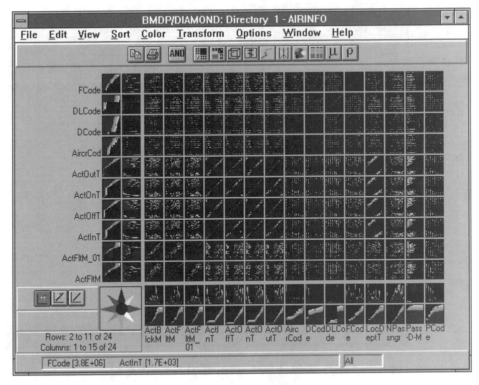

Figure 13.4 Scatterplots for the air delay model.

difference of fuel used by an aircraft (*Actual Burnoff*) compared to the projected amount of fuel use (*Total Flight Plan Burnoff*).

Creating the Hypercubes

Importing the Data

Data on over a thousand flights (for this size-limited case study) needed to be imported from the original Essbase model. The data was transferred via spreadsheet, which was practical due to the small number of records. (See Figure 13.5 to view a portion of the spreadsheet. For the entire view, open C:\TM1DATA\TRANS\AIRINFO.XLS, or the same file in the directory to which you installed the accompanying model if in a different location). Rekeying the data would be an unwieldy task, and the form of the data did not allow for simple "copying and pasting" from the spreadsheet to the multidimensional model (see the later section on sparsity for a hint as to why).

Microsoft Excel - AIRINFO.XLS

File Edit View Insert Format Tools Data Window TM/1 Help

Geneva 10 B I U $ % , 75%

A1 Flight

	A Flight	B Date	C Aircraft	D Pilot	E timeblok	F Delay Type	G Flight Departures	H Local Departure Time	I Total Passengers	Sched
1	Flight	Date	Aircraft	Pilot	timeblok	Delay Type	Flight Departures	Local Departure Time	Total Passengers	Sched
2	100/MIA/EW	96/06/01	463	649	1900	LWA	1	1920	74	
3	100/MIA/EW	96/06/02	463	292	1900	No Delay	1	1920	86	
4	100/MIA/EW	96/06/03	463	179	1900	No Delay	1	1920	112	
5	100/MIA/EW	96/06/04	463	295	1900	No Delay	1	1920	54	
6	100/MIA/EW	96/06/05	469	239	1900	No Delay	1	1920	60	
7	100/LGA/EV	96/06/06	461	393	2200	PAS	1	2217	96	
8	100/MIA/LG	96/06/06	461	393	1900	No Delay	1	1920	130	
9	100/MIA/EW	96/06/07	469	204	1900	LQM	1	1920	74	
10	100/MIA/EW	96/06/08	464	207	1900	No Delay	1	1920	63	
11	100/MIA/EW	96/06/09	463	292	1900	EQM	1	1920	79	
12	100/MIA/EW	96/06/10	463	179	1900	No Delay	1	1920	54	
13	100/MIA/EW	96/06/11	467	295	1900	LQM/LWA	1	1920	46	
14	100/MIA/EW	96/06/12	463	239	1900	No Delay	1	1920	45	
15	100/EWR/LG	96/06/13	462	UNK	2300	No Delay	1	2350	45	
16	100/EWR/LG	96/06/13	462	393	1900	MTM	1	1920	122	
17	100/MIA/EW	96/06/14	462	583	2200	LQM	1	2220	51	
18	100/EWR/LG	96/06/14	462	583	1900	EQM/PAS	1	1920	129	
19	100/EWR/LG	96/06/15	469	UNK	2200	LQF	1	2220	67	
20	100/MIA/EW	96/06/15	469	207	1900	PAS	1	1920	126	
21	100/EWR/LG	96/06/16	469	UNK	2200	No Delay	1	2205	62	
22	100/MIA/EW	96/06/16	469	292	1900	PAS	1	1905	65	
23	100/EWR/LG	96/06/17	465	UNK	2200	LOA	1	2200	64	
24	100/MIA/EW	96/06/17	465	179	1900	LDS	1	1905	55	
25	100/EWR/LG	96/06/18	460	204	2200	LQM/LQI	1	2210	40	
26	100/MIA/EW	96/06/18	460	204	1900	MTM/FDI	1	1905	93	
27	100/MIA/EW	96/06/19	461	393	1900	PAS	1	1905	78	
28	100/EWR/LG	96/06/20	467	390	2200	LWA/LQF	1	2210	0	
29	100/MIA/EW	96/06/20	467	390	1900	LWA/PRF	1	1905	42	

9606EAGL.TXT

Ready NUM

Figure 13.5 Portion of an imported spreadsheet.

However, the spreadsheet interface to TM/1 allows spreadsheet formulas to link cells into hypercubes, which makes the process much simpler. (We could have used a linking process that would read an ASCII table, but the data was already in a spreadsheet so the formulas were more convenient. The data is all in a type one table, while the "database send" formulas transfer a single cell of data at a time. The linking methodology as described in Chapter 7 was employed. For each hypercube, we created a formula that linked a variable in the spreadsheet to its corresponding member in the hypercube. The formula combined cell references with member names contained in the rows and in the columns, essentially creating one column-member link and five or six row-member links, depending on the hypercube. We used the "fill down" command in Excel to copy the equation across all the thousand flights. Then, we used the "fill across" command to create the remaining column-member links for all the applicable variables. We recalculate the spreadsheet then imported all the data into the TM/1 hypercubes.

Dealing with Sparsity

Based on the ratio of the product of the number of members in each dimension it appears that the database will be very sparse. For the fuel cube, we're

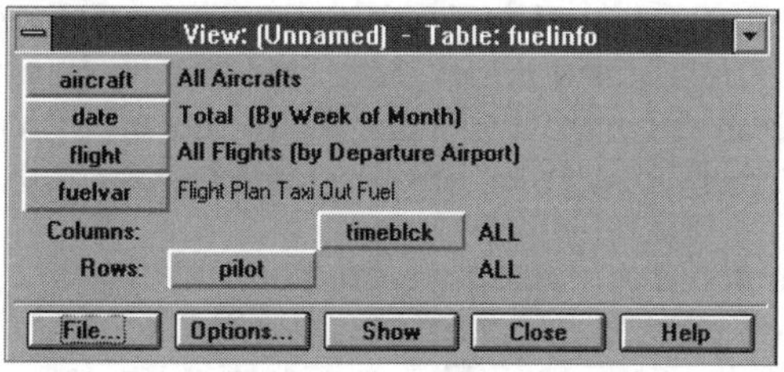

Figure 13.6 TM/1 browse box.

importing information for about a thousand flights, for each of the 13 variables—producing about 13,000 data points. However, in the fuel cube, the aircraft dimension has 14 members, the date dimension has 30, the flight dimension 107, the pilot dimension 57, the timeblck dimension 4—and there are 13 fuel variables. This creates 133,202,160 intersections, which is 10,000 times the number of data points! How will this affect the model?

Base-Level Views

Let's examine what our cubes will look like. For each hypercube, TM/1 creates a browse box by which we can define views of the hypercube (see Figure 13.6).

Viewing the Fuelinfo Hypercube

We will now open the *fuelinfo* browse box. Click on <u>TM/1</u>, then click on the <u>Tables</u> subheading.

[TM/1 - Tables Menu]

Click on <u>Browse</u>.

[Select Table to Browse]

Click on <u>fuelinfo</u>, then click <u>OK</u>.

[View: (Unnamed) - fuelinfo]

This is the *fuelinfo* browse box. If you wish minimize the browse box, click on the arrow in the upper-right corner. To bring it back after you've minimized it, double-click on it.

The dimension "tags" are listed in three columns. The dimension(s) in the first column (*aircraft*, *date*, *flight*, and *fuelvar*) define the "page" of the view, with a particular member selected for each (in this case, *All Aircrafts, Total (By Week Of Month), All Flights*, and *Flight Plan Taxi Out Fuel*, respectively). The dimension(s) in the second column (*pilot*) will be placed down the rows of the view; the dimension(s) in the third column (*timeblck*) will be set in the columns of the view.

How sparse does sparse get? Let's examine the base-level (nonaggregated) values in our hypercube for one of our variables (we'll choose *Flight Departures*). We'll choose a particular aircraft (*293*), on a particular date (*96/06/01*), for a particular flight (*501/AUS/FLL*), and we'll view the pilots and timeblocks in the rows and columns.

Examining Base-Level Hypercube Data in Fuelinfo

[View: (Unnamed) - Table: fuelinfo]

Click on aircraft.

[Select One Element of Dimension: aircraft]

Click on 293, then click OK.

[View: (Unnamed) - Table: fuelinfo]

Click on date.

[Select One Element of Dimension: date]

Click on 96/06/01, then click OK.

[View: (Unnamed) - Table: fuelinfo]

Click on flight.

[Select One Element of Dimension: flight]

We want to select an individual flight. Click on Drill. Click on Aus (depart), then click on Drill. Click on 501/AUS/FLL. Click OK.

[View: (Unnamed) - Table: fuelinfo]

Click on fuelvar.

[Select One Element of Dimension: fuelvar]

Click on Flight Departures, then click OK.

[View: (Unnamed) - Table: fuelinfo]

Click Show. The display should now appear as in Figure 13.7.

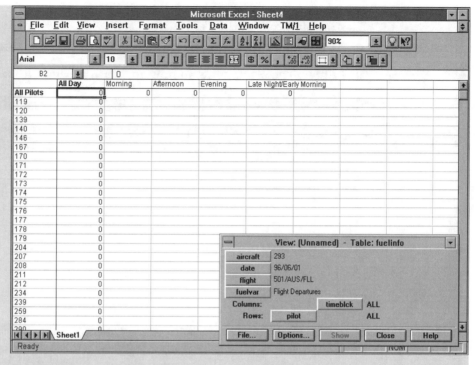

Figure 13.7 View of (sparse) base-level data.

Most of the view is blank, with a few zeros! TM/1 sums up a series of blanks to zero, so essentially there's no data here. The sparsity has a profound effect on our viewing; with only 1 out of every 10,000 intersections containing data, most base-level examinations of the data will return empty-handed.

Aggregated Views

Will our aggregations be meaningful in such a sparse matrix? Let's examine the effects of aggregating departure information. Instead of just looking at flight 293, we'll look at *All Aircrafts*.

Viewing Data Across All Aircrafts

[View: (Unnamed) - Table: fuelinfo]

Click on <u>aircraft</u>.

[Select One Element of Dimension: aircraft]

Click on <u>All Aircrafts</u>, then click <u>O</u>K.

[View: (Unnamed) - Table: fuelinfo]

Click <u>Show</u>. The display should now appear as in Figure 13.8.

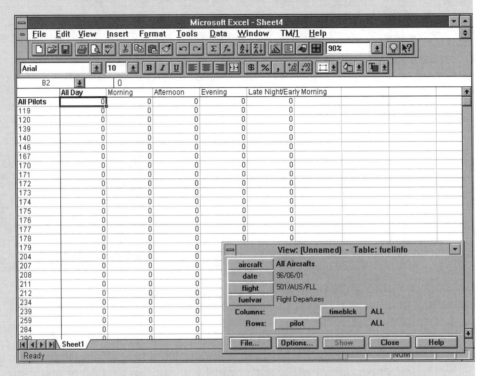

Figure 13.8 View of (sparse) aggregated departure data.

Everything is all zeros, which for this variable means the inputs are still blank. Instead of looking at just *96/06/01*, let's look the entire month.

<u>**Viewing All Aircrafts and All Dates**</u>

[View: (Unnamed) - Table: fuelinfo]

Click on <u>date</u>.

[Select One Element of Dimension: date]

Click on <u>Total (by week of month)</u>, then click <u>OK</u>.

[View: (Unnamed) - Table: fuelinfo]

Click <u>Show</u>. Your display should appear similar to Figure 13.9.

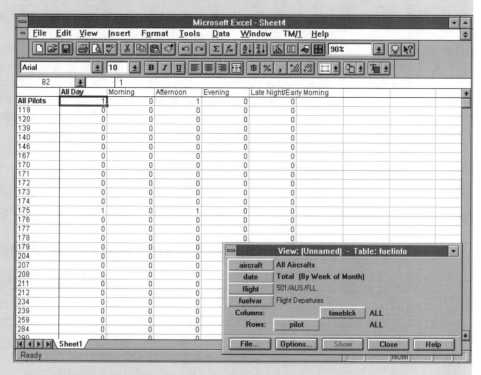

Figure 13.9 View of (sparse) more-aggregated departure data.

At least we have a value for pilot 175, but even so it's still incredibly sparse. Let's do one final aggregation, viewing departure data for all flights.

All Aircrafts, Dates, and Flights

[View: (Unnamed) - Table: fuelinfo]

Click on <u>flight</u>.

[Select One Element of Dimension: flight]

Click on <u>All Flights</u>, then click <u>OK</u>.

[View: (Unnamed) - Table: fuelinfo]

Click <u>Show</u>. Your display should appear as in Figure 13.10.

By combining departure information from all flights we have a sufficiently dense matrix with which we can make meaningful observations. We can see that most of our flights happen in the afternoon. We have almost no late night flights. We can also see the time of day each pilot usually flies.

Essentially, as we aggregate, our views become less and less sparse, producing higher-level aggregations that are analytically useful.

Performing Calculations

How does sparsity affect the way we perform calculations? There is both the fact of the sparsity and the way in which the tool deals with it. Let's look at

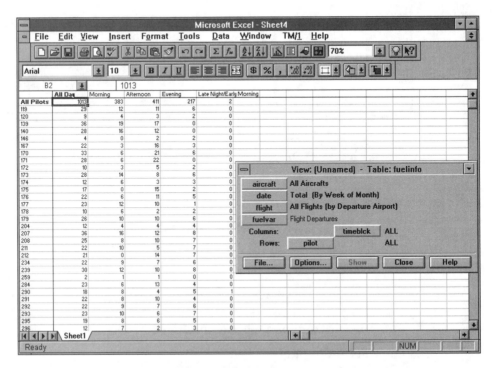

Figure 13.10 View of sufficient aggregation to cover sparsity.

the two most common types of calculations, sums and averages. For example, when evaluating delay times (which are used in both hypercubes), we shall be interested in both the sum of delays (Total Delay Minutes) and average delay (Average Delay Minutes).

As we have seen, the data set is quite sparse. TM/1 treats empty cells as containing 0. Whether TM/1 treats empty cells as contributing nothing to the aggregation or as each containing zero, the sum will be the same either way. There are two distinct interpretations of average available, however: averaging over all available values and averaging over all cells. When averaging over all available values, blank cells will not contribute to either the sum of values or their count. When averaging over all cells, though (which is what the conversion of blank to zero leads to), each blank cell will contribute to the count of cells but not their sum. This will leave our calculated average much lower that the true average; with less that 1 out of 10,000 intersections having nonzero value, almost all of the average delay values would be less than a second.

Also, it is not enough to just average the nonzero values. *Some of these zeros represent meaningless intersection, but some of them reflect data points for actual flights whose delay was 0 minutes*. We don't want to throw these out.

We need to know how many of these values correspond to actual flights. We can determine this through the use of the flight departures variable. This variable tracks how many flights actually took place in a given set of flight intersections. This variable has a value of 1 for each individual flight. Thus, we can divide our total delay by this value to calculate the correct average:

Average Delay = Total Delay / Flight Departures

Essentially, we have to use a lower level control over our aggregation processes and explicitly aggregate the count and sum components. This type of modification allows us to factor sparsity correctly into the aggregations we perform.

Limitations of Analysis with Sparse Data Sets

Although you have seen how to count and sum data correctly in a sparse environment, not all analyses can be equally well performed. Analyses that require cardinally ordered identifier dimensions, such as regression analysis, cannot be properly performed in a sparse environment. Just imagine trying to calculate a regression coefficient for a time series variable such as "sales" when only 1 in 10,000 time periods was defined. If you collapsed the missing time periods, you would be left with a modified time dimension that no longer had the cardinal properties required for the regression analysis. (More on this in Chapter 15.)

Creating Formulas (Rules)

Once we imported the data, the next step was to create the variable rules. Let's examine the variable rules for the *fuelinfo* cube.

Examining/Creating Rules

Click Close on the *fuelinfo* browse box. To view the rules worksheet, click on TM/1, then the Rules Subheading.

[TM/1 - Rules Menu]

Click on Open.

[Select Rules Worksheet]

Click on fuelinfo, then click OK.

[FUELINFO.XRU]

The worksheet shown in Figure 13.11 should be displayed. This worksheet contains all the rules for the delay cube. We can open any rules worksheet in the same manner.

These rules allow us to calculate variables that are derived from other variables. We used several rules of thumb to create these rules.

Precedence Rules

In this regard, the models are quite straightforward. Outside of the dimensional aggregations, there are only three rules in the *fuelinfo* hypercube and five in *delayinf*. Of these eight formulas, only one requires any special attention to dimensional precedence.

Passenger-Delay-Minutes takes the amount of time that a flight is delayed and multiplies it by the number of passengers who are on that flight. For a given flight, we want the rule:

$$Passenger\text{-}Delay\text{-}Minutes = Total\ Passengers\ *\ Total\ Delay\ Minutes$$

However, we have to be careful about how we have the hypercube calculate this rule for nonleaf (consolidated) members. For example, imagine that flight A has 10 people and a 10-minute delay (100 passenger-delay-minutes). Flight B has 20 passengers and a 5-minute delay (another 100 passenger-de-

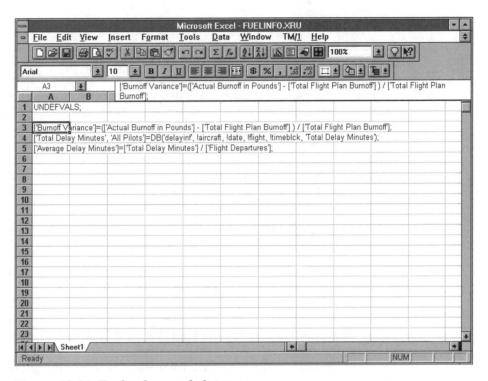

Figure 13.11 Fuel rules worksheet.

lay minutes). Suppose there is a consolidated member AB, which is the parent of the two flights.

What is the total passenger delay for AB? It should be 200 total passenger-delay-minutes. But using our dimensional aggregation formulas, the total number of passengers for AB is 30, and total delay minutes is 15. If we applied the above rule on the consolidated level, passenger-delay-minutes would be 30 * 15 = 450!

Essentially, we want our passenger-delay-minutes rule to have precedence over dimensional aggregation. We want to calculate passenger-delay-minutes at the leaf level first (10 * 10 = 100, 20 * 5 = 100), and <u>then</u> aggregate the values (100 + 100 = 200). We do not want it to aggregate first and then calculate passenger delay; otherwise, we get incorrect values as before. In TM/1 the rule is as follows:

*['Passenger-Delay-Minutes'] = N: [Total Delay Minutes'] * ['Total Passengers'];*

The *N:* tells TM/1 to use the formula for leaf (nonconsolidated) members only. The dimension structure will by default compute the aggregated (consolidated) members.

Intercube References

Let's discuss the fuelinfo rule for Total Delay Minutes. (If you wish, open the FUELINFO.XRU rules worksheet.) The Total Delay Minutes variable was imported into the *delayinfo* cube for delay analysis. However, it is also necessary for fuel analysis. We could have imported a separate copy in the *fuelinfo* dimension, but we'd rather not have duplicate variable information. If we do, every time we add new flight information, we will need to copy the data. In addition to the effort required, we may make errors that will produce inaccurate and inconsistent data. Instead, we choose to exploit the multicube structure of the model and *link* the hypercubes, so that the *fuelinfo* cube simply uses the Total Delay Minutes data from the *delayinf* cube. This lets us store the data in one place. The formula in TM/1 is:

['Total Delay Minutes', 'All Pilots']

=DB('delayinf', !aircraft, !date, !flight, !timeblck, 'Total Delay Minutes');

Because the delay cube information is not broken down by pilot, we link the information to the *All Pilots* member (which will have a useful sum, even if from just one pilot). The "DB()" tells the hypercube that it needs to reference a different cube—in this case, *delayinf*. We need to select "Total Delay Minutes" from the *delayvar*, and we want this rule to apply for every aircraft, date, flight, and timeblock.

Once we've created the necessary rules in both cubes, our model is complete and we can start performing analysis.

Analyzing the Data

The multidimensional structure allows us to analyze the data from any perspective we are interested in. Let's begin by looking at delay information, then looking at fuel consumption.

Delay Analysis

Let's evaluate the delay information that we have on our June flights. We'll begin with examining delays by time block, then look at delays by date and by flight.

By Timeblock

At what times of day are we having the most delay problems? Let's view the variables *Flight Departures*, *Average Delay Minutes*, *Total Passengers*, and *Passenger Delay Minutes* across each timeblock. In terms of our multidimensional tool, we want to set aircraft to *All Aircrafts*, date to *Total (By Week Of Month)*, flight to *All Flights (by Departure Airport),* and view the selected delay variables in the rows and the timeblocks across the columns.

Viewing Delays by Timeblock

Open the *delayinf* cube, following the same procedure as given for opening the *fuelinfo* cube.

[View: (Unnamed) - Table: delayinf]

The *aircraft* dimension is already set to *All Aircrafts*, the *date, flight,* and *timeblck* dimensions are set correctly as well. Click on delayvar.

[Edit Subset: ALL of Dimension: delayvar]

Control-click on the members Total Passengers, Flight Departures, Average Delay Minutes, and Passenger Delay Minutes to select them all. Click OK.

[View: (Unnamed) - Table: delayinf]

Click Show. This will take a minute or two; be patient. You should see the view shown in Figure 13.12.

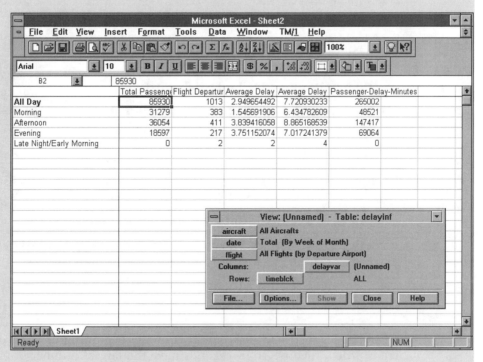

Figure 13.12 Delay information by time block.

Looking at Figure 13.12, the *Late Night/Early Morning* flights have no passengers, so there are no corresponding passenger-delay minutes. Notice that the average delay per flight is much lower in the morning than in afternoon or evening; it is clearly the best time to fly. We see that there are fewer passengers and flights to deal with in the morning, which could contribute to the lack of delays. Days could also start off on time, with delays accumulating as each day wears on.

Compare *Afternoon* and *Evening*. Even though they have similar average delay minutes, the passenger-delay-minutes are much greater in the afternoon. Many more people are traveling then, making the delays more significant.

Thus, out of all the timeblocks, it appears most productive to invest in improving afternoon air travel.

By Date

Suppose we're interested in analyzing these variables across different days of the week. With a few clicks of the mouse, we can now examine the data from this new perspective.

Viewing Delays by Date

[View: (Unnamed) - Table: delayinf]

Drag *timeblck* to the left-most column; it should set itself to *All Day*. Drag *date* to the middle column. Click on date.

[Edit Subset: ALL of Dimension: date]

Click on Total (By Day Of Month), then click Keep. Click on Drill. You should see all seven weekdays listed. Click OK.

[View: (Unnamed) - Table: delayinf]

Click Show. This step takes several minutes on a 133 MHz Pentium; be patient. The view shown in Figure 13.13 should appear.

Look at Figure 13.13. It seems that at the beginning of the work week, there is little difficulty. The weekends have the largest number of passengers and correspondingly the largest delays. In particular, we need to invest more in improving Friday air travel.

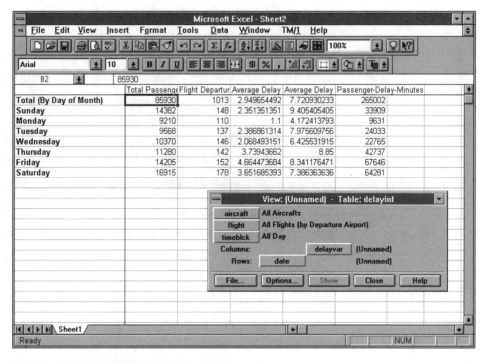

Figure 13.13 Delays by day of the week.

By Flight

In New York, we operate in two airports, *JFK* and *LGA*. Given the relatively high amounts of travel and delay during weekends, which of these airports do we want to route people out of for weekend travel? Let's examine the departure information for the two airports on Friday and Saturday.

Viewing Delay by Departing Flight

[View: (Unnamed) - Table: delayinf]

Drag *flight* to the middle column, beneath *date*. Click on flight.

[Edit Subset: ALL of Dimension: flight]

Click on All Flights (By Departure Airport), then click on Keep. Click on Drill. Control-click on JFK (depart) and LGA (depart). Click OK.

[View: (Unnamed) - Table: delayinf]

Click on <u>date</u>.

[Edit Subset: ALL of Dimension: date]

Hold down the Control key and click on <u>Friday</u> and <u>Saturday</u>. Click <u>OK</u>.

[View: (Unnamed) - Table: delayinf]

Click <u>Show</u>. This will be much faster than the last two views. The view shown in Figure 13.14 should appear.

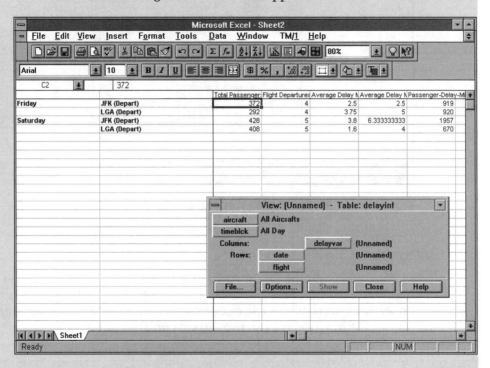

Figure 13.14 Delays by selected airports.

Look at Figure 13.14. We see on Friday that, even though JFK has a greater number of total passengers, it has a smaller average delay. It is clearly the better place to route people through on Friday. However, on Saturday, even though they have approximately the same number of passengers, it seems that JFK has a much larger average delay and higher passenger-delay-minutes, so LGA clearly looks better.

Summary of Delay Analysis

While the choice of dimensional structure for the data has led to a very sparse hypercube, it also supports useful analyses of the given information by providing a rich set of aggregation combinations by which we can understand the given flight information. In particular, being able to easily separate time of day from date has proven quite useful.

Fuel Analysis

Let's now examine the fuel cube.

Viewing Fuelinfo

[View: (Unnamed) - Table: delayinf]

Click Close.

Within the spreadsheet, click on TM/1, then click on the Tables menu choice.

[TM/1 - Tables Menu]

Click on Browse.

[Select Table to Browse]

Click on fuelinfo, then click OK.

[View: (Unnamed) - Table: fuelinfo]

We are now ready to view the *fuelinfo* cube.

By Aircraft

Let's examine the burnoff variance information across all of the different aircraft to see which ones are the least efficient. Delays will increase a plane's fuel usage, so we want to view average delay time as well.

Viewing Fuel Consumption by Aircraft

[View: (Unnamed) - Table: fuelinfo]

Drag *aircraft* to the middle column. Click on date.

[Select One Element of Dimension: date]

Click on <u>Reset</u>. Click on <u>Total (by week of month)</u>. Click <u>OK</u>.

[View: (Unnamed) - Table: fuelinfo]

Click on <u>flight</u>.

[Select One Element of Dimension: flight]

Click on <u>Reset</u>, then click on <u>All Flights (By Departure Airport)</u>. Click OK.

[View: (Unnamed) - Table: fuelinfo]

Drag *fuelvar* to the right-most column. Click on <u>fuelvar.</u>

[Edit Subset: ALL of Dimension: fuelvar]

Control-click on <u>Burnoff Variance</u> and <u>Average Delay Minutes</u>. Click <u>OK</u>.

[View: (Unnamed) - Table: fuelinfo]

Drag *pilot* into the left-most column. Drag *timeblck* into the left-most column. Click <u>Show</u>. This will take a couple of minutes. The view shown in Figure 13.15 should appear.

In Figure 13.15, notice that plane 293 has by far the highest variance, but it also seems to have high delays. AirTran will probably want to further investigate the reason for these delays; if its delays are caused by gate problems then it may need maintenance, but if it is spending its time on the runway or in holding patterns then it may be fine. Now, look at aircraft 463 and 465. They have a higher-than-average burnoff variance, yet they are experiencing below-average delay times. They appear to be less fuel efficient than the rest of the fleet, so we should target them for additional maintenance.

By Pilot

Now let's examine the fuel burnoff variance by pilot. We need to factor in which aircraft they are flying—if they happen to be flying planes that are possibly fuel inefficient (that is, 463 and 465) or stuck in traffic (293). Let's view the variance for each pilot on all aircraft and on 263, 463, and 465. We'll move pilots to the rows and aircraft to the columns because the pilot dimension is fairly large, and we want to fit as many as we can on the screen.

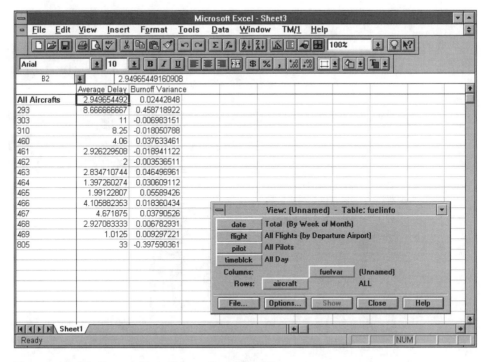

Figure 13.15 Burnoff variance by aircraft.

Examining Fuel Consumption by Pilot

[View: (Unnamed) - Table: fuelinfo]

Drag *fuelvar* into the left-most column. Click on <u>fuelvar</u>.

[Select One Element Of Dimension: fuelvar]

Click on <u>Burnoff Variance</u>, then click <u>OK</u>.

[View: (Unnamed) - Table: fuelinfo]

Drag *pilot* into the middle column. Drag *aircraft* into the right-most column. Click on <u>aircraft</u>.

[Edit Subset of Dimension: aircraft]

Click on <u>All Aircrafts</u>, and Control-click on <u>293</u>, <u>463</u>, and <u>465</u>. Click <u>OK</u>.

[View: (Unnamed) - Table: fuelinfo]

Click <u>Show</u>.

In the spreadsheet, highlight the cells from *A3* to *D59*, and sort by the second column (the *All Aircrafts* column). This will create the view shown in Figure 13.16.

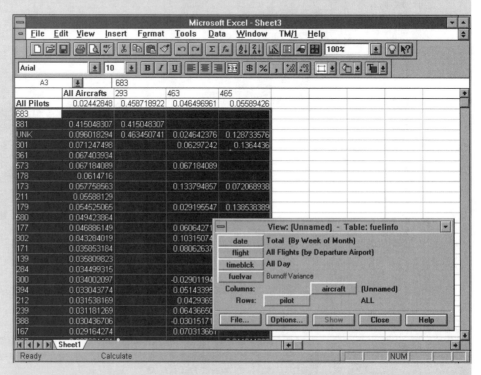

Figure 13.16 Sorted view of burnoff variance by pilot.

Note that pilots *UNK* and *301* come in the upper burnoff variances, but they also fly both of the suspect planes, which could explain why. Pilot *881* has the highest variance but is on the most-delayed plane. Now, look at pilots *301*, *178*, and *211*. They are among the highest in burnoff variances (all greater than 5 percent variance), but they are not using the fuel-inefficient planes (they each have zeros for planes 293, 463, and 465). This suggests further investigation into their flights and flying; they may be inefficient in their fuel use, and they may benefit from further training on fuel-conservation procedures.

Conclusion

In this chapter you have seen what it is like to work with a very sparse data set. Data that seemed useless at the base level acquired meaning during the aggregation process. You also saw the benefits of splitting multiple hierarchies in single dimension—time—into two dimensions: a date dimension and a time of day dimension.

Cost/Benefit Analysis for Infrastructure Investments

This hands-on case study takes you through the building and analysis of a multidimensional model that uses cost/benefit analysis to identify the type of water system investment projected to bring the greatest net benefit to the inhabitants of several regions in Indonesia. This chapter describes the process of transferring the water supply model from a spreadsheet to a multidimensional tool and of performing cost/benefit analysis from a multidimensional perspective. We will also compare the efficiency of how things are done using a multidimensional tool with how things are done using a spreadsheet. The model was originally created, using spreadsheets and geographic information systems, by GIS/Trans, which provides vendor-independent information technology (IT) solutions to infrastructure management agencies and corporations worldwide.

The Situation at GIS/Trans

GIS/Trans first became involved with this project as a subcontractor to Jonathan Stevens, a consultant working with a research grant from the World Bank to help the Indonesian government to analyze the impact of performance measurement on the effectiveness of operation and management (O&M) decisions in five sectors within the East Java Bali Urban Development Project: water supply, solid waste collection, roads, road drainage, and storm

381

drainage. Subsequently, GIS/Trans worked directly with the Indonesian government. The company evaluated the development and implementation of a user-based performance measurement approach, for use in the Performance-Oriented Maintenance Management System that is being implemented by the government of Indonesia to improve urban infrastructure management. The initial project focused on the water sector.

GIS/Trans Problems and Goals

Unlike the other case studies in this book, GIS/Trans does not currently use multidimensional technology to provide solutions, although one of its principals knew something about the technology from previous projects where he and I had collaborated. At this juncture, GIS/Trans wanted to explore the possibility of substituting OLAP products for spreadsheets as its primary numerical data store, analytical engine, and viewer. Toward that end, I duplicated one of its spreadsheet models in an OLAP tool and showed them its benefits, which you will learn about during this chapter:

1. Easier model definition
2. Easier formula creation
3. Easier analytical view reorganizations
4. Easier model expansion
5. Easier handling of increased formulaic complexity.

The government used an Excel spreadsheet to store and analyze health and cost information about the Denpasar water supply and the effects of investing in pipe repair. Open the spreadsheet *C:\TM1DATA\DENPASAR\WATER.XLS* and look at sheet 1. (All of the variables and terminology used in the spreadsheet will be explained in detail later.) This is the water supply spreadsheet.

At the top of the spreadsheet (rows 1–14) are the net benefits/costs of repairing the pipes. A portion of this is shown in Figure 14.1. These rows comprise the basic summary of the spreadsheet's data. Listed first are the net costs of PDAM repair, operation, and maintenance (columns C–F), then the net benefits calculated for each water consumer group (columns G–N). The net benefits are totaled at the end (columns O–Q). The numbers are measured in millions.

Next, the cost projections over the next five years are listed for each of the four subareas of Denpasar (rows 20–311). A segment of this is shown in Figure 14.2. The variables that are constant for all four subregions are listed in rows 21–29, columns A–L. Then, in each subarea, information about water consumption, supply costs, illness rates, and so on, are compiled to analyze the situation both in the status quo (without action, columns D–T) and if the pipes are repaired (with action, columns V–AL). This data is stored for each

Figure 14.1:

File Edit View Insert Format Tools Data Window TM/1 Help

A1 — BENEFIT-COST ANALYSIS - PDAM WATER SUPPLY O&M IMPROVEMENTS

BENEFIT-COST ANALYSIS - PDAM WATER SUPPLY O&M IMPROVEMENTS

ACTION: Repair Pipes 4.7 km   LOCATION:Denpasar   TOTAL NPV(mil. Rp):

Benefit Summary

Year	Cost of Action	Other PDAM O&M Costs w/o action	Other PDAM O&M Costs with action	Net Cost to PDAM	Domestic Households Low	Medium	High	Commercial Restaurant	Office	Store
1995	132.6			132.6	11.8	7.2	25.9	0.3	0.1	0
1996		471.0	447.5	-23.5	12.3	7.5	27.2	0.4	0.1	0
1997		471.0	447.5	-23.5	12.8	7.8	28.6	0.4	0.2	0
1998		471.0	447.5	-23.5	13.4	8.1	30.0	0.5	0.2	0
1999		471.0	447.5	-23.5	14.0	8.4	31.5	0.6	0.2	0
Total	132.6	1,884.0	1,790.0	38.6	64.3	38.9	143.1	2.3	0.9	4

BENEFIT DETAILS

Subarea 1:Dangin Puri
A. DOMESTIC USERS

(Average Consumption:	liter per person per day	Value of Time:	Rp per hr.	Unit Cost of Disease (Rp):	240,0
Low Income	120		300		
Mid Income	130		1200		
High Income	160		3600		
	average liter per establishment per month				
Commecial	24119				
Industrial	605340				
Hospital	51300				
1. Low Income	**Without Action**			550	550	24,195	761
	Number	% Use of Supply Source		Average Cost of Using Supply Source	1251.6 man. well

Sheet1 Sheet2 Sheet3 Sheet4 Sheet5 Sheet6 Sheet7 SH

Ready   NUM

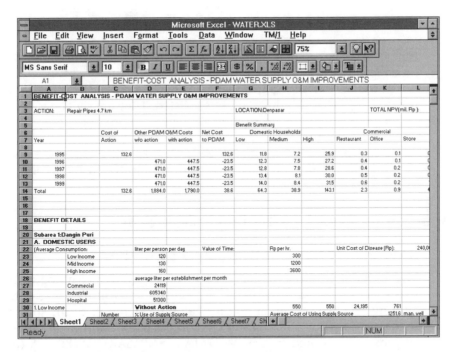

Figure 14.1 Net benefits/costs of repairing pipes.

Figure 14.2:

Microsoft Excel - WATER.XLS

File Edit View Insert Format Tools Data Window TM/1 Help

Arial   10   M46

Subarea 1:Dangin Puri
A. DOMESTIC USERS

(Average Consumption:	liter per person per day	Value of Time:	Rp per hr.	Unit Cost of Disease (Rp):	240,000)
Low Income	120		300		
Mid Income	130		1200		
High Income	160		3600		
	average liter per establishment per month				
Commecial	24119				
Industrial	605340				
Hospital	51300				

1. Low Income — **Without Action** — 550 | 550 | 24,195 | 761

	Number of Users	PDAM only	other piped	bottled	well/river	PDAM only	other piped	bottled	well/river	time cost	Cost
1995	10,229	56.5%	0.0%	0.0%	43.5%	139,225,385	0	0	148,364,349	4,449,615	292,039,349
1996	10,536	56.5%	0.0%	0.0%	43.5%	143,402,146	0	0	152,815,280	4,583,103	300,800,530
1997	10,852	56.5%	0.0%	0.0%	43.5%	147,704,211	0	0	157,399,738	4,720,597	309,824,545
1998	11,178	56.5%	0.0%	0.0%	43.5%	152,135,337	0	0	162,121,731	4,862,214	319,119,282
1999	11,513	56.5%	0.0%	0.0%	43.5%	156,699,397	0	0	166,985,382	5,008,081	328,692,860

2. Medium Income

	Number of Users	PDAM only	other piped	bottled	well/river	PDAM only	other piped	bottled	well/river	time cost	Cost
1995	3068	67.4%	0.0%	0.0%	32.6%	53,965,246	0	0	36,127,855		90,093,101
1996	3,160	67.4%	0.0%	0.0%	32.6%	55,594,203	0	0	37,211,691		92,795,894
1997	3,255	67.4%	0.0%	0.0%	32.6%	57,251,729	0	0	38,328,042		95,579,771
1998	3,352	67.4%	0.0%	0.0%	32.6%	58,969,281	0	0	39,477,883		98,447,164
1999	3,453	67.4%	0.0%	0.0%	32.6%	60,738,359	0	0	40,662,220		101,400,579

3. High Income

	Number of Users	PDAM only	other piped	bottled	well/river	PDAM only	other piped	bottled	well/river	time cost	Cost
1995	665	67.4%	22.0%	0.0%	10.6%	14,396,505	4,699,156	0	3,133,815		22,229,476
1996	685	67.4%	22.0%	0.0%	10.6%	14,828,400	4,840,131	0	3,227,830		22,896,361
1997	705	67.4%	22.0%	0.0%	10.6%	15,273,252	4,985,335	0	3,324,664		23,583,251
1998	727	67.4%	22.0%	0.0%	10.6%	15,731,450	5,134,895	0	3,424,404		24,290,749

Sheet1 Sheet2 Sheet3 Sheet4 Sheet5 Sheet6 Sheet7 SH

Ready   NUM

Figure 14.2 Cost projections.

type of consumer, then broken down by water type. The savings earned by pipe repair are stored in column AM.

At the bottom of the spreadsheet (rows 313–334), the information particular to hospital and industrial users is listed. They are separated from the rest of the regional data because they are regional costs that couldn't be broken down by subarea.

Spend a minute or two surveying the spreadsheet and examining its structure. How could this be recreated in a multidimensional tool?

From a Spreadsheet to an OLAP Solution

Determining General Hypercube Structure

The multidimensional model we constructed is provided along with the original spreadsheet. As with the other case studies, you have the option of examining the two models as you read along. References to the spreadsheet are made throughout the chapter; if you wish to examine it firsthand, the spreadsheet is stored in C:\TM1DATA\DENPASAR\WATER.XLS (during the default installation; you may have opted to place it in a different directory). If you choose not to use TM/1, you can just read through, ignoring the segments of the text with **bold and underlined headings**, such as the **Using TM/1: Getting Started** section below.

Please note: the directions for following through this case study will be more abbreviated than in the previous three studies. If you have worked through the detailed instructions of one or both of the previous studies, you should now be familiar with the basic operations in TM/1.

Using TM/1: Getting Started

As you follow along, you will be asked to open up different windows in the TM/1 program. Each time that you are supposed to see a new window on your screen, we will print the name of the window in [bold and bracketed] text. Text of note on the screen will be *italicized*. Everything that you will be asked to click on with your mouse will be underlined in the text. This tutorial assumes that TM/1 has already been installed, and the user has access to all directories. (To find out how to install TM/1, see Appendix I).

Within the spreadsheet, click on the TM/1 menu and then the Options menu choice.

[TM/1 PERSPECTIVES - OPTIONS]

> Make sure the database directory is set to *C:\TM1DATA\DENPASAR* (or the directory to which the model was actually installed, if different) and that the *Advanced Mode* option is checked. Click <u>OK</u>.
>
> **[TM/1 PERSPECTIVES]**
>
> (It should ask you "Do you want to update file: tm1.ini?")
>
> Click <u>Yes</u>. You are now ready to begin.

Our goal is to identify the model dimensions in the spreadsheet and use them to create an OLAP model for the same structure.

There are six main structural components to the spreadsheet:

1. *Regions:* Denpasar is broken down into four subareas in the spreadsheet, each with its own economic data.
2. *Endpoints (consumers and producers):* Each region is broken down into different types of water consumers.
3. *Water type:* Consumers purchase four different types of water; each type has unique advantages and disadvantages.
4. *Measures* Many different types of economic measures are used to determine costs and benefits.
5. *Years:* The model has a five-year time frame, from 1995 to 1999.
6. *Strategy:* The goal of the model is to compare two strategies: continuing with the status quo or investing in pipe repair.

These six components form the basis of the spreadsheet model and are used as the dimensions of our hypercube. A diagram of the multidimensional structure is shown in Figure 14.3.

Visualizing the Model

We also created an analytical visualization of the structure of this model which is described on the CD-ROM in Diamond\Data\Denp1.txt. Pointers to the image and data files are also contained therein.

Forming the Dimensions and Their Basic Aggregation Formulas

Region

The four subareas that compose Denpasar are *Dangin Puri*, *Pemecutan Kelod*, *Pemecutan Kaja*, and *Sanur*. Each one is a member of the dimension (see Fig-

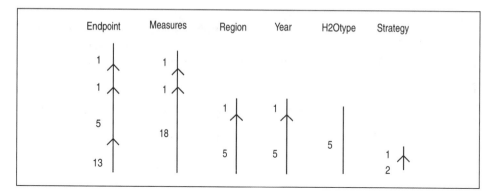

Figure 14.3 Diagram of multidimensional structure for water supply model.

ure 14.4). *We also created a member All Denpasar, containing all the information that cannot be broken down by subarea.* For example, the information on hospital and industrial water use is determined only on a regional level, not by

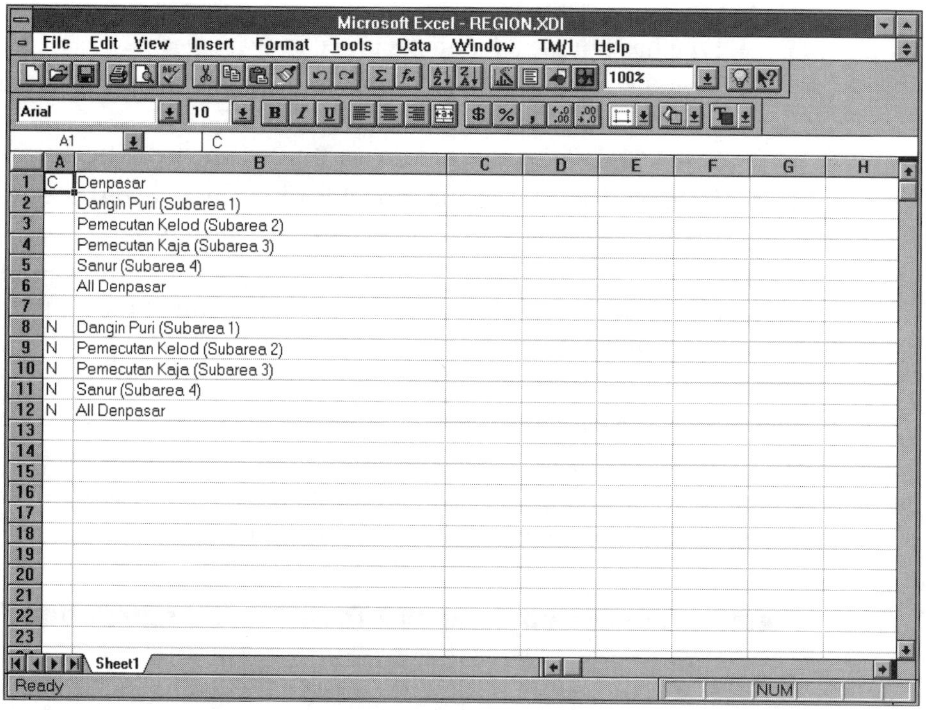

	A	B
1	C	Denpasar
2		Dangin Puri (Subarea 1)
3		Pemecutan Kelod (Subarea 2)
4		Pemecutan Kaja (Subarea 3)
5		Sanur (Subarea 4)
6		All Denpasar
7		
8	N	Dangin Puri (Subarea 1)
9	N	Pemecutan Kelod (Subarea 2)
10	N	Pemecutan Kaja (Subarea 3)
11	N	Sanur (Subarea 4)
12	N	All Denpasar

Figure 14.4 The region dimension.

subarea. We made *Denpasar* a consolidation (parent) of these five members. (In TM/1, all consolidated members are preceded by a "C," and nonconsolidated numeric members are preceded by an "N.") By default, values for the Denpasar level will be computed as the sum of the values from its child members.

Viewing/Editing a Dimension

Let's examine the region dimension in TM/1. From within the spreadsheet, click on the TM/1 menu, then the Dimensions menu choice.

[TM/1 - Dimensions Menu]

Click Open.

[Select Dimension Worksheet]

Click region, then click OK. The dimension worksheet of Figure 14.4 should appear.

[REGION.XDI]

This is the technique by which we view and edit dimensions. We can open any dimension using the same procedure.

Endpoints (Consumers)

The consumer population is broken down into four categories: household users, commercial users, industrial users, and hospitals. A portion of the dimension is shown in Figure 14.5. *Household* is broken down into *Low Income, Medium Income,* and *High Income. Commercial* is broken down into three types: *Restaurant, Office,* and *Store.* These three types of consumers, along with *Industrial*, purchase water for situations in which the quality of the water isn't significant (for example, dry cleaning) and situations where the water must be high quality (for example, food preparation in restaurants). Each type of consumer is broken down in *Quality-Sensitive* and *Nonquality-Sensitive* consumption. *Hospitals* is a separate member. The member *All Consumers* is used to associate any costs that don't break down into consumer groups. For example, the cost of repairing the pipes is a regional cost and is not particular to any consumer groups. *Total Consumers* is the consolidation of all these members. Each consolidation step is a simple sum of the component members.

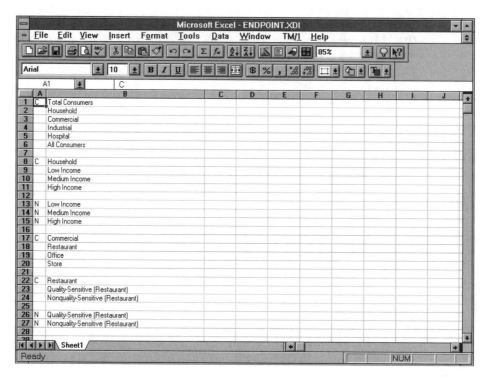

Figure 14.5 The endpoint dimension.

h2otype (Water Type)

There are four types or sources of water. *PDAM*, the local water authority in Denpasar, provides the majority of the water. *Other Piped, Bottled,* and *Well/River* are the other three types. They compose the consolidation *Non-PDAM water. All Water* represents information about the total water supply. In this model, it is *not* a consolidation of the four water types because its information is not always derived from combining values of the other members. For example, the total water consumption figures are researched information that is entered into the database; they are *not* calculated by summing the consumption figures of each of the different water types. No aggregation is built into this dimension.

Measures (Variables)

These are the variables in the water supply data. The variables enclosed in brackets were defined in the OLAP tool, not in the original spreadsheet:

❑ *Cost of Repairs:* The cost of investing in pipe repair.

- *Other PDAM/O&M Costs:* Additional costs (operational, maintenance, and so on) for PDAM.

- *Total PDAM Costs:* The sum of the above two costs.

- *Number of Consumers:* Number of people using a particular supply source.

- *[Growth Rate of Consumer Population]:* The rate at which the consumer population increases. This is not explicitly stored in the spreadsheet, but it used by the spreadsheet to project consumer population figures.

- *Percent of Consumers Using Supply Source:* The percentage of all consumers that use a particular water supply.

- *[Avg. Liters Used per Consumer (monthly)]:* The average number of liters purchased per consumer in a month. In the spreadsheet, some of these figures were taken as daily averages rather than monthly; they were converted to monthly averages in the multidimensional database to simplify creating global formulas.

- *Cost of Supply Source per Liter:* The cost of supplying a liter of water from a supply source.

- *Rp. per Hour:* The opportunity cost per hour (travel time), in rupees, for a person using well water. This cost is incurred only by low-income households; wealthier households would have well water that is directly accessible.

- *Man. Well Time Cost:* The total opportunity cost in a region for using well water.

- *Total Cost of Supplying Water:* The total cost of supplying water to an area.

- *Disease Incidence Fraction:* The average fraction of people who become sick from using a particular water source.

- *Total Water-Borne Disease Incidence:* Total number of people who become sick from a particular water source.

- *Cost per Person:* The total cost of water divided by the number of people consuming it.

- *Unit Cost of Disease:* The health costs for each person who contracts disease.

- *Net Present Value:* The present value of the total saving, taking discount rates into account.

- *Discount Rate:* The percentage discount that a future value is worth at an earlier time.

- *Total Cost of Illness:* Total costs incurred from sickness/disease.

- *Total Cost:* The sum of *Total Cost of Illness*, *Total Cost of Supplying* Water, and *Total PDAM Costs*.

Year

The members of this dimension are the years *1995-1999* and *Total Forecast*, which aggregates values over all five years.

Strategy

This is the essential purpose for creating an OLAP model: to determine what course of action Denpasar should pursue. *Status Quo* reflects the projected figure if the region does not invest in its water infrastructure; *Investment* in Pipe Repair is the scenario in which the water authority does invest. *Net Benefits/Costs of Repair* calculates the difference between the two options. For cost variables, a positive value at this member represents savings due to pipe repair, and negative values represent losses.

Benefits of Dimensional Formulas

Dimensional formulas simplify the process of creating aggregations. Rather than creating thousands or even millions of cell-based formulas, we simply define an aggregation formula in each hierarchical dimension. In Excel, this entails the following.

For *every* consumer group in *each* region we have to create a formula to calculate net benefits and costs, then "fill them down" to calculate the values for each year (see column T, rows 20–334 in Sheet1). With two strategies, four subareas, nine individual consumer groups per region, with each set of formulas requiring two steps (creation of the formula and then "fill down"), we have 144 steps at the start. Then we compare the cost figures from the two strategies to calculate the net benefits (*Total Cost Savings*) of pipe repair for each subarea, consumer group and year (row AM). To find the net benefits for each consumer group across all of Denpasar, we have to again create separate formulas for each consumer group to sum across all four regions (rows 1–14, columns G–L), then we have to add in hospital and industrial net costs (rows 1–14, columns M–N). Finally, we have to create a formula summing net costs across all consumer groups (see rows 1–14, columns O–Q). Each of these equations needed to be "filled down" across all five years. There are more than 200 steps in this entire process, with great potential for error. (It may be possible to help automate this by creating some spreadsheet macros to assist the process, but they will be quite inflexible and must themselves be created and debugged.)

In the OLAP tool, you define the following:

- *Denpasar* as the consolidation of the four subareas
- *Total Consumers* as the consolidation of all the consumer groups
- *Net Benefits/Costs of Repairs* as the difference between *Status Quo* costs and *Investment in Pipe Repair Costs*

This takes but *three* steps; and it produces the same calculations.

Furthermore, additional aggregated values are created by virtue of the dimensional structure. For example, the total amount of each water type consumed in all of Denpasar is automatically calculated in the multidimensional tool by virtue of these dimensional consolidations; in the spreadsheet we would need to set up a whole new set of formulas. *Total Cost of Illness* is calculated by region, by consumer group, by year and by water type. We also calculate the *Net Benefits/Costs* for these values, informing us of how much is saved in illness costs. It would take a significant amount of work to set up additional formulas in the spreadsheet for each of these.

As we try to expand the spreadsheet calculations, it becomes extremely difficult to keep things in a structured, comprehensible form. *The problem (with the spreadsheet) is that we are trying to define a six-dimensional model in a two-dimensional medium.*

Defining the Hypercube

Once the dimensions have been created, you can combine them to form the hypercube. In TM/1, for example, you simply list the desired dimensions for your hypercube (see Figure 14.6; we have called the hypercube "h2oinfo"), and the cube is created.

Transferring Data to the Hypercube

Once the cubes are constructed (with the associated dimensional aggregation formulas), we need to import the data from the spreadsheet. In this small example, our strategy is to "copy and paste." We use Excel to copy a segment from the spreadsheet and then paste that segment onto the corresponding

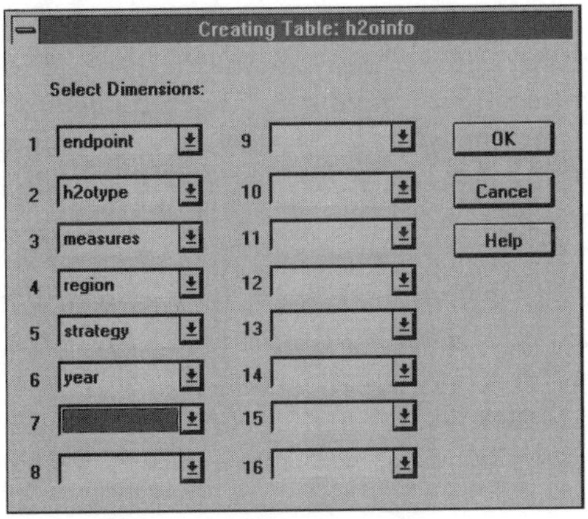

Figure 14.6 Defining the hypercube's dimensions.

view of the hypercube. (In the last chapter, we looked at importing data through table import facilities.)

Transferring Only Input Data and Arranging Multidimensional Views to Match Data to Be Copied

One simplifying factor is that we don't need to copy any calculated, or "derived," data. Once we copy the "base" data into the cube, the formulas we created will calculate the derived values. For example, we don't copy over *Total Water Borne Disease Incidence* values; once we've transferred the *Disease Incidence Fraction* and *Number of Consumers* information, the formulas in the multidimensional model will calculate *Total Water Borne Disease Incidence*.

Another feature that we can use to our advantage is that multidimensional tools allow us to display hypercubes in any dimensional orientation. In the case of TM/1, which is designed to use a spreadsheet as its interface, if we can arrange a view to match the layout of a section of data, we can copy the data out of the given spreadsheet and paste it directly into the view, then update the TM/1 database with the pasted values.

Arranging a View

Let's reexamine the spreadsheet. The two main segments of "base data" are rows 20–311, where the information broken down by region is stored, and rows 313–334, where the information on industrial users and hospitals is stored. We enclosed these two main segments on *Sheet2* and *Sheet3* of the Excel workbook. Examine *Sheet2*. A portion of this sheet is shown in Figure 14.7. The rows contain the regions, consumers, and years; the columns contain the strategies, measures, and water types. All the derived measures (for example, total cost, total illness) have been deleted because we don't need to copy them. Examine *Sheet3*. *The rows here contain consumers (Industrial Users and Hospitals) and years; the columns contain the strategies, measures, and water types.*

Using the browse box, we reorganized the multidimensional view to match this structure. The browse box layout of the dimensions is shown in Figure 14.8, and the resulting display from the prebuilt multidimensional model is shown in Figure 14.9. Notice that the view in Figure 14.9 is structured to match *Sheet2* in the spreadsheet. With the view arranged this way, we simply copied that data from

Microsoft Excel - WATER.XLS

File Edit View Insert Format Tools Data Window TM/1 Help

Arial   10   B I U $ %

I4   0.435

	A	B	C	D	E	F	G	H	I	J	K
1						Without Action				With Action	
2						% Use of Supply Source				% Use of Supply Sour	
3						PDAM only	other piped	bottled	well/river	PDAM only	other pipe
4	Subarea1	Low		1995		56.5%	0.0%	0.0%	43.5%	57.3%	0.(
5				1996		56.5%	0.0%	0.0%	43.5%	57.3%	0.(
6				1997		56.5%	0.0%	0.0%	43.5%	57.3%	0.(
7				1998		56.5%	0.0%	0.0%	43.5%	57.3%	0.(
8				1999		56.5%	0.0%	0.0%	43.5%	57.3%	0.(
9		Med		1995		67.4%	0.0%	0.0%	32.6%	74.9%	0.(
10				1996		67.4%	0.0%	0.0%	32.6%	74.9%	0.(
11				1997		67.4%	0.0%	0.0%	32.6%	74.9%	0.(
12				1998		67.4%	0.0%	0.0%	32.6%	74.9%	0.(
13				1999		67.4%	0.0%	0.0%	32.6%	74.9%	0.(
14		High		1995		67.4%	22.0%	0.0%	10.6%	68.4%	22.(
15				1996		67.4%	22.0%	0.0%	10.6%	68.4%	22.(
16				1997		67.4%	22.0%	0.0%	10.6%	68.4%	22.(
17				1998		67.4%	22.0%	0.0%	10.6%	68.4%	22.(
18				1999		67.4%	22.0%	0.0%	10.6%	68.4%	22.(
19		Restaurant	Qual	1995		100.0%	0.0%	0.0%	0.0%	100.0%	0.(
20				1996		100.0%	0.0%	0.0%	0.0%	100.0%	0.(
21				1997		100.0%	0.0%	0.0%	0.0%	100.0%	0.(
22				1998		100.0%	0.0%	0.0%	0.0%	100.0%	0.(
23				1999		100.0%	0.0%	0.0%	0.0%	100.0%	0.(
24		Office	Qual	1995		100.0%	0.0%	0.0%	0.0%	100.0%	0.(
25				1996		100.0%	0.0%	0.0%	0.0%	100.0%	0.(
26				1997		100.0%	0.0%	0.0%	0.0%	100.0%	0.(
27				1998		100.0%	0.0%	0.0%	0.0%	100.0%	0.(

Sheet1 **Sheet2** Sheet3 Sheet4 Sheet5 Sheet6 Sheet7 Sh

Ready   Calculate   NUM

Figure 14.7 The spreadsheet layout.

the spreadsheet onto the multidimensional view. We repeated this same process for *Sheet3*. After that, all we needed to do was transfer a few cost variables (rows 21–29). These variables were copied into their corresponding members in the hypercube and filled across all the other dimensions.

To confirm the transfer, we checked to see that the basic consolidation values matched those in the spreadsheet.

View: (Unnamed) - Table: h2oinfo

measures   Percentage of Consumers using supply source

Columns: strategy   (Unnamed)
                  h2otype   (Unnamed)

Rows: region   (Unnamed)
         endpoint   (Unnamed)
         year   (Unnamed)

File...   Options...   Show   Close   Help

Figure 14.8 Browse box layout of the dimensions.

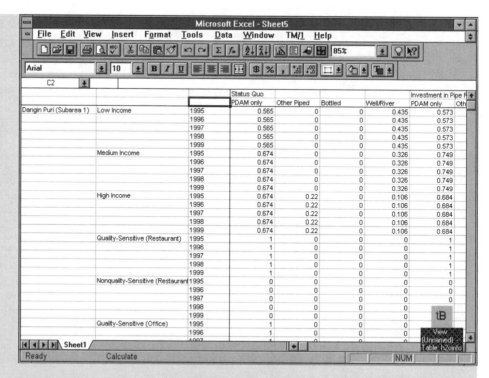

Figure 14.9 Multidimensional display matches spreadsheet layout.

Defining Variable Formulas and Aggregating

Once all the base data has been transferred, you need to define the variable formulas to compute the derived data. This involves going through the variables and determining formulas for the derived ones. Over 95 percent of the cells used in the spreadsheet are calculated based on other cells in the spreadsheet; there are literally thousands of formulas on this spreadsheet. All of these formulas are condensed into the dimensional-based aggregations and about 30 *additional formulas* in the multidimensional model.

For example, *Total Cost of Illness* is a derived value, for which one would create a formula using the enclosed multidimensional tool like the one below:

['Water Borne Disease Incidence'] = N:['All Consumers', 'Disease Incidence Fraction', 'All Denpasar'] * ['Number of Consumers'];

(The *"N:"* tells TM/1 that this rule applies only to nonconsolidated members.)

The *Disease Incidence Fraction* is associated with *All Consumer* and *All Denpasar* intersections (the information is not known by consumer group or subarea) so the rule tells TM/1 to look in those fields for the value. It is then multiplied by the *Number of Consumers*.

Viewing/Editing a Rule

[View (Unnamed) - Table: h2oinfo]

Click Close.

From the spreadsheet menu, click on TM/1 and the Rules menu choice.

[TM/1 - Rules Menu]

Click Open.

[Select Rules Worksheet]

Double-click on h2oinfo.

[H2OINFO.XRU]

This contains all the TM/1 Rules. The rule we're interested in is in row 35.

The rule is listed on row 35 of the rules worksheet (see Figure 14.10).

Let's examine the first instance of this formula in the Excel spreadsheet. Click on Sheet1, cell N33, which contains the Total Water-Borne Disease Incidence for Low Income Households from PDAM water in Dangin Puri (sub-area 1) in 1995. We see the equation:

$$N33 = C33 * \$D33 * \$N\$30$$

This is much harder to understand and work with. The use of member names in multidimensional tools makes formula writing, testing, and correction clearer and simpler. (A spreadsheet's named ranges are useful for blocks of cells, but they do not offer this flexibility.)

Second, in the spreadsheet, this formula needs to be recreated for each water type, for every consumer group, in every subarea, for both strategies. There are four regions, and nine subareas in each region, and two strategies, requiring the creation of 72 formulas. Then there are industrial users and hospitals, in both strategies, bringing the formula count to 76. Each of these

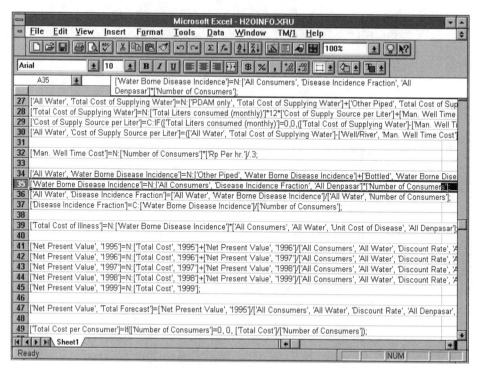

Figure 14.10 The rules worksheet.

needs to be "filled down," to create the formula for each of the five years (another 76 operations), and "filled across" to cover each the water types (another 76). This bringing the total to 228 operations, and the formula appears in 1,520 cells. With the global formulas created in the multidimensional approach, this equation needed to be created only *once*!

Formula modification is also much simpler. Imagine if we wanted to change the way we calculated *Water-Borne Disease Incidence*; we'd have to change 1,520 formulas in the spreadsheet, rather than changing one formula with the multidimensional approach.

The Advantages of the Multidimensional Approach: Viewing and Analysis

View Reorganization and Browsing

Suppose that you wished to examine the total costs of supplying water to medium-income households in Dangin Puri (subarea 1), broken down by wa-

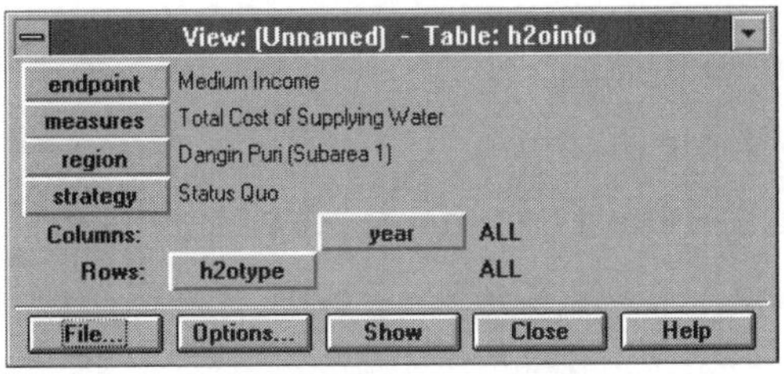

Figure 14.11 Arranging costs by water type by time.

ter type given the status quo. The information is stored in Sheet1, rows 41–45, columns H–K, M. (Refer back to Figure 14.2.) Compare this with how you view things in a multidimensional environment. Set endpoint to *Medium Income*, measure to *Total Cost of Supplying Water*, region to *Dangin Puri* (subarea 1), strategy to *Status Quo*, set h_2otype as the rows, and *year* as the columns (see Figure 14.11).

Dangin Puri Water Supply Cost for Medium-Income Users

Let's reopen the hypercube's browse box.
    Now let's reorganize the view to match the spreadsheet view.

<u>**Matching the Spreadsheet View**</u>

[View (Unnamed) - Table: h2oinfo]

Click on endpoint.

[Select One Element of Dimension: endpoint]

Click on <u>Medium Income</u>, then click <u>OK</u>.

[View (Unnamed) - Table: h2oinfo]

Click on <u>measures</u>.

[Select One Element of Dimension: measure]

Click on <u>Total Cost of Supplying Water</u>, then click <u>OK</u>.

[View (Unnamed) - Table: h2oinfo]

Click on <u>region</u>.

[Select One Element of Dimension: region]

Click on <u>Dangin Puri (subarea 1)</u>, then click <u>OK</u>.

[View (Unnamed) - Table: h2oinfo]

Drag *strategy* into the left-most column. Click on <u>strategy</u>.

[Select One Element of Dimension: strategy]

Click on <u>Status Quo</u>, then click <u>OK</u>.

[View (Unnamed) - Table: h2oinfo]

Drag *h2otype* to the middle column.

Click <u>Show</u>.

We now have a view of water supply costs for Dangin Puri (see Figure 14.12).

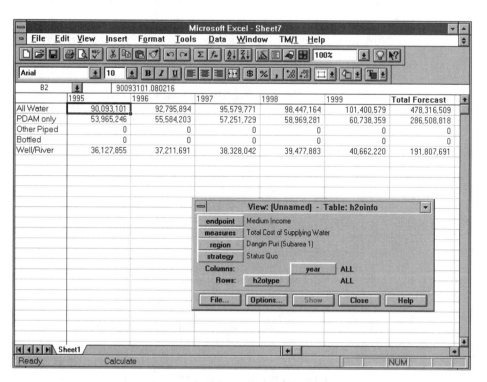

Figure 14.12 A view of water supply costs for Dangin Puri.

We're interested in how these figures compare with those of the other sub-areas. Let's examine the status quo 1995 medium-income household water supply costs across *all four* subareas. With our multidimensional tool, we simply reorganize the view by switching the region dimension tag with the year tag.

Viewing Costs by Subarea

[View (Unnamed) - Table: h2oinfo]

Drag the <u>year</u> dimension into the left-most column. It is already set to *1995*. Drag the <u>region</u> dimension to the right-most column. It is already set to display all regions.

Click <u>Show</u>.

We can now examine this view in the multidimensional model (shown in Figure 14.13). How can we examine this view in the spreadsheet?

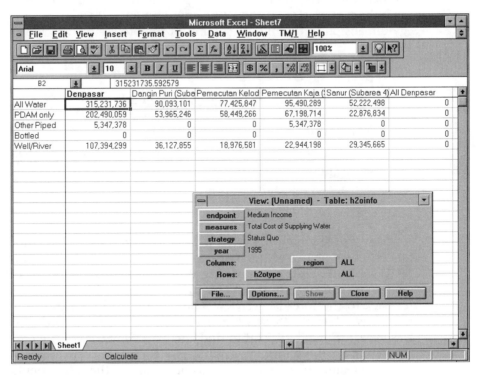

Figure 14.13 An analytical view.

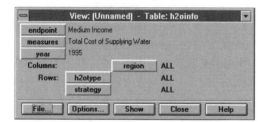

Figure 14.14 Positioning the strategy dimension across the rows.

First try to find the figures in the spreadsheet. They aren't neatly packed together in our spreadsheet view. They're in columns H–K, M, in rows 41–45, 113–117, 185–189, and 257–261. Do we try to scroll up and down the spreadsheet trying to remember the numbers as we move from one section to another; do we try to cut and paste all of them onto another spreadsheet? Either way, it's much more difficult.

Let's go one step further. Our main concern is how these cost figures would be affected by repairing the pipes. Let's reorganize the display again to compare the costs and benefits of supplying water to medium-income housing in both strategies. In the OLAP environment, all we do is move the strategy dimension to the middle column of the browse box (as shown in Figure 14.14).

Viewing Costs by Scenario

[View (Unnamed) - Table: h2oinfo]

Drag the strategy dimension beneath *h2otype* in the middle column. Click Show.

Now we see something interesting (see Figure 14.15). Even though the total cost of supplying all the water goes down (Net Benefits/Costs of Repair of All Water), the costs of supplying PDAM water (PDAM only of All Water) seem to increase significantly! This information is critical for our analysis. Refer back to the spreadsheet view, and attempt to locate this same information. The relevant information is scattered throughout the spreadsheet in this view, making it difficult to find and extremely complicated to analyze.

Return to the multidimensional model. Is this cost increase that we've seen in medium-income households occurring in the total population? Let's

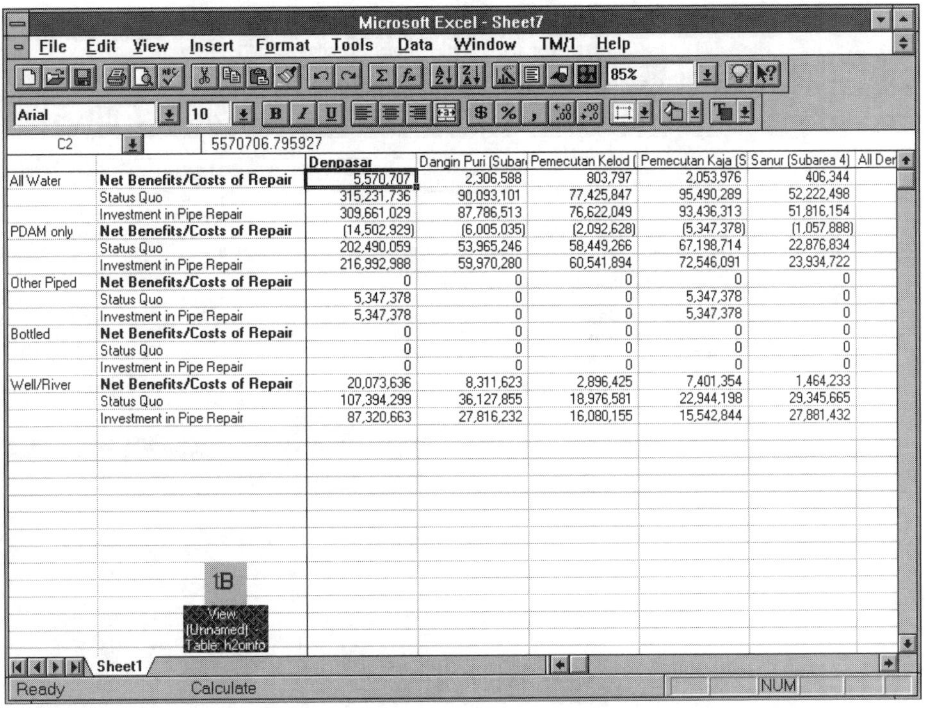

		Denpasar	Dangin Puri (Subar	Pemecutan Kelod (	Pemecutan Kaja (S	Sanur (Subarea 4)	All Der
All Water	**Net Benefits/Costs of Repair**	5,570,707	2,306,588	803,797	2,053,976	406,344	
	Status Quo	315,231,736	90,093,101	77,425,847	95,490,289	52,222,498	
	Investment in Pipe Repair	309,661,029	87,786,513	76,622,049	93,436,313	51,816,154	
PDAM only	**Net Benefits/Costs of Repair**	(14,502,929)	(6,005,035)	(2,092,628)	(5,347,378)	(1,057,888)	
	Status Quo	202,490,059	53,965,246	58,449,266	67,198,714	22,876,834	
	Investment in Pipe Repair	216,992,988	59,970,280	60,541,894	72,546,091	23,934,722	
Other Piped	**Net Benefits/Costs of Repair**	0	0	0	0	0	
	Status Quo	5,347,378	0	0	5,347,378	0	
	Investment in Pipe Repair	5,347,378	0	0	5,347,378	0	
Bottled	**Net Benefits/Costs of Repair**	0	0	0	0	0	
	Status Quo	0	0	0	0	0	
	Investment in Pipe Repair	0	0	0	0	0	
Well/River	**Net Benefits/Costs of Repair**	20,073,636	8,311,623	2,896,425	7,401,354	1,464,233	
	Status Quo	107,394,299	36,127,855	18,976,581	22,944,198	29,345,665	
	Investment in Pipe Repair	87,320,663	27,816,232	16,080,155	15,542,844	27,881,432	

Figure 14.15 Total cost of PDAM goes up.

examine the 1995 Total Consumer costs, broken down by strategy, region, and water type.

Examining Costs for the Total Population

[View (Unnamed) - Table: h2oinfo]

Click on endpoint.

[Select One Element of Dimension: endpoint]

Click on Total Consumers, then click OK.

[View (Unnamed) - Table: h2oinfo]

Click Show.

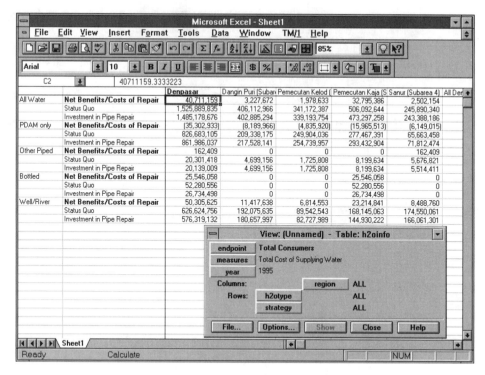

Figure 14.16 PDAM water costs increase.

We see these same characteristics at the total population level; total costs decrease, but the PDAM water costs increase (See Figure 14.16). Why do the costs of supplying water go up after we've repaired the pipes? *Could it be that when the pipes and resulting water flow are improved, more people switch over to using PDAM water, thereby increasing total costs?* To test this hypothesis, we need to see the changes in consumer population and costs per consumer of PDAM water, broken down by strategy, region, and water type.

Examining Changes in Consumer Population

[View (Unnamed) - Table: h2oinfo]

Click on measures.

[Select One Element of Dimension: measure]

Click on Number of Consumers, then click OK.

[View (Unnamed) - Table: h2oinfo]

Click on Show.

The number of PDAM consumers does significantly increase after the pipes are repaired (See Figure 14.17). We know that, for PDAM, total supply costs are increasing, as the total number of consumers. But, we still need to discover—when all the cost factors are taken into account (cost of supply, cost of repairs, cost of illness)—if the average cost *per person* is increasing or decreasing?

Costs per Consumer

[View (Unnamed) - Table: h2oinfo]

Click on measures.

[Select One Element of Dimension: measure]

Click on Total Cost per Consumer, then click OK.

[View (Unnamed) - Table: h2oinfo]

Click Show.

The cost per consumer does decrease for all water, and for PDAM in particular! Thus, even though the total water supplying costs increase due to increased PDAM water consumption, the decrease in the cost per consumer shows that it is a good investment. The steps of this analysis were considerably simplified using the enclosed multidimensional tool.

Aggregate Analysis

The aggregations defined in the dimensions will allow us to examine the total net benefits of pipe repair across the entire region. This view corresponds to the original view that we had when we first opened the hypercube (refer back to Figure 14.8). We see total cost in both strategies, then the net benefits/costs. The net benefits/costs can be seen in the spreadsheet in column P, rows 9–14; however, the total costs for each individual strategy are never actually calculated in the spreadsheet.

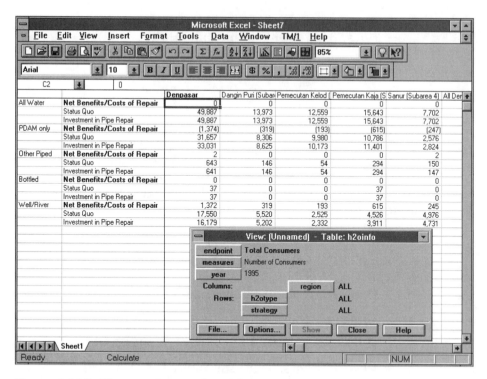

Figure 14.17 Changes in number of consumers.

We see that in the first year, there is a net loss (which is due to the fact that all of the pipe repair costs are in the first year). However, over the next four years, there is a net benefit, and in the *Total Forecast* we see a large cumulative savings over five years.

Let's examine how this breaks down by region. In the multidimensional model, you need to set the strategy dimensions to *Net Benefits/Costs of Repair* and place the region dimension in the rows. The browse box would be arranged as in Figure 14.18.

View: original - Table: h2oinfo

endpoint	Total Consumers
h2otype	All Water
measures	Total Cost
strategy	Net Benefits/Costs of Repair

Columns: year ALL
Rows: region ALL

File... Options... Show Close Help

Figure 14.18 Browse box for net benefits/costs.

<u>**Viewing Net Benefits by Subarea**</u>

We wish to view the dimensions arranged as in the browse box shown in Figure 14.18.

[View (Unnamed) - Table: h2oinfo]

Drag <u>region</u> to the middle column. Drag <u>strategy</u> to the left-most column. It should be set to *Net Benefits/Costs of Repair*.

Click <u>Show</u>. (This operation may take a few seconds; be patient if it does.)

In the spreadsheet, total costs were not calculated by subarea. We would have to create a completely new set of formulas for each region to determine these values. In the multidimensional approach, global dimensional formulas apply across every member in every level of other dimensions' hierarchies. The multidimensional tool has total cost by region, by water type, by strategy, by year, and by consumer group; the spreadsheet doesn't have breakdowns by any of these. It would take hundreds and hundred of spreadsheet formulas to determine all these values.

Figure 14.19 shows the values broken down by subarea. The cost in *All Denpasar* reflects the regional costs incurred by the PDAM water authority (for example, pipe repair, operation, and maintenance). Notice that most of the savings occur in *Pemecutan Kaja* (subarea3). Instead of repairing pipes throughout all of Denpasar, it may be more cost-effective to invest in pipe repair solely in Pemecutan Kaja, with remaining capital invested more effectively in some other way.

Figure 14.20 is a map of the Denpasar region with the relative location of different income groups highlighted and a bar chart of the benefits accruing to different income groups in each subarea positioned over the map. Notice the disparity in how income groups in different areas fared.

The Advantages of the Multidimensional Approach: Database Modification

Example: Adding a Consumer Group

We are likely to expand our model of the Denpasar water supply costs at some point. How can we do that with the multidimensional database versus

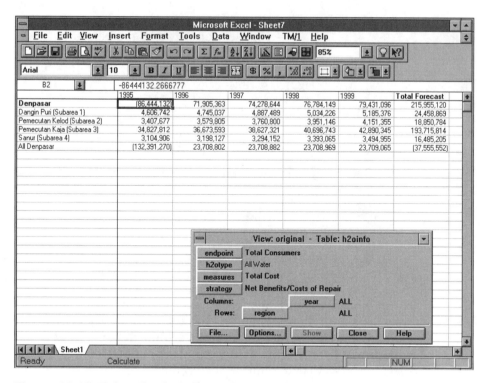

Figure 14.19 Values broken down by area.

the spreadsheet? Suppose that the utility companies in each subarea have significantly different consumption rates than the other industrial users, and we want to define a new endpoint called *Utilities*. How would we do that in the spreadsheet?

First, in *each* of the four subareas we would have to add a section for *Utilities*. Then, all the formulas that are used to make cost calculations for a consumer group have to be recreated. The cost variable unique to the utilities will have to be added. Then, we have to rewrite all the total cost calculations to include the utility values. Then, we would have to check *extensively* for errors. Realistically, this will take hours to do correctly, and that estimate doesn't even address bringing in the data.

With an OLAP tool, you just modify the endpoint dimension. In TM/1, you would open the endpoint dimension, add *Utilities* as a member, and then add it to the consolidation *Total Consumers* (see Figure 14.21, row 2 and row 9). *Nothing else would need to be changed.* You've made the same modifications, which would take hours with a spreadsheet, in about one minute.

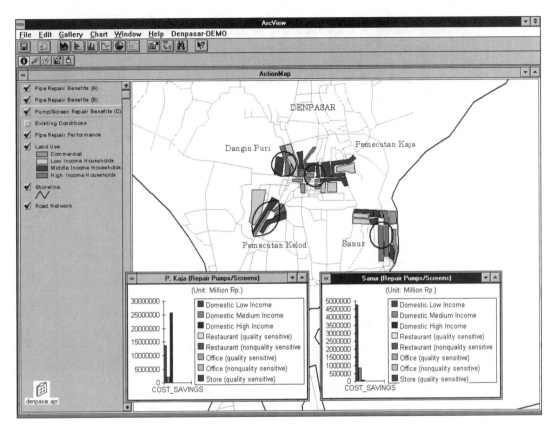

Figure 14.20 The benefits accruing to different income groups.

Example: Variable Economic Factors

Suppose that we want to improve our use of economic factors. For example, in the spreadsheet model it is assumed that things such as population growth rate, unit cost of disease, and discount rate are constant over time. Suppose you want to capture their changes.

In the spreadsheet you need to create a space to store all these values. And, as the number of economic variables factored in increases, we'll likely place these values on separate sheets and link them in. Every formula involving each of these variables will have to be changed, in every region, in every subgroup. This will take a long time.

We have already made these modifications in the TM/1 model. All it entailed was adding members to the variables dimension. Then we changed a few global formulas, as opposed to the hundreds of cell formulas in the spreadsheet.

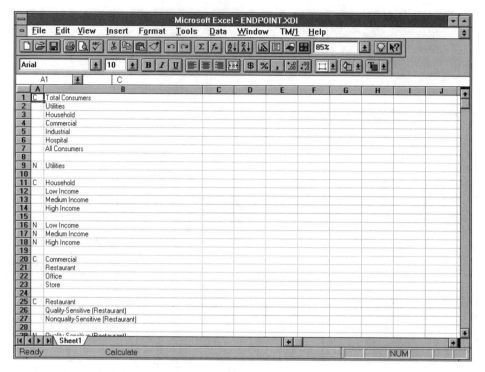

Figure 14.21 Modifying the endpoint dimension.

The Advantages of the Multidimensional Approach: Database Expansion

Additional Strategies

We may want to consider strategies other than pipe repair. Suppose that we were considering water filtering, that is, investing in improving the quality of the Denpasar water supply. We would now have four total strategies: *Status Quo, Water Filtering, Investment in Pipe Repair*, and *Pipe Repair and Filtering*. Going from two potential strategies to four will double the size of each model. Take a couple of minutes to reexamine the spreadsheet and think about how to make this expansion.

First, we would need to completely remodel the spreadsheet format; it's currently designed for only these two strategies. We might choose to use multiple sheets. The complexity of the spreadsheet will increase dramatically. Second, *for each strategy, in every consumer group, in every region, in every year, for every water type, every variable formula calculation must be recreated.* There

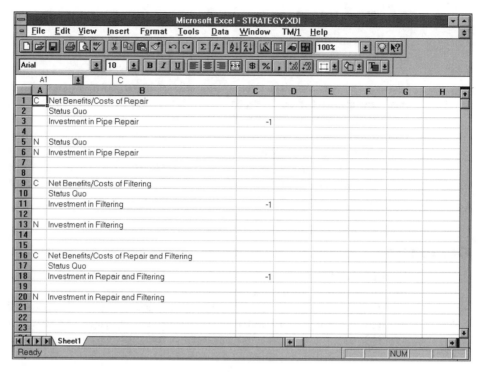

Figure 14.22 Adding members to the strategy dimension.

are thousands of formulas to be considered on this spreadsheet. We would likely make a copy of this sheet onto another sheet and attempt to reuse most of the formulas. Regardless of what method we choose, this is an enormous undertaking, fraught with potential for errors. Then, we would need to create all the aggregate values for each strategy and create methods of comparing the different strategies. Between this entire process and error checking/correction, you would be lucky if this process took only a day (with this simplified model).

With a multidimensional approach, you just open the strategy dimension and add the two additional members *Water Filtering* and *Pipe Repair and Filtering*. Then, add the two consolidated members *Net Benefits/Costs of Water Filtering* and *Net Benefits/Costs of Pipe Repair and Water Filtering* (as shown in Figure 14.22). Each of these consolidations would compare their corresponding strategies to the Status Quo. This would allow us to examine which strategy had the highest net benefit. No variable formulas need to be recreated! We won't need to think through a restructuring of our database—the multidimensional framework is especially suited for making such additions. It is a clear, swift process.

Additional Sectors

Finally, remember that the full goal of the Indonesian government is to create a performance monitoring system across five different infrastructure sectors. Investment choices are also intersectoral. The water supply model was just for starters. Adding the same kinds of information (though not the same base variables) for each sector would get out of control pretty quickly in a spreadsheet environment. But in a multidimensional environment, you could add a sector dimension to the hypercube. Because the base variables are different from sector to sector, it is better to use a multicube approach that maintains one hypercube with sector-specific variables for each sector and one hypercube with intersectorally comparable service-level indicators (quantity, quality, reliability, and coverage indicators).

Conclusion

In this chapter, you saw how much easier it is to define and analyze OLAP models using a multidimensional tool than using a spreadsheet. GIS/Trans was very impressed with the power and flexibility of the multidimensional environment (not to mention its ability to leverage existing spreadsheets) and is looking for ways to integrate this technology in future projects.

Section IV

Further Issues

Why should it be possible to have grounds for believing anything if it isn't possible to be certain?

—Ludwig Wittgenstein

Dimensional Modeling and Analysis

Throughout this book, we have explored dimensions in a variety of senses or contexts:

1. Screen representations, where we saw two-, three-, and multidimensional grid displays
2. Logical modeling, where we saw identifier dimensions and variables
3. Analysis, where we saw dimensions as numerators and denominators
4. Physical implementations, where we saw arrays, tables, B-trees, hashing, and Z-keys

The purpose of this chapter is to pick up and extend some of the modeling and analysis threads that were begun in Chapter 4. We will build toward a deeper view of hypercubes where they are seen as analytical systems of variably interdependent mixed type variables and not just as collections of numbers and formulas. Toward that end, we will pass through a number of intermediate stages.

First, the differences between identifiers and variables will be explained and justified in more detail than they were earlier in the book. If you already subscribe to them and are not interested in exploring counter-arguments, you may safely skip this section.

Second, metadata-resident, data-set-independent dimensions will be introduced as the underlying commonality between identifiers and variables. This allows us to think in terms of identifier dimensions and variable dimensions. Identifier dimensions and variable dimensions are then definable in

413

terms of objective criteria. This is important because it is the key to flexible modeling and because analytical attributes such as ordering, which are discussed later, apply directly to dimensions.

Third, we will look at different ordering properties that may be ascribed to dimensions, such as nominal and cardinal. We will show how they are inherited by identifiers and variables, we will point to some of the analyses that can be performed with each type, and we will show how the process of analysis can alter the ordering of (or amount of embedded information in) the data. This is important because all analytical techniques are data- and dimension-structure-specific.

Finally, identifier and variable dimensions will be connected to the basic analytical notions of independent and dependent variables, as found, for example, in algebra and statistics. Here, we will look at the need for the independent variables (a.k.a. identifier dimensions) to be independent of one another when there are more than one, how you can test for their independence, and what you should do when they are not totally independent.

Because this is the last section of the book, I have allowed myself to include slightly more philosophical content than elsewhere. Specifically, there is some etymological information on the main concepts "dimension" and "analysis" and more attention is paid to refuting possible counterexamples where appropriate. (I, for one, am never convinced of an argument until all reasonable attempts to refute it are laid to rest.) You may safely skip these parts if you wish.

Dimensions: Identifier and Variable

Etymology of the Term "Dimension"

The word "dimension" is a very rich, and for that reason, semantically loaded term. During most of its 2,500 year history, it was used predominantly by mathematicians and carried a largely geophysical or three-dimensional meaning. With the advent of abstract geometries and algebras over the last few centuries, that meaning has expanded into spaces that are more than three-dimensional, or multidimensional.[1]

Etymology of the Term "Dimension"

Today's practical discussions of how dimensions and variables (as a generalization of the concept of measure) should be treated in a multidimensional system have their roots going back over two millennia. The term "dimension" traces back through the old French of the time of Descartes to the Latin "dimetiri," meaning a way of measuring (though many dictionaries translate "dimetiri" simply as "to measure"), which in turn traces back to the Greek.

The Greeks had two very different terms for "dimension" and "measure." To the Greeks, these were two very different concepts. The concept of measure was a very practical concept, and the Romans, being a very practical people, easily adopted the concept. But the concept of "dimension" was another story. The Greeks were great contemplators. They espoused myriad ontologies. The Romans, in contrast, were not known for their philosophical enterprises. And, I imagine, the Greek word for "dimension" may have confused them. For the Romans, there was nothing to think about. To the translators of the time, the Greek word for "dimension" must only have had meaning in the concrete sense of measuring.

Thus the Latin term for the Greek concept of "διατάσειδ" became wedded to the concept of measurement. And, in fact, for the next 2,000 years, with the exception of geometers who maintained a distinction between the meaning of "dimension" and the meaning of "measure," the term "dimension" became synonymous with the concepts of measurement and number. The dimension of an object referred to its size, as it does today when we talk about the dimensions of a refrigerator, or the dimension or magnitude of a problem.

In Chapter 3, we discussed the "multi" aspect of multidimensionality more than the "dimensional" aspect. Do you remember how we distinguished between logical and physical dimensions? Angle-based dimensions as found in a cube are physical dimensions[2] and are spatially limited to three. In contrast, logical dimensions apply to any situation and have no inherent upper limits. The key to understanding the "multi" aspect of multidimensionality is understanding the difference between logical and physical dimensions.

The "dimensional" aspect is just as important as the "multi" aspect. What makes something dimensional or a dimension? How do we identify the dimensional structure of a data set? Are columns in a flat file always dimensions? In a business sense, the term is frequently used to mean a perspective. (But what exactly is a perspective?[3]) All this could make it seem that a dimension is a property of the organization of a data set because, as we saw in Chapter 3, the same data can be organized in multiple ways. In that case, the dimensionality is in the eye of the beholder. Or, is the dimensionality of a data set somehow a property of the data, independent of how it is organized? It certainly seemed that dimensions were equated with groups of things, such as all the departments or stores or employees in a company, and that such things are to some degree observer independent. But if dimensions equate with groups, are all groups dimensions?

The "dimensional" aspect of multidimensionality was not treated as thoroughly as the "multi" aspect in Chapter 3. Terms were introduced and used without being fully defined or justified. Of course, my hope was that the terms were being used in a sufficiently intuitive way that they wouldn't need formal definitions, at least in Chapter 3. To attain a deeper understanding of the dimensional aspect of multidimensionality, we will return to the distinction between identifiers and variables that was drawn in Chapter 3. After justifying their differences and clarifying what they mean, we will be prepared to explore their commonality. Once you understand how identifiers and variables are the same and how they are different, we can move on to explore dimensional analysis.

Distinguishing Between Variables and Identifier Dimensions

As we saw briefly in Chapter 3, and will see in more depth here, the basis for the distinction between identifier and variable dimensions arises from a combination of the activity of describing (and manipulating) events and the events themselves. If you were happy with the distinction between identifiers and variables and are not interested in exploring it any further, you may skip this section.

Look at the urban commercial planning data in Figure 15.1. It shows a table containing data about times, neighborhoods, stores, and sales. Can you visualize the data source? Let's say that the data came from a small-sized city neighborhood and the stores that do business within its boundaries. Figure 15.2 shows a map of the neighborhood and the location of its stores and their type. The urban planning authorities monitor the neighborhood once a month.

Months	Neighborhood	Store	Sales	Foot traffic
Jan	Pearl Square	C1	200	4000
Feb	Pearl Square	C1	75	2000
Mar	Pearl Square	C1	125	2250
Apr	Pearl Square	C1	150	3000
:	:	:	:	:
:	:	:	:	:
Dec	Pearl Square	C1	225	5000

Figure 15.1 Urban planning data.

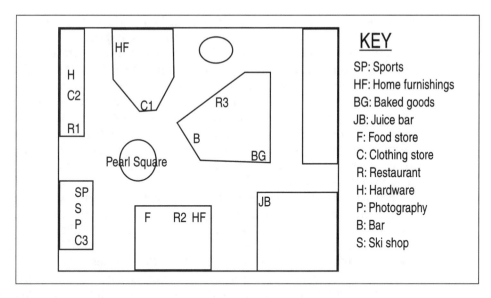

Figure 15.2 Pearl Square neighborhood.

What You Need to Take into Account

If you had the responsibility for building a commercial monitoring system for a senior analyst with the urban planning authorities, what aspects, components, or factors of the neighborhood's situation would you need to know or take into account (assuming all the neighborhoods' businesses were cooperative)?

Variables Certainly, you would have to take store sales into account or you couldn't talk about having a commercial monitoring system. And unless you are exceptionally clairvoyant, you can do this only by tracking, measuring, or otherwise recording the fact that something was sold for each time and place that a sale is made. Everything that you track in a situation is called a variable (in that situation). The collection of all the variables you track for a particular situation is called a *variables dimension*.

By way of comparison, in a financial situation, line items or accounts usually function as variables. In a manufacturing situation, worker productivity and error rates may serve as variables. And in a transportation situation, passenger miles, cost, and revenue per passenger mile may serve as variables.

Note how the urban planner's variables reflect what the urban planner is trying to do. A different entity with different purposes may track different variables in the same situation. For example, *given the same events within which the urban planner is tracking sales, a local resident might be tracking what stores he or she enters and how much money he or she spends per store.*

Now let's say you've gone and accumulated some instances of your sales variables and it is time to analyze and report on them. What might you want to know? You might want to know the value for a particular instance of a particular variable, say the sales variable for the dry cleaners in January. Or you might want to know how sales compared between two times, say last week and this week. Or you might want to know how many sales go to young customers compared to old customers. Or you might want to know which businesses are doing the best and the worst in the neighborhood. You might want to know many things.

But what could you ever know unless you could differentiate or identify each of the variables you originally measured? You wouldn't be able to ask for the first measurement taken or the measurements taken from store *x* or the measurements made Tuesday, or the measurements of product *y* sales, or even the first sequential measurement in data storage. You would never be able to formulate any questions about your variables, not even a question about their total or average, for even a question about totals assumes it is possible to identify all the variables in question from other variables or information that may be in storage. Strictly speaking, unless your variables have identity tags, they are totally and completely useless.

Dimensions Of course, you would never measure a series of variables without retaining the ability to identify them somehow. In the example given above, and if you were tracking sales, it is likely that the sales measurements would be identified by time, store, and product. Each set of identifying factors, that is, the set of all stores, the set of all times, or the set of all products, is an identifier dimension of the situation.

An identifier dimension is a set of variable-identifying factors of the same type. In contrast with variables, the identifier dimensions of a situation have values that you already know. Refer back to Figure 15.1, the simple row and column layout of commercial data. Ask yourself the following question, "What are the months for which I am tracking sales?" Don't you somehow know this? Don't you need to know this to specify a particular report? If Figure 15.1 was what you wanted to see, it must be that it represents the response to a command, such as "Show me the sales for January through June in the green neighborhood," or the answer to a question such as "What are the sales for January through June?" However phrased, the time values January through June identify which sales instances you are interested in seeing.

Because identifier dimensions have values you already know, a stream of identifier dimension values to which no other information was attached couldn't possibly tell you anything new. (See "Possible Counter-examples to the Need for Identifiers and Variables.") Identifier dimensions are as meaningless without variables as variables are meaningless without identifier dimensions. Luckily, you would never think to build a model without including them both.

Variables and dimensions are at the core of a multidimensional modeling taxonomy (regardless of whether variables are given any special status in the multidimensional product that you use). They are not types of dimensions in the way that stores, times, employees, clients, geography, and scenarios are dimensions.[4] They are basic classes or roles that dimensions may fill. (As you will see below, any specific dimension, such as stores, time, products, and so forth, can play the role of either identifier or variable.) Rules and scripts, objects, entities and relationships, generalized blackboards, and logic denote data modeling taxonomies in their respective domains. Modeling taxonomies are at the heart of what the AI community calls knowledge representation.[5]

Possible Counter-examples to the Need for Identifiers and Variables

Possible Counter-example 1

As a possible counter-example to the need for identifier and variable dimensions, consider a situation where you are given a commercial model for which you didn't even know what the dimensions are, much less their values. You could start your queries into the model with the question "What are the dimensions of my model?"; the response might be "months, stores, products, and customers." (Note that this is how the metadata discovery of the OLAP Council's MD-API actually works.) Following this, you could formulate the question "For what months do we have commercial data?"; t the response might be "January, February, and March." Thereafter, you could formulate more typical queries, such as "What are the sales for January, February, and March?". Even though this might seem like a counter example to the assertion that we need to know the values of our dimensions, closer inspection reveals otherwise.

Recall that a dimension is only a dimension relative to a variable. Nothing is inherently a dimension or a variable. Time, which usually serves as a dimension, can just as easily serve as a variable. For example, in a model that tracks the average amount of time between feeding sessions for humans, time would be the variable, and age, culture, or geography might be dimensions.

When you asked the question "What are the dimensions of my model?", the term "dimension" served as a variable and the term "model" served as a dimension. Imagine that you had several models, not just a commercial model. Questions such as "Are there any dimensions in my commercial model that are shared by my finance model?" or "What are the dimensions of my human resources model?" all treat "model" as an identifier or dimension for the term "dimension" that is acting like a variable and whose unknown values are what these "meta" models are tracking.

When you asked the question "What are the time values for which I have commercial data?" (which could be rephrased as "What are the members of the time dimension in my commercial model?"), the term "members" served as a variable and the term "dimension" served as a dimension. Here, in other words, you are tracking sets of member values as identified by their dimension name. The set of members in a dimension varies from dimension to dimension.

The counter-example isn't a counter-example because there isn't a single model—there are three models. Model 1 is the commercial model we've been talking about all along. Its variables are sales and costs; its dimensions are time, store, and product. To ask questions about particular sales values, you have to know the value of the time, store, or month whose sales values you want to know. Model 2 is a metadata model. Its variables are dimension members; its dimensions are dimension names. To ask questions about the members of a dimension, you have to know for what dimension you are asking the question. Finally, model 3 is also a metadata model. Its variables are dimension names; its dimensions contain model names. To ask questions about the names of dimensions in a model, you have to know for what model you are asking the question.

Possible Counter-example 2

Of course, you can imagine extreme cases where a seemingly pure one-dimensional stream of dimension values constitutes useful information. For example, consider a model that just tracked, for a moment in time, which products were being carried. Table 15.1 shows such a model. It would appear to contradict the rule that both a variable and nonvariable dimension are required for a useful model. Kimball, in his book, *The Data Warehouse Toolkit*, called this a factless fact table.[6]

However, the seemingly one-dimensional model is not really one-dimensional. In addition to the product dimension, there is an implicit second dimension bearing one member that acts as a variable. That dimension might be called an "existence" dimension. Its

Table15.1 List of Products Carried

Products
Sniglets
Foozbars
Dingbots
Foodles
Smuglets
Grimples

one member might be called "status." The status variable has a logical or Boolean type capable of two values—yes, meaning the product is available, and no. The model consists of the intersection of the product and the existence dimensions. The cell values would thus contain the binary values, yes and no, as shown in Table 15.2. Notice how all the values are yes. In other words, the only products listed in Table 15.2 are the available ones. It is this convention (as opposed to showing all products that did or could ever exist along with their existence value of yes/no) that eliminates the need to explicitly show the *existence dimension*. Table 15.3 shows what the model would look like with all products available and unavailable.

The concept of an implicit dimension is analogous to the concept of an implicit part of speech. The interjection "wow," for example, seems to carry meaning when used in a real-world situation, yet apparently violates the need for a subject and predicate. Of course, implicitly, "wow" parses into a subject-predicate form meaning approximately "This thing/event here now is unusual."

Table 15.2 Revealing the Existence Dimension

Products	Status
Sniglets	yes
Foozbars	yes
Dingbots	yes
Foodles	yes
Smuglets	yes
Grimples	yes

Table 15.3 List of Products and Their Status

Products	Status
Sniglets	yes
Tugles	no
Foozbars	yes
Bonkles	no
Dingbots	yes
Foodles	yes
Jimbas	no
Smuglets	yes
Grimples	yes
Nerplas	no

Benefits to Thinking in Terms of Variable and Identifier Dimensions

By this point you should be convinced that there is no escaping identifier and variable dimensions. What would you be giving up by not making the distinction? Maybe it's no worse than not distinguishing cabernet sauvignon grapes from merlot grapes when ordering wine. If all you want is red wine, it is an unnecessary distinction.

As stated at the beginning of this chapter, the difference between identifier dimensions and variables will be secured and then deepened. The reason for doing this is because all further development of multidimensional analysis depends on this distinction. Because not all products single out variables, there is some feeling that variables are somehow optional or that they are just another dimension like products. As I have mentioned elsewhere, you can ignore the distinction between identifiers and variables for the purposes of display, but not for analysis.

Identifiers and variables are to modeling behavior as gravity is to physical behavior. In the same way that you live your life in cognitive ignorance of gravity but your physical being cannot ignore or break the laws of gravity, you can live your life in cognitive ignorance of the difference between identifiers and variables but your cognitive being cannot ignore or break the laws of identifiers and variables. Incidentally, these kinds of laws should not be confused with politically based laws such as tax rates, gun control, habeas corpus, and highway speed limits. You can break only human laws. What follows is a brief description of the benefits to thinking in terms of identifier and variable dimensions.

More Intuitive Modeling   The goal of most, if not all, data modeling efforts over the years has been to mimic real-world structure. Of course, as Kant pointed out, mimicking real-world structure amounts to mimicking human perception.[7] Variables and identifiers are a crucial component of any modeling effort because they stem from the way we structure thoughts (hence the connection to logic). *The major reason why multidimensional systems appear intuitive is because they do their business the way we do ours.* For this reason, variables and identifiers need to be a supported by any multidimensional modeling tool.

Better Connection to Logic and Analysis   Identifier dimensions, as opposed to variables, provide the logical notion of uniqueness, identity, object, or reference. In database terms, this is called a key. The concept of key is a central, and logically grounded, tenet of the relational model. In fact, it is law number one in the relational model, version 2.[8]

Multidimensional models need this distinction for the same reason that relational models need it. It provides a criteria for meaningful and meaningless statements. In other words, a database, multidimensional or relational, is just a fancy word for a big collection of statements capable of being true, false, missing, and meaningless. A necessary, though not sufficient, condition for meaningfulness is the coexistence of an identifier, or key, and a variable, or nonkey, attribute. Furthermore, when it comes to handling missing and meaningless data, keys or identifiers get handled differently from nonkeys or variables. (Missing keys, for example, are not allowed in the relational model whereas missing attributes are allowed.[9]) There is no way to handle missing and meaningless data properly without at some point making the distinction. As you will see in the remainder of this chapter, all analysis from time series to regressions makes use of the distinction between identifiers and variables.

More Efficient Data Mining   Distinguishing identifiers and variables allows for mining programs to scan for interesting patterns within a restricted search space. Without this distinction, any dimension element could just as easily be analyzed against any other. For example, imagine just two dimensions, a time dimension and a variables dimension. Without any dimensional distinction it makes just as much sense to look at how a particular variable, such as sales, changes over time as it does to look at how a particular time, say January, changes over variables. Without any dimensional distinction, it makes just as much sense to talk about the average or total sales across time as it makes sense to talk about the average or total Monday across all variables. Thus, without these distinctions and left to its own devices, a tool will spend needless resources uselessly exploring meaningless relationships.

The Dimensional Grounding of Identifiers and Variables

We have just described identifier dimensions and variables and how they are both a necessary part of any dimensional model. But where does that leave us with dimensions? What was the point of adding the term "dimension" to the description of identifiers and variables?

The point was to prepare the way for understanding the common root of identifiers and variables. As you will see, that difference isn't one of kind but rather one of use. Identifiers and variables represent different uses of a dimension. Furthermore, any dimension can be used either as an identifier or as a variable. Here now we shall explore the dimensional underpinning of identifiers and variables.

First of all let's look at a simple two-column table of time and sales, as shown in Table 15.4.

Table 15.4 represents a simple sales table. The time column is the key column or identifier dimension. Sales is the attribute column or variable. The table shows how many sales were made for each time period. Normally, each column would be defined in terms of a previously declared type, as illustrated in Table 15.5.

The declaration of time and sales as shown in Table 15.5 is a metadata structure. It defines the limits of what could be a value for the dimension or

Table 15.4 A Simple Sales Table

Identifier: Time (hour)	*Variable: Sales (100s of dollars)*
10:00	5
11:00	3
12:00	4
13:00	4
14:00	4
15:00	6
16:00	3
17:00	3
18:00	4
19:00	2

Table 15.5 Metadata Definition of the Time and Sales Dimension

Possible Time Values	*Possible Sales Values*
Any integer > 0 representing a number of minutes	Any integer > 0 representing sales in dollars

any use of that dimension. An analogous concept is that of domain or data type. Table 15.4 is an instantiation of the metadata-based dimensions where one dimension, time, is used as an identifier and another dimension, sales, is used as a variable.

Notice how, at the metadata level, the variable sales is treated as a dimension in the same way as time. If time and sales are treated the same at the metadata level, what makes them different at the data-set level? So far (in Chapter 3 and in the previous section), we appealed to common sense in what was otherwise a private argument for distinguishing variables and identifiers. We saw the subjective basis for distinguishing variables (what's being tracked) and identifiers (how the data is organized). What about a more objective criteria for differentiating identifiers and variables? Is there one? It turns out that there is a more public or objective way of distinguishing between identifiers and variables that is consistent with the common-sense definition given earlier.

Variables and identifiers can be objectively or logically distinguished based on the relationships between the distribution of their values in a data set and their definition at the metadata level. As you will see, in most cases there is a clear difference in the distributions between the dimensions in a data set, and thus a clear indication of which dimensions are being used as identifiers and which are being used as variables. Sometimes, though, there is no difference between the distributions. When that is the case, there is no logical way of distinguishing variables from identifiers.

The more a dimension is usable as an identifier in a table, the more the unique values of the dimension in the table are in one-to-one correspondence with a contiguous range of the values of the dimension's definition in metadata, and the more the number of instances of each dimension value in the table is a constant.

Apart from being defined in terms of a metadata-based dimension, there is no equivalent criteria for being a variable because anything could be a variable. Essentially, whatever is not used as an identifier is a variable. Now, on average, the distribution of the values of a dimension being used as a variable in a table does look different from that of an identifier. Namely, the values of the dimension in the table are not in one-to-one correspondence with a contiguous range of the values of the dimension's definition in metadata. Of

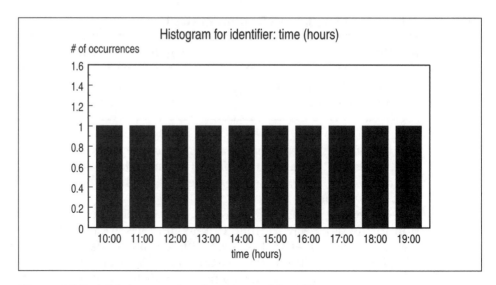

Figure 15.3 A histogram for time as an identifier.

course, when all table dimensions look like their metadata definitions, there is no way to tell what's going on just by looking at the data. (The dimensions could be interdefined, or there could be an interesting and nondefinitional correlation.) This means that there can always be data sets where there are no natural identifiers or variables.

An easy way to see whether a dimension is more naturally used as an identifier or as a variable is to inspect a histogram of the dimension's values as found in the data set. If the histogram for a dimension, like the time dimension in Table 15.4, shows a constant height for frequency, the dimension has the form of (and should be used in analysis as) an identifier. This is shown in Figure 15.3. If the histogram for a dimension, like the sales dimension in Table 15.4, shows a nonconstant, or even better, an interesting distribution, the dimension has the form of (and should be used in analysis as) a variable. This is shown in Figure 15.4.

To drive home the point that dimensions can be used as either identifiers or as variables, let's look at some nontypical data sets that, nevertheless, stem from the same sales and time metadata you saw in Table 15.5. The first one will show sales as an identifier with time as a variable. The second will show time as both an identifier and as a variable. For both tables, a histogram will be shown for each dimension.

Imagine a sales-based fund-raising effort whose goal is to raise $10,000. And, for the first $1,000, the time that each increment of $100 was raised was recorded so as to indicate the rate of progress and what times were more effective for fund raising than others. A table with this information is pre-

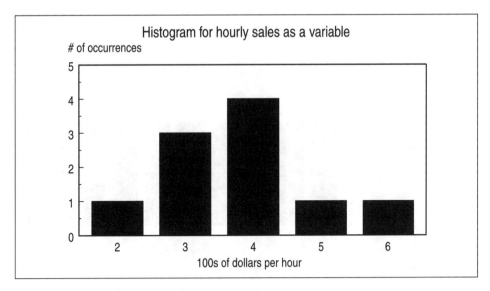

Figure 15.4 A histogram for sales as a variable.

sented in Table 15.6. The sales column represents hundred dollar intervals (of fund-raising sales); the time column represents the time when the sales amount was achieved. The elapsed time column represents the amount of time elapsed since the last $100 increment.

Table 15.6 Table of Time by Sales

Sales ($100s)	Time	Elapsed Time
0	9:00	0
1	9:30	30
2	10:00	30
3	10:15	15
4	10:30	15
5	11:30	60
6	12:30	60
7	1:00	30
8	1:30	30
9	1:45	15
10	2:15	30

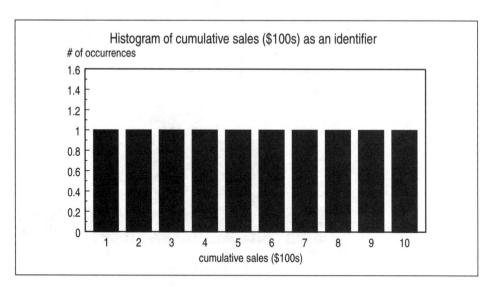

Figure 15.5 Histogram for sales as an identifier.

Notice how the sales histogram in Figure 15.5 is the one with the constant frequency while the histogram for time in Figure 15.6 is the one whose frequency follows a more typical distribution.

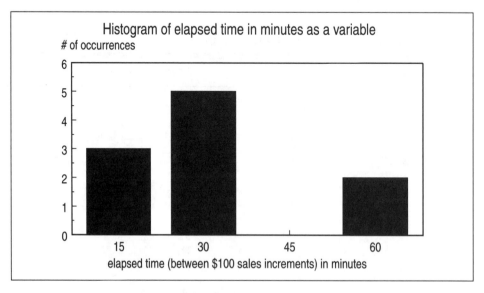

Figure 15.6 Histogram for time as a variable.

Table 15.7 Table of Spacecraft Time by Earth Time

Earth time	Space Time	Elapsed Time (Earth)	Elapsed Time (Space)
10:00	10:00	N/A	N/A
10:10	10:10	10	10
10:20	10:20	10	10
10:30	10:30	10	10
10:40	10:38	10	8
10:50	10:46	10	8
11:00	10:52	10	6
11:10	10:54	10	2
11:20	10:56	10	2
11:30	10:56	10	0

Finally, let's look at an example where the time dimension, in the same sense of clock-measured time, is used as both an identifier and a variable in the same table. Consider Table 15.7. The first time column represents the time on Earth taken at fixed intervals. It is used as a basis for the identifier. The second time column represents the time taken on a spaceship as it is leaving Earth. Imagine that the speed of the spacecraft is precisely known so that the distance of the spacecraft from Earth can be calculated from the time it has been gone, and that Earth sends a signal to the craft at fixed intervals, as measured by Earth. The spacecraft records the time it received each signal and (after correcting for its distance from Earth and other factors) records its local time for each signal reception. Assuming we are close to possessing Warp technology (that is, the ability to travel at or near the speed of light), the purpose of the recording is to test whether, and if so by how much, time slows down as the spacecraft approaches the speed of light. The third and fourth columns represent elapsed time on Earth and on the spaceship, respectively. Entirely derived from columns 1 and 2, the elapsed time columns are what actually get graphed.

Notice how the Earth time column has an identifier-like appearance. This is shown in its constant frequency histogram in Figure 15.7. Meanwhile the same time dimension, albeit in a different use as spacecraft time, shows a variable-like character. Time seems to be slowing down with a limiting point at 10:56, as shown in the histogram in Figure 15.8 .

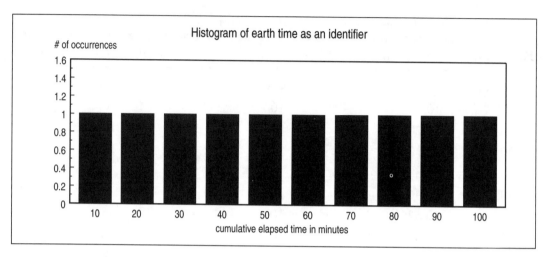

Figure 15.7 Histogram of Earth time as identifier.

From the above examples we have seen three important things:

❑ The distinction between identifiers and variables in a data set represents different uses of a metadata-based dimension. A dimension that is used as an identifier in one situation may be used as a variable in another.

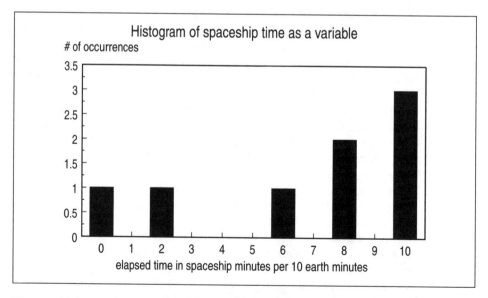

Figure 15.8 Histogram of spacecraft time as variable.

❏ When a dimension is used as an identifier in a table, its values exist in 1-to-1 correspondence with the values of (a contiguous range of) the dimension in its metadata definition.

❏ When no dimension, or all the dimensions, in a table has values that exist in 1-to-1 correspondence with the metadata dimension values, no identifier can be picked out from among the dimensions in the data set based purely on its values.

That Thing Called a Value or Data Dimension

The view that data is beyond the dimensional structuring of a model is quite common.[10] It can be summarized in the following formula template, which will be discussed later in this chapter:

data = f(dimension1, dimension2, ...dimension n)

Most frequently, this view is espoused when a type zero table (remember from Chapter 3 that a type zero table has all the variables listed as values within a column called variables plus an additional value or data column) is connected to a hypercube. The data column is not treated as a dimension. For example, a table whose columns are time, store, products variables, and data would define a four-dimensional cube. Analytically it would be represented in the following way:

data = f(time dimension, store dimension, product dimension, variable dimension)

As shown in Figure 15.9 there is no dimensional grounding for the data. It is extra-systemic. On the other hand, if the same data were represented in a type one table, as shown in Figure 15.10, every piece of the table is accounted for in the dimensional structure. Its corresponding formula would look like this:

sales dimension = f(time dimension, store dimension, product dimension)

actual value of sales dimension = f(actual value of time, store, product dimensions)

It would appear that the form of the data table (that is, type zero or type one) determines which parts of the model are grounded and which are not. This is not very clean. As shown in this section, every element in a table needs to be dimensionally grounded.

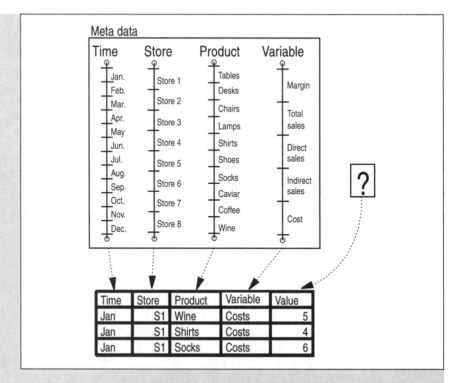

Figure 15.9 No dimensional grounding for the value column.

It is easy to resolve the dilemma by recognizing that in a type zero table, the data or value column is implicitly a dimension in its own right. For simplicity's sake, the resulting cube is called four-dimensional, but then again, it is only for simplicity's sake that we refer to a

In this section on dimensions, we saw that multidimensional models are collections of identifiers and variables and that identifiers and variables represent different uses of dimensions that may be similarly structured. This is why we referred to identifiers as identifier dimensions and to each variable as a variable dimension. We tried several different ways to get around thinking in terms of variables and dimensions, but we could not. Even when we thought we had got rid of variables, they surfaced under the guise of a value or data dimension. Some of the benefits to thinking with identifiers and variables were described. Thinking in terms of variables and identifiers is the first precondition for analysis. We saw the distinction made in a common-sensical way and in a quantitative way.

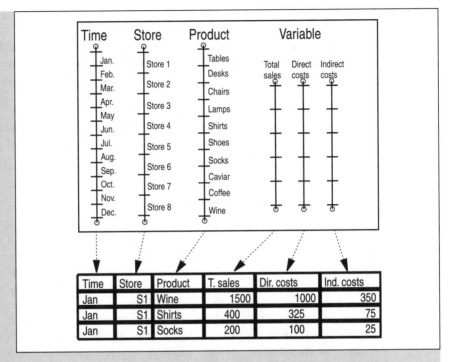

Figure 15.10 The type one table is fully grounded.

group of variables as members of a single variables dimension. It is ultimately more descriptive to refer to, say, a collection of 125 variables, each of which is organized according to the same five dimensions, than to speak simply of a six-dimensional model.

Dimensions in Analysis

Etymology of Analysis

Analysis relates to modeling as a building relates to its foundations. The multidimensional modeling terms introduced in this book such as dimension, identifier, variable, member, hierarchy, and formula are the raw materials and serve as the basis for all analyses.

Analysis, like so many abstract terms, traces back through Latin into Greek. It originally meant to take apart, as opposed to put together. Thinking required both analysis and synthesis. These days, it is common for the term "analysis" to refer both to traditional (decompositional) analysis and to synthesis.

Analysis, in this modern sense, is thus a very broad term. Think of all the things that commonly fall under the purview of analysis: interest rates, mortgage applications, sporting events, political campaigns, elections, mechanical designs, software architectures, sales and marketing activity, financial liquidity, voting patterns, demographics, GNP, unemployment figures, science in general, and any kind of trend. My French dictionary identifies no fewer than 25 categories of analysis, each one with a different set of primitive "analytical elements."[11] Anything can be analyzed.

Dimensions and Ordering

Regardless of the area, most analyses are performed with the aide of mathematics such as algebra, calculus, statistics, geometry, and sets. Different mathematical analyses have different requirements that the data needs to meet in order for the analysis to be performed. For example, given a list of 500 persons and their political affiliation, it makes no sense to calculate the average political party of the group. Political parties are values of a categorical or nominal variable. There is no way to take the average of a categorical variable because you cannot add or divide categories. You could, however, count the number of persons in each political party and create a histogram of those counts from which you could sort the political parties by their count and identify the mode, or the political party having the highest count.

In this section, we look at the interplay of ordering and analysis. We explore how the ordering of identifier dimensions and variables affects the types of analyses that can be performed. We will look at how the process of analysis changes the ordering of the identifiers and variables (which, in turn, changes the types of analyses that can subsequently be performed).

Let's review some of the basic ordering distinctions that you may remember from Statistics 101: nominal, ordinal, and cardinal. In a typical statistics book, these distinctions are commonly made with respect to variables or data.[12] Here in a multidimensional environment, orderings apply to dimensions. Thus, they affect both identifiers and variables. For example, cardinally organized nominal variables, such as a time series of the political party of the President, would be analyzed differently from a nominally organized cardinal variable, such as the average income of registered voters per political party.

Statisticians frequently use the term variable as a synonym for what we have been calling dimension. They speak of dependent and independent variables, whereas we would speak of variable dimensions and identifier dimensions. The term "case," which refers to the instances of a variable, means something analogous to record number or a one-dimensional identifier. You should be aware of this, especially if you have a background in statistics. I will continue to use the terms dimension, identifier, and variable.

Nominal Dimensions

Nominally ordered dimensions are dimensions where the only relationship between the members of the dimension is one of difference. Political parties, gender, color, markets, products, employees, and distribution channels are typically found in nominally ordered form. When the number of members is small and when the dimension is playing the role of variable, as is typical with gender, political party, and color, it is sometimes (in the statistics world) also called a *category variable*. Notice that all the examples given of nominally ordered dimensions were composed of string or character data. This is not necessary, but it is typical. You can perform counts and create histograms and bar charts with nominal data; you can't perform sums, averages, ranks, sorts, or differences.

Ordinal Dimensions

Ordinally ordered dimensions are dimensions where it is possible to rank the members of the dimension from least to most. Race finish (that is, first place, second place, and so on), city size rankings, and sales rankings are examples of ordinally ordered dimensions. Even though, with an ordinal dimension, you know which members are adjacent to any other member, you cannot compare the relationships. There is no way to compare whether the size difference between the third and fourth largest cities is greater than, equal to, or less than the size difference between the fourth and fifth largest cities. Note that many OLAP products use ordinal dimensions by default, but the ordering principle is based on the chronological order in which the dimension members were first loaded into the software. Unless this is a meaningful ordering for you, the dimensions are essentially nominal.

Cardinal Dimensions

Cardinally ordered dimensions have members whose relationships can be quantified. Any integer dimension such as sales in dollars, weight in pounds, temperature in degrees Celsius, height in inches, time in seconds, and defects in units is cardinally ordered. In general, you can sum, difference, average, multiply, and divide cardinal data values. Of course, whether it makes sense to perform a particular operation will depend on the specific dimension and units. Volume divides meaningfully into mass to get density, but sales does not divide meaningfully into angle.

Nonlinear and Nonrectilinear Dimensions   When we think of cardinally ordered dimensions, most of us probably think of equal-sized-interval or linear dimensions. Every day is the same size as every other day. But cardinal dimensions do not need to be linear. Logarithmic scales like the Richter scale are still cardinal.

When we think of models composed of cardinal dimensions, most of us probably think of the Euclidean or rectilinear forms we were exposed to in high school. Here again, there is nothing inherently Euclidean about a model composed of multiple cardinal dimensions. Just think of the longitudinal and latitudinal lines that traverse a globe. They are cardinal and spherical. Geographic information systems (GIS) are just a special case of multidimensional systems where the identifier dimensions are cardinal and fixed (longitude, latitude, and altitude).

Pseudo-cardinal Dimensions   In addition to cardinally ordered dimensions, there exist what I call *pseudo-cardinal dimensions*—dimensions that have numerical values but whose values do not coexist in a quantitatively specifiable relationship. IQ tests are the classic example. There is no basis for comparing a one-point difference in IQ between an IQ of 59 and 60 with an IQ of 139 and 140. Gymnastics scoring (and other judged scoring) is another classic example of a pseudo-cardinal dimension. Scores go from zero to 10 in increments of one hundredths. The higher the score, the better. But how much better is a score of 9.2 than a score of 9.1? And is the difference between a score of 9.2 and 9.1 the same as the difference between a score of 8.6 and 8.5? Is a score of 8 twice as good as a score of 4? The scoring doesn't have to be linear to be cardinal, but it does have to be consistent. There needs to be a rule for comparing value differences. If you've ever watched a gymnastics event, you can see that, although the scores are treated as cardinal (team scores get added), the scores are more realistically somewhere between ordinal and cardinal.

Continuous and Infinite Dimensions   Most of the higher math that is taught in schools treats cardinal dimensions, generally focusing on rational and real number systems, as continuously differentiable. Continuous differentiability allows us to use the differential and integral calculi; it usually allows us to use infinitesimal and infinite series as well. Taylor series, McLauren series, the derivation of e, pi, irrational numbers, the square root of 2, limit functions, the central limit theorem, all make use of the theorem of continuity. Continuous differentiability also assumes that the cardinality, or number of members, in a dimension is infinite. As useful an assumption as this is for some types of mathematics, there is nothing inherently true or better about assuming that dimensions are continuously differentiable. In fact, a significant body of mathematics assumes just the contrary: namely, that all dimensions have a finite cardinality and their members are specifiable. This doesn't mean giving up infinity, just the Cantorian notion of infinity as a completable series.[13] (See Thomsen and Shavel [1993] for a detailed discussion of this issue.)[14]

Most OLAP tools implicitly work according to a discrete-world hypothesis. A part of the dimensional specification process is usually the explicit identification of each member of the dimension either by enumeration or formulaically. Even when the members of a dimension, typically time, are formulaically defined, each member has a specifiable or finite value. Many physical optimizations are based on the awareness of the relative cardinalities of the various dimensions in combination with other dimensions.

Ordering and OLAP

Typical OLAP models are composed of nominally ordered identifier dimensions such as products and stores (or rather the way products and stores are typically treated), one cardinally ordered identifier dimension, time, and cardinally ordered variables such as sales and costs. This is due to the domains where OLAP usage has sprung up and to the limitations of OLAP products.

As OLAP usage becomes more commonplace, its analyses will need to make greater use of cardinally ordered identifier dimensions and nominally ordered variables. Cardinally ordered identifier dimensions are critical for analysis of variance, and nominally ordered variables are very common. Most OLAP products are not suited for analyzing variances beyond time series because they do not support cardinal dimensions beyond time. And few products are suited for analyzing changes and correlations with nominal variables.

Orderings Change During the Analytical Process

An important part of the analytical process is the incorporation of newly learned information into the model. In other words, you may start off with a nominally ordered list of countries and the per capita incomes in each country. Then, if you want to compute the per capita income for the region you will need to find out the population of each country so that you can create correctly weighted average incomes. In doing this, however, you have added information to your country dimension. Instead of just a list of names you now have a list of absolute sizes (in population) attached to those names. A list of population-weighted countries is a cardinal dimension. You can quantify the relationship between any two countries. Country A is twice the size of country B, and so on. This means that for any variable you believe is correlated with country population, it makes sense to explore what that relationship is through the use of correlations and regressions. For example, it might be that you want to predict what the demand for roads or schools will be in a new country of a known population.

Sometimes we need to transform variables by scaling the values of a variable so that they fit between zero and one or by taking the log of a set of values because that correlates better with something. For example, the log of a typical bacteria count has a nice, clean relationship with time.

Sometimes these new weightings, scalings, or logarithms permanently stick to the dimension. When they become incorporated, we get to use the new ordering to view and analyze yet other information. Table 15.8 presents a matrix of identifier orderings by variable orderings. For each intersection,

Table 15.8 Ordering Combinations and the Analyses That Work with Them

		Identifier Dimension		
		Nominal	*Ordinal*	*Cardinal*
Variable dimension	Nominal	majority political party by district .... Count Histogram, mode	majority political party by town income rank	majority political party in town *x* by time .... Logistic regression (LR), multiple LR
	Ordinal	party finish by town .... Ordinal rank Percentile rank Median Kruskal-Wallis test Wilcoxon two-sample test	Party finish by town income rank .... Kendall's correlation coefficient of rank	party finish by time ....
	Cardinal	sales by store .... Sum Chi-square test* Mean(fn)	sales by stores ranked by size .... Running mean	sales by time .... Standard deviation Regression

such as nominal dimension by ordinal variable, a data set that exhibits those characteristics is described in the upper region of the cell, and the names of standard statistical analyses that require at least that amount of ordering (if there are any) are listed in the lower region. The statistical terms are described below the table. (Note that statistical routines can always work on data sets that are more ordered than the minimum amount of required ordering.)

Note that "means" assume that the elements that were summed and whose count needs to be taken to complete the calculation of the mean are of equal size for the purposes of the calculation.

Description of Analysis Terms

- ❑ *Count*: Compute the number of instances of each value. This is perhaps the most general operation. It works with nominal data. You can count colors, genders, races, and religions. And it doesn't assume anything about how the instances are ordered.

- ❑ *Histogram*: Graphical technique of plotting the counts associated with each value. Ordinal and cardinal dimensions may indicate relevant relationships among the various counts.

- ❑ *Mode*: Determines the most frequently occurring value.

- ❑ *Ordinal rank*: Assigns a relative ranking to the data values (as in assigning medals to race times at a track meet).

- ❑ *Percentile rank*: Like an ordinal rank, but carries additional proportion-of-set information, as the percentile rank for a value in the set is the percentage of values in the total set that the value of interest is greater than.

- ❑ *Median*: Finds the "middle" value for the given values of the variable. The values of the variable generate the ordering required; hence, it can be used with nominally ordered dimensions.

- ❑ *Kruskal-Wallis test*: Tests for differences in rank location of data that is grouped by some single classification. This lets you see if there is some significance to the relative rankings that the values get, based on the classification.

- ❑ *Wilcoxon two-sample test*: Tests to see if there are significant differences between two sets of data based on their ranks.

- ❑ *Kendall's correlation coefficient of rank*: Computes a coefficient of correlation between ordinal data values and their ordinal position within a dimension. Any correlation activity is correlating values of a "dependent" variable with their locations along an "independent" dimension, hence the need for this operation to use ordinal data in an ordinal dimension.

❑ *Sum*: Adds together all the values for the variable. Ordering of the dimension should have no effect on the sum obtained.

❑ *Chi-square test*: Tests the significance of differences in values of a variable distributed across nominally divided baskets. Note that if this is performed on variables organized by an ordinal or cardinal dimension, the dimension must be divided into essentially nominal sets for the test to work.

❑ *Mean*: Computed by dividing the sum of the values by the count of the values. As with sums, the ordering of the dimension has no effect on the average obtained. However, when you are averaging *aggregates* of unequal size (like averaging per capita income across several countries), you will generally want to weight the averages by the size-determining factor of the aggregates.

❑ *Standard deviation*: Computed using the mean of the values and the values themselves. Describes the variation between the values. Because it depends on the mean, it requires its input values to be suitable for means.

❑ *Regression*: Computes the coefficients of a function connecting the values of cardinal variables to their position along the dimension. The dimension needs to be cardinally ordered, so that change in variable per change in dimension position can make sense as an operation.

❑ *Logistic regression*: Computes the correlation between changes in the values or state of nominal variables and a cardinal independent dimension. Basic logistic regression assumes one binary state variable. Other forms work with multistate variables and multiple variables.

Whereas analyses need to discover and cultivate relationships or dependencies between variables, preparation for analysis needs to discover and cultivate independent dimensions. Dependencies between dimensions distort (or, as statisticians would say, bias) correlation calculations between variables.

Independent Dimensions

Part of analysis involves understanding variables in relation to other variables. How do sales relate to costs? How does education relate to productivity? How does nutrition relate to education? Part of analysis involves understanding patterns in the set of instances for a variable. Are sales increasing? When will our run rate reach $1 million per month? Will it rain tomorrow?

Put the two parts together, and you get dimensional analyses such as "How are costs varying relative to sales over time and from region to region?"

Table 15.9 A Cube Collection of $y = f(x)$ Statements

	x	x	x	x
y	$y = f(x)$	$y = f(x)$	$y = f(x)$	$y = f(x)$
y	$y = f(x)$	$y = f(x)$	$y = f(x)$	$y = f(x)$
y	$y = f(x)$	$y = f(x)$	$y = f(x)$	$y = f(x)$
y	$y = f(x)$	$y = f(x)$	$y = f(x)$	$y = f(x)$

These analyses can be put in the form of $y = f(x)$ functions. They are simple and powerful mechanisms. It can be useful to think of a collection of these $y = f(x)$ statements as forming a cube as shown in Table 15.9. The y is the dependent variable; the x is the independent variable.

With a multidimensional data structure representation like the one in Figure 15.11, it is easier to show all the x dimensions and reinforce the fact that individual y's are dimensions and equate with whole sets of x's.

In practice, we are always viewing and analyzing variable dimensions (y's) with respect to identifier dimensions (x's). We may view the value of a sales variable for some product dimension value and some time dimension value. Or we may analyze changes in sales as a function of changes in product or time.

All analysis can be built from these simple beginnings. Viewing or specifying the change in a variable as a function of changes in a dimension is

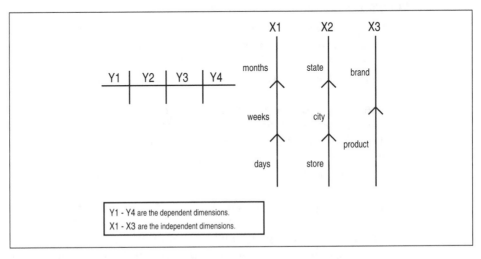

Figure 15.11 A multidimensional data structure representation of $y = f(x)$.

equivalent to defining a partial derivative for the variable's function. Add a little complexity, and you can specify the second-order derivative as the change in change of a variable with respect to the change in change of a dimension. Going further, you can specify the ratio, or change in ratio, or change in change of ratio between two or more variables, still for a dimension, change in dimension, or change in change in a dimension. In other words, all views and analyses of variables are relative to some dimension value or location. This location serves the role of framework for viewing and analysis.

Now what happens if you try to analyze for some customer how sales to that customer varied across stores in a sales data set where store and customer are identifier dimensions, and it turns out that customer and store are correlated? What would it mean to analyze for some customer how sales to that customer varied exclusively across stores? You might get an answer such as sales were at some value for one store and zero for all other stores. This isn't meaningful information about sales trends per customer. (Would you now go about trying to increase sales across the stores that experienced zero sales to that customer? Probably you would not take such a course of action.)

Rather, the information confirms that the customer shops at a particular store (which is to say that customer IDs are correlated with store IDs) and that changes observed for the variable "sales" are not totally attributable to changes in store. You will not be able to look at an accurate partial derivative of customer sales on store until the influence of stores' correlation with customers has been totally compensated for, if not eliminated.

Independence Between Dimensions

For the purposes of dimension-specific analysis of variance, it is important that changes in the values of any identifier dimension are uncorrelated with changes in the values of any other identifier dimension. To the degree that the identifiers are interdependent, they can no longer serve as separable factors.

The independence or dependence between different identifier dimensions is a function of the use of the dimensions in a particular data set. In other words, two dimensions that may be independent in one data set can be dependent in another. The best way to look at the degree to which your dimensions are independent is to examine the data sets from whence they came.

In general, and always relative to a particular data set, two dimensions can be coexistent and independent, coexistent and interdependent, or noncoexistent. To discover the degree to which your dimensions are independent, I suggest drawing a diagram of the cross-product of the two dimensions. If the two dimensions are totally independent, every one of the possible intersections

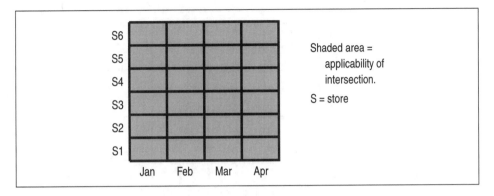

Figure 15.12 Independent dimensions.

will be valid, as shown in Figure 15.12. If there are some dependencies between the two dimensions they will show in a reduction of the number of valid intersections, as depicted in Figure 15.13. If the two dimensions are totally dependent, their relationship will appear as a line within the matrix, as shown in Figure 15.14.

Parallel coordinates, which you saw in Chapters 6 and 13, can also be used to picture the degrees of independence between several identifier and variable dimensions at the same time.

For example, Figure 15.15 shows a parallel coordinates view of a set of idealized identifier and variable relationships. The Store, Time, and Product dimensions show M*N relationships with each other (the M*N relationship between product and store requires color to bring out, since they are separated by Time). The relationship between Product and Returns, being more regular on the Product side and more chaotic on the Returns side, indicates a

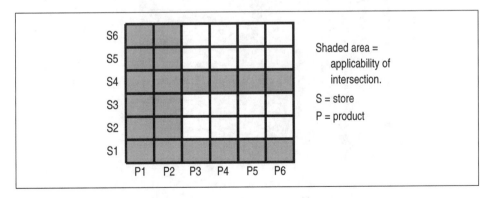

Figure 15.13 Some dependencies between dimensions.

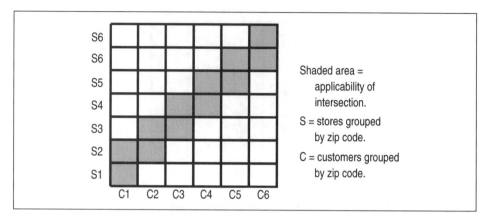

Figure 15.14 Interdependent dimensions.

transition between an identifier and a variable while the chaos of the relationship between Returns and Costs is typical between two variables. The relationship between Costs and Sales is an example of perfectly correlated variables.

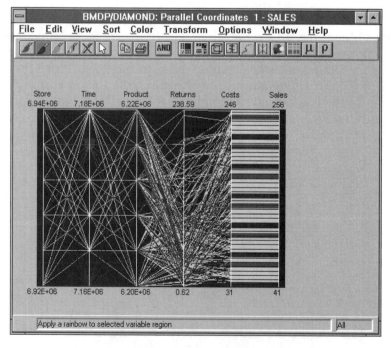

Figure 15.15 Idealized view of parallel coordinates.

Now let's focus on just two dimensions. If the dimensions are independent of each other, they can both be used as identifiers. When there is interdependence any one should be used as identifier and the other one as variable. For example, if store and customer are correlated, you can treat stores as the dependent dimension, with customer as the independent dimension or vice versa. You might look at store facts per customer as a function of customer facts. This tells you information about the stores that different types of customers like. Or you can treat customers as the dependent dimension with stores as the independent dimension. Here you would look at customer facts per store, like the income and education distribution of the customers for store x.

By treating customer and store as interdependent, you succeed in squeezing a maximum amount of information from your data set. Of course, things get more complicated as the number of dimensions increases because the degree of independence of two dimensions may be a function of the values of the other dimensions. Furthermore, dimensions may be independent of other dimensions for only a subset of their possible values. Some products may be correlated with some stores. Some customers may be correlated with some products. And some stores may be correlated with some times. Nevertheless, the principle of looking at interdependencies remains the same.

Conclusion

In this chapter analysis was presented as a movement, played out between variables and identifiers; both variables and identifiers were grounded in the same notion of dimension, ordering, and independence.

Endnotes

1. It wasn't until the early nineteenth century that mathematicians such as Mobius, Cauchy, and Clifford began theorizing about abstract geometrical spaces independent of the three-dimensional limitations of physical space. See David Smith, *A Source Book in Mathematics* (New York: Dover Publications, 1959), pp. 525–545.

2. The term "orthogonal" has been used in the industry to mean generic as in if all dimensions are generically the same, they are orthogonal. This is an unfortunate misuse of the term. The term's real use, as defined by its mathematical origins, has to do with the concept of independence between dimensions, which, as we saw in the text, is an important concept in the OLAP world.

3. Even in a business sense, the term *perspective* has a subtly complex meaning. What exactly does it mean to say that we need to examine our busi-

ness from a customer perspective? It means that we need to look at all noncustomer aspects of the business, such as all types of sales of all types of products at all different times, in terms of how any of that varies as we look at different groups of customers. For example, how have sales evolved over the last 12 months to persons under 30 versus persons over 30? In addition, and instead of being arbitrarily grouped, the members of a dimension may be ordered. There may, for example, be an income ordering placed on customers. You could then define how sales varies as a function of changes in customer for customers ordered by personal income.

4. *The OLAP Report*, for example, treats variables as just another "dimension" alongside products, time, and scenarios, pp. 41–51.

5. See, for example, these sources:

   Marvin Minsky, "A Framework for Representing Knowledge," in P. H. Winston (ed.), *The Psychology of Computer Vision* (New York: McGraw Hill, 1975), pp. 211–277.

   Douglas B. Lenat and R. V. Guha, *Building Large Knowledge-based Systems* (Reading, MA: Addison-Wesley, 1990).

   Paul Cohen, Edward Feigenbaum, Avron Barr, *The Handbook of Artificial Intelligence,* vol. I (Reading, MA: Addison-Wesley, 1986).

6. Ralph Kimball, *The Data Warehouse Toolkit* (New York: John Wiley & Sons), pp. 143–151.

7. Kant, "Critique of Pure Reason, Perception of Space and Time."

8. E. F. Codd, *The Relational Model for Database Management, Version 2* (Reading, MA: Addison-Wesley, 1991) p. 460.

9. *Ibid.*, p. 176. Incidentally, it is inconsistent for Dr. Codd simultaneously to propose that all dimensions are generic and to formally handle missing data per the rules of *The Relational Model, Version 2* because the definitions of missing and meaningless have to do with the relationship between nonkey attributes, or variables, and keys, or identifiers.

10. Maurice Frank, "A Drill-Down Analysis on Multidimensional Databases," *DBMS,* July 1994:

11. See Paul Robert [1967].

12. Stat1

13. Cantor on the actual infinite

14. Erik Thomsen and Shavel, "A Tractarian Basis for Number Theory," Wittgenstein Symposium on the Philosophy of Mathematics.

Toward a Logic-Grounded Model for OLAP

Throughout this book, you have read about many aspects of multidimensional software technology. You have seen its need, its basic and advanced features and benefits, how it is instantiated in storage and access routines, how it is deployed across a network, how it is implemented by corporations, and, perhaps most important of all, you have had the chance to experience OLAP in practice. One thing, however, remains to be seen: an underlying data model. And, if you read this chapter, I need to warn you such a data model will still remain to be seen. A well-grounded comprehensive data model for OLAP is beyond the scope of this book, requiring a small book in its own right (as would a detailed critique of the limits of the Relational model and Canonical logic). However, I think it is useful to outline the challenges of articulating an OLAP data model and where such a data model could be grounded. At the very least, it will give you a deeper understanding of the foundations of OLAP. Perhaps it will encourage you to look further into some of the questions raised in this chapter.

Products, Data Models, and Foundations

A *data model* consists of structuring and operational definitions (frequently called a data definition and manipulation language) that apply to all the data that could ever be described or manipulated by software adhering to the model. Data models benefit the community of users, product developers, and researchers by providing a common language of expression independent of any particular tool and in terms of which any tool may be easily understood. In addition, for researchers especially, the language gets reified, thus becoming a thing to be thought about independently of any particular product or problem. A data model is like a map one can reason with distinctly from the terrain it depicts. This is the essence of abstract data model based research. When the data model integrates elements from logic, it provides a basis for the design of deductive databases where, given any database state, some other set of states may be logically deduced.

Let's contextualize the concept of data model by considering the spectrum of levels relevant to data models. Figure 16.1 is an illustration of that spectrum. There is a products level, which refers to all the software products available in the marketplace that one can use, a common product language level, which refers to any industry-standard API specification, a data model level, which refers to things like the Relational model, and, finally, a logico-mathematical level, which refers to things like matrix algebra and predicate calculus. When you consider this spectrum from a broad perspective, it becomes clear that a data model is sandwiched between individual products and standard APIs on one end, and math and logic on the other.

For example, SQL database products, such as those produced by Oracle, Sybase, and Informix, can be driven through ODBC (an industry standard

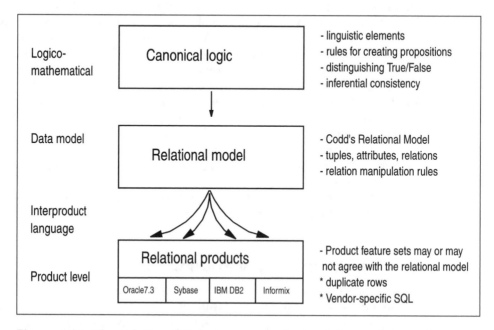

Figure 16.1 The relationship between products, data models, and foundations.

API specification). These are all grounded in a common logical data model—the "Relational model" of data. The Relational model was first introduced by E. F. Codd in his seminal 1970 paper "A Relational Model of Data for Large Shared Databanks."[1] It introduced a set of primitive data structures including domains, relations, tuples, and attributes. It also introduced a set of primitive operations including joins, products, restrictions, and projections. These primitive structures and operations are grounded on the primitive structures and operations of Canonical logic (and theory of relations) including functions, arguments, and connectives. It is interesting to note that the Relational model was developed and debated before any products were created that claimed to be relational.

Logic and the Relational Model

Logic, of any provenance, is concerned with information elements, which are the smallest bearers of meaning. In the same way that all molecules and compounds are composed of physical elements, all data sets and publicly exchanged thought are composed of information elements. While logic offers a theory of how any one information element can be true or false, and how arbitrary groups of information elements may connect and be operated on in a truth-state consistent manner, the Relational model focuses on a particular group of information elements called relations, and how relations may be operated on in such a way that the output of any relational operation performed on a relation is always another relation. This is crucial to the Relational model, because the benefits of the model derive from the benefits of representing data in terms of relations.

Chief among the benefits is the preservation of truth-states or consistency across update operations. In other words, no edit operation to a relational table should ever unintentionally add, remove, or unintentionally change the value of any existent information. Because relations are groups of information elements, the laws of logic must apply to them.

Canonical logic[2] is the name for that body of primitives which is accepted by a majority of practicing logicians and analytical philosophers. Most current logical procedures (with the exception of those going back to Aristotle) can be traced to the turn-of-the-century symbolic innovations of Gottlob Frege's *Begriffsschrift*[3] and the *Principia Mathematica*[4] by Bertrand Russell and Alfred North Whitehead. The Relational model is based, in large part, on Canonical logic.

Features of an OLAP Model

Consider the following questions. Is there a multidimensional model of data separate from that of the Relational model? If there is not, then how do multidimensional structures and operations follow from relational primitives? If there is, what is it, and how does it relate to Canonical logic? Lastly, can Canonical logic support a multidimensional model, or are new foundations required?

Chronologically speaking, multidimensional products were developed in the absence of any standard data model. There was, of course, geometry, which had become multidimensional in the early 1800s, and the matrix algebra which appeared later. These probably were a part of the awareness of individuals who created OLAP products.

Ex post facto, one should at least be able to construct a standard data model of what all these products have in common. And within that collection of common structures and operations, one can distinguish basic or primitive features from ones that are constructed. This would allow researchers, developers, and users to speak a common language and think about issues independently of particular products. The task is not as simple as it might sound because different products differ substantially over fundamental issues, for example, whether all dimensions are equivalent or whether variables should be treated differently and whether multiple levels are a part of the same dimension or whether they each belong in a separate dimension.

From my perspective, the basic features of any multidimensional model need to include:

❑ multilevel dimensions,

❑ formulas that attach to dimension members for intra- and interdimensional operations,

❑ procedures for handling logical sparsity, and

❑ the ability for data to flow in any direction within the model.

These features can be used as a litmus test to distinguish if a particular item is in fact a multidimensional data model. But, as I will briefly describe below, most of these features are hard, if not impossible, to provide given the features offered by the relational model.

Multidimensional Features Are Not Directly Supported by the Relational Model

The relational model focuses on structural operations more than data operations (the basic operations of relational algebra, such as joins, Cartesian products, projections, and restrictions, are all structural operations), and on base data more than derived data. The mathematical functions used to define the values of one attribute of a relation in terms of the values of another attribute of the same relation attach to columns. Functions in the relational model apply most naturally in a relation- and column-specific sense.

Oddly enough, the main differences between the relational model and a multidimensional model have nothing to do with the multiple dimensions. From the moment you have multiple columns in a relation, the relation is multidimensional. The key differences are that the multidimensional model focuses on hierarchical relationships (that is, its dimensions have a multi-level structure), and that it focuses on efficiently defining data derivations by attaching formulas to dimension members. Let's look at these differences more closely.

Consider the multidimensional system shown in Figure 16.2. It represents a by now familiar four-dimensional model consisting of stores, time, products, and variables. Note the hierarchical structure in each of the nonvariable dimensions. Assume, for the moment, that all the hierarchies define simple aggregations. Thus, any user of the information can calculate and view any combination of derived values simply by asking for or navigating to them. The aggregations are built in, so to speak, in the definition of the dimensions. In the relational world, these aggregations would have to be defined on a view-by-view basis and sales sums across stores and time would have to be restated for each aggregate sales table created.

Nearly all multidimensional products offer a variety of methods for specifying functions, including both dimension-based and cell-based products. It is crucial for the efficient specification of large numbers of derived values, and is not directly supported by the relational model. It would take a shift from attribute-oriented formula specifications (where formulas are attached to columns in a table) to unique domain value-oriented formula specifications (where formulas are attached to rows in a table or to all rows containing a particular value) for the relational model to provide the same efficiencies for specifying derivations.

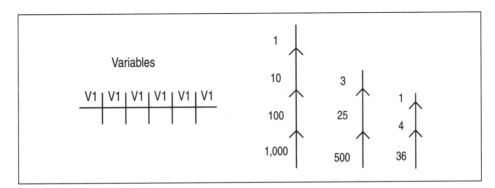

Figure 16.2 A familiar multidimensional system.

As was described in Chapter 2, for example, the relational algebra is not equipped to define intra-dimensional comparisons because they are generally performed between rows within a column. It is far more suited to defining inter-attribute calculations (which generally involve inter-column comparisons). SQL is so weak on this point that in order to perform inter-row calculations in SQL, people frequently transform, in a roundabout fashion, the inter-row problem into an inter-column problem, and then solve the inter-column problem.

Thus, core features of multidimensional products are not directly supported by the relational model. This is illustrated in Figure 16.3. Now, does the presence of these features make any multidimensional model irreconcilable with the relational model, or is there some way both models can be united?

Multidimensional Features Are Not Directly Supported by Canonical Logic

The question remains, "Are core multidimensional features supported by Canonical logic?" If they are, then, to the degree that the Relational model is as complete as the Canonical logic, multidimensional features should be de-

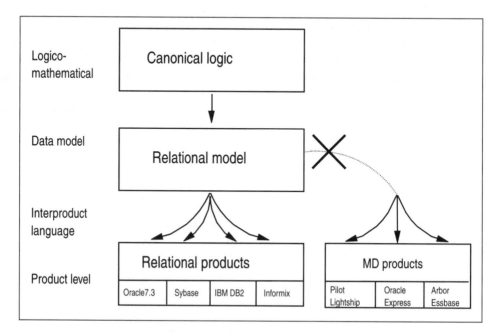

Figure 16.3 The Relational model does not adequately support multidimensional features.

rivable from the relational model. If they are not, then some other logic is needed to ground multidimensional features.

The biggest problem that C,anonical logic has trying to support uniquely multidimensional features is its lack of multilevel dimensions. In addition, canonical logic lacks a theory of meaning capable of being used as a procedure for parsing missing and inapplicable data. This creates problems for the relational model (where debate is still ongoing as to how best to process invalid data) as much as for OLAP where sparsity, as we saw in Chapter 7, is a significant issue. Note, in the discussion that follows, set theory will be treated synonymously with (or as extensionally equivalent to) logic.

Multiple Levels

On the one hand, it could be argued that level or resolution is the principle ordering feature of set theory, characterizing as it does the primitive relationship between element and set. On the other hand, multiple iterations of a many–one relationship do not generate a resolutional order. Thus, for example, set theory has no way to distinguish between a 1–6 hierarchical relationship, such as a state and its political subunits, and a 1–6 relationship that defined an object, such as a table and six sibling-like neighbors such as chairs. It is precisely the primitive nature of the set–membership function that obstructs the construction of a resolutional axis for relating elements, sets, and sets of sets. In addition, the set–membership relation isn't transitive: to be a member of a set is not, by virtue of that relation, to be a member of a set of that set.

Mereology

Mereology is the only school of axiomatic set theory that even addresses these concerns. Specifically, mereology treats of part–whole relations, modifying the standard theory in such a way as to capture some aspects of resolutional relationships. The basic modifications are simple: the *singleton* (unit class) is postulated as the primitive element; the *parts* of a class (or set) are defined to be all and only its subclasses. Classically, because transitivity was not an automatic feature of the set–element relation, part–hole relations (where transitivity is a given) were detached from and subordinated to the broader context of set–membership. David Lewis, in his *Parts of Classes*,[5] inverts this and treats part–hole relations as the more primitive. In his calculus, x is a member of a class y only when x is a member of a singleton that is a part of y. Moreover, we can adapt standard iterative set theory to formally characterize this relationship.

What is clear is that the distinction made in the multidimensional world between ancestral relationships of parent and child versus sibling relationships is not made in Canonical logic.

Handling Sparsity: Theory of Meaning

Canonical logic also has a problem defining what constitutes an information element or unit of meaning. Typically speaking, valid information elements are defined according to some syntactic conditions wherein only certain (or *well-formed*) formulas are considered valid. All, and only, valid formulas possess a truth value, which, in the classical two-valued case, may be either true or false. The problem is that there are many seemingly valid syntactic expressions which do not appear to possess any meaning, or which appear to be both true and false. Logicians call the latter expressions paradoxes. The liar paradox, which many readers may have seen in college, is one such example. A modern version of it is "This sentence is false." If the sentence is true then it is false; but if it is false, then it is true.

The lack of an adequate theory of meaning is a problem for Canonical logic that appears in all applications, not just OLAP. In the OLAP world, as we saw in Chapter 7, for example, a hypercube typically defines many empty cells (it is important to know which cells are empty and meaningless, and

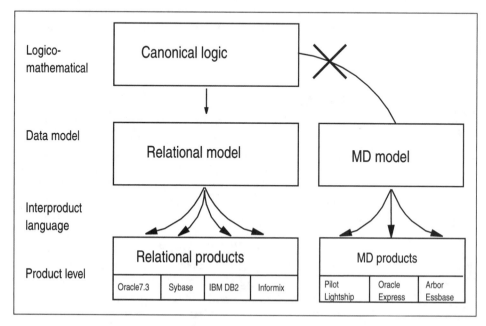

Figure 16.4 Canonical logic does not support a multidimensional model.

which cells are empty and missing). In the relational world, it is clear that canonical logic has nothing to say about handling invalid propositions. This is why, as described in Chapter 6, the debate continues in the relational world between advocates of two-, three-, four- and many-valued logics. There is no Canonical way to decide the issues. So Canonical logic, with its inability to define levels or account adequately for meaning, does not provide a comprehensive foundation for multidimensional models.

A Tractarian Approach

The term "Tractarian" refers to any of several approaches to language and logic based on the *Tractatus Logico-Philosophicus*,[6] by the Austrian philosopher Ludwig Wittgenstein. Wittgenstein wrote the work in the early part of the century, shortly after his studies and collaboration with Bertrand Russell at Cambridge. The final goal of his book was to delineate clearly what can be expressed by means of propositions, these being the proper subject matter for logical treatment. Along the way, it laid a groundwork for distinguishing propositions from nonpropositions, by means of usage- or functionally-based criteria. Perhaps because of the difficulty of the work, few of his innovations were incorporated within the main body of Canonical logic, though he is remembered as having been the inventor of the truth tables. Although it goes beyond the scope of this book to dive into and do serious battle for his ideas, I felt the need to at least minimally describe an approach to logic possessing the requisite properties for supporting multidimensional functionality (as well as Relational functionality) and for resolving the problems that plague Canonical logic.

L-C logic is the name given to a tractarian-based logic that resulted from research conducted over the past 15 years by a number of individuals, including me. You might remember (from Chapter 7) that the method for handling missing and inapplicable data was attributed to something called "L-C logic."

Overview of L-C logic

The below-described multidimensional-relevant features of an L-C logic are

1. It distinguishes positional and resolutional adjacencies in dimension structures.
2. It handles sparsity by incorporating a mechanically grounded model for distinguishing propositions from nonpropositions, and works only on valid propositions.
3. It supports omni-directional data flows.

L-C Dimension Structures

L-C logic articulates a principle for ordering propositions that translates into the multidimensional world as a primitive topology for dimensions. This principle is grounded in the primitive concept of adjacency. There are two primitive types of adjacency: *position*, such as between two cities or persons or between two measurements made in meters, and *resolution*, such as between cities and a state or measurements made in meters with measurements made in angstroms.

The Relevance of Resolution or Scale to Logic

Traditionally, canonical logic has ignored these distinctions, since it claims to treat only the combinatorial connections between propositions (and, or, not, etc.), irrespective of their meaning. And surely concerns about *adjacency* must belong to their semantics, or meaning. However, the logical treatment of two propositions p and q cannot be the same when the meaning of q is part of the meaning of p, as when the two are inferentially independent. This is more evident in the case of predicate logic, which treats specifically of the cardinality relationships between sets and members. According to the L-C way of thinking, to say that something is a part of something else (in the resolutional sense of *part*) is to express a tautology. Similarly, the relationship between an operation and its results (as used, positionally speaking, to express a series of integers) is also tautologous. And tautologies are precisely the domain of logic. Ignoring the relevance of adjacency means the logician must abstain from specifying any criteria for well-formedness (i.e., the use of those p's and q's in real world situations).

Note how this parallels the multidimensional distinction between hierarchical (or root–leaf) relationships, such as parent–child, and nonhierarchical (or branch–branch) relationships, like inter-sibling. The combination of position and resolution adjacencies constitutes a minimally sufficient set of types for creating any possible specification or statement. In other words, any adjacency relation is determined by mixing from the two *pure* adjacency types (wherein, *pure* position measurements are resolution-specific, while *pure* resolutional measurements are position-specific) in the same way that a location on the globe is determined by mixing from a pure set of longitude, latitude, and altitude measurements.

Meaning and Sparsity

Traditionally, the term "proposition" has been used in one way or another to indicate the *meaning* of a sentence, following on the observation that two or more sentences may mean the same thing, or (though less often recognized) that the same sentence can have two or more meanings. However, the claim that a consistent logic and a viable theory of representation somehow follow from a theory of propositions is not widely acknowledged.

Canonical logic treats sentences, propositional tokens or signs, well-formed formulas, character strings, and propositions indiscriminately (according to various definitions of well-formedness). Historically, the sentence/proposition distinction has only been invoked in the evident cases where a sentence does not uniquely specify a proposition, or an apparently well-formed sign doesn't yield a proposition at all. One reason is that logicians are inclined to believe meaningfulness can be ascertained from the sign itself—otherwise, by what criteria would we call a system formal? A second reason is that the very notion of proposition has never been well-defined.

Aristotle characterized logic within the context of an affirming/denying game (the *dialectic* in its original sense), and defined propositions as the primitive units of this game. He further diagnosed a certain compositeness of type as their defining character, distinguishing that which an assertion was asserting from that of which the assertion was being made. Yet since Aristotle equated these types with the grammatical distinctions of predicate and subject respectively, he thereby sanctioned the subsequent focus on indicative sentences.

Logicians ever since have been devising ways of preserving that focus. Bertrand Russell, who early on recognized that grammatical form does not always indicate logical form, is a case in point. His theory of descriptions was an attempt to uncover the hidden logical form of sentences whose grammatical subject no longer exists, and thus maintain their place in the truth-functional calculus. Otherwise, well-formed but meaningless (i.e., non-truth-functional) sentences might infect the calculus as a whole. The insight behind Tractarian logic is that well-formedness on the page, however it is defined, does not sufficiently determine meaning.

In contrast to the referential approach in Canonical logic, where both the "grammatical" Aristotelian and "logical" Russellian subjects and predicates are distinguished referentially (i.e., by reference to individual substances and universals, for the former, and to individuals of acquaintance and sense-data-properties for the latter), the regulating principle of an L-C logic is a *functional* distinction of types. To this end, it distinguishes two primary or *prototype* functions necessary and sufficient for determining a proposition: location specification and content specification. (For a detailed treatment of these functions please see Thomsen and Shavel [1990].) Remember these two functions from Chapter 15? There we saw type structures used as identifiers or locators, and as variables or content.

> The terminology is somewhat reversed in logical parlance, where the term "variable" is usually reserved for the locator (the x of a propositional function $f(x)$). In an L-C logic, however, both prototype functions (content and location) are expressed by variables (the f and x respectively of quantified expressions).

The prototype specification has quite a lot to say about which sentences enter the calculus, regulating the possible substitutions for the variables p, q, r, . . . in a logical schema. This is of no small consequence since, even as canonical logic recognizes, not all well-formed sentences determine propositions.

The self-referentially interpreted, "This sentence is false" (which if true, is as it claims, false; but if false, is thereby true) is a case in point. It is on all accounts well-formed; but if allowed into the calculus, it would undermine the "complementarity" requirement of truth and falsity. Both L-C and Canonical logic, then, begin with the insight that certain well-formed sentences do not take a truth value. L-C, however, reasons about these sentences without having to reason with them—that is, without bringing them into the calculus. Because sentences are themselves located contents (as perceptible facts: character strings, tokens, etc.), it is possible to mechanically parse their representational forms *from the outside. One distinguishes the genuine from the putative propositions by attempting to make the terms perform their prototype functions.*

Within a two-valued propositional calculus, then, the only presupposition is that propositions alone are treated; and it is expressed in the following manner: propositions occur in other propositions only as the *arguments* of truth-functions. "p is false" is identical to the truth-function $\sim p$ *(or not p).* So, even in the case of "This very proposition is false," however strongly the phrase "this very proposition" insists that it is a proposition, it fails the L-C compositeness query. Nor can one retreat to the claim that the phrase *names* a proposition ("this very proposition is false,") because this string of tokens has to submit to the same query: what proposition? Neither "this very proposition" nor the entire "this very proposition is false" are (on the standard reading of these terms) possible values of p in "p is false" (that is, neither can be its own truth-argument in the logical formula $\sim p$).

In L-C logic, then, meaninglessness never infects a logical formula, since it never enters the calculus. Despite appearances, "If the square root of 2 is blue, then Bill is in the bar" is not an instance of "if p then q." It is not the logical formula that is called into question (as if its applicability were no longer global), but the substitution of a nonproposition for the propositional variable *p*. And if an element of a proposed molecular compound fails the test, the element may be eliminated, generally without having to delete the entire expression. Thus, L-C logic takes a firm stand on the issue of invalid propositions, and can serve as a useful support for the OLAP (and relational) requirements of logical sparsity handling (as it did in Chapter 7).

Data Flows

The position and resolution structuring of the L-C dimensions relativizes all statement locations, and paves the way for data to flow from anywhere to anywhere. Allocations and inferences are as natural as aggregations. In contrast, Canonical logic, as evidenced by Russell's empiricism, logical atomism, and Theory of Descriptions (a decompositional approach to transforming ordinary language into collections of quantified logical statements and assertions of primitive sense data) all tacitly assume that data enters at some base level and then propagates upward. Of course, as you've seen throughout this book, it is highly desirable for a data model to permit data to flow in any direction, for it is easier to ground OLAP features in a logic for which these data flows already occur.

Summary: Tractarian Support for an OLAP Logical Model

The OLAP notions of sibling and ancestor are directly supported by the L-C notions of position and resolution. The OLAP notion of derivation is directly supported by the Tractarian notion of proposition combined with the L-C notion of data flows. And the ability to differentially process missing and inapplicable data, crucial to the proper handling of sparse data sets, is directly supported by the L-C method for defining and operating on propositions. The Tractarian approach to logic thus serves as a better foundation for an OLAP features and an eventual data model than either the Relational model or Canonical logic. Much work remains to be done in this area.

Endnotes

1. E. F. Codd, "A Relational Model of Data for Large Shared Data Banks," IBM Research Laboratory, San Jose, CA, February 1970.

2. More precisely, by "Canonical" I mean "standard," nondeviant, predicate logic (Principia-like) and axiomatic set theory (Zermelo-Fraenkel-like) with intended reference to W. V. Quine's "canoncial notation" for refining scientific discourse. In the context of this (rather skeletal) overview, I refer to predicate logic and set theory interchangeably (such that *Fx* can be ex-

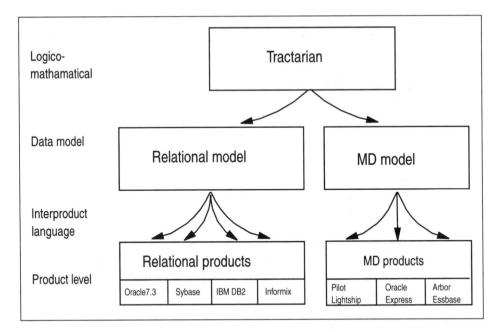

Figure 16.5 A multidimensional model is grounded in a Tractarian approach to logic.

pressed as $x \in F$ and vice versa). Also, I use "set" and "class" interchangeably. ("Set" is usually given as a restricted version of class; but the reasons for these restrictions are precisely the ones addressed in L-C logic as found in Thomsen and Shavel [1990].)

3. Begriffsschrift, a formula language, modeled upon that of arithmetic, for pure thought. Gottlob Frege 1879. reprinted in *A Source book in Mathematical Logic*, 1879–1931. Edited by Jean van Heijenoort. Copyright 1967 by the President and Fellows of Harvard College. (Cambridge, MA: Harvard University Press).

4. Bertrand Russell and A. N. Whitehead, *Principia Mathematica*.

5. David K. Lewis, *Parts of Classes* (Oxford: Oxford University Press), 1991.

6. Wittgenstein, Ludwig, *Tractatus Logico-Philosophicus*. First published 1921. English edition copyright 1961. This edition printed 1977. (London: Routledge & Kegan Paul).

17

Comprehensive Guidelines

If you have arrived at this last chapter after having read the rest (or at least most) of the book, then you have explored multidimensionality from a variety of perspectives: logical, physical, conceptual, and applied. In Chapters 3 and 4, explanations of basic functions were arranged in order of ease of assimilation. In Chapters 6 and 7, explanations of advanced functions were arranged in order of expected use frequency. In Chapter 10, explanations of how to use multidimensional functions were arranged in the way that functions would likely be used for building and analyzing models.

In this chapter, multidimensional functions are arranged (with minimal explanation) in structural or reference order to be used for trying to evaluate or compare multidimensional tools, for thinking about application requirements, or simply for organizing, summarizing, and, to a small degree, extending what you have learned in this book. (The wording is tool-oriented in the sense that I describe tool features or ask questions about tool features. But you can, in most cases, easily rephrase tool questions as application questions.) Organizationally, logical features are distinguished from physical features. Core features are distinguished from application features. Structural features are distinguished from operations and representational features. (These distinctions are discussed below.)

The guidelines are written in terms of questions and statements about features. Only where I feel that further elucidation is necessary, do I offer an explanation. (Mostly this is to reinforce key points made earlier in the book.) Where relevant, I add some contextual discussion. There are a few spots in this chapter—always demarcated as a further issue—where I introduce feature/concepts that go beyond what vendors currently offer. Within what is a fairly formal organization, I try to be as informal as possible. Sometimes there are no questions, and sometimes there are no statements. (This is because descriptive statements, such as "You should make sure that the tool can support the largest dimension you think you'll need," can be stated as tool questions, such as "What is the maximum number of members that the tool supports in a dimension?" or as application questions, such as "What is the maximum number of members your application requires in a dimension?")

Multidimensional Guidelines

Remarks

The purpose of these feature guidelines is to describe the key areas of multidimensional functionality in terms of functional categories that any tool must provide and in terms of functionality that tools may or may not provide. When appropriate, within each functional category, features are ordered in terms of how basic or advanced they are. While any tool should support basic functionality in all functional categories (and most do), it is not necessary for any tool to provide advanced functionality in all areas.

Rather, it is important that you evaluate your needs and align those needs with the features offered in a tool. If your application is budgeting, you may require real-time computation capabilities. If your application is route analysis for a shipping company, you may require very large dimension support and excellent sparsity management. If your application involves financial reporting across a basket of currencies, you may wish to use a tool that understands currency translations.

The guidelines assume that you have read about practical steps for building an OLAP model in Chapter 10 and thought about some of the questions that you can ask yourself to assess your needs. The descriptions and questions in this chapter are meant to fine-tune your awareness.

The guidelines are divided into two broad categories: logical features and physical features. Logical features can be described independently of any particular hardware platform, operating system, number of users, physical storage methods, or network properties. Dimensions, hierarchies, formulas, links, and views are examples of logical attributes.

Physical features can be described independently of any particular model that might be defined or analyzed. Physical features include how a product distributes computations across a network, how it stores and retrieves data, and what hardware and software platforms it can run on. (As with most categorizations, there are borderline cases.)

Outline

At an overview level, the guidelines are structured as follows:

1   **Logical**
    1.1   **Core**
        1.1.1   Structure
        1.1.1   Operations
        1.1.3   Representations
    1.2   **Application**
        1.2.1   Knowledge-oriented
        1.2.2   Process-oriented
2   **Physical**
    2.1   **Internal**
        2.1.1   Storage/access
        2.1.2   Computation
    2.2   **External**
        2.2.1   Client server
        2.2.2   Platform

Core Logical Features

The three principal categories of core logical features described below are *structure, operations,* and *representations.* How models and dimensions are defined and the types of relationships that can exist between members of a dimension are examples of structural issues. How data flows through a cube, the types of links that can be created, and the types of formulas that can be defined are examples of operational issues. How multidimensional data is displayed and browsed in either matrix or graphic form are examples of representational issues.

This organization is similar but not identical to the relational model which is usually defined in terms of data structure, data operations, and data integrity.[1] Some of you may have, correctly, noticed that I have not used the definite article "the" in conjunction with the term "model" as in "*the* multidimensional model." This is because OLAP products were built and deployed in the absence of any formal models. In contrast, *the* relational model was defined as a data model before any products were built that attempted to embody relational principles. Although I believe there is an articulatable formal model that OLAP products could adhere to, which is alluded to in Chapter 16 and whereupon we would be able to speak about "*the* multidimensional model," one does not currently exist.

A Comparison of the Organization of the Relational Model and a Multidimensional Model

The structural aspects of the relational model consist of domains, attributes, tuples, relations, and schemas. In the multidimensional world, they are composed of dimensions, hierarchies, cubes, and models (schemas). Clearly, any type of data model needs to define some types of structures.

The operational aspects of the relational model cover the relational algebra and the relational calculus. Joins, Cartesian products, and projections are common examples of relational operations. These operations may be called structural operations in that they manipulate the structure of relations. In contrast with these structural operations are what may be called data operations such as sum, max, order by, and so forth. The relational model and relational database products tend to focus more on structural operations than on data operations.

In the multidimensional world, the major focus of operations is in data operations. How data flows through a cube and the types of formulas that can be defined in a cube are data-operational issues. Multidimensional products offer a range of data operations that go significantly beyond what is defined in the relational model. On the other hand, they have less to say about structural operations. Forming a cube from a set of dimensions, which has no name in the multidimensional world is, in the relational world, akin to taking the Cartesian product of the separate dimensions. Although they are different, it makes sense to compare multidimensional and relational approaches to operations.

Notice that we didn't even mention integrity as a component of the definition of a multidimensional model, but we did include representations, which are absent from descriptions of the relational model.

Integrity can be thought of in two parts: definitional integrity and data integrity. In the relational world, the fact that the value of a certain attribute, say salary, is drawn from the domain of possible salary values is a matter of definitional integrity. The fact that the values of a foreign key in one relation match the values of a primary key in another relation is a matter of referential data integrity. And the fact that no employee's salary may be greater than his or her manager's is predicate-based data integrity.

Multidimensional models certainly deal with the issue of integrity in the sense of filtering. Agents deployed in a multidimensional model are essentially integrity or data value testers. But there isn't the notion of domains, at least in any common sense, in the multidimensional world and, thus, the definitional notion of integrity is lost in the multidimensional world. For this reason, I choose to leave out integrity as a part of the definition of a multidimensional model. However, filtering or data integrity testing is certainly an important part of multidimensional modeling and is included as a part of applications.

Representation is a major issue for multidimensional models. How multidimensional data is displayed and browsed in either matrix or graphic form is an example of a representation issue. The closest counterpart to representation in the relational world is probably views.

Structure

Dimensions

The four main factors are cardinality, hierarchies, versioning, and regularity.

Cardinality   The key issue to consider is how many members can be in any one dimension.

- ❑ Be especially careful if your application has one or more very large dimensions (a dimension with millions of members).
- ❑ Make sure a candidate product works efficiently with the largest dimension you need for your application.

Hierarchies

1. Can the tool support hierarchical dimensions?
2. Can it support multiple hierarchies within a single dimension?
3. Do all the members of a dimension have to be connected or can members of a dimension be unconnected?
4. Does it support named levels?
5. Does it support ragged hierarchies?

These are the basic questions you should be able to answer. Just make sure you have thought through your application needs. For example, if your roll-ups are irregular and frequently changing, as may be the case with product or organizational hierarchies, you need a tool that supports ragged hierarchies. If you need to specify equations that make use of relative orderings between members such as lagged variables in a time series equation, you need a product that supports named levels.

Further Issues

1. How would you aggregate week-level data, for which no daily totals existed, into calendar months?

2. How would you apportion demographic data that entered a cube spatially dimensioned by county into data that was spatially dimensioned by voting district?

3. How would you aggregate city level data for a city, such as Kansas City, that spanned two states?

The answer to all these questions is the same. You need to fractionally apportion the values associated with a member across two different parents. Few tools support connecting children to multiple parents in a single hierarchy. And it can certainly get you into trouble because it makes it very easy to double-count. However, it is the easiest way to solve the apportioning problem

Versioning   When there are multiple data cubes in a model, or when dimensions can be created, maintained, and updated independently of cubes, the same dimensions frequently appear in more than one cube and questions arise as to how the multiple instances of a dimension are to be kept synchronized. There are times when it makes sense for the multiple instances of a dimension to vary slightly between cubes.

1. It may be that different departments use different names for the same products, in which case you can handle the variation by assigning aliases to dimension names.

2. Or it may be that different cubes need to use different subsets of the same product dimension.

3. Or it may be that different cubes (or a cube and its dimension) need to be updated at different times. Think about the case where the marketing department is responsible for maintaining the official list of products and this list changes every quarter. Sales analysts can't analyze the quarter's sales until the quarter has ended. So ideally they work on last quarter's product dimension until they have finished their analysis, at which point their product cube is updated to reflect the changes made by the marketing department. If this is the case, the tool needs to support dimension versioning.

How OLAP Tools Define and Differentiate Dimensions

How OLAP Tools Define a Dimension

Some tools permit only one aggregation path per dimension. For these tools each aggregation path, such as stores aggregated by region and by size, would constitute a separate dimension.

Some tools define a dimension as a single level of a hierarchy. Weeks would describe one dimension. Months would describe another dimension. Quarters would define a third dimension, and so on. Although this last class of tools might seem to be the simplest or weakest, their implicit definition of dimension is actually closest to the geometrical definition of dimension.[2]

Some tools insist that all dimensions be composed of named levels. Store, city, state, and region could be named levels of a geography dimension. Named levels are harder to work with when hierarchies are irregular and dynamic. Time has commonly used named levels.

How OLAP Tools Differentiate Dimensions

Some tools treat all dimensions in the same way. They do not distinguish between variables and identifier dimensions. Typically, they provide additional features available to all dimensions but are likely to be used only by dimensions playing the role we have, up until now, called variables. In popular jargon, this way of defining dimensions is called orthogonal.

Some tools explicitly treat "variables" as a special dimension and attach it to other nonvariable dimensions to form a cube. Most relationally based OLAP tools work in this way. In addition, relational/OLAP tools usually require that the variables dimension be physically represented by database columns because the measures members generally have the most complicated formulas and SQL processors permit more sophisticated column math than row math.

Some tools treat variables separately from dimensions. To form cubes, a variable is organized or dimensioned according to some (but not necessarily all) of the dimensions in a model. Tools of this type have been called *series multicubes*.[3]

Cubes

Because most of the properties of cubes follow from the properties of their components, such as dimensions and formulas, the key cube-specific questions are quantitative.

1. What is the maximum number of dimensions per cube? Most tools provide sufficient coverage here. Possible exceptions might be tools that do not support hierarchical dimensions or multiple hierarchies per dimension. In these cases, a model that might only require 6 multipath hierarchical dimensions could need 30 or more nonhierarchical dimensions.

2. What is the maximum number of intersections per cube? If you have very sparse models where the dimensions are extremely large, you may bump up against some limits.

3. What is the maximum number of input data values per cube?

4. What is the maximum number of stored data cells per cube?

Further Issue: Regularity   Generally speaking, the dimensions of a hypercube form a regular grid. This means that every dimension intersects at every point in the hypercube. The real world isn't quite so regular. The dimensionality of data points represented within a single hypercube may vary across different parts of the hypercube. For example, in a cube defined in terms of products, time, and measures, certain products may be differentiated by color. Instead of embedding color attributes in the product dimension, color can be factored (dimensioned) out. But it doesn't make sense to have a separate color dimension at the cube level because only a small subset, say 20 out of 200 products, wants to be dimensioned by color. The answer is to dimension only those 20 products by color by defining a color dimension that exists only for the 20 relevant products.

Models

1. Is your model composed of a single hypercube, or of multiple interactive cubes?

2. Are all your variables dimensioned in the same way?

Some tools treat all dimensions as components of a "single hypercube." For example, whereas in Chapter 6 we described the sales and employee data as belonging to two separate logical cubes, hypercube tools would have defined both data sets as belonging to the same hypercube if they needed to exist within the same model. Tools of this type generally have developed efficient methods for storing what are frequently very sparse cubes of data. While some would argue that it is easier to understand a hypercube than several linked cubes, I believe that the more complicated the data being modeled, the more difficult it is to understand with a hypercube metaphor. It helps to see things broken out. Also, hypercubes make it more difficult to keep track of different types of sparsity.

Some tools allow dimensions to be shared between one or more interreferenceable cubes (frequently called multicubes). They do not force the designer to define multiple cubes, but by permitting data to reside in more than one cube they allow the designer to define multiple cubes for a particular model.

Data Types or Domains

Data values are limited by the type from which they are drawn. In the relational world, for example, fields draw their actual values from a domain that defines their potential values. With multidimensional tools, defining a variable as a character string versus an integer delimits the potential values that the member could have. At a minimum, any OLAP tool supports real numbers.

1. Does it support character strings as data values?
2. Does it support other media such as images?
3. Does it support data types on a variable-by-variable basis?
4. Does it recognize nominal, ordinal, and cardinal series?
5. Or is sorting just an option for formatting?
6. What is the range of data types supported by the tool?

Further Issues: Data Types

1. Does the tool support user-defined data types?

In advanced applications, such as simulation models, there is a need for domain concepts as well as data type concepts. Having a domain in an OLAP context would amount to defining the potential values that a datum could take. For example, a survey may have five possible responses. To model it, it would be useful to define a domain of possible responses and to make sure that the responses actually recorded came from the defined domain. This is also necessary for defining categorical variables and performing analysis with them.

Further Issue: Dimension Orderings

In Chapter 15, we took a detailed look at orderings and how they applied to identifiers and variables. Recall that the members of a dimension are always ordered in some way. The question is how are they ordered. At one extreme, the members of a dimension have no particular order, not even a base ordering. They could, for example, have a machine-generated order that changes in unpredictable ways as a function of system requirements. At the other extreme, the members of a dimension could have a completely specified distance function relating each member with its neighbor-members.

1. Does the tool allow you to assign distance functions between dimension members (thus creating unit intervals)? Can you write formulas that involve the notion of the following:

1.1 Previous member, next member (opening balance = previous time balance)

1.2 First member, last member (closing price = last time price)

1.3 Distance between two members (cycle length = distance between min and max)

2. If so, can you do it for dimensions other than time? (Recall that clock-based time is "naturally" ordered, as is ruler-based space. For other dimensions, the ordering needs to be made explicit as when ordering the members of a product's dimension by product price ranking.)

3. If so, how do you define orderings for other dimensions?

Operations

Data Flows

An operation such as summing or averaging can be looked at as taking a set of inputs from some place in the hypercube and transforming that data into an output form that "flows" in some direction to an output location in the hypercube. For example, whether data can enter anywhere in a cube or whether data can enter only at the leaves is a question of pathways, or allowable data flow directions.

All OLAP systems provide for input leaf data to aggregate up the various hierarchies.

1. Many, but not all, allow data to enter anywhere in the cube and to flow in any direction. Allocation calculations, for example, begin with data that is input at a high level and then distributed down the cube toward the leaves. Managerial estimates may enter the cube midway up the hierarchy and then aggregate.

2. Does data have to enter at the leaf level? If not, and there exist formulas for rolling up the leaf level data, can the user control when these aggregation formulas are overridden by manually entered data?

3. Can formulas reference data from anywhere in the cube? If so, do references need to be explicit as in *store contribution = store sales/city sales*, or, preferably, can references also be relative as in *contribution (at any level) = sales/parent sales*?

4. Can formulas reference data from multiple cubes?

Precedence

In Chapter 3 (and again in the hands-on case studies), you saw that for some dimensional formulas, the order in which they are combined affects the calculated results.

1. You should find out what the default logic is for any tool you may acquire.
2. Does it create precedence based on user declaration of data type or on default formula precedence?
3. Can you set precedence on a dimension-by-dimension basis?
4. Can you override them on a cell-by-cell basis or member basis?
5. Does the tool provide facilities for testing the impact of using different precedence?

Exceptions

Hypercubes define regular spaces that do not always correspond to real-world jaggedness. Most OLAP tools provide methods for defining exceptions.

1. Does the tool provide for formula exceptions?
2. If so, can they be:
   2.1 Position-based?
   2.2 Data-based?
3. How are they defined?
   3.1 Vectors based on selecting one or more members of one or more dimensions?
   3.2 On a cell-by-cell or cell-region basis?

Variables

1. Are variables treated any differently than other dimensions? Given a simple variables dimension with sales and costs that both sum over stores, and given a price variable that needs to average, you would want to attach the fact that the price variable averages across stores directly to the price variable instead of attaching it to every nonleaf node of the stores dimension.
2. Can dimensional aggregation formulas attach to variables?
3. Can you declare variable types, and inherit formulaic or type properties from variables?
4. Does the tool support nonnumeric variables?

Sparsity

Hypercubes are frequently sparse with less than 1 cell in 100 actually containing any data. That sparsity may be indicative of missing, meaningless, or zero-valued data. The two most common forms of sparsity are meaningless and zero-valued data. As discussed in Chapter 7, different types of sparsity need to be processed differently.

An OLAP tool processes sparsity with its variable logic, which is generally a component of its formula language. Most OLAP tools provide very little support for processing missing and meaningless data.

The more you have multiple types of sparsity within single cubes, the more you want robust sparsity processing.

Can the tool distinguish between the following:

1. Cube intersections whose data is missing and whose values are otherwise unknown

2. Intersections for which data would be meaningless

3. Intersections whose data, while not entered, is known to be equal to zero

4. If yes, does the tool process missing data differently from meaningless data?

    4.1 Can the tool substitute data where data is missing? How is this done?

    4.2 Does it use a fixed value, or a lookup table, or proxy functions, or interpolation?

    4.3 Can the tool substitute meaningful variables where a variable is meaningless?

Formulas

1. At a minimum, an OLAP tool needs to provide for full algebraic formulas that attach to the members of a variables dimension.

2. Does the tool allow any algebraic formula to be assigned to any member of any dimension?

3. A powerful OLAP tool will also provide for logical functions, set functions, and simultaneous equations. Can the formula compiler detect simultaneous equations? If they are detectable, can the system resolve them? If not, are they treated as circular? How about circular references—can they be detected? If not, what happens?

4. Further issue: An OLAP tool well integrated with SQL databases would interpret SQL views and carry out their corresponding computation within the OLAP engine. An OLAP tool that tied directly into a GIS system would provide dimensional structures that allow for cardinal relationships.

There is no right or wrong here. Make sure the tool provides what is needed.

Formula Interface

1. Does the tool provide for point-and-click choices when creating statements, or does the user have to write in functions?
2. Sometimes you need to write formulas that reference a number of other member names and you either do not remember the full name of the member or you want to avoid typing. Partial term-matching facilities ease the task. Does the tool provide a partial term-matching facility? Does it show you a list of possibilities when there are more than one?

Links

Multidimensional models receive the majority of their data from external database files that need to be linked to the multidimensional model. Links were discussed in Chapters 4 and 7.

1. Can a dimension be defined in terms of parent-child tables?
2. Can a dimension be defined in terms of SQL tables where each column in the table represents a level in a dimensional hierarchy?
3. Can data and metadata be brought into a model from a single table?
4. Can the links parse a type two table?
5. Can the links parse a type one table?
6. Are the links persistent? If so, how are changes detected in the external data source?
7. Can data from external tables be aggregated in a multidimensional model without first duplicating the data?
8. Can data from a multidimensional model be sent back to an external table? If so, what kinds of tables can the tool generate?
9. Can formulas that are stored in external tables be referenced from within formulas in a multidimensional model?
10. Can data from external tables be joined with data in cubes via a command/query sent to the cube?

Automation

As OLAP systems are connected to large data sources that refresh on a regular, if not nightly, basis, the process of propagating changes from the source to the cube requires a lot of work that is best automated.

1. Can data automatically be fed into a cube via links and then (re)computed?

2. Can changes to model structure defined in external tables be brought automatically into a model and used for recomputation?

3. Are changes to member names automatically propagated throughout all formulas where the member name is used?

For OLAP tools that precompute data, initial computation usually occurs in batch at load time.

1. Can recomputes be scheduled?

2. When multiple cubes and dimensions are scheduled together for recompute, is there an intelligent queue manager to optimize the ordering of recomputed items such as computing dimensions before cubes?

Optimizations/Efficiencies

A lot of work is taking place here. There is rich cross fertilization between traditional database researchers and OLAP researchers.

1. At a minimum, an OLAP tool allows a model builder to assign default aggregation operations to dimensions. For example, if in a stores dimension all the members roll up neatly into their respective higher-level categories, it should be possible to assign the operator "sum" to the entire dimension or to some node below which all other members behave the same way.

2. At a more advanced level, an OLAP tool should be able to detect all types of changed values and trigger the minimal recalculation required to propagate the changes. Minimal recalc requires that the OLAP tool track dependencies between data cells. Very few, if any, OLAP tools currently provide full dependency tracking.

3. What is recalculated during a minimal recalc?

   3.1 Variable vectors (that is, all stores, products, and times for some variable)

   3.2 Whole level intersections

   3.3 All dependents

   3.4 Whatever was identified in a range

4. Is it possible for the hypercube to be left in an inconsistent state as a result of a partial recalculation?

5. Does the tool allow an administrator to specify which aggregates get precomputed and stored and which get computed at request time? Is this then transparent to the end user?

6. Can the tool automatically figure out what aggregates are best to pre-compute and compute on the fly?

7. In a client/server implementation, can calculations be designed on the client? If so, what range of calculations can be client-defined?

8. Can the tool figure out where a computation should take place—client or server

Representations

This is an important area in multidimensional information systems. Rules of thumb for setting up screens were presented in Chapter 3. The hands-on case studies all made use of view reorganizations. When evaluating tools, make sure you sit down and use them. There are real differences in terms of how you browse and reorganize views.

Views

At a minimum, an OLAP tool must provide some form of matrix viewing. All matrix viewing mechanisms must provide for any model dimension to be mapped to any row, column, or page display dimension.

1. In addition to matrix views, an OLAP tool should provide for graphical views. Many tools do provide the minimum in graphic viewing, which is to say standard two- and three-dimensional graphs. This is also basic OLAP functionality.

2. Tools that allow for the creation of multiple linked cubes should provide for multicube viewing. Recall, from Chapter 6, that multicube viewing shows the dimensions which are shared between two or more cubes as nesting dimensions on a display device. Nested within those shared dimensions are each of the sets of nonshared dimensions. It is a nontrivial exercise to do this correctly. Very few viewers currently do. This is advanced OLAP functionality.

3. Also at the advanced end of the spectrum, OLAP tools should provide for multidimensional graphical views. Specific techniques were discussed in Chapter 6.

Navigating

Most tools provide endpoint navigation; this is basic functionality. Endpoint navigation is useful if you know where you want to go, but it frequently requires leaving the view screen to enter a dimension editor in which you select the desired new endpoint, click, and see your choice in the view screen.

The endpoint approach is less direct than directional navigation such as clicking on a cell to send the directional navigation command to "drill down" or move in the direction of increased granularity. Keeping directional commands in dimensions that have multiple aggregation paths or in models that have multiple cubes gets increasingly complicated. It is advanced functionality.

1. Ideally, an OLAP tool should provide for both directional and endpoint navigation across, as well as up and down, dimensional hierarchies.

Variable Representation Formatting

OLAP models are shared by users, and used to communicate decision-oriented information. Yet OLAP tools frequently have only very limited ability to define how to display a variable, and so they leave that to each user to perform themselves. Ideally, an OLAP tool allows a default display format of a variable (such as a currency value, percentage, rounded to hundredths, and so on) of a variable to be associated with the variable itself, so that users don't need to rediscover this every time they wish to create a view or a report.

Noncore Logical Issues

Noncore logical issues are broken down into knowledge and process-oriented domains.

Knowledge Domains

Common areas which a multidimensional tool possesses knowledge are time, currency, and foreign languages.

Time

Time is an aspect of any situation and most data sets.

1. Does the tool have any special time knowledge?
2. Does it understand calendars: fiscal, project, retail?
3. Can it compare time series of different periodicities?
4. Can it algorithmically generate time series positions?
5. If it offers time knowledge, can you still create you own time dimensions?
6. Can there be more than one time dimension in a single cube?

Currency

If your work spans multiple countries, you may want a currency translation module.

1. Does the tool recognize currencies?
2. Can it perform currency translations?
3. Can these be based on average exchange rate, last day, first day, lowest, highest?

Foreign Language Support

If your organization exists in multiple countries and they do not all speak English, you may want to consider an OLAP tool with explicit support for multiple interface languages.

1. What languages does the tool support?
2. How much of the program is translated? Are the menu options, error messages, and help translated?

Process-Oriented Domains

Process-oriented domains are more activity-centric than knowledge-oriented domain-centric activities.

Application Building

If you intend to use the same tool to write your own applications, especially across multiple domains, you should explore the type of application-building environment offered by the tool.

1. Does the tool provide a complete application development environment?
2. What functions are covered by the application environment?
   2.1 Analysis, links, model creation, or reporting?
3. To what degree is it declarative or procedural, textual or graphic?
4. Does it offer debugging facilities?

Data Mining

Although data mining is not a multidimensional phenomena (some OLAP vendors who sell a data mining product opt to make it run on SQL tables), I believe multidimensional models offer a rich exploratory environment for mining when the dimensional structures are intentionally ordered, as discussed in Chapter 15. In addition, mining today is still largely passive. You need to specify what is being mined for and you need to know a lot about your data to mine successfully. Mining would benefit from the same transition toward type-based searches as agents.

1. Does the tool offer data mining facilities? If not, does it have an interface to work with data mining packages?

2. Does the mining work with cube data alone, base data held in SQL tables alone, a combination of the two, or something else?

3. Do you need to perform any preliminary transformations (such as type conversion or scaling) on the data?

4. Do you have to input the types of patterns you are looking for? (Does it offer neural net-style mining?)

5. Does the tool scan for patterns and report what it has found? (Does the tool offer more rule-based mining?)

Agents and Exception or State Tracking

Currently, intelligent agents generally provide automation of routine queries. Specific variables are monitored or tracked; values detected in predefined ranges trigger predefined responses. This is extremely useful because it automates otherwise time-consuming processes.

In some high-paced areas like financial trading, agents have for some time been involved not just with the monitoring but also with the actions taken as a result of the monitoring. For example, program traders are intelligent agents that make decisions such as what stocks to buy or sell as a result of price and volume conditions that they monitor in real time.

Intelligent agents are evolving toward type-sensitive agents rather than the value-sensitive agents that currently exist (though I am not aware of any currently on the market). Type-sensitive agents need to work with a dictionary or thesaurus to continually interpret new measurements to decide what category they fall into and thus how to react. For example, a type-sensitive system might be programmed to look out for stocks that appear risky. Such an agent would have to know the warning signs of riskiness, such as fluctuating earnings, the appearance of new players in the market, changes in the economy or in the price and availability of raw materials.

1. Does the tool offer agents or value tracking?

2. How are monitored values defined?

3. What kinds of values are tracked?

4. Can queries run on the server?

5. Can they run in the background?

6. Can alerts be broadcast to a list of users?

Multiuser Security

OLAP systems have the same security needs as any multiuser data environment. Even if the system is a layer on top of a SQL database and thus not a persistent data store, you still want to be able to define access privileges in multidimensional terms. Recall the discussion in Chapter 3.

1. Does the tool offer security for both reads and writes?

2. Is security defined in a dimensional language?

3. To what level of granularity can security be defined: model, cube, dimension members, cells?

4. If a data cell is secured to some level, are all its dependents automatically assigned the same level of security?

5. Can the system record when (and by whom) attempts were made to access or write secure data?

6. Can the user see the members for cells to which he or she has no access?

7. Is access granted or revoked or both?

8. Can security be associated with individuals and/or groups of individuals?

DBMS Facilities

DBMSs protect against data loss and data inconsistency due to power, hardware, or software failure. These integrity features are critical for any OLAP software that manages data regardless of whether that software provides a persistent store.

1. What kind of backup facilities does the tool offer?

2. What happens if system software goes down?

3. What happens if there is media failure?

4. Is there a transaction log? Can partially finished transactions be rolled back?

5. Can the system ever wind up in an inconsistent state?

Friendliness Features

User friendliness was one of the requirements for OLAP described in Chapter 1. Many interface issues were addressed throughout the book, such as interfaces for browsing and for defining formulas. In addition, there are some general issues of user friendliness you may want to consider.

1. Does the tool prompt the user for confirmation before performing large operations, such as deleting a cube?

2. Does the tool warn the user when an expensive query has been requested as with, "This query will take 45 minutes to compute. Do you really want to do this?"?

3. Can the user stop a query in progress?

4. Is there an undo feature? How far back does it go?

5. Can the user have multiple interactive windows open simultaneously? Are changes to the model made through one window propagated to the other windows?

Physical Features

Physical features are independent of the domain of the OLAP model. They are most closely related to its size and performance.

Internal Features

Internal features are independent of any network configuration. You would come across these issues even if your entire OLAP system ran on a single machine.

Storage/Access

This material was discussed in Chapter 8.

1. Are current session data stored on the client and/or server?

2. If on the client, is there a buffer pool on the client?

3. Where can current session data exist?

  3.1 In RAM structures?

  3.2 In source databases?

  3.3 In disk storage?

  3.4 In indexes?

4. Do pointers/indexes need to be stored in RAM? If they do, what happens to performance when the indexes can no longer fit in RAM?

5. Can you configure the way current session data is stored between optimized disk, RAM, and external (SQL) tables?

6. If so, what level can you control?

7. How are missing, meaningless, and zero-valued data stored?

8. How much space does it take to store 1 million, 10 million, and 100 million actual numbers?

9. How much overhead is there per stored number?

10. How does the ratio of empty cells to actual values affect storage?

11. Are there any access performance benchmarks that show how long it takes to retrieve a screenful of precomputed numbers from a database of 1 million, 10 million, and 100 million numbers?

Computations

You want to make sure that any tool under consideration is suited for the types of calculations you are likely to make. Some tools may be fast for simple calculations but slow on the more complex ones. Others may work best with smaller numbers of dimensions. These issues were discussed in Chapter 8.

1. How long does it take to compute a screenful of numbers (50–100) where each number is a function of perhaps 1,000 other, nonoverlapping, numbers?

2. What happens to compute time when functions reference complex sets of inputs?

3. How much temporary RAM/disk storage is needed for server calculations?

External

External physical issues are concerned with how data and processing may be distributed across physical devices (usually within the framework of a client/server architecture) and how this affects overall system performance. What's the point of query response time on the server of less than a second if network overhead adds another 30? External physical issues were discussed in Chapter 9.

Client/Server

1. What computations can be defined by the client to be computed on the server?

2. Can the system (client and/or middle tiers and/or server) figure out the most efficient way to distribute computations between the client (any middle tiers) and the server?

3. What is the maximum number of concurrent client readers?

4. Can multiple client sessions share the same server data?

5. Can the administrator set the buffer sizes?

6. Are buffers persistent between table requests?

7. Does the tool support multiuser write?

8. What happens if two users with write authority attempt to write to the same cell(s) at the same time?

9. If one user is writing to a cube, at what level is the cube locked against concurrent writes?

10. Can clients browse the data cube at the same time that the cube is being recomputed?

11. What levels of data isolation are available to the client?

11.1 Dirty read?

11.2 Repeatable read?

11.3 Real-time synchronization concurrent with other users' updates?

Platform

Platform issues fell beyond the purview of this book. Topics range from operating systems to hardware architectures. The following questions should serve to at least get you started.

1. What operating system(s) does the rest of your analysis-based decision-oriented environment run on?

2. What operating systems does the tool need to run on?

3. What physical machine types does the tool need to run on?

4. Can the tool take advantage of SMP for load, query, and/or compute?

5. Can the tool take advantage of MPP for load, query, and/or compute?

Endnotes

1. Chris Date, *An Introduction to Database Systems*, 6th ed. (Reading, MA: Addison-Wesley), pp. 57, 77.

2. In geometry, a dimension is akin to an axis. A multidimensional data point is defined by the intersection of two or more axes. The relationship between different levels of a hierarchy is thought of in terms of quantitative transformations between dimensions.

3. *OLAP Report*, vol. 1, p. 52.

APPENDIX

The Relationship Between Data Warehousing and OLAP

The terms "OLAP" and "data warehousing" (DW) each describe some aspects of analysis-based decision-oriented processing (ABDOP). Because they emerged independently of each other, it is understandable that their relationship is more accurately described as a difference in emphasis within the same category than a difference in function. In other words, there is a lot of overlap between typical descriptions of OLAP and of data warehousing. Beyond these overstated descriptions, however, there are some genuinely complementary differences.

Let's begin by looking at data warehousing from the perspective of data warehousing. Table A.1 shows the relationship between operational processing and data warehousing, as described by Bill Inmon, a prominent advocate for data warehousing.[1] The table looks pretty similar to Table 1.1, which showed the essential differences between operational information processing and ABDOP.

Compare this with Table A.2, which shows the relationship between operational information processing and OLAP as described by Jeff Stamen, senior vice president for Oracles OLAP division and a prominent advocate for OLAP.[2] This table also looks pretty similar to Table 1.1.

Just how similar are they? Remember, neither of these tables is meant to be taken as a complete exposition. They are broad-stroke descriptions. Let's see what happens when we try to superimpose the two tables. Notwithstanding that the two tables have a different number of rows, use different terms, and are ordered differently, they can still be integrated relative to a common set of criteria that they both used to compare themselves with OLTP (implic-

483

Table A.1 A Definition of Data Warehousing Relative to OLTP from a Data Warehousing Perspective

	Operational data	DSS data
1	Detailed	Summarized
2	Current	Time series
3	Clerical	Managerial
4	Repetitive	Nonrepetitive
5	Processing requirements understood	Not understood
6	Unit at a time	Set at a time
7	Application-oriented	Subject-oriented
8	Nonredundant	Redundant
9	Static	Dynamic
10	Supports day to day operations	Strategic support

itly or in the case of Table A.2, more explicitly). This is shown in Figure A.1, which superimposes the operations and decision information relative to a common set of criteria. Thus, each criteria row, such as amount of information per query or model basis, or data granularity, has at least one entry from Table A.1, the DW table, and from Table A.2, the OLAP table. In the case of query characteristic, there are three entries from the DW table because the different entries make roughly the same point. In other words, managerial queries tend to be more strategic than clerical queries and the requirements for managerial queries are less understood than those of clerks.

Table A.2 A Definition of OLAP Relative to OLTP from an OLAP Perspective

		Application	
	Characteristics	**Transaction Processing**	**End-user Computing**
1	Data per transaction	Little	Lots
2	Orientation	Records	Attributes
3	Screens	Unchanging	User-defined
4	Typical operation	Update	Analyze
5	Data level	Detail	Aggregate
6	Age of data	Current	Historical, current, projected

Characteristics	Operations		ABDOP
Model basis	OLAP 2	records	attributes
	DW 7	application-oriented	subject-oriented
Data granularity	OLAP 5	detail	aggregate
	DW 1	detailed	summarized
Data time range	OLAP 6	current	historical, current, projected
	DW 2	current	time series
Data redundancy	OLAP *	No*	Yes*
	DW 8	nonredundant	redundant
Views	OLAP3	unchanging	user-defined
	DW 4	repetitive	nonrepetitive
Amount of data acessed per query	OLAP 11	little	lots
	DW 6	unit of a time	set at a time
Query characteristics	OLAP 4	update	analyze
	DW 3	clerical	managerial
	DW 5	proc. req. understood	proc. req. not understood
	DW 10	day to day	strategic

* Means that the row was not contained in the original table. The values represent what would have been included

Figure A.1 A comparison of data warehousing and OLAP relative to OLTP.

In words, this is how to read, for example, the "amount of data accessed per query" row in Figure A.1. In row 1 of the OLAP table it was stated that typical operational processing uses little data per transaction, whereas typical decision-oriented processing uses lots of data per transaction. In row 6 of the DW table it was stated that typical operational processing is unit at a time in contrast with typical decision-oriented processing which is set at a time. Row 1 of the OLAP table thus says the same thing as row 6 of the DW table.

On the surface, at least, it would appear that OLAP and data warehousing are very similar, if not identical. But as I said earlier, these articulations emerged independently of one another. In such cases, given that they were both implicitly aimed at the ABDOP category, it is understandable that their purviews may have become somewhat overstated.

The bottom line is that although data warehousing and OLAP may mention the same things, if you compare the products that position themselves in the data warehousing category such as metadata extraction tools, data cleansing tools, and warehouse databases, with the products that put themselves in the OLAP category, essentially multidimensional servers and desk-

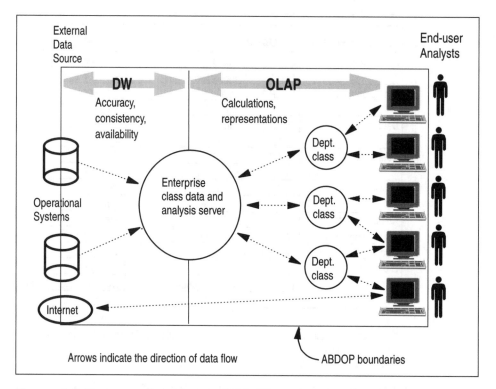

Figure A.2 Data warehousing and OLAP: two parts of the same process.

top client tools, they focus on different things. The same could be said for a comparison of data warehousing literature and OLAP literature.

Whereas data warehousing focuses on the processes required to make data accurate, consistent, and available to end users without getting into too much detail about the end user's analytical requirements, OLAP focuses on the end user's analytical requirements and the modeling and computation processes necessary to fulfill them without detailing the processes involved to make the raw data available or to ensure the accuracy of raw data. This is illustrated in Figure A.2, which shows overall the ABDOP process divided into a data warehousing region and an OLAP region.

Data Warehousing

In a popular book called *Building the Data Warehouse*, published in 1992, Bill Inmon identified some of the main problems that arose from allowing end users to initiate analysis-oriented activities on unstructured extracts taken from transactional databases. Finding the data pertinent to a strategic query was frequently a problem. And because every time a piece of information (such as overhead per department) got used in a different report it was regenerated from transaction tables, data inconsistency frequently occurred between different reports of the same phenomena.

Inmon coined the term "data warehouse" and suggested that the goal of the data warehouse is to make accurate data, which is consistent across the enterprise, accessible to end users in an efficient way that could not happen if the data were residing on an operational database. The popularity of data warehouses grew rapidly. Several conferences, and even an institute, are devoted to data warehouses.[3]

As companies found out when trying to implement a data warehouse, a data warehouse isn't a piece of software that you buy—it is a process of reengineering the information flow within the organization. For this reason, I prefer to use the process term "data warehousing" instead of the static term "data warehouse," which carries with it the unnecessary connotation of data storage. Remember, the value of the warehousing effort is in the information delivered to the end user, not in the amount of data stored in some repository. Aaron Zornes, a prominent industry analyst, called these monolithic data stores "data jailhouses." Data warehousing implies all the functions that, taken together, support the creation and maintenance of easy access for end users to consistent and enterprise-wide data. This includes metadata capture and management, data replication, data refinement, and data cleansing. The following sidebar briefly describes a variety of key terms relevant to data warehousing.

Glossary of Key Data Warehousing Terms

Metadata: Metadata is data about data. Metadata falls into several different categories. Essentially we have descriptive metadata, usage metadata, source metadata, and structural metadata. **Descriptive metadata** includes a description of what the data means, including the units if the data is quantitative. **Usage metadata** typically includes who created the data, who has authorization to change the data, when the data was last updated, who uses the data, whether the data was measured or derived, and if derived, what formula was used. **Source metadata** typically includes the names of the logical databases, tables, and physical devices where the data came from, along with refresh characteristics for the data. **Structural metadata** includes dependency relationships such as linkages and parent-child relationships.

Replication: Replication is the copying of data from one place to another. At the simplest level, it represents the wholesale copying of tables from one database to another. This is sometimes referred to as duplication. At a more sophisticated level, it represents change management where all that is replicated across databases are changes. Replication can be one way or bidirectional. And it can take place between databases of the same type—called homogeneous replication—as in from Oracle to Oracle, or between databases of different types—called heterogeneous replication—as from Oracle to Sybase.

Refinement: Data refinement refers to the integration of names, units, and forms required for the creation of global data sets. For example, a furniture chain that grew through the acquisition of individual stores, and that is transforming parts inventory management from the individual store to the chain level, may need to unify the way it labels and represents parts such as shelves. In one store, a data table for shelves may have a column recording shelf width which is called "shlf_w" measured in units of centimeters and represented internally as a single precision float. In another store, the equivalent data table for shelves may have a column for shelf width that is called "shlfwd" measured in units of inches and represented internally as an integer. None of the data is incorrect. Each store had, internally speaking, a perfectly acceptable method for representing data. It is just that for global purposes, the stores need to adopt a consistent method of representing the same information.

Cleansing: Data cleansing refers to the process of discovering and repairing anomalous data within data tables. One common form of anomaly is a column that contains data other than what the column was intended to contain as defined by its header. For example, an address column in a customer database may contain, for some customer, the customer's phone number instead of or in addition to the customer's address. Another common form of anomaly occurs where the same logical entity, such as a customer, appears more than once in a database. This frequently occurs in customer databases where the same customer may have multiple records: one for each spelling of his or her name or one for each address.

Endnotes

1. William H. Inmon, *Building the Data Warehouse* (New York: Wiley, 1992).

2. Jeffrey P. Stamen, "Structuring Databases for Analysis," *IEEE Spectrum 30* (October 1993).

3. DCI, based in Andover, Massachusetts has organized four data warehousing conferences per year since 1994. And the Data Warehousing Institute, based in northern Virginia, organizes at least one per year.

4. In a speech made at the DCI Data warehousing conference in Orlando, Florida, in February 1995.

APPENDIX

Further Issues of Invalid Data

Treatment of Missing and Inapplicable Data

Computations in arithmetic and logic require valid data in order to be performed. The computational engine of a data model must deal with problems that crop up when not all data and relationships are equally valid everywhere. For full control, data validity needs to be tracked at an elemental level.

An adequate data definition language needs to provide formulas with explicit validity operators to use on variables and expressions, allowing substitutions to be made for both inapplicable types and for missing data. Where substitutions are not made, the Dynamic Data Link needs to offer a parsing mechanism for converting expressions containing missing and inapplicable data into sets of expressions consisting only of valid data capable of being processed via traditional two-valued logic.

The example shown in Figure B.1 involves monthly sales reports sent from stores to the home office. At the end of March 1994, the home office wants to calculate how many shoes were sold across all stores, for the first quarter of 1994, in order to refine plans for the second quarter. Where actual figures are not available, an estimate must be used to facilitate the planning process.

On February 1, 1994, as part of a specialization program, the Buckley store stopped selling shoes. The Ashmont and Painesville stores have not, as of March 31, 1994, reported their sales for March.

The available data types per store and month, as highlighted in Figure B.1, indicate that the Buckley store needs to be eliminated from any calcula-

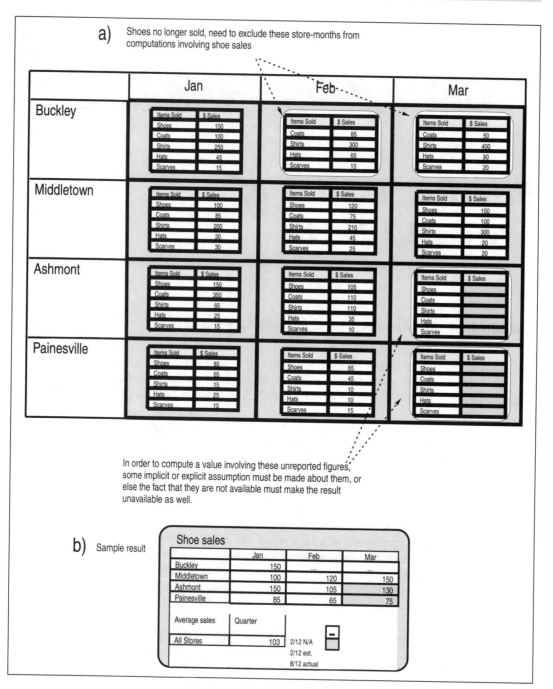

Figure B.1 Handling inapplicable versus missing data.

tions involving February and March. By maintaining applicability information, this is easily done.

The available data per store and month, as highlighted in Figure B.1, requires that March figures for the Ashmont and Painesville stores be estimated because the measurements are applicable but are as yet unavailable.

Consider the following formula to calculate the average monthly shoe sales applied across all stores in the company for the first three months of 1994:

```
Shoe sales = average, over stores and months, of:

    if shoe sales is applicable and present in the store/month,
        then use it;

    if shoe sales is applicable and missing for that
        store/month, then use the shoe sales from one year ago
        (if any) times a projected increase factor;

    if shoes sales is not applicable, contribute nothing to the
        average and skip this store/month in its count of sales
        values.
```

Wherever the shoe sales variable is inapplicable, such as in the Buckley store in February and March, no substitution will be made for those locations. Where the shoe sales variable is applicable but data is missing, such as Painesville in March, the formula will create an estimate based on sales for the same period in the prior year. If there were no approximation clauses in the formula to deal with missing data, or if they, in turn, were missing, then the formula as a whole would be unevaluable.

The rules presented here for handling incomplete expressions apply to logical as well as computational formulas. In this book, computational formulas were used because they can be stated in terms of numbers and tend to be more familiar to the typical business reader.

Logical formulas such as "if conditions x and y are true then raise a status flag" (or, to a logician, "if (p and q) then r"), though not as familiar, are just as frequent because they occur anytime a query is posed to a database. No matter what the terms of the formula may be—sales figures, salaries, manufacturing errors, labor hours—the formula's evaluation always depends on the existence of truth values for each of its terms.

In traditional logic there are only two truth values, true and false. This means we can only substitute the values true and false into each component term of the expression. The problem is what to do when some of the terms are invalid, that is, when it is unknown whether condition x is true or false or whether it even makes sense.

Three-Phase Procedure for Evaluating Expressions Containing a Mixture of Valid and Invalid Data

Within the context of something that became known as LC logic (and which is consistent with a Tractarian approach to logic—see Chapter 16 for a more detailed treatment of these logical approaches), I devised a method for evaluating formulas that contain a mixture of valid and invalid data. These procedures are outlined below and illustrated in Figure B.2.

The following procedure is repeated for each variable in the expression or formula. The application and the formula together determine the strategy for deciding what to do when variable inapplicability or missing data are encountered. The procedure takes place per identifier dimension intersection and per variable reference within the expression.

Phase 1: Test for Applicability

Determine whether the variable is applicable to this location. If not, then refer to the evaluation strategy for what to do: substitute another variable or value, drop the variable, or consider this computation to be invalid and stop. Substituted terms follow the same rules as do other expressions, so, if substituting a variable, bring it in and restart phase 1 with it. If not, proceed to phase 2.

Phase 2: Test for Missing Data

Determine whether the variable has a known value for this location. If not, then refer to the evaluation strategy for what to do: substitute another expression, drop the variable, or consider this computation to be invalid and stop. Substituted terms follow the same rules as other expressions, so if substituting a term involving variables, bring the substitute term in and restart it at phase 1.

Phase 3: Evaluation

At this stage, values are presented for computation.

Note that ranges of values as well as individual values may be substituted for invalid data. When logical data (truth-values) are missing, the result may be, for the purposes of logic, true or false, essentially a range of values from false to true. Computing a result from this, at a logical level, would be equivalent to creating two scenarios: computing one result as though the value were true, computing a second result as though the value were false, and then comparing the results—if both outcomes are the same, then it didn't matter that the data was missing, and that result can be used. If the outcomes

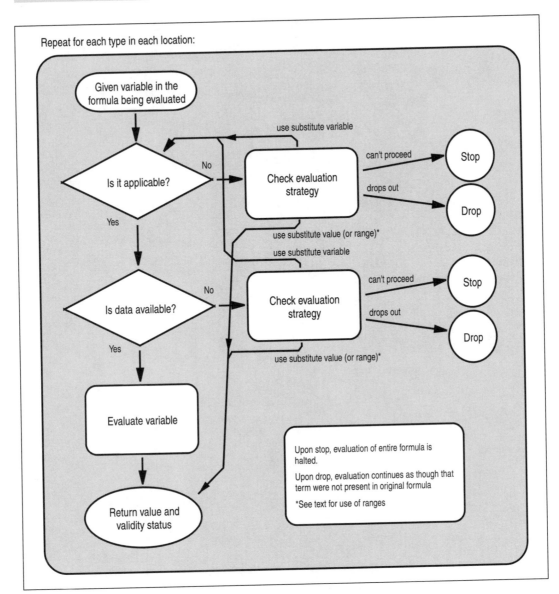

Figure B.2 Procedure for handling invalid/missing information.

are different, then the missing data is significant, and the result is still un-known (pending further substitutions, of course). Simplifications can be made to the process so as to avoid the requirement that a computer actually process all possible outcomes, but the logic remains the same.

Codd's 18 Rules or Features

Although multidimensional concepts have been applied to computing for over 30 years (the APL language used multidimensional arrays in 1964), the term OLAP first arose in September 1993 when Codd, Codd & Salley wrote a white paper entitled "Providing OLAP (On-Line Analytical Processing) to User-Analysts: An IT Mandate." You can obtain a copy of this paper by contacting Arbor Software.

Due to Dr. Codd's renown as the founder of the relational data model, the white paper generated a lot of attention. However, the attention was not unanimously positive. There were several problems with the paper.

Originally published in *Computerworld*[1] as if it were the product of unbiased research, the paper's credibility was severely damaged when it was discovered that it had been funded by one particular company, Arbor Software, and, if taken at face value, purported to show that only Arbor's product met a significant percentage of Codd's "Twelve Rules."[2] *Computerworld* later wrote a retraction stating that it was a mistake to have published the article as if it were unbiased research.[3]

The paper attempted to leverage Codd's original definition of the relational model which began with a list of 12 rules (later expanded to more than 300). One of the central tenets of the relational model was the need to separate logical issues, such as the relational schema of a model, from issues of physical implementation, such as how the various relations should be stored and accessed on a computer. The relational model was a logical model.

A cube considered as a logical structuring of data is the same regardless of whether it is instantiated in relational tables on disk using a Star schema, or whether it resides in a server buffer as a RAM cube, or whether it sits on a client tool, or whether it is partitioned between several physical devices.

Codd's white paper, however, clearly confused logical issues with physical issues. One of the original 12 rules, for example, states that a product needs to have physical facilities for handling sparse matrices. (There is nothing wrong with taking a stand on physical issues, but physical issues must be distinguished from logical issues. And if you're going to mention physical issues, you need to be systematic about it. You need efficient array processing and data access as much as you need efficient handling of sparsity.)

The 12 rules for OLAP, as originally published, followed 10 pages of background information. In one crucial area, multidimensional aggregation, the background pages distinguished between variable and nonvariable dimensions (actually nonvariable dimensions were called parameters). It is certainly reasonable to suppose that the 12 rules were intended to represent the crystallization into rule form of a more prosaic description of the same issues. Yet in the body of the 12 rules, rule number 6, for example, stated that all dimensions were equivalent in both structure and operational capabilities.

The advocacy of generic dimensionality would seem to contradict the background material that preceded it. And it clearly did not follow from the work Dr. Codd performed in the late 1970s on issues of aggregation. In 1978, for example, Dr. Codd published a paper entitled "Extending the Database Relational Model to Capture More Meaning."[4] This paper attempted to define a minimal set of constructs required to generate all types of semantic abstractions. At no point did the paper even attempt to reduce the set to a single, generic dimension.

Another problem with the paper, if read as an academic work, which is how the paper presented itself (though that is no longer how it is treated), is Codd's definition of a dimension. On page 11 of the original 1993 paper, Codd defines a dimension in the following way: "The highest level in a data consolidation path is referred to as that data's dimension." This would imply that each consolidation path in a multipath hierarchy is a separate dimension because there is a top level for each consolidation path. If a given set of leaf nodes, say stores, connects to three different consolidation paths, cities, store-types, and store-sizes, do stores belong to three dimensions, or do the three consolidated dimensions share the same base level, in which case the dimension does not include the leaf nodes? At the very least, Codd's notion of a dimension is not clearly defined.

Reservations notwithstanding, Codd's efforts certainly brought a substantial amount of mass attention to multidimensional problems and tools and assigned the easily pronounceable buzzword, OLAP, to the ensemble. In any event, the 12 original rules, later reclassified as features, were expanded to 18 in May 1995 (although you had to pay to be exposed to them) and they deserve to be mentioned, if only for their historical interest. What follows is a brief discussion of Codd's 18 features They are shown categorized according to Codd's May 1995 categories.

Basic Features

Feature 1: Multidimensional Conceptual View

Codd states that the user's view of the enterprise is multidimensional in nature and thus the user-analyst's conceptual view of OLAP models should also be multidimensional in nature. In an informal way, this is certainly true. It is fine as a loose requirement, but it assumes that the term "dimension" has been defined.

Feature 2: Intuitive Data Manipulation

Referring to consolidation path reorganization, drilling down and across, and so on, Codd advocated direct action on the cells of a model as the preferred method of intuitive data manipulation. People do not all share the same concept of intuitive. Tools should allow for a variety of interaction methods, from mouse gestures to dialogue boxes and command lines. (At Power Thinking Tools, the first prototypes of our client tool made use of a joystick for browsing.)

Feature 3: Accessibility

According to Codd, the OLAP tool should present a single logical view of enterprise data originating from a variety of sources. The source of the data in the OLAP model should be transparent to the user. I agree with this, but I would add that end users may also be a source of data.

Feature 4: Batch Extraction Versus Interpretive

Codd advocates that an OLAP tool should be able to work either as a data store or as a vehicle for accessing data stored in external databases (generally relational). The latter capability is frequently called "live reach-through." It is most useful as a means for an OLAP tool to seed its base level with aggregates taken from a relational data warehouse. When someone is browsing the base level of the OLAP model and wants to drill down even further, the connections exist to allow the user to "reach through" to the underlying relational data.

Feature 5: OLAP Analysis Models

Codd states that OLAP products should support his four analysis models: exegetical, categorical, contemplative, and formulaic. Because Codd gives no examples, it is hard to know exactly what he means, but I would interpret (using the formula classifications presented in Chapter 10) exegetical as descriptive, categorical as explanatory, and then contemplative and formulaic as not being clearly distinguished.

Feature 6: Client/Server Architecture

Codd states that an OLAP product should be capable of running on the server in a client/server architecture and that client tools should be able to hook up to the server with a minimal amount of effort. For OLAP servers, the latter requirement makes sense, though it begs the question of interoperability standards. (If the OLAP API gets adopted, the latter requirement, at least for browsing, should be easier to fulfill.)

Feature 7: Transparency

Codd states that an OLAP product should act as a transparent support to the end user's customary front-end tool. While I agree with the goal of minimizing the learning curve of new users of an OLAP product, and while it is admirable to leverage as much as possible from existing client tool investments, literally speaking, transparency is a myth. The way an OLAP server hooks up to a client tool such as spreadsheet is via an add-in menu box offering function selections such as drill down, dimension member selection, cascade, and pivot which are meaningless concepts within the spreadsheet paradigm.

Feature 8: Multiuser Support

According to Codd, OLAP tools should support concurrent read/write operations, integrity, and security. I agree with this view.

Special Features

Feature 9: Treatment of Nonnormalized Data

Codd suggests that calculations made within an OLAP product should not affect the external data that serves as the source. It is certainly useful to be able to close the loop between external databases and an OLAP tool whereby the results of calculations generated in the OLAP tool are exported back to the external database. For example, an OLAP tool might be used to compute optimal seat-pricing schemes for an airline. The data for the OLAP tool would be sourced from an external, production database. And the results of the OLAP computations could wind up back in the same production database as overwrites to the original pricing data.

Feature 10: Storing OLAP Results

Write-capable OLAP tools should not be deployed on top of transactional systems. Depending on exactly what he means by this, I may or may not agree.

Feature 11: Extraction of Missing Values

Missing values are to be treated as specified by the relational model, version 2. In the relational model, version 2, missing values are distinguished from zero and from meaningless values. The problem with the relational model, version 2, is that Codd advocates the use of four-valued logic. Four-valued logic creates all sorts of problems for logical inferencing (see Chapter 7 and Chapter 16). A version of two-valued logic, which handles all the unusual cases that four-valued logic is intended to handle without introducing any of the problems introduced by three- or four-valued logic, is presented in Chapter 7.

Feature 12: Treatment of Missing Values

Missing values are to be ignored by the OLAP analyzer regardless of their source. As described in Chapter 7, you should not simply ignore missing values. Missing values require proxies. (It is possible for the proxy to be "eliminate.")

Reporting Features

Feature 13: Flexible Reporting

Codd seems to be advocating the ability to display a cube's dimensions mapped to any combination of rows, columns, and pages. However, Codd treats rows, columns, and pages equally, which is not possible. While Codd states that any subset of the members of a dimension should be able to be mapped to any row, column, or page, as shown in Chapter 4, it is possible only to display a single member at a time in the page dimension. To do otherwise would be to convert the "page" into a row or column.

Feature 14: Consistent Reporting Performance

Here, Codd suggests that reporting performance should remain constant as the number of dimensions or size of the database increases. However, there are limits to reporting performance unless the data is all precomputed and stored in RAM. Assuming the data is disk-based (a rational assumption if the question is how to maintain consistent reporting as the size of the database increases), all data is clustered in some way on disk. Thus, there will always be some queries that necessitate more disk accesses than others. Also, absolute speed is more of a factor than consistency. There could be a performance degradation of three orders of magnitude between different types of queries and different database sizes (a factor of 1,000), but if the range of speeds was from one one-thousandth of a second to one second, you might not even notice this huge inconsistency in performance. If the range was from 5 seconds to 50 seconds, a mere factor of 10, the same users might complain about the longer queries.

Feature 15: Automatic Adjustment of Physical Level

I agree with Codd that, in an ideal situation, the physical organization of the data should reflect real data characteristics. And as the data characteristics change over time, so too should the data's physical organization.

Dimension Control

Feature 16: Generic Dimensionality

Codd states that each dimension must be equivalent in both its structure and operational capabilities and that additional operations may be granted to selected dimensions. Beyond the fact that the definition is internally inconsistent (once additional operations have been granted to certain dimensions they are arguably no longer equivalent), I have voiced elsewhere my disagreement with this feature.[5]

Feature 17: Unlimited Dimensions and Aggregation Levels

I consider this to be a pretty vacuous feature. Aside from the fact that anything implemented on a finite computer is ipso facto limited, many OLAP servers have technical limits that far exceed user's practical needs as well as the practical limits of the tools.

Feature 18: Unrestricted Cross-Dimensional Operations

I agree with Codd where he states that OLAP tools' DML "must allow calculation and data manipulation across any number of data dimensions and must not restrict or inhibit any relationship between data cells regardless of the number of common data attributes each cell contains." As a cautionary note, in a world of cross-dimensional calculations, it is very easy to define member-specific formulas that, when combined at a cell, produce a meaningless cell formula. Beyond the simple summations and ratios, it is also easy to imagine dimension-specific formulas for which there is no "correct" precedence ordering when the formulas are combined across dimensions.

Endnotes

1. "He's Back," Computer World, September 1993.

2. On-Line Analytical Processing: An IT Mandate, distributed by Arbor Software, p 18.

3. Editorial page, Computerworld, October 1993.

4. Codd [1978].

5. Letter to the editor, DBMS.

Glossary

Aggregate: From the Latin term "aggregare" meaning to collect in a flock. As a verb, it refers to the process of combining two or more data items into a single item. Summing a series of numbers is a typical example of aggregating. As a noun, it refers to any data item that is the result of an aggregation process, such as a total or average.

Ancestor: Within a hierarchy, an ancestor of a member is found along the path between the member and the root (that is, parent, grandparent, and so on)

Antecedent: *See also* ancestor.

API: Acronym for Application Programming Interface. An API provides services that a software developer can write applications to use. ODBC and the OLAP Council's MD-API are examples of APIs. They generally consist of a specified set of callable functions and data structures that may be exchanged with the functions.

Applicable: Whether a variable makes semantic sense at a given coordinate (or location). For example, if a single hypercube's measure dimension contains members for both inventory and employee measures, and an organizational dimension contains members for both product categories and job classifications, the inventory measures are inapplicable at job-classification-related cells, and the employee measures are inapplicable at the product-category-related cells. A measure can be considered missing only at a cell in which it is considered applicable.

Array: A storage method where the elements of the array are placed sequentially in a contiguous region of storage (disk or RAM). Element 1 is followed by element 2, is followed by element 3, and so on. When all elements are the same size (as is usually the case), then the location for any element in the array can be directly computed by multiplying the size of an element by the array index number for the element; it can then be accessed by skipping ahead that many units from the beginning of the array. This is a fundamental structure for computers; the memory of a computer is modeled as an array of bytes, pages of records in databases are frequently organized as an array of records, and so on.

Attribute: Information associated with an object, frequently with the members of a dimension. Address, for example, may be an attribute of a store dimension.

B-tree: A hierarchical indexing technique. Each node represents a range of indexed values, and each level of the hierarchy starting at the top focuses in on a progressively smaller set of index values, so an entry may be looked up by zeroing in on its value from the top down. Unlike a binary tree, a parent element in a B-tree can have many children. It has many variations, including the B+-tree and the B*-tree, which place index information differently within the same basic structure.

Buffer: A region of memory that holds information being transferred from one place to another. In database terms, a buffer can hold information transferred from the disk or other storage medium. Because a computer can operate only on data held in RAM, some form of buffer is required to operate on data in a database. *See also* buffer cache.

Buffer cache: A set of buffers that hold information that is either also on disk or is slated to be placed on the disk. The set of buffers is cached in memory so that further accesses to the information will not require reading it from disk, but can simply be read from memory. If the data is slated to be placed on the disk, another reason to hold it in a buffer first is to allow the disk to be used for other tasks (perhaps other reads) before writing the data out.

Cell: For OLAP vendors, the intersection of one member from each dimension in a hypercube.

Child: In a hierarchy with distinct leaves and roots, a child of a member is any member one hierarchical unit toward the leaves from the given member.

Cleansing: The process of discovering and repairing anomalous data within data tables.

Consolidate: As a financial term, used to refer to complex aggregations involving intracompany eliminations (to avoid double counting) and frequently currency translations as well.

Descendent: Within a hierarchy, a given member's descendents include any members found along the path between the member and the hierarchy's leaves.

Dimension: A collection of members, positions, or units of the same type. Synonyms from different disciplines include factor, axis, and attribute. In a multidimensional data set, every data point is associated with one and only one member from each of multiple dimensions. Dimensions are frequently organized into one or more hierarchies in OLAP applications, though this is not a logical requirement.

Dimensional formula: A formula attached to the member of a dimension. For example, the formula *Profit = Sales – Costs* when attached to the profit member of a variables dimension is a dimensional formula.

Domain 1. *Relational*: The data type from which an attribute is drawn. For example, "sales" may be drawn from the domain of positive integers. **2.** *General and AI*: A topic or subject matter as in the domain of chemistry versus the domain of economics. The term "multidomain" generally has this second sense as well.

Drill up/down: Navigating toward/away from the root of a hierarchy.

Form-based meaning: When the meaning of a symbol, such as a number, is a function of the form of the symbol.

Generation: A hierarchical distance measured from a member toward the leaves. *See also* level.

Granularity: *See* resolution.

Hash index: A technique whereby the key for a record in a database is converted to a number (through the use of what is called a *hash function*), which can then be used as an offset into an array of record locations to find the actual location of the record. Because all information in a computer (including text) may be treated as numbers, it becomes possible to treat the key values as a number or set of numbers that can be combined. This technique is much faster than using trees to index a set of records, but it scrambles the order so it is not useful to, say, find all of the records whose product name begins with "A" and look them up in alphabetical order.

Hierarchy: An organization of members into a logical tree structure, with each member having at most one "parent" member and an arbitrary number of "children" members.

Hypercube: A multidimensional construct formed from the cross-product of a number of dimensions. In a regular hypercube, every cell is defined by one member from each dimension.

Identifier: Within the context of a data set, dimensions can be used as identifiers or keys *or as variables or things that get tracked.*

Index: A structure used to facilitate the process of locating values. Optimum indexes vary as a function of many things including value set sizes, frequency of usage, and ratio of updates to accesses.

Instance: An identifiable coordinated (or located) value for a measurement. In OLAP terms, the contents of a cell. Contrast with value: Each instance is separately identifiable from any other instance, but multiple instances may all have the same value.

Inverted table: A table where all the fields have been indexed.

Leaf: Any bottom-most member of a hierarchy (a member without children).

Level:

1. *Named set of equally weighted members*: In some OLAP products, a level is specified as a subset of the members of a dimension, with the property that all members in each level are entirely above all the members in the next level down and entirely below the members of the next level up. For example, all members in a time dimension corresponding to minutes will be at a particular level, entirely above all members corresponding to a seconds level and entirely below all members corresponding to an hours level.

2. *Measure of hierarchical distance*: In some OLAP products, a level is specified as the hierarchical distance or number of hierarchical steps from either a root member of the hierarchy or from the leaf members of the hierarchy to a particular member. These products may use the term "level" to mean members measured in one direction (from the hierarchy lead members or root) and "generation" to mean members measured in the other direction.

Location-based meaning: When the meaning of a symbol, such as a point, is a function of where it is on a display.

Meaningless: Cells in a hypercube for which no data would ever exist are meaningless or inapplicable.

Measure: A unit-bearing data type. Though literally it refers to measured data such as measured temperature or measured sales, the term has been used by several OLAP vendors as synonymous with the term "variable" which also includes the notion of derived or nonmeasured values. *See also* variable.

Member: An element, position, or unit within a dimension.

Metadata: Data about data. Metadata falls into several different categories. The most common categories are descriptive, usage, source, and structural.

Missing: Cells in a hypercube for which data is applicable but does not currently exist.

Multicube: A multidimensional construct formed from two or more hypercubes, which each share one or more dimensions in common.

Nest: With respect to row and column displays, nesting one dimension under another means that all the members of the nested dimension will appear for each member of the nesting dimension. Another way to look at it is the nesting dimension represents the primary sort while the nested dimension represents a secondary sort.

OLAP: An acronym that stands for OnLine Analytical Processing. It is meant to contrast with OLTP. The key aspects are that OLAP is analysis-based and decision-oriented.

OLTP: An acronym meaning OnLine Transaction Processing.

Orient: The mapping of structural dimensions to the screen dimensions of row, column, and page.

Override: Dimensional formulas and precedences that apply to many cells sometimes need to be overridden for a subregion of cells.

Page (disk): A unit of information that can be read from a disk or written to a disk. While a disk is theoretically capable of transferring just a single bit at a time to or from memory, in practice bytes are written and read some multiples at a time. On IBM PC-compatibles and UNIX systems, the operating system may transfer 512 bytes in one operation, while on a mainframe computer the number might be 8192 (8K) bytes. Because this has an impact on the efficiency of transferring information between memory and disk, database programs will transfer pages of information to and from disk as well. A database program may use pages of data that are the same size as the pages the operating system use, or pages that are a multiple of the size of the operating system's.

Page dimension: The set of dimensions in a hypercube that are not displayed across either the rows or columns but that are necessarily displayed as pages where one and only one member of each page dimension is displayed at a time.

Parent: In a hierarchy with distinct leaves and roots, the parent of a member is the member one hierarchical unit toward the root from the member.

Peer: In a hierarchy, all members at the same level are considered to be peers. Note the multiple definitions for *level*; depending on the definition of level used, the peer group will be different.

Pivot: Rearranging the orientation of structural dimensions on the screen.

Precedence: When multiple formulas defined in different dimensions intersect at a cell, the precedence of each formula determines the order in which it is calculated, or in the case where only one formula is actually applied to the cell, which formula is applied.

Refinement: The integration of names, units, and forms required for the creation of global data sets.

Replication: A form of data duplication where only changes are propagated from place to place.

Resolution: A level whose members are defined in terms of a common scale or granularity.

Root: The top-most member of a hierarchy. In a dimension with multiple hierarchies, there will be multiple roots.

Scale: *See* resolution.

Siblings: All children of the same parent.

Star schema: An arrangement of tables in a relational database where a central "fact" table is connected to a set of "dimension" tables, one per dimension. The name "star" comes from the usual diagrammatic depiction of this schema with the fact table in the center and each dimension table shown surrounding it, like the points on a starburst.

Tree: Synonym for hierarchy. A binary tree is a tree where each node may have zero, one, or two children. A B-tree (see definition) is a hierarchically structured search index.

Type one table: A table where one dimension (usually the variables dimension) has its members placed across the columns as column headings and all the other dimensions have their names as column headings and their members defined down the rows.

Type zero table: A table where all the dimensions have been placed as the headers of columns whose data runs down the rows and a "value" dimension becomes the heading for the one data column.

Value: The quantity for a single instance of a variable. For example, $30 could be a value for a sales variable.

Variable: A unit-bearing data type, either measured or derived. Sales, costs, profit, and interest rates are typical variables. Depending on the OLAP tool, variables may be treated on an individual basis and kept separate from the dimensions according to which they are organized, or they may be collected together in a single "variables" dimension.

Virtual memory: A technique for allowing software in a computer to address more memory than is installed in the system. This allows programs that require a large amount of RAM to operate on systems that have only smaller amounts of RAM. Data that will not fit into actual RAM is moved onto or off of disk as needed, without the software being aware that the disk was involved. Generally, this is a feature of the operating systems that is transparent to the programs running on it.

Case Study and Software Providers

Case Study Providers

Elkins Economics

2 Appletree Square suite 438
Minneapolis, MN 55425
phone: 612-853-0070
email: elkinsecon@aol.com

Founded by Steve Elkins in 1992, Elkins Economics assists its clients, which include companies in the hotel, car rental, and airline industries, in the selection, design, and implementation of decision support systems, with a focus on yield management and marketing analysis. Steve, one of the travel industry's leading experts on the use of OLAP software to generate marketing business intelligence, is currently researching a comprehensive guide covering over three dozen OLAP software products that will be published in 1997. Steve also publishes a quarterly newsletter, *High Yield*, which discusses topical issues in the field of travel industry decision support systems.

GIS/Trans, Ltd

8555 16th Street, suite 320
Silver Spring, MD 20910
phone: 301-495-0217

GIS/Trans provides vendor-independent Information Technology (IT) solutions to infrastructure management agencies and corporations worldwide. The firm specializes in Geographic Information Systems for Transportation and carries out a range of consulting and software development activities in other related areas of infrastructure management. Their growing list of clients includes federal and state Departments of Transportation (DOTs), Ministries of Public Works, the World Bank, major railways, and numerous regional and urban government agencies.

MIS AG

325 Columbia Turnpike
Florham Park, NJ 07932
phone: 201-765-0405
fax: 201-765-0305

Tracy Peck, the developer of the TM/1 application in Chapter 12, is a software specialist with MIS AG in Florham Park, New Jersey. MIS AG is a software and distribution firm for TM/1 OLAP and ancillary software tools. They support their clients through formal training, technical support, building prototype applications, and "coaching" their clients on the development and use of TM/1 for their applications. Their clients range from BMW to Saatchi & Saatchi, and from Deutsche Bank to Merck. The application described in the book mimics the typical decision support solution MIS AG's customers develop using TM/1 OLAP.

Planning Technologies Group (PTG)

The Planning Technologies Group, Inc. (PTG) based in Lexington, Massachusetts, is a strategy management consulting firm which assists clients in achieving their full potential by helping them streamline and improve the quality of strategic decision making through powerful information tools and techniques.

PTG specializes in the areas of corporate strategic planning, scenario-based planning, global planning and resource allocation, mergers and acquisitions, regional sales and marketing, and operations improvement. PTG combines traditional strategy consulting, bringing extensive experience from such firms as McKinsey and Co., Boston Consulting Group, and Bain & Company, with cutting edge technology tools to affect change in the client organization.

Software Providers

TM/1 Software (now a division of Applix)

TM/1 Software, now a division of Applix, was the provider of Perspectives, the OLAP tool used throughout the case studies. They can be reached at the following address

TM1/Software
513 Warrenville Road
Warren NJ 07059
phone: 908-755-9880
fax: 908-755-9230
email: individual only
web: http://www/tm1.com
contact person: Lawson Abinanti

SPSS

SPSS was the provider of Data Diamond, the visualization tool used in Chapters 12, 13, 14 and 15. They can be reached at the following address.

444 N. Michigan Avenue
Chicago, IL 60611
phone: 1-800-543-2185
fax: 1-800-841-0064
email: http://www.spss.com
contact person: Stacy Hicks

APPENDIX

The OLAP API

The OLAP Council's MD-API

The MD-API, created through a cooperative effort of the members of the OLAP Council, was proposed in early 1995 to address the issue of multidimensional client and server interoperability. Its goal is to provide a common programming interface so that a program can create multidimensional queries and fetch resulting data sets without regard to the actual product in which the data is stored. In this way, it is similar to ODBC (a standard API for interacting with SQL databases). Version 1 of the API was readied for public review by the OLAP Council in September 1996, and implementation in products that support the API ought to become available during 1997.

The chief benefit that MD-API provides to developers of OLAP client software is a standard programmatic interface. A developer can write his or her software using the same set of functions that all behave the same way, regardless of the database platform with which the application actually communicates. This, in turn, should open the doors for both packaged software vendors and custom application developers to exploit OLAP technologies in a wide set of applications.

Additional benefits for OLAP tool developers include the following:

❏ A standardized metadata model, which provides a developer with a clear, consistent view of the components of a multidimensional model. This reduces the need for a developer to make the program handle one set of structures if running on one vendor's server and another set of structures if on another vendor's server. It also reduces the need for a developer to learn multiple sets of product terms for the same concepts.

517

❏ Support for simple report formatting as well as query formation, to assist the developer in presenting results to users. The primary purpose of the tools it has been designed to support are interactive browsing of data, which has information display as a major component.

In addition, it has been designed to be easy to administer by both database administrators and end users, which facilitates the deployment of OLAP models and tools throughout a large organization.

Important limitations on the API in its first version include the following:

❏ The metadata supported may be a subset of a server's capability, thus not exploiting the server fully. Given the lack of standardization in the OLAP servers themselves and the design requirement that the API support the greatest common subset of features, the lack of completeness is unavoidable. The similarities between products are strong enough that applications may derive significant benefit from the common API nonetheless.

❏ No means are defined to modify metadata (add or remove members, define dimensions and cubes, and so on). Furthermore, if a model's structure changes on the server, the client will not notice the change until it logs off from the server and then logs back in. Given that the majority of users of OLAP tools only browse existing structures, and that those structures are not very dynamic, this is not a major lacking. As has been demonstrated in the body of this book, though, model definition is part of analysis, and the ability to define new variables and aggregations is important to furthering analysis.

❏ Along the same lines, there is no standard way to discover the formulas that are used to compute a particular data value or other factors in a value's history.

❏ In keeping with the read-only nature of the API, no way is provided to update data values (for example, to enter a corrected sales value or to place an estimated sales total into a what-if simulation).

Although some desirable capabilities are not available in the MD-API, the OLAP Council was careful to consider what the impact would be of adding various features in the future, so the evolution of the API to add these features should be a clean process from a technical point of view.

The API provides services for identifying and connecting to a source of multidimensional information (called a "multidimensional schema"), querying metadata about the multidimensional schema, forming queries, and fetching results from those queries. "Filters" and "sorts" are the principal elements of queries; filters describe rules that filter in certain members of dimensions and filter out others, while sorts describe the order in which the members of each dimension appear in the result space. The container that represents each query and its results is a "cube" view. The filters and sorts are "applied" to the cube to add their conditions and actions to the query that the cube represents.

If you are familiar with ODBC, you know that in ODBC a client sends SQL statements to the database and gets back columns of data and a "cursor" that allows the rows returned by the query to be stepped through one at a time in a linear order. The MD-API presents a different style of defining queries and providing results to the programmer, that help to overcome three major programming issues: lack of a standard language, dynamic and incrementally modified queries, and simplicity of programming style.

Rather than using a standard textual language (as ODBC does with SQL), the MD-API represents all query elements as data objects. Each filter and sort is a discrete object representing some rule, like "direct sales > 5 in Kalamazoo, 1995, All products, actual." As an object, it does not have a textual representation that the programmer must put together. This sidesteps the issue of forming a chunk of code in some query language that means the same thing. The API (actually, a piece of driver code supplied by a vendor) is responsible for turning all of the applied objects into an appropriate query suitable for the actual database product being queried.

In a typical OLAP session (examples of which appear in the case studies of Chapters 11 to 14), a user will set up a view of the information, tweak one aspect while leaving the others alone, then tweak another aspect, and so on. Each aspect of the view (orientation of dimensions on the screen, the particular members selected for each dimension or the criteria for their selection, how they are ordered on the screen) corresponds to some state of some object in the API. If a textual query language like SQL were in use, a client program would need to generate a query for each (re-)configuration of the view. Given a highly interactive interface, the program would need to examine all of the elements of the interface that correspond to elements of a query or view format in order to generate the query and place the results on the screen. Those elements are the very objects that the MD-API provides! While a standard textual language would provide a common description of queries and views that would be easily saved (and printed and read), there would still be a gap between the language and the features that assist a user in an interactive analysis session.

For canned queries, such as a report that is run every month, this does not provide an advantage over any given textual language. (Actually, it ends up being more work for a program because saving and restoring the objects is more work than just storing a text string. A good library of additional functions to do this work can make it just about as easy for the programmer, though.) Apart from hiding the complexity of storing a query in multiple languages, though, it simplifies the process of creating interactive multidimensional browsers as opposed to a textual language. Each query object, once created, can be individually modified and reapplied to a cube view to change its part of the overall cube view's definition. Several separate views can be defined that share some query components and not others, for example.

All metadata (dimensions, hierarchies, levels, members, and attributes) are also represented as objects. A client tool needs to create a structure of the metadata that more or less corresponds to the API's given structure of metadata, but the client only needs to worry about maintaining "handles" (roughly equivalent to pointers) to the metadata, while the API takes care of managing all of the information about a piece of metadata.

In a trade of ultimate scalability for simplicity of programming (and in contrast to ODBC), the MD-API does not use cursors to exchange multiple pieces of information with a client. Rather, information is exchanged with the API in arrays. Metadata is queried from the API by first querying how many pieces of metadata there are of a given type (dimensions within a multidimensional schema, hierarchies within a dimension, and so on), then requesting that the API fill in an array of handles to that type of metadata. If the array can hold fewer handles than there are pieces of metadata, then only an arbitrary subset that will fit in the array will be returned. Because metadata must be queried in order to get the handles used in filters and sorts, the ability to navigate a model will depend on how a client queries the metadata and the size of a multidimensional schema. Querying the set of leaf members in a customer dimension could be quite storage-intensive (and take some time), but navigating down to a set of particular customers either by name or by drilling down from the top levels of the dimensional hierarchy should be reasonable in terms of storage consumed and response time.

Arrays of handles are also sent to the API as well as queried from it. For example, to specify the set of dimensions that map to the row edge of a cube view, an array of dimension handles would be used.

Although there are resource implications for the use of arrays that are not present in a cursor-based database API such as ODBC, the style of programming is relatively simple, so a developer can spend relatively less time focusing on the mechanics of exchanging information with the API itself as opposed to manipulating the exchanged information.

At the time of this writing, the MD-API is still more potential than actual. I hope that it has opened up a new phase in the use of multidimensional applications and OLAP, by simplifying the task of creating highly interactive multidimensional tools and increasing their application across servers of multidimensional information.

What's on the CD-ROM

There are two software packages on the CD-ROM enclosed with the book: TM/1, a multidimensional database engine from TM/1 Software, and Diamond, an analytical data visualization program developed by IBM and resold through SPSS. The software packages are used in conjunction with the hands-on case studies found in Section III of the book. All the case studies, plus the multidimensional testing in Chapter 5, are fully developed models included on the CD-ROM. You will also find an introduction to TM/1 in Appendix I and an introduction to Diamond within the Diamond program.

The CD-ROM contains the two software packages, all relevant application files, some visual images produced with Diamond and referenced in the case studies that do not appear in the book, introductions to both software packages and a list of OLAP vendors along with brief descriptions of their products.

Directory Structure of the CD-ROM Software Files

The following is the directory structure for the software files on the CD-ROM.

```
D:\
    Readme.TXT
    TM1Intro.DOC  (intro manual for TM1, MS-Word 6.0 format)
    Vendors.WRI   (list of vendors and products)
    DiaData\
        (Diamond data files for book)
    DiaSetup\
        (all setup files for installation of SPSS Diamond)
```

```
TM1Data\
    Chapter5\
        (data files for Chapter 5)
    Denpasar\
        (data files for Chapter 14)
    Fords\
        (data files for Chapter 12)
    Fordsnew\
        (data files for Chapter 12)
    PTG\
        (data files for Chapter 11)
    Transport\
        (data files for Chapter 13)
TM1Setup\
    (all setup files for installation of TM1)
```

Both TM/1 and Diamond setup programs work as is from their respective directories. To install Diamond, simply double click on the setup.exe file in the DiaSetup directory. The setup program will create the sample data directories that are normally associated with the applications. If you want to transfer the data files to your hard drive, you can do this by explicitly copying the data. For Diamond, this would consist of copying the files in the Dia-Data directory to the destination suggested to be the Data directory, (c:\Diam_le\data), that the Diamond setup creates.

There are two options for installing TM/1:

1. Setup.exe works the same way as the Diamond setup program. By double clicking on the setup.exe file in the setup directory, TM/1 will install on your hard drive. The setup program will create the sample data directories that are normally associated with the applications. If you want to transfer the data files to your hard drive, you can do this by explicitly copying the data. This consists of copying the subdirectories found in the TM1Data directory on the CD ROM to the appropriate directory on your hard drive suggested to be the TM1Data directory (i.e., c:\TM1data), that the TM/1 setup creates. If you are short for space on your hard drive, the advantage of running setup.exe is that you can copy model files into your hard drive on an as-needed basis. The disadvantage is that the files are copied in as read-only. You will have to convert the files to read/write in order to make changes to the models either for your own purposes or to follow along with some of the manipulation-oriented parts of the tutorials.

2. Setup2.exe will install TM/1 and all the data files automatically. Assuming you can afford the 3 MB that the data files require, this is definitely the easier option. In addition, setup2.exe will install the data files as write-capable. So you won't have to fiddle with system settings to convert the files to read/write status.

IMPORTANT NOTE

The version of TM/1 enclosed with this book, version 2.5, is not the same as the version used to produce the tutorials and screen shots. Those were produced with version 2.0. There are a number of reasons for this, the main ones being 1) that at the time these tutorials were created, version 2.5 (version 2.5a, to be exact) was not yet sufficiently stable while version 2.5c was only made available after the manuscript was sent to the publishers and 2) version 2.0 does not work with Excel 7 which, by now, I assume many, if not most of you have installed on your machines.

As it turns out, the two versions are virtually identical in the way they appear to the user. Here I will warn you of the few places where they differ and thus where the screen shots you see in the book differ somewhat from what you see on your computer screen.

1. Version 2.5 uses the term "cube" in every place that version 2.0 used the term "table". Thus, for example, the book talks about clicking on the TM/1 Table Open command whereas you will need to click on "cube" instead of "table". There are some slight differences in the look of the options dialogue box in version 2.5, but the two essential elements, namely the text edit bar where you type in the name of the directory you wish to make active and the check box where you check 'advanced mode' are identical. So you can do the same things in version 2.5 as in version 2.0.

2. Version 2.5's menu bar for working with cubes, has one less step than (but is otherwise identical in all respects to) version 2.0. In version 2.5, you will see the options 'browse, create, save and clear' as sub options in the menu stemming from the item 'cube' whereas in version 2.0, you would select them from a dialogue box (shown in the book's screen shots) that opened after selecting 'table'.

3. Version 2.5's menu bar for working with dimensions, has one less step than (but is otherwise identical in all respects to) version 2.0. In version 2.5, you will see the options 'open, new, and save' as sub options in the menu stemming from the item 'dimension' whereas in version 2.0, you would select them from a dialogue box (shown in the book's screen shots) that opened after selecting 'dimension'.

4. Version 2.5 will sometimes show N/A and sometimes show blanks where there are meaningless intersections in a model. In the screen shots taken with version 2.0, there are zeroes.

Vendor List and Descriptions

The purpose of this appendix is to let you know who is in the OLAP space, what they are doing in it, and how you can get in touch with them. The material contained here represents vendor's uncut responses to a questionnaire I sent out. In many cases, the vendor's response was substantially greater than the brief description I had requested. It didn't make sense to me to perform selective editing. Caveat emptor.

Arbor Software Corporation

Arbor Software Corporation
Corporate Headquarters
1325 Chesapeake Terrace
Sunnyvale, CA 94089
800-858-1666
Phone: 408-727-5800
Fax: 408-727-7140
E-mail: info@arborsoft.com
World Wide Web: http://www.arborsoft.com

Company Mission

Arbor Software Corporation develops, markets, and supports Essbase client/server multidimensional database software for business planning, analysis, and management reporting. Arbor is committed to supporting customers worldwide by providing quality Essbase products, support, and services.

OLAP Products

Essbase Analysis Server

Essbase (version 4.0 currently shipping) is a multidimensional database optimized for business planning, analysis, and management reporting applications such as profitability analysis, budgeting, forecasting, planning, financial consolidations, sales analysis, and EIS. Based on a true client/server architecture, Essbase supports multi-user read and write access, large-scale data capacity, robust analytical calculations, flexible data navigation, and consistent, rapid response times. The Essbase server's open architecture supports direct data access using standard spreadsheets or leading third-party query, reporting, and EIS tools. Essbase scales from a single-user version to an enterprise OLAP solution serving thousands of users with databases that are hundreds of gigabytes in size. Essbase enables robust OLAP applications directly accessing transaction-processing systems or serves as a data mart in a data warehousing strategy. Essbase operates on Windows NT, OS/2, UNIX and AS/400 servers across all major networks connected to Windows, Macintosh, and UNIX clients.

Essbase Spreadsheet Client

The Essbase Spreadsheet Client enables users with a variety of third-party front ends, including Microsoft Excel (Windows and Macintosh) and Lotus 1-2-3 for Windows to connect and seamlessly interact with Essbase. Users work within the spreadsheet interface to activate special Essbase features through mouse clicks and familiar drag-and-drop operations.

Essbase Application Manager

This product is used to build, modify, and manage analytical models, calculations , data access security, data-loading rules, and dimension-building functions. Essbase's powerful data-loading and dimension-building features ensure that applications are built rapidly with tight links to OLTP or data warehouse repositories.

Essbase Application Tools

Essbase Web Gateway is a multithreaded server application that enables high-speed, interactive, read and write access to the Essbase multidimensional database server over the World Wide Web. The Essbase Web Gateway delivers essential Essbase features including data drill-down/up/across, pivot, slice and dice, and interactive online update to corporate users through forms-compatible Web browsers and Web servers.

Currency Conversion converts financial data using any currency exchange rate scenario. The Currency Conversion module lets you model the impact of exchange rates and perform ad hoc conversions directly from a spreadsheet or custom application. This module is FASB52-compliant.SQL Interface provides access to more than 20 PC and SQL relational databases such as Oracle, Sybase, Informix, and DB2, by making the Essbase Server operate as an ODBC client. The SQL interface moves data from diverse sources into the Essbase Server for access and analysis.

Extended Spreadsheet Toolkit includes more than 20 macros and VBA functions, letting you build custom Microsoft Excel or Lotus 1-2-3 applications that tightly integrate with Essbase.

Application Programming Interface (API) lets you use standard tools to create custom Essbase applications that take advantage of the robust data storage, retrieval, and analytical capabilities of Essbase. The API supports Visual Basic, PowerBuilder, C, or C++ and works with Windows, Macintosh, Windows NT, OS/2, and UNIX.

SQL Drill-Through provides tight links between the summary data in Essbase and the detail data in OLTP and data warehouse relational databases. SQL Drill-Through automatically creates the SQL query that corresponds to the Essbase data in your spreadsheet, executes the query, and effortlessly returns the detail data to your spreadsheet.

First release date

May 1992

Number of Installed Sites

700+ Essbase customers worldwide

Characteristics of Typical System Implementations

Essbase application development averages three to four months for the first application, with the second application averaging two months' development time. On average, one to two people (FTE) support/maintain Essbase customer applications.

❑ Deal size by revenue averages $100K.

❑ For example, for server products, you may wish to say something about the number of end users per server, the number of application builders required to support the end users (the type of skills required to be an application builder), the price and its breakdown into product and consulting, and the length of time required for implementation. You may wish to break this down by deal size—that is, typical characteristics of small, medium, and large deals.

Business Objects Americas

Business Objects Americas
2870 Zanker Road
San Jose, CA 95134
Phone: 408-953-6000
Fax: 408-953-6001
E-mail: jboehm@busobj.com
World Wide Web: www.businessobjects.com
Jeff Boehm

Company Mission

The company's mission is to provide leading decision support technology to corporations while maintaining a high level of customer satisfaction.

OLAP Products

BusinessObjects 4.0

An integrated query, reporting, and OLAP solution, BusinessObjects 4.0 provides an end-user decision support solution for accessing and integrating data from relational, multidimensional, flat file, and personal data sources. BusinessObjects 4.0 includes an end-user toolset and an IS toolset for setting up, deploying, and maintaining the solution.

First Release Date

BusinessObjects 4.0 was released in April 1996.

BusinessObjects 3.x, which provided query, reporting, and limited analysis capabilities, was released in 1994.

Number of Installed Sites

3,200 customer sites, 185,000 users

Characteristics of Typical System Implementations

For example, for server products, you may wish to say something about the number of end users per server, the number of application builders required to support the end users, the type of skills required to be an application builder, the price and its breakdown into product and consulting, and the length of time required for implementation. You may wish to break this down by deal size (i.e., typical characteristics of small, medium, and large deals).

For client tools you may wish to specify the size ranges of deals, price per size range, and what they included such as training. BusinessObjects is installed in a wide variety of sites, from 10 to 10,000 users. Because of the strong IS design and deployment tools, implementation time is measured in days or weeks rather than weeks or months.

Business Objects provides comprehensive product training and has a network of certified consulting and training partners around the world.

Cognos

Cognos
67 South Bedford Street
Burlington, MA 01803-5164
Phone: 617-229-6600
Fax: 617-229-1839
E-mail: brittanie.balloch@cognos.com

Company Mission

Cognos's vision is to deliver value to commercial and government enterprises by supplying software tools that give them a competitive advantage. It is achieving this through its market-leading business intelligence tools, Power-Play and Impromptu; its application development environments, Power-House and Axiant; and with its latest break-through technology, RealObjects. Supported by a worldwide network of business intelligence partners, Cognos is at the forefront of business computing technology.

OLAP Products

PowerPlay is a Windows-based, multidimensional reporting and analysis tool used to provide corporate data to business users. It is used by managers to probe and explore data in graphical or numerical format, and to produce key reports on the factors driving their business. Impromptu enables Windows users to create sophisticated reports from corporate databases without knowing SQL, database structure, or network navigation. At the same time, it gives corporate administrators full control over database access, security, and networking impact.

PowerPlay and Impromptu are used extensively to provide solutions for sales analysis, financial analysys, customer service, quality control, and other applications. Both products have proved to be faster, more cost-effective methods of accessing corporate data than standard EIS (Executive information system) and DSS (decision support system) applications. With over a quarter of a million seats installed worldwide, PowerPlay and Impromptu consistently service the widest range of users across corporate, department, workgroup, personal, and mobile applications. The products support over 100 relational and OLAP data sources and are available in seven languages.

First Release Date

January 1990

Number of Installed Sites

There are 163,917 users worldwide

Characteristics of Typical System Implementations

The Cognos PowerPlay solution has historically distinguished itself by being able to bring multidimensional analysis to most decision makers in an organization, with minimal implementation overhead and training. The intuitive nature of the product, combined with a standard Windows interface, has allowed business managers to adopt the product quickly and effortlessly and to derive immediate competitive advantage.

Installations have typically been 25–50 Windows-based clients operating on a LAN, with a multidimensional PowerCube (or third-party cube) at the file server and/or subcubes local at the client PC. The ability to provide subcubes at the PC allows far faster processing, with the feature that managers can disconnect from the LAN and do multidimensional analysis anywhere, at any time.

PowerPlay is a highly scaleable product, where installations can go from a few users up to several thousand. With release 5.0 of PowerPlay, PowerCubes can be created at the PC or on Unix servers. They can be created as files within the file system or alternately stored as tables inside a relational database such as Oracle or Sybase. Corporations involved in data warehousing can now store their multidimensional data within their relational structure and employ the data and resource manageability of PowerPlay to deploy true enterprise-wide business intelligence solutions.

In a typical installation, one person is assigned the administrative role for the system. The time involvement will largely depend on the size of the system. Quite often, this person is the Business Analyst, who is supported by the DBA.

Rarely is there a static view of a solution. To this end, PowerPlay supports an iterative and cyclical approach in an application implementation. Clients will go through a prototype (3–10 days), then pilot (10–35 days) before they usually get to their final solution (30–90 days). This allows them to refine their direction as they are developing and to accommodate new needs as they discover new capabilities in the product. This is most important, as it also allows them to accommodate change in their business as well.

While the company recommends training for all users of an installation, usually the process is to train an on-site trainer, who then trains the rest of the users at the site. (Many sites, however, will launch a PowerPlay capability without any training from Cognos.) This serves to better acquaint the person for the administrative role, as well as provide an on-site authority to handle local problems and requests for enhancements. That said, Cognos offers a full range of user, administrator, and train-the-trainer courses.

Comshare, Inc.

Comshare, Inc.
555 Briarwood Circle
Ann Arbor, MI 48108
Phone: 313-994-4800
Fax: 313-994-5895
E-mail: bhartlen@comshare.com
djankowski@comshare.com
Brian Hartlen, Dan Jankowski
Director, Marketing Communications

Company Mission

Comshare's mission is to provide customers with successful planning, analysis, and reporting applications and to improve customers' productivity, decision making, and competitiveness.

OLAP Products

Comshare's DSS Product Portfolio

Consumer Packaged Goods. BOOST* Sales and Margin Planning is designed exclusively for marketing finance, and sales executives in consumer packaged goods manufacturing who wish to grow market share, volume, and profitability through more efficient planning.

BOOST* is a brand and customer planning system for large CPG manu-facturers that uses proven technology built on Comshare's successful mer-chandise and store planning application for retailers.

BOOST* integrates marketing's brand plans with sales' customer forecasts and finance's margin goals, to produce consistent cross-functional plans.

BOOST* helps decision-makers build more targeted plans that make the best use of promotional and advertising resources, product assortments, new product introductions, and pricing.

BOOST* instantly illuminates the effects of alternative plan scenarios on product, brand, customer, region, channel, and consolidated margins, to produce more profit-focused plans.

Unlike generic budgeting tools, BOOST* has CPG industry expertise built-in to help sales, marketing, and finance executives plan their total busi-ness more efficiently. Unlike spreadsheets and personal forecasting tools, BOOST is an integrated system that dramatically shortens planning cycle times and removes the pain and effort of sharing plan data across the func-tional silos.

Executive Information Systems. Commander Decision is a dynamic new deci-sion-support product for analysts, managers, and executives—anyone whose strategic and tactical decisions affect the success of an organization. It's a planning, analysis, and reporting system that promotes innovative thinking, identifies alternative courses of action, and monitors progress.

Commander Decision is an entirely new, state-of-the-art decision-support software product that was designed from the ground up using Visual C++ and the Microsoft Foundation Class libraries. Commander Decision is a 32-bit software product that can accommodate Windows 95, Windows NT 3.5, and Windows 3.1 (Win32s) desktop users all within a single application. It ex-ploits the latest technologies, including OLE2 and OCXs, for openness.

Its desktop interface presents business information in five ways: graphi-cally with charts; geographically with an integrated mapping system; visu-ally, with color-coded exception reporting; analytically with ad hoc queries and calculations; and proactively with Comshare's innovative alert system, Detect and Alert. Such flexibility allows executives to view business informa-tion in a way that makes sense— without compromising speed and effi-ciency.

Perhaps Commander Decision's most intriguing component is Com-share's innovative Detect and Alert software. It allows a user to establish per-sonalized monitors based on custom performance criteria. Software agents—called "robots"—inform the user when conditions occur that meet the prespecified criteria. This allows an executive to direct his or her time and effort at analyzing problems, rather than searching for them.

Detect and Alert contains another Comshare exclusive—*NewsAlert.* It's an electronic newspaper that can routinely monitor news services such as Dow

Jones and Reuters, text sources such as Lotus Notes, internal custom sources, and all the multidimensional application databases created with Commander Decision*. This feature automatically identifies important intelligence that requires the user's attention.

Financial Reporting Applications. Typical users of Comshare's financial reporting applications are corporate and group finance departments that have the vision to perceive financial data as more than just the aggregate of a set of numbers. These departments have realized the data's value as a corporate asset, which if stored in a financial decision-support database can provide vital management information. Comshare's Commander FDC and Commander Budget are particularly valuable for such uses.

Commander FDC is a schedule-based application that handles collection, consolidation, and reporting of financial data for public, statutory, and management reporting on networked personal computers. It's a comprehensive solution for the common problems associated with international currency translations, intercompany eliminations, account reclassifications, and changing reporting needs. Commander FDC collects financial data from general ledgers, spreadsheets, and other sources; manages the data in a shared, secure database; produces financial reports; and delivers the data and reports to business professionals.

Commander Budget, an enterprise solution for budget planning, has features that aid in financial modeling and forecasting. Its open architecture, multi-user database allows access to all authorized users and can fulfill the needs of a wide range of sizes and types of companies. The application tracks the status of data input from budget areas, allows user to perform easy multidimensional analysis, and produces summary and detailed reports to support the preparation of a budget at all levels of an organization. Commander Budget can share the underlying database and functions of Commander FDC, enabling dynamic reporting of actual-to-budget variances.

With their Execu-View/Finance option, both Commander FDC and Commander Budget users have point-and-click access to interactively browse, report, graph, and analyze the database created by these applications.

With the Commander Prism data modeling application, both Commander FDC and Commander Budget have a point-and-click multidimensional modeling tool that allows the user to do such complex functions as allocations, "Goal Seeking," and forecasting.

Retail Decision-Support Applications. Comshare is the world leader in decision-support applications for the retail industry. From merchandise planning to detailed performance tracking, Comshare's family of Arthur products enhances the ability of retailers to provide their customers with the right merchandise, at the right time, at the right place, and the right price

The Arthur product family gives Comshare Retail customers access to the applications required to effectively plan, allocate, and track merchandise across the retail enterprise, regardless of location or number of stores. Comshare Retail products include the following:

- ❑ Arthur Planning—A powerful merchandise planning, decision-assist application that enables retailers to create detailed plans they can use to act on, analyze valuable information, and test merchandise strategies before resources are committed. Arthur Planning helps retailers treat each store as if it were their only store.

- ❑ Arthur Allocation—A client/server application that enables users to easily determine which stores should receive merchandise to generate the highest sales and maximum margins. By accessing information from virtually any source, Arthur Allocation reviews historical or planned data from lines of business, products, distribution channels, sales and promotions, and other critical dimensions. Arthur Allocation is another illustration of Comshare Retail's dedication to providing retailers with the best in retail decision-support applications.

- ❑ Arthur Tracking—A sophisticated application that gives retailers the detailed, up-to-date merchandise performance information they need in seconds to spot trends and opportunities while there is still time to act. Arthur Tracking brings retailers closer to their customers, so they can keep them satisfied.

- ❑ Arthur Plan Monitor—An advanced client/server-based performance tracking application designed to support a wide range of users, from executives to individual planners and field personnel. Arthur Plan Monitor delivers advanced capabilities ranging from retail executive information systems to merchandise/store sales analysis and general reporting, along with planning system administration.

First Release Date

Among the current client/server products, Commander OLAP was released March 17, 1994. The company's very first OLAP product, System W, was released in 1983 for mainframe computers.

Number of Installed sites

The company has more than 3,000 customers in 40 countries worldwide.

Characteristics of Typical System Implementations

The characteristics of its implementations are the following:

- ❑ Data warehouse integration
- ❑ Multidimensional analysis

- Large data volumes
- Efficient design
- Fast, iterative response
- Read/write environment
- SQL drill-through
- Scenario building
- Information visualization
- Monitoring
- Open
- Fast implementation

Dimensional Insight, Inc.

Dimensional Insight, Inc.
111 South Bedford Street
Burlington, MA 01803
Phone: 617-229-9111
Fax: 617-229-9113
E-mail: mary@dimins.com
Mary A. Finn
E-mail: mike@dimins.com
Mike Sullivan
World Wide Web: http://www.dimins.com

Company Mission

Dimensional Insight is dedicated to developing cross-functional, cross-platform data analysis and reporting software that works quickly and is incomparably easy to implement and use. Its software is designed to help business professionals transform their corporate data into useful information for better, more rapid decision making.

OLAP Products:

DI's CrossTarget provides users with a fast, easy way to analyze their corporate data and generate reports. The server module, Builder 3.2, accepts data from any source and indexes it to create a multidimensional model. It has been tested with up to 20 million rows of input data. Diver 5.0, the client module, is a powerful graphical user interface that allows users to "slice and dice" their data any way they please. It supports a wide variety of tabular and graphical formats, including mapping, and automatic report generation.

DI's DataFountain (version 1.0) is a Web-based analysis and reporting tool, allowing users to perform OLAP functions over the Internet or a corporate intranet.

First Release Date

1990

Number of Installed Sites

There are more than 300 sites worldwide.

Characteristics of Typical System Implementations

DI's products run on a wide variety of platforms, including Windows (and Windows 95), Macintosh OS, OS/2, Windows NT, all major Unix platforms, MVS, and VMS. Many of its customers have mixed computing environments and need to pull data from several different systems for analysis. DI takes care to design its software so that it will migrate with its customers' evolving system architecture, providing the greatest possible flexibility, while maintaining a common user interface that is quick and easy to use.

Holistic Systems, Inc.

(North American headquarters):
Holistic Systems, Inc.
510 Thornall Street, Suite 217
Edison, NJ 08837
Phone: 908-321-6500
Fax: 908-321-6504
(International headquarters):
Holistic Systems, Ltd.
Suite C, 2nd Floor
7 High Street
Ealing, London W5 5DB
Phone: 011-44-181-566-2330
Fax: 011-44-181-579-2279

Holistic Systems, a Seagate Software company, is a member of the Seagate Software Information Management Group, having been acquired by Seagate in June 1996.

Company Mission

The mission of Holistic Systems, Inc. is to be the most respected provider of business intelligence tools and solutions through leadership in innovation, quality, efficiency, and customer satisfaction and by the unwavering commitment to excellence by its staff, mindful that it is its people who make the unassailable difference.

OLAP Products

Holistic Systems is entirely dedicated to marketing and supporting only one product, Holos. Holos is a purpose-built application development and delivery environment for enterprise business intelligence applications. Holos incorporates EIS, DSS, and OLAP functionality in a thin client, three-tier architecture designed to address large-scale business requirements. Tightly integrated with all popular relational databases, Holos is available on a variety of Unix, VMS, and NT servers and supports Windows, Windows NT, and Macintosh clients. A core strength of Holos is its broad, robust analytical layer, providing the most comprehensive data analysis and exploration tools in the business intelligence market today. A neural network-based data mining capability, integrated with the Holos analytic layer, has been introduced in version 5.0.

First Release Date

Holos version 1.0 was released in 1988. The current release is Holos 5.0, and there are more than 1,100 installations of Holos worldwide.

Number of Installed Sites

Holistic Systems customers include the Global 2000 corporations and major governments worldwide. A typical Holistic Systems customer is involved in high-value business intelligence applications with a significant user population and complex analytical requirements Holos usage ranges from as few as a dozen or so users to more than 5,000 users on one or more servers per customer installation. Holos development teams are typically small, averaging three people per team, and are multidisciplinary in their composition. That is, Holos development teams typically have representation from IT, end user, and business analyst functions, and this balanced, combined point of view is vital to the ultimate success of Holos applications. The real knowledge required for successful application development has more to do with a clear understanding of the data and the business application being developed, not the technology being utilized. Holos is currently available in the North American market starting at $88,000 for a license for eight concurrent users. Pricing varies internationally. Consulting services are available either from Holistic Systems or from a wide range of consulting partners who have developed a high level of expertise in Holos and ancillary technologies and techniques. Implementation periods vary depending on the specific requirement.

Hyperion Software

Hyperion Software
900 Long Ridge Road
Stamford, CT 06902
Phone: 203-703-3000
Fax: 203-968-9319
E-mail: info@hysoft.com

Company Mission

"Hyperion Software's mission is to deliver the world's best business software solutions focusing on budgeting and planning, accounting, multisource consolidation, and business analysis."

OLAP Products

Hyperion offers three OLAP products:

- ❏ Hyperion OLAP v.2.5. General-purpose business analysis application that provides modeling, ad hoc analysis, production reporting, drill-down, and Web access. Includes "smart dimensions" that provide financial better/worse reporting, time series intelligence encompassing special treatment of accounting flow, balance, ratio, and statistical elements, and currency translation. Runs as both client/server and client-only.

- ❏ Hyperion Enterprise v.4. Specialized OLAP application focusing on complex, multisource financial consolidation applications. Built-in capabilities handle statutory, legal, and management consolidations including FASB currency conversion, complex ownership, journal processing, intercompany eliminations, detailed allocations, and more. Also provides ad hoc analysis, production reporting, drill-down, and Web access. Runs as both client/server and client-only.

❏ Hyperion Pillar v.2.5. Specialized OLAP application focusing on detailed budgeting and planning applications. Built-in capabilities handle line item budget detail that varies by user, input by unit and rate, automatic spreading of inputs, "adjust, push, and pull" tools for modifying plans, allocations, and more. Also provides ad hoc analysis, production reporting, drill-down, and Web access. Runs as client-only application with built-in distribution and data collection capabilities (can run in a multiuser network environment).

First Release Date

1991.

Number of Installed Sites

More than 2,700 corporations have the above products installed.

Characteristics of Typical System Implementations

Hyperion solutions are specific to each customer. Implementation skills, time frames, and costs can vary greatly based on many parameters. While over 50 percent of the Fortune 100 rely on Hyperion solutions, smaller companies can also benefit from them ("smaller" is defined to be companies in the U.S. $100 million annual revenue range). For additional information, please contact Hyperion Software directly.

Information Advantage, Inc.

Information Advantage, Inc.
7401 Metro Boulevard
Minneapolis, MN 55439
Phone: 612-820-0702 US Toll Free: 800-959-OLAP
Fax: 612-820-0712
E-mail: marketing@infoadvan.com
World Wide Web: www.infoadvan.com
Karen Drost

Company Mission

Information Advantage is recognized as the leading provider of thin-client, server-centric relational OLAP business analysis applications for data warehouses and data marts that can start small (tens of GBs and tens of users) and grow to very large enterprise environments (terabytes of data and ten-thousands of users). DecisionSuite includes DecisionSuite Server and four front ends running under Windows that provide varying levels of functionality. WebOLAP extends DecisionSuite by allowing organizations to put their data warehouse on the Internet or corporate intranet and perform analysis using standard browsers. Information Advantage was the first company to introduce the integration of the Web with relational OLAP in February 1996 with a presentation at the DCI Data Warehouse Conference and live demonstrations of WebOLAP along with user references.

OLAP Products

❑ DecisionSuite 3.6. DecisionSuite is an integrated set of business analysis applications that perform relational OLAP analysis directly against data warehouses and data marts in a thin-client, server-centric environment. With automated analysis, detect and alert agents, workflow and desktop integration as well as collaborative computing, workgroups and the enterprise interactively exchange "live" work resulting in more consistent, timely decisions. With a notebook-style interface, users point and click to identify trends and exceptions, draw comparisons, perform calculations, share enterprise data, and get answers fast. Users independently create business calculations and filters to draw conclusions from the data warehouse. Triggers, agents, and alerts run continuously on the server in background, notifying users on a need-to-know basis via e-mail, beeper, telephone, or the Internet.

❑ WebOLAP 2.0. WebOLAP is an extension of DecisionSuite that allows organizations to put their data warehouse on the Internet or corporate intranet, then perform relational OLAP analysis on structured database contenting via standard Web browsers. WebOLAP dynamically transforms content into interactive HTML documents and lets users drill on report dimensions, append messages, pivot, and collaborate with others. Information is not distributed as static text documents; rather, users can analyze online databases and create dynamic interactive reports. WebOLAP is server-resident, runs on all major Unix platforms, providing a thin-client architecture, and is completely RDBMS-independent. WebOLAP does not require additional server hardware.

First Release Date

1990

Number of Installed Sites

It is difficult to say exactly how many sites Information Advantage has. Its client base is composed of mostly Fortune 1000 companies and large government institutions. It is very common for a client to purchase an enterprise license, therefore having hundreds or thousands of user sites around the world. Both DecisionSuite and/or WebOLAP are proven in productions environments at clients such as MasterCard International, Land O' Lakes, Cargill, 3M, Northwestern Mutual Life, U.S. Customs, Dayton Hudson Corporation, Mervyn's, Target Stores, Neiman Marcus, HE Butt Grocery, GreenTree Financial, SuperValu, Tandy, Tyson, Sears, University of Minnesota Hospitals, Nabisco, Quaker Oats, Sara Lee, TJ Lipton, Birds Eye Walls, and Shoppers DrugMart. For example, right now four of its WebOLAP clients have licensed WebOLAP for more than 27,000 users collectively. Other WebOLAP clients account for more than 50,000 users.

The implementation at MasterCard is the largest known data warehousing application of its kind, with a 1.5-TB data warehouse available to 22,000 member financial institutions. With 452 million credit and debit cards in circulation, 13 million acceptance locations, and more than 11 million transactions per day, MasterCard provides access and analysis capabilities to its member institutions never before available in the payment services industry.

Member banks want information on cardholder purchasing patterns so that they can better focus their marketing activities. Previously when a request for information was made, it took several days as data was gathered from multiple systems, processed by IT, and delivered as static reports. Now, they simply use a graphical point-and-click interface to get dynamic, consistent information about purchasing trends by merchant category, geographic location, or card performance as well as benchmarks against other lenders' performance. Member banks comment that this approach has increased efficiency, eliminated waste by offering only those promotions that are of interest to the customer, and has proven to help retail customers through relevant, timely offers.

For MasterCard, selecting a graphical front end along with a relational OLAP (ROLAP) engine was critical because ease of use and scalability could make or break the project. After extensive research, Information Advantage was chosen because it met the grueling analysis demands. Users point and click to collaborate quickly and flexibly, analyzing large amounts of customer-centric data that posed challenges that only DecisionSuite could address, said MasterCard. The agent technology can be used to analyze and continuously monitor the environment to proactively alert decision makers when certain conditions exist. As an extension of DecisionSuite, WebOLAP, which allows the data warehouse to be analyzed using Web browsers, opens up endless opportunities for future offerings. MasterCard specifically sought powerful server functionality and a product that was proven to scale with thousands of users and a data warehouse in the multiterabyte range. The entire effort from inception to roll-out took only six months. This was the largest implementation effort delivered at MasterCard in the shortest amount of time.

Characteristics of Typical System Implementations

Information Advantage was the first vendor to promote thin-client, server-centric relational OLAP with the release of its first products in 1990. The products, DecisionSuite and WebOLAP, consist of a server-based relational OLAP (ROLAP) engine with Windows or Web front ends. The ROLAP engine employs intelligent optimization strategies to distribute the OLAP processing and optionally performing the joins, aggregations, and OLAP calculations outside of the RDBMS when it is appropriate for optimum performance. This strategy generates SQL to request only the desired level of summary warehouse data and then, based on rules defined in metadata, dynamically decides the optimum place to perform the join, aggregation, and OLAP calculation—either in the RDBMS or the ROLAP engine. Data is held in memory only during the processing of the report. Once complete, memory is released as the system awaits the next user request. Processing occurs near the data, minimizing network traffic between the client and server. The ability to perform joins in the RDBMS makes it a good fit for sparse data models and large dimension tables. It also supports all OLAP calculations because the ROLAP engine is not bound by the limitations of the RDBMS. Additionally, on-the-fly groupings of virtual dimension and attribute items that are effectively redefined at run time without requiring updates to the database or additional calculation definition to compensate for a new aggregate level.

One of the most important benefits is its ability to scale—both users and data warehouse size—potentially starting with tens of GB and a few users to support for a large number of active, interactive users up into the ten thousands and data warehouses in the multiterabyte range. (Information Advantage currently has customers in production with similar configurations.) By distributing the OLAP processing across both the RDBMS and the ROLAP engine, IT is provided with a number of metadata-driven SQL strategies to help manage and control the use of temporary database tables, system memory, and network traffic. Leveraging these options can maximize application performance and functional requirements based on factors such as data size, data model, number of users, user activity, hardware configuration, RDBMS, and system architecture. Information Advantage is the first vendor to address the grueling demands of customer-centric data warehouses and is recognized as a leader with this technology.

Informix Software, Inc.

Informix Software, Inc.

4100 Bohannon Drive

Menlo Park, CA 94025

Phone: 415-926-6300

fax: 415-926-6593

World Wide Web: http://www.informix.com

Company Mission

Informix Software, based in Menlo Park, California, provides innovative database technology that enables the world's leading corporations to manage and grow their business. Informix is widely recognized as the technology leader for corporate computing environments ranging from workgroups to very large OLTP and data warehouse applications. Informix's database servers, application development tools, superior customer service, and strong partnerships enable the company to be at the forefront of many leading-edge information technology solution areas.

With the acquisition of Illustra Information Technology's completely extensible database technology, Informix is now positioned as the first information management company capable of meeting the market's exploding need for a sophisticated database engine that combines enterprise scalability, robustness, and parallel processing with the ability to store, retrieve, manage, and manipulate virtually any kind of rich content data.

OLAP Products

❑ INFORMIX-MetaCube V2.1. The sophisticated analysis engine, transforms the Informix Online Dynamic Server into a full-featured, high-performance OLAP server. MetaCube provides full multidimensional capabilities while leveraging customers' investment in open relational technology.

❑ INFORMIX-MetaCube Explorer. Ad-hoc DSS software for end users. MetaCube Explorer offers end users a simple drag-and-drop interface for powerful data warehouse access, reporting, charting, and integration with common desktop productivity applications.

❑ INFORMIX-MetaCube Warehouse Manager. A graphical tool for administering the metadata that describes your data warehouse in a logical, user-friendly view.

❏ INFORMIX-MetaCube Warehouse Optimizer. Automatically analyzes your data warehouse to recommend optimal aggregation and performance strategies.

❏ INFORMIX-MetaCube for Excel. Extends the popular spreadsheet environment to provide direct "wizard" access to the data warehouse.

❏ INFORMIX-MetaCube Agents. Perform user queries and administrative tasks on the database server in the background.

First Release Date

February 1995

Number of Installed Sites

The number of installed sites is unknown.

IQ Software Corporation

IQ Software Corporation
3295 River Exchange Drive, Suite 550
Norcross, GA 30092
Phone: 770-446-8880; 800-458-0386
Fax: 770-448-4088
E-mail: info@iqsc.com
World Wide Web: www.iqsc.com

Company Mission

The company's mission is to empower end users with data access, analysis, and reporting tools for transforming corporate data into useful information.

OLAP Product

IQ/Vision, Version 4

First Release Date

June 1992

Number of Installed Sites

There are approximately 50 installed sites.

Characteristics of Typical System Implementations

IQ/Vision is a front-end OLAP tool for both multidimensional and relational databases.

For MDDB installation this is a plug-and-play product. For relational databases, additional tools are required to build the data sets.

Installation time varies depending on database type and setup requirements. The product can support more than 200 users, and typical installations are in companies with large databases and large numbers of users.

Kenan Systems Corp.

Kenan Systems Corp.

One Main Street

Cambridge, MA 02142-1517

Phone: 617-225-2200

Fax: 617-225-2220

E-mail: johno@kenan.com

John O'Rourke

World Wide Web: http://www.kenan.com

Company Mission

Kenan Systems Corporation is a leading provider of strategic software products and services to the Fortune 1000. With headquarters in Cambridge, Massachusetts and offices throughout the United States, Europe, and Asia, the company delivers powerful software solutions targeted at the operations and decision-support needs of large organizations in the telecommunications, financial services, retail, and manufacturing industries.

OLAP Products

Acumate Enterprise Solution (ES) Version 1.31, includes the following products:

- ❑ Acumate Server. A powerful database and application development environment, featuring a multidimensional stored procedure language (MSPL), advanced analysis tools, and the industry's leading production-proven multidimensional database. The server also includes a set of powerful data-loading tools for accessing heterogeneous transaction data stores and data warehouses. Acumate Client. Standard APIs to access the database functionality and a set of programmable Visual Basic Extensions (VBXs). This also includes a powerful spreadsheet interface to the Acumate Server for analysts who want to access subsets of multidimensional data in a spreadsheet environment.

❏ Acutrieve. A customizable decision-support application optimized for analysts and other data-intensive end users, providing a powerful decision-support application for turning data into information.

❏ Acumate Workbench. A graphical front end to Acumate's multidimensional stored procedure language (MSPL). Workbench enables OLAP application developers to take advantage of the Windows environment as well as powerful OLAP application logic—all from the client.

❏ Acumate Web. HTML generator and CGI parsing engine that can be used to enable static and ad hoc reporting using Web browser technology. Acumate Web's toolkit allows users to build HTML-based, customized Web applications.

First Release Date

March 1994

Number of Installed Sites

The company has 185 sites and more than 3,000 users.

Characteristics of Typical System Implementation

Kenan Systems focuses its efforts around Acumate ES on the development of customer-centric business intelligence solutions for large organizations in the telecommunications, financial services, retail, and manufacturing markets. With a high level of customer focus, it specializes in solving business problems in the areas of marketing and customer analysis applications. This includes sales analysis, sales forecasting, product profitability, promotions evaluation, customer analysis, and segmentation. Typical implementations may start with a small number of users, beginning at 25 in a pilot project, and may grow into an enterprise-wide application supporting thousands of users. Kenan Systems offers product training, installation services, and implementation consulting services, and it is dedicated to providing whatever level of services are required to ensure its customers' success. Kenan Systems also offers a packaged customer analysis application for the telecommunications industry, called Strategist.

Micro Strategy, Inc.

Micro Strategy, Inc.
8000 Towers Crescent Drive
Vienna, VA 22182
Phone: 703-848-8600
Fax: 703-848-8610
E-mail: info@strategy.com
World Wide Web: http://www.strategy.com/

Company Mission

The company's mission is to become the preeminent provider of merchant decision support software to corporations and consumers worldwide by 2000.

OLAP Products

Relational OLAP Engine

- ❑ DSS Server 4.0 — Relational OLAP Server

End User Interfaces

- ❑ DSS Agent 4.0. Relational OLAP client interface
- ❑ DSS Objects 4.0. OLE API for custom client application development
- ❑ DSS Web 4.0. Relational OLAP client interface for the World Wide Web

Developer Tools

- ❑ DSS Architect 4.0. DSS client design tool
- ❑ DSS Administrator 4.0. Client data warehouse and DSS management tools
- ❑ DSS Executive 4.0. EIS client design tool

First Release Date

September 1993 (DSS Agent 1.0)

Number of Installed Sites

The company has 150 sites and 15,000 end users.

Characteristics of Typical System Implementations

MicroStrategy provides clients with the most comprehensive array of high-performance relational OLAP solutions. Project implementation, therefore, varies according to individual client needs. MicroStrategy supports an open architecture, allowing integration with all major relational databases. Because this architecture does not include a proprietary multidimensional database, projects may scale from a few gigabytes of data to multiterabytes. End-user communities are similarly able to range from a few dozen individuals to thousands. With the advent of DSS Web, projects are currently envisioned for mass consumerization, utilized by millions of end users.

VLDB drivers optimize query performance, allowing for such potentially large-scope projects. Likewise, query processing occurs directly on the data warehouse to leverage superior RDBMS calculation capabilities and minimize network traffic. Performance will ultimately vary according to hardware and system demands; however, the vast majority of analyses may be processed within a matter of a seconds.

Projects are typically supported by 4–20 application developers with knowledge of the relevant business area and an understanding of the RDBMS environment. Few developers are required to support the end-user community as applications are managed completely through GUIs. Limited engagement consulting offered by MicroStrategy typically supplements project implementation, as does MicroStrategy education. Primarily offered to developers and power end users, education courses are offered on a variety of product-specific and OLAP-general topics. Project development varies in time from approximately two weeks to two months, depending on scope.

NetCube Corporation

NetCube Corporation
115 River Road, Suite 831
Edgewater, NJ 07020
Phone: 201-941-6200
Fax: 201-941-3103
E-mail: NetCube.Sales@THINKinc.com
World Wide Web: http://www.THINKinc.com
Jim Carlisle (e-mail: Jim.Carlisle@THINKinc.com)

Company Mission

The company's mission is to provide profitable business intelligence solutions to innovative managers.

Profitability comes from speed to market with new applications, flexibility to adapt to changing user requirements, open architecture to ensure compatibility with many products, ease of use to enable large user populations, and Distributable DataCubes to facilitate Internet and intranet publishing solutions as well as efficient, high-performance use on an untethered laptop.

NetCube provides next-generation products and services to end-user organizations, to channel resellers, to systems integrators, and to database publishers.

OLAP Products

NetCube Product Suite is its primary OLAP product. It is a high-performance product designed to transform relational data into multidimensional DataCubes or DataMarts, with extreme speed, scalability, ease of use, and flexibility.

- ❑ It is scaleable to handle dozens of primary dimensions, each of which can be very complex. It can rapidly build DataCubes or DataMarts directly from one or many relational databases containing up to billions of transaction-level records, with no custom programming per DataCube. This eliminates the need to program, compute, and maintain large tables of aggregate numbers from which to build cubes or answer user questions.

- ❑ Flexibility derives from storing the business knowledge separately from the data, making it easy to reorganize dimensions and define clever, custom hierarchies. Dimensional elements can be defined using complex functions and multiple variables in the source database.

- ❑ Speed of automatic DataCube building makes it easy to allow end users to automatically generate their own cubes, to build large families of DataCubes (e.g., for a population of salespeople, stores, or customers), and to update DataCubes nightly.

- ❑ NetCube takes advantage of high-performance parallel processing in both SMP and MPP architectures as well as the parallel options of RDBMS software to minimize DataCube or DataMart generation time.

- ❑ Interoperability with other OLAP products is ensured by NetCube's capability to generate DataCubes in various formats, including NetCube Compressed Array (NCA) format, ROLAP Star Schema tables, or .CSV format. This allows end users to analyze rapidly built and updated DataCubes using a wide range of OLAP client/server products. NCA

DataCubes can be viewed via the Cognos PowerPlay application. Building into a standard OLAP format is planned for the future.

❑ This is a "high-end" product for demanding applications in which speed to market and large cost savings on hardware and technical support are important.

❑ NetCube is a third-generation architecture, taking advantage of direct computation from source-level data and allowing use via untethered laptops and set-top devices, in support of database publishing (data push distribution) via Internet and intranets. Many of the performance, scale, and distributed use limitations of second-generation OLAP and ROLAP products are overcome by NetCube.

The NetCube Product Suite components include the following:

❑ CubeFactory (version 6.2). The CubeFactory is the heart of the NetCube product. It builds MetaCubes (business knowledge databases) as well as DataCubes and controls the program execution process. It runs on a Unix server and consists of three applications: MetaCube Builder, CubeAgent Builder, and CubeFactory Controller. After CubeAgents are built, they also become logically contained in the CubeFactory.

   • The MetaCube Builder processes MetaCube Definition Files as input and transforms them into a MetaCube, which is the logical "Hyper-Cube" that represents a comprehensive, multidimensional analysis space. While the MetaCube "represents" this HyperCube, the product suite typically never builds this HyperCube. This ensures that the product is scaleable to a very large number of potentially large dimensions.

   • NetCube users have defined and used MetaCubes with HyperCube spaces exceeding the 10 to the 20th power against databases with billions of source records and continually changing dimension hierarchies and definitions.

   • The CubeFactory Controller governs the processes within the Cube-Factory. This series of control programs creates and executes CubeAgent programs to build new DataCubes, update existing Data-Cubes, and restart a cube build if a database problem should occur before completion.

   • The CubeAgent Builder builds CubeAgents based on Cube Request specifications and MetaCube definitions, mappings, and rules.

❑ MetaCubeDesigner (version 6.2). MetaCubes are the knowledge base of a NetCube data warehouse. Much more than mapping dimensions to fields in the relational tables, these object databases contain a wealth of sophisticated information about how each dimension element is defined, how to handle missing values, compute rollups, derive complex measures (such as "target market share"), and optimize parallel processing queries in cube building.

- The MetaCubeDesigner is a Windows client application that is used to build and maintain this knowledge base. It is used, by a data or application administrator, to enter database definitions, dimension definitions, multidimensional data, functions and calculation rules. The MetaCubeDesigner is used to map the user's view of the analysis space to the underlying, source-level, relational Data Warehouse. The outputs of this application are MetaCube Definition files that are used to define and build the MetaCube on the server.

❑ CubeDesigner (version 6.2). NetCube's notion of a DataCube is what some would call a small DataMart. The CubeDesigner is a Windows client application that allows a nontechnical end-user to select elements of a MetaCube that he or she would like to analyze and rapidly build a customized DataMart or DataCube. The input to the Cube-Designer is the MetaCube. The output of the CubeDesigner is a Cube Request, which is used first to build a CubeAgent and ultimately the desired DataCube.

❑ The Designer allows highly-efficient selections from lists of natural language dimensional elements. For example, a user can quickly select all "leaf nodes" on a dimension, all children of a "node" down a specified number of levels, or selected children of selected parents throughout a hierarchy. Rollups, "all other" logic, and dependent variable selection are handled automatically.

❑ 4. CubeViewer (version 6.2). The CubeViewer is a Windows client application that is used to analyze and view data contained in DataCubes. This application can rapidly create views to display multidimensional data as a table or chart. CubeViewer has the ability to save views, load previously created views, and export the data contained in a view as a comma separated (.CSV) data file.

NetCube add-on products include the following:

❑ NetPlay NetCube PowerPlay .DLL (version 6.2). This .DLL allows end users to analyze data stored in NetCube Compressed Array (NCA) Data-Cubes using the Cognos PowerPlay product (version 5.0). This is available as a site license to augment existing PowerPlay site licenses or as a fully supported, value-added package from NetCube.

❑ CubePress (version 6.2). CubePress is a server application that allows DataCubes to be transformed (or "pressed") into a variety of ASCII and database table formats. CubePress allows end users to define the specific data elements to be transformed and the target format(s). Target formats currently include star schema (aggregate tables and associated dimension tables), .CSV files, and Oracle or DB2 relational database tables. Custom target formats, such as any OLAP or ROLAP data format, as well as customized mapping functions, are available from NetCube on request. CubePress specifications are defined at the time of each DataCube request, using the CubeDesigner application.

❏ NetCube API (version 6.2). The NetCube API allows developers to create their own applications to read data from its NCA DataCubes and to use its CubeEngine object classes. The API currently consists of C++ classes, which will be expanded into C and Java classes in the near future.

First Release Date

The NetCube product suite was first installed in a production environment for a Fortune 100 company in 1992.

Number of Installed Sites

There are currently two customer installations, with fully paid licenses. NetCube is working with several additional "development partners" to expand and target the capabilities. The product is fully operational and is available for license, but it is not yet "formally released."

Characteristics of a Typical System Implementation

NetCube typically works in conjunction with a relational database, such as Oracle or DB2, implemented on a parallel processing Unix server.

The databases are typically large, ranging from a 100 million records up to billions of records. Data is efficiently indexed, so that overhead for indexing is as low as 5–10 percent.

Data are typically stored at the source- or record-level. Examples are phone calls, prescriptions, subscriptions, automobile purchases or service transactions, credit card purchases, retail item purchases, and Web site clickstream detail. NetCube can store aggregate values as well, if that is all that are available, but it does not require them.

Customers are typically sales and marketing managers, data warehouse managers, or information publishers.

The automatic DataCube building and updating allows customers to "publish" DataCubes to a large number of users, such as a sales force, customer or supplier population, dealers, or stores.

Frequent changes in the dimension hierarchies and the definitions of DataCubes of interest typically lead to large, complex, constantly changing, MetaCubes. For example, a dimension might hold a list of employees or customers in a Fortune 100 company; a long, elaborate hierarchy of products (such as drugs, auto parts, or grocery items); time to the hour level; dates organized by calendar month, fiscal month, promotion period, down to the day; separate geographies for customers, retailers, and manufacturer of each item sold; demographic variables; purchase histories; and predictive marketing model scores.

The NetCube CubeFactory is typically used to rapidly and reliably generate complex extracts for use by other marketing analysis and data mining products.

Customers typically receive several days of administrator training, spend a few day or a few weeks defining the MetaCube dimensions, and then load the database and begin building DataCubes immediately. End users receive an hour or two of training, mostly focused on explaining all the new data and analysis options available, with a brief orientation to using the very manager-intuitive Market Advantage application.

Customers typically add additional source-level databases more quickly than the initial implementation.

No customization is required to the software to read data from different industries or in different relational formats. Some customization may be needed or valuable to optimally handle different relational database configurations and hardware platforms.

This is a "high-end" product for demanding applications, in which speed to market and cost savings on hardware and technical support are important.

Pilot Software, Inc.

Pilot Software, Inc.
One Canal Park
Cambridge, MA 01241
Phone: 617-374-9400
E-mail: rclayton@pilotsw.com
Richard Clayton

Company Mission

Pilot Software, Inc., a company of The Dun & Bradstreet Corporation, develops interactive decision-support software for managers and analysts in large organizations who need to make time-critical decisions based on quantifiable information.

OLAP Products

Pilot's flexible solution provides several analysis metaphors including ad-hoc navigation for analysts, graphical analysis for managers, and summarized briefings for executives. It consists of five components and can be installed as a single-user, workgroup, or distributed configuration. The client components support Windows 95, Windows NT, and Windows 3.1, and the server components are available for NT and six leading Unix platforms.

The Pilot Decision Support Suite includes the following:

❑ Pilot Desktop. A single-user environment for interactive business analysis with a complete set of dimensional tools that allow users to drill down, rotate, and pivot through consolidated data. Pilot Desktop provides intuitive tables, charts, and maps for graphically navigating and understanding data. It includes a built-in time intelligent multidimensional engine and tools for ranking and exception analysis. Within minutes, users can create dimensional models from leading relational databases or any other ODBC-compliant data source.

❑ Pilot Analysis Server. Pilot's scaleable multiuser OLAP server provides a rich array of analytical modeling capabilities including its unique support for time-based analysis and dynamic dimensions that enable advanced analysis capabilities on large amounts of data without the need to preconsolidate. It includes a library of built-in functions supporting dozens of forecasting techniques, correlation methods, and regression analyses. The Pilot Analysis Server connects to a wide range of relational databases and other ODBC-compliant data sources.

❑ Pilot Designer. The next generation of Pilot's award-winning design environment, formerly known as LightShip Professional, has been enhanced to provide a comprehensive tool set for creating all types of visual decision-support applications ranging from simple executive information systems (EIS) front ends to complex OLAP applications. It includes a complete set of dimensional objects, geographic mapping, an integrated scripting language that is compatible with Visual Basic, and support for industry standards including OLE, ODBC, and MAPI. Pilot Designer also includes Pilot Desktop so applications can be tested and validated and a software developer kit for designers who wish to integrate Pilot into applications built with other client/server development tools.

❑ Pilot Analysis Library. An optional library of analysis modules that allow users to accelerate the implementation of advanced decision-support solutions. These include modules for 80/20 Pareto analysis, time-based ranking, BCG quadrant analysis, trend line analysis, and statistical forecasting. These prebuilt modules can be customized or extended with Pilot Designer.

❏ Pilot Excel Add-in. An optional component that allows Excel users to seamlessly integrate the capabilities of the Pilot environment into their Excel solutions. It provides a dimensional selection object, plus drill-down and rotate facilities to access information in multiple dimensional models from Excel.

First Release Date

Pilot Analysis Server, formerly LightShip Server, was first released in 1992.

Number of Installed Sites

With operations in more than 25 countries worldwide, Pilot has more than 1,500 corporate customers.

Characteristics of Typical System Implementations

Pilot is a full-service vendor, offering training, consulting, ongoing support, and maintenance services. Pilot's approach to solution implementation is to help the customer achieve self-sufficiency as quickly as possible. This approach is embodied in Pilot's Rapid Development Methodology, an approach to delivering solutions in the OLAP marketplace focused on rapid delivery of value to business users. Typical implementations start delivering information to users in two to four weeks, with incremental application functionality and additional information added to the solution on an ongoing basis. Typical solution implementations include several key steps:

❏ Identifying and specifying the multidimensional business model

❏ Locating appropriate source data

❏ Building production procedures to build and maintain multidimensional model(s)

❏ Data administration and cleansing issues

❏ Customized application development

The time for implementation of a solution depends largely on the data issues—locating, accessing, and cleaning data sources—unique to each client. After the initial delivery, clients with some programming background can easily customize analyses—developing custom EIS screens, for example—and continually expand the information universe handled by the system.

Typical Pilot solutions include multiple components of the Pilot Decision Support Suite. Typical configurations include one or more multiuser analysis servers, 50–1000 client systems, and application libraries for immediate delivery of enhanced analysis. A typical 50-user solution including add-ins lists for approximately $100,000, including training classes, initial consulting, and one-year support and maintenance. Services are available in unbundled fashion.

PLATINUM Technology, Inc.

PLATINUM Technology, Inc.

1815 South Meyers Road

Oakbrook Terrace, IL 60181

Phone: 617-647-2912, 800-442-6861

Fax: 708-691-0710

E-mail: lrobinson@platinum.com

Lisa Robinson

Company Mission

PLATINUM's goal is to be the leading provider of software for the open enterprise.

OLAP Product

PLATINUM InfoBeacon 3.1 is a next-generation online analytical processing (OLAP) product. The distributed three-tier architecture of InfoBeacon delivers performance and functionality that, to date, have only been available in OLAP products based on proprietary multidimensional databases, while also providing enterprise scalability and an open architecture not found in these proprietary solutions. InfoBeacon 3.1 also overcomes the shortcomings of other relational OLAP (ROLAP) products by providing rapid response, full analytical processing calculation capabilities, database write-back capabilities, schema flexibility, and complete security.

The distributed three-tier client/server architecture of InfoBeacon consists of industry-standard relational data warehouses or data marts acting as the data store, the InfoBeacon application server that provides a "virtual cube" or VCube that interacts directly with the relational database and performs the analytical processing functions, and the InfoBeacon client tools for analysis, reporting, and administration. In addition to advanced analytical processing, InfoBeacon also provides proactive agent capabilities. Server-based agents can be created to notify users of opportunities or problems, or they can even automate an entire series of analytical processes.

InfoBeacon Web is a multithreaded server application that brings the power of online analytical processing to the Internet/intranet environment. InfoBeacon Web turns a Web browser into a client tool capable of delivering a full range of advanced OLAP capabilities to the knowledge worker. InfoBeacon Web provides the ability to: run and modify any analysis in a "live" manner, dynamically drill down/up on data from within the browser, and create and run server-based agents that can automate entire analytical processes. InfoBeacon Web provides the performance and capabilities needed to deliver interactive business analysis to the knowledge worker over the World Wide Web via any Web browser on any client platform.

First Release Date

PLATINUM's OLAP product was originally developed by Prodea Software Corporation in 1993 and was named ProdeaBeacon. PLATINUM acquired Prodea in February 1996; at that time the product's name was changed to InfoBeacon.

TM/1 Software

TM/1 Software
513 Warrenville Road
Warren, NJ 07059
Phone: 908-755-9880
Fax: 908-755-9230
E-mail: individual only
World Wide Web: http://www/tm1.com
Lawson Abinanti

Company Mission

TM/1 Software is committed to the worldwide proliferation of its multidimensional database products through direct and indirect channels, including VARs, strategic partners, and application software companies. The company strives to provide quality products at a fair price while continuing to set the standard for real-time analytical processing—the ability to calculate large data sets on-demand, in real-time. It strives to delight its customers with products that enhance insight and competitive advantage during enterprise-wide planning, reporting, and analysis.

OLAP Products

TM1 Server 6.0 is the latest version of TM/1 Software's proven scaleable, real-time multidimensional OLAP server/engine. Each server can support as few as 5 to more than 100 users and deal with databases of up to 200 million numbers. A typical 3-user system costs $6,000 in the United States; a 50-user system, $55,000.

Summary of Specifications: Up to 16 dimensions per table. Up to 2 billion elements per dimension. Data from any number of tables may be combined in a worksheet. Automatic aggregation, consolidation, and comparison defined in dimensions. No limit to levels of consolidation. One dimension may be used in any number of tables. Database size limited only by available memory and disk resources.

TM1 Client 2.5 provides cost-effective connectivity to TM1 Server 6.0 using the a familiar Excel or Lotus 1-2-3 spreadsheet interface to provide real-time OLAP. U.S. pricing starts at less than $400.

TM1 Perspectives 2.5 is a self-contained, real-time multidimensional, single-user server. As a stand-alone, it is ideal for rapid application development (RAD). In addition, TM1 Perspectives is a completely portable OLAP environment that can be carried in a notebook computer for remote work, on-site prototyping, or presentations. With a dial-up connection to your network, it offers all the client functionality of TM1 Client 2.5. U.S. pricing starts at about $800 per copy.

TM1 ShowBusiness is a graphical presentation tool that makes it easy to produce focused views of multidimensional data stored in TM1 client/server applications. It offers the functionality of point-and-click OLAP in graphical applications that can be distributed enterprise-wide very cost-effectively. U.S. pricing starts at $345 per user and drops to $139 per user for 1,000 users. A developer license costs $1,595.

TM1 API (Applications Programming Interface) permits universal client access to the TM1 engine through programming languages such as Visual Basic, C, C++, PowerBuilder, and Delphi.

First Release Date

1984

Number of Installed Sites

There are 1,300 installed sites.

Characteristics of Typical System Implementations

Implementation of full solutions with TM1 generally requires about two man-months. This will obviously vary with factors such as scope of the project, availability of good source data, prior familiarity with TM1, and so on. The skills required for implementation vary through the different stages. During the initial development/setup stage, the required skill is similar to those of an IT programmer/analyst. It requires general knowledge of TM1 to define what data is needed, and it requires knowledge of the data source to understand how to get that data.

Once the data is obtained, it is straightforward for the IT person to import the data into TM1. No actual programming is required, just a mapping between the data source and the TM1 dimensions. Once the data is in TM1, the setup stage is complete. Generally, the "power users" in the end-user community can perform all maintenance including adding/editing dimensions and cubes and creating libraries of reports. No special language must be learned for this—it is all accomplished through visual manipulation with drag-and-drop features.

TM1 operates with a concurrent user model. For example, a 10-concurrent-port server means that only 10 people may be logged on at the same time, although 30 users might have TM1 clients on their machine. A server is quite easy to administer, and after the initial setup is done, it can be easily maintained by a "power user."

Pricing starts at $6,000 for a three-port server. The price does not include training. A two-day training class for developers usually is sufficient. End users do not really need training—if they already know how to use their spreadsheet application, they can be trained on TM1 in one hour.

Because TM1 is so scaleable, many customers begin implementation with a proof of concept. They can quickly develop a prototype application to get buy-in from everyone. This can generally be done in one week, often in a few days. When this proof of concept has been carried forward to a real stand-alone application, it can be turned into a TM1 client/server application by merely copying the appropriate files to the server. Many TM1 customers start with a few users and quickly expand usage throughout the enterprise. A large TM1 implementation is one where hundreds of users can connect to numerous distributed TM1 servers, and where the cubes at each TM1 server communicate with each other to distribute the data appropriately close to the users.

Bibliography

Abbott, Edwin, *Flatland*, HarperCollins Publishers, Inc., New York, 1983

Bentley, Jon L., "Multidimensional Binary Search Trees in Database Applications," IEEE, 1979

Berebson, Mark L., and Levine, Daniel M., *Basic Business Statistics: Concepts and Applications*, Prentice-Hall, Inc., Englewood Cliffs, NJ, 1979

Celko, Joe, *Instant SQL Programming*, Wrox Press Ltd., Chicago, 1995

Codd, E. F., "Extending the Database Relational Model to Capture More Meaning," Association for Computing Machinery, 1979

Codd, E. F., "Missing Information (Applicable and Inapplicable) in Relational Databases," Association for Computing Machinery, SIGMOD Record, vol. 15, no. 4, December 1986

Codd, E. F., *The Relational Model for Database Management: Version 2*, Addison-Wesley Publishing Company, Inc., Reading, MA, 1991

Codd, E. F., "A Relational Model of Data for Large Shared Data Banks," IBM Research Laboratory, San Jose, CA, February 1970

Codd, E. F., and Date C. J., "Much Ado About Nothing," *Database Programming and Design*, vol. 6, no. 10, October 1993

Cunto, Walter, Lau, Gustavo, and Hlajolet, Philippe, "Analysis of *KDT-trees: KD*-trees Improved by Local Reorganizations"

Dahl, Veronica, "A Three-Valued Logic for Natural Language Computer Applications," Departmento de Matematica, Facultad de Ciencias Exactas, 1980

Dahl, Veronica, "Quantification in a Three-valued Logic for Natural Language Question-Answering Systems," Departmento de Matematica, Facultad de Ciencias Exactas, Buenos Aires, Argentina, 1979

Date, Chris J., *An Introduction to Database Systems,* 6th ed., Addison-Wesley Publishing Company, Reading, MA, 1995

Editors, Proceedings of the 21st International Conference on Very Large Data Bases, Morgan Kaufmann, San Francisco, CA, 1995

Errman, Lee D., and Lesser, Victor R., "A Multi-level Organization for Problem Solving Using Many, Diverse, Cooperative Sources of Knowledge," Computer Science Department, Carnegie-Mellon University, 1975

Frank, Maurice, "A Drill Down Analysis on MDDBs," *DBMS,* July 1994

Freeston, Michael, "The BANG File: a New Kind of Grid File," European Computer-Industry Research Center (ECRC), Munchen, West Germany, 1987

Gray, Jim, Bosworth, Adam, Jayman, Andrew, and Pirahesh, Hamid, "Data Cube: A Relational Aggregation Operator Generalizing Group-By, Cross-Tab, and Sub-Totals," Microsoft Research, Advanced Technology Division, Microsoft Corporation, Technical Report, October 4, 1995

Gries, David, and Gehani, Narain, "Some Idea on Data Types in High-Level Languages," Association for Computing Machinery, 1977

Gupta, Ashish, Harinarayan, Venky, and Quass, Dallan, "Aggregate-Query Processing in Data Warehousing Environments," IBM Almaden Research Center, Stanford University, 1995

Guttag, John, "Abstract Data Types and the Development of Data Structures," Association for Computing Machinery, 1977

Harinarayan, Venky, Rajataman, Anand, and Ullman, Jeffrey D., "Implementing Data Cubes Efficiently," Standford University, CA

Heath, Thomas, ed., *The Thirteen Books of Euclid's Elements*, Dover Publications Inc., New York, 1956

Inmon, W. H., *Building the Data Warehouse*, Wiley New York, NY, 1992

Johnson, Theodore, and Shasha, Dennis, "Hierarchically Split Cube Forests for Decision Support: Description and Tune Design"

Kant, Perception of Space and Time.

Keller, Peter R., and Keller, Mary M., *Visual Cues*, IEEE Computer Society Press, Los Alamitos, CA, 1992

Kimball, Ralph, "Data Warehouse Insurance," *DSMS,* vol. 8, no. 13, December 1995

Kimball, Ralph, "The Database Market Splits," *DSMS,* vol. 8, no. 10, September 1995

Kimball, Ralph, "The Problem with Comparisons," *DSMS*, vol. 9, no. 1, January 1996

Kimball, Ralph, "SQL Roadblocks and Pitfalls," *DSMS*, vol. 9, no. 2, February 1996

Kimball, Ralph, *The Data Warehouse Toolkit*, John Wiley & Sons, Inc, New York, NY, 1996

Lauwerier, Hans, *Fractals: Endlessly Repeated Geometry Figures*, Princeton University Press, Princeton, NJ, 1991

Ledgard, Henry F., and Taylor, Robert W., "Selected Papers from the Conference on Data: Abstraction, Definition, and Structure," Association for Computing Machinery, 1977

Manning, Henry P., *The Fourth Dimension Simply Explained*, Munn & Company Inc. New York, NY, 1919

Mansfield, Edwin, *Statistics for Business and Economics*. 2nd ed., W. W. Norton & Company, Inc, New York, NY, 1983

Martin, Daniel, *Advanced Database Techniques*, The MIT Press, Cambridge, MA, 1985

McGoveran, David, "Classical Logic: Nothing Compares 2U," *Database Programming and Design*, vol. 7, no. 1, January 1994

McGoveran, David, "Nothing from Nothing (Or, What's Logic Got to Do With It?)," *Database Programming and Design*, vol. 6, no. 1, December 1993

McGoveran, David, "Nothing from Nothing: Can't Lose What You Never Had," *Database Programming and Design*, vol. 7, no. 2, February 1994

McGoveran, David, "Nothing from Nothing: It's in the Way That You Use It," *Database Programming and Design*, vol. 7, no. 3, March 1994

Mendenall, W., Ott, L., and Larson, R. F., *Statistics: A Tool for the Social Sciences*, 3rd ed., Duxbury Press, Boston, MA, 1983

Orenstein, Jack A., "Spatial Query Processing in an Object-Oriented Database System," Computer Corporation of America, 1986

Osborn, Sylvia L., and Heaven, T. E., "The Design of a Relational Database System with Abstract Data Types for Domains," The University of Western Ontario, London, Ontario, 1986

Pendse, Nigel, and Creeth, Richard, *The OLAP Report (Norwalk, CT: Business Intelligence Inc.)*, 1995

Rich, Charles, "Knowledge Representation Languages and Predicate Calculus: How to Have Your Cake and Eat It Too," The Artificial Intelligence Laboratory, MIT, Boston, 1982

Robert, Paul, *Petit Robert: Dictionaire Alphabetique et Analogique de la Langue Francaise*, Societe du nouveau Littre, Paris, 1967

Sarawagi, Sunita, and Stonebraker, Michael, "Efficient Organization of Large Multidimensional Arrays," Computer Science Division, University of California at Berkeley

Shavel, Steven, and Thomsen, Erik C., "A Functional Basis for Tractarian Number Theory," Power Thinking Tools, Inc., Power Thinking Tools: Academic Background, Northampton, MA

Shipman, David, "The Functional Data Model and the Data Language DAPLEX," 81 Transactions on Database Systems, vol. 6, no.1, March 1981

Smith, David Eugene, *A Source Book in Mathematics*, Dover Publications, Inc., New York, NY, 1959

Smith, Henry C., "Database Design: Composing Fully Normalized Tables from a Rigorous Dependency Diagram," Association for Computing Machinery, 1985

Smith, John Miles, and Smith, Diane C. P., "Database Abstractions: Aggregation and Generalization," Association for Computing Machinery, Inc., 1977

Sokal, Robert R., and Roglf, F. James, *Biometry: The Principles and Practice of Statistics in Biological Research*, 3rd ed., W. H. Freeman and Company, New York, NY, 1995

Stamen, Jeffrey P., "Structuring Database for Analysis," *IEEE Spectrum*, vol. 30, no. 10, October 1993

Stigler, Stephen M., *The History of Statistics*, The Belknap Press of Harvard University Press, Cambridge, MA, 1986

Stonebraker, Michael, ed., *Readings in Database Systems*, Morgan Kaufmann, San Francisco, CA, 1993

Thomsen, Erik, "A Tractarian Approach to Information Modeling," Power Thinking Tools, Proceedings of the International Wittgenstein Symposium on the Foundations of Logic, 1989, Kirchberg, Austria, 1989

Thomsen, Erik C., "Synthesizing Knowledge from Large Data Sets: The Need for Flexible Aggregation," Power Thinking Tools, IT Europe, 1992, London, England, 1992

Thomsen, Erik, and Shavel, "A Tractarian Basis for Number Theory," Power Thinking Tools, Proceedings of the International Wittgenstein Symposium on the Philosophy of Mathematics, Vienna: Verlag Holder Pichler Tempsky

Thomsen, Erik and Shavel, On Three-Valued Logic, Power Thinking Tools, Proceedings of the International Wittgenstein Symposium on Cognitive Science Vienna Verlag Holder Pichler Tempsky, 1993, Kirchberg, Austria, 1993

Tillman, George, *A Practical Guide to Logical Data Modeling*, McGraw-Hill, Inc., New York, NY, 1993

Tufte, Edward R., *The Visual Display of Quantitative Information*, Graphic Press, Cheshire, CT, 1983

Index